GENDER AND HISTORY IN CANADA

D0861079

NeW
CANADIAN
READINGS
SERIES EDITOR
J. L. GRANATSTEIN

Titles currently available

GENDER AND HISTORY IN CANADA

Edited by
JOY PARR
Simon Fraser University

and

MARK ROSENFELD

Copp Clark Ltd.
Toronto

ISBN: 0-7730-5541-X

publisher: Jeff Miller
managing editor: Barbara Tessman
editor: Bay Ryley
design: Susan Hedley, Liz Nyman
cover: Anthony Leung
typesetting: Marnie Benedict
printing and binding: Metropole Litho Inc.

Canadian Cataloguing in Publication Data

Main entry title:

Gender and history in Canada

(New Canadian readings)
Includes bibliographical references.
ISBN 0-7730-5541-X

1. Sex role - Canada - History.   2. Women - Canada - History.   3. Canada - Social conditions.   I. Parr, Joy, 1949–   .   II. Rosenfeld, Mark.   III. Series
HQ1453.G45 1996.   305.3'0971   C95-933379-7

COPP CLARK LTD.
2775 Matheson Blvd. East
Mississauga, ON
L4W 4P7

Printed and bound in Canada

1 2 3 4 5   5541-X   00 99 98 97 96

FOREWORD

o

Gender history is a relatively new field of historical investigation in Canada, so new in fact that several of the articles in this first collection on the subject have never before been published. There can be no doubt that the field has much of interest to students and researchers alike. Where else in one place can one find articles on males and females, straights and homosexuals, honeymooners at Niagara Falls, baseball, fatherhood in northern British Columbia, and crossdressing woman warriors?

History is now and always has been the most all-inclusive subject with room under its capacious tent for all subjects. But what could be more important than gender? Everyone of us everyday operates within the boundaries laid down for us by the past and the rapidly changing attitudes of the present, and gender is one of the key determinants of life. That historians generally, and Canadian historians in particular, have been slow to examine the subject takes away nothing from its importance.

The articles in this pathbreaking collection, gathered together by two of the leading scholars in the field, show how rich the study of gender can be. This is one field in Canadian history that is about to explode into the mainstream, and this volume demonstrates that, while much has already been accomplished, we have much to which we can still look forward.

J.L. Granatstein
General Editor

CONTENTS

○

INTRODUCTION

○

In the past two decades, the study of gender has become an important feature of historical writing. Historians researching gender have looked at neglected dimensions and challenged previous interpretations of Canada's past. The title of this volume, *Gender and History in Canada*, signals the three key considerations that have shaped this collection and Canadian historical writing on gender in general.

First, the concept of *gender* informs each contribution to the collection. Gender is a term feminist theorists developed to explain how being male or female is not simply the result of biology but is socially constructed and reconstituted. Gender is shaped by social interaction. Gender identities—masculinity and femininity—acquire meaning in relation to one another. Theoretical and empirical studies of gender are concerned with examining this relationship, particularly the inequalities and hierarchies of authority and power that have underpinned relations between women and men.

The concept of gender has directed researchers to explore the specific context where gender relations have been shaped. Paid and unpaid work, family, popular culture, and government policy have been some of the more common contexts investigated by scholars attempting to understand the dynamics of gender. Sexuality has also been a notable focus of study, revealing a dimension of gender relations that previously received relatively little attention. The ambition of gender studies, however, has not been to explore these locations in isolation from one another but rather to attempt to understand the totality of gender relations. Consequently, scholars have also recognized the need to integrate the relations of class, race, and ethnicity, with gender in their investigations. Gender studies assume that masculinity and femininity are not only interrelated but are identities that have been shaped by those of race, ethnicity, and class. The study of gender therefore looks to the diversity of experience while attempting not to lose sight of the commonalities which might unite women or men.

The second consideration shaping the collection is the recognition that gender has a *history*. Gender relations and identities are not static but have changed over time. Seventeenth-century conceptions of masculinity and femininity differ from those of the twentieth century. Major economic transformations, such as the Industrial Revolution, crises such as war, and periods of great ideological ferment had major implications for the way gender relations, and the understanding of those relations, developed in the past.

Historical studies of gender are part of an inter- and intradisciplinary field of inquiry. Historians have drawn on the insights and observations of anthropologists, sociologists, psychologists, political scientists, as well as literary and linguistic theorists. Concepts and methods borrowed from these disciplines, however, have been used in ways that reflect the historian's concern about context and change. Within the discipline of history, the examination of gender relations has drawn on the research of its many sub-disciplines, particularly women's history, as well as the work of labour, ethnic, and family historians, and historians of sexuality.

Historical research has allowed practitioners to reinterpret the past in ways that bring to light hidden but influential assumptions about gender. Studies of the nineteenth-century legal system, for example, reveal how the development of married women's property law was shaped by male judges who believed that freeing women from their subordinate legal status would undermine family stability. Investigations of the development of the twentieth-century welfare state have shown that public policy was premised on the assumption that male breadwinning and female dependence were the norm.

The final consideration shaping this collection is a focus on the history of gender in *Canada*. While the history of gender relations of different countries might have much in common, there are significant differences. The contributions in this volume look at the historical development of gender in specific Canadian regions and locales. Yet, the collection is not parochial in its concerns. The study of gender relations is an international endeavour and the essays that comprise the collection have been influenced by, and represent a dialogue with, gender histories written elsewhere.

The collection contains eighteen essays that illustrate the concepts, methodologies, and analytical frameworks found in some of the most recent work in gender history. The essays reflect many of the research interests of gender historians and the current state of historical knowledge about gender relations in Canada. Contributors have considered traditional documentary sources, such as newspapers, company and government records, diaries, and contemporary literature, for what they reveal about gender relations and identities of the past. Some have also employed less conventional sources, such as oral history, to explore the emotional texture of gender relations of the more recent past.

The essays are grouped thematically and highlight the importance of gender to our understanding of racism, sexuality, national identity, popular culture, and family in Canadian history. They also highlight the importance of gender to our understanding of paid work, class conflict, and government policy. Some of the concerns explored in one thematic section are further explored through a different lens in another section. Many of the essays look at how the experience of gender acquired particular and selective meanings over time. The majority specifically focus on the different historical representations and practices of masculinity or femininity.

Chronologically, the articles span the period from seventeenth-century New France to the 1960s, although the majority of contributions focus on the decades of the late nineteenth and early twentieth century. An attempt has been made to cover most of geographic regions of the country, therefore allowing the reader to see how particular local economies, cultures, and social settings have shaped gender relations.

The writing of gender history has its own history. Joy Parr's historiographical essay traces the evolution of gender history in Canada. She identifies both the major influences on the practice of gender history and the understandings that gender history brings to the study of the past. Her discussion sets the context for the remaining articles in the collection.

Sarah Carter and Elizabeth Vibert explore the way in which European traders' and settlers' representations of Native people reflected the dominant gender and racial ideology of the period. Carter investigates the political and economic consequences of negative representations of Native women in nineteenth-century western Canada. She observes that images of these women as dissolute and dangerous were deliberately propagated by state officials and settlers and became central to the Canadian government's segregationalist policies toward Aboriginal people. Vibert analyzes the relationship between early nineteenth-century British fur traders conception of their own and Aboriginal hunters' masculinity. Her study highlights how fur traders' construction of their gender identity depended on particular images of Aboriginal manliness.

The intersections of race, gender, and class are also taken up in Agnes Calliste's essay on Canadian immigration policy toward Caribbean blacks, and Madge Pon's study of a Toronto newspaper's construction of Chinese masculinity in the early decades of the twentieth century. Both contributions show how particular depictions of the sexuality of racial minorities were central to the way the dominant culture constructed gender identities and formulated racist ideologies.

National icons and symbols have often reflected gender-specific imagery and a particular historical understanding of gender relations. Cecilia Morgan's study of Laura Secord, and Colin Coates' essay on Madeleine de Verchères explore the way these symbols of English and French Canadian nationalism were constructed and reshaped to advance the claims of late nineteenth- and early twentieth-century feminists for greater participation in the public sphere. Both authors underline the way in which the historical significance of such symbols could be recast to reassert or remake existing gender boundaries.

Historians have used the concept of sexualized space to explore the development of sexual and gendered meanings that are acquired in certain environments or locations. They have also looked at how men and women have attempted to appropriate these spaces for their own use. Karen Dubinsky examines the construction of Niagara Falls as a place of romance, sex, and danger in the popular imagination of its nineteenth-century visitors. Her study underscores how the historical analysis of gender relations and sexuality can reveal aspects of social life not usually considered in the history of tourism. Drawing on the insights of gay history, Steven Maynard looks at the appropriation of public places such as lavatories, parks, and laneway by men seeking sex with other men in late nineteenth- and early twentieth-century Toronto. He portrays a complex dynamic between police surveillance of sexual activity between men and the creation of a homosexual subculture in the city.

The organization of institutional sports and leisure has been historically grounded in distinct social relations—competition and hierarchy among men and the exclusion or domination of women. Colin Howell's contribution, excerpted from his social history of Maritime baseball in the nineteenth and twentieth century, focuses on baseball in the Victorian era and shows that the game was enmeshed in the period's class and gender relationships. Different conceptions of manliness that were articulated by baseball promoters, players, and social reformers, were central to the history of the game and profoundly shaped its development. Judith Fingard investigates another site that historically played an important role in determining gendered identifications among men—the men's club. Her study of an African-Canadian Masonic Lodge and a veterans' society in late nineteenth-century Halifax details the role of each association in maintaining a positive masculine identity. Gender was central to the way these associations negotiated racial and class divisions, fostering an illusion of equality.

A gendered structure of hierarchy and competitiveness has also figured prominently in the workplace. The sexual division of paid and unpaid labour has both reflected and reinforced gender differences. However, such differences have not only been reinforced by sex-segregated workplaces. Even in integrated workplaces, gender differences have been reproduced. The contributions by Shirley Tillotson, Eric Sager, and Steven Penfold pursue the links between paid work and gender. Each examines how working-class men have used their gender identities to assert privilege and combat employers in the workplace or community. Tillotson looks at the early twentieth-century urban commercial telegraph offices as a case study in the link between gender and definitions of skill. She demonstrates that the connection between masculinity and skill was established through the craft culture of telegraph operators and company policy and then redefined in the face of technological change that threatened to undermine these skilled workers' status and wage levels. Sager's contribution, which is taken from a larger oral history of merchant seafarers employed between 1920 and 1950, depicts the reinforcement of the sexual division of labour by ideology and work rhythms in the seafarers' work and family lives. Penfold investigates the way in which gender was woven into the texture of social relations in the Cape Breton coalfields in the 1920s and coloured the class conflict between the miners' community and employers.

Historically, the Canadian state has played an important role in the regulation of reproduction, both promoting and delimiting the role of women and families in childbearing and childrearing. State regulation of reproduction has also taken some unusual but revealing turns, some of which are ingeniously explored by Mariana Valverde. Her study of the Ontario government's control over the famous Dionne Quintuplets and its handling of another well-known case of the Great Depression, the Toronto Stork Derby, cautions against simple historical generalizations about the state's role in the administration of reproduction.

The state has actively regulated the sexuality of its citizens too, defining as legitimate certain sexual practices and criminalizing others. Punitive state sanctions have not only been directed at men or women caught in sexual situations deemed illegitimate, however. Gays and lesbians have been targeted simply because of their sexual orientation. Daniel Robinson's and David Kimmel's essay documents the elaborate lengths to which the Canadian government went during the 1950s and 1960s to root out suspected homosexuals employed inside and outside of government.

Gender relations have not been static. There have been significant generational differences as well as changes in the life cycle that have influenced how gender was experienced and perceived. For example, notions of appropriate behaviour for men have often depended on age. Older men could openly express feelings that would be considered a sign of weakness in younger men. Both Suzanne Morton's and Robert Rutherdale's case studies specifically look at the relationship between particular stages of the life cycle and gender. Morton's contribution, part of a larger study on domestic life in a Halifax working-class suburb during the 1920s, looks at the way old age could differ for women and men. She finds, however, that despite these differences the common vulnerability and dependence of the elderly could overcome important gender distinctions. Rutherdale's article investigates the experience of fathers with young families in a small northern city in British Columbia during the two decades following World War II. Like Sager, he uses oral history to explore some of the emotional dimensions of masculinity, and details how the men he interviewed saw their role as husbands and fathers, and extended notions of parenting into their community. Specifically, he analyzes the relationship between the experiences and practices of husbands and fathers, and the socially prescribed gender ideals that shaped these men's perceptions of the past.

All the essays in the volume open new ways of thinking about gender history and Canadian history. Readers are encouraged to supplement this collection with related studies, for example two other volumes from Copp Clark, *Rethinking Canada: The Promise of Women's History*, and *Canadian Family History*. A Further Reading section at the end of the volume provides a list of selected readings for those who wish to pursue the themes of gender history in greater depth.

section 1

GENDER AND HISTORY

o

GENDER HISTORY AND
HISTORICAL PRACTICE [*]

JOY PARR

○

I remember some years ago sitting waiting for a faculty seminar to begin, when a well-published colleague entered, bemused. In a newly arrived packet of reviews his most recent offering was being described, and to his mind dismissed, as definitive. "What they mean," he muttered, "is that I have laid to rest interest in the topic for at least a generation." We all tittered, but no one was minded to dispute his conclusion.

We each had a repertoire of settled certainties strung out along clear chronologies. These were our stock-in-trade in the lecture hall. We had learned, when called upon by the media or by legal counsel, to be succinct, declaratory, and unambiguous. We understood these strategic artifices of expertise to be companionable and saving necessaries at the lectern, before the camera, in the witness box.[1] But equally we agreed, at least then, that as scholars the "definitive" would remain for us elusive, always at some distance beyond our reach.

We began from certain ordinary old-fashioned premises. As the historical record is never complete, the practice of our craft, no matter how refined, will never allow us entirely to reclaim the past worlds that are the focus of our historical imaginings. It is no mark of good scholarship to claim that the histories we write are definitive, or to write in ways that disguise the limitations of the portraits we render, so that others make false claims to definitiveness on our behalf. Such stances refuse the invitation to revise which as scholars we perpetually are obliged to extend. Scholarship is to open rather than extinguish questions, to discomfit rather than enshrine both settled certainties and the collective practices they sustain. In this we,

[*] Canadian Historical Review 76, 3 (1995): 354–76. Reprinted by permission of University of Toronto Press Incorporated.

in that seminar room, shared a carefully schooled, if thus paradoxical, consensus. Lately, historians' ranks appear to be dividing on these matters. These honourable traditions in the historians' craft have been called into question by senior members of our profession in their responses to the work of a younger generation of scholars in gender history, cultural studies, and the "newest" of the new social history.

The vehemence of the response by older colleagues to this new work and their claims that such studies will be the undoing (to take up only selected recent suggestions) of the nation, or of feminist politics, or of academic freedom, are surprising. As scholars our work has always been with indeterminant qualities rather than solid substance, our published studies a series of interim reports from an ongoing search, crafted to resist closure. Our knowledge is not definitive but, as Walter Benjamin argued in the 1930s, always so much more like "a memory as it flashes up at a moment of danger" than a thorough reclamation of the past "the way it really was."[2] The English historian Carolyn Steedman catches this obligation well: "The writing of history, which does indeed come to conclusions and reach ends . . . actually moves forward through the implicit understanding that *things are not over*, that the story isn't finished, can't ever be completed for some new item of information may alter the account as it has been given. In this way the writing of history represents a distinct cognitive process precisely because it is constructed around the understanding that things are not over, that the story isn't finished: that there is no end." While historians share the stated objective of exhaustiveness, she notes, "they proceed upon the path of refutation by pointing to exceptions and to the possibility of exception. The practice of historical inquiry and historical writing is a recognition of temporariness and impermanence."[3]

The practice of gender history has focused attention on this temporariness and impermanence. Herein lies its greatest contribution, and the source of its most sustained, invested, and determined opposition. For the interpretive possibility it engages, that manliness and womanliness are socially constituted and continually reconstrued in specific historical conjunctures, goes "all the way down" to the body itself,[4] featuring biological knowledge as culturally constructed, drawing interpretations of the natural into the historian's domain, and eroding the ground that once sustained absolute and universal claims for a "human nature" existing transhistorically.

Historians have a long-standing fascination with claims based in nature, with arguments that certain political systems and military organizations were *naturally* superior, that certain classes or races were *born* to rule. It has been an indispensible and honourable part of the historian's work to take human activities presumed eternal, or inevitable, or natural, and to trace the processes by which they have been made and changed through time. This task has included attempts to understand why and how universal and absolute truths have been invoked, how certainty is made out of uncertainty, and to what historical effect. Yet lately this historical inquiry into the construction of the ahistorical, the search to understand how, by whom, and in whose interest some parts of the contemporary are established as beyond temporality, rather than being accepted as integral to the historian's work, has been called corrosive of the historical project, and the historical subject, itself. Highlighting the partialness of our understanding of the past, and the artifices through which certain beliefs and practices have been selected and elevated as absolutes and universals, has been called dangerous.

THE CRITIQUES OF GENDER HISTORY

The ferociousness and the hostility of the response to recent work in gender history by some traditional political and social historians, and by some historians of women, is political, generational, and, at root, epistemological. Historians for some time have dwelt in boundary lands, impelled both by the humanist ancestral memories of our craft to seek out and invoke enduring properties of human nature, and by more recent social science allegiances to chart the social forces that make change through time. Gender history, by historicizing the biological foundations of sexual difference and refusing assertions about universals in human nature more generally, reorders the balance in the epistemology of history between the humanities and the social sciences, and makes life in these boundary lands exponentially more difficult. For if what is human is constructed specifically in time and space, the common interests that we might as scholars have invoked as explanations, whether Canadians' consciousness of themselves as a people,[5] or women's experience of oppression as females,[6] or historians' confidence that they were recovering the past essentially as it was,[7] seem less definitive answers than hexes scaring away important questions.

The political threat that such work has been seen to pose is variously described. Michael Bliss, in his much cited article "Privatizing the Mind: The Sundering of Canadian History, the Sundering of Canada," argues that the new social history is a negative force in national politics. He contends that the attempt to understand why "a unified conception" of Canadian national identity was asserted as transcending the experiences of region, ethnicity, class, family, and gender was part of the undoing of the nation: "the sundering of a sense of Canadian history thus became part and parcel of the sundering of Canadians' consciousness of themselves as a people."[8] By this reasoning, Gail Cuthbert Brandt says that "too much history, or more accurately, too much history of the wrong kind," a history which challenges settled definitions and resists being definitive, which studies the problem, has been taken to be the problem itself.[9]

J.R. Miller, a former editor of the *Canadian Historical Review*, has argued that cultural and feminist studies, cultural and women's history, pose another kind of political threat, a threat to the hard-won protections of academic freedom which many of us (perhaps faintly) hope will guard us as we pursue our unsettling and wilfully inconclusive work. Miller contends that the methodologies of cultural and feminist historians will compromise academic freedom, "the freedom from constraint and retribution that responsible researchers enjoy no matter where their inquiries lead them."

For Miller, the ideas that cultural and feminist historians entertain which cast them outside the circle of responsible researchers, "the infection that new methodologies bring to this essential condition [academic freedom] is found in the implication that there is no single truth that can be uncovered by inquiry."

Miller wants to cleave close to the roots of history in the humanities, to the belief that there is a human condition, absolute, enduring, and universal, which is the proper subject of scholarship in the humanities.[10] He takes as his guide Leopold von Ranke, the nineteenth-century German historian, who asserted that we could recover the past "wie es eigentlich gewesen,"[11] essentially as it was. The younger scholars he calls dangerous turn rather to Ranke's countryman Walter Benjamin, whose 1930s musings in *Illuminations* acknowledge the contingency and partialness of our historical acts of reclamation, that "every image of the past that is not recognized by the present as one of its own concerns threatens to disappear irretrievably."[12]

For Miller it is the elaboration of the social science elements in the historical tradition which poses the threat. "If everything is socially or otherwise humanly constructed," he argues, "then inquiry can never lead to truth," and "the sole justification for academic freedom" as a protection for "free and unfettered investigation" is undermined.[13]

Within women's history, the new methodologies are also seen as a political danger, particularly when such studies place the unitary concept of woman under scrutiny. Joan Hoff, co-editor of the *Journal of Women's History*, has argued that "by highlighting linguistic signs of difference among women," such work destroys any collective concept of women upon which a political movement can be organised,"[14] a position similar to Bliss's characterization of the Canadian case in its linking of the study of difference with the creation of politically disabling dissention. Some feminists have responded to the criticism that interrogating the "solid substance" of the category woman will erode the solid ground on which to found feminist political work by invoking the "Riley paradox": that only by recognizing the diversity among women can effective ties among women be forged.[15] Others, among them Joan Scott, have argued that the study of diversity, rather than being a threat to political work, is an activity in need of, and which merits, political protection: "There can be no democracy worthy of the name that does not entertain criticism, that suppresses disagreement, that refuses to acknowledge difference as inevitably disruptive of consensus, that vilifies the search for new knowledge."[16]

Thus, the critique of gender history, and the newest cultural and social history of which it is a part, is both epistemological (a resistance to the shift in the balance of historians' allegiances away from the humanities and towards the social sciences), and political (a contention that differences are less disabling strategically if they are suppressed rather than expressed). Not incidentally, the critique is also a cry from amidst, and against, a generational transition, as Bliss, Miller, and Hoff acknowledge. Bliss locates himself "as a member of a generation that was privileged to grow up in one of the world's more humane, open and successful societies," one that "had no insecurities about our identity or about Canada as a country."[17] Miller candidly writes of himself as being among historians "in mid-career" and "of a certain age," trained in "the comfortable nineteenth-century intellectual world on which until the past quarter-century academic tradition in the Humanities unquestioningly reposed," a world now shaken by methodologies "that strike at the heart" of that intellectual edifice.[18] Hoff reminds us that she is part of "the pioneer generation of historians of women" that "constitutes the same generation that participated in the formation of the Second Women's Movement."[19] These locations frame the way our colleagues see the world around them, and the historical project we must continue to share, but they are not the only locations from which the struggle to reclaim the past can be launched.

This recent enterprise expands the historian's compass, by broadening the range of concepts and activities understood to be made and changed through time, but is not a threat to "the historian's presumption to authority."[20] We should be intrigued rather than resistant if "race, like gender and the power of the state, turns out to be an indeterminant quality rather than a solid substance, an elusive disguise rather than a fixed identity."[21] The dawning understanding that there is more historical work to be done, that more which had seemed "solid" can be made more intelligible if scrutinized through the historian's lens, is not to be lamented. This desire, as historians, to know more—this suggestion that there are new terrains where historical knowledge can be made—is not, as Miller suggests, "agnostic."[22] Rather than be discomfited, we should agree that the "definitive" must be elusive, that as scholars we are not entitled to be comfortable.[23]

Perhaps our colleagues in preceding generations made their peers uncomfortable when they worked to understand the social processes by which human beliefs in religious freedom and democratic liberty were forged or constructed. Perhaps the historicizing of these truths was once taken as an affront to their worth as ideas, as a reproach to those who wrote their histories. But this is no longer the case. The writing hand has moved on. Surely our forming hypotheses about the historicity of race, gender, and the power of the state are within this tradition, and confirm rather than deny the worth of the historical project, of the historian's work.

The topical space where this generational battle has been engaged has significance. This work is not new, and the unease it causes does not seem to be rooted in the widening of the historical landscape. So long as the cultural and women's historians were off in distant precincts, pushing out the perimeter, all was well. There is something about the return of cultural and women's historians to the metropolis, and the fact that these historians return with theories and methodologies that appear to bind together the study of nationality, race, gender, ethnicity, and the power of the state, which seems to be causing the problem. When insights from cultural and feminist studies make historical the once firmly forged fractures between the political and the social, make historical the once presumed natural markings of national, racial, ethnic, and sexual difference and the truths that sustain hierarchies of power, then alarm bells sound.

BEYOND MASTERY

No reasoned invocations will salve the unease this seeming surfeit of diversity and temporality has caused. Rather, we must find ways to think ourselves into a sense of safety even as we acknowledge that single truths and solid substance are illusory; we must hear into speech differences we wish to deny. In a thoughtful meditation on a related theme, the effect of the search for personal authenticity upon the possibility of political community, the McGill philosopher Charles Taylor argues that the challenge the acknowledgment of difference poses is "to combine in some non-self-stultifying fashion a number of ways of operating," to be "continually recreating a balance between requirements that tend to undercut each other, constantly finding new solutions as old equilibria become stultifying," knowing that "there can never be, in the nature of the case, a definitive solution."[24] Elsa Barkley Brown uses the analogy of African American women's quilt-making, where representations are crafted through asymmetry, to suggest this habit of mind: "It is not merely a question of whether or not we have learned to analyse in particular kinds of ways, or whether people are able to intellectualize about a variety of experiences. It is also about coming to believe in the possibility of a variety of experiences, a variety of ways of understanding the world, a variety of frameworks of operation, without imposing consciously or unconsciously a notion of the norm."[25]

That this variety needs to be acknowledged as existing historically, not only between people who showed similarities but also within individuals who had been definitively classified in their day, calls for a tolerance of ambiguity that presses many of our colleagues' patience to the limit. This notion entails an inherent instability in identities—that being simultaneously a worker, a Baptist, and a father, one is never solely or systematically any of these. The more readily accessible resolution here is to ask what circumstances would bring this man's religious faith to precedence, would make him comport himself essentially as a Baptist. The more vexed query, but the one that helps us to understand more of the landscape before us, remains with the man in the ordinariness of his multiplicity, and attempts to understand him there. Between these two strategies lies a battle "between the impulse and desire to impose order and a tolerance for ambiguity," a division Carol Berkin aptly characterizes as a conflict "between a sense of mastery and the burdens of modesty."[26]

WHY GENDER HISTORY?

Disputes within historical practice, over how much of what is human changes through time (is historically constructed) and how stable and unified are people's perceptions of themselves and the world around them within time, are central to gender history, and account for its existence distinct from women's history. The premise of women's history was that hierarchical social, economic, and political contexts rather than biology, history rather than nature, created woman. This insight, that the characterization "natural" had the power to make specific historical differences seem eternal and unchangeable, had become commonplace among North American historians of women before many on this continent had read Foucault.[27] Early on, studies of the social relationships that had crafted womanliness began to reveal the historical moorings that anchored other distinctions, between the public and the private, between activity counted as inside and outside the market, that had not seemed to be strictly or solely "about women." In time it became apparent that questions framed to be about women alone could entail their answers in their asking. A question posed about "woman" called forth responses selectively. These responses always to some degree isolated woman from the social relationships which created her, and presumed that woman existed in certain ways. "Tell me about woman" always to some degree meant "Tell me about someone who will be recognizable to me as a woman."

Thus, as Mariana Valverde has suggested, women's history was not sufficient, or "self-sufficient, because it [could] fall into the trap of presupposing the object of its inquiry."[28] The self-conscious move towards the study of gender, rather than woman, instead began from the poststructuralist premise that identities were made in relationships. Gender history assumes that masculinity and femininity do not exist in isolation from each other or from contemporary assumptions about, for example, race, ethnicity, or sexuality.[29] Gender history made masculinity and femininity commensurably problematical historically, while insisting that neither could be well understood without companion inquiries into the other hierarchies with which they were mutually entwined.[30]

From this position it followed that gender could not be taken *ex ante* as the primary form of identity, although in certain historical conjunctures it might emerge to be so. Both the character and the precedence of gender relations need to be put as historical questions. As gender history is practised, "in historical context, the social positions women and men occupy are specified in multidimensional terms, and femininity and masculinity are not cultural universals but vary with other forms of power and markers of difference."[31] This emphasis on social positions as multidimensional and specific rather than universal or totalizing is at the core of poststructuralist theory.[32] In historical studies, these understandings about the simultaneity and heterogeneity of identities were nurtured within a monographic research tradition that emphasizes context, contingency, and specificity. Thus, analyses in gender history and poststructuralist theory have proceeded together, "if not always hand-in-hand."[33]

EXPERIENCE

The first sunderings of the confines that limited history to the doings and beings of men in parliament and men in the news were tied closely to the recognition that many people's experience of the past was not well understood by analogy with the experience of newsmakers and parliamentarians.

In important ways the experience of women was not like the experience of men, the experience of first nations was not like the experience of colonizers, the experience of workers was not like that of bosses, the experience of those who lived outside the "happy bonds of matrimony" was not like those so bound. "Reclaiming" these experiences became a central part of the social historian's work. Experience became the foundation on which much historical inquiry of the 1970s and 1980s was lodged, the place from which to begin to understand what difference was and how it infused hierarchies of power.

And yet the thorny question remained: Among all the sensations which passed before the eye and the ear, which caused the mind and the body pleasure and pain, why were some remarked and some suppressed? What sorted these sensations into those recalled and those repressed? What made some stick in the mind and become defining of the moment, while others remained outside ken? What made some parts of experience remarkable and left others unmarked, as fleeting distinctions from which no difference was consciously or unconsciously distilled?

Historical portraits of experience told us much, but unmistakably these *were* portraits. They were rendered in the style of their time, products of hierarchically ordered understandings rather than pristine data against which those understandings could be definitively tested. They were interpretations, reclamations of sensations which first had been organized and then claimed as experience. Experiences were claims, not irrefutable foundations upon which claims could be lodged. Like the questions about women which only invoked answers that recognized the concept of woman, experiences were framed from elements the contemporary mind recognized. The eye "only let in" what it "had been taught to see."[34]

Experience was not foundational or originary. It did not come from "outside the loop." Meaning preceded experience, and people had experiences, sorted and selectively registered sensations, through learned systems of meaning. Reclaiming experience was a key part of the historical project, but a work which was itself *not finished*. The forging of an experience was itself an outcome of social processes that made and hierarchically organized meanings. Experience was "not the origin of our explanation, but that which we want to explain."[35]

DISCOURSE

Experiences are formed through webs of connected meanings. They are organized by understandings about what parts of life have influence on one another and what parts are elements from some other story. They are made of combinations known in advance to be fitting or anomalous, fortuitous or forbidden. Experience, this is to say, is formed through discourses. Experiences are not made *by* discourses, but discourses are the medium through which experiences are comprehensible. The study of discourses is the study of how events are made sensible. It is through these connections to "social institutions, aesthetic productions, political systems, popular cultures, economic structures," to ideological belief systems and the material circumstances of life, that experiences come to life.[36] Experience is "the linguistically shaped process of weighing and assigning meaning to events as they happen."[37] Thus the study of the elements from which experience is constituted is not a diversion from the analysis of power, but a way to understand how power works.

The analysis of discourses can tell us much that is useful about how power works. It can also tell us how power is dismantled, how hierarchies are subverted. Evelyn Brooks Higginbotham makes this case well in her discussion of "African-American Women's History and the Metalanguage of Race." She notes that racial meanings were never internalized by Blacks and whites in an identical way. The language of race was "double voiced" and was made an instrument for change. Drawing upon Bakhtin she argues: "The word in language is half someone else's. It becomes "one's" own when the speaker populates it with his [or her] own intention, his [or her] own accent, when he [or she] appropriates the word, adapting it to his [or her] own own semantic and expressive intention." Thus did Blacks take race and empower its language with their own meaning and intent.[38] Similarly, as Judith Walkowitz has shown in her study of narratives of sexual danger in late Victorian London, although women were "bound imaginatively by a limited cultural repertoire, forced to reshape cultural meanings within certain parameters," what was plausible and possible looked different from different cultural and social settings. Crusading journalists and women reformers could disassemble and refeature their circumstances, and thus mobilize actions, "even if the outcomes of their actions were not always or only what they had intended."[39] So, too, the German women workers Kathleen Canning has studied, "armed with the consciousness of their multiple subject positions as workers, wives and mothers, succeeded in contesting the terms of the discourses that defined them."[40]

Because people historically have existed severally, holding within themselves different and contending conceptions of their place in the world, experience is formed dialectically, as the meanings made from these several parts collide.[41] Human life, as Charles Taylor argues, is "fundamentally *dialogical*," both individual and social: "We become full human agents, capable of understanding ourselves, and hence defining an identity, through our acquisition of rich human languages of expression. . . . It's not just that we learn the languages in dialogue and then can go on to use them for our own purposes on our own." But "important issues such as the definition of our identity," we frame "always in dialogue with, sometimes in struggle against, the identities our significant others want to recognise in us."[42] The analysis of the discourses through which experience is construed must be simultaneously, as Joan Sangster shows in her study of women's pardon tales before Peterborough magistrate's court, about how "certain discourses came to dominate precisely because they reflected class and patriarchal power," and about the "inventive tactics and rebellious justifications" through which the hierarchies these discourses sustained might be undermined.[43]

MASCULINITY

The study of masculinity through poststructuralist techniques has raised particular concerns among feminists. Bliss and Miller worried that the nation and the power of the state might dissolve as their unassailable, ahistorical foundations were portrayed as contingent and historical. Similarly, feminists have worried that poststructuralism might perform "a vanishing trick on questions of agency and responsibility"[44] in sexual politics, so fragmenting masculine power that it becomes elusive to strategy and apparently politically benign.[45]

The late gestation of studies of masculinity within gender history, and the early emphasis within these studies on the diversity among men rather than the privileges of dominance shared by men, contributed to these concerns. For a decade, research into the historical construction of woman proceeded apace, and man remained outside. This differential feminist focus on the temporality of woman inadvertently enhanced the conceptual capacity of man to stand for all that was enduringly human.[46]

Of the many ways to account for this delay, two seem most noteworthy. First, the world of men had for so long been the principal, almost exclusive, subject of historical inquiry that it seemed strange to claim renewed priority for this area of study, to feature it as neglected or ignored. Second, while women were drawn to study the history of women as a way to understand their legacy of subordination and to alter their contemporary condition, what men might gain by undoing the artifices that sustained masculine privilege as ordinary, fair, or unquestionable was more elusive.[47]

Masculinity had been naturalized so effectively that it seemed without names of its own. The words to describe its properties always seemed to attach more readily to something else, to the artisan's skill, the colonial administrator's burden, the pastor's wisdom, or the entrepreneur's acumen. As Steven Maynard has noted, even fine recent Canadian histories of working men he considers, Craig Heron's *Working in Steel* and Ian Radforth's *Bushworkers and Bosses*, analyse how men's identities were made by their class position and through the labour process, with only "an obligatory gesture toward the study of gender." These gestures do not entrain an analytical frame through which to track masculinity as a historically constitutive part of these working men's identities, but rather have the contrary effect, of invoking "a very narrow and essentialist notion of masculinity" that makes their gender identities seem "natural or given."[48] Maynard regrets that Heron and Radforth had not noted the pervasiveness of turn-of-the-century appeals to manliness, and argues for "a crisis approach" that would recognize that as industrial capitalism unfolded, "it not only altered class relations, but also shifted gender relations, precipitating a crisis in masculinity."[49] The reservation itself is well placed, but the raising of a "crisis" alert each time masculinity is found to be mutable or to exist in mutuality with other parts of the social life, when "change" or "response" might seem adequately to serve as descriptors, shows how ordinary and common-sensical the fixity of masculinity has remained even among those who have undertaken its critical study.

In Canada the early emphasis in historical and ethnographic accounts of masculinity on the diversity among men, rather than the privileges of dominance shared by men, may have been partly methodological in origin. The three works of this type frequently cited, Mark Rosenfeld's "She was a hard life," Thomas Dunk's *It's a Working Man's Town*, and my own *Gender of Breadwinners*, rely centrally for their evidence on some mix of oral history and participant observation. Rosenfeld was interested in marital relationships, but interviewed married couples together.[50] Dunk in some measure rejoined a group of chums from his young manhood in a town where they all continued to live and work, and where his own class privileges were accumulating while the lot of his friends remained more stable. As a younger women mindful of the respect older men, especially craftsmen, were due, I interviewed them in a period when their town was weathering calamitous economic transitions and the problems of work and community were at the fore of everyone's mind. In none of these settings were men likely to be candid about the ways they handled threats to their standing as "the man of the house"; in each case, our distinctiveness from the men whose stories we heard may have amplified our perceptions of their distinctiveness as men.

But in the international literature on masculinity, these tendencies, to privilege distinctiveness among men and to look away from dominance, are also apparent, which suggests that some more complex patterns are also at work. Michael Roper and John Tosh, and also David Morgan, in examining the British case, argue that these tendencies arise from the connections between histories of masculinity and contemporary sexual politics. Historians of masculinity usually have been feminist men who, through understandings of the personal as political, have come to see masculinity as a deformation of their "true self." This has made the reformation of masculine identity into an intensely personal struggle to acknowledge guilt and complicity and to make a commitment to change. It has also given rise to an "over-socialised model of man,"[51] where gender is recognized "more as an oppressive social structure 'out there' than as a set of relations which is reproduced psychically and socially in daily living,"[52] a feature of a patriarchy that is both "everywhere and nowhere."[53] In both Britain and the United States, where published studies in the history of masculinity are more numerous than in Canada, attention has been focused on the prescriptive processes by which masculine identities were inculcated, largely in institutional settings, private schools, voluntary organizations, and places of work, where women were, at least physically, largely absent.[54] In these situations, becoming a man could seem to be a personal journey, an individual accomplishment achieved in solidarity with some men, and in distinction from others, but relatively abstracted from relations with women. In one sense, then, this pattern in histories of masculinity, the emphasis on the heterogeneity of manliness and men's individual distinctiveness one from another, should not surprise us. Our conventional meaning for the word "masculinity," formed within the emerging concept of the self in Early Modern Europe, is "a quality of an individual," a personal rather than a social attribute.[55] And in the rising North Atlantic democracies of the modern period, while differences in men's political effectiveness might be attributed to differences in their propertied wealth, education, or talent, women were more uniformly (if not entirely) cast outside politics on the basis of their gender.[56]

Two recent collections of essays on the history of masculinity in Britain and the United States, Mark Carnes and Clyde Griffen's *Meanings for Manhood* (1990) and Michael Roper and John Tosh's *Manful Assertions* (1991), work against these individualistic analyses of men autonomous from women. They aim to understand differences in masculinity between men and across time in ways that make the social influence on individual responses plain, and an individual's implication in social hierarchies apparent. Reacting against two unities, that man stands for all that is universally human and that man is essentially oppressive, they report on the "telling evidence of the historical diversity of masculinity,"[57] their emphasis in the investigation of masculinity being "on identifying the variety of adaptations for different social groups in different settings."[58]

The readiness with which masculinity has fractured into heterogeneity, when historians' acknowledgement of heterogeneity within femininity was both wary and nettlesome, has invoked comment. Nancy Cott, in a sense, sees this as a benefit historians of masculinity have accrued from their late start; they learned from historians of women how to avoid falsely universalizing analyses of gender. But she notes as well that, "where historians of women may be predisposed to assume that gender was the significant determinant of whatever they investigate, in men's history other, more familiar, competing categories—politics, race, region and class, to name just a few—crowd the frame of reference in any consideration of motivation or causation." Cott welcomes this circumstance, arguing that the long-acknowledged precedence of these other aspects of identity "cross-cutting the category of male gender induce a healthy, constructive skepticism," forcing historians to be specific about which men in which historical circumstances are the focus of their critique.[59]

Other commentators have been more guarded. If, historically, naming has been a privilege of power, the traits of gender identity being more often featured as socially inscribed upon women and individually achieved by men, it is not surprising that, historically, men more readily acknowledged their differences or that these differences have been more accessible to study by historians. Morgan, in a query which may seem to echo Joan Hoff and Michael Bliss, wonders: "In the ever-proliferating multiplication of masculinities, is there a danger of losing a sense of dominance, of patriarchy and of control?" His reply, like that of Lynne Segal, is to note a regularity within these diversities in masculinities,[60] that "men's relative power, authority, and status compared to women . . . seem to stay the same." Thus the question becomes: What is it about men *"which makes them different from women in ways that confirm privilege, power and authority?"*[61] Segal argues that rather than equating a unitary masculinity with male dominance, we are better to attend to the ways in which the "varieties of masculinity" find similar superordinant positions in many different kinds of social relationships,[62] to consider whether masculinity might be a trait of dominance rather than dominance a trait of masculinity. This would certainly be a way to be sure that studies of the readily documented heterogeneity within masculinity not lose sight of male dominance, but the strategy risks limiting study to hegemonic masculinities and definitionally excluding masculinities subordinated in their relationships to other masculinities. As Bob Connell suggests in his sketch "The Big Picture: Masculinities in Recent World History," the history of gender relations must include studies of how hegemonic masculinities emerge, and also of the ways in which some masculinities are marginalized among the powerful. Some masculinities historically have been subordinated by their association with subordinated class and race identities, even as men occupied dominant positions within these groups.[63] It is probably as important to leave open the possibility that some forms of masculinity have not been defined by their difference from femininities, but by their difference from other masculinities, that, as in the case of the Norrland woodsworkers Ella Johansson has studied, gender may be more a relationship of complementarity and similarity than of difference.[64]

GENDER HISTORY AND KEATS'S NEGATIVE CAPABILITY

The poet John Keats recommended "not knowing" as a habit of mind through which to learn. This stance, the willingness to wait, attentive and deliberating, seeking but not foreclosing the search for an answer, he called negative capability.[65] Gender history is practised from this stance, and has tended and is intended to make the question "What is *this* about?" less constrained in the asking. It has offered a healthy reminder that the discursive field of which the "this" is a part is best not assumed in the question, that these constituting elements need rather to be located and their influence appraised. It is our task "to brush history against the grain."[66] From the moment the archives boxes are opened, this habit of mind alerts the researcher to be self-checking: "What am I expecting?" "What has my eye been taught to see?" "What is here, that my specification of the problem might lead me to dismiss?"

Valverde's study of the Dionne quintuplets is a clear example of this process in play. Reflexively, the story of state intervention in the lives of these five baby girls born in the 1930s appears to be about the "regulation of children and motherhood in the context of an emerging welfare state." Yet the diction in the provincial guardianship documents so consistently figured them as "a nationally owned resource" that their place in another story became starkly apparent to one open to see it thus. Much of government decision-making, which seemed peculiar as child welfare policy in a time when self-help was the watchword of a state in desperate fiscal crisis, made sense if the quints were understood less as children in need of help than as children whom tourists would spend their way over long distances through the province to see.[67]

If stories might not be the ones conventional categories most readily seemed to frame, through time the logic that organized a tale also might change. This is what Sylvie Murray, in an article on the women's auxiliaries of the International Association of Machinists, urges us to consider. Through their early years, the auxiliaries had been valued and necessary supports for the union's struggles. This women's work was tied centrally to the class struggles for recognition and fair compensation in which the men of their households were also engaged. After the Second World War, the women's focus changed to community building and welfare work, a change that, in terms of the priorities of the 1930s, could well be construed as a retreat from class politics into the sheltering anonymity of the nuclear family. Yet to define the auxiliaries by what they were not—that they were no longer centrally engaged in running soup kitchens during strikes or augmenting strike funds—is to miss what they were. The work in recreational organizations and the community chest, where cross-class alliances were more notable, may not have been a wilful and wistful blurring of class differences, but a recognition of where in the 1950s working-class interests most urgently needed to be represented.[68]

Much of this emphasis within gender history on the different meanings that may attach to practices and regulations which show ostensible similarities between places and across time may seem indistinguishable from long-accepted contextualizing practices within the historian's craft. And indeed it is so. Yet after three decades in which the influence of social science has led historians increasingly to seek out patterned regularities and to immobilize them as structures, to think cross-culturally in ways that rinse out local colour, the renewed attention to specificity and to the implications of the ornery exceptions is not misplaced.

Recent studies of the changing regulation of married women's property are a telling case in point. The establishment of separate marital property in the nineteenth century was an achievement along the road to attaining separate personhood for female citizens. Yet in mid-nineteenth century Ontario, Lykke de la Cour and her colleagues suggest, a legal system "highly reluctant to give married women any autonomy from their husbands" bowed to the necessity of separate property "when class relations developed to the point at which creditors needed the legal ability to sue women running small businesses."[69] By the late nineteenth century, Peter Baskerville's closely textured study of "enterprising" women in Victoria and Vancouver shows separate property facilitating entrepreneurial activity, home-based activity which in practice called the ideology of separate spheres into question.[70] Bettina Bradbury, Peter Gossage, Evelyn Kolish, and Alan Stewart, after noting that the choice of separate property became more common in bourgeois marriage in the same decade in nineteenth-century Quebec when propertied women were losing the franchise, suggest that the instrument was chosen more to secret husbands' assets from the reach of creditors than to secure women's rights within marriage. Given the slow progress of the woman movement later in Quebec, they are led to wonder whether the privatization of this choice, far from being an advantage, "may have held back legal change in this area until well into the twentieth century."[71]

Increasingly, research in gender history has come to include studies in public policy and of policy-makers. Rather than framing questions that would observe and thus sustain the divisions between the home and the legislature, the voluntary and the professional, practice and policy, gender historians have sought out analytical orientations that would "bridge the categories of the private and the public."[72] These studies of the "meaning of gender as power," as Roper and Tosh argue, offer striking potential "for convergence with the interests of traditional historians."[73]

It has become possible to "investigate how sexual and moral questions became part of the discourse of economic decline, development and nation building," to see "changes, both real and imagined, in gender and sexual relations" as a dimension of nation building.[74] These bridges between the public and the private were most readily apparent to those studying maternal welfare policies. Both in countries of emigration, where declining population might be framed as a question of national survival,[75] and in more recently settled regions where dependent mothers and children unsettled cherished national-building notions of a self-sufficient citizenry,[76] family policies by definition transgressed the divisions between the state and the home. But gendered assumptions about entitlement to waged labour, as studies by Ruth Roach Pierson and Ann Porter have shown, so centrally informed the planning and implementation of unemployment policy that these programs, too, confound assumptions about a homogeneous citizenry equally entitled before the state.[77] It is also possible to track the ways in which gendered hierarchies of strategic precedence influenced economic policy, privileging certain kinds of consumption through import and exchange controls and access to credit to the derogation of others, and lending heavy moral force to a persistently problematic division between consumption and production.[78] Increasingly, the discourses which classify the purchase of a washing machine as consumption and the purchase of a smoke stack scrubber as investment, which measure sales of composters among quixotic retail activities and of home computers within the deliberate domain of the wholesaler, have become part of the analysis of how the economy has and has not worked.

CONCLUSION

The implications of gender history for historical practice are not resolved. This, too, is a story that *is not finished*. The ways in which gender history makes a departure at the level of evidence and analysis are clear enough. This is work that begins by acknowledging diversity and instability rather than searching out unity and solidity. The recognition that gender was made by history rather than nature began a cascade of temporality. If gender was made in circumstance, it was likely to vary within time as well as across time, for the circumstances that framed gender were not always the same, and did not always form gender alone.

Thus were identities in fact severalties, multiple, evokable, scrutable, but settled in contingency rather than certainty. Knowing this meant not "knowing what was," but knowing what was brought to the fore and forced into congruence, both seeking the circumstances which made this precedence and symmetry plausible and reckoning the contradictions which could be its undoing. This knowing is less agnostic than pantheistic, seeking explanation by inclusion rather than excision. And like all historical knowledge, this knowing is interim, expectant, augmentable, recombinant.

What is not so clear is how this knowing will affect how we write. Until now, historians' acknowledgement that the story *was not finished* has in practice been deferred, made a feature of the ever elusive last instance, certain presently to be compromised by some exigency. Always there has been the degree, the job, the contract, the loss of appetite or will, to occasion closure, to impel the forging of some seamless illusion from the happily fragmentary. Is this artifice to be resilient, this persistent refeaturing of unruly elements we know into the lean clear line we tell? Are we to embrace these definitive fictions as a saving secret of our craft? Or is it possible that once we know that the woman we wish to know cannot be featured by one name alone, we will seek instead for a way to go to her and to tell her story there?

NOTES

1. On this complexity, in the case of expert witness testimony in women's history, see Ruth Milkman, "Women's History and the Sears Case," *Feminist Studies* 12 (1986): 375–400; "Women's History Goes on Trial: EEOC v. Sears, Roebuck and Company," *Signs* 11 (1986): 751–79; Alice Kessler-Harris, "Equal Employment Opportunity Commission v. Sears, Roebuck and Company: A Personal Account," *Radical History Review* 35 (1986): 57–79; Joan Scott, "Deconstructing Equality versus Difference: Or, the Uses of Poststructuralist Theory for Feminism," *Feminist Studies* 14 (1988): 33–50.

2. Walter Benjamin, "Theses on the Philosophy of History," in *Illuminations*, ed. Hannah Arendt, trans. Harry Zohn (New York: Schocken, 1969), 255.

3. Carolyn Steedman, *"La théorie qui n'en est pas une*; or Why Clio Doesn't Care," in Ann-Louise Shapiro, *Feminists Revision History* (New Brunswick: Rutgers, 1994), 91, 92.

4. Linda Nicholson, "Interpreting Gender," *Signs* 20 (1994): 83.

5. Michael Bliss, "Privatizing the Mind: The Sundering of Canadian History, the Sundering of Canada," *Journal of Canadian Studies* 26 (1991): 14.

6. Joan Hoff, "Gender as a Postmodern Category of Paralysis," *Women's History Review* 3 (1994): 158.

7. J.R. Miller, "'I can only tell what I know': Shifting Notions of Historical Understanding in the 1990s," presentation to the Authority and Interpretation Conference, University of Saskatchewan, 19 March 1994, 7.

8. Bliss, "Privatizing the Mind," 15. This article had its origins in the Creighton Centennial Lecture delivered during the 100th anniversary celebrations of the University of Toronto history department.

9. Gail Cuthbert Brandt, "National Unity and the Politics of Political History," *Journal of the Canadian Historical Association* 1992, 5. See also Ruth Roach Pierson, "Colonisation and Canadian Women's History," *Journal of Women's History* 4 (1992): 147, for a portrait of the context in which this debate arose.

10. Miller, "I can only tell," 2, 22.

11. Ibid., 2, 7, 8.

12. Benjamin, "Theses on the Philosophy of History," 255.

13. Miller, "I can only tell," 23.

14. Joan Hoff-Wilson, "The Pernicious Effects of Poststructuralism on

Women's History," *Chronicle of Higher Education*, 20 October 1993, 21–22. I am grateful to my colleague Jack Blaney for drawing this article to my attention. See also Sonya O. Rose, "Gender History/Women's History: Is Feminist Scholarship Losing Its Critical Edge?" *Journal of Women's History* 5 (1993): 89–101.

15. Denise Riley, *"Am I That Name?" Feminism and the Category of 'Women' in History* (Minneapolis: University of Minnesota Press, 1988), 4, 98.

16. Joan Scott, "The Campaign against Political Correctness: What's Really at Stake," *Radical History Review* 54 (1992): 66. I am grateful to Christina Simmons for this reference.

17. Bliss, "Privatizing the Mind," 8, 16–17.

18. Miller, "I can only tell," 1, 3.

19. Hoff, "Gender as a Postmodern Category of Paralysis," 161.

20. Miller, "I can only tell," 7.

21. Ibid., 8.

22. Ibid., 7, 9.

23. On the question of entitlement to comfort, I draw upon an intervention by Margaret Conrad during the Creating a More Inclusive History session at the Teaching Women's History conference, Trent University, August 1993.

24. Charles Taylor, *The Malaise of Modernity* (Concord, ON: House of Anansi 1991), 50, 52, 74, 110, 111.

25. Elsa Barkley Brown, "African-American Women's Quilting: A Framework for Conceptualising and Teaching African-American Women's History," *Signs* 14 (1989): 921, 929.

26. Leora Auslander, "Feminist Theory and Social History: Explorations in the Politics of Identity," *Radical History Review* 54 (1992): 175; Joy Parr, *The Gender of Breadwinners: Women, Men, and Change in Two Industrial Towns, 1880–1950* (Toronto: University of Toronto Press, 1990), 245; Elsa Barkley Brown, "Womanist Consciousness: Maggie Lena Walker and the Independent Order of Saint Luke," *Signs* 14 (1989): 631–32; Carol Berkin, "'Dangerous Courtesies': Assault on Women's History," *Chronicle of Higher Education* 11 December 1991, A44.

27. Kathleen Canning, "Feminist History after the Linguistic Turn: Historicizing Discourse and Experience," *Signs* 19 (1994): 370.

28. Mariana Valverde, "Comment," *Journal of Women's History* 5 (1993): 124.

29. Lykke de la Cour, Cecilia Morgan, and Mariana Valverde, "Gender Regulation and State Formation in Nineteenth-Century Canada," in Allan Greer and Ian Radforth, *Colonial Leviathan: State Formation in Nineteenth-Century Canada* (Toronto: University of Toronto Press, 1992), 165.

30. Ava Baron, "On Looking at Men: Masculinity and the Making of a Gendered Working-Class History," in Shapiro, *Feminists Revision History*, 149, 153.

31. Editorial, *Gender and History* 6 (April 1994): 3.

32. Chris Weedon, *Feminist Practice and Poststructuralist Theory* (Oxford: Basil Blackwell, 1987), 19–42.

33. Canning, "Feminist History after the Linguistic Turn," 371.

34. Minnie Bruce Pratt, "Identity: Skin Blood Heart," in her *Rebellion: Essays 1980–1991* (Ithaca: Firebrand, 1991), 34. I am grateful to Barbara Herbert of Boston City Hospital for urging me to read and reread this text.

35. This discussion draws upon Joan Scott, "The Evidence of Experience," *Critical Inquiry* (1991): 773–97, especially 785, 787, 793–97; Ruth Roach Pierson, "Experience, Difference, Dominance and Voice in the Writing of Canadian Women's History," in Karen Offen, Ruth Roach Pierson, and Jane Rendall, *Writing Women's History* (Bloomington: Indiana University Press, 1991), 79–106; and Joy Parr, "The New Social History—

Twenty Years On," in *Labouring Children: British Immigrant Apprentices to Canada, 1869–1924*, 2nd ed. (Toronto: University of Toronto Press, 1994). See also Scott, "The Campaign against Political Correctness," 72, 74. Miller's cry against "the experiential emphasis of feminist approaches" seems simultaneously to acknowledge and to refuse the feminist critique of experience; "I can only tell," 13, 14. The last quote is from Scott, "Evidence," 797.

36. Louise M. Newman, "Critical Theory and the History of Women: What's at Stake in Deconstructing Women's History," *Journal of Women's History* 2 (1991): 62.

37. William Sewell, "Gender, History and Deconstruction: Joan Wallach Scott's *Gender and the Politics of History*," CSST Working Paper, no. 34, cited in Canning, "Feminist History after the Linguistic Turn," 376.

38. Evelyn Brooks Higginbotham, "African-American Women's History and the Metalanguage of Race," *Signs* 17 (1992): 267.

39. Judith Walkowitz, *City of Dreadful Delight: Narratives of Sexual Danger in Late-Victorian London* (Chicago: University of Chicago Press, 1992), 9–10.

40. Canning, "Feminist History after the Linguistic Turn," 384.

41. Leora Auslander, "Feminist Theory and Social History," 175, on the dialectic of epistemic breaks.

42. Taylor, *Malaise of Modernity*, 33.

43. Joan Sangster, "'Pardon Tales' from Magistrate's Court: Women, Crime, and the Court in Peterborough County," *Canadian Historical Review* 74 (1993): 196, 197.

44. Frank Mort, "Crisis Points: Masculinity in History and Social Theory," *Gender and History* 6 (1994): 128.

45. Those who see discourse analysis as displacing the study of ideology, rather than an inquiry that includes ideology among its constituting

parts, share similar concerns. For example, see Joan Sangster, "The Softball Solution: Female Workers, Male Managers and the Operation of Paternalism at Westclox, 1923–60," *Labour/Le Travail* 32 (1993): 172, 198.

46. For the influence of this chronological difference on working-class history, see Baron, "On looking at Men," 149–53.

47. David Morgan, *Discovering Men* (London: Routledge, 1992), 29.

48. Steven Maynard, "Rough Work and Rugged Men: The Social Construction of Masculinity in Working-Class History," *Labour/Le Travail* 23 (1989): 159, 161, 166.

49. Ibid., 159.

50. Mark Rosenfeld, "'She was a hard life': Work, Family, Community, Politics and Ideology in the Railway Ward of a Central Ontario Town" (PhD dissertation, York University 1990); Thomas Dunk, *It's a Working Man's Town: Male Working-Class Culture in Northwestern Ontario* (Montreal and Kingston: McGill-Queen's University Press, 1991), Parr, *Gender of Breadwinners*.

51. Morgan, *Discovering Men*, 39.

52. Michael Roper and John Tosh, "Historians and the Politics of Masculinity," in their *Manful Assertions* (London: Routledge, 1991), 6.

53. Morgan, *Discovering Men*, 39.

54. Roper and Tosh, *Manful Assertions*, 3; Clyde Griffen, "Reconstructing Masculinity from the Evangelical Revival to the Waning of Progressivism," in Mark C. Carnes and Clyde Griffen, *Meanings for Manhood* (Chicago: University of Chicago Press, 1990), 184.

55. R.W. Connell, "The Big Picture: Masculinities in Recent World History," *Theory and Society* 22 (1993): 606.

56. Thanks to Ruth Roach Pierson for elaborating the relevance of this point. She directed my attention to Michele Le Doeuff, "Pierre Rousel's

Chiasmas: From Imaginary Knowledge to Learned Imagination," *Ideology and Consciousness* 9 (1982/3): 39–70. Recent writing by Linda Kerber supports this same contention. See her "'I have don . . . much to carry on the warr": Women and the Shaping of Republican Ideology after the American Revolution," *Journal of Women's History* 1, (1990): 231–43; "The Paradox of Women's Citizenship in the Early Republic: The Case of Martin vs Massachusetts, 1805," *American Historical Review* 97 (1992): 349–78; and "Women and Individualism in American History," *Massachusetts Review* 20 (1989): 589–609.

57. Roper and Tosh, "Historians and the Politics of Masculinity," 1.

58. Griffen, "Reconstructing Masculinity," 184.

59. Nancy Cott, "On Men's History and Women's History," in Carnes and Griffen, *Meanings for Manhood*, 206.

60. Morgan, *Discovering Men*, 46.

61. Lynne Segal, "Changing Men: Masculinities in Context," *Theory and Society* 22 (1993): 626.

62. Ibid., 635, 638.

63. Connell, "The Big Picture," 610–12.

64. Ella Johansson, "Beautiful Men, Fine Women and Good Workpeople: Gender and Skill in Northern Sweden, 1850–1950," *Gender and History* 1 (1989): 200–12, and Cynthia Cockburn, "Forum: Formations of Masculinity," ibid., 162.

65. John Keats, *Letters*, ed. Maurice Buxton Forman (London, 1935), 71–72.

66. Benjamin: "Theses on the Philosophy of History," 257.

67. Mariana Valverde, "Representing Childhood: The Multiple Fathers of the Dionne Quintuplets," in Carol Smart, *Regulating Womanhood* (London: Routledge, 1992), 120–21, 143.

68. Sylvie Murray, "Quand les ménagères se font militantes: La Ligue auxiliaire de l'Association internationale des machinists, 1905–80," *Labour/Le Travail* 29 (1992): 182–83.

69. de la Cour, Morgan, and Valverde, "Gender Regulation," 168.

70. Peter Baskerville, "'She Has Already Hinted at Board': Enterprising Urban Women in British Columbia, 1863–96," *Histoire sociale/Social History* 26 (1993): 224–26.

71. Bettina Bradbury, Peter Gossage, Evelyn Kolish, and Alan Stewart, "Property and Marriage: The Law and the Practice in Early Nineteenth Century Montreal," *Histoire sociale/Social History* (1993): 13, 35.

72. Cott, "On Men's History and Women's History," 208.

73. Roper and Rosh, "Historians and the Politics of Masculinity," 8.

74. Karen Dubinsky, *Improper Advances: Rape and Heterosexual Conflict in Ontario, 1889–1929* (Chicago: University of Chicago Press, 1993), 145.

75. Anna Davin, "Imperialism and Motherhood," *History Workshop Journal* 5 (1978): 9–66; Denise Riley, "The Free Mothers: Pronatalism and Working Women in Industry at the End of the War," ibid., 11 (1981): 59–119; Yvonne Hirdman, *Att Lagga Livet Till Ratta—studier i svensk folkemspolitik* (Stockholm: Carlssons, 1989), in an abridged version in English as "Utopia in the Home," *International Journal of Political Economy* (1992).

76. Marilyn Lake, "The Independence of Women and the Brotherhood of Man: Debates in the Labour Movement over Equal Pay and Motherhood Endowment in the 1920s," *Labour History* 63 (1992): 1–24; Nancy Fraser and Linda Gordon, "A Genealogy of *Dependency*: Tracing a Keyword in the U.S. Welfare State," *Signs* 19 (1994): 309–36; Margaret Hillyard Little, "The Regulation of Ontario Single Mothers during the 'Dirty' Thirties," paper presented to the Canadian Historical Association Annual Meeting, Charlottetown, 1992; Suzanne Morton, "Women on Their Own: Single Mothers in

Working-Class Halifax in the 1920s," *Acadiensis* 21 (1992): 90–107.

77. Ruth Roach Pierson, "Gender and Unemployment Insurance in Canada 1934–40," *Labour/Le Travail* 25 (1990): 77–104; Ann Porter, "Women and Income Security in the Post-War Period: The Case of Unemployment Insurance, 1945–1962," ibid., 31 (1993): 111–44.

78. Joy Parr, "Women and Consumer Policies in Postwar Canada and Sweden," unpublished paper, Schlesinger Library Anniversary Conference, Radcliffe College, 6 March 1994; Avner Offer and Sue Bowden, "Gratification and Prudence: The United States and Britain, 1945–1989," unpublished paper, Rutgers Center for Historical Analysis, 4 November 1991.

section

2

REPRESENTATIONS
OF FIRST NATIONS

○

CATEGORIES AND TERRAINS OF EXCLUSION: CONSTRUCTING THE "INDIAN WOMAN" IN THE EARLY SETTLEMENT ERA IN WESTERN CANADA ◊

SARAH CARTER

○

In 1884 Mary E. Inderwick wrote to her Ontario family from the ranch near Pincher Creek, Alberta, where she had lived with her new husband for six months.[1] The letter provides a perspective on the stratifications of race, gender, and class that were forming as the Euro-Canadian enclave grew in the district of Alberta. Mary Inderwick lamented that it was a lonely life, as she was twenty-two miles from any other women, and she even offered to help some of the men near them to "get their shacks done up if only they will go east and marry some really nice girls." She did not consider the companionship of women such as "the squaw who is the nominal wife of a white man near us," and she had dismissed her maid, who had become discontented with her position as a servant. Inderwick had disapproved of a ball at the North-West Mounted Police (NWMP) barracks at Fort Macleod, despite the fact that it was "the first Ball to which the squaws were not allowed to go, but there were several half breeds." Commenting on the Aboriginal population that still greatly outnumbered the new arrivals, Inderwick wrote that they should have been "isolated in the mountains," rather than settled on nearby reserves, and that the sooner they became extinct the better for themselves and the country.

At the time of Mary Inderwick's arrival in the West the consolidation of Canada's rule was not yet secure. The Metis resistance of 1885 fed fears of a

◊ Reprinted courtesy of *Great Plains Quarterly* 13 (Summer 1993): 147–61.

larger uprising, and an uncertain economic climate threatened the promise of a prosperous West. There was a sharpening of racial boundaries and categories in the 1880s and an intensification of discrimination in the Canadian West. The arrival of women immigrants like Mary Inderwick after the Canadian Pacific Railway was completed through Alberta in 1883 coincided with other developments such as the railway itself, the treaties, and the development of ranching and farming that were to stabilize the new order and allow the recreation of Euro-Canadian institutions and society. The women did not introduce notions of spatial and social segregation, but their presence helped to justify policies already in motion that segregated the new community from indigenous contacts.[2] The Canadian state adopted increasingly segregationist policies toward the Aboriginal people of the West, and central to these policies were images of Aboriginal women as dissolute, dangerous, and sinister.

From the earliest years that people were settled on reserves in western Canada, Canadian government administrators and statesmen, as well as the national press, promoted a cluster of negative images of Aboriginal women. Those in power used these images to explain conditions of poverty and ill-health on reserves. The failure of agriculture on reserves was attributed to the incapacity of Aboriginal men to become other than hunters, warriors, and nomads.[3] Responsibility for a host of other problems, including the deplorable state of housing on reserves, the lack of clothing and footwear, and the high mortality rate, was placed upon the supposed cultural traits and temperament of Aboriginal women. The depiction of these women as lewd and licentious, particularly after 1885, was used to deflect criticism from the behavior of government officials and the NWMP and to legitimize the constraints placed on the activities and movements of Aboriginal women in the world off the reserve. These negative images became deeply embedded in the consciousness of the most powerful socio-economic groups on the Prairies and have resisted revision.

The images were neither new nor unique to the Canadian West. In "The Pocahontas Perplex" Rayna Green explored the complex, many-faceted dimensions of the image of the Indian woman in American folklore and literature. The beautiful "Indian Princess" who saved or aided white men while remaining aloof and virtuous in a woodland paradise was the positive side of the image. Her opposite, the squalid and immoral "Squaw," lived in a shack at the edge of town, and her "physical removal or destruction can be understood as necessary to the progress of civilization."[4] The "Squaw" was pressed into service and her image predominated in the Canadian West in the late nineteenth century, as boundaries were clarified and social and geographic space marked out. The either/or binary left newcomers little room to consider the diversity of the Aboriginal people of the West or the complex identities and roles of Aboriginal women. Not all Euro-Canadians shared in these sentiments and perceptions. Methodist missionary John McDougall, for example, in 1895 chastised a fellow missionary author for his use of the term "squaw": "In the name of decency and civilization and Christianity, why call one person a woman and another a squaw?"[5] While it would be a mistake to assume a unified mentality among all Euro-Canadians, or, for example, among all members of the NWMP, it is nonetheless clear that the negative stereotype not only prevailed but was deliberately propagated by officials of the state.

EURO-CANADIAN SETTLEMENT OF THE WEST

Following the transfer of the Hudson's Bay Company territories to the Dominion of Canada in 1870, the policy of the federal government was to clear the land of the Aboriginal inhabitants and open the West to Euro-Canadian agricultural settlement. To regulate settlement the North-West Mounted Police (later Royal North-West and then Royal Canadian Mounted Police) was created and three hundred of them were dispatched west in 1874. A "free" homestead system was modeled on the American example, and a transcontinental railway was completed in 1885. To open up the West to "actual settlers," seven treaties with the Aboriginal people were negotiated from 1871 to 1877, and through these the government of Canada acquired legal control of most of the land of the West. In exchange the people received land reserves, annuities, and, as a result of hard bargaining by Aboriginal spokesmen, commitments to assist them to take up agriculture as their buffalo-based economy collapsed. A Department of Indian Affairs with headquarters in Ottawa was established in 1880, and in the field an ever-expanding team of Indian agents, farm instructors, and inspectors were assigned to implement the reserve system and to enforce the Indian Act of 1876. The people who had entered into treaties were wards of the government who did not have the privileges of full citizenship and were subject to a wide variety of controls and regulations that governed many aspects of life.

Much to the disappointment of the federal government, the West did not begin rapid development until the later 1890s. There were small pockets of Euro-Canadian settlement, but in 1885 in the district of Alberta, for example, the Aboriginal and Metis population was more than 9500 while the recent arrivals numbered only 4900.[6] All seemed hopeless, especially by the mid-1880s when immigration was at a near standstill. Years of drought and frost and problems finding suitable technique for farming the northern Plains account in part for the reluctance of settlers, and the 1885 resistance of the Metis in present-day Saskatchewan did little to enhance the image the government wished to project of the West as a suitable and safe home.

RESISTANCE TO SETTLEMENT

The Metis were people of mixed Aboriginal and European ancestry who regarded the Red River settlement (Winnipeg) as the heartland of their nation. It was here in 1869–70, under the leadership of Louis Riel, that the Metis first resisted Canadian imperialism, effectively blocking Ottawa's takeover of the West until they had been guaranteed their land rights, their French language, and their Roman Catholic religion. But the victory negotiated into the Manitoba Act of 1870 soon proved hollow as the Canadian government adopted a variety of strategies to ensure that the Metis did not receive the lands promised them, and many moved further West.[7] In their new territories the Metis again demanded land guarantees but when the Canadian government largely ignored their requests, they asked Louis Riel to lead another protest in 1884. The Canadian government dispatched troops west and defeated the Metis at Batoche in May 1885. Riel was found guilty of treason and was hanged, as were eight Aboriginal men convicted of murder.

Despite desperate economic circumstances and deep resentment over government mistreatment, few of the treaty people of the West joined the Metis resistance, although at a settlement called Frog Lake, in present-day Alberta, some young Cree men killed an Indian agent, a farm instructor, and seven others, and in the Battleford district two farm instructors were killed. This limited participation became a rationale for the increasingly authoritarian regime that governed the lives of the treaty people. Anxious to see western development succeed in the face of all of the setbacks of the 1880s, the Canadian government restricted the Aboriginal population in order to protect and enrich recent and prospective immigrants.

DEVELOPMENT OF STEREOTYPES

Particularly irksome to many of the recently-arrived "actual settlers" was Aboriginal competition they faced in the hay, grain, and vegetable markets. Despite obstacles, many Aboriginal farmers had produced a surplus for sale. Settlers' particularly vocal and strident complaints led the government to curtail farming on reserves. To explain why underused reserves had become pockets of rural poverty, Indian Affairs officials claimed that Aboriginal culture and temperament rendered the men unwilling and unable to farm.

Plains women were also responsible: according to government pronouncements they were idle and gossipy, preferring tents to proper housing because tents required less work to maintain and could be clustered in groups that allowed visiting and gossip. Reports of the Superintendent General of Indian Affairs claimed that Indians raised dust with their dancing and the women's failure to clean it up spread diseases such as tuberculosis. Administrators blamed the high infant mortality rate upon the indifferent care of the mothers. The neglected children of these mothers grew up "rebellious, sullen, disobedient and unthankful."[8] While men were blamed for the failure of agriculture, women were portrayed as resisting, resenting, and preventing any progress toward modernization. As an inspector of Indian agencies lamented in 1908, "The women, here, as on nearly every reserve, are a hindrance to the advancement of the men. No sooner do the men earn some money than the women want to go and visit their relations on some other reserve, or else give a feast or dance to their friends. . . . The majority of [the women] are discontented, dirty, lazy and slovenly."[9]

The unofficial and unpublished reports of reserve life show that officials recognized that problems with reserve housing and health had little to do with the preferences, temperament, or poor housekeeping abilities of women. Because of their poverty the people were confined in large numbers in winter to what were little better than one-room and one-story huts or shacks that were poorly ventilated and impossible to keep clean, as they had dirt floors and were plastered with mud and hay. Tents and tipis might well have been more sanitary and more comfortable. One inspector of agencies noted in 1891 that women had neither soap, towels, wash basins, nor wash pails, and no means with which to acquire these.[10] Officials frequently noted that women were short of basic clothing but had no textiles or yarn to work with. Yet in official public statements, the tendency was to ascribe blame to the women rather than to draw attention to conditions that would injure the reputation of government administrators.

"LICENTIOUSNESS" AND GOVERNMENT OFFICIALS

Officials propagated an image of Aboriginal women as dissolute, as the bearers of sinister influences, to deflect criticism from government agents and policies. This image was evoked with particular strength in the wake of an 1886 controversy that focused upon the alleged "brutal, heartless and ostentatious licentiousness" of government officials resident in Western Canada.[11] The remarks of Samuel Trivett, a Church of England missionary on the Blood reserve in present-day southern Alberta, became the focus of the controversy. To a special correspondent for *The Mail* of Toronto, Trivett said that Indian women were being bought and sold by white men who lived with them without legally marrying them and then abandoned the offspring to life on the reserve.[12]

Trivett strongly hinted that some government agents were involved in licentious behavior, an accusation seized upon by critics of the administration of Indian affairs in western Canada. In the aftermath of the Metis resistance of 1885, opponents of John A. Macdonald's Conservatives amassed evidence of neglect, injustice, and incompetence and were delighted to add immortality to this list. In the House of Commons in April of 1886, Malcolm Cameron, Liberal Member of Parliament, delivered a lengthy indictment of Indian affairs in the West, focusing upon the unprincipled and unscrupulous behavior of officials of the Indian department. Cameron quoted Trivett and further charged that agents of the government, sent to elevate and educate, had instead acted to "humiliate, to lower, to degrade and debase the virgin daughters of the wards of the nation." He knew of one young Indian agent from England, unfit to do anything there, who was living on a reserve in "open adultery with two young squaws . . . revelling in the sensual enjoyments of a western harem, plentifully supplied with select cullings from the western prairie flowers."[13]

Cameron implicated members of the NWMP in this behavior, wondering why it was that over 45 percent of them were reported to have been under medical treatment for venereal disease. Cameron was not the first to raise the matter of police propriety in the House. Concern about possible improper relations between the police and Aboriginal women long predated the Trivett scandal and was one aspect of a larger debate in the press and in the House in the late 1870s over charges of inefficiency, lack of discipline, high desertion rates, and low morale in the force. Lieutenant-Governor of the North-West Territories David Laird alerted NWMP Commissioner James Macleod in 1878 that reports about immoral conduct were in circulation: "I fear from what reports are brought me, that some of your officers at Fort Walsh are making rather free with the women around there. It is to be hoped that the good name of the Force will not be hurt through too open indulgence of that kind. And I sincerely hope that Indian women will not be treated in a way that hereafter may give trouble."[14]

Although Macleod and Assistant Commissioner A.G. Irvine denied that there was "anything like 'a regular brothel'" about the police posts, such reports persisted. In the House of Commons in 1880 Joseph Royal, a Manitoba Member of Parliament, claimed that the NWMP was accused of "disgraceful immorality" all over the West. Royal had evidence that at one of the police posts that winter there had been "an open quarrel between an officer and one of the constables for the possession of a squaw . . ." and that one officer slapped another "in the face on account of a squaw." Royal had been informed that "many members of the force were living in concubinage with Indian women, whom they had purchased from their parents and friends."[15] In 1886 public attention was once again drawn to police behavior. *The Mail* informed its readers that between 1874 and 1881 the police had "lived openly with Indian girls purchased from their parents" and only the arrival of settlers had compelled them to abandon or at least be "more discreet in the pursuit of their profligacy."[16]

There is little doubt that Trivett and other critics based their accusations of both the police and government officials on some foundation, but remaining evidence is scanty and scattered. Missionaries depended to a large extent on the goodwill of government and were rarely as outspoken as Trivett or John McLean, a Methodist missionary on the Blood reserve near Fort Macleod, who in 1885 characterized many reserve employees as utterly incompetent and urged the government to employ only married men, "of sterling Christian character."[17] But missionaries were instructed in 1886 by Edgar Dewdney, lieutenant-governor of the North-West Territories, not to voice their accusations to the newspapers "even if allegations against public officials were true," as this would do more harm than good, would affect mission work, and could be used to stir up political strife.[18] Government officials generally investigated reports of government misconduct themselves and this functioned to cover up or to mitigate such allegations. Similarly members of the NWMP themselves looked into any complaints about the force's behavior.

MARRIAGES OF ABORIGINAL WOMEN AND NWMP MEMBERS

There were members of the NWMP, especially among the earliest recruits of the 1870s and early 1880s, who formed relationships with Aboriginal and Metis women, as did a great many other male immigrants of these years. Some of these were marriages of long-standing, sanctioned by Christian ceremony or customary law. Lakota author/historian John O'Kute-sica noted that six "Red Coats" of the Wood Mountain Detachment in the early 1880s, married Lakota women from Sitting Bull's band, and most of the couples, such as Mary Blackmoon and Thomas Aspdin, lived together to old age and death. One couple, Archie LeCaine and Emma Loves War, separated because she did not wish to move to Eastern Canada.[19]

Other relationships were of a more temporary nature. Of course there were children. Cecil Denny for example, while a sub-inspector at Fort Macleod, had a daughter with Victoria Mckay, a part-Piegan woman who was the wife of another policeman, constable Percy Robinson.[20] Denny was forced to resign from the force in 1881 as a result of his involvement in a series of court cases that Robinson brought against him for "having induced his wife to desert him and also having criminal connections with her."[21] The child was raised by her mother on the American Blackfoot reservation. Assistant Surgeon Henry Dodd of the NWMP had a daughter who lived on one of the Crooked Lake reserves in the Qu'Appelle Valley. There is a record of this in the police files only because Dodd was granted leave to attend to her when she was very ill in 1889.[22]

D.J. Grier, who served three years with the NWMP beginning in 1877 at Fort Macleod, married Molly Tailfeathers, a Piegan woman, and together they had three children.[23] By 1887, however, Grier had remarried a white woman. For a short time the children from his first marriage lived with their mother on the Piegan reserve, but the two eldest were taken from her and placed in the care of Grier's parents, who had also settled in Fort Macleod. Grier was one of the most prominent men of the West. Renowned as the first commercial wheat grower in Alberta, he also served as mayor of Macleod for twelve years from 1901 to 1913.

ABUSE OF ABORIGINAL WOMEN

John O'Kute-sica wrote at length about one unsuccessful Wood Mountain customary marriage, that of his aunt Iteskawin and Superintendent William D. Jarvis, who had been with the original contingent and who was dismissed from the force in 1881. According to O'Kute-sica his aunt consented to marry Jarvis (who hailed from a prominent Toronto family) because he promised that her brothers and sisters would have something to eat twice a day, and all of her people were in want and suffering. After only a few weeks of marriage Jarvis, in a jealous rage, publicly assaulted Iteskawin at a Lakota "Night Dance," an incident that strained relations between the two communities, and she immediately left him.[24] On most of the few occasions that Aboriginal women laid charges against policemen for assault or rape, their claims were hastily dismissed as defamation or blackmail.[25]

Some government employees resident on reserves clearly abused their positions of authority. In 1882, for example, Blackfoot Chief Crowfoot and his wife complained that the farm instructor on their reserve demanded sexual favors from a young girl in return for rations, and when an investigation proved this to be the case the man was dismissed.[26] Both the documentary and oral records suggest that several of the government employees that the Crees killed at Frog Lake and Battleford in the spring of 1885 were resented intensely because of their callous and at times brutal treatment of Aboriginal women. The farm instructor on the Mosquito reserve near Battleford, James Payne, was known for his violent temper—he once beat a young woman and threw her out of his house when he found her visiting his young Aboriginal wife. The terrified and shaken woman, who was found by her father, died soon after, and her grieving father blamed Payne, whom he killed in 1885.[27] Farm instructor John Delaney, who was killed at Frog Lake in 1885, laid charges against a man by the name of Sand Fly in 1881 so he could cohabit with Sand Fly's wife. Delaney first claimed that Sand Fly had struck him with a whip, and when this charge did not result in the desired jail sentence, Delaney claimed that the man had beaten his wife. The farm instructor then lived with Sand Fly's wife, and the general feeling in the district, shared by the local NWMP, was that "Mr. Delaney had the man arrested in order to accomplish his designs."[28] As a Touchwood Hills farm instructor told a visiting newspaper correspondent in 1885, the charges of immortality among farm instructors on reserves were in many instances too true, as "the greatest facilities are afforded the Indian instructor for the seduction of Indian girls. The instructor holds the grub. The agent gives him the supplies and he issues them to the Indians. Now you have a good idea of what semi-starvation is . . ."[29]

BLAMING ABORIGINAL WOMEN

The most vocal response to the accusations of Trivett and other critics was not to deny that there had been "immorality" in the West but to exonerate the men and blame the Aboriginal women, who were claimed to have behaved in an abandoned and wanton manner and were supposedly accustomed to being treated with contempt, to being bought and sold as commodities, within their own society. In defending the NWMP in 1880, the Toronto *Globe* emphasized that Aboriginal women had "loose morals" that were "notorious the world over" and that "no men in the world are so good as to teach them better, or to try to reform them in this respect." These sentiments were echoed again and again in the wake of the 1886 controversy. The editor of the Fort *Macleod Gazette*, a former NWMP, argued that whatever immorality there might have been came from the women themselves and from the customs of their society. They were prostitutes before they went to live with white men, who did not encourage this behavior but were simply "taking advantage of an Indian's offer." *The Mail* told readers that Aboriginal males had sold their wives and children in the thousands to soldiers and settlers since the time of the French fur trade in exchange for alcohol, and that with the arrival of the police a great deal had been done to end this situation.[30]

The *Gazette* stressed, incorrectly, that there was no marriage in plains societies, simply a little lively bartering with the father and a woman could be purchased for a horse or two. The argument that Aboriginal women were virtual slaves, first to their fathers, and then to their husbands, was called upon by all who wished to deflect criticism from government officials and the NWMP. In the House of Commons in April 1886 Sir Hector Langevin defended the record of the government against Cameron's charges of immorality. Langevin claimed that to Indians marriage was simply a bargain and a sale and that immortality among them long predated the arrival of government agents in the North-West.[31]

The government published its official response to the criticisms of Indian affairs in the North-West in an 1886 pamphlet entitled "The Facts Respecting Indian Administration in the North-West." A government official had again inquired into accusations about the misconduct of employees of the Indian department and, predictably, had found no evidence. The investigator, Hayter Reed, assistant commissioner of Indian affairs, was one of those unmarried officials who had been accused of having Aboriginal "mistresses" as well as a child from one of these relationships.[32] The pamphlet boldly asserted that Trivett was unable to come up with a shred of actual evidence, although the missionary vehemently denied this.[33] The pamphlet writer admitted that some men had acquired their wives by purchase, but claimed that this was the Indian custom, and that "no father ever dreams of letting his daughter leave his wigwam till he has received a valuable consideration for her." If the government stopped this custom, there would be loud protests, over and above the Indians' "chronic habit of grumbling." "The Facts" insisted that it was not fair to criticize the behavior of the dead, such as Delaney and Payne, who had "passed from the bar of human judgment."[34]

ENDANGERED WHITE WOMEN

The real danger was not to Indian women but to white women, who might again be dragged into horrible captivity if critics encouraged Indians in their exaggerated, misled notions. Two white women, Theresa Delaney and Theresa Gowanlock, had been taken hostage by Big Bear's band following the events at Frog Lake. There were a great number of Metis and Aboriginal women (and men) hostages as well, but outrage and indignation did not focus upon them. Although Delaney and Gowanlock were fed and housed as well as their captors, and released unharmed, the government publication played up the perils, hazards, and threat to the safety of these women and others who might move west. The women's account of their two months of captivity stressed the "savagery" of their captors, and the ever-present danger of "the fate worse than death."[35]

Following the period of heightened tensions within the Euro-Canadian community after the events of 1885 there was an increased emphasis upon the supposed vulnerability of white women in the West. Rumors circulated through the press that one of Big Bear's wives was a white woman being held against her will.[36] After a girl of about nine with fair hair and blue eyes was spotted on the Blackfoot reserve by an English artist accompanying Canada's governor general on a tour across the continent, in 1889, the story of a "captive" white child attracted international attention and calls for a rescue mission. Indignant outrage was expressed, especially in the Fort Macleod newspaper, which called for prompt action to rescue the girl from "the horrible fate that is surely in store for her." The NWMP and Indian affairs officials assigned to look into the case knew all along that the child was not a captive at all but resided with her mother on the reserve. The captivity story functioned, however, to reaffirm the vulnerability of white women in the West and to provide a rationale for those wished to secure greater control over the Aboriginal population.[37]

THE IMAGE OF THE "SQUAW MAN"

The use of the term "squaw man" to denote men of the lowest social class became increasingly frequent during the later 1880s. There was disdain for those within the community who did not conform to the new demands to clarify boundaries. Police reports blamed "squaw men" for many crimes such as liquor offenses or the killing of cattle. S.B. Steele of the NWMP wrote from the Fort Macleod district in 1890 that the wives of these men "readily act as agents, and speaking the language, and being closely connected with the various tribes, their houses soon become a rendezvous for idle and dissolute Indians and half breeds, and being themselves in that debatable land between savagery and civilization possibly do not realize the heinousness and danger to the community. . . ."[38] The *Moosomin Courier* of March 1890 blamed the "squaw-men" for stirring up trouble with the Indians in 1885 and prejudicing them against policies that were for their own good.[39]

LIVES OF ABORIGINAL WOMEN

The overwhelming image that emerged from the 1886 "immorality" controversy was that of dissolute Aboriginal women. They, and the traditions of the society from which they came, were identified as the cause of vice and corruption in the new settlements of the prairie West. This was not an image shared or accepted by all Euro-Canadians in the West at all times, nor did the image bear resemblance to the lives of the vast majority of Aboriginal women. Women were not commodities that were bought, sold, or exchanged at will by men. Plains marriage practices entailed mutual obligations between the families of the couple and an on-going exchange of marriage-validating gifts.

Aboriginal oral and documentary sources suggest that in the early reserve years, particularly in the aftermath of the events of 1885, women provided essential security and stability in communities that had experienced great upheaval. In these years of low resources and shattered morale, the work of women in their own new settlements was vital, materially as well as spiritually. Cree author Joe Dion wrote that when spirits and resources were low on his reserve in the late 1880s "much of the inspiration for the Crees came from the old ladies, for they set to work with a will that impressed everybody."[40] Aboriginal women also provided considerable assistance to new immigrants, particularly women. They were important as midwives to some early immigrants and they helped instruct newcomers in the use of edible prairie plants and other native materials.[41] Aboriginal women formed what was described as a "protective society" around the women and children hostages in Big Bear's camp in 1885, keeping them out of harm's way, but this aspect of the drama was absent from the headlines of the day.[42]

CONSTRAINTS ON ABORIGINAL WOMEN

It was the image of Aboriginal women as immoral and corrupting influences that predominated in the non-Aboriginal society that was taking shape. Authorities used this characterization to define and treat Aboriginal women, increasingly narrowing their options and opportunities. Both informal and formal constraints served to keep Aboriginal people from the towns and settled areas of the prairies and their presence there became more and more marginal. While they may not have wished to live in the towns, their land-use patterns for a time intersected with the new order and they might have taken advantage of markets and other economic opportunities, but townspeople believed that Aboriginal people did not belong within the new settlements that were replacing and expelling "savagery."[43] Their presence was seen as incongruous, corrupting, and demoralizing. Classified as prostitutes, Aboriginal women were seen as particular threats to morality and health. An 1886 pamphlet of advice for emigrants entitled "What Women Say of the Canadian Northwest" was quick to reassure newcomers that Aboriginal people were seldom seen. The 320 women who responded to the question "Do you experience any dread of the Indians?" overwhelmingly replied that they rarely saw any. Mrs. S. Lumsden, for example, thought they were "hundreds of miles away with sufficient force to keep them quiet."[44]

Following the events of 1885, government officials as well as the NWMP made strenuous efforts to keep people on their reserves. A pass system required all who wished to leave to acquire a pass from the farm instructor or agent declaring the length of and reason for absence. A central rationale for the pass system was to keep away from the towns and villages Aboriginal women "of abandoned character who were there for the worst purposes."[45] There is evidence that some Aboriginal women did work as prostitutes.[46] Cree chiefs of the Edmonton district complained to the prime minister in 1883 that their young women were reduced by starvation to prostitution, something unheard of among their people before.[47] Officials attributed prostitution not to economic conditions but to what they insisted was the personal disposition or inherent immorality of Aboriginal women.[48] Classified as prostitutes, Aboriginal women could be restricted by a new disciplinary regime. Separate legislation under the Indian Act, and, after 1892, under the Criminal Code governed Aboriginal prostitution, making it easier to convict Aboriginal women than other women. As legal historian Constance Backhouse has observed, this separate criminal legislation, "with its attendant emphasis on the activities of Indians rather than whites, revealed that racial discrimination ran deep through the veins of nineteenth century Canadian society."[49]

The pass system was also used to bar Aboriginal women from the towns for what were invariably seen as "immoral purposes." Women who were found by the NWMP to be without passes and without means of support were arrested and ordered back to their reserves.[50] In March of 1886 the Battleford police dealt with one woman who refused to leave the town by taking her to the barracks and cutting off locks of her hair. Two years later the Battleford paper reported that

> during the early part of the week the Mounted Police ordered out of town a number of squaws who had come in from time to time and settled here. The promise to take them to the barracks and cut off their hair had a wonderful effect in hastening their movements.[51]

Accustomed to a high degree of mobility about the landscape, Aboriginal women found that the pass system not only restricted their traditional subsistence strategies but also hampered their pursuit of new jobs and resources. Government officials further limited the women's employment and marketing opportunities by advice such as that given by one Indian agent, who urged the citizens of Calgary in 1885 not to purchase anything from or hire Aboriginal people, so as to keep them out of the town.[52] The periodic sale of produce, art, and craftwork in urban or tourist areas could have provided income to women and their families, as did such sales for Aboriginal women in eastern Canada. Studies of rural women in western Canada suggest that in the prairie boom and bust cycle the numerous strategies of women, including the marketing of country provisions and farm products, provided the buffer against farm failure.[53] Aboriginal women were not allowed the same opportunities to market these resources.

The mechanisms and attitudes that excluded Aboriginal women from the new settlements also hampered their access to some of the services these offered. Jane Livingston, the Metis wife of one of the earliest farmers in the Calgary district, found that whenever there was a new policeman in Calgary, he would ask her and her children for passes and make trouble because of their appearance. On one occasion when a child was sick and she needed medicines from downtown Calgary, she rubbed flour into her face and "hoped I looked like a white Calgary housewife" so that the new police constable would not bother her about a pass.[54]

MURDERS OF ABORIGINAL WOMEN

Community reactions to the poisoning of one Aboriginal woman and the brutal murder of another in the late 1880s in southern Alberta reflect the racial prejudices of many of the recent immigrants. In 1888 Constable

Alfred Symonds of the NWMP detachment of Stand Off was accused of feloniously killing and slaying a Blood woman by the name of Mrs. Only Kill by giving her a fatal dose of iodine. The woman had swallowed the contents of a bottle given to her by Symonds that apparently held iodine and had died the next morning. The same day she had also eaten a quantity of beans that had turned sour in the heat. Although Only Kill died on Wednesday morning, the matter was not reported to the coroner until late on Friday night. The coroner claimed that by this time the body was too decomposed for post mortem examination, and the coroner's jury decided that the deceased had come to her death either from eating sour beans or from drinking the fluid given to her by Symonds, who was committed to trial and charged with having administered the poison.[55] Constable Symonds was a popular and jocular cricketer and boxer, the son of a professor from Galt, Ontario.[56] In his report on the case, Superintendent P.R. Neale of the NWMP wrote to his superior, "I do not think any Western jury will convict him." Symonds appeared before Judge James F. Macleod, former commissioner of the NWMP, in August of 1888 but the crown prosecutor made application for "Nolle Prosequi," which was granted, and the prisoner was released.[57]

During the 1889 trials of the murderer of a Cree woman identified only as "Rosalie," who had been working as a prostitute, it became clear that there were many in Calgary who felt "Rosalie was only a squaw and that her death did not matter much."[58] Instead the murderer gained the sympathy and support of much of the town. The murder was a particularly brutal one, and the accused, William "Jumbo" Fisk, had confessed and given himself up to authorities, yet there were problems finding any citizens willing to serve on a jury that might convict a white man for such a crime. The crown prosecutor stated that he regretted having to conduct the case, as he had known the accused for several years as a "genial, accommodating and upright young man."[59] Fisk was a popular veteran of 1885, and he was from a well-established eastern Canadian family. At the end of the first of the Rosalie trials the jury astoundingly found the accused "Not Guilty." Judge Charles Rouleau refused to accept this verdict and he ordered a re-trial at the end of which Rouleau told the jury to "forget the woman's race and to consider only the evidence at hand," that "it made no difference whether Rosalie was white or black, an Indian or a negro. In the eyes of the law, every British subject is equal."[60] It was only after the second trial that Fisk was convicted of manslaughter and sent to prison for fourteen years at hard labor. The judge intended to sentence him for life, but letters written by members of parliament and other influential persons who had made representations to the court as to his good character, combined with a petition from the most respectable people of Calgary, persuaded him to impose the lesser sentence.

The people of Calgary tried to show that they were not callous and indifferent toward Rosalie by giving her "as respectable a burial as if she had been a white woman," although several months later the town council squabbled with the Indian Department over the costs incurred, as the department did not think it necessary to go beyond the costs of a pauper's funeral. As a final indignity Rosalie was not allowed burial by the priests in the mission graveyard, although she had been baptized into the Roman Catholic Church, because they regarded her as a prostitute who had died in sin. The lesson to be learned from the tragedy, according to a Calgary newspaper, was "keep the Indians out of town."[61]

ABORIGINAL WOMEN AND ANGLO-SAXON MORAL REFORMERS

There was an intensification of racial discrimination and a stiffening of boundaries between Aboriginal and newcomer in the late 1880s in western Canada. In part this may have been because the immigrants exemplified the increasingly racist ideas and assumptions of the British toward "primitive" peoples.[62] Like the Jamaica Revolt and the India Mutiny, the events of 1885 in western Canada sanctioned perceptions of Aboriginal people as dangerous and ungrateful and justified increased control and segregation.[63] Aboriginal women presented particular perils and hazards. The Metis of the Canadian West had fomented two "rebellions" in western Canada, so authorities wanted to discourage such miscegenation, which could potentially produce great numbers of "malcontents" who might demand that their rights and interests be recognized.[64]

A fervor for moral reform in Protestant English Canada also began to take shape in the later 1880s. Sexual immorality was a main target and racial purity a goal of the reformers.[65] There were fears that Anglo-Saxons might well be overrun by more fertile, darker, and lower people who were believed not to be in control of their sexual desires. Attitudes of the moral reformers toward the inhabitants of the cities' slums were similar to categorizations of "savages" as improvident, filthy, impure, and morally depraved. The 1886 accusations of Malcolm Cameron about the extent of venereal disease among the NWMP had led to an internal investigation of the matter, and although this proved that Cameron's claims were exaggerated, they were not entirely incorrect.[66] The concerns of the moral reformers, however, justified policies segregating Aboriginal and newcomer communities.

THE INVALIDATION OF MIXED MARRIAGES

Also at issue in the West at this time was the question of who was to control property and capital, who was to have privilege and respectability, and who was not. The possibility that the progeny of interracial marriages might be recognized as legitimate heirs to the sometimes considerable wealth of their fathers posed problems and acted as a powerful incentive for the immigrants to view Aboriginal women as immoral and accustomed to a great number of partners. With the arrival of Euro-Canadian women, Aboriginal wives became fewer, and there is evidence, just as Trivett had suggested, that in the 1880s husbands and fathers were leaving their

Aboriginal wives and children for non-Aboriginal wives. D.W. Davis, for example, began his career in Alberta as a whiskey trader at the infamous Fort Whoop-Up, but by 1887 was elected as the first Member of Parliament for the Alberta district. He had a family of four children with a Blood woman by the name of Revenge Walker, but in 1887 he married an Ontario woman, Lillie Grier (sister of D.J. Grier), with whom he had a second family. Although Davis, like Grier, acknowledged the children of the earlier marriage and provided for their education, they were excluded from the economic and social elite in the non-Aboriginal community.[67]

While the validity of mixed marriages according to "the custom of the country" had been upheld in Canadian courts earlier in the nineteenth century, this changed with the influential 1886 ruling in *Jones v. Fraser*. The judge ruled that the court would not accept that "the cohabitation of a civilized man and a savage woman, even for a long period of time, gives rise to the presumption that they consented to be married in our sense of marriage."[68] In 1899 the Supreme Court for the North-West Territories decided that the two sons of Mary Brown, a Piegan woman, and Nicholas Sheran, a founder of a lucrative coal mine near Lethbridge, were not entitled, as next of kin, to a share of their father's estate, as the judge found that Sheran could have but did not legally marry Brown while they lived together from 1878 until Sheran's death in 1882.[69]

HAUNTED BY AN IMAGE

Negative images of Aboriginal women proved extraordinarily persistent. Their morality was questioned in a number of sections of the Indian Act. If a woman was not of "good moral character" for example, she lost her one-third interest in her husband's estate, and a male government official was the sole and final judge of moral character. As late as 1921 the House of Commons debated a Criminal Code amendment that would have made it an offense for any white man to have "illicit connection" with an Indian woman. Part of the rationale advanced was that "the Indian women are, perhaps, not as alive as women of other races in the country to the importance of maintaining their chastity." The amendment was not passed, as it was argued that this could make unsuspecting white men the "victims" of Indian women who would blackmail them.[70] By contrast, any critical reflections upon the behavior of early government officials and the police in western Canada did not survive beyond the controversy of the 1880s. Ideological constraints, combined with more formal mechanisms of control such as the pass system, succeeded in marginalizing Aboriginal women and in limiting the alternatives and opportunities available to them.

Local histories of the prairies suggest that by the turn of the century many of the settlements of the West had their "local Indian" who was tolerate on the margins or fringes of society and whose behavior and appearance was the subject of local anecdotes. "Old Dewdney" for example, an ancient, often flamboyantly dressed man, was a familiar sight in Fort Macleod. Local people exchanged stories about the exotic past of the old man and of their generosity and kindness toward him.[71] "Nikamoos" or the Singer camped each summer by herself on the trail to the Onion Lake reserve agency in Saskatchewan. Among the white community it was reputed that as a girl Nikamoos had run away with a policeman but that he had been compelled to leave her. The child she bore died and Nikamoos went insane.[72]

A solitary Indian woman known only as Liza camped on the outskirts of Virden, Manitoba, for many years until her disappearance sometime in the 1940s. By then Liza was thought to have been well over one hundred years old. She lived winter and summer in an unheated tent by the railroad tracks although she spent the long winter days huddled in the livery stable and also at times crept into the Nu-Art Beauty Parlour, where she sat on the floor in front of the window, warming herself in the sun. Liza smoked a corncob pipe as she shuffled about the streets and lanes of Virden, rummaging in garbage tins. She bathed under the overflow pipe at the water tower, sometimes clothed and sometimes not, and dried off by standing over the huge heat register in Scales and Rothnie's General Store. To an extent she was tolerated and even assisted; town employees shoveled out a path for her when she was buried under snow, and it was thought that the town fathers supplied her with food from time to time. Children were half fascinated and half frightened by this ancient woman. Old-timers believed that Liza was there well before the first settlers, that she was among the Sioux who had escaped the pursuing American army in 1876, that she received regular checks from the United States, and that she was capable of fine handwriting, where learned, no one knew.[73]

The presence of Liza, and the stories told about her, served to sharpen the boundaries of community membership and to articulate what was and what was not considered acceptable and respectable.[74] Liza was the object of both fascination and repugnance as she violated norms of conventional behavior, dress, and cleanliness, representing the antithesis of "civilized" prairie society. Although economically and socially marginal, Liza was symbolically important. Her role attests to the recurrent pattern through which the new society of the West gained in strength and identity and sought to legitimate its own authority by defining itself against the people who were there before them. Liza was a real person, but what she represented was a Euro-Canadian artifact, created by the settlement. The narratives circulated about Liza were not those she might have told herself—of the disasters that had stripped her of family and community, or perhaps of her strategies in adopting the character role—and this folklore reflected less about Liza than about the community itself. Her solitary life was unique and in contrast to the lives of Aboriginal women; Liza was not representative of a Lakota woman within Lakota society. Yet her presence on the margins of the settlement was tolerated and encouraged in the way these women were not, as she appeared to fit into the well-established category of the "squaw" that still served to confirm the Euro-Canadian newcomers in their belief that their cultural and moral superiority entitled them to the land that had become their home.

NOTES

1. Mary E. Inderwick, "A Lady and Her Ranch" in *The Best From Alberta History*, ed. Hugh Dempsey (Saskatoon: Western Producer Prairie Books, 1981), 65–77. In 1882 the North-West Territories were divided into four provisional districts named Assiniboia, Saskatch-ewan, Alberta, and Athabasca.

2. For an examination and critique of the argument that European women introduced segregation, see Margaret Strobel, *European Women and the Second British Empire* (Bloomington: Indiana University Press, 1991). See also essays by Ann Laura Stoler, "Carnal Knowledge and Imperial Power: Gender, Race and Morality in Colonial Asia" in *Gender at the Crossroads of Knowledge: Feminist Anthropology in the Postmodern Era*, ed. Micaela di Leonardo (Berkeley: University of California Press, 1991), 51–101, and Stoler, "Rethinking Colonial Categories: European Communities and the Boundaries of Rule" in *Colonialism and Culture*, ed. Nicholas B. Dirks (Ann Arbor: University of Michigan Press, 1992), 319–52.

3. See Sarah Carter, *Lost Harvests: Prairie Indian Reserve Farmers and Government Policy* (Montreal: McGill-Queen's University Press, 1990).

4. Rayna Green, "The Pocahontas Perplex: The Image of Indian Women in American Culture" in *Unequal Sisters: A Multicultural Reader in U.S. Women's History*, ed. Ellen Carol DuBois and Vicki L. Ruiz (New York: Routledge, 1990), 15–21.

5. John McDougall, "A Criticism of 'Indian Wigwams and Northern Camp-Fires'" (n.p.: 1895), 12–13.

6. P.B. Waite, *Canada, 1874–1896: Arduous Destiny* (Toronto: McClelland & Stewart, 1971), 149.

7. D.N. Sprague, *Canada and the Metis, 1869–1885* (Waterloo, ON: Wilfrid Laurier Press, 1988).

8. Canada, *Sessional Papers*, Annual Report of the Superintendent General of Indian Affairs for the year ending 30 June 1898, xix, for the year ending 31 Dec. 1899, xxiii, xxviii, 166; *The Mail* (Toronto), 2 March 1889; Pamela Margaret White, "Restructuring the Domestic Sphere—Prairie Indian Women on Reserves: Image, Ideology and State Policy, 1880–1930" (PhD thesis, McGill University, 1987); quote taken from W.H. Withrow, *Native Races of North America* (Toronto: Methodist Mission Rooms, 1895), 114.

9. Canada, *Sessional Papers*, Annual Report of the Superintendent General of Indian Affairs for the year ending March 1908, 110.

10. Inspector Alex McGibbon's report on Onion Lake, Oct. 1891, National Archives of Canada (NA), Record Group 10 (RG 10), records relating to Indian Affairs, Black Series, vol. 3860, file 82, 319-6.

11. *The Globe* (Toronto), 1 Feb. 1886.

12. *The Mail* (Toronto), 23 Jan. 1886.

13. Canada, House of Commons *Debates*, Malcolm Cameron, Session 1886, vol. 1, 720–21.

14. As quoted in E.C. Morgan. "The North-West Mounted Police: Internal Problems and Public Criticism, 1874–1883," *Saskatchewan History* 26, 2 (Spring 1973): 56.

15. Canada, House of Commons *Debates*, 21 April 1880, Joseph Royal, Fourth Parliament, Second Session, 1638.

16. *The Mail*, 2 Feb. 1886.

17. John Maclean, "The Half-breed and Indian Insurrection," *Canadian Methodist Magazine* 22, 1 (July 1885): 173–74.

18. Edgar Dewdney to the Bishop of Saskatchewan, 31 May 1886, NA, RG 10, vol. 3753, file 30613.

19. John O'Kute-sica Correspondence, collection no. R-834, File 17(b), 15, Saskatchewan Archives Board (SAB).

20. *Blackfeet Heritage: 1907–08* (Browning: Blackfeet Heritage Program, n.d.), 171.

21. A.B. McCullough, "Papers Relating to the North West Mounted Police and Fort Walsh," Manuscript Report Series no. 213 (Ottawa: Parks Canada, Department of Indian and Northern Affairs, 1977), 132–33.

22. L. Herchemer to Comptroller, 23 May 1889, NA, RG 18, vol. 35, file 499–1889.

23. Personal Interview with Kirsten Grier, great-granddaughter of D.J. Grier, Calgary, 19 May 1993. See also *Fort Macleod—Our Colourful Past: A History of the Town of Fort Macleod from 1874 to 1924* (Fort Macleod, AB: Fort Macleod History Committee, 1977), 268–69.

24. O'Kute-sica Correspondence, 3.

25. See for example S.B. Steele to Commissioner, Fort Macleod, 20 July 1895, NA, RG 18, vol. 2182, file RCMP 1895 pt. 2, and Gilbert E. Sanders Diaries, 20 Oct. 1885, Edward Sanders Family Papers, M1093, file 38, Glenbow Archives.

26. F. Laurier Barron, "Indian Agents and the North-West Rebellion" in *1885 and After: Native Society in Transition*, ed. F. Laurie Barron and James B. Waldram (Regina: Canadian Plains Research Center, 1986), 36.

27. Norma Sluman and Jean Goodwill, *John Tootoosis: A Biography of a Cree Leader* (Ottawa: Golden Dog Press, 1982), 37.

28. Hugh A. Dempsey, *Big Bear: The End of Freedom* (Vancouver: Douglas & McIntyre, 1984), 117. See also *Saskatchewan Herald* (Battleford), 14 and 28 Feb. 1881.

29. Newspaper clipping, "Through the Saskatchewan," n.p., n.d., N.A. William Henry Cotton Collection.

30. The Globe, 4 June 1880; *Macleod Gazette* (Fort Macleod, AB), 23 March 1886; *The Mail*, 2 Feb. 1886.

31. Canada, House of Commons *Debates*, Session 1886, vol. 1, 730.

32. William Donovan to L. Vankoughnet, 31 Oct. 1886, NA, RG 10, vol. 3772, file 34983.

33. *The Globe*, 4 June 1886.

34. *The Facts Respecting Indian Administration in the North-West* (Ottawa, 1886), 9, 12.

35. Theresa Gowanlock and Theresa Delaney, *Two Months in the Camp of Big Bear* (Parkdale: Parkdale Times, 1885).

36. *Manitoba Sun* (Winnipeg), 7 Dec. 1886.

37. Sarah Carter, "'A Fate Worse Than Death': Indian Captivity Stories Thrilled Victorian Readers: But Were They True?" *The Beaver* 68, 2 (April/May 1988): 21–28, *Macleod Gazette* quoted p. 22.

38. Canada, *Sessional Papers*, Annual Report of the Commissioner of the North West Mounted Police for 1890, vol. 24, no. 9, 62.

39. *Moosomin Courier*, 13 March 1890.

40. Joe Dion, *My Tribe the Crees* (Calgary: Glenbow-Alberta Institute, 1979), 114.

41. See Sarah Carter, "Relations Between Native and Non-Native Women in the Prairie West, 1870–1920," paper presented to the Women and History Association of Manitoba, Winnipeg, Feb. 1992.

42. Elizabeth M. McLean, "Prisoners of the Indians," *The Beaver*, Outfit 278 (June 1947): 15–16.

43. David Hamer, *New Towns in the New World: Images and Perceptions of the Nineteenth Century Urban Frontier* (New York: Columbia University Press, 1990), 17, 213.

44. "What Canadian Women Say of the Canadian North-West" (Montreal: Montreal Herald, 1886), 44.

45. L. Vankoughnet to John A. Macdonald, 15 Nov. 1883, NA, RG 10, vol. 1009, file 628, no. 596-635.

46. S.W. Horrall, "The (Royal) North-West Mounted Police and Prostitution on the Canadian Prairies," *Prairie Forum* 10, 1 (Spring 1985): 105–27.

47. Clipping from the *Bulletin* (Edmonton), 7 Jan. 1883, NA, RG 10, vol. 3673, file 10 986.

48. Canada, *Sessional Papers*, Annual Report of the Superintendent General of Indian affairs for the year ending 1906, 82.

49. Constance B. Backhouse, "Nineteenth-Century Canadian Prostitution Law: Reflection of a Discriminatory Society," *Histoire sociale/Social History* 18, 36 (Nov. 1985): 422.

50. Canada, *Sessional Papers*, Annual Report of the Commissioner of the North-West Mounted Police Force for the year 1889, reprinted in *The New West* (Toronto: Coles Publishing, 1973), 101.

51. *Saskatchewan Herald* (Battleford), 15 March 1886, 13 March 1888 (quoted).

52. *Calgary Herald*, 5 March 1885.

53. See for example Carolina Antoinetta J.A. Van de Vorst, "A History of Farm Women's Work in Manitoba" (MA thesis, University of Manitoba, 1988).

54. Lyn Hancock with Marion Dowler, *Tell Me Grandmother* (Toronto: McClelland & Stewart, 1985), 139.

55. *Macleod Gazette*, 18 July 1888.

56. John D. Higinbotham, *When the West Was Young: Historical Reminiscences of the Early Canadian West* (Toronto: Ryerson Press, 1933), 260–61.

57. R.C. Macleod, *The North-West Mounted Police and Law Enforcement, 1873–1905* (Toronto: University of Toronto Press, 1976), 145. See also NA, RG 18, vol. 24, file 667–1888.

58. Donald Smith, "Bloody Murder Almost Became Miscarriage of Justice," *Herald Sunday Magazine*, 23 July 1989, 13. Thanks to Donald Smith, Department of History, University of Calgary for allowing me to draw upon his sources on this case.

59. James Gray, *Talk To My Lawyer: Great Stories of Southern Alberta's Bar and Bench* (Edmonton: Hurtig Publishers, 1987), 7.

60. Rouleau quoted in Smith, "Bloody Murder,"15.

61. *Calgary Herald*, 24 July, 10 Sept. (quoted), 27 Feb., and 8 March (quoted) 1889.

62. See Christine Bolt, *Victorian Attitudes to Race* (Toronto: University of Toronto Press, 1971); Philip D. Curtin, *The Image of Africa: British Ideas and Action, 1780–1850* (Madison: University of Wisconsin Press, 1964); V.G. Kiernan, *The Lords of Human Kind: European Attitudes Toward the Outside World in the Imperial Age* (Middlesex: Penguin Books, 1972); Douglas A. Lorimer, *Colour, Class and the Victorians* (Leicester University Press, Holmes and Meier Publishers, 1978); and Philip Mason, *Patterns of Dominance* (London: Oxford University Press, 1971).

63. Walter Hildebrandt, "Official Images of 1885," *Prairie Fire* 6, 4 (1985): 31–40.

64. This is suggested by Backhouse, "Nineteenth-Century Canadian Prostitution Law," 422.

65. Mariana Valverde, *The Age of Light, Soap, and Water: Moral Reform in English Canada, 1885–1925* (Toronto: McClelland & Stewart, 1991).

66. NA, RG 18, vol. 1039, file 87–1886, pt. 1.

67. Beverley A. Stacey, "D.W. Davis: Whiskey Trader to Politician," *Alberta History* 38, 3 (Summer 1990): 1–11.

68. Sylvia Van Kirk, *"Many Tender Ties": Women in Fur Trade Society, 1670–1870* (Winnipeg: Watson and Dwyer Publishing, 1980), 241, and Constance Backhouse, *Pettitcoats and Prejudice: Women and the Law in*

Nineteenth-Century Canada (Toronto: Osgoode Society, 1991), chap. 1.

69. Brian Slattery and Linda Charlton, ed., *Canadian Native Law Cases* 3, 1891–1910 (Saskatoon: Native Law Centre, 1985), 636–44.

70. Canada, House of Commons *Debates*, Session 1921, vol. 4, 26 May 1921, 3908.

71. Fort Macleod History Committee, *Our Colourful Past*, 217–18.

72. Ruth Matheson Buck, "Wives and Daughters," *Folklore* 9, 4 (Autumn 1988): 14–15.

73. "Talk About Stories," *Anecdotes and Updates: Virden Centennial, 1982* (Virden: Empire Publishing, 1982), 57–59

74. Diane Tye, "Local Character Anecdotes: A Nova Scotia Case Study," *Western Folklore* 48 (July 1989): 196.

REAL MEN HUNT BUFFALO: MASCULINITY, RACE AND CLASS IN BRITISH FUR TRADERS' NARRATIVES ⬥

ELIZABETH VIBERT

o

British fur traders arrived in the Plateau region of northwestern North America early in the nineteenth century to find the indigenous peoples living in an "unhallowed wilderness," supporting themselves by fishing, hunting, and gathering—living, as one trader phrased it and all presumed, in a "rude state of nature." In their writings from the region the traders ranked Plateau societies, casting those they identified as "fishing tribes" as indolent, improvident, and suffering periodic starvation. Those described as hunters, by contrast, were cast as brave, industrious, stoic—in a word, manly. In this essay I probe the gendered nature of traders' representations of "the Indian buffalo hunter." The aim is to expose the cultural logic by which this hunter was constructed and became the standard-bearer of manly Indianness.[1] Integral to the project is the illumination of the process by which middle-class British masculinity, in its fur trade variant, was constructed as the norm and elevated above Indian manhood.[2] This was not a simple feat, even in the realm of narrative. The masculinity of the traders

⬥ Reprinted by permission of Blackwell Publishers, from *Gender and History* 8, 1 (1996). This research builds on a larger project funded primarily by the British Council (Commonwealth Scholarship programme) and the Social Sciences and Humanities Research Council of Canada. My thanks to the Hudson's Bay Company Archives, Winnipeg, Canada, for permission to quote from its collection. I am grateful to Terence Ranger, Megan Vaughan, Glyndwr Williams, Keith McClelland, and two anonymous reviewers for suggestive comments on an earlier version of this essay. I especially thank Todd Hatfield and Lynne Marks for their careful criticism and support.

was never secure, defined as it was in a local context of gender, race, and class conflict and resistance.

The rude state in which Plateau peoples were said to dwell was not new to these early nineteenth-century observers. The British had been encountering "natives" abroad for centuries, inscribing them as savages both noble and ignoble.[3] Fur traders produced their own voluminous, and in many ways distinctive, cultural commentaries. The ideological baggage they carried with them from their British and colonial homes functioned as a kind of coordinating grid in the travellers' encounters with "the Indian." The outline of the grid was defined by an imagination which was white, male, middle-class and British.

While inherited discourses were influential, they were not intractable. A large part of the project of analysing traders' narratives is to assess how their cultural knowledge was produced, reproduced, and reordered in the North American Plateau in the period 1807 to 1846.[4] Cultural meanings were surely open to inventive refashioning. The traders' purpose was to carry on a profitable, and therefore peaceable, trade with indigenous peoples; many lived for years in this "Indian country" (if generally behind insulating walls) and married indigenous women. They were surely subject to that "jarring of meanings and values" which one cultural theorist so convincingly portrays as the consequence of inhabiting the liminal spaces of interacting cultures. The images that arose were shifting and contradictory, vacillating between what was already "known" about the Indian and what was in need of anxious repeating.[5] With these observations in mind, I will place the traders not only in the context of their own shifting ideological heritage but also in their fluid North American setting.

The unpacking of trader narratives is of more than merely academic interest. As the earliest "ethnographic" records of the indigenous societies of northern North America, traders' accounts have been extensively, and far too often uncritically, mined for data. The construction of these texts demands analysis.[6] In addition, the narratives present an early rendering of "the Indian" which proved to be extraordinarily potent and enduring. So powerful was the image of the buffalo-hunting Indian that by the late nineteenth century, he had displaced his eastern woodlands cousins (Hiawatha, Pocahontas, and their vaguely Algonquian kin) as *the* Indian of the Euro-american imagination. In casting the buffalo hunter as the quintessential manly Indian, traders' narratives anticipated generations of popular iconography.[7]

In casting Plateau buffalo hunters as industrious and praiseworthy, traders' narratives also departed from what is often taken to be a basic theme of the colonial encounter, the representation of indigenous hunters as wasteful, lazy, and far from manly. By the eighteenth century the hunting way of life was clearly associated with a backward social state: witness its position as the most rudimentary phase in Adam Smith's four-stage theory of social development. In settler commentaries from the eastern woodlands of North America at this time, hunters—indigenous or white—were frequently condemned as indolent and improvident. Fur trader narratives from farther west rarely praised Indian hunters. David Thompson expressed a general view in his 1785 account of subarctic hunter-gatherers. In the regions to the south and west of Hudson Bay, a relatively mild climate and abundance of game assured the hunters of a "manly appearance," Thompson wrote. But they could not tolerate hard labour, a weakness Europeans frequently ascribed to the natives of the colonies. The hunters' very choice of activity was evidence of their degeneracy. These lazy people would rather rove for six hours over rough terrain "than work one hour with the pick axe and spade." Thompson concluded that "naturally [the Indians] are not industrious."[8]

Similar commentaries may be found in many other colonial settings in the later eighteenth and early nineteenth centuries. However, the most harshly condemning images of wasteful, cruel, and unmanly hunters gained ascendency only as colonizer and colonized came into intense competition for access to wildlife, other resources, and land.[9] Earlier travellers' impressions of indigenous hunters were more mixed; still, their perceived indolence was a common theme. To take just one example, in the early period of white exploration in interior southern Africa, game constituted an essential resource for expansionist Europeans. British travellers in the Cape interior relied heavily on Khoikhoi hunters, in particular, for subsistence. Such dependence led to at least a grudging acknowledgement of native skills, and at best a measured admiration.[10] Yet "indolence" and "idleness" were frequently called upon to describe the Khoikhoi way of life. Interestingly, Afrikaners (Boers) were described in much the same terms. As one student of African colonial literatures has put it, the mobile hunting and mixed subsistence patterns of both white Afrikaners and black Africans were regarded as a rejection of British ethics of discipline and labour: "the fruits of the earth are enjoyed as they drop into the hand, [and] work is avoided as an evil."[11] As a growing British presence brought the Cape Colony into the international capitalist economy, local animal resources began to be studied for science and hunted for sport. By the 1820s, the increasing tendency to view the Cape as a hunting estate had led to a hardening of discourse about indigenous hunters; now, as well as indolent, they were described as wanton, cruel, or cowardly.[12] In North America a similar hardening came when the fur trade gave way to settlement and "roving" hunters became an obstacle to those who sought to pre-empt their lands.

Fur traders' glowing accounts of Plateau buffalo hunters, which quite explicitly depicted them as industrious, appear all the more exceptional against this background. This positive view was restricted to buffalo hunting, however; the neighbouring "fishing tribes" were "indolent and lazy to an extreme." As I have argued elsewhere, the traits of the fishers were defined quite clearly *in contrast to* those of the buffalo hunters.[13]

In much of North America the fur trade preceded settlement by several decades (and longer in the east). At base the fur trade entailed the exchange of European manufactures for furs and hides produced by indigenous peoples. The traders whose writings concern us here were the men on the ground in the extractive industry on which Canada and much of the northern U.S. was founded. Beginning in the late 1500s, the fur trade brought French, British, Dutch, Spanish, Russian and other mercantile interests to the continent. Beaver pelts were the principal inducement, for the felt demanded by the European clothing and hatting industries.[14] After a long history of imperial and commercial jockeying for power, by the early nineteenth century the fur trade of British North America was presided over by arch-rival enterprises, the London-based Hudson's Bay Company and the Montreal-based, Scots-dominated North West Company. The NWC, having established itself west of the Rocky Mountains ahead of its rival, was able to monopolize the trade of the Plateau and the larger Columbia district until economic pressures forced the companies to amalgamate in 1821.[15] Until the early 1840s, the Hudson's Bay Company remained the only effective non-native presence in the region; in that decade growing numbers of American settlers and missionaries began to arrive over the Oregon Trail.

In the context of the Plateau fur trade, "British" included men of Scots, English, Welsh and Irish background. The traders' personal histories prior to joining the North West and Hudson's Bay companies are generally not well known. The interaction of class and ethnicity created a distinctive and taut hierarchy in the North West Company which persisted in the Plateau region throughout the period under study. Promising Scots and Englishmen and their colonial counterparts were recruited in their teens to the rank of clerk, their advancement all but assured by the patronage of a real or fictive kin member in the position of senior officer.[16] Many of these young clerks appear to have come from tenant farming or trades families. The fur trade offered these men opportunities which simply were not available at home. Not only could the thrifty among them put aside sufficient funds to return to Britain or the eastern colonies much wealthier than when they had left; within fur trade society itself, they achieved a social rank far beyond that from which most had come. They cultivated this status with some finesse. Those of other ethnic backgrounds, principally French Canadians, peripheral Scots,[17] Métis (literally "mixed," the offspring of traders and their country wives), Aboriginals, and Hawaiians, faced less attractive prospects. They entered the North West Company as boatmen and labourers, the "servants" of the trade. Upward mobility was the exception for these men.

Members of the officer class, the clerks included, styled themselves the "gentlemen" of the trade. The most immediate referent for this self-identification was "the men," the company servants; but there were many others against whom the gentlemen defined themselves. Rituals to mark off their exclusive social space were highly formalized. Dining arrangements, for instance, spoke to class, ethnic, and gender hierarchies. Gentlemen and servants dined separately, and local Indians were rarely found at either mess table. By the early nineteenth century, however, virtually all the traders had Aboriginal or Métis wives. The women ate after the men.[18]

Alexander Ross described the dining practices of the North Westers with a touch of irony. "[Y]ou take your seat," Ross wrote, "as a Chinese Mandarine [sic] would take his dress, according to your rank." Even the common beverage was class-specific: there were three grades of China leaf tea, and as many of sugar. Such boundary-defining exercises were widespread and officially sanctioned. In a policy directive of 1822, the governing council of the reorganized HBC decreed that the "line of distinction" between gentlemen and servants needed highlighting. To this end, a prohibition was issued on guides and interpreters dining with the officers. These men were in the upper ranks of the servant class, but they also tended to be French Canadian or native. Their occasional presence in the gentlemen's hall had apparently become a threat.[19]

Recent research indicates that the early nineteenth century was a period of hardening social distinctions throughout fur trade society. For instance, whereas in the eighteenth century tradesmen (the "labour aristocracy" of the fur trade) and common labourers had generally lived together in barracks-style accommodation at HBC posts, by the early 1800s tradesmen and labourers were housed in separate buildings. Similarly, married and unmarried men were segregated. And whereas senior and junior officers had often shared a single officers' bastion, senior officers now enjoyed detached residences.[20] The advent of private family dwellings for the elite of the fur trade echoes developments in middle-class housing in Britain at the time. As Leonore Davidoff and Catherine Hall have shown, acquisition of a comfortable private home was the "utmost ambition" of middle-class families by the turn of the nineteenth century. Not only was the home a symbol of status, proof that one had arrived; it was a sanctuary from external pressures.[21] Surely it performed this function in fur trade country, where added to the class and gender pressures of daily working life were those of an alien environment, alien peoples, and perceived threats to the civilized, white order.

The gentlemen traders' attempts to draw boundaries around themselves in order to secure their particular brand of masculine identity were not entirely successful. The refuge which they sought to construct was rooted in a cultural and political setting shot through with the antagonisms of class, gender and ethnicity. And there was a profound ambivalence at the heart of the project. As noted above, virtually every officer in the Columbia, and most servants, had Aboriginal or Métis wives. Throughout fur trade country Indian women had from the early years been taken as wives "by the custom of the country." As Métis daughters of these liaisons became numerous, they displaced Indian women. Their upbringing in fur trade communities and their tutelage at their fathers' knees was believed to have fitted them perfectly for the role of wife and servant of the trade. Indian or Métis, these women were important to their husbands for economic and diplomatic purposes and for the "many tender ties" which softened life at the posts. As George Barnston, a long-time Columbia trader observed, as long as there was love "within doors . . . many a bitter blast may be born from without."[22]

Ultimately, though, marriages to women of the country came to be seen as a threat to the traders' gentlemanly self-fashioning. The arrival of missionaries in the territories east of the Rockies in the 1810s, and the introduction by the 1830s of British women to the fur trade scene, led to attacks on the morality and social acceptability of country unions. High-ranking company officers were first to follow the missionaries' admonitions to avoid mixed-race marriages, which one man of the cloth described as "the snare which has ruined many of our countrymen."[23] With this new model of racial and social etiquette in place, it was no longer seemly for men of the officer class to take indigenous wives. By the 1830s, the racial hierarchies encoded in traditional fur trade practice—hierarchies which had seen Métis women displace Aboriginal women, and which had given rise to occasional epithets such as "his bit of brown"—erupted into full view. The possession of an imported British wife became a key marker of proper fur trade manhood.[24]

The man personally responsible for the introduction of white "ladies" to fur trade society was the Hudson's Bay Company's overseas governor, George Simpson. His return from England in 1830 with his young bride, Frances, prompted instant imitation by a number of officers.[25] Simpson, a proud Highland Scot with solid London connections, cut a very manly figure. He was precise in defining the qualities expected of his officers: "zeal," "hard work," "firmness," and "restraint" were pet phrases. Simpson's own zeal is legendary. He was a tirelessly competitive man, who earned both notoriety and reverence among fellow traders for his habit of pushing his canoe brigades to eighteen-hour days as he travelled about the region under his control, all the while clad in top hat and dress coat. On his first trip up the Columbia River in 1825, Simpson noted the "hard marching" of his canoes, and boasted that their pace "beats anything of the kind hitherto known in the Columbia."[26]

Simpson prided himself on striking the right balance between "firmness" and "restraint." These traits marked his handling of business matters (he arrived in the Columbia Department bent on "economy" and the reduction of "wasteful extravagance") and his perception of how best to manage both company servants and Indians.[27] John McLoughlin, chief of Columbia operations, set out the accepted practice. The "proper management" of the Indians entailed treating them with "apparent openness and confidence" (restraint) while maintaining their respect (firmness).[28] Hence the juxtaposition of pipe-smoking and gift-giving ceremonies at the trade posts, with fortifications, well-armed brigades, and the perpetual readiness to use force.

Contemporary notions of the manly behaviour befitting fur trade gentlemen are spelled out in the officers' narratives and form a strong undercurrent in their commentaries on indigenous men. For example, in the midst of a passage praising the clean and handsome dress of Plateau hunters, John Work drew attention to a lapse:

> The young, and especially the males . . . occupy no inconsiderable portion of the morning decorating themselves[;] in point of time, and the degree of pains taken to ornament their hair, paint their faces &c they may compete with the more accomplished fops in the civilised world.[29]

The resonance with early nineteenth-century middle-class notions of respectable manhood is striking. For the new man of enterprise such affectations were a waste of time, and invoked the decadence of an idle and self-absorbed aristocracy. The alternative model implied here would seem to be one of serious manhood, modesty, and self-restraint. The emergence of this new man in Britain, in an era of burgeoning urban capitalism and ascendent Evangelical religion, has been convincingly portrayed by Davidoff and Hall. Masculinity was redefined in terms of a harsh work ethic, independent enterprise, piety, sobriety, and dedication to family.[30] This model of manhood had more significance, perhaps, for the traders' self-image than for their imaginings of buffalo hunters. However, the two are closely intertwined. While the texts considered here are explicitly about manly buffalo hunters, implicitly they are about white middle-class men.

Simpson's own model points to the paradoxes that marked fur trade manhood in this period. Simpson was very much the sober man of business, yet he also sought to prove his worth in more physical pursuits. His pride in the success of his canoes drew on a sporting code more closely associated with the gentry, the very social class whose notions of masculinity the middle class in this era so vigorously rejected. Perhaps fur trade country provided an irresistible arena for such physical tests of manhood. Certainly, buffalo hunters provided an irresistible challenge to British men.

Trader commentary on Plateau hunters was a transparently masculine discourse. The masculinity that traders imagined the buffalo hunters to possess was complex, conceived as it was in the encounter with cultural difference. These hunters were at once brave and martial, savage and technologically backward. Difference was defined in trader narratives in cultural terms, as a matter of "customs," "manners" and "habits" rather than organic or biological difference. The formal questionnaire on "Natural History" which the London Committee of the Hudson's Bay Company began circulating to its trade posts in the mid-1820s, for instance, asked after the Indians' "habits," "usual occupations" and practices.[31] In keeping with dominant eighteenth- and early nineteenth-century assumptions about the universal brotherhood of man and the perfectibility of the "backward" races, British traders believed in the potential of the Indian for improvement. The doctrine of perfectibility was, however, a double-edged sword: encoded within it were both equality and difference. If Indian hunters were *potentially* just like British men, even the most noteworthy of them were not there yet. Assumptions of essential difference—or more accurately, essential inferiority—frequently rose to the surface in trader narratives.

All this attention to the symbolism in traders' texts is not meant to down-play the material logic; the trade itself shaped traders' perceptions of the manly and the good. The furs and hides produced by Plateau buffalo hunters, particularly the Salish Flathead and Kutenai, were critical to the profits of the trading companies in the Columbia Department. Between 1825 and the late 1840s, the only period for which reliable records exist, the trade district which included outposts in Salish and Kutenai territories produced, on average, 52 percent of total fur returns from the Columbia Interior (about 18 percent of fur returns for the entire region west of the Rockies). The buffalo hunts of these peoples were also vital to Columbia operations, providing leather for pack cords, portable hide lodges, and horse gear, as well as welcome infusions of fresh and dried meat for the local posts and travel food. Material concerns loomed large, then, in the traders' valorization of the buffalo hunters. But there was far more than instrumental logic to this imagery.

The principal distinguishing feature of the Plateau buffalo hunt, as traders depicted it, was the premium it placed on bravery. As the Salish chief known as Cartier told David Thompson, "when [we] go to hunt the Bison, we also prepare for war."[32] Hunting by Plateau groups in the parklands of the Rocky Mountains and the Plains to the east brought them into pitched competition with their longstanding Plains foes, the members of the Blackfoot Confederacy. Traders based in the Plateau favoured local hunters in these confrontations, not least because the Blackfoot had so resolutely resisted traders' attempts to penetrate their territory en route to the Plateau in the opening years of the nineteenth century.

Traders endowed the buffalo hunting of Plateau groups with a lofty moral significance. In his ethnographic summary of these peoples, Ross Cox emphasized that those qualities which "ranked among the virtues" were most conspicuous among the buffalo hunters. He singled out the Salish and Upper Kutenai for special praise:

> Their bravery is pre-eminent; a love of truth they think necessary to a warrior's character. They are too proud to be dishonest, too candid to be cunning. Their many avocations leave them no leisure for gambling; and their strict subordination, joined to the necessity of exerting all their energies against the common enemy, prevents them from quarrelling.[33]

Burdened as it is by Cox's taste for purple prose, the passage captures well the perceived nobility of these hunters. What are the implications of the form of masculinity affirmed here for men of Cox's station? The answer is not readily gleaned from his narrative. Cox does on occasion admit to insecurity in the presence of armed Indian warriors. But it seems that he aspired to a rather different model of manhood. In another passage he depicts himself "Hunting, fishing, fowling, horse-racing," enjoying the classic sporting pursuits of the man of leisure.[34] Cox's social aspirations were consistent with his design to make his book attractive to a British travel literature audience, many of whom would have been members of the leisured classes. His buffalo hunter presents an alternative image of manhood. Here is the noble savage in all his glory: brave to a fault, proud, morally upright, diligent, and warlike.

Warrior imagery pervades traders' accounts.[35] The Plateau hunters' exploits against the Blackfoot were rendered in gripping detail in a number of the narratives. Thompson's account made very explicit the link between buffalo hunting and war. By 1811, three years after their first trade of muskets from the North West Company, the Salish and Kutenai had regained much of the buffalo territory they had long claimed as their own. The following summer, a massed war party of about 350 Salish, Kutenai, Kalispel, Spokane, and others set off to extend their hunting territory onto lands claimed by the Piegan, members of the Blackfoot confederacy. Thompson was impressed with the sentiments expressed in the council that preceded the battle. Although they would prefer peace, it could not be relied upon in present circumstances, so the Plateau hunters would go to war. Chief Cartier urged the warriors, in Thompson's rendition, to "show ourselves to be men, and make ourselves respected."[36]

At the appointed time in August, when the buffalo bulls were in best condition for the kill, the Plateau party proceeded to the Plains:

> [T]he hunting was carried on with cautious boldness into the lands of their enemies, this insult brought on a battle . . . [the Piegan] advanced singing and dancing, the Saleesh saw the time was come to bring their whole force into line . . . they also sung and danced their wild war dance; the Peegans [sic] advanced to within about one hundred and fifty yards, the song and the dance ceased, the wild war yell was given, and the rush forward; it was gallantly met, several were slain on each side, and three times as many wounded, and with difficulty the Peegans carried off their dead and wounded and they accounted themselves defeated.[37]

In Thompson's eyes, the Salish and their allies had indeed shown themselves to be men. What began as courageous hunting soon developed into its natural extension, war. Here two of the most enduring and powerful images of idealized masculinity in the European tradition, the hunter and the warrior, form a potent combination.

Thompson's account betrays the tensions and ambiguities inherent in the valorizing of indigenous buffalo hunters. The traits which define their exceptional masculinity are the very traits which mark them as Indian, and therefore inferior to their British observers. The boundary between the heroic culture of hunter-warrior and savage nature is a brittle one in trader discourse. What starts as a display of masculine bravery ends in a display of the primitive natural world—the "wild war dance" and the "wild war yell"—played out in the enmity of two savage peoples. The account reveals just how close the noble savage is to his ignoble alter ego, how quickly the brave hunter can become the murderous brute. Governor Simpson slipped into similarly essentialist assumptions. On one occasion he extolled the Kutenai as fine hunters; on another, he scorned them as treacherous barbarians bent on plunder.[38] The buffalo hunter might be manly and noble but he was, still, representative of a savage race. The tensions inherent in hunter-warrior imagery ran very deep.

Quite apart from the warfare it entailed, the buffalo hunt was seen as requiring courage of another sort. The buffalo itself epitomized savage nature in this region. Buffalo herds presented an awesome spectacle. Alexander Ross reported seeing one herd that numbered at least ten thousand. With his customary flourish, and with the Victorian adventure reader in mind, he asserted that there was no animal more fierce than a buffalo bull in rutting season: "Neither the polar bear nor the Bengal tiger surpass that animal in ferocity." Ross's allusion to other British colonial possessions places his work squarely in the tradition of the imperial adventure tale, which was just coming into full flower at the time his narratives were published.[39]

According to traders' accounts, when not mortally wounded the buffalo was known to turn on its hunter. It fairly defied man to kill it. Yet so savage was this beast that, in Thompson's words, it was "never pitied." Ross recounted how a badly wounded animal propped itself on front legs and stared him down until he and his colleagues had pumped ten balls into its mass. Even then, they kept their distance, "for such is their agility of body, their quickness of eye, and so hideous are the looks of the beast, that we dared not for some time approach him."[40] In this instance Ross himself donned the mantle of heroic hunter. In doing so, Ross may well have been influenced by the model of manhood presented by Indian hunters. Cultural theorist Homi Bhabha observes that representation of cultural others always involves an ambiguous process of projection and introjection, of condemnation and desire.[41] In casting himself in the role of manly buffalo hunter pitted against the west's most savage foe, Ross is momentarily united with the Indian hunter of his imagination.

But again this imagery is complex. In his big-game hunting exploits, Ross has another point of identification which lies closer to his own ethnic home. Generations of more privileged men in Britain had routinely sought to prove their manhood and their social status in the pursuit of this most excellent sport. By the early nineteenth century the hunting cult of the British upper classes was being extended to the colonies, and to men who in Britain might have had no claim to gentility. By the time Ross published his Plateau narratives at mid-century, growing numbers of British traders, army officers, colonial administrators and others were testing their masculine mettle against the big game of Africa, India, and to a lesser extent North America. "Shooting madness" was an increasingly common affliction which Ross could be sure his readers would appreciate. The emerging class, national and gender connotations of big-game hunting go some way toward explaining Ross's proud portrayal of his encounter with a buffalo and his invocation of Bengal tigers and polar bears.

A central feature of Victorian hunting discourse was its preoccupation with the masculinity of *British* hunters. In pointing up the exceptional manliness of white sportsmen, Victorian hunting ideology tended to emphasize the cowardliness and wastefulness of indigenous hunters. The pattern is clearly revealed in the narratives of British sport hunters in Africa and India in the mid- and late nineteenth century.[42] Ross sought to cast his lot with these imperial hunters, but he stopped short of representing indigenous hunters as inferior. This peculiarity of trader accounts may have arisen because the men were operating in a very different political-economic context than later, imperial hunters. Fur traders were in the advance guard of colonialism. They did not compete with Aboriginal people for land and resources; rather, they were dependent on them for access to those resources. Not until the fur trade gave way to the settlement frontier would material competition lead to a hardening of colonial discourse and a systematic refiguring of the Indian hunter as wasteful brute.[43]

The buffalo hunt, with its dual challenge of Plains enemies and savage beasts, represented the supreme test of the courage and fortitude of manly Indian hunters. In facing such challenges, Plateau hunters distinguished themselves yet again through their successful application of the tools of European technology. And once again, the tensions implicit in making these hunters into heroes come to the surface. By Cox's account, Salish hunters had been brave even before they acquired firearms from the traders. They had yearly marched to the buffalo plains with nothing to oppose the Blackfoot "but arrows and their own undaunted bravery." This bravery had the whisper of a fatal flaw. The Salish were frequently routed by their better-armed foes, but despite their losses appeared unable to restrain themselves. What was at the root of this destructive obsession? It was the love of the hunt, what Cox called their "unconquerable hereditary attachment" to the chase.[44] The Salish were brave—braver, perhaps, than Cox could ever hope to be—but that bravery was itself a mark of their Indianness. Their desire to hunt was unreasonable, an expression of primitive nature. As is so often the case in such colonial discourses, in the midst of a passage praising the virtues of the Indian comes a forceful—perhaps an anxious—reminder of his difference.

Thompson recalled the joy of Salish elders in 1810 at seeing the "alacrity" with which the younger men went off to the Plains with their new guns. A dogged proponent of European technology, Thompson reasoned that without guns, the Salish would have been "pitiful," "defenceless," forced to operate in the Plains "by stealth." Stealth, in his view, was the mode of cowards; real men would "hunt boldly and try a battle."[45] The image of these hunters as possessors of new, progressive power over the forces of nature and human foes is most pronounced in Thompson's writings. His devotion to the theme is not surprising, given his personal commitment to the technologies of the day. During his twenty-six years in fur trade country, Thompson's principal interest was exploration, scientific survey, and observation; he produced a series of remarkably accurate maps of the vast area between Hudson Bay and the Pacific Ocean, south to the Columbia River. Thompson's activities are in many ways emblematic of his culture's increasing confidence in the capacity of humans to delve into and master the secrets of the natural world. His views on the salutary effects of firearms were registered in his account of improvements in Salish and Kutenai hunting. He was convinced that guns allowed these hunters greater technical mastery. Their flint-headed arrows "broke against the Shield of tough Bison hide . . . their only aim was the face; these [bows and arrows] they were now to exchange for Guns, Ammunition and Iron headed arrows," the better to face both beasts and men.[46] Thompson's optimism about the superiority of firearms for buffalo hunting was overstated. His views may have moderated had he stayed in the Columbia beyond 1812, and seen that bow and arrow remained in wide use long after guns became available.[47]

Implicit in all this discussion of bravery in the face of beastly foes and technology in the service of men is a whole set of European ideas about the human capacity to dominate nature. Contemporary discourse on the subject, and on the relationship between the state of a society and its physical environment, is too complex to rehearse here.[48] By the measures of the day, Plateau peoples dwelt in the state of nature, the rudimentary "hunter" stage. It would require a rash leap of logic to suggest that British traders equated the killing of buffalo by Indian hunters with the perceived domination of nature by European culture. But a critical aspect of the presumed relationship between humans and their environment was its mutability. Progress out of the rude state of nature was possible, indeed many would say inevitable. In the minds of the traders, the first imperative of that progress was mastery of the tools of a superior technology. The native skills of the buffalo hunters enabled them to master those tools and to extend their authority over nature.

The perception that buffalo hunters were rendered more manly and more powerful by the possession of firearms at once reinforced and checked their imagined masculinity. Many remarked that those they defined as hunters (in contrast to "fishermen") were better equipped to cope with the demands of this new and powerful European technology. Writing of the Salish and Kutenai, Thompson noted that their long practice at hunting deer from horseback made them adept with bow and arrow and prepared them well for the change to muskets. Another trader made a similar observation about the Cayuse, remarking that their experience as hunters gave them a "singular dexterity." Interestingly, Thompson described the skill of the Plateau hunters as superior to that of their Plains foes.[49] This observation probably says more about traders' biases against the Blackfoot than it does about relative hunting abilities.

In an intriguing inversion of such reasoning, the gun also served as a marker of the native hunters' inferiority. Whether the hunters were heroic or "pitiful" before the gun, they were all rendered dependent on the traders for its benefits. The narratives speak volumes about the confidence this advantage bestowed. In his first winter in the Plateau (1811), Ross found his musket to be of profound practical and symbolic benefit. It gave him a sense of security in the face of a wolf attack, an event which he recalled had terrified the Indians. The gun also afforded a symbolic dominance over the Indians, who, according to Ross, were awed by this technology. After killing a wolf at a distance he claimed to be five arrow shots, the trader enthused that "nothing but [the Indians'] wonder could exceed their admiration of this effect of firearms." Ye-whell-come-tetsa, a prominent Okanagan leader, appears in the narrative thanking Ross for his assistance and proclaiming "we have nothing to fear . . . I shall always love the whites."[50] Manly as the hunter-warriors might be, they were in the end representatives of a primitive race. Their manliness was always constrained, in trader discourse, by the assertion that they lacked certain attributes which only the British traders could supply.

This rhetorical strategy had the added benefit, of course, of securing the traders' masculinity. The "warrior" nature of Plateau hunters at times posed a serious threat to the traders, who had to live safely among these people if they were to succeed in their venture and retain their own manly identities. Ross penned what must be the most self-conscious assertion of imperial masculine hegemony in the whole of the Plateau record. Recounting the 1818 building of Fort Walla Walla, a strategic post on the Columbia River, Ross mustered his considerable narrative skills. A formidable structure was needed to protect traders and to tame the "many war-like tribes that infest the country." Fort Walla Walla was the only North West Company post protected by a double wall; Indian traders were admitted through the outer wall and had to conduct trade through a small aperture in the inner one, which shielded the company dwellings and storehouse. The whole was surrounded by six-metre palisades and fortified towers, and defended with cannons and muskets. Ross's enthusiasm at the building of the fort exposes the symbolic function of such a structure for the traders.[51] Dubbed "the Gibraltar of the Columbia," it kept "savagery" at bay:

> as if by enchantment, the savage disposition of the Indians was either soothed or awed, a stronghold had arisen in the desert, while the British banner floating over it proudly proclaimed the mistress of a vast territory; it was an example of British energy and enterprise, of civilization over barbarism.[52]

The imperial discourse is loud and clear, and surely tailored to Ross's intended Victorian readership. Britannia prevails over a race which may be martial and powerful, but is at base savage. The remark that the Indians are perhaps "soothed" by this assertion of British power even hints that they are aware of their own inferiority. The masculine discourse is embedded in and inseparable from the imperial.[53] The war-like tribes are subdued by the appearance of this hulking fortress, and British traders have proven their worth, both as traders and as men. They have prevailed over the threat from these potential enemies, and exhibited their manliness in the very act of erecting the fort. It stands as a symbol of their "energy and enterprise," ultimate masculine virtues in the idioms of early nineteenth-century capitalism and the fur trade alike.

As it turned out, control over these groups was elusive. Ross soon resumed complaining about the "insolence" and "independence" of the people around Walla Walla, and his successors voiced similar sentiments.[54] But the historical accuracy or inaccuracy of Ross's account is not the point. The gap between his initial, confident assumption of British male authority and his later accounts of continued challenges to that authority speaks to the gap that probably will always exist between imagined and lived masculine identities. Ross anxiously hoped that British traders would prevail over Indian hunters in this desert "wilderness." The reality, it seems, was continual challenges to British manhood, continual contests between variant expressions of masculine identity. Still, Ross's writings reveal the gendered nature of traders' relationships with indigenous men and the ways in which the traders' discourse was constituted through hierarchies of gender, class and race.

NOTES

1. The quotations are from Alexander Henry's "Journal," in *New Light on the Early History of the Greater Northwest . . . vol. 2: Alexander Henry's Journal*, ed. Elliott Coues (Ross and Haines, Minneapolis, 1897), 707. The terms "Indian," "hunter," and "fisherman" are used here as categories employed by the traders. "Indian" refers throughout to the discursive Indian, the indigenous male (for traders wrote mainly about men) inscribed in trader narratives. On the rhetorical displacement of indigenous peoples implicit in the use of the label "Indian," see Carrol Smith-Rosenberg, "Captured Subjects/Savage Others: Violently Engendering the New American," *Gender and History*, 5 (1993), 177–95. The terms "hunter" and "fisherman" set up artificial categories. The seasonal rounds of all Plateau societies were far more complex, and based on a more diverse range of gathered, hunted, and fished resources, than such labels imply. Women's production was critical to the subsistence base. See Elizabeth Vibert, *Traders' Tales: British Fur Traders' Narratives of Cultural Encounters in the Plateau, 1807–1846* (Oxford University D.Phil. dissertation, 1993; revised and forthcoming, University of Oklahoma Press, 1996).

2. This essay focuses on relationships between British trader and Plateau hunter masculinities. Traders' relationships with Plateau femininities are explored in Vibert, *Traders' Tales*, ch. 3. Differences of national identity among traders were eroded in the North American fur trade, where men's identities and interests came into line with the agendas of British-run overseas trading companies. Men of "gentleman" or officer rank became an "imagined community," collaborating across divisive boundaries and internal hierarchies. Benedict Anderson's notion of "horizontal comradeship" seems especially appropriate in this context. See his *Imagined Communities: Reflections on the Origins and Spread of Nationalism* (Verso, New York, 1983).

3. For discussions of the complexity and ambivalence of European attitudes toward the indigenous peoples of the Americas, see Hugh Honour, *The New Golden Land: European Images of America from the Discoveries to the Present Time* (Pantheon Books, New York, 1975); Tzvetan Todorov, *The Conquest of America: The Question of the Other* (Harper and Row, New York, 1984); Robert Berkhofer, *The White Man's Indian* (Vintage, New York, 1978); Mary Louise Pratt, *Imperial Eyes: Travel Writing and Transculturation* (Routledge, London, 1992); Anthony Pagden, *The Fall of Natural Man: The American Indian and the Origins of Comparative Ethnology* (Cambridge University Press, Cambridge, 1986); Fredi Chiapelli (ed.) *First Images of America: The Impact of the New World on the Old*, 2 vols. (University of California Press, Berkeley, 1976); P. J. Marshall and Glyndwr Williams, *The Great Map of Mankind: Perceptions of New Worlds in the Age of Enlightenment* (Harvard University Press, Cambridge, 1982); Antonello Gerbi, *The Dispute of the New World: The History of a Polemic, 1750–1900* (University of Pittsburgh Press, Pittsburgh, 1973).

4. These dates mark, respectively, the entry of North West Company traders into the Plateau region, and the establishment of the international boundary between U.S. and British North American possessions west of the Rockies. By 1846 political events and swelling numbers of settlers were pointing to the demise of the fur trade in the region.

5. Homi Bhabha, *The Location of Culture* (Routledge, London, 1994), 162.

6. These days, traders' writings are routinely pillaged for information about Aboriginal land use patterns

by those involved in land-claims cases before the British Columbia and federal courts. In a controversial recent decision, Chief Justice Allan McEachern of the B. C. Supreme Court, finding against the Gitksan and Wet'suwet'en plaintiffs, privileged traders' accounts as "fact" while dismissing Aboriginal elders' oral histories as "cultural belief." There are as yet very few studies of the social construction of fur traders' narratives. The best recent analysis, on a limited theme, is Mary Black-Rogers's "Varieties of 'Starving': Semantics and Survival in the Subarctic Fur Trade," *Ethnohistory*, 33 (1986), 353–83. It should be noted that most, though not all, of the writings under scrutiny here were prepared specifically for publication; this shaped their production in particular ways, and distinguished them from daily fieldnotes, journals, letters, and annual post reports. See Ian MacLaren, "Exploration/Travel Literature and the Evolution of the Author," *International Journal of Canadian Studies*, 5 (1992), 39–67. For broader discussion of the implicit demands imposed on authors and publishers by travel literature audiences, see Paul Carter, *The Road to Botany Bay: Landscape and History* (University of Chicago Press, Chicago, 1987); Pratt, *Imperial Eyes*; Billie Melman, *Women's Orients. English Women and the Middle East, 1718–1918: Sexuality, Religion and Work* (University of Michigan Press, Ann Arbor, 1992); Stephen Greenblatt, *Marvellous Possessions: The Wonder of the New World* (University of Chicago Press, Chicago, 1991); Germaine Warkentin, "Introduction," in *Canadian Exploration Literature: An Anthology*, ed. Germaine Warkentin (Oxford University Press, Toronto and Oxford, 1993), ix–xxi.

7. On the process whereby the buffalo-hunting Indian became *the* Indian of popular imagination, see Rayna Green, "The Tribe Called Wannabee: Playing Indian in America and Europe," *Folklore*, 99 (1988), 30–43,

and John Ewers, "The Emergence of the Plains Indian as the Symbol of the North American Indian," *Annual Report of the Smithsonian Institution* (1964), 531–55.

8. David Thompson, "Narrative," in *David Thompson's Narrative of his Explorations in Western America, 1784–1812*, ed. J. B. Tyrrell (Champlain Society, Toronto, 1916), 80.

9. See John MacKenzie, *Empire of Nature: Hunting, Conservation and British Imperialism* (Manchester University Press, Manchester, 1988); Mahesh Rangarajan, "Hunting and Conservation in India," Oxford University D.Phil. dissertation, 1992; William Beinart, "Empire, Hunting, and Ecological Change in Southern and Central Africa," *Past and Present*, 128 (1990), 162–86; E. P. Thompson, *Whigs and Hunters: The Origin of the Black Act* (Allen Lane, London, 1977). On hunting in North America, see R. M. Ballantyne, especially *The Buffalo Runners: A Tale of the Red River Plains* (Nisbet, London, 1891) and *Away in the Wilderness* (Nisbet, London, n.d.).

10. MacKenzie, *Empire of Nature*, 86–95; Beinart, "Empire, Hunting," 163, 167, 174; Richard Grove, "Scottish Missionaries, Evangelical Discourses, and the Origins of Conservation Thinking," *Journal of Southern African Studies*, 15 (1989), 163–87.

11. J. M. Coetzee, *White Writings: On the Culture of Letters in South Africa* (Yale University Press, New Haven, 1988), 32.

12. MacKenzie, *Empire of Nature*, 95; Beinart, "Empire, Hunting," 163.

13. Hudson's Bay Company Archives D.3/1, fos.61–62. All HBC documents, housed at the Provincial Archives of Manitoba, Winnipeg, are denoted hereafter by the prefix HBCA. For a more nuanced account of perceptions of Plateau fishing groups, see Vibert, *Traders' Tales*, ch. 3 & 4.

14. For accessible overviews of the North American fur trade see Glyndwr Williams, "The Hudson's Bay Com-

pany and the Fur Trade, 1670–1870," special issue of *The Beaver*, 314 (1983); E. E. Rich, *The Fur Trade and the Northwest to 1857* (McClelland & Stewart, Toronto, 1967). For an international perspective, see Eric Wolf, *Europe and the People Without History* (University of California Press, Berkeley, 1982), ch. 6.

15. The NWC faced fierce competition from the American Fur Company in the period 1811–13; otherwise, it had the land-based fur trade of the region to itself. The Plateau, or "Columbia Interior" in fur trade parlance, comprised the interior reaches of the Columbia Department. This latter name applied to the entire administrative district west of the Rocky Mountains: present-day British Columbia, Washington State, and portions of Oregon, Idaho, and Montana.

16. The best treatments of fur trade social history remain Jennifer S.H. Brown, *Strangers in Blood: Fur Trade Company Families in Indian Country* (University of British Columbia Press, Vancouver, 1980), and Sylvia Van Kirk, *"Many Tender Ties": Women in Fur-Trade Society, 1670–1870* (Watson and Dwyer, Winnipeg, 1980). While most NWC officers were Scots, those whose writings are canvassed here were more diverse: Thompson was of Welsh parentage; Cox and Work were Irish.

17. The Orkneys and Hebrides were popular recruiting grounds for "stout" and "serious" young men with few economic alternatives. They were never figured as Scots by their superiors, although they were less "other" than French Canadian, Métis, Aboriginal or Hawaiian men. Given the relatively favourable discourse about Orcadians, they could be said to have functioned as what Spivak calls "self-consolidating" others. Gayatri Spivak, *In Other Worlds: Essays in Cultural Politics* (Methuen, London, 1987).

18. After a long period of institutional resistance, and counter-resistance by company employees, by the nineteenth century unions made in the custom of the country were sanctioned by "immemorial custom" as proper marriages. HBCA B.223/b/21 fos.4–12.

19. Ross Cox, *The Columbia River, or Scenes and Adventures . . .*, ed. E. I. Stewart and J. R. Stewart ([London, 1831]; repr. University of Oklahoma Press, Norman, 1957), 230, 360; Alexander Ross, *Fur Hunters of the Far West*, ed. K. A. Spaulding ([London, 1855]; repr. University of Oklahoma Press, Norman, 1956), 7–10, 19–20; R. Harvey Fleming, (ed.) *Minutes of Council Northern Department of Rupert Land, 1821–31* (Champlain Society, Toronto, 1940), 25–26; HBCA B.223/b/4 fo.31.

20. See Michael Payne, "Daily Life on Western Hudson Bay 1714–1870: A Social History of York Factory and Churchill" (Carleton University PhD dissertation, 1989), 389–90. A similar pattern developed in the Plateau. See, for example, Cox, *The Columbia*, 230.

21. Lenore Davidoff and Catherine Hall, *Family Fortunes: Men and Women of the English Middle Class, 1780–1850* (University of Chicago Press, Chicago, 1987), 17, 357 and ch. 8.

22. Quoted in Van Kirk, *"Many Tender Ties,"* 136.

23. Rev. William Cockran, quoted in Van Kirk, *"Many Tender Ties,"* 172.

24. On the shifting processes of racial and class ranking associated with Aboriginal, Métis and British women in fur trade society, see Van Kirk, *"Many Tender Ties,"* and Brown, *Strangers in Blood*.

25. Some traders privately denounced the callousness with which Simpson had treated his country wife, Margaret Taylor, and remained committed to their own wives and families. See Van Kirk, *"Many Tender Ties,"* and Christine Welsh, "Voices of the Grandmothers: Reclaiming a Métis Heritage," *Canadian Literature*, 131 (1991), 15–25.

26. George Simpson, "Journal 1824–25," in *Fur Trade and Empire: George Simpson's Journal . . . 1824–25*, ed. Frederick Merk (1931; repr. Harvard University Press, Cambridge, 1968), 140; HBCA D.3/1 fo.102.

27. HBCA D.3/1 fo.24.

28. These are persistent themes in fur trade records. See HBCA B.223/b/30 fo.49, McLoughlin to the Governor and Committee, 15 Nov. 1843; E. E. Rich, ed. *The Letters of John McLoughlin*, Vol. 1, 48; HBCA D.5/6 fos.173–74.

29. HBCA B.45/e/2 fo.5.

30. Davidoff and Hall, *Family Fortunes*, 108–18.

31. HBCA, PP 1828-1, "Queries Connected with the Natural History of the Honorable Hudson's Bay Company's Territories."

32. Thompson, "Narrative," 533.

33. Cox, *The Columbia*, 264, 267.

34. Cox, *The Columbia*, 93–94, 215.

35. Cox, *The Columbia*, 81; Ross, *Fur Hunters*, 200; HBCA B.69/a/1 fo.3. For similar observations see Alexander Ross, *Adventures of the First Settlers on the Oregon or Columbia River* ([London, 1849]; repr. Lakeside Press, Chicago, 1923), 243, 268; John Work, "Journal No. 4," fo.166, original in British Columbia Archives and Records Service, Victoria, B.C.

36. Thompson, "Narrative," 548–52.

37. Thompson, "Narrative," 548–52.

38. HBCA D.3/1 fo.11; HBCA D.3/2 fo.93.

39. Ross, *Fur Hunters*, 243, 283. Although his service in the Plateau ended in the mid-1820s, Ross's two Plateau narratives were not published until 1849 and 1855.

40. Ross, *Fur Hunters*, 243, 283; Thompson, "Narrative," 432.

41. Bhabha, *The Location of Culture*, ch. 3 & 4.

42. MacKenzie, *Empire of Nature*.

43. An expansion of this argument can be found in Vibert, *Traders' Tales*, ch. 7.

44. HBCA B.69/a/1 fos.3,6; Cox, *The Columbia*, 134; HBCA B.45/e/3 fos.12–13.

45. Thompson, "Narrative," 411, 420, 424.

46. Thompson, "Narrative," 411, 463.

47. Vibert, *Traders' Tales*, ch. 4 & 6.

48. See Ludmilla Jordanova, "Earth Science and Environmental Medicine: The Synthesis of the Late Enlightenment," in *Images of the Earth: Essays in the History of the Environmental Sciences* (British Society for the History of Science, Chalfont St. Giles, 1979) and Jordanova, *Sexual Visions: Images of Gender in Science and Medicine* (Harvester Wheatsheaf, Hemel Hempstead, 1989); Richard Grove, *Conservation and Colonial Expansion* (forthcoming, Cambridge University Press, Cambridge); Marshall and Williams, *The Great Map of Mankind*.

49. Thompson, "Narrative," 411, 420, 424, 463, 549; Phillip Rollins (ed.) "Journey of Mr. Hunt and His Companions . . . ," in *The Discovery of the Oregon Trail* (Edward Eberstadt, New York, 1935), 303.

50. Ross, *Fur Hunters*, 48–52, 114.

51. His enthusiasm apparently got the better of him. Archaeological evidence indicates that the fort was rather smaller than Ross recalled. See Theodore Stern, *Chiefs and Chief Traders: Indian Relations at Fort Nez Percés, 1818–1855* (Oregon State University Press, Portland, 1993), ch. 1.

52. Ross, *Fur Hunters*, 119–20, 144–46.

53. For recent studies analysing nineteenth-century British imperialism as a profound historical expression of British masculinity, see Graham Dawson, "The Blond Bedouin: Lawrence of Arabia, Imperial Adventure, and the Imagining of English-British Masculinity," and other essays in *Manful Assertions:*

Masculinities in Britain since 1800, ed. Michael Roper and John Tosh (Routledge, London and New York, 1991); Catherine Hall, *White, Male and Middle Class: Explorations in Feminism and History* (Polity and Routledge, London and New York, 1992); J. A. Mangan and James Walvin (eds.) *Manliness and Morality: Middle-Class Masculinity in Britain and America, 1800–1940* (Manchester University Press, Manchester, 1987); Lynne Segal, *Slow Motion: Changing Masculinities, Changing Men* (Virago, London, 1990), esp. ch. 7; Mrinalini Sinha, "Gender and Imperialism: Colonial Policy and the Ideology of Moral Imperialism in Late Nineteenth-Century Bengal," in *Changing Men: New Directions in Research on Men and Masculinity*, ed. Michael S. Kimmel (Sage, London, 1987). Also suggestive are Helen Callaway, *Gender, Culture, and Empire: European Women in Colonial Nigeria* (University of Illinois Press, Urbana, 1987); Chandra Talpade Mohanty, "Introduction: Cartographies of Struggle," in *Third World Women and the Politics of Feminism*, ed. Chandra Talpade Mohanty, Ann Russo and Lourdes Torres (Indiana University Press, Bloomington and Indianapolis, 1991).

54. Ross, *Fur Hunters*, 154–55; HBCA B.146/a/1,2; HBCA B.223/b/11 fo.49.

section 3

RACE

○

RACE, GENDER AND CANADIAN IMMIGRATION POLICY: BLACKS FROM THE CARIBBEAN, 1900–1932 ◇

AGNES CALLISTE

◯

INTRODUCTION

The history of the labour migration of Caribbean blacks to Canada in the early 1900s has been largely ignored in social science research in favour of the Oklahoma black migration to the prairies and the recent movement from the Caribbean.[1] This study examines two migrations of Caribbean blacks to Canada between 1900 and 1932 from a political economy perspective. The first group of Caribbean immigrants went to Nova Scotia, especially to Sydney, to work in the steel mills and coal mines. The second group comprised female domestic workers recruited from Guadeloupe and the British Caribbean to help fill the demand for cheap domestic labour in Quebec, Ontario, and the Maritimes.[2] This paper provides insight into Canadian immigration policy and official attitudes towards blacks, particularly black women, in Canada between 1900 and 1932. It also offers a background for understanding immigration policies relating to other groups of black men and women, and facilitates the general analysis of Canada's racialized and gendered immigration policies from an historical perspective.

Canada's immigration policy regarding Caribbean blacks between 1900 and 1932 was structured by a dialectic of economic, political, and ideological relations: employers' demand for cheap labour to do unskilled and domestic work was set in tension with the state's desire to exclude blacks as perma-

---

◇ Reprinted with permission from *Journal of Canadian Studies*, 28, 4 (Winter 1993–94): 131–48.

nent settlers.[3] Caribbean blacks provided a reserve army of labour; they were employed in a split labour market where they were paid less than white workers for doing the same work.[4] For example, in 1910–11, Caribbean domestics in Quebec were paid less than half the monthly wage received by their white counterparts, though employers reported favourably on their performance. In the submerged, split labour market operating in the Sydney steel plant, blacks were restricted to working around the coke ovens or blast furnaces, relegated to the hottest, most physically demanding, and lowest paid jobs in the plant.[5] This situation demarcates a colour line beyond which only white workers are able to advance.[6] During economic contraction in the early 1900s, blacks were the first to be fired by most employers. As W.D. Scott, Immigration Superintendent, stated to the minister of immigration in 1918, "Coloured labour is not generally speaking in demand in Canada and it is not only regarded as the lowest grade, but it is the last to be taken on and the first to be discharged in most enterprises."[7] These discriminatory hiring practices demonstrated blacks' subordination in economic, political, and ideological relations and helped to fuel Canada's discriminatory immigrant policy against blacks. In turn, this policy further reinforced the subordinate status of black workers.

International labour migration was spurred by the uneven development associated with European colonialism and imperialism.[8] The development was marked by the massive accumulation of capital and the concentration of productive resources in some countries, together with underdevelopment and dependence on those countries by others. For the Caribbean countries, the economic legacy of colonialism and slavery in the early 1900s was underdevelopment; a single cash crop of sugar was the extent of development in most of the islands. High levels of unemployment, limited opportunities, and low wages in Caribbean economies, coupled with a demand for cheap labour in the more developed capitalist countries like Canada, resulted in long traditions of emigration for Caribbean women and men.[9] Caribbean governments and agencies encouraged emigration as a means of reducing their respective surplus populations and unemployment, stimulating economic growth through remittances sent home by emigrants, as well as improving the economic conditions of emigrants and their families. For example, in 1923 and 1924 the governor of the Leeward Islands asked Canada to take in 1000 Antiguans as migrant harvesters in order to relieve Antigua's unemployment.[10] Moreover, in 1928, Jamaica's Young Women's Christian Association (YWCA) proposed to the Canadian government that an "intelligent, superior class of domestics" be trained with the understanding that the Canadian government would recruit them.[11]

While the Canadian state regarded immigration as a way of resolving labour shortages and a source of future permanent citizens, its definition of suitable permanent citizens was structured by race, class, and gender. Section 38 of the 1910 Immigration Act empowered the governor-in-council to prohibit entry of immigrants belonging to "any race deemed unsuited to the climate or requirements of Canada, or of immigrants of any specified class, occupation or character."[12]

Blacks were stigmatized as mentally, morally, physically, and socially inferior and a potential social problem in Canada. It was feared that any influx of black immigrants would cause economic and race-relations problems similar to those experienced in the United States.[13] Immigration officials thus sought to avoid the problem by restricting the entry of black settlers. They argued that the importation of black labour as a temporary expedient to meet unusual demand pressures was not in the country's long-term interest if the immigrants were to remain permanently in Canada.[14] As Scott argued in 1915,

> It seems to me that Canada would be adopting a very short-sighted policy to encourage the immigration of coloured people of any class or occupation. At its best it would only be a policy of expediency and it is altogether unnecessary, in view of the present upheaval in Europe, which will unfortunately throw upon the labour market a large number of women of a most desirable class, who can be utilized for the permanent advantage of Canada ... [;] the Department is determined to shut down on any class of immigration which constitutes a serious problem and ... these coloured domestics ... are bound to meet with difficulties.[15]

Scott's statement indicated that the process of racialization and the ideologies of racism, sexism, and classism played a key role in the state's decision to restrict the entry of Caribbean blacks. Unlike British domestics who were expected to be prospective wives and mothers for the ideal Canadian home and thus contribute to Canada's "nation-building" enterprise, Caribbean women were seen as economic and social liabilities.[16]

The racialized, class-oriented, and gendered immigration policy concerning black people was based on the assumptions that they were biologically incapable of adjusting to the Canadian climate, incapable of assimilating themselves into Canadian society, and incapable of succeeding in its competitive, capitalist economy.[17] As late as 1955, the director of immigration argued against the immigration of Caribbean domestics, rehearsing an argument familiar during the period 1900 to 1932. In his words

> It is from experience, generally speaking, that coloured people in the present state of the white man's thinking are not a tangible asset, and as a result are more or less ostracized. They do not assimilate readily and pretty much vegetate to a low standard of living ... [;] many cannot adapt themselves to our climatic conditions. To enter into an agreement which would have the effect of increasing coloured immigration to this country would be an act of misguided generosity since it would not have the effect of bringing about a worthwhile solution to the problem of coloured people and would quite likely intensify our own social and economic problems.[18]

Another assumption in Canada's immigration policy was that working-class Caribbean women were "immoral," likely to become single parents, and eventually public charges.[19] These stereotypes of the "bad" black woman were used to justify the restriction and exclusion—even deportation—of Caribbean domestics. For instance, in July 1911, eight Guadeloupean domestics were denied entry to Canada when it was judged that they were likely to become a public charge because they were single parents. The immigration officer surmised that they were likely to become pregnant again and would probably become a drain upon the public purse. In that year, the domestic scheme (which had encouraged the immigration of Guadeloupean women to Quebec) was closed to further entries on the grounds that they were morally and physically unfit.[20]

These racialized, patriarchal, and class-based assumptions encouraged the belief that the economic and social cost of black immigration far outweighed the economic benefits. Thus, the entry of black immigrants was severely restricted except when there was an urgent demand for their labour. For example, in 1916 the Dominion Iron and Steel Company in Nova Scotia was given permission to import 1000 Caribbean labourers because suitable labour was not available from other sources. As Scott explained to the Inspector of Immigration Agencies in the Maritimes," The production of steel and coal must go on even at some expenses to the country, and the concession is made on the principle of being the lesser evil. You can readily understand how unwilling we would be here to make the concession under any but the strongest reasons."[21] However, the evidence suggests that most of the labourers were recruited from among "Austrians" released from the Ontario and Quebec internment camps. From 1915 to 1918 only 177 Caribbean blacks were admitted to Canada.[22]

The main source of data for this paper is the files of the immigration branch which exercised control over migration to Canada between 1900 and 1932. These files give an indication of the state's aim in forming immigration policy and the actual practices of state officials. Given that these documents were not initially intended for public consumption, they provide a more accurate picture of social processes than the public documents of state agencies.[23] However, they offer an incomplete picture of the extent of deportation of Caribbean domestics.

The discussion is organized as follows: the paper examines Canada's immigration policy and the migration of Caribbean blacks to Nova Scotia, particularly to Sydney. Second, it investigates the migration of Caribbean domestics.

IMMIGRATION OF CARIBBEAN BLACKS TO NOVA SCOTIA

Caribbean blacks began migrating to Canada in very small numbers at the turn of the century. They travelled on schooners that traded in the Caribbean and landed in Halifax, Nova Scotia and other Maritime ports. The schooner captains increased their profits by selling passage on the return run for $20 to $30, the passengers providing their own food and hammocks. Since they had no difficulty meeting immigration regulations— "good" character, physical, and mental health, and the $25 fee—they were admitted. The collector of customs at Port Hawkesbury described those arriving at his port as members of "the better class"; most of them had trades such as carpentry and mechanics. Many were Barbadians whose transportation costs were subsidized by their home government.[24]

Despite their skills, most of them were restricted to jobs in the Sydney mines and the steel plant's coke ovens because of the segregated workforce and the myth that blacks could withstand the heat better than whites. Some Caribbean blacks worked in service occupations (restaurant waiters and domestics), in trades, and in the shipyards in Halifax and Collingwood, Ontario. Their numbers were small, however, and there was no indication that any became public charges. Those who did not find work in Nova Scotia soon migrated to Boston.[25] The chief of police in Sydney, where the majority of Caribbean blacks found employment, spoke of them in 1909 as "always well-dressed and as being very civil in their manners."[26] Condescending as this acknowledgement was, it indicated that there was no cause for concern.

The Dominion Iron and Steel Company (DISCO) also imported Caribbean blacks to work in the mines and around the steel plant's coke ovens. The company relied on cheap and controllable immigrant labour to reduce its costs in order to compete effectively with American iron and steel producers. However, its isolated location, low wages, undesirable working and "wretched" living conditions made it difficult for the company to maintain a steady supply of cheap labour, particularly during busy periods of full employment. For example, Alabama blacks recruited by DISCO in 1899 to work around the coke ovens left Cape Breton shortly after their arrival.[27] Thus, from time to time, the company sent ethnic agents to recruit fellow immigrant workers. Between 1912 and 1914, management sent two Barbadian steel workers to Barbados to recruit labourers. The company paid the workers' transportation costs, which were later deducted from their wages. In the fiscal years from 1912 to 1915 more than 200 Caribbean blacks were admitted to Canada annually, predominantly to Nova Scotia. In 1920–21, DISCO also recruited 61 labourers from the Caribbean to work in the mines.[28]

Despite favourable reports about Caribbean blacks and employers' continuing demands for their cheap labour, the immigration branch was determined to exclude black immigrants who were deemed "undesirable." As Scott stated in 1914,

> The government does not encourage the immigration of coloured people. There are certain countries from which immigration is encouraged and certain races of people considered as suited to this [country] and its conditions, but Africans, no matter where they come from are not among the races sought, and hence, Africans no matter from what country they come are in common with the uninvited races, not admitted to Canada.[29]

In order to stop Caribbean blacks from entering the Maritimes, the immigration branch decided to tighten up local inspections by means of strict enforcement of immigration regulations. When this strategy failed, immigration agents were privately advised to exclude Caribbean blacks even when they compiled with the Immigration Act. As the Inspector of Immigration Agencies in the Maritimes suggested to Scott, "every obstacle is to be put in their way, and if everything else fails . . . reject them under subsection (g) of Sec. 3 of the Act, as "likely to become a public charge."[30] Caribbean blacks who complied with every immigration condition—health, money, assured employment, and relatives in Canada—were rejected as liable to become a public charge, particularly during the 1914–15 economic recession. It was reported that hundreds of Caribbean blacks were employed by DISCO while thousands of steel workers, including scores of Caribbean blacks, were laid off. Blacks were identified as potential public charges because of economic reasons and racism in immigration policy and employment. Blacks were more likely than whites to be unemployed during economic recession. At the same time they were blamed for taking away jobs from Canadians.[31] The immigration branch justified the exclusion of Caribbean blacks on the grounds that the government was encouraging only farmers and domestics to immigrate rather than those "whose presence in Canada would tend to add to the congestion of our towns and cities."[32]

However, the immigration department's concern over unemployment was partly an argument designed for public consumption. Immigration officials were unwilling to permit the entry of black immigrant labour even when there were labour shortages in Canada. For example, in January 1916, Scott refused to give DISCO permission to import 150 Caribbean blacks to fill labour shortages in its mines in Springhill and Sydney. He concluded that there "was absolutely no hope" of bringing blacks from the Caribbean or anywhere else, and suggested the company recruit miners from Newfoundland.[33] As for farmers, he argued that the record of American blacks showed that very few blacks did farming in Canada and they were generally unsuccessful. Though they were in demand as domestics, they were not likely to succeed in Canada. Thus, Caribbean blacks were excluded partly because of humanitarianism. After "years of experience," the state "decided not only in the interest of Canada, but also in the interest of coloured people themselves, not to encourage their settlement in this country."[34] The immigration branch was trying to stop Caribbean immigration while making it appear that they were not making decisions based on race.

In addition to barring blacks at the port-of-entry, the immigration branch tried to stop black immigration at its source. Steamship agents were strongly urged to discourage Caribbean immigration (for example, to stop selling tickets to blacks except merchants, students, and tourists), and they were expected to comply. Apart from the risk of having to return immigrants rejected at the port-of-entry, steamship agents could be liable for the cost of detaining passengers and returning deportees within three years (five in 1919) of their arrival in Canada.[35] Nine Caribbean blacks who arrived on the *Chaleur* at Saint John in July 1914 were detained as likely to become public charges. Despite protests from the Royal Mail Steam Packet Company that the passengers left the Caribbean before the immigration branch asked the shipping agencies to discourage black immigration, and the agency's promise to obtain guaranteed employment for the men, all nine appeals against deportation were dismissed. Scott argued that the assurance of employment was insufficient reason for admission, given acute unemployment. The jobs could be filled by Canadians. This incident and information from immigration officers that they were instructed to reject all blacks led steamship companies to conclude that the risks of having to return rejected immigrants, the cost of detaining passengers, and the cost of returning deportees after three years were too great. Thus, they refused to sell tickets to Caribbean blacks unless they had a "permit" from the Canadian government.[36]

This discriminatory immigration policy antagonized Caribbean people. The *Barbados Advocate* and Guyana's *Demerara Daily Chronicle* protested against Canada's "illegal discrimination."[37] They argued that it was likely to hinder Caribbean-Canadian relations. Though the governor-in-council had authority under Section 38 of the 1910 Immigration Act to prohibit the entry of immigrants deemed undesirable, there was no regulation prohibiting the entry of blacks. The exclusion of black settlers was illegal. *The Demerara Daily Chronicle*'s editor further argued that, since Caribbean people were fighting in France to defend the British Empire, they could adapt to Canadian climate and society. He suggested that if the Canadian government did not give a satisfactory explanation for excluding Caribbean people, the Guyana Chamber of Commerce should abolish the reciprocity treaty and institute a trade boycott against Canada.

These reports dismayed influential institutions with interests in Canada. For example, members of the West Indian League, which included corporations with trade interests and investments in the Caribbean, were particularly concerned. The league's secretary complained to Scott that the immigration branch's actions would hurt Canadian–Caribbean trade. He warned that immigration officials must take steps to clear up the impression that Canada did not want black immigrants. Some employers also expressed concern. For example, DISCO argued that it had an urgent demand for Caribbean miners in Springhill and Sydney.[38]

The mulattoes or "coloured" people, who occupied an intermediary position between whites and blacks in the colour stratification in the Caribbean, were alarmed about Canada's discriminatory immigration policy. They asked what "degree of mixture in the blood" would qualify an individual for admission? As Rev. Cropper from Guyana's Presbyterian Church explained:

> These coloured people are to all intents and purposes white, and would rank as such in a community where the racial question was not raised . . . the situation is not helping forward the relations between Canada and these Colonies where so large a section of the population is of mixed blood of every variety of degree and where the white man from England and Scotland does not hesitate to marry the coloured lady of education and refinement.[39]

These complaints were to no avail. Before the 1950s, Caribbean blacks did not have the economic and political power resources to hinder

Canadian investments and Canadian–Caribbean trade. The immigration branch denied that it discriminated against Caribbean blacks.[40] However, Scott sought to avoid further criticisms by advising his officers to be more diplomatic in public. He wrote

> I notice in a number of Board cases the cause of rejection includes the statement that the person rejected is a Negro and that instructions have been received to prevent the entry of Negroes in every possible way. While it is true that we are not seeking the immigration of coloured people . . . I do not think it is advisable to insert any notice of the instructions or policy of the Department in a Board decision or any other correspondence. . . . I am sure you will appreciate the view I have expressed and will understand the reason therefor.[41]

In the immediate post-war years, Canada enacted more restrictive immigration regulations because of the country's high unemployment rate, instances of labour unrest (for example, the Winnipeg General Strike), and the desire to restore the Anglo-Saxon character of the population. One of the most effective regulations used to restrict Caribbean blacks and other people of colour from the British Empire was Order-in-Council P.C. 717 of 1922, which prohibited the landing of immigrants except farmers, farm labourers and domestics, the wives and children of residents in Canada, and British subjects from white English-speaking countries (Britain, Australia, Newfoundland, New Zealand, and South Africa), and American citizens.[42] Since blacks were stereotyped as not adaptable to farming, the regulation excluded Caribbean blacks except "dependents" and domestics slated for assured employment. Caribbean blacks were continuously rejected at Maritime ports under P.C. 717 of 1922. For example, seven Caribbean blacks, including five who travelled first-class on the *Caraquet*, and whom the steamship agent thought were qualified under the regulations, were detained entrance at Saint John, in September 1922. Thus, the Royal Mail Steam Packet Company concluded that it was unsafe to bring Caribbean blacks regardless of class, occupation, or gender.[43]

Caribbean people's concerns regarding Canada's discriminatory immigration policy were exacerbated by the five-day detention in 1925 of a 16-year-old Jamaican woman in Montreal who did not obtain a "permit" to enter Canada. It was reported that she had a nervous breakdown after being treated like a prisoner while in detention. A stinging editorial in the September *Daily Gleaner* of that year argued that Canada's lack of frankness about its immigration policy was likely to cause a protest against Canadian–Caribbean trade and Canadian investments in the Caribbean. As the *Daily Gleaner* put it

> We need the Canadian market and Canada needs our market quite as much. Canada is doing us no favour to trade with us on a preferential basis, for unless Canada received a preference in the British West Indies she would be completely shut out of our markets. Canadian banks are established here, and it is well-known that a

large amount of West Indian capital is sent by these banks to Canada for the development of Canadian agriculture. We have no doubt that, if all the facts were known, it would be seen that West Indian capital was doing more to develop Canada than Canadian capital was doing to develop the West Indies; consequently there is no reason why the British West Indies should assume towards Canada a spaniel's attitude, or why Canada should imagine that it is conferring more benefits upon these colonies than we confer upon the Dominion. This being so, we should always approach trade questions in a practical and sensible manner, and emigration questions in a similar fashion. We for one do not confuse the two.[44]

Though Caribbean blacks did not have the power to pressure Canada to liberalize its discriminatory immigration policy, Canadian trade commissioners in the Caribbean felt embarrassed when dealing with complaints from prospective immigrants, particularly middle-class mulattoes who satisfied the requirements of the immigration act. The commissioners' real problem was how to tell Caribbean people that they would not be treated as desirable immigrants while the Canadian government was advocating a closer relationship between Canada and the British Caribbean. The trade commissioner in Jamaica, made this clear in posing several questions to the deputy minister of immigration in 1925:

Just what are your requirements in regard to immigrants from Jamaica to Canada? . . . It is doubtless very convenient to place the responsibility on the intending immigrant, but it puts me in a very awkward position here when they come and complain. All the time the people are reading that Canada wants desirable immigrants, and a closer rapprochement between Canada and the British West Indies is loudly advocated. Can I tell Jamaicans that they are not wanted in Canada? The situation is doubtless difficult. . . . What I want is something cut and dried, so that I do not have to continue hedging.[45]

The deputy minister was blunt in his reply: appeasement of Caribbean blacks was unnecessary. He replied that if the commissioner must be frank, he should tell Jamaicans that Canada was seeking closer trade relations with the Caribbean; she was not seeking immigration; and non-whites were not wanted.[46] However, the immigration branch was more diplomatic when dealing with influential people in the Caribbean who could jeopardize Canadian–Caribbean trade. For example, when a retired American businessman in Jamaica advertised in Canada for capable and willing Jamaican domestics for an advanced $150 fee, the assistant deputy minister of immigration asked the Department of External Affairs to inform him diplomatically that Canada did not encourage black immigration.[47]

In sum, immigration of Caribbean black settlers to Canada was severely restricted even when there was a demand for cheap unskilled labour. Caribbean blacks protested against this discriminatory immigration policy.

Because of unequal economic and political power relations between Canada and the Caribbean, Canada furthered its economic interests in the British Caribbean while strongly discouraging immigration of Caribbean blacks.

IMMIGRATION OF CARIBBEAN DOMESTICS

To return to the matter of domestics Caribbean women began migrating to Canada at the turn of the century. By 1909 there were several Caribbean women working as domestics in Nova Scotia. Some were recruited as cheap and dependable workers by employers who visited the Caribbean.[48] Like other immigrant women, they were in great demand as domestics since few Canadians were attracted to this work; indeed, most Canadians left such work as soon as possible because of deplorable working conditions—low pay, long hours, hard labour, low status, isolation, and lack of independence and respect. Unlike European women, most Caribbean women remained in domestic service since other areas of employment were closed to them.[49]

In 1910–11 the first Caribbean Domestic Scheme, which involved 100 Guadeloupean women, helped to fill the demand for cheap labour in Quebec. These Guadeloupean women were recruited by J.M. Authier, a former American consul in Guadeloupe, on behalf of Quebec's middle class. The $80 fare to Canada for these women was pre-paid by their employers in return for two years of service at a monthly wage of five dollars compared to the wage of $12–15 paid to other domestics.[50] Even with the transportation costs from Guadeloupe to Quebec, Caribbean domestics were cheaper to employ.

The first group of 16 domestics arrived in Montreal in September 1910 to work in Trois-Rivières, Montreal, and Quebec City and seemed to have attracted little attention.[51] However, the expected arrival of two larger groups in 1911 prompted the immigration branch to take action to prevent "too much" black immigration. New York and Montreal immigration officials were instructed to examine the women very carefully and make detailed reports in order to determine their desirability as immigrants and their likelihood of success as domestics. Fifty-eight women from Guadeloupe arrived in Montreal on 7 April 1911. Many were experienced domestics. They were strong, healthy, and intelligent; over 70 percent were literate. Immigration officers also described them as "a good class" of immigrants who were likely to succeed, given the demand for domestics.[52]

About the same time that the western boards of trade were petitioning the federal government to stop American blacks from taking up Canadian homesteads, the *Montreal Herald* reported that the 58 "dark-skinned" domestics were the advanced guard for others to follow.[53] Forty-eight Guadeloupean women were expected on the next trip.[54] Evidently, some Canadians were opposed to what they perceived as an influx of undesirable women and future "unfit" mothers. As an Albertan wrote to C.A. Magrath, Member of Parliament,

Are there many negro women who are desirable immigrants, they will certainly all be mothers some day? We may not be able to forbid negroes from entering Canada, though we do stop Chinese, Japs and E. Indians, but importing them wholesale, paying their passages, finding places for them is another matter.[55]

Such a stereotypical statement implies the devaluation of black women as mothers, a view that had its origin in slavery. The dominant ideology of motherhood ("purity" and making and caring for children within the context of the "ideal" nuclear and patriarchal family) constructed some locations within social relations of race, class, and citizenship that were more appropriate for motherhood than others. The portrayal of black women as undesirable immigrants and as less deserving of motherhood reinforced their subordination.[56]

In keeping with the stereotype of black women as immoral, *Collier's Magazine* reported in 1911 that Guadeloupean domestics were met at the Windsor Station by red-light district women who spirited them away to serve as prostitutes. However, a special policy investigation found the story unfounded. Actually, the domestics were met at the train station by their employers, "some of the best ladies in Montreal" who brought them warm coats. None of these women were employed in the red-light district.[57]

The immigration branch did a half-hearted survey of the 96 employers of the Guadeloupean domestics only two months after their arrival to find out whether they were satisfied with their new employees' performance and conduct and whether further immigration of Caribbean domestics was desirable. Of the 55 replies in the departmental files, most employers expressed satisfaction with their employees because they were cheap, intelligent, industrious, devoted, fond of children, docile, polite, submissive, and, unlike some white domestics, "they knew their place." Moreover, they were devout Catholics and spoke French. A Supreme Court judge commended his two employees for reading and learning English during their spare time.[58] One employer frankly wrote

I am happy to reply that the two servants whom I had brought over from Guadeloupe, give me entire satisfaction in every respect; they are clean, docile, attentive to their work, and their moral conduct leaves nothing to be desired. There is a great difference between the service that they give us and that we have from the greater number of the whites who have been in our employ during the last 30 years. The fact is that housework has become almost impossible with regard to the whites, the intelligent girls work in the shops and factories and there remain for us a small number, at exorbitant prices, of prostitutes and imbeciles who spoil everything. . . . The importation of the creoles is a benefit and the Government should favour their importation.[59]

Employers' responses indicated the demand for exploitable domestic labour. They also reflected stereotypes about black women (for example, the "black mammy"), the maternalistic mistress-servant relationship, and the fragmentation of gender along racial and class lines. Employers ranked the personality of the domestic worker and the kinds of relationships they were able to establish with them as important or more important than job-performance considerations. As Judith Rollins points out, the personal relationships between employer and domestic worker make domestic work more "profoundly exploitative than other comparable occupations."[60]

Employers suggested that the scheme be continued as a solution to the "servant problem" and that men be included to work as coachmen and domestics. An employer was so satisfied with her employee's performance, she sent for two male domestics.[61] However, some added the proviso that Caribbean women remain in the country as domestics; they should be carefully selected because there were rumours that some had "illegitimate" children. One of the domestics who had a baby shortly after her arrival in Montreal was dismissed from her first job because her employer felt she spent too much time with her new-born baby. However, she was subsequently employed by a city physician, who was pleased with her work.[62]

A few employers were dissatisfied with their employees' performance and conduct. For example, one complained, "I do not believe that these girls will ever be capable of rendering any good service to our Canadian families or others, they do not wish to submit, have not a good will and are very exacting."[63] Another fired his employee after a month's trial, "having established the fact that her climatic indolence was backed by a strong dose of bad will which rendered her quite unsuitable."[64]

Despite favourable reports from most employers, Scott recommended to Frank Oliver, the immigration minister, that the Caribbean Domestic Scheme should be discontinued because the women were "not all of good moral character."[65] Such a view clearly demonstrated the conflict between the demand for cheap and controllable domestic labour and the state's racialized, gendered, and class-based immigration policy. Given that domestic labour was not part of capitalist production, immigration branch officials thought that the admission of Caribbean domestics was unnecessary. Scott also emphasized to Oliver the need to exclude black immigrants, especially Americans going to Saskatchewan and Alberta as homesteaders.

The immigration branch sought legislation in order to exclude blacks. An Order-in-Council, P.C. 1324, was passed in 1911 under Section 38 of the 1910 Immigration Act to prohibit black immigration for one year. However, the order was cancelled for political reasons.[66] Such an order would have raised undesirable diplomatic problems with the Caribbean and American governments. It would have antagonized black voters in Ontario and Nova Scotia who had traditionally supported Liberal candidates. Moreover, the informal restrictions instituted by the department were probably considered sufficient to exclude blacks.[67]

In June 1911, Scott rejected Authier's application for the admission of 150 Guadeloupean domestics to meet the increasing demand. However, since he had already given him permission to bring in a smaller group, those emigrants would be admitted if they arrived before 30 June 1911.

Scott warned him that if any further domestics arrived after that date, they would be rejected if that action could be taken legally.[68] In July 1911, 10 domestics from Guadeloupe arrived in New York destined for Quebec. All were rejected as likely to become a public charge—two for medical reasons and eight because they were single parents.[69] The scheme was closed to further immigration with the excuse that the Guadeloupean women were physically and morally undesirable.[70]

Some of the Guadeloupean domestics were subsequently deported as likely to become public charges because of "tuberculosis, insanity, and immorality."[71] Evidently, some were deported because they had "illegitimate" children in Canada. Some Caribbean domestics who had lost jobs could not find work during the 1914–15 recession when it was reported that there were scores of unemployed Canadian women in cities and towns willing to do domestic work. In addition to expelling immigrants deemed "undesirable," deportation helped the state to reduce costs for social services (such as child rearing and education) and maintenance of unemployed Caribbean domestics by redirecting these costs back to the Caribbean. In 1913–15, Caribbean blacks had the highest deportation rate in Canada: 91 were deported.[72] For decades, such statistics were used to justify the restricted entry of Caribbean blacks, particularly women.[73] Behavioural and physical characteristics such as mental disorder and tuberculosis, which were associated with such structural and psychological factors as isolation, loneliness, stress, and poor living and working conditions, were attributed to racial characteristics. Except for the YWCA which assisted some Jamaican domestics in the late 1920s, immigration societies did not provide social services for Caribbean domestics as they did for British ones. Unlike the latter who were regarded as preferred immigrants, and thus likely to be "fit" mothers who would contribute to the material, ideological, and physical reproduction of the Empire, Caribbean women were recruited solely for their labour power.[74]

The evidence suggests there were fewer deportees among Caribbean miners and steel workers in Cape Breton than among Caribbean domestics. During the 1914–15 recession, some Caribbean miners and steel workers returned to the Caribbean until they were recalled for work.[75] Thus, they were in effect migrant workers. This concealed migrant-worker system offered significant economic and political advantages to employers and the state. In a migrant-labour system, the costs of renewing the work force are passed on to the sending countries while the receiving country is responsible for maintaining workers only during periods of employment. Moreover, mining and steel production were capital-producing industries and considered more important than domestic service which was not regarded as productive work. Thus, Caribbean domestics were more expendable. Miners and steel workers also had support systems: their families, neighbourhoods, and black political and social organizations (for example, by 1921 Saint Philips African Orthodox Church and two branches of the Universal Negro Improvement Association).[76] Since immigration officers were instructed to exclude all Caribbean blacks even when their applications were in compliance with the immigration act, the number of unwarranted deportation cases is unknown.

The demand for Caribbean domestics, particularly in the rural areas, increased during World War I as Canadian women increasingly left domestic service to work in the war industry, replacing the men who had joined the military. The supply of British domestics was also cut off during the war. The superintendent of immigration in New Brunswick, James Gilchrist, pleaded with Scott, Ottawa's superintendent, to allow the importation of Caribbean domestics:

> Our rural districts are simply starved for the want of domestic help. While there is a fair supply in our cities and towns, it is impossible to get a girl to work in the farm house, no matter what the conditions or pay, as they are determined to stay in the towns, and I am positive that if we had one hundred of these coloured girls in the country districts, they would not displace any of our own help, but would be a great blessing to our women in general.[77]

However, the immigration of Caribbean domestics continued to be strongly discouraged, particularly since the state expected an influx of British domestics after the war. Some employers asked their members of Parliament to assist them in getting permission to recruit Caribbean domestics. Scott explained to a member that if the immigration branch allowed all blacks entry, there would be a black domestic in every other home.

> The Department has always depended on the national spirit of our people to assist in keeping this country for the classes best-suited and most wanted here. I trust that those who are pressing you to assist them in getting coloured help from the West Indies will take a wider view of the situation and decide to support the policy . . . which I am sure appeals to the good judgment of Canadians generally.[78]

Thus, he expected Canadians to "suffer some little inconvenience" until the end of the war, rather than admit Caribbean domestics who would be a permanent problem.[79]

When the anticipated influx of British domestics did not occur, there was active recruitment and encouragement of domestics from continental Europe. However, employers continued to request permission to recruit cheap domestic labour from the Caribbean, particularly with the return of prosperity in 1923. The number of Caribbean domestics admitted to Canada increased from 24 in 1924–25, to 67 in 1927–28, to 152 in 1929–30. Between 1927 and 1931, domestics comprised 78 percent of the 499 black Caribbean immigrants.[80] The national immigration and travellers' aid secretary reported in 1928 that employers in Toronto were very satisfied with the performance and conduct of Jamaican domestics. However, some Jamaican domestics in Toronto who tried to negotiate a contract that specified the working conditions they wanted (for example, "no washing," "no children," "all evenings off") were facing at that time keen competition from

Finnish domestics who seemed willing to accept any kind of domestic work.[81] With the beginning of the Depression in 1930–31, only 89 Caribbean domestics were admitted because of restrictive immigration regulations. During the Depression itself immigration almost ceased. For example, only 15 Caribbean immigrants, including two domestics, arrived in 1931–32.[82]

CONCLUSION

This study of Canada's immigration policy regarding Caribbean blacks between 1900 and 1932 supports the view that immigration policy was structured by a dialectic of economic, political, and ideological relations: the demand of employers for cheap labour and the state's desire to exclude blacks as permanent settlers. The immigration branch perceived black people as likely to cause difficult economic and race-relations problems in the country. Thus, the immigration of Caribbean blacks was severely restricted. Only 2378 Caribbean blacks were admitted to Canada between 1904 and 1932 mostly as labourers to work in the steel plant and coal mines in Nova Scotia and as domestics.[83] Given the historical importance of the domestic service for black women in Canada, further research is needed on the lives of these early Caribbean domestics and the impact of that labour migration on the black community.

NOTES

1. See I. MacKenzie, "Early Movements of Domestics from the Caribbean and Canadian Immigration Policy," *Alternate Routes* (1988): 124–28; J. Schultz, "White Man's Country," *American Review of Canadian Studies* 12.1 (1982): 53–64.

2. Public Archives of Canada (PAC), Immigration Branch Records, RG 76, Vol. 475, File 731832; Vols. 566–7, File 810666.

3. R. Miles, *Racism and Migrant Labour* (London: Routledge and Kegan Paul, 1982); V. Satzewich, *Racism and the Incorporation of Foreign Labour* (London: Routledge, 1991).

4. E. Bonacich, "A Theory of Ethnic Antagonism," *American Sociological Review* 37 (1972): 547–59; "Advanced Capitalism and Black/White Relations in the United States," *American Sociological Review* 41 (1976): 34–51.

5. PAC, RG 76, File 731832, Regimbal to W.D. Scott, 10 April 1911; *The Montreal Herald*, 7 April 1911; W.

Ruck, "Nova Scotian Blacks in the Canadian Mosaic," *Canadian Black Studies*, ed. B. Pachai (Halifax: Saint Mary's University, 1979), 212–13.

6. Bonacich, "A Theory of Ethnic Antagonism."

7. PAC, RG 76, Vol. 566, File 810666, Scott to W. Cory, 25 April 1918.

8. Burawoy; Miles.

9. G. Beckford, *Persistent Poverty* (New York: Oxford University Press, 1972); B. Richardson, "Caribbean Migrations, 1838–1985," *The Modern Caribbean*, eds., F. Knight and C. Palmer (Chapel Hill: University of North Carolina Press, 1989), 203–28.

10. PAC, RG 76, Vol. 567, File 810666, E. Bart to the Governor General of Canada, 28 March 1924.

11. PAC, RG 76, File 731832, Kingston YWCA, "Domestic Training Scheme" (c. 1928); W. Hutchinson to M. Burnham, 16 February 1928.

12. "An Act respecting Immigration," 9–10 Edward VII, Chap. 27, 4–5.

13. PAC, RG 76, Vol. 556, File 810666, Scott to J. Webster, 16 May 1916; H. Troper, *Only Farmers Need Apply* (Toronto: Griffin House, 1972), 121–45; R. Winks, *The Blacks in Canada* (Montreal: McGill-Queen's University Press, 1971).

14. PAC, RG 76, File 731832, Scott to Hone and Rivet, 11 May 1915; RG 76, Acc. 83-84/349, Pt. 1, Box 107, File 5750-5, the Director of Immigration to Hon. Crerar, Minister of Immigration, 17 April 1942.

15. PAC, RG 76, File 731832, Scott to Hone and Rivet, 11 May 1915.

16. B. Roberts, "'A Work of Empire,'" in *A Not Unreasonable Claim*, ed. L. Kealey (Toronto: Women's Press, 1979), 188.

17. PAC, RG 76, File 731832, Scott to F. Oliver, 2 June 1911; Vol. 566, File 810666, Scott to Webster, 16 May 1911; Scott to Cory, 16 November 1916; Winks, *Blacks in Canada*.

18. PAC, RG 76, Vol. 830, File 522-1-644, the Director of Immigration to the Deputy Minister, 14 January 1955.

19. The ideological construction of black women as immoral developed during slavery. See J. Walvin, "Black Caricature: The Roots of Racism," cited in Satzewich; A. Davis, *Woman, Race and Class* (New York: Vintage Books, 1983).

20. PAC, RG 76, File 731832, W. Klein to Scott, 21 July 1911; Scott to Oliver, 2 June 1911; Vol. 566, File 810666, Scott to Harrison, 1 June 1917.

21. PAC, RG 76, Vol. 566, File 810666, Scott to L. Fortier, 10 August 1916.

22. Department of Citizenship and Immigration, 1954; PAC, RG 76, Vol. 498, File 775789, A. MacDonald to J. Lantalum, 22 July 1916; Lantalum to Scott, 26 July 1916; MacDonald to Scott, 5 May 1917; C. Heron, *Working in Steel* (Toronto: McClelland and Stewart, 1988), 76.

23. Satzewich.

24. PAC, RG 76, Vol. 566, File 810666, F. Williams to Scott, 29 June 1909; J. Douglas to J. Young, 3 December 1914.

25. Ibid., Williams to Scott, 29 June 1909; R. Ripley, "Industrialization and the Attraction of Immigrants to Cape Breton County, 1893–1914" (M.A. thesis, Queen's University, 1980), 54; Winks, *Blacks in Canada* 334.

26. PAC, RG 76, Vol. 566, File 810666, Williams to Scott, 29 June 1909.

27. PAC, RG 76, File 775789, D. McDougall to the Acting General Superintendent, Employment Service of Canada, 29 September 1919; F. Blair to J. Smith, 29 November 1920; Heron; Winks, *Blacks in Canada* 300.

28. Canada, Department of Immigration and Colonization, *Annual Report*, 1921; Department of Citizenship and Immigration, Annual Report 1954; Department of the Interior, *Annual Reports*, 1912–15; Heron; H. Potter and D. Hill, "Negro Settlement in Canada, 1628–1965" (April 1966); Ripley; Ruck.

29. PAC, RG 76, Vol. 566, File 810666, Scott to Pickford and Black, 14 November 1914.

30. Ibid., Fortier to Scott, 30 June 1914.

31. Ibid., Scott to Pickford and Black, 21 July 1914; Scott to W. Thompson, 31 July 1914; Fortier to Scott, 27 July; 8 and 12 August 1914; *The Sydney Daily Post*, 22 July 1914.

32. PAC, RG 76, Vol. 566, File 810666, Scott to E. Mauser, 29 August 1914.

33. Ibid., Scott to MacDonald, 11 January 1916.

34. Ibid., Scott to J. Smith, 26 January 1917; Scott to C. Horton, 2 April 1917.

35. "An Act respecting Immigration" (1910), Section 46, 24; "An Act to amend The Immigration Act," 9–10 George V, Chap. 25 (1919), Section 17, 9.

36. PAC, RG 76, Vol. 566, File 810666, Pickford and Black to Scott, 21 July 1914; The Royal Mail Steam Packet Co. to Scott, 30 and 31 July 1914; Scott to W. Thompson, 31 July 1914; F. Ohara to Scott, 17 July 1917.

37. *Barbados Advocate*, 26 June 1917; *Demerara Daily Chronicle*, 4 August 1916.

38. PAC, RG 76, Vol. 566, File 810666, E. Mauser to Scott, 29 August 1914; 3 September 1914; MacDonald to Scott, 3 May 1915; R. Winks, *Canadian-West Indian Union* (London: Athlone Press, 1968).

39. PAC, RG 76, Vol. 566, File 810666, R. Mackay to Scott, 7 September 1917.

40. Ibid., Scott to Cory, 16 November 1916.

41. Ibid., Scott to L. Barnstead, 29 July 1914.

42. PAC, RG 76, Acc. 83-84/349, Box 107, File 5750, Pt. 1, The Director of Immigration to Crerar, 17 April 1942. D. Avery, *"Dangerous Foreigners": European Immigrant Workers and Labour Radicalism in Canada, 1896–1932* (Toronto: McClelland and Stewart, 1979); J. Cameron, "The Law Relating to Immigration" (LL.M. thesis, University of Toronto, 1943); House of Commons, *Debates*, 1922, Vol. 3, 2514–2517; V. Malarek, *Haven's Gate: Canada's Immigration Fiasco* (Toronto: Macmillan, 1987).

43. PAC, RG 76, Vols. 566–7, File 810666, the Royal Mail Steam Packet Co. to Scott, 7 September 1922; the Royal Mail Steam Packet Co. to F. Blair, 5 February 1923; the Deputy Minister of Immigration to J. Pope, 24 April 1924.

44. *The Daily Gleaner*, 23 and 24 September 1925.

45. PAC, RG 76, Vol. 567, File 810666, J. Cormack to W. Egan, 9 April 1925.

46. Ibid., Egan to Cormack, 24 April 1925.

47. PAC, RG 76, File 831832, Hutchinson to Burnham, 16 February 1928; Burnham to Blair, 24 February 1928; Blair to O. Skelton, 26 March 1928.

48. PAC, RG 76, Vol. 566, File 810666, William to Scott, 29 June 1909; Scott to Cory, 9 September 1915; Scott to F. Knight, 25 April 1916.

49. PAC, RG 76, File 731832, M.D. to Fortier, 22 May 1911; Vol. 566, File 810666, J. Gilchrist to Scott, 1 April 1915; M. Barber, "The Women

Ontario Welcomed," *Ontario History* 72 (1980): 148–72; G. Leslie, "Domestic Service in Canada, 1880–1920," *Women at Work*, ed. J. Acton, P. Goldsmith and B. Shepard (Toronto: Canadian Women's Educational Press, 1974), 71–125.

50. *The Montreal Herald*, 8 April 1911; *La Patrie*, 7 April 1911; PAC, RG 76, File 731832, R. Morin to Scott, 22 May 1911; Regimbal to Scott, 10 April 1911.

51. PAC RG 76, File 731832, G. Elliott to Scott, 10 September 1910.

52. Ibid., Assistant Superintendent of Immigration to Oliver, 3 April 1911; E. Robertson to Klein, 3 April 1911; J. Stafford to Klein, 7 April 1911; Regimbal to Scott, 10 April 1911.

53. House of Commons, *Debates*, 1911, Vol. 4, 6524-27; Troper, 137–38; Winks, *Blacks in Canada* 308–9.

54. *The Montreal Herald*, 7 April 1911.

55. PAC RG 76, File 731832, C. Godsal to C. Magrath, 10 April 1911.

56. D. Roberts, "Punishing Drug Addicts who Have Babies: Women of Color, Equality, and the Right of Privacy," *Harvard Law Review* 104.7 (1911): 1436-9.

57. PAC, RG 76, File 731832, J. O'Keefe to the Chief of Police, Montreal, 14 June 1911; A. Swars to J. Monahan, 15 June 1911; *Collier's Magazine*, 3 June 1911.

58. PAC, RG 76, File 731832, Scott to F. Oliver, 2 June 1911; G. Boudrias to Scott, 23 May 1911; G. Marsolais to Scott, 20 May 1911; E. Dufresne to Scott, 20 May 1911; C. Laurendeau to Scott, 23 May 1911; R. Morin to Scott, 29 May 1911.

59. Ibid., M.D. to Fortier, 22 May 1911.

60. J. Rollins, *Between Women: Domestics and Their Employers* (Philadelphia: Temple University Press, 1985), 156.

61. Ibid., A. Rivet to Scott, 22 May 1911; E. Morin to Scott, 25 May 1911; F. MacKay to Scott, 31 May 1911; C. Boudrias to Immigration, 27 July 1911.

62. Ibid., G. Boudrias to Immigration, 23 May 1911; H. Provost to Fortier, 15 June 1911.

63. Ibid., W. Tremblay to Fortier, 29 May 1911.

64. Ibid., P. Couture to Scott, 17 June 1911.

65. Ibid., Scott to Oliver, 2 June 1911.

66. PAC, RG 2/1, Vol. 769, P.C. 1324, 12 August 1911; Vol. 772, P.C. 2378, 5 October 1911.

67. House of Commons, *Debates*, 1911, Vol. 1, 608; R. Brown and R. Cook, *Canada 1896–1921* (Toronto: McClelland and Stewart, 1974), 62; Troper, 281.

68. PAC, RG 76, File 731832, Scott to A. Dion, 16 June 1911.

69. Ibid., Klein to Scott, 21 July 1911.

70. Ibid., Scott to Elliott, 21 July 1911; Scott to Boudrias, 4 August 1911; Vol. 566, File 810666, Scott to Harrison, 1 June 1917.

71. PAC, RG 76, Vol. 566, File 810666, Scott to Mauser, 8 September 1914; Scott to Harrison, 1 June 1917.

72. *Canada, Dominion Bureau of Statistics, The Canada Year Book 1915* (Ottawa: Dept. of Supply and Services, 1916), 114.

73. PAC, RG 76, Vol. 566, File 810666, Scott to Harrison, 1 June 1917; RG 76, Acc. 83-84/349, Box 107, File 5650-5, Pt. 1, the Director of Immigration to Crerar, 17 April 1942.

74. PAC, RG 76, File 731832, Hutchinson to Burnham, 16 February 1928; Roberts, "'A Work of Empire,'" 188.

75. PAC, RG 76, Vol. 566, File 810666, Scott to Pickford and Black, 17 March 1915; Scott to Harrison, 1 June 1917.

76. Burawoy; Winks, *Blacks in Canada* 354, 416.

77. PAC, RG 76, Vol. 566, File 810666, J. Gilchrist to Scott, 1 April 1915.

78. Ibid., Scott to Webster, 16 May 1916.

79. Ibid., Scott to Ames, 11 October 1916.

80. Canada, Department of Immigration and Colonization, *Annual Report*, 1924–1931; House of Commons, *Debates*, 1929, Vol. 2, 1940–41; PAC, RG 76, Vol. 566, File 810666, Scott to Webster, 16 May 1916; Scott to Ames, 11 October 1916.

81. PAC, RG 76, File 731832, Hutchinson to Burnham, 16 February 1928. Lindstrom-Best points out that Finnish domestics took almost any work first. Subsequently, with the support of Finnish employment agencies, they shopped around until they found a suitable domestic job. V. Lindstrom-Best, "'I Won't Be a Slave!'" *Looking into my Sister's Eyes*, ed. J. Burnet (Toronto: Multicultural History Society of Ontario, 1986), 44.

82. Canada, Department of Immigration and Colonization, *Annual Report*, 1930–1932; House of Commons, *Debates*, 1929, Vol. 2, 1940–41; *Canada, Dominion Bureau of Statistics, The Canada Year Book 1931* (Ottawa: Dept. of Supply and Services, 1931), 192.

83. Department of Citizenship and Immigration, 1954.

LIKE A CHINESE PUZZLE: THE CONSTRUCTION OF CHINESE MASCULINITY IN JACK CANUCK [*]

MADGE PON

o

A Yellow Liar belongs to the yellow variety of man. Some persons are so utterly selfish, contemptible and cowardly, that we say they have a yellow streak running all through them.[1]

Jack Canuck, 14 October 1911.

When these statements were made in the Toronto newspaper *Jack Canuck*, Chinese men were not mentioned. But, according to the Myth of the Yellow Peril, no men were more tainted with the yellow stain than the Chinese. While yellow men were not women, neither were they considered to be men. The language, imagery, and metaphors used to create, and express, anti-Chinese racism were loaded with cultural values that hinged upon intersecting notions of race, class, and gender. The Myth of the Yellow Peril was distinctly tailored to fit the western construction of Oriental Chinamen as cunningly deceitful, morally dangerous, and peculiarly feminine. Co-existing with the idea of "yellow" and "unmanly" Chinamen was the contradictory belief that Chinese men posed a moral and sexual threat to white women.

A recurring theme in *Jack Canuck*, a muckraking "people's" paper, was that Chinese men deviously hid their corruption, their vice, and their sexual hunger for white women behind a façade, or a partition. This partition metaphor stigmatized Chinese men's work in laundries and restaurants and

[*] This article has not been previously published. I thank Bettina Bradbury, Amanda Glasbeek, Varpu Lindström and Gordon Pon for their comments on various drafts of this essay.

fragmented Chinese men's sexuality. White Canadians argued that Chinese men lured white women behind the partition erected in all laundries and restaurants. Once hidden from view, Chinese men were accused of ravishing white women and plying them with wine and opium. Similarly, white Canadians' racism was fuelled by a belief that beneath the veneer of the smiling, harmless Chinaman lurked an evil so deep and so incomprehensible that assimilation was impossible. This partition took on symbolic resonance because it signified the insurmountable distance between the white and the yellow races. The notion that the partition was erected by the Chinese, and not by Canadian society, furthered the belief that Chinamen were devious and opposed to assimilation. According to *Jack Canuck*, Chinese men were tainted with yellowness and would inevitably be outdone by their own cunning. They were to be destroyed by the weight of their own partitions crashing down upon them.

Although the Chinese formed less than half a percent of Toronto's population in 1911, writers for *Jack Canuck* argued that the Yellow Peril was nigh.[2] Once Toronto was "swarmed" and "teeming" with yellow men, there would be no recourse. How was it that, given the relatively few Chinese actually in the city, citizens wrote about this invasion as if it were fact?[3] What mechanisms created this sense of crisis? How did the partition metaphor validate white Canadians' resentment and suspicion of Chinese immigrants in Toronto?

THE RHETORICS OF RACISM: WOULD A DECENT GIRL MARRY A CHINK?

In the Canadian historical literature on anti-Chinese racism, the emasculation and feminization of Chinese men, as a form of racial and gender oppression, have either been ignored or glossed over.[4] Most scholars have focused upon the racist stereotypes of Chinese men as sojourners, cheap labourers, opium fiends, and bachelor immigrants.[5] By looking at Chinese men as gendered,[6] as well as racialized and class-defined subjects, we can better understand the complexity of racist myths and discourses. Although images of emasculated Chinese men in western thought have been noted by historians, these images, and their attendant assumptions concerning manhood and womanhood, have not been closely analyzed. Peter Ward, for example, has stated that white Canadians were not concerned with Chinese men's sexuality, whereas "attitudes toward blacks were highly charged with sexual imagery."[7] Ward assumed, however, that interest or concern over men's sexuality was only manifested in language and imagery that denoted traditional western manliness. But the feminization of a race or a group of men cannot be interpreted as a sign of disinterest. It is apparent from the diametrical constructions of yellow and black masculinity that sexuality is a common ingredient in racist ideology.[8]

Since, in the 1910s, most of the Chinese in Toronto were men, white women were seen as the dangerous liaisons between the white and yellow races. In 1912, under a column called "Please Tell Us," *Jack Canuck* asked its readers "if a girl, with good home influences, would ever think of marrying a Chink?"[9] In the same year, *Saturday Night* published an article condemning interracial marriages between whites and Asians. According to the writer, such unions were crimes against nature that threatened the mental health of white women:

> Evidence that nature is opposed to the intermarriage of persons of different colors is to be found in the physical and moral degeneracy of half-caste races everywhere, and a specially pertinent example of the evils of this form of "mixed marriage" is shown by the fact that at Los Angeles, Cal., within the past twelve months, five white women who had married Japanese husbands have been sent to the insane asylum.[10]

The writer concluded that, given their choices in partners, these women were mentally unstable even before their interracial marriages.

According to Emily Murphy, a police magistrate in Edmonton, opium addiction was a prime cause of social evils and interracial mixing. This "grey peril,"[11] as Murphy described opium addiction, was superimposed upon the Yellow Peril, and the spread of opium smoking in Canada was blamed on Chinese immigration.[12] In her 1922 treatise against opium, Murphy argued that addiction led to the breakdown of boundaries between social classes and racial groups. Race mixing, according to Murphy, was an inevitable corollary to drug addiction:

> A man or woman who becomes an addict seeks the company of those who use the drug, and avoids those of their own social status. This explains the amazing phenomenon of an educated gentlewoman, reared in a refined atmosphere, consorting with the lowest classes of yellow and black men.[13]

In Murphy's war against drugs, she stipulated that opium was initially an aphrodisiac but that prolonged addiction resulted in sexual impotence. Opium addiction would, in the long run, extinguish Chinese and black men's sexual libidos. The danger, however, was that these lower classes of men were turning white women into addicts and robbing them of their childbearing abilities. According to Murphy, opium addiction was a national problem because it endangered the fertility of the British Empire. With falling birth rates, the British race would soon be outrun by Germans, the prolific Russians, and the "still more fertile yellow races."[14] Victorian era social reformers, including Emily Murphy, were bent upon cleansing their world of the dark evils that threatened to dilute the white purity of Canadian society. In Toronto, this intensive project involved penetrating the dark slums that were festering in the city, as well as saving the rest of society from moral and physical contagion.

This equation between darkness and public morality was made in a 1911 Toronto report on slum conditions. According to this document, dark rooms were one of the twenty-five health problems that inspectors discovered.[15] They concluded that health, morality, and decency were threatened by the slums of Toronto:

> The following conditions peculiar to great cities are found to be present to a lamentable extent: rear houses, dark rooms, tenement houses, houses unfit for habitation, inadequate water supply, unpaved and filthy yards and lanes, [these] have become a public nuisance, and a menace to public health, a danger to public morals, and, in fact, an offence against public decency.[16]

The report concluded that surveillance, through official inspections and stringent regulation, could stave off the "pressing evils" found in Toronto slums. The spread of darkness could be checked and in its place there would be "plenty of fresh air, sunshine, and sanitary homes."[17] Residences were not the only targets of reform. City officials and concerned citizens in Toronto also claimed that Chinese laundries, and their proprietors, violated sanitary and moral regulations.

Ironically, although Asians were vilified for being filthy and dirty, most Chinese in Toronto were involved in the laundry business. Between 1901 and 1908, the number of Chinese hand laundries increased from 95 to 237.[18] In the discourse built up around Chinese laundries, we see the process of breaking down, or increasingly fragmenting, the binaries between cleanliness and dirtiness, purity and impurity. Though Chinese men were involved in the business of cleaning, their manner of cleanliness was deemed inferior and even unsanitary. Chinese men were said to fill their mouths with water that they squirted onto clothing before ironing.[19] They were also accused of spreading their own diseases through handling white people's laundry. One citizen wrote to *Jack Canuck*, describing the "frightful, loathsome, nameless" horrors of Chinese laundries. He feared for the health of his family and sympathized with the "decent married woman having to run the gauntlet of the class of Chinamen who usually run laundries."[20]

THE CHINESE PARTITION: THE MOST FRUITFUL SOURCE OF DANGER

After an expedition into the dark side of Vancouver's Chinatown, Emily Murphy described "that queer district where men seemed to glide from nowhere into nothing." Chaperoned and guarded by two "dope cops," Murphy crossed the partition into a Chinese opium den:

> In passing up a narrow staircase of unplaned boards, one detective walked ahead and one behind me, each carrying a flashlight. . . . [T]he head man stopped about mid-way up, and inserted a long key into a board when, to my amazement, a door opened where no door had been visible. Here, in a small cupboard, without a window—a kennel of a place—lay four opium debauchees. . . . The hole was absolutely dark and the men slept heavily.[21]

This unseen door, like the Chinamen's partition, obstructed the "searchlight"[22] of truth and moral purity. When Murphy and her cops cast their light into this small room, they were working on the assumption that privacy was a privilege that white Canadians dared not extend to the yellow races. It was not only the privilege of whites to observe and monitor the Chinese, but it was also their moral obligation.

Michel Foucault argues that "themes of surveillance" are often prompted by desires to regulate, monitor, and control sexuality and sexual practices.[23] He states that the construction of spaces are imbued with political tensions and are always contested areas of control between people with differing degrees of power. He argues that in Europe, beginning in the late eighteenth century, there was a growing quest for a "transparent world."[24] There was a fear of dark zones, "of the pall of gloom that prevent[ed] the full visibility of things, men and truths."[25] Penetrating and destroying these darkened areas demanded increasingly sophisticated and unrelenting means of surveillance. Foucault's analysis can be directly applied to the construction of anti-Chinese racism in *Jack Canuck*.

Writers for *Jack Canuck* called for the police to break down the doors of Chinese dens of iniquity and infamy, "kept for the purpose of ruining young Canadian girls."[26] They argued that "a certain class"[27] of white girls needed to be "saved" from frequenting Chinese "joints," and criminal charges had to be laid against the foreigners.[28] The police and all decent men were to "step beyond the line" drawn by the "fiends"; to look beyond the "entertaining and attractive exterior" of Toronto's Chinatown in order to expose the "unbelievable crime and vice behind its doors."[29] Though incidents of white women being lured into these "dens of iniguity" for the purposes of prostitution were rarely mentioned in anti-Chinese articles, this crime was implied.

The Myth of the Yellow Peril interwove all of the predominant concerns that plagued decent citizens in the early twentieth century. Accusations of vice, gambling, interracial seduction, drug use, and other "moral offences" were made regularly against the Chinese in Toronto. In the myth spun by *Jack Canuck*, writers frequently evoked images of the Chinese partition as a dangerous barrier that obstructed the public's ability to monitor Chinese activities. The partition metaphor, as it was created by writers, was constructed in two sites: in the businesses operated by Chinese men and within the minds and bodies of the men themselves. *Jack Canuck* described the partitions that existed in laundries and restaurants as barriers purposefully used to hide the real goings-on that transpired behind the storefront. This idea of a partition was also superimposed onto the character of Chinese men. Writers for *Jack Canuck* argued that Chinamen hid their devious depravation beneath a veneer of a cheery, smiling good nature. But beneath this façade, or behind the partition, Chinese men mocked white society and secretly hungered for white women.

The construction of the partition metaphor is consistent with Michel Foucault's hypothesis that the architectural construction of spaces become focal points of contention between the "eye of power" and the subjects of this gaze. *Jack Canuck* articles, which condemned Chinese businesses, focused on the architectural characteristics of laundries and restaurants. In the first article, published in September 1911, the partition metaphor was introduced and later became a recurring theme in anti-Chinese writing:

There are no less than 25 Chinese stores, laundries and restaurants in the block bounded by King, Queen, Yonge and York Streets. . . . One need only stroll through the above mentioned block and notice the throngs of Chinamen lounging in the streets and doorways to realize that the "Yellow Peril" is more than a mere word in this city. The average citizen would stand aghast did he but realize the awful menace lurking behind the partitions or screens of some of these innocent appearing laundries and restaurants.[30]

In its next issue, *Jack Canuck* again used the existence of a physical partition in Chinese businesses to construct a metaphor alluding to the dangers posed by the Chinese: "The Chinese restaurant[s] that abound so thickly in the downtown districts are the most fruitful source of danger. The majority of restaurants are subdivided along one side into small rooms where one can secure as much privacy as desired."[31] In these anti-Chinese articles, writers expressed an outrage that Chinese were audacious and presumptuous enough to erect these partitions. One aim of these articles was to expose the ineptitude of police officials who allowed the Chinese to engage in vice and crime "more or less openly."[32]

Toronto newspapers argued that the Chinese had ruined San Francisco, New York, and South Africa. Since Chinese people had been banned from Australia and England, it was argued, they should not be allowed into Canada either.[33] One writer for *Saturday Night* argued that white Canadians were responsible for keeping Canada white: "[Canada] was once ranged by red men, but we took it from them, and it is ours, if we can keep it."[34] An important component of the Myth of the Yellow Peril was the idea that a trickle of Chinese immigration would lead to a swarming, teeming onslaught of the "scum of the Orient."[35] *Jack Canuck* suggested that any citizens who were naive enough to disregard or underestimate the threat of the Chinese should take a trip to Toronto's Chinatown:

Visit Vancouver or go into the Chinese quarters in New York and see the Yellow Peril in all its aggravated forms; let him go no further away than his own city, Toronto the Good. A visit to the gambling haunts, the heavily curtained, evil smelling opium joints into which white girls are lured. . . . A peep behind the scenes of such places would make him think that this article was inspired—not by the Devil—but by god, in the interests of humanity.[36]

This idea of a partition stigmatized the work Chinese men did in laundries and restaurants. It was implied that Chinese men were involved in these businesses precisely because they would be convenient "fronts" for nasty deeds. And, until immigration laws and head taxes effectively stopped the yellow men "from pouring in,"[37] the Chinese needed to be policed and constantly observed.[38]

The strands of thought woven into the Myth of the Yellow Peril included the belief that men of colour were incapable of controlling their sexual desires.[39] According to historian G.J. Barker-Benfield, a general feature of western sexual attitudes in the nineteenth century was the dichotomous division made between mind and body. These two parts were arranged hierarchically, with the power of the mind dominating the functions of the body.[40] This binarism was superimposed onto Chinese men and writers for *Jack Canuck* argued that the diminutive, smiling façade of the "quaint" Chinamen hid the true essence of their character. The partition metaphor was, thus, used to describe the dangers of Chinese laundries and the deceitful nature of the men themselves.

Adjectives such as "quaint," "bland," and "smiling," described the various disguises donned by Chinamen. But, argued *Jack Canuck* writers, decent citizens should beware of this seemingly harmless façade. Having visited the Chinatown in New York City, Fred Jarrett (a name linked with a large number of anti-Chinese articles) claimed to have the "inside" scoop on the Chinese. Jarrett argued that Toronto's Chinese, like those in New York, were beginning to congregate and to multiply at an alarming rate. He warned the good citizens of Toronto to "get past the first partition"[41] of the Chinamen's smiling exteriors:

> Our Chinaman is very polite; we may "lookee in his store" or question him all we wish, but he answers wisely, and no one can fathom the depths behind that smiling face. . . . Our Chinese population exists in a quarter through which thousands of our own girls must pass daily—and nightly—and be subjected to the temptations and wiles of a race of people that are loathsome in every respect, and cunning beyond belief.[42]

Jarrett postulated that all Canadians were naturally fascinated by Chinamen because of the quaint customs and mysterious looks of the Chinese.[43] This curiosity, however, could not blind Canadians to the perils wrought by the Chinese. Left unchecked, Toronto would be swarmed with "clubs, stores, chop-suey houses, gambling dens and other attachments to Chinese life."[44] The inevitable result would be a "Chinatown where murders are small account and thousands of white girls are dragged down to the lowest depths of degradation."[45]

There was an overriding assumption in *Jack Canuck* articles that white women were particularly partial to the smiling Celestials. Not only were women more susceptible to Chinese charms and persuasions, but they also paid the greatest price once deceived:

> The bland smiling Oriental and his quaint pidgeon English does not appear very formidable to the young woman who enters his store for a weekly wash. She does not notice the evil leer lurking in the almond eyes as she accepts the silk handkerchief or other trifling Oriental knick-knack "just flor a plesant." A few weeks later she is induced to drink a cup of "leal Chinese tlea" whilst examining his Oriental treasures. A drowsy feeling and when she returns to her senses the evil deed has been consummated. One more victim of the Chinese pitfall so thickly strewn in Toronto the good.[46]

This idea that Chinese men threatened the racial and sexual purity of white womanhood contradicted yet co-existed with the emasculating images of Chinese men as "unmanly," "bland," "cowardly," and "yellow." With the use of drugs and deceit, the cunning Chinamen would spread "immorality among young girls" and lead white women to "utter demoralization."[47]

Because the Chinese were "cunning beyond belief," commentators urged their readers to believe the very worst.[48] So hateful and irreverent were the Chinese that they would even pretend to abandon their heathen gods. But the pretence of Christianization was yet another deceitful disguise donned by the Chinese. Mortals could, however, take comfort in the fact that Chinamen's only virtues, being good cooks and launderers, would not get them past heaven's gates.[49] While God would not be fooled by Chinamen, white women's gullibility was cause for concern. The process of Christianizing the "yellow heathen" was dangerous because it brought Chinamen into contact with white women. According to the *Toronto Daily Star*, there was "Trouble in Sunday Schools": "The Chinese veneer of Christianity is not an absolute guarantee of protection to the white girls. . . . Their [Chinese men's] instinct of centuries is stronger. We should not let the girls associate with the riff-raff of the Orient."[50]

Fred Jarrett, writing for *Jack Canuck*, stated that "decent minded Canadian girls" should be stopped from teaching Chinamen in Sunday schools.[51] Contact between yellow men and white women was not safe until the Chinese were made into "honorable gentlemen." But, according to Jarrett, this transformation would not occur for a very long time. In the meantime, he claimed, "the Chinaman will need watching as much to-day as yesterday, and until he has succeeded in throwing off the taint of bygone generations."[52]

As a culmination of its articles on the Chinese, *Jack Canuck* published a "testimony" by a white woman who had fallen victim to a Chinaman's "degrading embrace." In keeping with previous articles, this one interwove all of the recurring themes of a woman's horrific downfall including the partition metaphor, the opium bait, and the Christian veneer. The woman who was shamed had originally struck up an innocent, conversational relationship with the Chinaman who operated a local laundry. He began offering her small gifts, for a "Clismas plesant," and eventually lured her behind a partition to see his rooms. Being innocent, being naive, and above all, being curious, she complied. She thought she was safe because he had been Christianized and was known to be an attentive student at Sunday school. Christian or not, this Chinaman turned out to be a fiend. With the purpose of examining his Chinese idol, which the man kept as a reminder of his "foolish" pagan past, she ventured behind the partition:

> As I entered the room, a faint indescribable odor seized me. . . . One corner of the room was draped off. A colored lamp suspended from the ceiling gave barely enough light to see the hideous, monkey-like object executed out of what seemed ivory when he pulled the drape to one side. The odor became almost unbearable. . . . I became

faint. . . . Some time after I came to my senses. The Chinaman had
me clasped in a fervent embrace. The horror and shame I endured
at that moment almost drove me crazy.[53]

This woman became an opium addict. Too ashamed and addicted to return
home, she stayed with "her" Chinaman. She fled when he tried to sell her to
another Chinaman. She then wandered from one "joint" to another, seeking
only to find solace in the pipe. She concluded that her only escape was to
follow the path taken by other victims of these yellow fiends: to "make a
hole in the Bay some day."

CONCLUSION

Mariana Valverde states that according to middle-class reformers, working-
class men could attain masculine virtues through their sobriety and honesty.[54] By avoiding drink and embracing hard work, even poor white
Canadians could rise above the limitations of their class. Chinese men, however, were not granted any saving graces. The ways in which Chinese masculinity was constructed and fragmented made it impossible for men to
acquire the virtues of white manhood. The Chinese were ridiculed and condemned for their hard work; attempts at assimilation through Christianity
were seen as ploys; opium addiction, gambling, and lying were construed
as natural extensions of Chinese character. When Chinese men tried to cross
the language barrier, they were mimicked and mocked for speaking "pidgeon English."

Even the term "yellow" was invested with cultural meanings that were
emasculating. According to *Saturday Night*, yellow men were those who
"exhibited that cowardly 'welching' spirit," hence the phrase, "he has a yellow streak somewhere in his makeup."[55] Yellowness was not "somewhere"
in Chinese men's character, it was constructed as the very essence of
Chinese manhood. The terms "yellow fiend," "yellow devil," and "yellow
Chinamen" referred to degrees and gradations of masculinity, and not
only to skin colour. Yet running contrary to all these allusions to the emasculated Chinese man was the recurring "lure of the Chinaman" theme.
Miscegenation, white women's addiction to opium, and their resultant
infertility and debauchery, were all dreaded as the inevitable outcomes of
contact between Chinese men and white women.

The screen in the Chinese laundry was interpreted as a threatening
"partition" because it obstructed the white dominant gaze. In circumventing
this barrier, Canadians constructed a narrative about the evils that transpired behind the partition and within the hidden minds and souls of
Chinese men. This master narrative was ugly. Repeatedly, articles in *Jack
Canuck* described the cunning ways in which the Chinese veiled their evils
from white society. This idea of a partition, between Chinese and Canadians,
warned against trusting the yellow race and against flimsy surveillance. The
construction of anti-Chinese racism in *Jack Canuck* relied heavily upon the
readers' racist imaginations and their pre-existing notions about the differences between the classes and between the sexes.

The partition metaphor was an effective racist construct because it operated like a Chinese puzzle. The Canadians who despised the yellow race argued that no matter what was already known about the Chinese, there were missing pieces to the picture. Those missing pieces would always be more horrific, more dangerous, and uglier than what was already seen and known. The Yellow Peril took on mythic proportions because it was shrouded in secrecy, cloaked in darkness, and hidden from plain view.

Despite *Jack Canuck*'s use of the partition metaphor to validate and fuel anti-Chinese racism, the partition was also used as a gauge against which standards of white manhood were measured. As white Canadian men constructed their images of Chinamen, they were simultaneously constructing their own self-image. Concepts of "other" were not shaped within a vacuum but were forged within, and as part of, a self-indulgent process of comparing and contrasting. While Chinese men were described as lounging, lurking, and lying, white men were honest men of decisive action, men who could "molest"[56] and "raid" the Chinese. An essential component of the myth was that Chinese men could not attract white women without the "opium bait" or a "pinch or drop of some subtle Oriental drug."[57] The belief that white women had to be lured by opium and tricked into lovemaking protected white men's virility and their heterosexual dominance. The "luring theme" also revealed certain assumptions about the weak nature of white womanhood. While Chinamen were not manly enough to acquire the attentions of white women without deceit and drugs, neither were these women considered astute enough to see the supposed danger lurking behind the Chinese façade.

o

"The smiling Chinamen"—writers often used this phrase to describe Chinese men's deceitful and servile nature. White Canadians were so intent upon dehumanizing and desexualizing the Chinese that they did not stop to consider why Chinamen smiled as they did. As providers of services, as "house boys," and as labourers, these smiles were crucial for earning a livelihood. They were the smiles of those who had to survive within and under an oppressive social system. In the white man's eyes, however, these smiles were not only dangerous façades, but they were further proof of Chinamen's "unmanly humility."[58] There was also the suspicion that these smiles were outward signs of mockery, a smug contempt for white society that the Chinese were too cowardly—too "yellow"—to express in any other way. But it was not their subservient race or their questionable masculinity that explained Chinese men's cheery exterior. Material circumstances, their vulnerability and exploited class standing in Canadian society, explained why Chinese men had to smile when middle-class, white men might have grimaced, frowned, or growled.

The language, imagery, and metaphors used in the Myth of the Yellow Peril simultaneously gendered, racialized, and stigmatized the Chinese as the "lowest class of men." The partition metaphor was a powerful discursive creation because it was vague, yet concrete enough to symbolize perceived differences between white Canadians and Chinese people. *Jack Canuck* warned its readers that Chinese businesses were, in fact, dens of iniquity and infamy. No doubt, the decent citizens of Toronto the Good would have been disappointed with the banal kitchens that Chinese men kept behind their storefronts.[59] Chinese men were not ravishing white women behind the partition. Behind the screens, in the privacy of their own space, Chinese men cooked and ate their meals. While white Canadians speculated about, and prescribed the activities that transpired behind the partition, Chinese people knew the truth. On the other side of the partition, the "hidden" side, Chinese men took nourishment, made themselves strong, and made themselves whole.

NOTES

1. "Liars—Yellow, Red, and Black," *Jack Canuck*, 14 Oct. 1911, 6. According to this article, "red liars are so indifferent to human suffering that they exhibit a Satanic delight in twisting the dagger which they have thrust into the vitals" and "the black liar is the most dangerous foe with which humanity has to deal. He is conceived in sin and born in iniquity."

2. Toronto's total population in 1911 was 327 753, out of which there were 1001 Chinese men and 35 Chinese women. Census figures compiled from *Census of Canada*, 1911, vol. 2, Table X, "Origins of People, male, female, by districts," 355–56. Interestingly, Chinese women were not mentioned in the *Jack Canuck* articles.

3. Toronto newspapers published articles about the Chinese in western Canada and the United States, referring to the global declension wrought by Chinese immigration. Headlines prophesied impending doom for Toronto: "Ten Chinamen Shot in Boston," *Toronto Daily Star*, 3 Aug. 1907, 1; "Orientals Threaten to Burn the City [Vancouver]," *Toronto Daily News*, 11 Sept. 1907, 4; "Chinamen are Cause of White Man's Ruin," *Toronto Daily Star*, 8 Sept. 1913, 3; and "Yellow Men are Coming Here," *Toronto Daily Star*, 5 July 1907, 3.

4. For discussions on the feminization of Chinese American men, see, for example, Cheng-Tsu Wu, *"Chink!"* (New York: The World Publishing Company, 1972); Maxine Hong Kingston, *China Men* (New York: Alfred A. Knopf, 1977); Frank Chin et al., eds., *Aiiieeeee!* (New York: Penguin Books, 1991); William Wei, *The Asian American Movement* (Philadelphia: Temple University Press, 1993).

5. See, for example, James Morton, *In the Sea Of Sterile Mountains* (Vancouver: J.J. Douglas, 1974); Peter Ward, *White Canada Forever* (Montreal: McGill-Queen's University Press, 1978); Edgar Wickberg ed., *From China to Canada* (Toronto: McClelland & Stewart, 1982); Anthony Chan, *Gold Mountain* (Vancouver: New Star Books, 1983); Peter S. Li, *The Chinese in Canada* (Toronto: Oxford University Press, 1988); Patricia Roy, *A White Man's Province* (Vancouver: University of British Columbia Press, 1989); Kay J. Anderson, *Vancouver's Chinatown* (Montreal: McGill-Queen's University Press, 1990).

6. There are few studies on gendered masculinity in Canadian historiography. See, for example, Michael Kaufman, *Beyond Patriarchy* (Toronto: Oxford University Press, 1987); Gary Kinsman, *The Regulation of Desire* (Montreal: Black Rose Books, 1987).

Joy Parr's *The Gender of Breadwinners* (Toronto: University of Toronto Press, 1990) stands out as the foremost example of a gendered analysis of class and labour relations. While there are several important studies on American masculinity, most scholars have, thus far, chosen to examine the gendered experiences of white, middle-class men. Some exceptions are: Clyde W. Franklin's "Surviving the Institutional Decimation of Black Males" in Harry Brod, ed., *The Making of Masculinities* (Winchester: Allen & Unwin, 1987). There are two useful essays in Harry Brod and Michael Kaufman, eds., *Theorizing Masculinities* (Thousand Oaks, CA: Sage Publications, 1994): Pierrette Hondagneu-Sotelo and Michael A. Messner, "Gender Displays and Men's Power: The 'New Man' and the Mexican Immigrant Man," 200–18; Harry Brod, "Some Thoughts on Some Histories of Some Masculinities: Jews and Other Others," 82–96. For studies on white masculinity see Peter Filene, *Him/Her Self* (Baltimore, MD: Johns Hopkins University Press, 1974); Mark Carnes and Clyde Griffen, eds., *Meanings for Manhood* (Chicago: University of Chicago Press, 1990); E. Anthony Rotundo, *American Manhood* (New York: Basic Books, 1993). For examples of British work on gender and masculinity see Sonya Rose, *Limited Livelihoods* (Berkeley: University of California Press, 1992); Catherine Hall, *White, Male and Middle Class* (New York: Routledge, 1992).

7. Ward, *White Canada Forever*, 175.

8. See bell hooks, *Ain't I a Woman?* (Boston: South End Press, 1981) for a discussion on myths of black hypersexuality.

9. "Please Tell Us," *Jack Canuck*, 18 May 1912, 9.

10. *Saturday Night*, 10 Aug. 1912, 2.

11. Emily Murphy, *The Black Candle* (1922; Toronto: reprint, Coles Publishing, 1973), 42.

12. Murphy, *Black Candle*, 188.

13. Murphy, *Black Candle*, 17.

14. Murphy, *Black Candle*, 46–47.

15. On the issue of darkness, the inspectors stated: "Dark rooms are dangerous to health. . . . Practically all of them are used for sleeping apartments, a dangerous practice," *Report of the Medical Health Officer Dealing with the Recent Investigation of Slum Conditions in Toronto, Embodying Recommendations for the Amelioration of the Same* (Toronto: Department of Health, 1911), 10.

16. *Report of the Medical Health Officer*, 4.

17. *Report of the Medical Health Officer*, 24. The report also listed the "nationalities" of the families living in the areas designated as "slums." According to the report, there were thirteen Chinese "families" living in Toronto's slums, 16–17.

18. Richard H. Thompson, *Toronto's Chinatown* (New York: AMS Press, 1989), 41.

19. *Jack Canuck*, 6 July 1912, 11.

20. *Jack Canuck*, 23 Dec. 1911, 12.

21. Murphy, *Black Candle*, 29–30.

22. Mariana Valverde, *Age of Light, Soap, and Water* (Toronto: McClelland & Stewart, 1991), 35.

23. Michel Foucault, "Eye of Power" in *Power/Knowledge*, ed. Colin Gordon (New York: Pantheon Books, 1980), 150.

24. Foucault, "Eye of Power," 152.

25. Foucault, "Eye of Power," 153.

26. "For a Better Toronto," *Jack Canuck*, 25 Nov. 1911, 13.

27. "Yellow Peril," *Jack Canuck*, 30 Sept. 1911, 12.

28. *Jack Canuck*, 14 Oct. 1911, 11; "Ottawa in the Limelight," *Jack Canuck*, 20 July 1912, 14.

29. Fred Jarrett, "The Chinese Question," *Jack Canuck*, 28 Oct. 1911, 11.

30. *Jack Canuck*, 16 Sept. 1911, 10.

31. *Jack Canuck*, 30 Sept. 1911, 12.

32. "Alf. Cuddy After the Chinks," *Jack Canuck*, 6 July 1912, 11. The term "Chinaman" has been used as a euphemism describing ineptitude and incompetence, as evident in the phrase "a Chinaman's chance." In a tirade against Hamilton officials, a *Jack Canuck* writer said the police "messed more live things up, than a lot of Chinamen could," *Jack Canuck*, 19 Oct. 1912, 13.

33. See, for example, *Jack Canuck*, 10 Feb. 1912, 9; *Jack Canuck*, 27 Jan. 1912, 2; *Saturday Night*, 22 Dec. 1906, 1; *Toronto Daily Star*, 5 July 1907, 3; *Toronto Daily Star*, 10 Sept. 1907, 3.

34. *Saturday Night*, 27 Oct. 1906, 1.

35. *Saturday Night*, 22 Dec. 1907, 1.

36. *Jack Canuck*, 10 Feb. 1912, 9.

37. "Yellow Men Are Coming Here," *Toronto Daily Star*, 5 July 1907, 3.

38. See, for example, *Jack Canuck*, 14 Oct. 1911, 11; 25 Nov. 1911, 13; 28 Oct. 1911, 11; 9 March 1912, 12; *Saturday Night*, 25 May 1907, 2.

39. Valverde, *Age of Light, Soap, and Water*, 32.

40. G.J. Barker-Benfield, *Horrors of the Half-Known Life: Male Attitudes Toward Women and Sexuality in Nineteenth-Century America* (New York: Harper Colophon Books, 1976), xiii.

41. Fred Jarrett, "The Chinese in Canada," *Jack Canuck*, 27 Jan. 1912, 2.

42. Fred Jarrett, "The Chinese Question," *Jack Canuck*, 28 Oct. 1911, 11.

43. Fred Jarrett, "The Chinese Question," *Jack Canuck*, 28 Oct. 1911, 11.

44. Fred Jarrett, "The Chinese Question," *Jack Canuck*, 28 Oct. 1911, 11.

45. Fred Jarrett, "The Chinese Question," *Jack Canuck*, 28 Oct. 1911, 11.

46. "The Yellow Peril in Toronto," *Jack Canuck*, 16 Sept. 1911, 10.

47. *Jack Canuck*, 16 Sept. 1911, 12

48. Fred Jarrett, "The Chinese Question," *Jack Canuck*, 28 Oct. 1911, 11.

49. "The Devil is in Jack Canuck," *Jack Canuck*, 10 Feb. 1912, 9.

50. "Bar Chinamen from Hiring White Girls," *Toronto Daily Star*, 8 April 1914, 5.

51. "The Chinese Peril in Toronto," *Jack Canuck*, letter to the editor, 9 March 1912, 12.

52. Fred Jarrett, "The Chinese in Canada," *Jack Canuck*, 27 Jan. 1912, 2.

53. "The Yellow Peril," *Jack Canuck*, 28 Oct. 1911, 9.

54. Valverde, *Age of Light, Soap, and Water*, 78.

55. "The Yellow Streak," *Saturday Night*, 26 Aug. 1911, 21.

56. "Alf. Cuddy After the Chinks," *Jack Canuck*, 6 July 1912, 11: "Although gambling has been going on more or less openly in the Chinatown blocks for the last two years, the gamblers were not molested til Chief Cuddy took the reigns of office."

57. "Yellow Peril," *Jack Canuck*, 30 Sept. 1911, 12.

58. *Saturday Night*, 8 Sept. 1906, 1.

59. Valerie Mah, "The 'Bachelor' Society: A Look at Toronto's Early Chinese Community from 1878–1924," unpublished independent research paper, University of Toronto, 1978, 23.

section 4

NATIONAL SYMBOLS

○

"OF SLENDER FRAME AND DELICATE APPEARANCE": THE PLACING OF LAURA SECORD IN THE NARRATIVES OF CANADIAN LOYALIST HISTORY*

CECILIA MORGAN

o

To most present-day Canadians, Laura Secord is best-known as the figure-head of a candy company, her image that of a young, attractive woman wearing a low-cut ruffled white gown.[1] Some may even harbour a vague memory from their high-school courses in Canadian history of her walk in 1813 from Queenston to Beaver Dams, to warn British troops of an impending American attack. From the mid-nineteenth century, the story of that walk has been told by a number of Canadian historians of the War of 1812 in Upper Canada. Its military implications in assisting the British during the War of 1812 have been the subject of some rather heated debate. Did Laura Secord actually make a valuable contribution to the war? Did her news arrive in time and was it acted upon? However, another and as yet little-discussed issue is the way in which late-nineteenth and early twentieth-century historians attempted to transform Secord into a heroine, a symbol of female loyalty and patriotism in this period's narratives of Loyalist history.

* Reprinted with permission from *Journal of the Canadian Historical Association* NS 5 (1994): 195–212. Much of the research and writing of this paper was conducted with the financial assistance of Canada Employment. I would also like to thank Colin Coates, Mariana Valverde, and the *Journal's* anonymous readers for their much-appreciated suggestions and encouragement. The members of the gender, history, and national identities study group have provided invaluable comments and support: Lykke de la Cour, Paul Deslandes, Stephen Heathorn, Maureen McCarthy, and Tori Smith.

As historian Benedict Anderson argues, the formation of modern national identities has involved more than the delineation of geographically defined boundaries and narrow political definitions of citizenship. Nations, Anderson tells us, are "imagined political communities," created by their citizens through a number of political and cultural institutions and practices: shared languages, newspapers, museums, and the census. Furthermore, as Anderson (and others) have emphasized, it is also within narratives of "the nation's" history that these imagined communities are formed and national identities are created.[2] To the promoters of late-nineteenth century Canadian nationalism and imperialism, such narratives were of critical importance in understanding Canada's link to Britain and British political, social, and cultural traditions. As Carl Berger argues in *The Sense of Power*, "history in its broadest cultural sense was the medium in which [these traditions were] expressed and history was the final and ultimate argument for imperial unity."[3] Those who wrote these historical narratives also worked diligently to create national heroes who symbolized loyalty and the preservation of the imperial link. Historians interested in early nineteenth-century Ontario history found that a cast of such figures lay conveniently close to hand: Major-General Sir Isaac Brock and the Upper Canadian militia, the colony's saviours during the American invasion of 1812.

But Brock and the militia were not the only significant figures to be commemorated and celebrated, for it was during this period that Laura Secord became one of the most significant female symbols of Canadian nationalism. As feminist historians have pointed out, the formation of imagined national communities has been frequently, if not inevitably, differentiated by gender. While Anderson's work has been extremely influential on historians' understanding of national identities, he fails to recognize "that women and men may imagine such communities, identify with nationalist movements, and participate in state formations in very different ways."[4] And, in their use of iconography, monuments, or written narratives of the nation's history, proponents of nationalism have frequently relied upon gender-specific symbols and imagery.[5] Yet in these textual and visual representations of nationalities, gender as an analytic category has also varied according to its context and has been influenced by other categories and relationships, particularly those of race, class, religion, and sexuality. By looking at the process whereby Secord became a national heroine and at the narratives that were written about Secord's walk, we can further our understanding of the links between gender, race, and imperialism in late nineteenth-century Canadian nationalism and feminism.[6]

Secord became part of the narratives of Loyalist self-sacrifice and duty to country and Crown primarily—although not solely—because of the attempts of women historians and writers who, from the 1880s on, strove to incorporate women into Canadian history and to dislodge the masculine emphasis of the nineteenth-century Loyalist myths of suffering and sacrifice. Women such as Sarah Curzon, the feminist writer, historian, and temperance advocate, insisted that white Canadian women, past and present, had something of value to offer the nation and empire and that their contribution as women to the record of Canadian history be acknowledged and valued. Secord, she (and others like her) argued, was not outside the narrative of Canadian history and she (and other women) therefore had a place in shaping the "imagined communities" of Canadian nationalist and imperialist discourse. Unlike that of other, potentially unruly and disruptive women in Canadian history, Laura Secord's image could be more easily domesticated to accord with late-Victorian notions of white, middle-class femininity.[7] It could also be moulded by feminists to argue for a greater recognition of the importance of such femininity to Canadian society. Moreover, Laura Secord was not an isolated figure. Ranged behind and about her was a whole gallery of women in Canadian history, from Madeleine de Verchères of New France to the anonymous, archetypal pioneer woman of the backwoods of Upper Canada; women, these "amateur" historians insisted, who were historical figures as worthy of study as their male contemporaries.[8]

Before discussing the writing of Laura Secord into Loyalist history, however, it is crucial to outline the gendered nature of the nineteenth-century narratives of the War of 1812. Historians who have studied Upper Canadian politics have duly noted that assertions of loyalty and sacrifice during the war became the basis for many claims on the Upper Canadian state, in the competition for land and patronage appointments and for compensation for war losses.[9] Donald Akenson, for example, has pointed to the way in which claims to loyal duty during the war were used in attempts to justify the access of some residents to certain material benefits. Such claims were also made to legitimate the exclusion of others from such rewards.[10] Yet what has not been included in these historians' analysis of sacrifice in the war as a bargaining chip in the struggle for material gains in Upper Canada, is the gendered nature of the narratives that were used. In Upper Canadians' commemorations of the War of 1812, the important sacrifices for Country and monarch were made by Upper Canadian men, frequently in their capacity as members of the militia who risked life and limb to protect women and children, homes and hearths, from the brutal rampages of hordes of blood-thirsty Americans. During the war, and in its aftermath, women's contributions to the defence of the colony were either downplayed or ignored, in favour of the image of the helpless Upper Canadian wife and mother who entrusted her own and her children's safety to the gallant militia and British troops.[11]

Personifying the whole, of course, was the masculine figure of Isaac Brock, the British commander who made the ultimate sacrifice for the colony when he died at the Battle of Queenston Heights in 1812. Brock provided those who shaped the history of the war with a dualistic image of nationalism, one that managed to celebrate both Upper Canadian identity and colonial loyalty to Britain. He was also a Christ-like figure, a man who had given both his troops and the colony beneficent paternal guidance and wisdom but who had not spared himself from the physical dangers of war—physical dangers that really only threatened men in the military. Those who contributed to the glorification of Brock claimed that he had provided an invaluable means whereby the colonists might resist the enemy's encroachments. Brock had inspired Upper Canadian men, who might emulate his deed of manly patriotism, and he had reassured Upper Canadian women that, come what may, they could look to their husbands, fathers, sons, and brothers for protection.[12]

This kind of narrative, which emphasized masculine suffering, sacrifice, and achievements, was not unique to that of the War of 1812. As Janice Potter-MacKinnon argues, the history of Upper Canadian Loyalism focussed on male military service and the political identification of male Loyalists with the British crown and constitution:

> Well into the twentieth century, loyalty was a male concept in that it was associated with political decision-making—a sphere from which women were excluded. The same can be said of the idea that the Loyalists bequeathed conservative values and British institutions to later generations of Canadians: women have had no role in fashioning political values and institutions. The notion that the Loyalists were the founders of a nation had obvious and unequivocal gender implications. The amateur historian William Caniff was right when he equated the "founders" with the "fathers."[13]

Admittedly there was no automatic and essential connection between military activities and masculinity in Canadian history for, as Colin Coates has pointed out, the woman warrior tradition was not unknown to nineteenth-century Canada.[14] But specific female images (or images of femininity in general) as symbols of loyalty and patriotism in Upper Canada are almost completely lacking in the discourses of the period, and they display a general reluctance to admit that women could have contributed to the war effort as civilians.[15] This silence about women and the feminine—except as helpless victims to which the masculine bravery of Upper Canadian men was inextricably linked—was quite the opposite of the discourses of the French Revolution, with their glorification of Marianne; the American Patriot's figure of the republican mother; or even the more conservative use of the British figure of Britannia.[16]

The earliest efforts to call attention to Secord's contribution to the war were made by her husband James, by her son, and by Laura herself. In a petition written February 25, 1820 and addressed to Lieutenant-Governor Sir Peregrine Maitland, James Secord requested a licence to quarry stone in the Queenston military reserve. After mentioning his own wartime service—he had served as a captain in the militia—his wounds, and the plundering of his home by American troops, Secord claimed that "his wife embraced an opportunity of rendering some service, at the risk of her own life, in going thru the Enemies' Lines to communicate information to a Detachment of His Majesty's Troops at the Beaver Dam in the month of June 1813."[17] A second, similar petition was turned down in 1827 but Maitland did propose that Laura apply for the job of looking after Brock's monument. It is not clear whether Maitland was aware of the gendered and nationalist symbolism of a Canadian woman care-taking the memory of a British general; he did, however, have "a favorable opinion of the character and claims of Mr. Secord and his wife."[18] However, Maitland's successor, Sir John Colborne, was apparently not as well-disposed toward the family and the job went to Theresa Nichol, the widow of militia Colonel Robert Nichol.[19]

When James died in 1841, Laura submitted two petitions to Governor Sydenham: one that asked that her son be given his father's post as customs' collector and another that asked for a pension. Both cited her poverty, her lack of support since her husband's death, and her need to support her daughters and grandchildren. While her petitions used the language of female dependency noted by Potter-MacKinnon in Loyalist women's submissions, they also featured her service to her country in 1813 and her new position as the head of a household.[20] Her son Charles' article, published in an 1845 edition of the Anglican paper, *The Church*, publicised her walk, calling attention to his mother's service to her country and the British Crown.[21] Eight years later Laura Secord wrote her own account of her trek to warn the British Lieutenant James Fitzgibbon, in a piece that appeared in the *Anglo American Magazine* as part of a larger narrative of the war. While this article would be used and cited by others from the 1880s on, it was written in a straightforward manner, with few of the rhetorical flourishes or personal details that would characterize later accounts. And, while Secord concluded her story with the observation that she now wondered "how I could have gone through so much fatigue, with the fortitude to accomplish it," she did not stress her need to overcome physical frailty in reaching Fitzgibbon.[22]

Secord achieved some success in her campaign for some financial recognition on the part of the state in 1860, when she presented her story to the Prince of Wales during his tour of British North America. She was also the only woman whose name appeared on an address presented by the surviving veterans of the Battle of Queenston Heights to the Prince, in a ceremony attended by five hundred visitors and at which a memorial stone was laid on the site where Brock fell. Her "patriotic services," claimed the *Niagara Mail* in 1861, were "handsomely rewarded" by the Prince with an award of £100.[23] One of her more recent biographies argues that the prince "provided the magic touch that transformed the 'widow of the late James Secord' into the heroine, Laura Secord."[24]

However, Secord did not become a heroine overnight. Her own efforts to draw attention to the service she had rendered to her country should not be seen as attempts to create a cult for herself, but rather as part of the Upper Canadian patronage game, in which loyal service to crown and country was the way to obtain material rewards.[25] Furthermore, she died in 1868, almost twenty years before her popularity began to spread. Still, references to Secord had begun to appear in a few mid-nineteenth-century accounts of the War of 1812. For example, the American historian Benson J. Lossing's *The Pictorial Field-Book of the War of 1812* devoted a page to Secord and the Battle of Beaver Dams. The page's caption read "British Troops saved by a Heroine," and Laura's own written account was the voice that supplied Lossing with his information.[26] The Canadian historian and government official, William F. Coffin, elaborated on her story by adding the cow—which, he claimed, she had milked in order to convince the American sentry to let her pass. While some regard Coffin's account as yet another example of a romantically-inclined nineteenth century historian playing fast and loose with the facts, his placing of Secord in a context of pioneer domesticity foreshadowed subsequent stories appearing two decades later.[27] Secord thus was not rescued from complete obscurity by Curzon and others in the 1880s and '90s; she was, however, given a much more prominent place in their narratives of the war and Upper Canadian loyalty.

Sarah A. Curzon has become known in Canadian women's history as a British-born suffrage activist and a founding member of the Toronto Women's Literary Society (which would later become the Canadian Women's Suffrage Association) and the editor of a women's page in the prohibition paper, the *Canada Citizen*. But she was also an avid promoter of Canadian history and was one of the co-founders of the Women's Canadian Historical Society of Toronto (WCHS) in 1885, along with Mary Agnes Fitzgibbon, a grand-daughter of Lieutenant James Fitzgibbon. Furthermore, Curzon and Fitzgibbon were supporters of Canada's "imperial connection" to Britain, a link which they believed would benefit Canada both economically and culturally.[28] Emma Currie was another major contributor to the campaign to memorialize Secord. Indeed, her book, *The Story of Laura Secord and Canadian Reminiscences*, was published in 1900 as a fund-raiser for a monument to the "heroine" of Upper Canada. Currie lived in St. Catharines, helped found the Woman's Literary Club in that city in 1892, and would later join the Imperial Order of the Daughters of the Empire (IODE). She too was a supporter of the Women's Christian Temperance Union and women's suffrage.[29]

But these women were not alone in their crusade to win recognition for Secord. Other Canadian nationalist writers like Charles Mair, Agnes Maule Machar, and William Kirby, praised Secord's bravery in their poetry and prose,[30] while local historical societies and those who purported to be "national" historians, such as Ernest Cruikshank, also published papers that focussed on the Battle of Beaver Dams and acknowledged Secord's role in it.[31] Much of their work, as well as that of Curzon and Currie, was part of late-Victorian Canadian imperialist discourse, which perceived the past as the repository of those principles (loyalty to Britain, respect for law and order, and the capacity for democratic government) that would guide the nation into the twentieth century.[32] As Berger has argued, the local history societies that spread in the 1880s and 1890s were part of this "conservative frame of mind" in which loyalism, nationalism, and history were inextricably linked.[33]

Tributes in ink comprised the bulk of this material but they were not the only efforts to memorialize Secord. As Currie's book indicates, printed material might be used to raise funds and spread awareness in order to create more long-lasting, substantive reminders, such as monuments and statues. On June 6, 1887, W. Fenwick, a grammar school principal in Drummondville, wrote to the *Toronto World and Mail* asking for better care for the Lundy's Lane graveyard, a national monument to be erected to honour those who had died there, and a separate monument to Laura Secord. Curzon joined in a letter-writing campaign, calling for the women of Canada to take up the matter, and petitions were presented to the Ontario Legislature. When these were unsuccessful, the Lundy's Lane and Ontario Historical Societies mounted fund raising drives for the monument, sending out circulars asking Canadian women and children to contribute 10¢ and 1¢ respectively to the cause.[34] A competition for the sculpture was held and won by a Miss Mildred Peel, an artist and sculptor who also would paint the portrait of Secord hung in 1905 in the Ontario legislature.[35] After fourteen years of campaigning, the monument was unveiled June 22, 1901 at Lundy's Lane. In 1911, the Women's Institute of Queenston and St. David's felt that the village of Queenston (site of the Secord home during the War of 1812) had not done enough to honour Secord's memory and built a Memorial Hall as part of Laura Secord school. The gesture that ensconced her name in popular culture came in 1913, when Frank O'Connor chose Secord as the emblem for his new chain of candy stores.[36]

While it was not suggested that celebrating Secord's contribution was the sole responsibility of Canadian womanhood, many aspects of this campaign were shaped by deeply gendered notions and assumptions about both past and present. The idea that women might have a special interest in supporting the subscription drive, for example, or petitioning the legislature, linked perceptions of both womanhood and nationalism, drawing upon the underlying assumptions of self-sacrifice and unselfishness that lay at the heart of both identities.[37] Groups such as the WCHS, with their "unselfish patriotism," were exactly what the country needed. Kirby told Mary Agnes Fitzgibbon upon being made an honorary member of the society, adding "let the women be right and the country will be might!"[38] Moreover, while male writers and historians certainly expressed an interest in Secord, it is important not to overlook the significance of the participation of Anglo-Celtic, middle- and upper-middle-class women in the writing of Canadian history, a task they frequently undertook as members of local historical societies. Such women scrutinized historical records in order to find their fore mothers (in both the literal and metaphorical sense).[39] However, they also were fascinated with the entire "pioneer" period of Canadian history, both French and English, and with both male and female figures in this context. For the most part, women members of historical societies researched and presented papers on as many generals and male explorers as they did "heroines."[40]

There was, however, a difference in their treatment of the latter. They insisted that Canadian women's contributions to nation-building be valued, even though they had not achieved the fame and recognition of their male counterparts. To be sure, they did not offer alternative narratives of early Canadian history and tended to place political and military developments at its centre. Nevertheless, they sought to widen the parameters of male historians' definitions of these events in order to demonstrate their far-reaching effects on all Canadian society. In the meetings of organizations such as Canadian Women's Historical Societies of Toronto and Ottawa, papers were given on topics such as "Early British Canadian Heroines" or "Reminiscences" of pioneer women.[41] Women such as Harriet Prudis, who was active in the London and Middlesex Historical Society during this period, believed that while the history of the pioneer women of the London area

> records no daring deed . . . nor historic tramp, like that of Laura Secord, yet every life is a record of such patient endurance of privations, such brave battling with danger, such a wonderful gift for resourceful adaptability, that the simplest story of the old days must bear, within itself, the sterling elements of romance. While they took no part in the national or political happenings of the day, it may be interesting to us, and to those who come after us, to hear from their own lips how these public events affected their simple lives.[42]

Their efforts were shared by male novelists and historians who not only glorified Secord but also wished to rescue other Canadian women of her era and ilk from obscurity.[43] However, as more than one honorary member of the WCHS told Fitzgibbon, Canadian women should have a special desire to preserve records of their past. According to Mair, "the sacred domestic instincts of Canadian womanhood will not suffer in the least degree, but will rather be refreshed and strengthened" by the Society's "rescuing from destruction the scattered and perishable records of Ontario's old, and, in many respects, romantic home life."[44] The collection of material concerning this latter area, Mair and others felt, should be the special work of Canadian women.[45]

The extent to which this relegation of the "social" realm to women historians set a precedent for future developments, whereby "romantic home life" was perceived as both the preserve of women and the realm of the trivial and anecdotal, is not entirely clear.[46] Certainly it does not appear to have been Mair's intention that these areas be perceived as trivial or unworthy of male historians' attention, while women such as Mary Agnes Fitzgibbon were as eager to research battles and collect military memorabilia as they were concerned with "primitive clothing, food cookery, amusements, and observances of festivals attending births and wedlock or the Charivari."[47] Yet it was probably no coincidence that the first historian to seriously challenge the military value of Secord's walk was the male academic W.S. Wallace, who in 1930 raised a furor amongst public supporters of Secord with questions concerning the use of historical evidence in documenting her walk.[48]

This, then, was the context in which Laura Secord became an increasingly popular symbol of Canadian patriotism: one of feminism, history, patriotism, and imperialism. While many of these histories were, as Berger has pointed out, local and might seem incredibly parochial in their scope, their authors saw locally-based stories as having a much wider emotional and moral significance in the narratives of the nation.[49] Hence, narratives of Secord's contribution to the War of 1812 and to the colonial link with the British Empire were marked by the interplay of locality, nationality, and gender. First, Laura and James Secord's backgrounds were explored and their genealogies traced, in order to place them within the Loyalist tradition of suffering and sacrifice. For those writers who were concerned with strict historical accuracy, such a task was considerably easier for the Secords than for Laura's family, the Ingersolls. James' male ancestors had fought in the Revolutionary war for the British crown and the many military ranks occupied by the Secord men were duly listed and acclaimed. Moreover, the Secords could claim a history of both allegiance to the British Crown and a desire for the protection of the British constitution; they were descended from Huguenots who arrived in New York from LaRochelle in the late seventeenth century.[50]

But it was not only the Secord men that had served their country and suffered hardships. The loyalist legacy inherited by both Laura and James had, it was pointed out, been marked by gender differences. As Curzon told her audiences, James Secord's arrival in Canada had been as a three-year-old refugee, part of his mother's "flight through the wilderness," with four other homeless women and many children, to escape the fury of a band of ruffians who called themselves the "sons of Liberty." After enduring frightful hardships for nearly a month, they finally arrived at Fort Niagara "almost naked and starving." Curzon went on to comment that these were by no means "uncommon experiences." Frequently, she pointed out, Loyalist men had to flee "for their lives" and leave their women and children behind (as well as their "goods, chattels, estates, and money). Their loved ones were then left to endure the terrors of the wilderness:

> unprotected and unsupported, save by that deep faith in God and love to King and country which, with their personal devotion to their husbands, made of them heroines whose story of unparalleled devotion, hardships patiently borne, motherhood honourably sustained, industry and thrift perseveringly followed, enterprise successfully prosecuted, principle unwaveringly upheld, and tenderness never surpassed, has yet to be written, and whose share in the making of this nation remains to be equally honored with that of the men who bled and fought for its liberties.[51]

Unfortunately for Laura's popularizers, the Ingersoll family did not fit as neatly into the Loyalist tradition. Her father, Thomas, had fought against the British in 1776 and had seen his 1793 land grant cancelled as a result of British efforts to curb large-scale immigration of American settlers into Upper Canada.[52] As J.H. Ingersoll observed in 1926, Laura's inability to claim the United Empire Loyalist pedigree "has been commented upon." However, some historians argued that Thomas Ingersoll came to Upper Canada at Lieutenant-Governor Simcoe's request.[53] For those poets and novelists who felt free to create Laura's loyalism in a more imaginative manner, her patriotism was traced to a long-standing childhood attachment to Britain. They insisted that she chose Canada freely and was not forced to come to the country as a refugee.[54] Moreover, despite these historians' fascination with lines of blood and birth, they were equally determined to demonstrate that the former could be transcended by environment and force of personality. The loyal society of Upper Canada and the strength of Laura's own commitment to Britain were important reminders to the Canadian public that a sense of imperial duty could overcome other relationships and flourish in the colonial context.[55]

Accordingly, these historians argued, it should come as no surprise that both Laura and her husband felt obliged to perform their patriotic duty when American officers were overheard planning an attack on the British forces of Lieutenant Fitzgibbon.[56] However, James was still suffering from wounds sustained at the Battle of Queenston Heights and it therefore fell to Laura—over her husband's objections and concern for her safety—to walk the twenty miles from Queenston to warn the British troops at Beaver Dams. (Here the linear chronology of the narratives was frequently interrupted to explain out that Laura had come to his aid after the battle when, finding him badly wounded and in danger of being beaten to death by "common" American soldiers, she had attempted to shield him with her own body from their rifle butts—further evidence that Laura was no stranger to wifely and patriotic duty.[57])

Laura's journey took on wider dimensions and greater significance in the hands of her commemorators. It was no longer just a walk to warn the British but, with its elements of venturing into the unknown, physical sacrifice, and devotion to the British values of order and democracy, came to symbolize the entire "pioneer womanish experience in Canadian history."[58] Leaving the cozy domesticity and safety of her home, the company of her wounded husband and children, Secord had ventured out into the Upper Canadian wilderness with its swamps and underbrush in which threatening creatures, such as rattlesnakes, bears, and wolves, might lurk.[59] And even when Sarah Curzon's 1887 play permitted Laura to deliver several monologues on the loveliness of the June woodland, the tranquility of the forest was disrupted by the howling of wolves.[60]

But most serious of all, in the majority of accounts, was the threat of the "Indians" she might meet on the way. If Secord's commitment to Canada and Britain had previously been presented in cultural terms, ones that could be encouraged by the colonial tie and that might transcend race, it was at this point that her significance as a symbol of white Canadian womanhood was clearest. While her feminine fragility had been the subject of comment throughout the stories, and while her racial background might have been the underlying sub-text for this fragility, it was in the discussions of the threat of native warriors that her gender became most clearly racialized.[61] Unlike the contemporary racist and cultural stereotypes of threatening black male sexuality used in American lynching campaigns, however, her fears were not of sexual violence by native men—at least not explicitly—but of the tactics supposedly used by native men in warfare, scalping being the most obvious.[62]

To be sure, some stories mentioned that Secord had had to stay clear of open roads and paths "for fear of Indians *and* white marauders" (emphasis mine).[63] But even those who downplayed her fear of a chance encounter with an "Indian" during her journey were scrupulous in their description of her fright upon encountering Mohawks outside the British camp. Secord herself had stated that she had stumbled across the Mohawks' camp and that they had shouted "woman" at her, making her "tremble" and giving her an "awful feeling." It was only with difficulty, she said, that she convinced them to take her to Fitzgibbon.[64] As this meeting with the natives was retold, they became more menacing and inspired even greater fear in Secord. In these accounts, at this penultimate stage in her journey she stepped on a twig that snapped and startled an Indian encampment. Quite suddenly Secord was surrounded by them, "the chief throws up his tomahawk to strike, regarding the intruder as a spy."[65] In some narratives, he shouted at her "woman! what does woman want!" Only her courage in springing to his arm is the woman saved, and an opportunity snatched to assure him of her loyalty."[66]

Moved by pity and admiration, the chief gave her a guide, and at length she reached Fitzgibbon, delivered and verified her message—"and *faints*."[67] Fitzgibbon then went off to fight the Battle of Beaver Dams, armed with the knowledge that Secord had brought him and managed to successfully rout the American forces. In a number of narratives, this victory was frequently achieved by using the threat of unleashed Indian savagery when the Americans were reluctant to surrender.[68] While the battle was being fought, Secord was moved to a nearby house, where she slept off her walk, and then returned to the safety of her home and family. She told her family about her achievement but, motivated by fear for their security (as American troops continued to occupy the Niagara area) as well as by her own modesty and self-denial, she did not look for any recognition or reward. Such honours came first to Fitzgibbon.[69]

Women such as Curzon and Currie might see Secord's contribution as natural and unsurprising (given her devotion to her country) but they also were keenly aware that their mission of commemoration necessitated that their work appeal to a popular audience. These narratives were imbued with their authors' concerns with the relations of gender, class, and race and the way in which they perceived these identities to structure both Canadian society and history. For one, Secord's "natural" feminine fragility was a major theme of their writings. As a white woman of good birth and descent she was not physically suited to undertake the hardships involved in her walk (although, paradoxically, as a typical "pioneer woman" she was able to undertake the hardships of raising a family and looking after a household in a recently-settled area). Her delicacy and slight build, first mentioned by Fitzgibbon in his own testimony of her walk, was frequently stressed by those who commemorated her.[70] Her physical frailty could be contrasted with the manly size and strength of soldiers such as Fitzgibbon and Brock.[71] Nevertheless, the seeming physical immutability of gender was not an insurmountable barrier to her patriotic duty to country and empire. The claims of the latter transcended corporeal limitations. Even her maternal duties, understood by both conservatives and many feminists in late-nineteenth-century Canada to be the core of womanly identity, could be put aside or even reformulated in order to answer her country's needs.[72] While her supporters did not make explicit their motives in stressing her frailty, it is possible to see it as a sub-text to counter medical and scientific arguments about female physical deficiencies that made women, particularly white, middle-class women, unfit for political participation and higher education.[73]

Furthermore, there were other ways to make Secord both appealing and a reflection of their own conceptions of "Canadian womanhood," and many historians treated her as an icon of respectable white heterosexual femininity. Anecdotes supposedly told by her family were often added to the end of the narratives of her walk—especially those written by women—and these emphasized her love of children, her kindness and charity towards the elderly, and her very feminine love of finery and gaiety (making her daughters' satin slippers, for example, and her participation as a young woman in balls given by the Secords at Newark). Indeed, they went so far as to discuss the clothing that she wore on her walk. Her daughter Harriet told Currie that she and her sisters saw their mother leave that morning wearing "a flowered print gown, I think it was brown with orange flowers, at least a yellow tint...."[74] Elizabeth Thompson, who was active within the Ontario Historical Society and was also a member of the IODE, also wrote that Secord wore a print dress, adding a "cottage bonnet tied under her chin ... balbriggan stockings, with red silk clocks on the sides, and low shoes with buckles"—both of which were lost during the walk.[75]

For her most active supporters, the walk of Laura Secord meant that certain women could be written into the record of loyalty and patriotic duty in Canadian history, and female heroines could gain recognition for the deeds they had committed. In the eyes of these historians, such recognition had heretofore been withheld simply because of these figures' gender, for in every other significant feature—their racial and ethnic identities, for example—they were no different than their male counterparts. But such additions to the narrative were intended to be just that: additions, not serious disruptions of the story's focus on the ultimate triumph of British institutions and the imperial tie in Canada. Like her walk, Secord herself was constructed in many ways as the archetypical "British" pioneer woman of Loyalist history, remembered for her willingness to struggle, sacrifice, and thus contribute to "nation-building." These historians also suggested that patriotic duties and loyalty to the state did not automatically constitute a major threat to late-nineteenth-century concepts of masculinity and femininity. Secord could undertake such duties, but still had to be defined by her relations to husband and children, home and family. She did not, it was clear, take up arms herself, nor did she use her contribution to win recognition for her own gain.

In the context of late-nineteenth and early-twentieth century debates about gender relations in Canadian society, Secord was a persuasive symbol of how certain women might breach the division between "private" and "public," the family and the state, and do so for entirely unselfish and patriotic reasons. The narratives of Laura Secord's walk helped shape an image of Canadian womanhood in the past that provided additional justification and inspiration for turn-of-the-century Canadian feminists. These women could invoke memory and tradition when calling for their own inclusion in the "imagined community" of the Canadian nation of the late nineteenth century.[76] Furthermore, for those such as Curzon who were eager to widen their frame of national reference, Secord's legacy could be part of an imperialist discourse, linking gender, race, nation, and empire in both the past and the present.

NOTES

1. A Dorian Gray-like image that, as the company has enjoyed pointing out, becomes younger with the passage of time. See the advertisement, "There must be something in the chocolate," *Globe and Mail*, November 25, 1992, A14.

2. This term has been an invaluable methodological tool in thinking about the narratives of Secord. See Benedict Anderson, *Imagined Communities: Reflections on the Origin and Spread of Nationalism*. Revised Edition. (London and New York, 1991). See also Eric Hobsbawm and Terence Ranger, (eds.) *The Invention of Tradition*. (New York, 1983). Like Anderson's work, however, this collection does not address the complex relationships of gender, nationalism, and the "invented traditions" it analyses.

3. Carl Berger, *The Sense of Power: Studies in the Ideas of Canadian Imperialism 1867–1914* (Toronto, 1970), 78.

4. Catherine Hall, Jane Lewis, Keith McClelland, and Jane Rendall, "Introduction," *Gender and History: Special Issue on Gender, Nationalisms, and National Identities* 5: 2 (Summer 1993): 159–64, 159.

5. Recent work by historians of Indian nationalism explores the use of female images, particularly that of the nation as mother. See, for example, Samita Sen, "Motherhood and Mother craft: Gender and Nationalism in Bengal," *Gender and History: Special Issue on Gender, Nationalisms and National Identities*, 231–43. See also the essays in *History Workshop Journal. Special Issue: Colonial and Post-Colonial History* 36 (Autumn 1993) and Mrinalini Sinha, "Reading *Mother India*: Empire, Nation, and the Female Voice," *Journal of Women's History* 6:2 (Summer 1994): 6–44.

6. One of the few Canadian historians to point to these connections has been George Ingram, in "The Story of Laura Secord Revisited," *Ontario History* LVII: 2 (June 1965): 85–97. Other works tackling these questions have looked at such areas as social reform. See Angus McLaren, *Our Own Master Race: Eugenics in Canada, 1885–1945* (Toronto, 1990) and Mariana Valverde, *The Age of Light, Soap, and Water: Moral Reform in English Canada 1885–1925* (Toronto, 1991).

7. For a heroine who was not so easily domesticated, see Colin M. Coates, "Commemorating the Woman Warrior of New France: Madeleine de Verchères, 1696–1930," Paper presented to the 72nd Annual Conference of the Canadian Historical Association, Ottawa, June 1993; also Marina Warner, *Joan of Arc: The Image of Female Heroism* (London, 1981).

8. See, for example, the *Transactions* of both the Women's Canadian Historical Society of Ottawa and those of the Women's Canadian Historical Society of Toronto, from the 1890s to the 1920s.

9. David Mills, *The Idea of Loyalty in Upper Canada, 1784–1850* (Montreal and Kingston, 1988).

10. Donald H. Akenson, *The Irish in Ontario: A Study in Rural History* (Montreal and Kingston, 1984), 134.

11. See Cecilia Morgan, "Languages of Gender in Upper Canadian Politics and Religion, 1791–1850" (Ph.D. Thesis, University of Toronto, 1993), Chapter II. It is interesting that, while the militia myth has been challenged by many historians, its gendered nature has received very little attention. See, for example, the most recent study of the War of 1812, George Sheppard's *Plunder, Profit, and Paroles: A Social History of the War of 1812 in Upper Canada* (Montreal and Kingston, 1994).

12. Morgan, 56–60; see also Keith Walden, "Issac Brock: Man and Myth: A Study of the militia myth of the War of 1812 in Upper Canada 1812–1912" (M.A. Thesis, Queen's University, 1971).

13. Janice Potter-Mackinnon, *While the Women Only Wept: Loyalist Refugee Women in Eastern Ontario* (Montreal and Kingston, 1993), 158.

14. Coates, "Commemorating the Heroine of New France."

15. Morgan, chap II.

16. On the French Revolution, see Maurice Agulhon, *Marianne into Battle: Republican Imagery and Symbolism in France, 1789–1880* (Trans. by Janet Lloyd. Cambridge, 1981). For republican motherhood, see Linda Kerber, "The Republican Mother: Female Political Imagination in the Early Republic," in *Women of the Republic: Intellect and Ideology in Revolutionary America* (Chapel Hill, 1980); for Britannia, see Madge Dresser, "Britannia," in Raphael Samuel (ed.), *Patriotism, the Making and Unmaking of British National identity. Volume III: National Fictions* (London, 1989), 26–49.

17. The petition is reprinted in Ruth McKenzie's *Laura Secord: the legend and the lady* (Toronto, 1971), 74–75. To date, McKenzie's book is the most thorough and best researched popular account of the development of the Secord legend.

18. Ibid., 76.

19. Ibid., 76–77; also Sheppard, 221.

20. McKenzie, 84–85.

21. Ibid., 49ff.

22. Ibid., 91–92; also in Benson J. Lossing, *The Pictorial Field-Book of the War of 1812* (New York, 1869), 621.

23. McKenzie, 102.

24. Ibid., 103–4.

25. For an analysis of patronage in nineteenth-century Ontario, see S.J.R. Noel, *Patrons, Clients Brokers: Ontario Society and Politics 1791–1896* (Toronto, 1990).

26. Lossing, 621.

27. William F. Coffin, *1812: the War, and its Moral: a Canadian Chronicle* (Montreal, 1864), 148.

28. See Sarah A. Curzon, *Laura Secord, the Heroine of 1812: a Drama and Other Poems* (Toronto, 1887). For biographical sketches of Curzon and Fitzgibbon, see Henry James Morgan, *The Canadian Men and Women of the Time: A Hand-Book of Canadian Biography* (Toronto, 1898 and 1912), 235–36 and 400. Curzon's work is briefly discussed in Carol Bacchi's *Liberation Deferred? The Ideas of the English-Canadian Suffragists, 1877–1918* (Toronto, 1981), 26–27 and 44, but Bacchi's frame of reference does not take in Curzon's (or other suffragists') interest in history as an important cultural aspect of their maternal feminism and imperialism.

29. Morgan, 1912, 288–89; see also Mrs. G.M. Armstrong, *The First Eighty Years of the Women's Literary Club of St. Catharines, 1892–1972* (n.p., 1972); Emma A. Currie, *The Story of Laura Secord and Canadian Reminiscences* (St. Catharines, 1913).

30. Charles Mair, "A Ballad for Brave Women," in *Tecumseh: A Drama and Canadian Poems* (Toronto, 1901), 147; William Kirby, *Annals of Niagara*, ed. and intro. by Lorne Pierce (Toronto, 1927, first ed. 1896), 209–10. Kirby had been Currie's childhood tutor in Niagara and both she and Curzon

continued to look to him for advice, support, and recognition (Archives of Ontario [AO]), MS 542, William Kirby Correspondence, Reel 1, Curzon and Currie to Kirby, 1887–1906). Kirby and Mair were made honorary members of the WCHS (AO, MU 7837–7838, Series A, WCHS papers, Correspondence File 1, William Kirby to Mary Agnes Fitzgibbon, April 11, 1896, Charles Mair to Fitzgibbon, May 8, 1896). For Machar, see "Laura Secord," in her *Lays of the True North and Other Poems* (Toronto, 1887), 35. See also Ruth Compton Brouwer, "Moral Nationalism in Victorian Canada: The Case of Agnes Machar," *Journal of Canadian Studies*, 20: 1 (Spring 1985): 90–108.

31. See, for example, "The Heroine of the Beaver Dams," *Canadian Antiquarian and Numismatic Journal* VIII (Montreal, 1879): 135–36. Many thanks to Colin Coates for this reference. See also Ernest Cruikshank, *The Fight in the Beechwoods* (Lundy's Lane Historical Society: Drummondville, 1889), 1, 13–14, 19.

32. Berger, 89–90.

33. Ibid., 95–96.

34. Janet Carnochan, "Laura Secord Monument at Lundy's Lane," *Transactions of the Niagara Historical Society* (Niagara, 1913), 11–18.

35. Carnochan, 13.

36. McKenzie, 118–19.

37. Marilyn Lake has made a similar argument about Australian nationalist discourse during World War One. See her, "Mission Impossible: How Men Gave Birth to the Australian Nation—Nationalism, Gender and Other Seminal Acts," *Gender and History. Special Issue on Motherhood, Race and the State in the Twentieth Century* 4:3 (Autumn 1992): 305–322, particularly 307. For the theme of self-sacrifice in Canadian nationalism, see Berger, 217. The links between the discourses of late-Victorian, white, bourgeois femininity and that of Canadian racial policy have been explored by Valverde in

The Age of Light, Soap, and Water, in the contexts of moral reform, the white slavery panic, and immigration policies. See also Bacchi, *Liberation Deferred?*, ch 7. For gender and imperialism in the British and American contexts, see Vron Ware, *Beyond the Pale: White Women, Racism and History* (London and New York, 1992). The seminal article on imperialism and British womanhood is Anna Davin, "Imperialism and Motherhood," *History Workshop Journal* 5 (Spring 1978): 9–65.

38. WCHS papers, MU 7837–7838, Series A, Correspondence File 1, Kirby to Fitzgibbon, April 14, 1896.

39. See, for example, Mrs. J.R. Hill, "Early British Canadian Heroines," *Women's Canadian Historical Society of Ottawa Transactions*, 10 (1928): 93–98; Harriet Prudis, "Reminiscences of Mrs. Gilbert Ponte," *London and Middlesex Historical Society Transactions* (1902, pub. 1907): 62–64.

40. Harriet Prudis, "The 100th Regiment," *L & M H S Transactions*, V (1912–1913), n.p.; Agnes Dunbar Chamberlin, "The Colored Citizens of Toronto," *WCHS of Toronto Transactions*, 8 (1908): 9–15; also the biography of Brock by Lady Edgar, one of the first presidents of the WCHS [*Life of General Brock* (Toronto, 1904)].

41. See note 37 above.

42. Prudis, 62.

43. See Ernest Green, "Some Canadian Women of 1812–14," *WCHS of Ottawa Transactions* 9 (1925): 98–109.

44. WCHS papers, MU 7837–7838, Series A, Correspondence File 1, Mair to Fitzgibbon, May 8, 1896.

45. Ibid.; see also WCHS papers, MU 7837–7838, Series A, Correspondence File 1, John H. to Fitzgibbon, May 6, 1896.

46. As Linda Kerber argues, it was precisely this relegation that women's historians of the 1960s and '70s had to confront in their attempts to lift women's lives from the "realm of the trivial and anecdotal." See her

"Separate Spheres, Female Worlds, Woman's Place: The Rhetoric of Women's History," *The Journal of American History* 75: 1 (June 1988): 9–39, especially 37.

47. Mair to Fitzgibbon, May 8, 1896.

48. W.S. Wallace, *The Story of Laura Secord* (Toronto, 1932). For a response to Wallace, see "What Laura Secord Did," *Dunnville Weekly Chronicle*, 35 (1932), reprinted from Toronto *Saturday Night*, June 22, 1932.

49. Berger, 96. As M. Brook Taylor has pointed out about the work of nineteenth century writers such as John Charles Dent, Francis Hincks, and Charles Lindsey, "National historians were essentially Upper Canadian historians in masquerade." See his *Promoters, Patriots, and Partisans: Historiography in Nineteenth-Century Canada* (Toronto, 1989), 231.

50. Currie, 21–33.

51. Curzon, *The Story of Laura Secord, 1813* (Lundy's Lane Historical Society, July 25, 1891), 6–7.

52. See Gerald M. Craig, *Upper Canada: the Formative Years 1784–1841* (Toronto, 1963), 49, for a discussion of this shift in policy. McKenzie also argues that Ingersoll did not fulfill his settlement obligations (29). See also Currie, 38–39.

53. J.H. Ingersoll, "The Ancestry of Laura Secord," *Ontario Historical Society* (1926): 361–63. See also Elizabeth Thompson, "Laura Ingersoll Secord," 1. Others argued that Ingersoll was urged by Joseph Brant to come to Upper Canada (Ingersoll, 363). The Brant connection was developed most fully and romantically by John Price-Brown in *Laura the Undaunted: A Canadian Historical Romance* (Toronto, 1930). It has also been pointed out that Price-Brown picked up the story, "invented out of whole cloth" by Curzon, that Tecumseh had fallen in love with one of Secord's daughters. See Dennis Duffy, *Gardens, Covenants, Exiles: Loyalism in the Literature*

of Upper Canada/Ontario (Toronto, 1982), 61. In Price-Brown's account, Tecumseh proposes just before he is killed; Laura, however, disapproves of the match (259–69).

54. Price-Brown, 16–17, 180–82.

55. Just as French-Canadians could overcome other ties (see Berger, 138–39).

56. Thompson, 2; Currie, 48; Ingersoll, 362.

57. Price-Brown's "fictional" account is the most colourful, since one of the American officers who did not intervene to save the Secords was a former suitor of Laura's, whom she had rejected in favour of James and Canada (252–55). See also Currie, 53–54.

58. Norman Knowles, in his study of late-nineteenth-century Ontario commemorations of Loyalism, argues that pioneer and rural myths subsumed those of Loyalism ("Inventing the Loyalists: The Ontario Loyalist Tradition and the Creation of a Usable Past, 1784–1924," Ph.D. thesis, York University 1990). To date, my research on women commemorators indicates that, for them, both Loyalism (particularly people, places, and artifacts having to do with 1812) and the "pioneer past" were closely intertwined; both were of great significance and inspirational power in their interpretations of the past. See Elizabeth Thompson, *The Pioneer Woman: A Canadian Character Type* (Montreal and Kingston, 1991) for a study of this archetype in the fiction of Canadian authors Catherine Parr Trail, Sara Jeanette Duncan, Ralph Connor, and Margaret Laurence.

59. The most extensive description is in Curzon's *The Story of Laura Secord*, 11–12.

60. Curzon, *Laura Secord: The Heroine of the War of 1812*, 39–47.

61. While examining a very different period and genre of writing, I have found Carroll Smith-Rosenberg's "Captured Subjects/Savage others;

Violently Engendering the new American" to be extremely helpful in understanding the construction of white womanhood in the North American context. See *Gender and History* 5: 2 (Summer 1993), 177–95. See also Vron Ware, "Moments of Danger: Race, Gender, and memories of Empire," *History and Theory* Beiheft (1992): 116–37.

62. See Ware, "To Make the Facts Known," in *Beyond the Pale* for a discussion of lynching and the feminist campaign against it. Smith-Rosenberg points to a similar treatment of native men in Mary Rowlandson's seventeenth-century captivity narrative (183–84). While the two examples should not be conflated, this issue does call for further analysis.

63. Cruikshank, 13.

64. Secord in Thompson, 4–5.

65. See, for example, Blanche Hume, *Laura Secord* (Toronto, 1928), 1. This book was part of a Ryerson Canadian History Readers series, endorsed by the IODE and the Provincial Department of Education.

66. Ibid., 15.

67. Curzon, *The Story of Laura Secord*, 13.

68. See, for example, Cruikshank, 18.

69. Currie, 52–53. Fitzgibbon supposedly took full credit for the victory, ignoring both Secord's and the Caughnawaga Mohawks' roles (McKenzie, 66–67). He later became a colonel in the York militia and was rewarded for his role in putting down the 1837 rebellion with a £1000 grant (89–90).

70. Fitzgibbon in Thompson, 6.

71. Hume, 4.

72. For example, in Curzon's play Secord is asked by her sister-in-law, the Widow Secord, if her children will not "blame" her should she come to harm. She replies that "children can see the right at one quick glance," suggesting that their mother's maternal care and authority is bound to her patriotism and loyalty (34).

73. See Wendy Mitchinson, *The Nature of their Bodies: Women and Their Doctors in Victorian Canada* (Toronto, 1991), especially "The Frailty of Women."

74. Currie, 71.

75. Thompson, 3. Balbriggan was a type of fine, unbleached, knitted cotton hosiery material.

76. See Hobsbawm and Ranger, "Introduction: Inventing Tradition," particularly their argument that invented traditions are often shaped and deployed by those who wish to either legitimate particular institutions or relations of authority or to inculcate certain beliefs of values (9). In this case I would argue that the Secord tradition served very similar purposes, although it was used to both legitimate and, for certain groups of women, to subvert.

COMMEMORATING THE WOMAN WARRIOR OF NEW FRANCE, MADELEINE DE VERCHÈRES, 1696–1930 ⬦

COLIN M. COATES

○

Madeleine de Verchères, the child heroine of New France, was a cross-dressing woman warrior. In 1692, she led the defence of her family's fort at Verchères, near Montreal, against Iroquois attackers. In later accounts of her actions, she drew upon the long history of women warriors in the French and European traditions. Following the path laid out by such women as Joan of Arc, Jeanne Hachette, Catherine de Parthenay, and Philis de la Charce, Madeleine de Verchères tested the boundaries of gender roles in early modern society.

One analysis of the phenomenon of women warriors suggests that there are various factors that allowed women to modify the link between maleness and warfare. Women assumed military roles because of their social rank or religious beliefs, or because they found themselves in the midst of revolution or rebellion.[1] Verchères clearly fulfilled the first of these criteria, stepping into her father's role as defender of the seigneury during his absence. But other elements of the women warrior tradition were also apparent in her case. Women became warriors in emergency situations,[2] and they generally returned to the domestic sphere after the exploit. Often, the woman disguised herself as a man in order to participate in military matters.[3]

When she applied for a military pension in 1699, Madeleine de Verchères recognised that her previous actions had taken her beyond the usual bounds of her sex. In her lifetime and, later, as her story became a significant Canadian heroic narrative, the symbol of Madeleine de Verchères

---

⬦ This article has not been previously published.

became entangled in the fact that women did not usually fill military roles. As her story was swept up in the cult of commemorating the history of New France in the late nineteenth and early twentieth centuries, the fact that she had disguised herself as a man was suppressed. But the ambiguities of the woman warrior figure persisted, as both men and women reworked her story.

The first official report to the Minister of the Marine of the Iroquois raid did not mention Verchères' bravery or her male disguise. The governor wrote laconically that "the enemies killed and took prisoner some people at Verchères, absconded with some livestock and scalped a soldier at St. Ours."[4] Madeleine de Verchères' own accounts were, of course, much more compelling. She gave two versions of her exploit. The first, a letter to Mme de Maurepas, the wife of the Minister of the Marine, in 1699, was succinct and clear, and it explicitly situated the story in the context of other woman warriors. Verchères asserted that she was following an honorable French tradition: "I am aware . . . that there have been women in France during the late war who went forth at the head of their peasants to repel the attacks of enemies invading their province."[5] One of Verchères' first acts once she regained the seigneurial fort, after she narrowly escaped her intended rapist/assassin by leaving her *mouchoir de col* (scarf) in his hands, was to take off her headdress (*coëffe*) and don a soldier's cap. As she informed Maurepas, "I then transformed myself by donning the soldier's helmet."[6] Thus, Madeleine de Verchères claimed that she disguised herself as a soldier. Not only did Verchères look up all the (frightened) women, she displayed her male courage by shooting off a cannon.

Decades later, Madeleine de Verchères presented a second narrative of her heroism in a much longer epistle to the king. Written at the behest of Governor Beauharnois, this version (with all its lack of verissimilitude) provides most of the details taken up in later accounts. Instead of being 400 paces from the fort, Verchères was five arpents (about 300 metres) away in the second telling. The forty-five Iroquois chasing her did not manage to catch her, nor when they stopped running and began shooting did they hit her. Her scarf thus intact, Verchères made it to the fort, and closed the gates, repairing some of the breeches in the defences. She stopped a scared soldier from blowing up the munitions and the fort. Then throwing off her headdress and putting on a man's hat, she assumed command. Her younger brother and two frightened soldiers used their guns, but Verchères fired the cannon. As they held off what may have been a seige (though there is little indication in the narrative of Iroquois activity after all the firing), she opened the fort's gates three times: first to save Pierre Fontaine and his family who had arrived by canoe, second to allow the domestic animals back in, and third to recover the laundry. When lieutenant La Monnerie (Crisafy according to the historian P.-F.-X. Charlevoix) arrived to relieve the fort, Verchères and he engaged in gallant banter:

—Monsieur, you are indeed welcome. I surrender arms to you.
—Mademoiselle . . . they are in good hands.
—Better than you can imagine.[7]

Thus, the closure to the tale is realized in two ways: Verchères surrendered her arms to the "real" soldiers and La Monnerie, apparently unlike the Iroquois, recognised Verchères for what she was: a woman.

Two other versions of the story, written during Verchères' lifetime, invoked the image of the woman warrior. In his 1744 account, P.-F.-X. Charlevoix makes the transformation even more complete: she took off her headdress, knotted her hair, and donned a hat and a *juste-au-corps* (jerkin).[8] In his book, written by 1702 but not published until 1722, Claude-Charles de La Potherie recounts the story twice. In the initial version, which repeats Verchères' letter to Mme de Maurepas almost verbatim, he refers to Verchères as "une véritable Amazone."[9] The second story is essentially that of Verchères' second letter. Indeed, it is possible that La Potherie himself largely developed both versions of Verchères' exploits. He claimed to have helped her with the first letter justifying her petition for a pension, and later in life Verchères may have found La Potherie's other version suitable for her purposes.[10]

In Verchères' first version of the exploit, the cannon-shot ended the altercation with the Iroquois. Did her male disguise serve to protect the fort or was it the fire-power? Would the Iroquois have expected European women to eschew combat? Only two years previously, an undisguised Madame de Verchères had herself defended the fort. The Amerindians attacked numerous times, but Verchères' mother was always able to repulse them. According to Charlevoix, these Iroquois were "very ashamed of being obliged to flee by a woman."[11] The two defense narratives, fundamentally racist, probably say little of empirical value about the Iroquois. However, these stories do reveal something about gender ideology among Europeans.

Today, scholars disagree as to the broader significance of the phenomenon of cross-dressing. For some theorists, cross-dressers reinforce sex roles by their transgression. The woman warrior generally had to dress as a man in order to accomplish an act considered unsuitable for her sex. Although she momentarily allowed herself new freedoms, she did not fundamentally challenge traditional sex roles. For these reasons, the female transvestite became a stock figure in early modern European literature.[12] It is nonetheless possible to see female cross-dressers as proto-feminists, as they fulfilled their own individualistic desires for freedom.[13] For some, the phenomenon represents larger social dangers, since cross-dressing evokes the potential of sexual inversion and disorder.[14] Furthermore, transvestism serves to subvert both genders at once.[15] What if the cross-dresser belongs fundamentally to neither sex? What if resuming the original clothing does not lead one fully back to one's previous sexual identity? The treatments of Verchères heroism suggest that, for many commentators, cross-dressing indeed represents a challenge to fixed gender roles.

As the accounts of Charlevoix and La Potherie indicate, despite the wider social anxiety about cross-dressing, men could accept, even celebrate, temporary inversions such as Verchères'. This was because they could see Verchères as a specific case, not as a social icon. Two centuries later, men tended to be more disturbed by the image of women cross-dressers.

Thus, Madeleine de Verchères and her contemporaries cast her as a woman warrior—even, given her age, hinting at the similarities to *the* quintessential woman warrior, Joan of Arc, a fact which late nineteenth- and early twentieth-century authors would not fail to notice. They were both in their teens at the time of their famous exploits, and cross-dressed to achieve their aims. Both Joan of Arc and Madeleine de Verchères presented themselves as virgins, Verchères' dramatic action of leaving only her scarf in the Iroquois warrior's hand providing metaphorical evidence of her intact body. However, there were some important differences between the two. Unlike Verchères, Joan of Arc apparently never used her weapons. Unlike Joan of Arc, Verchères' actions were primarily defensive. Indeed, a few later commentators preferred to compare Verchères with Jeanne Hachette, who led the defense of Beauvais in 1472.[16] Of course, Verchères' closest Canadian counterpart was Dollard des Ormeaux, hero of the Battle of Long Sault. The cultural resonance of Dollard's story was as a narrative of "la survivance," and Madeleine de Verchères also fit this mould.[17] This survival ideology appealed both to French- and English-Canadians.[18] However, unlike both Dollard and Joan of Arc, Verchères did not have the good historical sense to die at the time of her bravery, therefore making it difficult to interpret her acts as the definitive moment of her life, a fact later historians would use to discredit her.[19]

In choosing to be a woman warrior, Madeleine de Verchères acquired a reputation for testing gender roles that remained throughout her life. She later married the military officer and seigneur Pierre-Thomas Tarrieu de LaPérade, and acted in a number of court cases against local priests, habitants, and seigneurs. As legal custom had it, she could not act in her own right, but only in the guise of her husband. The most public case occurred in 1730 when the priest of Batiscan, Gervais Lefebvre, took her to court to clear his name after she accused him of calling her a "whore."[20] At one point in the lengthy proceedings, the priest attempted to reassure himself that "God fears neither hero nor heroine,"[21] which suggests that Verchères was somewhat renowned for her act of bravery. Moreover, the "whore" epithet suggested that she, like so many other women warriors and warrior queens, experienced the other implications of gender-crossing: a presumption of wanton sexuality.[22]

In this way, the male disguise and the military action confused the issue of sex and sexuality in the person of Madeleine de Verchères during her lifetime. After her death, her story was never forgotten, but authors in the late eighteenth and early nineteenth centuries dealt with it in summary fashion, usually basing their writing on the account of Charlevoix, and being equally, if not more, interested in her mother's heroism.[23] It was not until the late nineteenth century that Verchères fully entered the pantheon of French-Canadian heroes.

By this time, of course, the historical context was different. The dominant cultural traits in Quebec of the late nineteenth and early twentieth centuries were conservative, nationalistic, and religious. Interest in the past led to increased production of historical works, and specific attention was lavished on the lives of the heroes and heroines of New France.[24] Military and religious figures were of particular importance.

Commemoration went far beyond the production of historical treatises in attempts to reach a broader audience. Artists produced paintings, engravings, and statues. Writers penned memorials to Verchères, including plays, poems, short stories, and historical accounts. Some forty writers dedicated poems, full narratives, or chapters in larger works to Verchères' memory.

Concurrently, men and women were facing challenges to rigid gender roles. The late nineteenth and early twentieth centuries were, at least in the major metropolises of the western world, a period of anxiety about proper gender roles and about sexual experimentation.[25] While Montreal was not London or New York, and certainly provincial Quebec (or Canada for that matter) was not in these same cultural networks, the influences were spreading. Important figures in this cultural ferment, such as Sarah Bernhardt and Oscar Wilde, visited Montreal. Moreover, women had been working outside the home for decades, and women's organizations were demanding new rights, in particular the vote, and this blurring of public space frightened many men.[26] This was as true of Quebec as elsewhere in Canada. Leading (male) social commentators of the time pointed out this "problem": Henri Bourassa reprinted a series of articles entitled, *Femmes-Hommes ou Hommes et Femmes?*, in which he attacked feminism. Describing the likely results of women's suffrage, he poured out his invective on "the woman-man, the hybrid and repugnant monster that will kill the woman-mother and the woman-*woman*."[27]

Such fears about challenges to gender roles were not unique to Bourassa. As a quick illustration, we can take the views of two men who themselves played important roles in commemorating Madeleine de Verchères. Politician Rodolphe Lemieux rejected women's suffrage because elected female representatives would have to vote on military matters, an untenable position given his belief that "Women . . . are unfitted for military service."[28] And Curé F.-A. Baillairgé wrote a pamphlet in 1925 warning of the dangers of North American modernity, including the confusion that would result if women dressed as men: "The idea, for a woman, to become a man acts against nature. . . . Why make only one [sex], when God desires that there should be two?"[29] One might have expected that a cross-dressing Madeleine de Verchères would pose a problem for such commentators.

Yet even in the most conservative circles, another cross-dresser was becoming popular. Joan of Arc underwent a renaissance that culminated in her sainthood in 1920 from the same church that had burnt her at the stake. Joan was tremendously popular in France, England, and the United States, and not only because of her patriotism and religious fervour. Her heroism appealed to feminists, as much as to conservatives.[30] In Quebec, statues were raised to her memory, and streets and hospitals were named after her.[31] French-Canadian nationalists made pilgrimages to Domrémy[32] and to Orléans.[33] This virginal military figure inspired interest in Madeleine de Verchères. In 1902, a writer in the popular magazine, *La Monde Illustré*, referred to her as "la Jeanne d'Arc du Canada."[34] The pictoral images of

Madeleine de Verchères reflect the comparison to Joan of Arc in emphasizing her femininity. These portraits downplay her military actions and present her as an innocent, young child (see figure 1).

F I G U R E   1   Madeleine de Verchères as innocent child, with her scarf intact and the Verchères fort in the background, by Gerald Hayward, 1915 (Arthur Doughty, *A Daughter of New France*. Ottawa: Mortimer Press, 1916).

Most of the prose retellings of her story took details from the longer, second letter Verchères wrote to the king, although some combined elements of her first letter to Mme de Maurepas as well. By 1900, both letters had been widely reprinted and made accessible. Very few of the retellings provide originality or in-depth research; these were not the strengths of popular history. Rather, the defining traits of popular history at this time seem to have been the retelling of a familiar story, imbued with moral values that surpassed the mere details of the narrative.

In theory, the fact that Verchères' story involved the testing of gender roles might be considered a problem for conservative commentators. Authors dealt with Verchères' disguise by ignoring it. Though many mentioned that she took off her headdress and donned a hat, few indicated the maleness of the apparel. Indeed, many did not suggest that Verchères changed her clothes, or even fired any weapons. Some placed emphasis on Verchères' virginity, a fundamental element of the Joan of Arc figure. The scarf incident, with its virgin imagery, was often repeated, even though most writers relied on Verchères' second letter, which did not include this detail. Continuing the comparison to Joan of Arc, Verchères was transformed into a standard-bearer rather than a fighter (figure 2).

F I G U R E   2   Madeleine de Verchères *not* fighting (Molson Advertisement, 1936)

Having made Verchères into a standard-bearer, many writers, particularly men, emphasized the virtues the heroine should embody. They could quote her own words for their patriotic resonance: "Let us fight to the death for our country and for our holy religion." In 1888, the editor of James LeMoine's version pointed out that the heroines of New France represented appropriate symbols for the youth of the day: "Like so many patterns for our young French-Canadian woman, like so many models of conjugal fidelity."[35] Historian Charles Colby suggested that, "she remains a bright, alluring figure, perennially young, like the maidens on Keat's Grecian Urn."[36] But English- and French-Canadian authors alike generally added contemporary nationalistic concerns. In 1916, Arthur Doughty published his study of Madeleine de Verchères in order to raise money for the Daughters of the Empire. Drawing a parallel between Iroquois and Germans that wartime readers could not miss, Doughty warned that "Savage tribes who had lorded over the continent for centuries were challenging the advance of European civilisation."[37] In a 1919 incident when some French-Canadian youths refused to answer a train conductor until he spoke to them in French, Pierre Homier applauded them. According to Homier, "It was their only response, but what a clear echo of the voice of the child of the fort of Verchères."[38]

Still, even with the cross-dressing episode suppressed, Verchères represented a potentially unruly female figure whom male writers had to tame. Poets William Chapman, Rev. Aen. McD. Dawson, and William Henry Drummond associated Madeleine de Verchères with the innocence and peacefulness of nature.[39] Curé F.-A. Baillairgé assured readers of his short study of Verchères' life, "Yes, Madeleine, who was strong, was nonetheless soft and sensitive."[40] In a collection of stories of heroism in New France, Thomas Marquis described the young woman: "Her delicate, active figure, soft, *spirituelle* face—intelligentforehead, brilliant eyes and well-cut lips—all bespoke gentle breeding (see figure 3)."[41]

F I G U R E   3   The Noble, Demure Madeleine de Verchères, by E.-Z Massicotte, 1900 (Henry James Morgan, ed., *Types of Canadian Woman and of Woman who are or have been connected with Canada*, vol. 1. Toronto: William Briggs, 1903).

Other writers were careful to ensure the closure of the story: the return to the status quo. Just as in Verchères' second narrative, these stories ended with Verchères surrendering arms to La Monnerie (or Crisafy). Lionel Groulx emphasized how Dollard's heroism surpassed that of Verchères'. Women's active roles could only be fortuitous: "They must sometimes fill in for men, but they must render them the arms for the battles that are more appropriate to them."[42] Other male writers shifted the narrative to the (male) soldiers' pursuit of the Iroquois and rescue of French prisoners.[43] Some added the apocryphal story, first apparently raised by Abbé François Daniel, that Verchères saved her future husband's life at the time of the Iroquois attack, and thus in marrying him became *his* conquest.[44] And both male and female writers emphasized that Verchères resumed her proper sex role following the incident. One journalist wrote in 1912 that "Magdelon [sic] was a perfect woman, as good a housekeeper as a mother."[45]

Women as well as men depicted Verchères' life in a heterosexual frame, mentioning her future marriage to M. de LaPérade. Literary critic Carolyn Heilbrun suggests that in the early twentieth century, female writers wanted their subjects to fulfill the important aspects of the "standard" woman's biography in which women, regardless of their desire to live a different life, ultimately placed men at the centre of their lives.[46] Nonetheless, women's versions had a different purpose than those of men. They used the story to stake out a feminist claim on Canadian history, and in some cases to justify the contemporary shifts in gender roles. Thus, Mary Sifton Pepper affirmed in 1901, "Many of them [the women of New France] would even nowadays be looked upon as 'emancipated' and 'advanced.'"[47] Many members of Women's Historical Societies were interested in the life of Madeleine de Verchères. Bellelle Guérin of Montreal, Emma Curie of St. Catharines, Teresa Costigan-Armstrong of Ottawa each presented papers on Verchères. In her address to the Women's Historical Society of Montréal, Louyse de Bienville (Mme Donat Brodeur) declared that she had considered speaking about early Canadian heroes, but turned her attention to heroines: "Since I am a woman, my sympathy turns first to women."[48] In a chapter of a book dedicated to Laura Secord, Emma Curie discussed Verchères' exploits, deploring (incorrectly) that her heroism, like Secord's, had been unjustly ignored when it came to the request for a pension because she was "only a woman."[49] Marie-Claire Daveluy was the clearest on the claim that Verchères' story permitted the insertion of women into history. In her 1920 short play, young girls at a convent school complain that, "history is mostly for boys . . . because of battles and soldiers." An older girl rebukes them, saying, "And Madeleine de Verchères? She was not a boy . . . and they talk about her in history."[50] Finally, Marie-Louise d'Auteuil tried to make the strongest link between nationalism and feminism, in proposing a "Journée de Madeleine de Verchères" for schoolgirls, to accompany the increasingly popular Dollard Day.[51]

It is interesting that women generally had less difficulty with Verchères' cross-dressing than did male writers. Mary Sifton Pepper judged Verchères' actions in this way: "With a thoughtfulness that seems almost incredible in one so young, she tossed aside her woman's head-gear and placed a man's hat upon her head, so that if the Indians saw her they would take her for a man and therefore a more formidable opponent."[52] Ethel Raymond supposed that Verchères "often wished that she had been born a boy."[53]

Only one early twentieth-century author explicitly interpreted Madeleine de Verchères' story as the narrative of a woman warrior. Frédéric de Kastner emphasized Verchères' noble lineage (an ancestry that the author was quick to point out he shared) and recognized Verchères as one in a line of "femmes guerrières." Indeed, he complained that most depictions portrayed her as too slight and wispish. He was clear, however, that she should not be seen as a burly, working-class woman.[54] His intervention is interesting, if only because it went unheeded by artists of the period.

A number of the authors complained about the lack of suitable memorials to Verchères. Some expressed the hope that a commemorative statue would be raised. In 1903, Henry James Morgan stated, "Singularly enough . . . no public statue has yet been erected by Canada to this the greatest of her heroines."[55] Within a decade, two separate initiatives—one led by the priest of Verchères and the other by the governor-general of Canada, Lord Grey—attempted to remedy the problem. Curé F.-A. Baillairgé wanted to raise the statue to Verchères as much to her memory as a way of putting the parish of Verchères on the map. However, the cost of raising a statue was far beyond the means of even a relatively prosperous agricultural parish. Baillairgé held tombolas to raise funds, and by July 1912 had raised over $2000 towards the statue.[56]

Meanwhile, the Montreal artist Louis-Philippe Hébert, sculptor of a number of other heroic statutes, had already crafted a statuette in her honour. It was, he recalled, a difficult figure to model, since he was afraid of turning her into a woman warrior: "Sometimes I felt that trying to translate all her beautiful energy, I would turn my young heroine into a virago."[57] Ultimately, the inspiration came from Louis Fréchette's poem, in which Verchères is compared to Jeanne Hachette. Coiffed by the soldier's hat, which appears to be a soft, leather cowboy hat, she clutches her gun nervously, if heroically, her skirts swirling in the wind.

Lord Grey saw Hébert's bronze statuette, purchased a copy for Rideau Hall, and encouraged politicians to erect a statue to her memory. In 1910, he gave Rodolphe Lemieux the mission to inspire his political colleagues. He hoped that Lemieux would "fire [Quebec Premier Lomer] Gouin with the desire to find such money as may be required to signify the great entrance to Canada by the erection on Verchères bluff of a figure which will tell the immigrant that the heroic virtues are the bedrock foundation of Canadian greatness."[58] Ultimately, it was the federal government rather than the Quebec provincial government that paid to commemorate the heroine. The cabinet earmarked $25 000 for the statue, which was erected in Verchères parish in September, 1913.

Although Curé Baillairgé had been swept aside in the planning for the statue, he was the president of the inauguration committee. Special trains and boats were leased for the pilgrimage to the statue on 20 September 1913. After numerous speeches by men, the mayor's wife (the one woman with a public role in the ceremony), unveiled the statue before the almost five thousand people in attendance.[59] The speeches reflected many of the themes apparent in the (male) literature on Verchères. Mgr Gauthier wished that other French-Canadian women could emulate Madeleine de Verchères, but he was quick to specify what kind of woman this represented: "There have been other Madeleines de Verchères lately, when French-Canadian [female] teachers preferred to lose their salaries rather than stop teaching French to their pupils." For his part, Wilfrid Larose compared Verchères with Joan of Arc: "If the kingdom of France was delivered and regenerated by Joan of Arc, this colony, then French in its cradle, was illustrated by Madeleine de Verchères."[60]

Gazing upon the statue (see figure 4), no one would mistake her for a man: the swirling dress, the feminine facial features, the long braids dangling down her back, the pubescent breasts, all precluded misinterpretation. Only her (men's) hat and massive gun hinted otherwise. For Maurice Hodent, who saw the statue in Paris where it was cast, there was no question whatsoever concerning Verchères' sex: "More than one Canadian seeing it as he sails up the St. Lawrence will say that there is no prettier girl under the blue sky."[61] The feminine icon apparently cloaked all traces of the cross-dressing Verchères.

FIGURE   4   Madeleine's Statute at Verchères: The First Girl Scout in the New World, by Louis-Philippe Hébert, 1913 (Pierre-Georges Roy, *Les Monuments commémoratifs de la Province de Québec*, vol. 2. Québec: Louis-A. Proulx, 1922).

Seven years later, in 1922, the first French-Canadian feature film— *Madeleine de Verchères*—premiered in Montreal. Like other contemporary commemorations, this film did not explicitly challenge gender ideologies.

English-Canadian and American entrepreneurs had already produced a film concerning the quintessential French-Canadian hero, Dollard des Ormeaux, in 1913. It is therefore not surprising that French-Canadian entrepreneurs should turn to Verchères' story for the first French-Canadian feature film.[62] In 1922, Joseph-Arthur Homier released the film to rather insipid critical acclaim. "It is a good picture," one critic wrote, "which should be seen as much as possible for its good history lesson."[63] According to a critic in *Le Devoir*, who nonetheless encouraged the development of a French-Canadian film industry, "One could describe it as man admiring an amateurish portrait of his ancestors. It is more a patriotic than an esthetic emotion."[64]

After a week in Montreal, the film made a tour of parish halls throughout the province, but its historical lustre could not compare with American silent films. The screenplay, written by Emma Gendron, combines romantic intrigue (involving Madeleine de Verchères and her future husband) with Verchères' act of bravery. Verchères is more than a soldier in this film; she also takes care of the wounded and encourages the defenders. La Monnerie finally relieves her, saying "You have saved the country." "I have only performed my duty,"[65] replies Verchères. Based on the remaining evidence of the film (some stills catalogued at the Copyright Office), no one mistook Madeleine de Verchères for a man in this movie (see figure 5). Becoming the Joan of Arc of Canada, she was seen to embody a militant, feminine ideal.

F I G U R E   5   Scene from the movie "Madeleine de Verchères," 1922
(NAC, MISA 16132)

Of course, Verchères could not live up to the historical virtues that she was expected to personify, if only because she outlived her exploit. About the same time that Verchères' narratives were reprinted, historians were setting the groundwork for the demolition of her reputation. The rediscovery of the court case concerning Curé Lefebvre's defamation of Verchères was particularly important in this matter. In 1900, an account of the 1730 trial appeared in the *Bulletin de recherches historiques*.[66] Lefebvre's testimony provided the necessary evidence of what the woman warrior persona suggested: wanton sexuality.

In 1922, Provincial archivist P.-G. Roy provided the first explicit attack on Madeleine de Verchères in a paper given to the Société Royale du Canada. Listing the court cases that involved Madeleine de Verchères after her marriage to Pierre-Thomas Tarrieu de LaPérade, Roy called her "une plaideuse enragée."[67] Were the court cases the result of her early heroism? Did her later actions flow logically from her military activity? What if, Roy posed in subtle fashion, Verchères had refused to return to the traditional woman's role?[68]

Thus, in the early twentieth century, at her time of greatest popularity, Madeleine de Verchères still represented a dangerous figure for some men. In momentarily choosing to be a woman warrior, Madeleine de Verchères challenged "proper" gender roles. She defended the seigneurial fort against Iroquois attackers in late October 1692. Two centuries later, as she became the subject of historical commemoration, popular historians would retell her story as a morality tale, emphasizing elements that fit their particular didactic purpose. For men primarily, this involved transforming her into an icon—a Joan of Arc figure—embodying nationalism and sacrifice. For women, Verchères, along with other religious and lay heroines, allowed them to enter the annals of Canadian history. This early form of women's history, the celebration of heroines, even cross-dressing ones, allowed elite women to establish an ancestry stretching back to the early colony, and helped to create a space where they could contribute their own view of history.

Madeleine de Verchères had clearly emerged as one of the most compelling female figures of the history of New France. Situating herself in the tradition of woman warriors, Madeleine de Verchères rejected strict gender roles. Her legacy was an ambiguous battleground for competing morality tales, nationalistic narratives, and gender ideologies.

NOTES

1. Louise Anne May, "Worthy Warriors and Unruly Amazons: Sino-Western Historical Accounts and Imaginative Images of Women in Battle" (PhD thesis, University of British Columbia, 1985), 21.

2. Megan McLaughlin, "The Woman Warrior: Gender, Warfare and Society in Medieval Europe," *Women's Studies* 17, 3–4 (Jan. 1990): 196–97; Rudolf M. Dekker and Lotte C. van de Pol, "Republican Heroines: Cross-Dressing Women in the French Revolutionary Armies," *History of European Ideas* 10, 3 (1989): 360–61.

3. Natalie Zemon Davis, "Women on Top" in *Society and Culture in Early Modern France* (Stanford, CA:

Stanford University Press, 1975), 124–51; Marina Warner, *Joan of Arc: The Image of Female Heroism* (New York: Alfred A. Knopf, 1981), chap. 7; Dianne Dugaw, "Balladry's Female Warriors: Women, Warfare, and Disguise in the Eighteenth Century," *Eighteenth-Century Life* 9, 2 (Jan. 1985): 1; Julie Wheelwright, *Amazons and Military Maids: Women Who Dressed as Men in the Pursuit of Life, Liberty and Happiness* (London: Pandora, 1989).

4. "Les ennemis avoient tué et pris prisonniers quelques personnes à Verchères, emmené les bestiaux dans le bois et levé la chevelure a un soldat a St Ours...." National Archives of Canada, Archives des Colonies, MG1 série C11A, Correspondance générale, Canada, Transcriptions, vol. 12, "Relation de ce qui s'est passé en Canada depuis le mois de septembre 1692 jusques au depart des Vaisseux en 1693," 358–420.

5. "Je sais, madame, qu'il y a en en France des personnes de mon sexe dans cette dernière guerre qui se sont mises à la tête de leurs paysans pour s'opposer à l'invasion des ennemis qui entraient dans leur province." The translations of Verchères' accounts are taken from Edouard Richard, ed., *Supplement to Dr. Brymner's Report on Canadian Archives by Mr. Edouard Richard* (Ottawa: King's Printer, 1901), 6–7. All other translations are the author's.

6. "Je me métamorphosai pour lors en mettant le chapeau du soldat sur ma tête."

7. —Monsieur, soyez vous le bien venu, je vous rends les armes.
—Mademoiselle ... elles sont en bonnes mains.
—Meilleures que vous no croyez.

8. P.-F.-X. de Charlevoix, *Histoire et description générale de la Nouvelle France* (Paris, 1744), 3: 123–25.

9. C.-C. Le Roy de Bacqueville de La Potherie, *Histoire de l'Amérique septentrionale* (Paris: 1722), 151.

10. André Vachon discusses the strong resemblance between La Potherie's

version and the second narrative in "Marie-Madeleine Jarret de Verchères" *Dictionary of Canadian Biography* (Toronto: University of Toronto Press, 1974), 3: 308–13.

11. "Bien honteux d'être obligé de fuir devant une Femme ...."

12. Dugaw, "Balladry's Female Warriors."

13. Wheelwright, *Amazons and Military Maids*, 15.

14. Davis, "Women on Top."

15. Marjorie Garber, *Vested Interests: Cross-Dressing and Cultural Anxiety* (New York: HarperCollins, 1993).

16. Louis Fréchette, *La Légende d'un peuple* (Trois-Rivières: Ecrits des forges, 1989 [1887]); Jacques Cézembre, "Les romans de la vie: Madeleine de Verchères, la Jeanne Hachette canadienne," *Dimanche-illustré* (14 Sept. 1930): 5.

17. Jacques Chevalier, "Myth and Ideology in 'Traditional' French Canada: Dollard, the Martyred Warrior," *Anthropologica* n.s. 21, 2 (1979): 144.

18. Ramsay Cook, *The Maple Leaf Forever: Essays on Nationalism and Politics in Canada* (Toronto: Macmillan, 1971), chaps. 8–9.

19. Marina Warner's comments on Joan of Arc's death are telling: "It is astonishing how many of Joan's apologists like her dead. Without this badge of blood, this self-obliteration in the ideal, her glory would be the less." *Joan of Arc*, 263.

20. I discuss this case in "Authority and Illegitimacy in New France: The Burial of Bishop Saint-Vallier and Madeleine de Verchères vs. the Priest of Batiscan," *Histoire sociale/ Social History* 22, 43 (May 1989): 65–90.

21. "Dieu ne craint ni héro ni héroine." Cited in Ibid.

22. Antonia Fraser, *The Warrior Queens* (New York: Alfred A. Knopf, 1989, 11–12.

23. D. Dainville (Gustave Bossange), *Beautés de l'histoire du Canada* (Paris:

Bossange frères, Libraires, 1821), 179–81. Philippe Aubert de Gaspé, a descendant of Madeleine de Verchères, briefly compares his gun-wielding aunt Agathe de Lanaudière to his "deux grand'tantes de Verchères" in *Mémoires* (Montréal: Fides, 1971 [1866]), 402–4; the discussion in F.-X. Garneau, *Histoire du Canada depuis sa découverte jusqu'a nos jours*, 2e édition (Québec: John Lovell, 1852), 313 is very short compared to that in the 8th edition (1944), 194–96.

24. Serge Gagnon, *Le Québec et ses historiens de 1840 à 1920: La Nouvelle-France de Garneau à Groulx* (Québec: Les presses de l'Université Laval, 1978); Fernande Roy, "Une mise en scène de l'histoire: La fondation de Montréal à travers les siècles," *Revue d'histoire de l'Amérique française* 46, 1 (été 1992): 7–36; Jacques Mathieu et Jacques Lacoursière, *Les Mémoires québécoises* (Sainte-Foy: Les Presses de l'université Laval, 1991), 319–23.

25. Elaine Showalter, *Sexual Anarchy: Gender and Culture at the fin de siècle* (Markham, ON: Penguin Books, 1990); Judith Walkowitz, *City of Dreadful Delight: Narratives of Sexual Danger in Late-Victorian London* (Chicago: University of Chicago Press, 1992).

26. Susan Mann Trofimenkoff, "Henri Bourassa and 'The Woman Question'" in Susan Trofimenkoff and Alison Prentice, eds., *The Neglected Majority: Essays in Canadian Women's History* (Toronto: McClelland & Stewart, 1977), 104–15; Susan Trofimenkoff, *The Dream of Nation: A Social and Intellectual History of Quebec* (Toronto: Gage, 1983), chap. 12; Andrée Lévesque, *La norme et les déviantes: Des femmes au Québec pendant l'entre-deux-guerres* (Montréal: Les éditions du remue-ménage, 1989).

27. "Le femme-homme, le monstre hybride et répugnant qui tuera la femme-mère et la femme-femme." Henri Bourassa, *Femmes-Hommes ou Hommes et Femmes? Études à bâtons rompus sur le féminisme* (Montréal: Imprimerie du Devoir, 1925), 41.

28. House of Commons, *Debates*, Session 1918, 1: 655.

29. "L'idée, pour une femme, de se faire homme est contre nature. . . . Pourquoi ne faire qu'un, là où Dieu veut qu'il y ait deux?" F.-A. Baillairgé, P.C., *Jeunesse et Folies* (Verchères: chez l'auteur, 1925), 40.

30. Eugene Weber, *Peasants into Frenchmen: The Modernization of Rural France, 1870–1914* (Stanford, CA: Stanford University Press, 1976), 111–12; Warner, *Joan of Arc*, chap. 13; Martha Vicinus, *Independent Women: Work and Community for Single Women, 1850–1920* (Chicago: University of Chicago Press, 1985), 266; Martha Hanna, "Iconology and Ideology: Images of Joan of Arc in the Idiom of the Action française, 1908–1931," *French Historical Studies* 14, 2 (Fall 1985): 215–39; Showalter, *Sexual Anarchy*, 29; Walkowitz, *City of Dreadful Delight*, 62.

31. On Joan of Arc's cult in Quebec, see *Nova Francia* 3 (1927–28): 381; and *Nova Francia* 4 (1929): 318.

32. On 19 August 1913, Joseph-P. Archambault [a.k.a. Pierre Homier of *L'Action française*] wrote to Dr. Gauvreau: "J'ai prié ce matin Jeanne, la bienheureuse et la vaillante, pour ceux qui, au Canada, luttent comme elle au service des traditions françaises et catholiques." Centre de recherche Lionel Groulx, Fonds Joseph Gauvreau, P39.

33. In 1907, Abbé Lionel Groulx visited Orléans, a city "pleine à déborder du souvenir de Jeanne d'Arc." *Mes Mémoires*, tome 1 (Montréal: Fides, 1970), 128.

34. L'annaliste, "M. Rodolphe Girard: L'homme du jour dans le domaine des lettres," *Le monde illustré*, 1 mars 1903, 1061; Frédéric de Kastner made the same comparison in *Héros de la Nouvelle France* (Québec: La Cie d'Imprimerie Commerciale, 1902); Charles Colby began his discussion of Verchères by saying that "New France had no Maid of Orleans." See *Canadian Types of the Old Régime, 1608–1698* (New York: Henry Holt and Co., 1908), 338.

35. "Comme autant de patrones [sic] pour nos jeunes canadiennes, comme autant de modèles de fidélité conjugale." J.M. LeMoine, *Les Héroines de la Nouvelle-France*, trad. de l'anglais (Lowell, MA: Raoul Renault, 1888), 23.

36. Colby, *Canadian Types*, 343.

37. Arthur Doughty, *A Daughter of New France* (Ottawa: Mortimer Press, 1916), 4.

38. "C'est leur seule réponse mais combien juste écho de la voix de l'enfant du fort de Verchères." Pierre Homier, "A travers la vie courante," *L'Action française* 3, 6 (juin 1919): 266.

39. Archives Nationales du Québec à Québec, P244, Fonds Tarieu de Lanaudière, vol. 2, W. Chapman à M. Lanaudière, 2 mai 1876 [copy of proposed poem]; Rev. Aen. McD. Dawson, "The Heroine of Verchères," *The Canadian Antiquarian and Numismatic Journal* (Montréal: Henry Rose, 1878) 6: 142–45; William Henry Drummond, *Phil-o-rum's Canoe and Madeleine Verchères* (New York: G.P. Putnam's Sons, 1898).

40. "Oui, Madeleine, qui était forte, n'en était pas moins douce et sensible." F.-A. Baillairgé, ptre, *Marie-Madeleine de Verchères et les siens* (Verchères: chez l'auteur, 1913), 30.

41. Agnes Maule Machar and Thomas G. Marquis, *Stories of New France: Being Tales of Adventure and Heroism from the Early History of Canada* (Boston: D. Lothrop Company, 1890), 216.

42. "On doit suppléer quelquefois les hommes, mais leur rendre les armes pour les batailles qui leur reviennent." Lionel Groulx, *Notre Maître, le passé, 1ère série*, 2e édition (Montréal: Librairie Granger Frères Limitée, 1937 [1924]), 61–69.

43. Chapman, "L'héroïne de Verchères"; LeMoine, *Héroïnes de la Nouvelle-France*, 16.

44. François Daniel, *Histoire des grandes familles françaises*, 519.

45. "Magdelon fut une femme parfaite, aussi habile ménagère que bonne mère de famille." T.G., "Magdelon la Canadienne," *Le Temps* (14 août 1912). "Magdelon" was a nickname for Verchères.

46. Carolyn Heilbrun, *Writing a Woman's Life* (New York: Ballantyne Books, 1988).

47. Mary Sifton Pepper, *Maids and Matrons of New France* (Toronto: George N. Morang & Co., 1902), 4.

48. "Puisque je suis femme, ma sympathie doit d'abord se porter vers des femmes." Madame Donat Brodeur, "Deux héroïnes de la Nouvelle-France," *The Canadian Antiquarian*, 3, 5 (1908): 65.

49. Emma A. Currie, *The Story of Laura Secord and Canadian Reminiscences* (St Catharines: n.p., 1913), 83.

50. "L'histoire, c'est fait surtout pour les garçons . . . à cause des batailles et des soldats."

"Et Madeleine de Verchères? Ca n'était pas un garçon . . . Et l'on en parle dans l'histoire." Marie-Claire Daveluy, "Le Cours Improvisé" [1920] in *Aux Feux de la Rampe* (Montréal: Bibliothèque de l'Action française, 1927), 11–12. Corinne Rocheleau makes a similar point in her play illustrating the roles of women in New France: "On dit que les peuples heureux n'ont pas d'histoire. Si cet épigramme s'applique aux individus, il faut croire que les premières Françaises établies en Amérique furent des femmes heureuses, car on n'en parle pas . . . ou si peu que c'est tout comme!" *Françaises d'Amérique: Esquisse historique* (Worchester, MA: La compagnie de publication Belisle, 1915), 3.

51. Marie-Louise d'Auteuil, "Vos Doctrines?," *L'Action française* 16, 6 (déc. 1926): 381.

52. Pepper, *Maids and Matrons*, 228–29.

53. E[thel] T. Raymond, *Madeleine de Verchères* (Toronto: Ryerson Press, 1929), 8–9.

54. Frédéric de Kastner, *Héros de la Nouvelle France*, 82–91. Another aristocratic author emphasising Verchères' social class was Thérèse de Ferron,

"Une héroïne de la Nouvelle-France: Marie-Madeleine de Verchères," *Revue hebdomadaire* (4 oct. 1924): 89–102.

55. Henry James Morgan, ed., *Types of Canadian Women and of Women who are or have been connected with Canada* (Toronto: William Briggs, 1903), 1: 80. De Kastner and Richard made the same point.

56. Archives nationales du Québec à Trois-Rivières, Fonds de la famille Baillairgé, Livre de compte personnel, 96–99.

57. "Tantôt je sentais que pour vouloir traduire toute sa belle énergie, j'allais faire de ma jeune héroïne une virago." Cited in M. Hodent, "Philippe Hébert: Le maître de la Sculpture Canadienne," *La Canadienne* (Paris) 11, 9 (sept. 1913): 164.

58. National Archives of Canada, MG27II D10, Fonds Rodolphe Lemieux, vol. 10, Lord Grey to Lemieux, 16 May 1910, 11878.

59. Women were thanked for organizing the brunch as well. The information in this paragraph comes from *Le Devoir*, 22 sept. 1913, 4–6.

60. "Il y en a eu d'autres Madeleine de Verchères dernièrement, alors que des institutrices canadiennes-françaises préférèrent perdre leur salaire plutôt que de ne pas enseigner le français à leurs élèves."

"Si le royaume de France fut délivré et réhabilité par Jeanne d'Arc, cette colonie, alors française à son berceau, fut illustrée par Madeleine de Verchères.

61. "Plus d'un canadien qui l'apercevra en remontant le fleuve dira qu'il n'est pas de plus jolie fille sous le ciel bleu." Hodent, "Philippe Hébert," 164.

62. Summary information on the film is provided in Peter Morris, *Embattled Shadows: A History of Canadian Cinema, 1895–1939* (Montreal: McGill-Queen's University Press, 1978), 48–49; Marcel Jean, *Le cinéma québécois* (Montréal: Éditions du Boréal, 1991), 17–19. D. John Turner provides a more extended analysis in "Dans la nouvelle vague des années 20: J.-Arthur Homier," *Perspectives* (de *La Presse*) 22, 4 (semaine du 26 jan. 1980).

63. "C'est une belle vue, qu'il faut faire voir le plus possible à cause de la bonne leçon d'histoire qu'elle donne." *La Presse*, 16 déc. 1922, 43.

64. "On dirait un homme qui admire le portrait de ses ancêtres—brossé par un artiste d'occasion. C'est une émotion plus patriotique qu'esthéstique." *Le Devoir*, 11 déc. 1922, 2.

65. "Vous avez sauvé le pays."

"Je n'ai fait que mon devoir."

66. Philéas Gagnon, "Le curé Lefebvre et l'héroïne de Verchères," *Bulletin de recherches historiques* 6 (1900): 340–45.

67. Pierre-Georges Roy, "Madeleine de Verchères, plaideuse," *Transactions de la Société Royale du Canada*, 3, 15 (1921): 63–72.

68. In 1946, after women had served in the armed forces, Jean Bruchési made a more explicit attack, using Verchères as an example, on "le renversement des rôles assignés à l'homme et à la femme, sinon par décret divin, du moins par la nature, voire par le bon sens." In "Madeleine de Verchères et Chicaneau," *Cahiers des Dix* 11 (1946): 25.

SEXUALIZED SPACE

○

"THE PLEASURE IS EXQUISITE BUT VIOLENT": THE IMAGINARY GEOGRAPHY OF NIAGARA FALLS IN THE NINETEENTH CENTURY◇

KAREN DUBINSKY

o

So much history has been written with such extreme accuracy that it can truthfully be called "dry as dust" and of interest only to a historian. In writing the story of Canadian history in such a way as to make it a tourist attraction, it would be well to remember that the details given are not nearly so important as the atmosphere created. . . .[1]

Wednesday, March 18, 1992 opened another chapter in the history of tourism at Niagara Falls. Canadian magician Doug Henning and his spiritual advisor/business partner, Maharishi Mahesh Yogi, announced at a press conference that day that Niagara Falls had been chosen as the site of their proposed New Age theme park, Veda Land. Veda Land will feature nature-themed hotels, a "Heaven on Earth" residential development, 33 rides, and the showpiece, a "Levitation Building" which will appear to be hovering 20 metres over a body of water.[2]

◇ Reprinted with permission from *Journal of Canadian Studies* 29, 2 (Summer 1994): 64–88. I am most indebted to local Niagara Falls historian Dwight Whalen for sharing his knowledge and his research with me, and to Stephen Connacher for helping me uncover more about Niagara history. Thanks also to members of my women's history group and sex history group, as well as Vince Sacco, Keith Walden, and anonymous reviewers, for their comments. Special thanks to my fellow excursionists and adventurers in post-tourism, Carol Whitehead, Gerard Coffey, and especially, Susan Belyea.

Henning was happy to combine two of his passions, magic and New Age spirituality, but he was not the only one smiling that day. Niagara Falls mayor Wayne Thompson declared Veda Land a "tremendous opportunity" for the town, and defended Henning and the Maharishi against alarmed local Christians. "These people" (the anticipated three million New Age tourists willing to pay the $18 admission charge), stated Thompson firmly, "do not smoke, drink or take drugs." If testimonials to the clean and sober New Age of the '90s didn't work, economics might. Mayor Thompson also noted at the press conference that tourists stay an average of six hours at the Falls, and that tourist business always plummets in the winter. Study after study has shown, explained the mayor, that the town needs a "major attraction."[3]

The choice of Niagara Falls for this venture fits well with many trends in the history of tourism in the region. The need to supplant natural physical wonders with those created by people and have nature "do tricks" for human amusement, the association of the Falls with near-mystical powers of healing and renewal, the appropriation of othered cultures as a spectacle for the enjoyment of North Americans, the concern on the part of the local establishment that the proper sort of person be visiting (which historically can be interpreted in stark class terms): all of these have deep roots in the history of Niagara Falls. The creators of Veda Land have made explicit what has been implicit in Niagara Falls tourism for almost 200 years: it's all an illusion.

It is true that there is a unique geographical phenomenon at one point in the Niagara River, which results in a mass of water cascading over cliffs. It is also true, though this is subjective, that this unique geographical phenomenon is powerful and beautiful to human eyes. (Yet even this is socially constructed. What we see as Niagara Falls today looks very different from the spectacle which awed millions of nineteenth-century visitors. Today's tourist sees the "limited edition" of the waterfall; more than one half of the water flowing down the Niagara River is diverted upstream to generate electricity in Canada and the United States). Beyond that, it's done with smoke and mirrors.

Like Oscar Wilde—the source of several *bon mots* about the place—who saw only a "vast unnecessary amount of water going the wrong way and then falling over unnecessary rocks," many have been disappointed by the illusion of Niagara. Those who deliver Niagara Falls to us have been castigated since the early nineteenth century for cheating us. The disappointment many tourists have felt after "doing" Niagara, only to realize, as one Canadian journalist put it in 1876, that "Niagara was doing me," led to a long series of moral panics about the harassment (financial and otherwise) of tourists and the ruination of Niagara.[4] Yet, as the remarkably candid 1947 assertion of the Ontario Travel and Publicity bureaucrat Mary Ainsly quoted earlier reveals—*all* tourism is about illusion, or perhaps more kindly, about the creation of "atmosphere." The history of tourism at Niagara Falls reveals the bizarre, the sublime, and at times, the ridiculous, but it is not *so* different from general trends in Western tourism throughout the past two centuries.

Recently, historians and sociologists have begun to explore tourism more analytically, focussing notably on the cultural significance of people's travel habits in the late nineteenth and twentieth centuries. Niagara Falls itself has been the subject of several historical and cultural studies that chart its broader social meanings for generations of tourists, artists, naturalists and industrialists. The best and most comprehensive of these, Elizabeth McKinsey's stunning visual history of changing artistic depictions of the Falls, *Niagara Falls: Icon of the American Sublime*, suggests a host of different identities assigned to the Falls over time: religious, natural and scientific, patriotic, sentimental and, of course, commercial. In Canada, historian Patricia Jasen has recently supplemented this work, arguing that there was never an "innocent" age of Niagara Falls tourism, by showing how even its earliest stages were fuelled by a combination of romantic and commercial values.[5]

Other scholars have attempted to deconstruct tourism by asking why sites and practices become designated as culturally desirable to "do," (such as Niagara Falls, the Canadian Rockies, Peggy's Cove or the West Edmonton Mall) and others (there are plenty of waterfalls, mountains, fishing villages and shopping malls in the world) do not. As John Urry suggests, in his influential study *The Tourist Gaze*, tourist attractions are never "natural"; even the most spectacular or unique phenomenon is packaged and acquires meaning through a number of possible signs.[6]

John Urry the sociologist, Mary Ainsly the post-war travel promoter, and Doug Henning the illusionist have all recognized that the tourist gaze is produced by binary divisions, particularly the separation between the ordinary and the extraordinary. It's relatively simple to point out that mass tourism is about a series of "constructed" experiences. The history of Niagara Falls alone yields a veritable treasure-trove of what the Niagara Parks Commission used to call "fakirs and squatters": Irish "Indians" selling local beadwork made in New York City (and later Japan), other entrepreneurs who sold jewellery made of "fossilized Niagara spray," tour guides, hack drivers, and hotel and museum owners who for generations have devised an impressive array of scams designed to help tourists spend money. There are a host of more significant, though less visible "fakes": the demonization of the scheming Niagara Falls hack driver in the nineteenth century displaced larger questions of who was profiting from tourism in the area, and the story of "how Niagara was made free" from the "bad old days" of commercial hucksters by the creation of provincial and state parks in the 1880s obscures the ongoing role of private interests, both during the park campaign and after. The biggest fake of all, perhaps, is the currently poisonous condition of the Niagara River.[7]

This paper will isolate one particularly popular Niagara feature—its identification with sexuality—to analyse the sexual meaning of Niagara Falls. Understanding the long-time association of Niagara Falls with the honeymoon is part of this project. There is, I have discovered, no definitive conclusion to be reached about the origins of this phenomenon, but I will raise several questions about the curious waterfall/honeymoon juxtaposition. Of all the possible gazes that could have been applied to the Falls, why did the area develop as a site for honeymooners in particular? How was the town of Niagara Falls packaged and promoted as the "Honeymoon Capital of the World" and how has this image been sustained and re-invented? Surprisingly little is known historically about the honeymoon as a specific institution of heterosexuality. The modern honeymoon has become a clichéd, risqué joke; the stuff of heart-shaped beds and hot tubs. When did honeymoons acquire this overtly sexual content? How did the meaning of the honeymoon change with shifts in conventional sexual mores and rules? I shall begin by discussing the institution of the honeymoon in the nineteenth century, then explore the popularity of Niagara Falls in this period as a tourist resort in general and a honeymoon site in particular.

THE HONEYMOON—ORIGIN AND MORES: "MY ONE HORROR IN LIFE IS AN EVIDENT BRIDE"

The modern honeymoon evolved from the nineteenth-century upper and middle-class custom of the bridal or wedding tour, during which the bride and groom, often accompanied by relatives, visited other relatives who could not attend their wedding. American historian Ellen Rothman suggests that by mid-century, wedding trips had become "the standard sequel to a middle-class wedding," but it was not until the 1870s that the notion of the honeymoon as a time of exclusive, romantic seclusion of the couple superseded "the need for affirming community ties" by visiting others.[8]

Sexual rituals did not figure prominently in the Victorian honeymoon. This had not, however, always been the case. Lawrence Stone finds the origin of the honeymoon in the bridal night of sixteenth and seventeenth-century England, an institution which contained several explicit sexual references. In upper and middle-class families, he explains "the pair were brought to the bedroom in state by relatives and friends, often accompanied with horseplay and ribald jests, and were only left alone (perhaps for the first time in their lives) once the curtains of the four-poster bed closed." The bride, he claims, went to bed with gloves on, and the removal of the gloves symbolized the loss of virginity.[9] Others have described the folklore of pre-industrial honeymoons, which contained similar public sexual references, mostly pertaining to the virginity of the bride. Paula Scher traces the origin of the word to pre-industrial Europe, when "those bawdy, Teutonic couples ran off into the night and drank a fermented honey drink, mead, for thirty days, or till the moon waned."[10] Such public sexual rituals ebbed at the end of the eighteenth century, when upper-class English couples began to regard as "vulgar and unnecessary" practices such as the firing of guns at weddings, the accompaniment of the couple into the bedroom to pull off the bride's garter, even the public kiss by the parson.[11]

Sexual advice manuals of the nineteenth century illustrate the "de-sexing" of the honeymoon, in ways consistent with hegemonic notions of gender and sexuality. *Searchlights on Health*, a popular turn-of-the-century text, warned husbands that consummation of the marriage immediately after the ceremony constituted "legalized rape." In most cases, noted Doctors Jeffries and Nichols, the bride is . . .

nervous, timid and exhausted by the duties of preparation for the wedding, and in no way in a condition . . . for the vital change which the married relations bring upon her. Many a young husband often lays the foundation of many diseases of the womb and of the nervous system in gratifying his unchecked passions without a proper regard for his wife's exhausted condition.

"Young husband," they exhorted, "prove your manhood, not by yielding to unbridled lust and cruelty, but by the exhibition of true power in self control and patience with the helpless being confided to your care!"[12]

Advice manuals also offer some clues as to why the public wedding tour was transformed into the private honeymoon. Since the 1880s, dispensers of advice decried the "harassing" wedding tour, which was deemed both immodest and physically debilitating to the bride. "To be hurried hither and thither, stowed in berth and sleeping-cars, bothered by baggage, and annoyed with the importunities of cabmen, waiters and hangers-on" wreaks havoc with the nervous system of the bride, wrote Dr. George Napheys in 1880. *Searchlights on Health* agreed, reminding the husband that "his bride cannot stand the same amount of tramping around and sight-seeing that he can."[13]

Yet it wasn't solely the bride's delicate physical condition which was at issue. Advice manuals all recommended that "the young pair should escape the prying eyes of friends and relatives at such a moment." It was horribly unpleasant for the bride to pass through "the ordeal of criticism and vulgar comments of acquaintances and friends" after the wedding. One young woman complained to Mary Wood-Allen, author of *What a Young Woman Ought to Know*, that she "did not want to be stared at or commented on by strangers" on her bridal tour. "Let us go to some quiet spot in the mountains or by the sea, and let us live with each other and with nature," she suggested as an alternative.[14]

American novelist William Dean Howells's fictional characters, Basil and Isabel March, illustrate well this attempt to combine public modesty with private romance. Howells's 1871 novel *Their Wedding Journey* follows Basil and Isabel on their tour from Boston through Niagara Falls and points east. The couple make their journey several weeks after their wedding ceremony, for which Isabel, especially, is extremely grateful. "How much better," she declared ". . . than to have started off upon a wretched wedding-breakfast, all tears and trousseau, and had people wanting to see you aboard the cars. Now there will not be a suspicion of honey-moonshine about us. . . ." Throughout their journey, Isabel reiterates her concern (amusedly tolerated by Basil) that "we shall not strike the public as bridal, shall we? My one horror in life is an evident bride."[15]

Even during the Victorian period, everyone—as Isabel March feared— knew what a honeymooning couple "stood for." In a culture which only considered sexual relations permissible within the institution of marriage, the wedding provided heterosexual couples with a social licence to become sexual beings. In earlier times this was acknowledged and celebrated as part of the post-wedding ritual. To young Victorian middle and upper-class couples of taste and refinement, however, the private wedding tour or honeymoon was firmly in step with late nineteenth-century prescriptions for public sexual modesty. Historians have identified the secluded honeymoon as one component of the trend towards private, romantic marriages in the nineteenth century. I would suggest that the quiet, contemplative and perhaps passionless honeymoon was also a means of reconciling the embarrassment of entering the public category of "sexual" with hegemonic ideas about physical decorum.

WHY NIAGARA?

A search through travellers' accounts, guidebooks by both travellers and local boosters, and promotional material generated by the tourist industry and, later, by government, reveals a curious paradox. The association of Niagara Falls with the honeymooning couple is almost as old as the "discovery" of tourism of the Falls itself, dating from the early nineteenth century. The legend, now a staple in Niagara Falls tourist promotion and local history, that the first honeymooners were Aaron Burr's daughter Theodosia and her husband, or Napoleon Bonaparte's brother Jérome and his wife (who visited in 1801 and 1803, respectively) has been challenged by historian Elizabeth McKinsey, who dates the origins of the "honeymoon craze" at Niagara to the late 1830s. Yet the first obvious "hard sell" of the region as the honeymoon destination did not occur until almost 100 years later. The 1920s saw the first stirrings of the widespread commodification of the Niagara Falls honeymoon.[16] The real selling of Niagara as a honeymoon haven—including the creation of honeymoon certificates by the tourist industry, "honeymoon hotels" and other promotional devices—did not begin until World War II. How do we understand, then, why huge numbers of honeymooning couples "voted with their feet" and visited the Falls in the nineteenth century, without being "told to" by anyone?

This raises the question, of course, of how certain sites become designated as popular places to visit, as well as how particular sites become invested with certain qualities. John Urry has traced the rise and demise of the British seaside resort through the nineteenth century with these questions in mind. The proximity of the sea to British cities and towns, and the development of relatively inexpensive railway travel, were not the only factors contributing to the popularity of the seaside resort. Most nineteenth-century British tourism, he argues, was based on the natural phenomenon of the sea, and its supposedly "health-giving" properties. In more recent years, in Britain as elsewhere, the sun has replaced the sea as the perceived provider of health and rejuvenation.[17] In Canada, "nature tourism," as Alexander Wilson describes it, has a long history, and was, like the British seaside resort, based on the notion that the woods provided a more "pure" environment. Ontario government promotional literature in the twentieth century made a concerted attempt to "sell" the province, especially the north, as a place of health, rest, and transformation.[18]

Places are more than simply locations; the spatial is also socially constructed. Social divisions are often spatialized, and places become labelled, much like "deviant" individuals. This combination of social divisions and spatial metaphors (e.g. the "wrong side of the tracks") becomes incorporated into what geographer Rob Shields calls "imaginary geographies," so much so that certain sites become associated with "particular values, historical events and feelings."[19] Tourist promoters can take these associations of places with values, events and feelings, and create successful enterprises from them. But social construction has its limits. As Michael Moore's documentary *Roger and Me* revealed, lots of money and grand planning could not turn the decaying industrial town of Flint, Michigan into a tourist mecca under any guise. For Niagara Falls to become a popular honeymoon spot— especially in the absence of massive promotion until the twentieth century—there must have been something there to begin with. Before considering the place of romance, sex, and danger in the imaginary geographies of countless Niagara Falls visitors, I shall briefly recount the history of tourism in the area during its first, "elite" phase.

"FIRST CLASS" TOURISTS: NIAGARA FALLS AS A NINETEENTH-CENTURY RESORT

Patricia Jasen dates the beginning of the modern tourist industry in Niagara Falls to the period immediately after the War of 1812. The first tourist entrepreneur, who was also the first of many businessmen to attempt to close public access to the Falls, was William Forsyth, who built the first hotel on the Canadian side. The opening of the Erie Canal in 1825 ushered in an era of widespread travel to Niagara, at least among the middle and upper classes. Easier access was also facilitated by the opening of the Welland Canal in 1832, and then by railroads and bridges linking the two countries that were built during the 1840s and 1850s.

    If tourism was the result of easier access, the industrial possibilities of the waterfall provided motivation for most of the investment in transportation. Backers of the Erie Canal saw visions of carding machines, grist and saw mills fuelled by power generated by the Falls, and such businesses indeed began to line the American side of the river shortly after construction of the canal. Niagara Falls, New York was renamed, for a brief period, Manchester, a telling indicator of industrial optimism. Tourism and industrial development co-existed in this period, though much to the chagrin of some visitors. While travellers have lamented the physical desecration of the Falls and surrounding area since at least the 1820s, the tourist industry has adapted to successive waves of industrial development with remarkable ease.

    By the late 1840s, the Falls hosted more than 40 000 visitors per year. From the late 1820s to the Civil War, it was especially popular with American aristocracy from the south, who wished to escape the summer heat on the plantation by attending the Niagara "Season." The grandest hotels in the area, Canada's Clifton House, and the American Cataract House and Frontier House (now a McDonald's restaurant), were constructed in the 1830s and by the 1860s there were 150 hotels on the American side alone. In this period, "everyone who could afford it" went to Niagara, often as part of the northern tour, the American equivalent of the European grand tour, which in North America included Boston and Quebec City.[20]

The waterfall was, of course, the main Niagara attraction, but there have always been plenty of sidelines. Battlefields were an important part of the early tourist experience. Travellers would hire guides, who claimed to have been survivors of the War of 1812, and be taken to Lundy's Lane, the monument to General Brock constructed in 1824, and to other famous war sites. Two of the most popular attractions were the American Cave of the Winds and the Canadian Table Rock tours, both begun in the 1830s, in which people can walk through the Falls, buffeted by wind and water, and end up viewing them from "inside." Another popular attraction, the Maid of the Mist steamer (named after a fake Indian legend of virgin sacrifice) began its journeys to the base of the waterfall in 1840. Thomas Barnett's museum of "rare and exotic" human and natural curiosities (such as deformed animals and artifacts from Native and Chinese cultures) opened in 1827, and the villages on both sides of the Falls boasted bathing palaces, billiard rooms, bowling alleys and botanical gardens. The "best" place from which to view Niagara was also constructed by private interests. The Terrapin Tower, built on the American Goat Island in 1833 (it collapsed in 1873) rivalled the Canadian Table Rock land formation (it collapsed in 1850), both privately owned. The view from various hotel balconies was also widely promoted.

Why did they come? Mass spectacles began drawing people to Niagara early on. The first major gathering occurred in 1827, when Canadian hotel owner William Forsyth had a condemned schooner, filled with live animals, go over the Falls. About 15 000 people—many of whom would have paid Forsyth and other landowners for the privilege of watching from their property—gathered for this event. Feats of human daring were also important (and massively advertised) spectacles; Sam Patch made his jump over the Falls in 1829, and the most famous Niagara Falls stuntman, the great "Blondin," performed his high-wire act over the Falls in 1859, repeating it the next year for another huge and appreciative audience, including the visiting Prince of Wales. Other tightrope walkers followed Blondin's lead, including an Italian woman, Maria Spelterini, who dazzled crowds in 1876 with her costume—a scarlet tunic, green bodice, and flesh coloured tights—with an added Canadian twist: her feet were encased in Niagara fruit belt peach baskets as she made her way across the wire. High-wire acts were eclipsed by the "barrel craze" begun in 1886 (by which time Niagara was already *passé* for the more prestigious holiday-goer). The first person who successfully went over the falls in a barrel was a woman, a widowed school teacher named Annie Taylor who plunged over in 1901 (and who has become the subject of misogynist lampooning in Niagara Falls tourist history ever since).

Niagara Falls was also sold in the popular and high culture of the period. As Elizabeth McKinsey's work demonstrates beautifully, Niagara Falls was the most frequently painted subject in early American art. Niagara Falls was the first example of Canadian scenery depicted on a movie screen, and remained a hugely popular subject for film-makers and photographers at the turn of the century.[21] It was also the subject of theatre and novels, as well as some inventive visual spectacles, in the U.S. and abroad. In New York, for example, a popular play, "A Trip to Niagara, or Travellers in America," took place in front of a moving panorama depicting the scenery between New York City and Niagara. In the 1840s, two museums, one in London, and P.T. Barnum's American Museum, exhibited scale models of the Falls. The most unusual spectacle was a moving panorama, a 1000-foot-long canvas based on 200 paintings of the Falls which took 1.5 hours to unroll; it toured the U.S. between 1853 and 1859.

Niagara Falls became a fashionable and desirable tourist resort in the early and mid-nineteenth century in part through mass spectacles and promotional gimmicks such as these, but also because, as a celebrity itself, the Falls was visited by a veritable who's who of nineteenth-century luminaries.[22] In this first period of prestigious tourism, celebrity tourists helped construct Niagara as a cultural icon. The literary-minded in their midst also helped create the proper sentiments and meaning of the Falls in the larger culture.

THE "IMAGINARY GEOGRAPHY" OF NIAGARA FALLS IN THE NINETEENTH CENTURY

Other diversions aside, the main part of the itinerary of visitors was quiet contemplation of the waterfall. To really "do" Niagara, one stayed for a long period of time, watched the Falls from different vantage points and in different lights, and contemplated life. "Words are powerless, guides are useless," wrote *London Times* correspondent Nicholas Woods in 1861, ". . . he who wishes to see and feel Niagara must watch it for himself."[23] We know a lot about what the nineteenth-century traveller felt and thought about Niagara, because a good many of them wrote it down. Literary celebrities published accounts of their visits to the Falls, as did a host of relatively unknown travel writers, poets and diarists. Guide and gift books also contained pages and pages of descriptive writings, sometimes quotes from the famous, but also the imaginative outpourings of (often anonymous) writers. The desire to express oneself about Niagara was institutionalized by the tourist industry; the proprietors of Table Rock House provided guest books in their sitting room, where people would write a few lines about their experience after taking the Table Rock tour under the Falls. At least two anthologies from the Table Rock *Album* were published as souvenir books in the 1840s and '50s.

What did people feel at Niagara? As McKinsey suggests, the effort to "read" the cataract was "earnest indeed" and a plethora of meanings were evident.[24] The nationalist meanings of Niagara are particularly interesting, perhaps especially so to Canadians. In paintings which depicted bald eagles, stars and stripes, and flag-draped young women standing before the waterfall, as well as in writings which proclaimed that "in no quarter of the globe are the majesty and loveliness of nature more strikingly conspicuous than in America," American writers appropriated the Falls for the spirit of their young country. Niagara, argues McKinsey, was ". . . read as a text of America's natural theology."[25] The fact that the Falls were shared by another nation, and that the Canadian Horseshoe Falls was in fact the larger and more physically unique of the two, was blithely ignored by most American writers. John Quincy Adams, one of the few who considered this question, turned the history of Canada/U.S. border battles into an act of God: "It is as though," he mused, "Heaven had considered this vast natural phenomenon too great for one nation."[26] A few Americans conceded that the Canadian Falls were a more interesting spectacle. William Dean Howells admitted that he watched the "mighty wall of waters" on the Canadian side "with a jealousy almost as green as themselves," and an anonymous scribbler in the Table Rock *Album* expressed the same sentiment in verse: "My pride was humbled and my boast was small, for England's King has got the fiercest Fall."[27] Canadian feminist Agnes Machar's delight that "our Canadian falls are the grandest" was a theme taken up by surprisingly few Canadian or British visitors.[28]

The waterfall also acquired an important religious identity. For many tourists, Niagara had all the trappings of a sacred shrine, a view which achieved official recognition in 1861 when Pope Pius IX established a "pilgrim shrine" at Niagara Falls.[29] Table Rock was invested with particular religious significance; many referred to it as a "cathedral," and others suggested it was "where God himself baptizes." "I feel as if I had entered a living temple of the Eternal," wrote one visitor, who invited others to "come and worship at the shrine of Niagara." Another wrote anonymously that he "dare not write my name where God has set his seal."[30] Poet Thomas Moore probably spoke for many when he wrote, in an 1804 letter to his mother, "Oh! Bring the atheist here, and he cannot return an atheist!"[31]

Such religious sentiment about the Falls helped construct another type of meaning: the moral power of Niagara. Niagara was the setting of several didactic Christian children's books, published in Britain and the United States in the nineteenth century, and the Canadian social purity movement in turn found Niagara Falls a powerful visual metaphor with which to illustrate its agenda. The "Mighty Niagara of Souls" was an image used by the Canadian Salvation Army to arouse concern for the plight of countless lost souls—the drunkard, the gambler, the sensualist, the society lady and her fallen sister—who were "fast being hurried over the 'Niagara' of life into the whirlpool of eternity."[32]

Nineteenth-century moralists conveniently found Niagara a powerful symbol to represent damnation and destruction because of another long-standing set of meanings evoked by the waterfall: its association with both pleasure and terror. From its first written description in 1683 by Father Louis Hennepin, who called it "the most Beautiful, and at the same time most Frightful Cascade in the World," such sublime ambivalence has characterized much writing about Niagara. "The pleasure is exquisite but violent," wrote one visitor in 1821. Yet, the lure of Niagara was as potent as its danger. As another early nineteenth-century traveller commented, he could "hardly consent to leave this seemingly dangerous, and enchanting spot."[33] In the remainder of this section, I want to consider the parallels between these images and feelings about Niagara, and nineteenth-century writings and feelings towards sexuality and gender.

Despite the voluminous writings about Niagara Falls, the task of describing the cataract was clearly considered quite difficult. "There is no term of our language too high, or idea of our imagination adequately comprehensive to describe this profound and impressive scene," wrote one anonymous guidebook author. Another Table Rock *Album* contributor agreed: "I came to see;/ I thought to write;/ I am but—dumb."[34]

Personification and the pathetic fallacy are two standard literary devices many writers used to describe the indescribable, attributing human feelings and emotions to the rushing waters. Some simply compared the waters to humans. One guide suggested that he would "submit to be shot at" rather than take the same leap as the Niagara waters, but others were more explicit in using human emotions to convey both the beauty and the terror evoked by and contained in the waterfall. Isabella Bird, an Englishwoman who visited in the 1850s, described the American rapids "rolling and struggling down, chafing the sunny islets, as if jealous of their beauty," rapids which then "flung [themselves] upwards, as if infuriated against the sky. . . . There is something very exciting in this view," she concluded; "one cannot help investing Niagara with feelings of human agony and apprehension."[35] Most others were less self-conscious than Bird in their use of personification, but no less prolific. The rapids were seen as "a symbol of life and human passion . . . [t]he helplessness of its frenzied sweep saddens your heart." Such imagery fills volumes of Niagara Falls prose, varying in mood and emotion. The rapids "gambol along in a sportive mood," then become "possessed by demons"; the mist is like "children of the air"; "greedy" waters evoke a "sullen majesty," a "haughty grandeur," or "dance and curl in rapture"; cliffs "frown"; billows are "angry"; shores are "sullen." Novelist Henry James saw the Horseshoe Falls as an exhausted swimmer, "shrieking, sobbing, clasping hands, tossing hair."[36] Niagara Falls, declared the Niagara Parks Commission, gave tourists the opportunity to see the "awe inspiring spectacle of nature in one of her turbulent moods."[37]

This last passage indicates another common descriptive device: the waters were not simply personified, they were gendered. And, overwhelmingly, they were gendered female. To almost all writers who gendered their descriptions, Niagara was female: the "Queen of the Cataracts," the "Water Bride of Time," and later, the "Daughter of History."[38] Niagara Falls has always been gazed upon as a specifically female icon.

When gender enters the imaginary geography of the physical landscape, what happens to the thoughts and feelings of spectators? Incorporating female imagery into their descriptions of Niagara, many writers also projected onto the landscape suitably gendered physical attitudes and emotional responses. Sometimes this took the form of simple flattery, particularly of the "costume" of the waterfall. Niagara "wears a garb that wins from man . . . wonder, awe and praise"; at "her" base, she "wrap[s] herself saucily in the rainbow robe of mist."[39] During the reign of "King Winter," Niagara dons a "coat of crystal" and sparkles like "a gem in the diadem of nature." One particularly poetic writer saw, in Niagara's winter scene, "trees . . . bowed down to the earth with their snowy vestments, like so many white nuns doing saintly homage to the genius of the place."[40] Others saw Niagara's mist as a veil; sometimes bridal, at other times ghostlike. The electrical illumination of the waterfall was also described in terms of fashion, though not always positively. Lady Mary McDowell Hardy was horrified to see Niagara "dressed up like a transformation scene in a pantomime. It was like putting a tinsel crown and tarlatan [sic] skirts on the Venus of Milo."[41]

To many who used similes, Niagara was *like* a woman; others who preferred the metaphor to the simile seem more literal-minded. William Russell claimed that "I never looked at it [the waterfall] without fancying I could trace in the outlines the indistinct shape of a woman, with flowing hair and drooping arms, veiled in drapery."[42] The invented tradition of the Indian "maid of the mist" who went over Niagara was fuel for many such fantasies. Promoters of Canadian Steamship Lines tours to the Falls in 1915 invited tourists to imagine that "instinctively we see the Indian maid in her flower-bedecked canoe approach the apex of the Falls, her body erect, her demeanor courageous." Images of naked Native women going over the waterfall adorned postcards, promotional brochures, as well as high Niagara Falls art, throughout the nineteenth and twentieth centuries.[43]

The positioning of the waterfall as female and the viewer as male enhanced the spectatorial pleasure of "doing" Niagara. It is not surprising, then, that sexual imagery abounds in descriptions of the Falls. The spray from the mist was often described as a "kiss," the sound of the water rushing as a "moan," islands rest on the "bosom" of the waterfall, and the "soft shales [of the cliff] gradually yield before the attack" of rushing water. The "clinging curves" of water "embrace" the islands, and water "writhes," "gyrates," and "caresses the shore"; the whirlpool is "passionate." Some recoil from the "mad desire" of the waters; for others, "no where else is Nature more tender, constrained, and softly clad." Niagara—"nature unclothed"—is "seductively restless," and "tries to win your heart with her beauty."[44]

Such images of the eternal feminine helped to construct sexualized responses to Niagara Falls. "Like a beautiful and true, an excellent and admirable mistress," wrote George Holley in 1872, "the faithful lover may return to it with ever new delight, ever growing affection."[45] Poets spoke of the "smooth, lustrous, awful, lovely curve of peril . . . cruel as love, and wild as love's first kiss!" Another evoked the image of Sappho "that immortal maid—enchantress sweet." One poem, published in a 1901 collection, is worth quoting at length, to illustrate the "exquisite pleasures" of Niagara:

Nymph of Niagara! Sprite of the mist!
With a wild magic my brow thou hast kissed;

I am thy slave, and my mistress art thou,
For thy wild kiss of magic is still on my brow.
I feel it as first when I knelt before thee
With thy emerald robe flowing brightly and free
Fringed with the spray-pearls and floating in mist
That was my brow with wild magic you kissed.

The author continues, describing how the waterfall has "bound" him:

. . . thy chain but a foam-wreath, yet stronger by far
Than the manacle, steel-wrought for captive of war . . .
While the foam-wreath will bind me forever to thee,
I love the enslavement and would not be free.

Nymph of Niagara! play with the breeze
Sport with the fawns 'mid the old forests trees . . .
I'll not be jealous, for pure is thy sporting
Heaven-born is all that around thee is courting
Still will I love thee, sweet Sprite of the mist
As first when my brow with wild magic you kissed![46]

Fictional treatments of visits to Niagara also reveal the magnetic sexual lure of the waterfall. Agnes Machar depicts Niagara as the first stop in her story about the holiday journey of several young Canadians. The protagonist, May, is joined at Niagara by her cousin Kate, and Kate's cousin Hugh, whom May had not met previously. Young May is initially shy around Hugh, but after their first look at the waterfall together (a "curving, quivering sheet of thundering surge . . . dazzlingly pure in its virgin beauty"), May looks at Hugh in a new light. She fells "much less shy" around him, and notices him physically for the first time. She is mesmerized by his "heightened colour" and the "absorbed expression of dark blue eyes." Hugh, it turns out, is also transformed by his view of the Falls: "I never felt," he tells May, "as if I had got so near the state of self-annihilation, the 'Nirvana' we read about." May experiences "much of the same feelings herself," though she is "too reserved to say it out." As the party continues their journey, across Lake Ontario and down the St. Lawrence River, the romantic tension between May and Hugh heightens, and by the end Hugh proposes marriage, asking May to "travel down the river of life together."[47]

Isabel March, the reluctant honeymooner in William Howells's *Their Wedding Journey*, is similarly transformed by Niagara, though she is rather more ambiguous about the feelings it evokes. Howells treats Isabel's determination not to reveal herself as an "evident bride" with gentle humour, particularly as she is one of countless evident newlyweds at Niagara Falls. The novel's parody of Victorian manners comes to a crescendo at Niagara, when Isabel, positioning the waterfall as a sexual male, confesses that she cannot contain herself any longer: ". . . I'm tossed upon rapids, and flung from cataract brinks, and dizzied in whirlpools; I'm no longer yours, Basil, I'm most unhappily married to Niagara. Fly with me, save me from my awful lord!"[48]

The waterfall could also—befitting a female of many moods—turn ugly. The "fatal lure" of the waters was commented on by many horrified but fascinated visitors. "As you gaze upon the rush you feel a horrid yearning in your heart to plunge in and join the mad whirl and see the mystery out," declared one.[49] Some suggested "scientific" explanations for this, positing that the sight of such a "frightful eminence" caused a rush of blood to the brain, which in turn produced a "partial derangement."[50] Yet most other descriptions relied less on "science" than on common discourses of feminine sexuality, depicting the waterfall as an alluring and enchanting female, bewitching and sometimes entrapping legions of male suitors. "With all this fear," wrote one promoter in 1856, "there is something so imposing in our situation as to render it pleasing. . . . We are in the presence of the enchanter." "The beautiful stream permits itself to be toyed with," wrote another visitor, "[i]ts smiling accessibility is most alluring, but is most dangerous. Every rock and ledge has its story of the fatal attraction of the waters." At the base of the waterfall, "man here is vanquished, and is captive, yielding willing homage to superior, presiding powers." Like a "designing woman," Niagara Falls often uses wiles to "trick" the unsuspecting. "One of the chief charms of the Falls of Niagara is the familiarity with which they can be approached, but beware of their relentless power."[51]

The dangers of Niagara were perhaps as widely promoted as its pleasures. As Patrick McGreevy has recently argued, the "metaphor of death is also manifest in the landscape that humans have created around the waterfall." Wax museums depicting famous criminals and monsters, war monuments, and emergency hotline telephones positioned at prime viewing areas all testify to the fascination people have found in the deadly potential of the waterfall.[52] Vivid descriptions of accidents, suicides and other deaths at the Falls have been a staple feature of Niagara guidebooks for two centuries. Twentieth-century promotional material focuses on the brave, heroic and happy; the tightrope walker, barrel jumper and, especially, the now legendary "miracle at Niagara," the story of a seven-year-old boy who went over the Falls in the summer of 1960 and lived. Nineteenth-century stories were decidedly more horrifying. Descriptions of the "hell of waters," their "angry fury," the "roar of ten thousand baffled demons" and the "hissing cauldron of spray" filled the accounts of nineteenth-century travellers. Niagara-area military history, evoked in many guidebooks, helped establish the context for dramatic tales of death. As one guidebook explained, "the lurid tales of conquest . . . have made the historical page of Niagara a record of blood."[53] The "fatal attraction" of the waters was thus promoted as part of the Niagara experience. Stories of babies accidentally swept over the Falls as their mothers looked on helplessly, construction workers falling off bridges, weak-minded souls (usually female) who jumped from the cliffs, and intoxicated men (usually Indians) going over in canoes, abound in guidebooks and obviously enhanced perceptions of the area's dangers. As one explained:

> You cannot tell when or where the next tragic affair will happen. Perhaps, reader, the polite stranger who has ridden with you . . . or

chatted with you at the hotel table, or who even now, at your side, leans over the bridge, is on the point of—but we forbear; it is not well to regard those about you as suicidal suspects, unless their conduct is manifestly suspicious.[54]

The most popular accident story in the nineteenth century was the tale of Charles Addington and Antoinette DeForest. The two were picnicking with their families on Luna Island in June of 1849. Addington, aged 22, grabbed DeForest, aged 8, and pretended to throw her in the current. She fell in and he jumped in after her. The two went over the Falls and did not survive. This most "melancholy of all Niagara tragedies" was recounted in lurid terms in guidebooks and travel writing over the next 50 years, but the way it was told varied markedly. Few guidebooks reported their ages; most told this as a story of two lovers who went over the Falls "locked in each others' arms."[55]

The point is not that guidebook writers, tourist promoters or travellers should be reprimanded for sloppy research; rather, as Mary Louise Pratt has explained in her analysis of European landscape and travel writing about Africa and South America, this genre reveals far more about the observer than the observed.[56] At Niagara, gendered, sexualized descriptive imagery, the perceived "fatal attraction" of rushing waters, tales of death and destruction, as well as invented stories of romance and tragedy, were all of a piece, and helped to create a highly romantic, erotic and somewhat scary image of Niagara Falls. Such imagery helped, in the nineteenth century, to fix an image of the Falls in the minds of North Americans as a place of forbidden pleasures.

And it wasn't just "in their heads." Accounts of two of the most popular Niagara Falls excursions, the Table Rock and Cave of the Winds tours, dramatically reveal how a visit to the Falls might *actually*, and not just imaginatively, heighten one's sensations of pleasure and danger. Before the advent of the elevator, the tours behind the Falls, through the tunnels at Table Rock, and inside the American Cave of the Winds were quite elaborate. At the entrance to each, women and men entered separate change rooms and completely disrobed ("down to the skin," as one traveller marvelled, "with no thought of retaining even your underclothes").[57] Both sexes donned a suit of flannel blouse and trousers, covered by an oilskin coat, and then followed a guide through the maze of rock and thundering spray. At their final destination, hearty travellers celebrated their accomplishment by frolicking in the waters. Upon their return, they were awarded with certificates that they had successfully completed this most dangerous tour.

The costume itself was enough to startle many visitors. One called it "the scantiest set of garments in which I have ever appeared in public." Others tried to take it in good humour; another commented that his party was "every way enlarged, with oiled cloth, india-rubber and tarpaulin," causing the women to look like "little, rosy Dutch butter women." That women and men wore the same dress caused some consternation to nineteenth-century visitors, so accustomed to rigidly gendered styles of clothing. Like many,

Isabella Bird balked at the idea of disrobing completely, and when she emerged from the dressing room her "appearance was so comic as to excite the laughter of my grave friends." In an effort to "upstage" Niagara, Sarah Bernhardt—another popular female icon of the late nineteenth century—proudly reported that she transformed the costume with a silver belt and a corsage of roses.[58]

As George Borrett recounted the Cave of the Winds tour:

> I cannot describe to you what a terrifying scene it was—how the waters roared around us—how the stifling spray beat upon our faces, so as to drive all the breath out of our bodies—how the wind, caused by the falling mass of water, blew about in a thousand blinding gusts . . . clashing the rain into our faces and chests, or driving it against our backs and legs. . . . I only know that I went down into this watery hell, and came up again uninjured, but very much out of breath and awfully frightened, half blinded, more than half deafened, and three-quarters drowned.[59]

For some, "natural" dangers were enhanced by human ones. Isabella Bird was horrified to find a "negro guide of the most repulsive appearance" waiting to take her through the Table Rock tunnels, and others recoiled as well at the Irish and French Canadians employed as guides. Table Rock House was owned by Saul Davis, one of the two most notorious "bad guys" of Niagara Falls tourism. A provincial inquiry into the business practices of Davis and his competitor Thomas Barnett (owner of the Niagara Falls Museum) investigated complaints that Davis used black guides to extort extra money from tourists. The claim that tourists trying to leave Table Rock House were stopped by five or six "negroes," using "profane language" and speaking "excitedly," who would attempt to charge them extra for leaving the area, was upheld by Commissioner Edmund Wood in 1873.[60]

Yet, after negotiating any number of possible "demons," both natural and human, the experience of cavorting through torrents of gushing water dressed in oilskin or rubber was indeed remarkable for many nineteenth-century travellers. The most pleasurable description of the experience comes from Frederic Almy, in 1896. He spoke of the water ". . . foaming and rushing about your knees, and lugging at you with an invitation that is irresistible. I have seen grave men frolic in the water, their trousers and sleeves swelled almost to bursting with the imprisoned air. . . . To play so with Niagara brings an exhilaration that is indescribable."[61] Others spoke of the "delightful, novel and strange sensation, of commingled terror and safety." Most agreed, even if they were less enthusiastic about the experience than Almy, that it was a "terrible ordeal, which no one should miss undergoing."[62]

Women and men alike make their appearance in this story of the imaginary geography of Niagara, and I have, to this point, not distinguished between male and female perceptions. There are, however, several places in which gender differences are revealed. In their writings (which are much fewer than those of men) women, more consistently than men, express disappointment and anger at the industrial and commercial "clutter" at

Niagara. Voteless women were claimed as staunch allies by some of the leaders of the Niagara preservation campaign in the 1880s.[63]

The place where we might expect to find the most obvious gender differences, particularly if we use feminist theory as our guide, is in the gendering and sexualizing of natural phenomena. The tendency to ascribe human, female and sexual characteristics to nature was by no means confined to travellers to Niagara Falls. The gendering of nature has been a staple feature of Western culture, which Annette Kolodny claims reached a zenith in the U.S. in the eighteenth and nineteenth centuries. Kolodny has found two dominant images of the "land-as-woman symbolization" in American life and letters. Early pioneers, explorers, and settlers experienced the land as a "nurturing, giving maternal breast" in part, she argues, "because of the threatening, alien and potentially emasculating terror of the unknown." To make the landscape female thus helped civilize it, "casting the stamp of human relations upon what was otherwise unknown and untamed." As the continent became less dangerous and more "known" through the nineteenth century, the bountiful mother image of the land gave way to a more sexualized, "seductive virgin" motif, an image which "invites sexual assertion and awaits impregnation . . . a field for exercising sexual mastery." While the gendering of landscape may help "civilize" the place, male fantasies of sexuality and conquest tell a much more sinister story. The "psycho-sexual dramas of men intent on possessing a virgin continent" can help us understand the continued "single-minded destruction and pollution" of the land.[64]

Kolodny argues that male sexualized imagery contrasts sharply with women's perceptions of the landscape. Pioneer women's fantasies and symbolism of their surroundings involved not massive exploitation and alienation, but rather, more modestly, "locating a home and a familiar human community within a cultivated garden." Women, in other words, both literally and imaginatively set about civilizing the frontier by making it homelike, planting gardens, dreaming of cottages, and otherwise projecting domestic ideals onto the wilderness.[65]

Does this argument hold true for Niagara Falls? When the "Queen of Beauty" meets the "King of Power" during the turn-of-the-century campaigns to "harness" the waterfall, the discourse of masculine domination clearly stands out. Canadian historian H.V. Nelles was struck by the ways hydro promoters used military metaphors to describe their attempts to "conquer" Niagara, turning the story of industrial development into a heroic and mystical epic of man against nature.[66] Let us not overlook, however, the specific gender configuration in this saga. After the construction of massive hydroelectrical plants at Niagara, travel writers enthused that "man has accomplished here, with Nature as his handmaiden, some of the greatest achievements of any age." The Canadian Steamship Lines celebrated the conquest of feminized nature together with Anglo-Saxon racial domination. The authors evoked the spirit of "yesterday's" Indian, the Maid of the Mist: "The hunting grounds of her fathers are peopled by a new race of strong, virile men. To them, the earth is their destiny, the things of the earth their heritage; this wonderful natural phenomenon but a potent natural force to be brought under human control."[67]

Men sexualized and tamed Niagara, and often spoke in the language of masculine conquer to express this. What about women? Like white men, white women used gendered and sexualized language in their descriptions of the waterfall; women, too, gendered Niagara female. Unlike men, not surprisingly, women—with the exception of Howells's fictional Isabel March—rarely positioned themselves as suitors wooing a seductive or restless icon. Indeed, note the contrast between the "Niagara-as-nymph" imagery cited earlier, and these lines, from "Niagara Above the Cataract," written by a woman: "Art thou not as quiet as an infant's dream/ Pure as its thought, unruffled as its brow/ When circled by its mother's arms in sleep."[68]

This asexual image of Niagara as a calm madonna with child could be read as evidence for Kolodny's view that women domesticate nature, while men eroticize and therefore conquer it. But there is an essentialist slippage in Kolodny's sexualization-equals-conquest formula, which tells only part of the story of sexuality and gender in the past. Kolodny does acknowledge that fantasies are not "blueprints for conduct, but contexts of imaginative possibility."[69] It is indeed true that women and men of the nineteenth century saw quite different imaginative possibilities in the sexual realm: women experienced sexuality as more problematic and more dangerous than men. Men, of course could eroticize conquest, and not just in campaigns to promote industrial development. But none of this negates other, more pleasurable sexual possibilities for either sex. Women, too, "played with Niagara," and romped about freely under its spray. Agnes Machar's May, while "reserved," also experienced the passion of heterosexual attraction when gazing at the waterfall.

The Niagara Falls honeymoon in the nineteenth century was not solely a creation of imaginary geographies. McKinsey notes that the popularity of the Niagara Falls honeymoon, at least for the middle and upper classes, was firmly established in American popular culture by the 1840s. Magazines, popular songs, fashion advertisements, and even Niagara Falls souvenirs themselves, depicted images of heterosexual romance with the Falls as a backdrop. Guidebooks and travellers' accounts also narrate tales of romance and honeymooners. Guidebooks directed travellers to islands above the waterfall that boasted secluded walks christened "Lovers Retreats." Travellers told stories of encountering flirting couples, even wedding ceremonies, in the "secluded, but much haunted groves" of Niagara's surrounding forests.[70]

The tradition of the Niagara Falls honeymoon was thoroughly popularized and commodified in the twentieth century, but it was not invented then. Many people have speculated about why Niagara Falls became associated with the honeymoon. It wasn't mere mimicry; it did not happen because famous people honeymooned there in the early nineteenth century. Nor does another popular answer—the falling water creates negative ions, which cheer people up and make them think about sex—get us very far.[71] Niagara Falls did, as I have argued, make people think about sex, but the creation of the place as a honeymoon mecca was a complex process which brought together several histories: its pre-existing status as an elite tourist resort: changing mores about the honeymoon itself in nineteenth-century social and family life; cultural depictions of Niagara as an icon of beauty, which were always understood in terms of gender and heterosexual attraction; and the forbidden pleasures of sexuality, romance and danger which countless travellers experienced while viewing, or "playing with" the waterfall.

POSTSCRIPT: THE TWENTIETH CENTURY HONEYMOON; CLASS, SEX, AND THE MODERN TOURIST

> To Niagara in a sleeper,
> There's no honeymoon that's cheaper
> And the train goes slow.
>
> Harry Warren and Al Dubin
> "Shuffle Off to Buffalo," 1938

It was in our century, and in particular in the late 1930s and 1940s, that the honeymoon took on two of the dimensions which currently define it: it became a truly mass heterosexual phenomenon, popular among most social classes, and it was re-sexualized, acquiring an overt sexual meaning in popular culture. The Niagara Falls honeymoon at mid-century reflected, and perhaps helped create, both of these trends. As Warren and Dubin's song popularized in the Hollywood musical "Forty-Second Street" indicates, "shuffling off to Buffalo" was a relatively affordable holiday trip, close to the Canadian and U.S. industrial heartland.

The creation of the honeymoon as a mass phenomenon owed much to a host of other changes in the twentieth century that lie outside the scope of this paper. Changes in transportation, leisure, and the social wage of advanced capitalist economies after World War II, and the "sexualization of love" in the twentieth century all form part of this story.[72]

Niagara Falls, however, had become a popular working-class resort long before the post-World War II travel boom. The region's status as an elite rendezvous for the southern American gentry had waned considerably by the 1870s. The creation of public parkland, which occurred on both sides of the waterfall in the 1880s, reflected the changing class composition of Niagara Falls tourists. The story of the campaign to "preserve" Niagara through the creation of public parks has been told as a story of far-sighted intellectuals acting to rescue the area from industrial and commercial interests. More cynically (and more accurately), Canadian historians have seen in the park campaign a story, familiar in our national past, of resilient businessmen negotiating with government to forge a consensus about the public interest which left untouched the basic structures of private capital accumulation.[73] Missing from both versions of this history, however, is the extent to which both racial and class fears were mobilized in the campaign to preserve Niagara. Indignation about "half-tipsy" Irish hackmen, "extortionist" black tour guides, Jewish museum owners, and "barbaric" Indian souvenir sellers (who were often, it was alleged, not even really Indian) had been part of the litany of tourist complaints about the area since the mid-nineteenth century. Concerns about the people who worked at Niagara Falls were more than matched by outrage over the people who went to Niagara, particularly as railroad and steamboat traffic increased in the 1870s and '80s. A petition organized by American, British and Canadian intelligentsia, demanding that the area immediately around the Falls be preserved as parkland, linked their concerns about the class of Niagara Falls visitors with their worries about commercial and industrial interference with nature. Niagara, claimed the petition, which included names such as Ruskin, Longfellow, Parkman and Emerson, "was now given up to second-class tourists and excursionists who are brought by the car load"; it was a "rare thing to find any of the best people" at the waterfall any longer. Tourists who "fetched their own tea and coffee and provisions and enjoyed a rollicking dance" at Niagara's shores failed to derive the proper moral benefit from the waterfall.[74] A leader in this campaign, the designer of the American park, was Frederick Law Olmstead, whose work 20 years previously created New York's Central Park. As an "urban safety valve" that brought warring classes and ethnicities together to enjoy common, refined amusement, Olmstead's Central Park inspired him to attempt the same vision at Niagara.[75]

It didn't really work, or at least, not as Olmstead might have hoped. The creation of public parkland at Niagara pushed back its commercialized, carnival-like trappings, but it by no means ended them. Niagara Falls simply became the bizarre and schizophrenic place it remains today: one part nature shrine, one part circus. As John Sears has argued perceptively, with the creation of the parks, "two versions of the Falls settled down side by side to vie for the attention of visitors."[76]

The crowning glory of Niagara fame in the mid-twentieth century was the film *Niagara*, released in 1953. How fitting that Marilyn Monroe, the most alluring sexual icon of North American popular culture in the twentieth century, played the role of Rose (a telling female/nature juxtaposition), the scheming, trampy wife of Joseph Cotton, a slightly deranged ex-serviceman. *Niagara* illustrates dramatically many of the strands of Niagara Falls' history, and helped at several levels to reinvent Niagara's image. The filming itself became a tourist attraction, and film-makers co-operated with the Chamber of Commerce, awarding a tour of the film set to the 10 000th couple to register for a honeymoon certificate on the Canadian side.[77] The film, and Monroe in particular, is alive with "dangerous" sexual imagery. The film is about sex and murder; the plot involves an unsuccessful attempt by Monroe's boyfriend to kill her husband, Cotton (on her behalf), the killing of Monroe herself by her husband, and finally, the death of Cotton as he falls over the waterfall in a boat. For the male viewer, it can be read quite openly as a tale of the awful powers of female (Rose/Niagara) sexual betrayal. In the opening scene, a distraught Cotton stands at the base of Niagara, railing at its power. The next scene shows Monroe laying naked in her bed, covered by a sheet, her legs spread apart (the "awful curve of peril"?), smoking a cigarette.

Niagara Falls has maintained this tawdry, low brow reputation, a reflection of both its sexual and class personae. A fascinating submission to the Niagara Post-War Planning Commission by local residents suggested a vast program of preservation, to restore the former historical glory of the area's buildings and streetscapes. Summer schools of art, chamber orchestras, historical pageants and outdoor plays were also suggested as fitting ways to attract tourists to the town, but these arguments fell on deaf ears at Niagara Falls.[78] It was Niagara-on-the-Lake, a few miles down the road, which became the beneficiary of middle-class cultural tourism and historical gentrification in the post-war era. The contrast between the two towns remains striking; they stand as vivid reminders of the differing class gazes of twentieth-century tourism.

A 1968 Chamber of Commerce survey concluded that over 60 percent of Niagara Falls visitors could be classified as working class. The same survey was one of many more since the 1960s which proclaimed the end of the honeymoon's popularity at the Falls; merely three percent of visitors surveyed were on their honeymoon.[79] The perception that the Niagara Falls honeymoon is over has resulted in an ever-frantic search for different, more widely appealing attractions. Few who gazed at Niagara in the nineteenth century would have understood the sentiment, expressed by a local tour promoter in 1990, that "the falls is a hook, a motivation, but it's not enough."[80]

NOTES

1. Mary Ainsly, Director of Publicity Branch, Dept. of Travel and Publicity, Ontario, 18 December 1947, responding to a complaint from a University of Western Ontario librarian about inaccuracies in a government promotional leaflet about the Rideau Canal.

2. *Toronto Globe and Mail* 18 March 1992.

3. CBC Radio News 20 March 1992, and CTV Dini Petty Show 21 March 1992. The eagerness on the part of local politicians to cosy up to Henning, or anyone else willing to spend money in the area, clearly has strong economic roots. The Niagara region has experienced devastating job losses through the early 1990s. According to a recent *Financial Post* report, tourism at the Falls has fallen by 40 percent in three years, and the winter of 1993 alone saw the closure of three major hotels and a large amusement park. See "Gloom Falls over Niagara," *Financial Post* 23 January 1993.

4. *Canadian Illustrated News* 14 Oct. 1876.

5. Elizabeth McKinsey, *Niagara: Icon of the American Sublime* (Cambridge: Cambridge University Press, 1985); Patricia Jasen, "Romance, Modernity and the Evolution of Tourism on the Niagara Frontier, 1790–1850," *Canadian Historical Review* LXXII, 3 (1991), 283–318. On Niagara Falls tourism history, see also John Sears, *Sacred Places: American Tourist Attractions in the 19th Century* (New York: Oxford University Press, 1989); Gordon Donaldson, *Niagara! The Eternal Circus* (Toronto: Doubleday, 1979); Ralph Greenhill and Thomas Mahoney, *Niagara* (Toronto: University of Toronto Press, 1969); Kiwanis Club of

Stamford, *Niagara Falls, Canada* (Niagara Falls: Kiwanis Club, 1967); Pierre Berton, *Niagara: A History of the Falls* (Toronto: McClelland and Stewart, 1992); Percy Rowe, *Niagara Falls and Falls* (Toronto: Simon and Shuster, 1978); and the many publications of George Siebel for the Niagara Parks Commission.

6. John Urry, *The Tourist Gaze—Leisure and Travel in Contemporary Societies* (London: Sage, 1990). On the social and historical construction of Maritimes tourism, see Ian McKay, "Twilight at Peggy's Cove: Toward a Geneology of Maritimicity in Nova Scotia," *Border/Lines* 12 (Summer 1988), and "Among the Fisherfolk: JFB Livesay and the Invention of Peggy's Cove," *Journal of Canadian Studies* 23, 1 and 2 (Spring/Summer 1988), 23–45, and "Tartanism Triumphant: The Construction of Scottishness in Nova Scotia, 1933–1954," *Acadiensis* XXI, 2 (Spring 1992), 5–47.

7. As John Phall, a Niagara region photographer, has pointed out, there is "an almost unbearable irony to the act of recording an achingly romantic meeting of shadowy forest and luminous water while suffering the stench of untreated sewer dripping nearby." Phall, John et al., *Arcadia Revisited—Niagara River and Falls from Lake Erie to Lake Ontario* (Albuquerque: University of New Mexico Press, 1988), 54. There are 164 hazardous waste disposal sites that line the shores of the Niagara River near the Falls. See Robert Malcolmson, "Niagara in Crisis," *Canadian Geographic* 107, 5 (Oct/Nov 1987). The devastation of the Niagara environment is also dealt with well in Kevin McMahon's NFB documentary film *The Falls* (1991).

8. Ellen Rothman, *Hands and Hearts: A History of Courtship in America* (New York: Basic Books, 1984), 175.

9. Lawrence Stone, *The Family, Sex and Marriage in England, 1500–1800* (Harmondsworth: Penquin, 1977), 223.

10. Paula Scher, *The Honeymoon Book* (New York: Evans and Co., 1981), 10.

11. John Gillis, *For Better or Worse—British Marriages, 1600 to Present* (New York: Oxford University Press, 1985), 138.

12. B.G. Jeffries and J.L. Nichols, *Searchlights on Health* (Toronto: J.L. Nichols, 1900), 202 and 204.

13. George H. Napheys, *The Physical Life of a Woman—Advice to the Maiden, Wife and Mother* (Toronto: Rose-Belford, 1880), 69, and Jeffries and Nichols, 200.

14. Napheys, 70, Jeffries and Nichols, 200, Mary Wood-Allen, *What a Young Women Ought to Know* (Philadelphia: Vir Publishing, 1928), 270.

15. William Dean Howells, *Their Wedding Journey* (Boston: Houghton Mifflin, 1871), 2.

16. Niagara Parks Commission promotional literature of this decade began to make claims aimed specifically at honeymooners, and one enterprising campground owner, taking advantage of highway access to the region, opened his "Honeymoon Huts in the Trees" autopark in 1920. *The Niagara Parks Commission Welcomes You,* circa 1920; Kiwanis Club, *Niagara Falls, Canada,* 54.

17. Urry, 16–37.

18. Alexander Wilson, *The Culture of Nature—North American Landscape from Disney to the Exxon Valdez* (Toronto: Between the Lines, 1991), 22–23.

19. Rob Shields, *Places on the Margin* (London: Routledge, 1990), 11 and 29.

20. This history of Niagara Falls is drawn from McKinsey, Jasen, Donaldson and Shields. Shields, 125.

21. McKinsey, 2. On Niagara in Canadian photography and film, see Patricia Pierce, ed. *Canada—the Missing Years* (Don Mills: Stoddart, 1985), 29, and Peter Morris, *Embattled Shadows: A History of Canadian Cinema, 1895–1939* (Montreal: McGill-Queen's, 1992), 8–9.

22. The roster of celebrity tourists in this period is quite impressive: Charles

Dickens, Frances and Anthony Trollope, Abraham Lincoln, Rupert Brooke, Oscar Wilde, Nathaniel Hawthorne, Mark Twain, Anna Jameson, Daniel Webster, Harriet Martineau, Margaret Fuller, H.G. Wells, Sarah Bernhardt, Jenny Lind, Henry James, Harriet Beecher Stowe, William Morris, Walt Whitman.

23. Nicholas Woods, *The Prince of Wales in Canada and the United States* (London: Bradbury, 1861), quoted in Charles Mason Dow, *Anthology and Bibliography of Niagara Falls* Vol. I. (Albany: J.B. Lyon, 1921), 273.

24. McKinsey, 87.

25. Joshua Shaw, *Picturesque Views of American Scenery* (Philadelphia, 1820), quoted in McKinsey, 101.

26. *A Souvenir of Niagara Falls* (Buffalo: Sage, 1864), 1.

27. William Howells, "Niagara First and Last" in William Howells et al. (eds.), *The Niagara Book: A Complete Souvenir of Niagara Falls* (Buffalo: Underhill and Sons, 1893), 9, and George Menzies, *Album of the Table Rock*, 1846.

28. Agnes Machar, *Down the River to the Sea* (New York: Home Book Co., 1894), 25. A few British visitors stated their preference for the Canadian side, but this was usually because of a perceived different social climate. British visitor William Howard Russell, for example, an abolitionist who hated the US, found Niagara Falls, New York "a lanky pretentious town, with big hotels, shops of Indian curiosities, and all the meagre forms of the bazaar life reduced to a minimum of attractiveness which destroy the comfort of a traveller . . ."—a description echoed in many other travellers' accounts of *both* villages. Russell, *My Diary, North and South* (NY: Harper, 1863). An American contributor to William Howells's *The Niagara Book* also commented on the different "temperments" of the two countries evident in the warning signs at the waterfall. "Canadians" wrote Frederic Almy, "are less considerate of the tender feelings of the dear public than with us. Mark the autocratic barbarity of the British declaration that persons throwing stones over the bank will be prosecuted according to law, as compared with the exquisite delicacy of the placards on [American] Goat Island: 'Do Not Venture in Dangerous Places,' . . . 'Stones Thrown Over the Bank May Fall Upon People Below.' On Goat Island, you always feel as if your mother were with you." Almy, "What to See at Niagara Falls," in William Howells, *The Niagara Book*, 41–42.

29. Patrick McGreevy, "Niagara As Jerusalem," *Landscape* 28, 2 (1985), 29.

30. Menzies, *Album of the Table Rock* (1846) and *Table Rock Album and Sketches of the Falls* (Buffalo: Thomas and Lathrop, 1856).

31. John Russell, ed., *Memoirs, Journal and Correspondence of Thomas Moore* (London, 1853) quoted in Greenhill and Mahoney, *Niagara*, 4.

32. "The Mighty Niagara of Souls," *War Cry*, 9 November 1895, quoted in Mariana Valverde, *The Age of Light, Soap and Water: Moral Reform in English Canada* (Toronto: McClelland and Stewart, 1991), 37.

33. McKinsey, 11 and 39.

34. *Niagara Falls Guide, With Full Instructions to Direct the Traveller* (Buffalo: J. Faxon, 1850), 32 and George Holley, *Niagara: Its History, Geology, Incidents and Poetry* (Toronto: Hunter Rose, 1872), 161.

35. Burke (1856), 19, Isabella Lucy Bird, *The Englishwoman in America* (London, 1856; Toronto: University of Toronto Press, 1966), 224.

36. George Curtis, *Lotus-Eating—A Summer Book* (New York: Harpers, 1852), reprinted in Dow, 254. See also Daniel Pidgeon, *An Engineer's Holiday* (London, 1882) quoted in Dow, 338; Mrs. S.D. Morse, *Greater Niagara* (Niagara Falls, New York: Gazette Printing, 1896), 12; J. Murray Jordan, *Niagara in Summer and Winter* (Philadelphia, 1904), and Peter Conrad, *Imagining America*

(New York: Oxford University Press, 1980), 16.

37. *The Niagara Parks Commission Welcomes You* (no date, circa 1950).

38. George Borrett, *Letters from Canada and the U.S.* (London, 1865), in Dow, 309; George Holley, 163; Canadian Steamship Lines, *Romantic Niagara*, 1940. The American and Horseshoe waterfalls were often referred to as "sisters."

39. Menzies, *Album of Table Rock*, 19; Curtis in Dow, 259.

40. Niagara Parks Commission, *Niagara Welcomes You* (1920); J. Murray Jordan (1904); H.T. Allen, *Tunis Illustrated Guide to Niagara Falls* (Niagara Falls, New York: Gazette Printing, 1877), 46.

41. Mary McDowell Hardy, *Between Two Oceans* (London: 1884), quoted in Dow, 342.

42. Russell in Dow, 318.

43. Canadian Steamship Lines, *Niagara to the Sea* (1915), 7. An insightful analysis of nineteenth-century depictions of native people in souvenirs is Ruth B. Phillips, "Consuming Identities: Curiosity, Souvenir and Images of Indianness in Nineteenth-Century Canada," David Dunston Lecture, Carleton University, Ottawa, 1991. See also the discussion of the "tourist Indian" in Daniel Francis, *The Imaginary Indian: The Image of the Indian in Canadian Culture* (Vancouver: Arsenal Pulp Press, 1992).

44. This compiled from Curtis in Dow, 257; J. Benwell, *An Englishman's Travels in America* (London, 1853), in Dow, 263; A.M. Ferree, *The Falls of Niagara and Scenes Around Them* (New York: 1876), 23; Pidgeon in Dow, 339; Edwin Arnold, *Seas and Lands* (New York: 1891), in Dow, 345; Howells, *The Niagara Book*, 130 and 15; *The Falls of Niagara Depicted by Pen and Camera* (Chicago: Knight and Leonard, 1893); R.R. Bell, *Diary of a Canadian Tour* (Coatbridge, England: Alex Pettigrew, 1927), 32;

Niagara Parks Commission Welcomes You (circa 1950).

45. Holley, 1.

46. Myron Pritchard, ed., *Poetry of Niagara* (Boston: Lothrop Publishing Company, 1901).

47. Machar (1894), 12–15 and 263.

48. Howells, *Their Wedding Journey*, 103.

49. Woods in Dow, 271.

50. F.H. Johnson, *Every Man His Own Guide at Niagara Falls* (Rochester: Dewey, 1852), 37. Visitors in the mid and late nineteenth century were consumed by the notion that the Falls made people want to kill themselves, but earlier visitors believed quite the reverse. Travellers in the 1830s were of the opinion that "the agitation of the surrounding air produced by the tremendous Falls, combines with the elevation and dryness of the soil" to produce "the most healthful [place] on the continent of North America." As proof of this, many noted that the "magic neighbourhoods" surrounding the Falls had remained untouched by the cholera epidemics of the 1830s. William Barham, *Descriptions of Niagara* (self-published, 1850); Burke's *Illustrated Guide*, 1856; Menzies, *Table Rock Album*, 1846. The association of water with curative powers continued through the nineteenth century in other places in Canada; a children's hospital was built on the Toronto Island in the 1880s for precisely these reasons. See Sally Gibson *More Than an Island* (Toronto: Irwin, 1984), 93.

51. Burke, 62; Charles Marshall, *The Canadian Dominion* (London: 1871) in Dow, 331; Ferree, 72; *Chisholm's Complete Guide to the Grand Cataract* (Portland: Chisholm Brothers, 1892), 14.

52. Patrick McGreevy, "Reading the Texts of Niagara Falls: The Metaphor of Death," in Trevor J. Barnes and James S. Duncan, eds., *Writing Worlds: Discourse, Text and Metaphor in the Representation of Landscape* (London: Routledge, 1992), 50–72.

53. *Chisholm's Complete Guide*, 12.

54. *Illustrated Guide to Niagara Falls* (Chicago: Rand McNally, 1897), 87.

55. *Complete Illustrated Guide to Niagara Falls and Vicinity* (Niagara Falls, New York: Gazette Publishing, circa 1880), 31; Isabella Bird, 225.

56. Mary Louise Pratt, *Imperial Eyes: Travel Writing and Transculturation* (New York: Routledge, 1992).

57. Frederic Almy, "What to See at Niagara," in Howells, *The Niagara Book*, 32.

58. Borret (1964) in Dow, 311; George Cousin, *Sketches of Niagara Falls and River* (Buffalo: Peck, 1846), 86; Bird, 232; Conrad, *Imaging America*, 17.

59. Borrett in Dow, 313.

60. Gerald Killan, "Mowat and a Park Policy for Niagara Falls, 1873–1887," *Ontario History* 70 (June 1975), 116–9; Menzies, *Album of the Table Rock*, 19.

61. Almy in Howells, *The Niagara Book*, 37.

62. *The Complete Illustrated Guide to Niagara Falls* (Niagara Falls, New York Gazette, circa 1880), 33; Edward Roper, *By Trace and Train Through Canada* (London: Allen, 1891), 418.

63. Thomas V. Welch, quoted in E.T. Williams, *Niagara, Queen of Wonders* (Boston: Chapple, 1916), 64.

64. Annette Kolodny, *The Lay of the Land* (Chapel Hill: University of North Carolina Press, 1975), 9, 67, 133.

65. Kolodny, *The Land Before Her* (Chapel Hill: University of North Carolina Press, 1985), xii–xv.

66. H.V. Nelles, *The Politics of Development* (Toronto: McMillan, 1974), 218–23.

67. Canadian Steamship Lines (1915), 8; Williams, *Niagara, Queen of Wonders*, 1.

68. Pritchard, *Poetry of Niagara* (1901), 70.

69. Kolodny, *The Land Before Her*, 10.

70. Russell in Dow, 328; Barham, *Descriptions of Niagara*, 35.

71. The ion story crops up a lot: see McKinsey, 183, Donaldson, 226, Dwight Whalen, *Lover's Guide to Niagara Falls* (Niagara Falls: Horseshoe Press, 1991). It also seems unlikely that, as H.G. Wells mused in 1905, the falling water was merely an alibi for honeymooners, a noisy "accessory to the artless love-making that fills the surrounding hotels." Conrad, *Imagining America*, 25.

72. For a useful analysis of changes in love and sexuality in America over the nineteenth and twentieth centuries, see Steven Seidman, *Romantic Longings—Love in America, 1830–1980* (New York: Routledge, 1991). I offer a preliminary examination of the commodification of the Niagara Falls honeymoon in the 1940s and 1950s in "Making Happy Heterosexuals: Sex, Class and the Post-War Honeymoon," paper presented at the Canadian Women's Studies Association / Canadian Sociology and Anthropology Association Annual Conference, June, 1993.

73. Gerald Killan's article "Mowat and a Parks Policy . . ." documents how Niagara land owners and entrepreneurs helped construct a parks policy consistent with their interests, and continued to involve themselves in the management and operation of the "public" Queen Victoria Park. See also Robert Welch, "The Early Years of the Queen Victoria Niagara Falls Parks Commission," M.A. Thesis, Queen's University, 1977.

74. James Carnegie Southesk, *Saskatchewan and the Rocky Mountains: a Diary and Narrative* (Edinburgh: Edmonton, 1875), quoted in Dow, 268. Petition quoted in Greenhill and Mahoney, 117.

75. On Olmstead's vision of landscape and social order, see Geoffrey Blodgett, "Frederick Law Olmstead: Landscape Architecture as Conservative Reform," *Journal of American History* LXII, 4 (March 1976). For a chilling look at how this reformist vision of public space has become as

"obsolete as Keynesian nostrums of full employment" in contemporary American cities, see Mike Davis, *City of Quartz: Excavating the Future in Los Angeles* (London: Verso, 1990).

76. Sears, 188.

77. "Film Stars Help Fete Honeymoon Couple at Falls," *Niagara Falls New York Gazette*, 2 June 1952.

78. *"Niagara Preserved and Restored" A Brief for the Realization of the Historical, Architectural and Cultural Values of the Town of Niagara Falls in Ontario* (1945).

79. *Niagara Falls Ontario Evening Review*, 26 February 1970.

80. "Niagara Falls seeks upscale tourist," *Toronto Star*, 27 May 1990.

THROUGH A HOLE IN THE LAVATORY WALL: HOMOSEXUAL SUBCULTURES, POLICE SURVEILLANCE, AND THE DIALECTICS OF DISCOVERY, TORONTO, 1890–1930 ⬧

STEVEN MAYNARD

○

"This is absolutely the last case of . . . gross indecency that I will try," declared Judge Morgan from the bench of the County Criminal Court in Toronto in 1913. In passing sentence on Patrick F, a single, thirty-year-old rubber worker, Judge Morgan continued: "I don't know whether it is the Morality Department that is stirring these things up or whether it is that the teaching of morals is lax, but the fact is that there is a tremendous increase in this kind of crime. I am thoroughly sick of it." In its coverage of the case, the *Evening Telegram*, in a story entitled "Not 'Toronto the Good,'" reported that Judge Morgan went on to say that "since he sat on the criminal bench he had been amazed at the city of Toronto, somewhat falsely characterized 'The Good,' and at the amount of indecency that had developed in it. It was as bad as Canal Street, New York."[1]

Patrick F was only one of many men brought before the Toronto courts on a charge of gross indecency, that is, for having had sex with another man. This article is based primarily on the case files of prosecutions for gross indecency in Toronto between the years 1890 and 1930.[2] The article is intended as a contribution to gay social history and, more generally, to the

⬧ Abridged from *Journal of the History of Sexuality* 5, 2 (1994). Reprinted with permission. For their very helpful comments, I would like to thank Ian McKay, Angus McLaren, Bryan D. Palmer, Mariana Valverde and the *JHS* readers. Earlier versions of this paper were presented to the Montreal History Group of McGill University in April 1993 and to the annual meeting of the Canadian Historical Association, Ottawa, June 1993.

history of sexuality, a relative newcomer to the field of Canadian social history and one pioneered by feminist historians of women's sexuality.[3]

In passing his judgment on sex between men, Judge Morgan described this "indecency" not as a natural (or even unnatural), timeless facet of human existence, but—choosing a word that betrayed a more historical understanding of the phenomenon—as something that "developed." Like many of his contemporaries, Morgan also believed that, whether in an auction room on Toronto's Yonge Street (the site of Patrick F's offence) or on Canal Street in New York, the historical development of indecency was intimately linked to the growth of the city. In the first section of the article I trace the spaces of a homosexual subculture[4] in the urban milieu of turn-of-the-century Toronto. The court records provide one way to begin outlining the contours of this emerging subculture. Testifying before the courts, both the men charged with gross indecency and constables policing such acts revealed the locations of sexual encounters between men, provided detailed descriptions of sexual relations and furnished information on the social characteristics of the men who participated in the homosexual subculture. This article focuses specifically on the men who helped to forge what has been described as the most "ubiquitous form" of the homosexual subculture, one revolving around "public" sex in parks, laneways, and lavatories.[5] Particular attention will be paid to aspects of the city-building process and the status of men as wage earners, both of which were important conditions of emergence for a homosexual subculture.

Judge Morgan's judicial diatribe also signals the important role of the police. He reminds us that in patrolling city streets the police did more than simply clamp down on men engaged in criminalized sexual activities, they played an active role, to use Morgan's words, in "stirring these things up." In this way, the police were implicated in what Foucault described as the historical process through which "sex became a 'police' matter"—a policing of sex based not solely on repression but on the productive regulation of sex through various technologies of surveillance.[6] The second section of the article looks in some detail at the Morality Department of the Toronto Police Force and its surveillance of sex between men. These police operations were, I argue, one of the modes through which a homosexual subculture was brought into existence.   *assumed to be in*

In the conclusion I offer a brief discussion of the relationship between the homosexual subculture and the practices of policing, a relationship marked by what I call the dialectics of discovery.[7] I also suggest how attention to the history of homosexuality can shed light on broader historical processes, such as the struggle over urban space or the rise of modern policing and other techniques of power.

IN PARK AND LANEWAY AND LAVATORY

On the evening of 23 May 1913, George C and George J were out walking after midnight in Memorial Square Park at the corner of Portland and Wellington Streets. As police constable McCoy testified before the Toronto

Police Court: "I saw George C laying on his right side with George J's face in his crotch. I watched there awhile. George J ordered George C to keep his leg higher up. When within 20 feet, George J got up. George C was laying on the ground with his pants open, his shirt up, his penis was slimy and had an erection." McCoy arrested the two Georges, escorted them to the patrol wagon and took them to the station.[8]

Sex in the city's parks occurred, of course, most often late at night, under the cover of darkness. In addition to Memorial Square, two of Toronto's central parks—Allan Gardens and Queen's Park—were popular sites for sexual encounters. The locations of homosexual activity often overlapped with the more general urban geography of sex and vice in Toronto. Allan Gardens was situated at the western end of Cabbagetown, Toronto's Anglo-Celtic, working-class neighbourhood and, as one historian has noted, "disorderly houses and houses of ill-repute were centred near the Cabbagetown region."[9] In contrast, Queen's Park, "beautifully laid out with walks, drives, lawn and garden" and surrounded by the University of Toronto, was more respectable and perhaps more effectively concealed what went on at night in and around its busy lavatory.[10] Parks associated with amusement areas, such as Sunnyside Beach and the Exhibition Grounds, were also frequented by men looking for sexual space. During the 1913 Canadian National Exhibition, for example, two young labourers, one aged nineteen, the other eighteen, were caught having sex. As the man who caught the two explained, I "was at the Exhibition on September 3rd" when, "at the rear of the fire hall" on the exhibition grounds, I "saw James C having Charles W's person in his mouth." At times, the parks could become rather busy sites of homosexual activity. As constable Christie explained, while patrolling Queen's Park "about 11:10 pm on Saturday" night, he "heard a sound like sucking." Christie said that not only did he observe a man "lying on his back and another man . . . kneeling with his mouth towards [his] privates," but beyond these men, behind a tree, there was "another couple who were there."[11]

In addition to parks, the nooks and crannies of Toronto's rapidly expanding built environment provided other sexual sites. In 1917, John P, a single, twenty-eight-year-old butcher, and Frank H, a single, thirty-two-year-old chef, took advantage of the space provided by the city's maze of laneways. As the police constable put it: "In a lane off 230 Yonge Street [the] defendant came in and took out his penis and after he got it stiff Frank H came in and held the penis and pulled it back and forwards."[12] The location of the laneway at the back of 230 Yonge Street was significant. Known as the Albert Street Lane, Albert Street was positioned within the city's central shopping and theatre district, as well as within close proximity to "the Ward," Toronto's immigrant and working-class Jewish neighbourhood. As Mariana Valverde has demonstrated, the Ward was constructed simultaneously as a slum and a sexualized area through a series of journalistic practices and social investigation techniques. In particular, the perception of overcrowding in the Ward's dwellings meant for many middle-class observers that incest was the "sexual secret of the slum."[13] But the slum harboured more than one sexual secret. In the Albert Street Lane, in the shadows cast by the factory, warehouse and department store buildings of the T. Eaton Company, men sought out other men for sex.[14] In fact, for men searching for sexual encounters with other men, as well as for the police, the Albert Street Lane was a well-known cruising area. During the month of April 1917, for example, twenty-eight men were arrested for having sex in the laneway. This sexual use of the Ward's streets must have done much to reinforce middle-class Torontonians' view that the Ward's "teaming back-streets and lanes were . . . breeding grounds for immoral activity."[15]

Lavatories were a third important site within the subculture of public sex. Police arrests indicate that men had sex in the lavatories of Queen's Park and Allan Gardens, but one could also find sex in the washrooms of certain hotels, Union Station, Sunnyside Amusement Park and the YMCA. In negotiating sex in public places such as the lavatory, men employed a variety of methods to make contact. Some men met somewhere first prior to going to the lavatory as is indicated by the police noting in cases such as George D's that the "prisoner came into the lavatory with a man." Other men waited inside the lavatory for another man to come into an adjacent compartment. As Henry B explained: "I was in the Lavatory at Union Station . . . about 4 pm when a man came in the next compartment." Once two men were in adjoining stalls connected by a hole in the partition, one man might put his hand through the hole to signal his interest or, in Henry B's case, the other man "looked through a hole in [the] partition and then took his penis out and put it through the hole" after which "he put his hand through the hole and grabbed my penis and took it in his mouth and sucked it." Yet another way was to proposition a man. In August 1919, Private Frank B recalled meeting Charles B when he came into the College Street YMCA. He "asked me to go to the toilet with him and he said he would give me a dollar. I went there and . . . [he] started to open the front of my pants." Unfortunately for Charles, the encounter ended at this point and Charles found himself before the Police Court charged with attempting to procure Frank for an act of gross indecency. It is not entirely clear from the case file whether Frank turned Charles in because he was shocked to discover what he was to do once he got to the toilet or because, once there, Charles failed to produce the promised one dollar, offering in its place the less than acceptable sum of fifty cents.[16]

Aspects of the city-building process, including the creation of urban spaces such as the park, laneway and lavatory, formed the "material base" of the subculture of public sex. Consider the example of lavatories. While men undoubtedly discovered long ago the potential of the public lavatory as a meeting place for sex, it is not a coincidence that evidence of a subculture of sex revolving around the lavatory appears in the court records in a significant way at the turn of the century. Beginning in the early 1900s, Toronto embarked upon something of a lavatory building boom. In 1905, the city engineer began to include in his annual report a special section on "Public Conveniences." The reports charted the locations and dates of lavatory construction and included statistics on lavatory use. For example, the city engineer noted that in the thirty-nine weeks since its opening on 8 April

1906, the new lavatory at Spadina and Queen Streets had an "average attendance" of 733 persons per day, 5136 persons per week, making for a total of 200 323 visitors since its opening.[17] Given that many of the city's houses lacked indoor plumbing, public lavatories were not merely "conveniences" but, like public bathhouses, necessities. Residents regularly petitioned their elected officials to erect lavatories in their neighbourhoods and parks. Alderman Weston was only one among many people during this period who proposed a motion that "proper sanitary lavatories" be constructed in Queen's Park.[18] One of the unintentional outcomes of the expansion of the city's system of lavatories was that it increased the number of public places men could meet for sex.

The men who found sex in the city's lavatories and laneways came from a range of backgrounds. Key to understanding the experience of these men, whether like Edward L you were a janitor at the Julian Sale Leather Goods Company or like Arthur H you were a clerk in the Cost Department of the Massey-Harris Company,[19] was their status as male wage-earners. Drawn from the ranks of both the skilled and unskilled, a majority of the men were working-class. Among skilled workers, numerous tailors, butchers, printers and illustrators reflected the predominance of the clothing, food and printing industries in Toronto, while among the unskilled, labourers were the most numerous. Lower middle-class men were also represented. Clerks, bookkeepers, sales workers and other office employees found work in the many jobs created by Toronto's administrative revolution in the first two decades of the twentieth century.[20]

The wages men earned provided many with the financial means to live apart from family. Residential status as revealed in the court records and in city directories indicates that a good proportion of the men lived apart from families. But class differences among the men shaped this experience in different ways. For a few middle-class men of means, it was possible to live alone in one of the city's apartment houses. Charles B, for example, lived at 121 Carleton Street in the "Allan Garden Apartments." George G, a single, fifty-year-old florist, had his own flat on Manning Avenue. In 1928, Arthur H, the single, thirty-two-year-old clerk at Massey-Harris, earned $1296 a year, more than the average annual budget for a working-class family of five. This meant Arthur could afford to board in a spacious suburban home where, as the case file indicates, "the landlady . . . like[d] him so well that she gave him the front downstairs room, where he keeps his piano."[21] This contrasted with the situation of working-class men. Toronto, lacking the large tenement districts of other urban centres such as Montreal, Chicago and New York, was predominantly a city of single family dwellings. For most working-class men, then, living away from home meant residing in other often crowded working-class households or boarding houses.[22] Thomas S boarded with Mrs. Margaret A on Simcoe Street and Harold F resided at Mrs. Daisy T's boarding house on McGill Street. In preparing the case file of Alfred J, a single, twenty-six-year-old stable keeper, the court clerk listed him as "boarding at 659 Bloor Street West."[23] The financial ability to construct an independent life meant that men could pursue sex with other men in their own apartments and boarding rooms, out from under the watchful eyes of family.[24] But for both lower middle-class and working-class men the presence of a landlady or the hustle and bustle of a crowded working-class household meant that sex often had to be found outside the confines of the household, in the lanes and lavatories of the city.

By tracing the relationship between a man's class background and place of residence with the location of his sexual encounter, it is possible to make some tentative observations on what I call the journey to sex.[25] The journey to sex differed for men according to class. For working-class men, sex generally took place in and around their own neighbourhoods, while for middle-class men there was often more of a distance to travel between their homes to the lavatories and laneways in the centre of the city. Victor H, for example, a single, die maker was in the Allan Gardens on a spring evening in 1920, sitting on a bench next to a labourer. According to the police constable, "I saw the other man take off his hat and stoop over [Victor] and suck his penis." Victor lived on Sherbourne, just down the street from the park. Similarly, Shirley B, a printer who resided on George Street had only to walk across the street when he wanted to find sex in the Gardens. In contrast, for middle-class men like Joseph B who had sex in the lavatory at Queen's Park and who owned his own house on Rhodes Avenue in the extreme eastern end of the city, there was quite a distance to journey between suburban homes and inner-city parks.[26]

For some men the journey to sex was a vehicle for movement through the class divided spaces of the city. Indeed, the vehicles of urban exploration themselves presented opportunities for sex. Toronto's notoriously overcrowded streetcars, for example, provided the setting for a sexual encounter. As Samuel H testified in Police Court in 1914, "on a streetcar . . . [the] defendant put his hands up my legs and in my privates. I got off and looked for an officer [but] I lost him."[27] Despite the increased mobility of urban dwellers, most middle-class Torontonians still "travelled" to the slum without ever leaving their living rooms; theirs was a literary journey made through the representation of the slum in the pages of the daily press. As one historian of Toronto has noted, the actual streets and laneways of the Ward were "an unknown territory to most middle-class citizens."[28] But gender could make a difference. For some men, relatively free to move at night through the city's sexual spaces, the journey to the slum was a more hands-on experience. Charles V, a forty-four-year-old married man met up with Robert C, a thirty-two-year-old working-class man, in the Ward's Albert Street Lane at 8:50 in the evening. Charles—a senior Salvation Army officer—probably made his journey to the laneway following a religious meeting, for the Salvation Army headquarters were located just around the corner. But regardless of his point of departure, the site of Charles's sexual encounter in one of the Ward's laneways contrasted sharply with his suburban and parkside residence on Indian Road in the western end of the city. The court description of Charles's sexual encounter incidently captured something of the danger involved in having sex in the busy backstreets of the Ward, particularly the risk of getting caught, not only by the police, but by passers-by: Charles V came into the laneway "and caught hold of Robert

C's privates and rubbed them. Charles V got his mouth towards Robert C's privates [when] . . . a man came and Charles V jumped." Not to be deterred from the task at hand "after he passed Charles V rubbed . . . Robert C's privates again."[29]

For other men the journey to sex was a move between immigrant communities and a site in the sexual subculture. The majority of men charged with gross indecency were white, Anglo-Saxons, most often born in Ontario, but Italian, Jewish and eastern European men were also involved in the subculture of public sex. Harry I, a Jewish man, ducked into the Albert Street Lane followed by another man where "they each got their penis out and each rubbed the penis of the other man." Harry's trial differed from that of most men for the judge in Harry's case was presented with a petition. Testifying to Harry's good character, the petition was signed by dozens of Jewish women and men, including the presidents of some of Toronto's major garment manufacturers. The petition is a vivid reminder that men arrested for "sexual crimes" with other men—whether in "public" or "private"—faced public exposure within their neighbourhoods and communities. But public exposure did not necessarily mean complete rejection by the community. Although the petition did not save Harry from six months at the jail farm, it is evidence that for some men, a tightly knit immigrant community, capable of organizing a collective response, was an important source of support. The petition probably also functioned as a collective defense of the Jewish community in the face of the repeated associations within the dominant cultural order of immigrant life with sexual "immorality."[30]

The journey to the slum was not only a physical movement through urban space, but also a sexual movement across class lines. The encounter between Charles and Robert was only one of many cross-class sexual liaisons that took place within the city's lanes and lavatories. Other historians have noted a similar class organization of homosexual behaviour. Jeffrey Weeks has written that sexual relations between middle-class and working-class men were "a major component of the subculture," noting the "upper-middle-class fascination with crossing the class divide."[31] Without necessarily disputing this, what this tends to ignore or overshadow is the existence of sexual relations between working-class men. Daniel L, for example, a twenty-two-year-old presser at the Lowndes tailoring company had sex in a laneway off Ontario Street with Clayton S, a young, single labourer who worked at the Gendron Manufacturing Company.[32] In fact, the court records indicate that working-class men in Toronto were as likely to have sex with other working-class men as middle-class men.

Men before the courts were often asked whether they knew each other and the answer was often, as Henry B replied, "I have never seen this man before."[33] While perhaps not surprising in the context of a court examination, such a denial must have been at times simply an indication that many sexual encounters in public spaces were quick and occurred between strangers. To focus on the parks, lavatories and laneways as spaces for anonymous sexual encounters, however, obscures the ways in which the sites of public sex were part of a more organized subculture. That the police staked out different places in the city and arrested a number of men in those sites over a period of time suggests that men knew of certain places in which to find one another. Albert Street Lane, as we have already seen, was one such place. To take another example, during the month of June 1919, there were six separate arrests involving fifteen different men at the lavatory in Queen's Park. How exactly men discovered or learned about the subculture is hard to say. Newspapers may have served as one travel guide to Toronto's sexual underground. Press accounts of gross indecency trials publicized the existence of the subculture, advertising the places within the city one might find sex with another man. In its coverage of a gross indecency trial in May 1921, the *Evening Telegram* noted that the offence was "committed in Allan Gardens" and, similarly, the *Telegram* reported that Arthur H had been found guilty "for committing an act of gross indecency in High Park."[34]

For some men, public sex was a recurrent feature of sexual life. In 1918, the police court column described the arrest and conviction of Alfred L as having "ridded Queen's Park of a man who has created a lot of trouble."[35] For Alfred, having several different charges of gross indecency against him, parks and lavatories represented not an isolated, one-time foray into the sexual underground, but a more regular element in his sexual life. Frequenting sites in the subculture on a regular basis meant that for some men it was a place of familiar rather than anonymous encounters. Consider two cases from 1926 in which four men were arrested in Allan Gardens. In the first case, the two men were arrested on 24 June and in the second case the other two men on 1 July. Although the offenses occurred a week apart, the men were brought into court together on the same day and one of the four men was described as "the ringleader" of the group, attesting to some degree of familiarity among the lot. That three of the four lived in close proximity to the park and worked in the printing trade suggests that sexual familiarity within the park was underscored by neighbourhood and occupational (perhaps workplace) ties as well.[36] In 1908, Alfred J got caught with his pants down in Queen's Park. About the man he had sex with Alfred told police that "he had met this man on a previous occasion," once again suggesting a degree of familiarity and organization to the homosexual relations of public urban space.[37]

Men who had sex with other men were discovered in a number of ways, often by family members and by others within households and neighbourhoods. The case of sex revolving around public spaces, however, posed regulatory problems. Having sex in a lavatory or in a park, often late at night, one was not likely to be caught by a family member or a neighbour. Other means of regulation had to be developed.

LADDERS, LIGHTS, LENSES, AND LOOKING

The Toronto police department employed a number of means to apprehend men who engaged in sex with other men. Many were caught by constables on the beat in working-class neighbourhoods, while others were taken into custody by park caretakers who were sworn in as "special constables" to patrol the parks.[38] The police also developed surveillance systems to monitor men in various sites of the subculture of public sex. Surveillance operations in and around the men's lavatories in Queen's Park and Allan Gardens between 1918 and 1922 detail the methods and machinery of the police gaze.

On 11 May 1922 just before midnight, Thomas P and James C were inside the lavatory at Allan Gardens. Thomas "was sitting on the toilet and his pants were unbuttoned and down and there was a hole cut through the partition between the compartments. He was looking through the hole then he put his hand through . . . to a man on the other side . . . James C was also sitting on the toilet at the same time with his pants unbuttoned and down. When Thomas put his hand through James stood up putting his rectum against the hole in the partition and Thomas then stood up and put his penis through the hole and started working towards James." Eventually, police officers came into the lavatory, opened the compartment doors, catching Thomas and James in the act. The two men were arrested, found guilty of gross indecency and sent to jail.[39]

During the trial one of the first questions concerned how it was that the police could see Thomas and James. The answer was to be found in the architecture of the lavatory. As the court heard, there were two basic lavatory designs, the "open lavatory" comprised of urinals and lavatories made up of "compartments" with "doors on each compartment." As Michel Foucault explained, surveillance of washrooms with stalls was facilitated by raising the bottom of the doors off the floor to allow for visual inspection.[40] But in our case, Thomas and James were not caught by someone looking underneath the stall doors. As the two police officers explained, "there is a hole in the wall at the back of the lavatory" and from the outside "you can look down into all the compartments . . . we have a platform built at the back so that we can." The officers climbed up onto the platform using ladders. From this platform, one of the lawyers asked, "could you see [the] two compartments clearly?" "Easily," replied one officer, "you could see them both at the same time." It is not clear whether the Morality Department was familiar with Bentham's panopticon, but here in miniature form was an example of what Foucault called "hierarchal observation" and "the perfect disciplinary apparatus"—that which "would make it possible for a single gaze to see everything constantly."[41]

Light was another element in the apparatus of surveillance. This could take a number of different forms. In trials involving sex in parks, the position of street lights was a crucial factor in determining whether there was enough light for a constable to have actually witnessed a sexual act from a distance. In lavatory cases, such as the one above, it was important to know whether "it was lit up . . . or not." In this instance there were "electric lights . . . a 75 candle power light" which police described as "good light." Naturally, men often sought out dark places away from any light. Detection in these cases was facilitated by advances in police technology. As early as 1886, in addition to his baton, handcuffs, whistle and revolver, a constable also carried a "small pocket lamp." By 1919, the chief constable noted that "electric flash-lights now form part of the equipment" of police constables.[42] Electric flash-lights were crucial in cases of sex in unlit lavatories. The following example comes from the Queen's Park lavatory where police had a surveillance set-up similar to the one in Allan Gardens. On the evening of 12 June 1919, Harry T and William M were inside the urinal-style lavatory at Queen's Park. According to constable Ward, the men "stood close together elbowing each other. Their elbows were moving." A third man came into the lavatory. "Norman T came in. Harry T went and stood one side of him and William M the other. All three defendants when I put the flash light on were standing with their hands crossed and their penis out." Ward's partner said that "when the light was flashed on they did not speak to each other . . . Ward had his head over their shoulders as the light was flashed."[43]

Police technology facilitated the surveillance of sex in other ways as well. Photography, for example, played an important role. In 1887, "the introduction of photography" and the "proper registration of criminals" were "among the features novel" to the Toronto police department. On numerous occasions the chief constable noted in his annual reports that "photography has played such an important part in the identification of

F I G U R E   1   The apparatus of police surveillance and the photo as state's evidence, Toronto, 1919 (Archives of Ontario, Crown Attorney Case Files, York County, 1919, Case 51).

criminals as to be indispensable. The plan of taking the photographs by an officer of the department continues to work satisfactorily."[44] But photography was not only used to identify criminals; the camera was also employed to provide a visual record of the scene of the crime. In at least two gross indecency cases the crown entered into evidence photographs of the police apparatus of surveillance and the interior of lavatory compartments. Fortunately, the photographs survived along with their case files (figs. 1 and 2). To make its case, the crown drew on the already well-established evidentiary status of the photograph to reveal the "reality" or "truth" of sex between men through a representation not of actual sexual activity but of the scene of the sexual crime.[45]

The ladder, the flashlight and the camera were all dependent on the police constable. At least as much as with the technology of surveillance, the courts were interested in the police and, in particular, they were preoccupied by the act of looking. About the two men special constable Christie found lying on the ground in the park he said, "I had them under observation for a few minutes before I flashed my light." "I watched there awhile"

F I G U R E   2   "Thomas S. was sitting on the closet seat and peeping through a small hole in the partition." (Archives of Ontario, Crown Attorney Case Files, York County, 1919, Case 51).

explained constable McCoy after he spied two men in a similarly compromising position. On one level, the court's attention to how much time was spent looking was necessary in order to establish that enough time had elapsed to witness a sexual act. But the line between looking and voyeurism was a thin one. Under cross-examination, defense lawyers questioned the police in such way as to suggest that perhaps they had looked too long:

Q. And you watched them for some time as a matter of fact?
A. Not a great while.
Q. But you watched them for a while?
A. Between one and two minutes.
Q. And then you called Sharp [another constable]?
A. [Yes.]
Q. And then you watched them again for a short time?
A. About a minute.

In giving testimony, the police themselves poorly disguised the element of voyeurism involved in spying on men in washrooms. "Look at this," one officer called to another, "come over here, wait till you see this." Sex between men as a spectacle for police surveillance and the spectacle made of sex between men in the court were both underlined during the trials by the repeated reference to the men's activities as a "performance." It is also important to note that against the gaze of the police, men under surveillance in the lavatory had their own "look." As Constable Midhurst put it: In Allan Gardens on 29 April 1921, "about 10:45 . . . I was looking into the lavatory. I saw Thomas S and another man Harold F. Thomas S was sitting on the closet seat and *peeping through a small hole in the partition*. I saw Harold F put his penis to the hole and Smith commenced to suck it after a few minutes. I was watching. I went to the door of the lavatory, opened the closet door where Harold F was—he was pulling away from the hole and sitting back on the seat. I then arrested" them (emphasis added).[46] Men in the washrooms did not realize of course that while they were looking they were also being watched.

As men bored holes in lavatory walls, more people—from city administrators to park attendants—were drawn into the sexual struggle over urban space. As one particularly interesting case reveals, even the holes themselves became a focus of struggle. Along with its verdict in the case of Allen M, the jury also submitted a series of recommendations. As the court clerk explained in a letter to the board of the Toronto Harbour Commission:

> From the evidence given in this case it appeared that the indecency charged was facilitated by a hole of about two inches square which had been made in the partition between two of the compartments, and the recommendation in this case was that attendants and other employees in or about the lavatories should be required to report immediately any such conditions so that they could be immediately remedied. This letter was directed to be sent to your Board for the reason that . . . this particular lavatory where the offence was said to be committed . . . is in the amusement area at Sunnyside, and might be under your jurisdiction.

In his return letter, the General Manager of the Harbour Commission wrote that he wished:

> to advise that since this trial metal sheets have been placed on the partitions between all the men's toilets which are under the control of this Commission at Sunnyside Beach. The attendants have been instructed to immediately report to the Park Supervisor if the partitions are tampered with, and we believe that we have taken the necessary precautions to prevent a recurrence.[47]

Holes made in the partitions of lavatory walls were evidence of the extent to which men who sought sex with other men appropriated public spaces for their own sexual uses.

Even when caught up in the surveillance systems of the police, men were not passive but devised a number of ways to resist arrest. Some managed to avoid arrest by running away. Explaining to the court why only one of two men he found having sex in the park appeared for trial, the police constable explained that during the arrest "the other man got up and ran away." Another case file noted simply: "co-offender escaped." In other instances, even after being physically apprehended by police, men might still attempt to get away. The officer who arrested Edward L said that Edward "bumped me under the chin with his head when he was trying to get away [but] I held on to him." When Howard F and Thomas S were arrested "Howard F denied it [and] Thomas S said nothing." Silence and denial were both common strategies. "It is absurd," was the response of one man to the charge that he had let another man suck him. Some men tried to avoid arrest by negotiating with police: William M told police that he "wanted to pay his fine now" because "he did not want to be exposed." Other men attempted to lie, explain and otherwise talk their way out of situations. Arrested in Allan Gardens, Walter L made up quite an elaborate story. The police constable told the court:

> I asked him where he lived . . . and he said he [was] from Detroit. I asked him what he was doing here and he was very nervous and confused and he said, 'I am just sitting in the park.' So I asked him what his business or occupation was and he said, 'I am a jeweler traveller, I am here in Toronto one day and I am all over.'

Walter did not entirely lie about his occupation—he was a timekeeper—but he was not from Detroit, nor was he in town on a one day business trip. Walter, as the court subsequently determined, lived at 11 Fulton Avenue, resident of Toronto. Thomas P tried several different excuses to explain why he had his penis through a hole in the lavatory wall. At the initial moment of arrest, Thomas said "I got an erection looking at a picture" but when asked by the constable where the picture was "he looked around and said 'I do not know'." Later at the station "when he was being searched and asked his name," a different officer asked "What happened to you Johnnie?" At first Thomas said "I am too excited to tell you anything," but later in the conversation he said that "he saw a hole in the partition and he got up just to see if his penis was big enough to go through the hole." And finally, to explain why he required the assistance of another man in the lavatory, Norman T said "he had been under medical treatment and that he could not properly urinate."[48] Many of the strategies and stories ultimately failed, but they are significant evidence that even under the oppressive conditions of police surveillance and arrest, many men did not remain silent but talked back. They are evidence of what George Chauncey, Jr. in his study of the "flamboyant, working-class street fairies" of New York City's Times Square calls "gay men's strategies of everyday resistance," strategies men developed to resist the policing of public space.[49]

CONCLUSION: THE DIALECTICS OF DISCOVERY

In laneways, parks and lavatories, men seeking sex with other men discovered one another. In doing so, men claimed public space and helped to construct a subculture of public sex. Aspects of the city-building process, along with the spread of wage labour, established some of the material conditions for the emergence of a subculture, while class and ethnic differences structured sexual relations between men and shaped their journey to sex.

As men discovered one another in the city's public spaces, they were also discovered by the police. One of the effects of the police surveillance and arrest of men was to help bring the subculture of public sex to the attention of a wider public. Consider the following two comments. In passing sentence on Walter F, a butcher at the St. Lawrence Market found guilty of having committed numerous acts of gross indecency in 1911, Judge Denton said: "The majority of people could hardly conceive of the offence which you have committed." In another case, this one involving lavatory sex, one man remarked that "he would never have believed the police statements had he not heard them with his own ears."[50] The practices of policing did much to alter this inability to conceive of or believe in the existence of sex between men. This was accomplished through the police techniques of surveillance, by making sex something you could see with your own eyes, by drawing it out of darkness into light, by providing photographic evidence of the signs of its existence. Foucault described this process with characteristic elegance:

> Side by side with the major technology of the telescope, the lens and the light beam, ... there were the minor techniques of multiple and intersecting observations, of eyes that must see without being seen; using techniques of subjection and methods of exploitation, an obscure art of light and the visible was secretly preparing a new knowledge of man.[51]

It was, I would argue, the reciprocal or dialectical relationship between the activity of the men and the maneuvers of the police that forged and contributed to the growth in knowledge of a sexual underground.

The Toronto evidence is also interesting in the way it highlights the shifting modes used to regulate homosexual relations. For much of the nineteenth century, the regulation of sex between men took place (in addition to within families and neighbourhoods) through generalized legal control and sporadic use of the courts. By the turn of the century, these regulatory strategies were complemented by a more pervasive individual surveillance carried out by disciplinary agencies such as the police. This is not to suggest that police supervision of sex between men only emerged at the turn of the twentieth century. Michel Rey, for example, has documented how as early as the 1700s police in Paris deployed undercover agents to entrap men engaged in homosexual activity.[52] But the technologies of surveillance used by the Toronto Morality Department to regulate homosexual activity represented relatively new forms of power that facilitated the extension of the local state into further realms of everyday life.[53] These new techniques and the way they were deployed against men who had sex with other men remind us of the role played by (homo)sexuality in helping to produce what Foucault identified as the broad historical shift in regimes of power from a punitive state to one that increasingly relied on individual discipline. We should be careful, however, not to overstate the completeness of these transformations. As a moment of transition away from coercion toward regulation, it was often rough and still quite repressive. Unevenness was rooted in the fact that these transformations were not accomplished without a struggle as men's attempts to claim public space and to resist arrest make clear.

I want to end with the lavatory wall. What can it tell us about the meaning of sex between men at the turn of the century? It depends, of course, on who was looking and through which hole. If you were peeping through the hole at the top of the wall into the stalls, sex between men was a site for sexual surveillance and discipline. If you were peering through the hole in the wall between the stalls, this was an act of possibility, a moment in the formation of a sexual subculture. That sight could simultaneously contain these seemingly contradictory meanings was part of the process whereby the dialectics of discovering "homosexuality" emerged in early twentieth-century Toronto.

NOTES

1. "Not 'Toronto the Good,'" Toronto *Evening Telegram*, 5 December 1913, 16.

2. The archival research upon which this paper is based was undertaken for my Ph.D. dissertation. My search through the court records, housed at the Archives of Ontario, turned up 313 cases of sexual "crimes" between men for Ontario in the period 1880 to 1930. Of that number, 113 cases were from Toronto. In this article, when I generalize about sexual relations and the social and economic backgrounds of the men, I am drawing on the total number of Toronto cases. Because the focus of this article is on those men who found sex in "public" spaces, when I refer to specific cases, I will draw mainly from the thirty-seven of the 113 cases that I have identified as involving "public" sex. An important distinction to keep in mind, particularly when reading the figures cited in the footnotes, is that between the number of cases and the number of men. For example, because each case involved at least two men, the 113 Toronto cases involved over 220 men. The case files for Toronto employed here

were created by the York County crown attorney. In order to be granted research access to the crown attorney's prosecution case files, I was required to enter into a research agreement with the Archives of Ontario. In accordance with that agreement, all the names of accused men have been anonymized. The crown attorney prosecution case files remain largely unprocessed and, as such, complete archival references do not exist. They are located within RG 22, Series 5890, but they are stored in temporary boxes. Rather than cite temporary box numbers, I will reference case files in the following way: Archives of Ontario (AO), Crown Attorney Case Files, York County, 1918, Case 10. Case numbers refer to my own numbering scheme and are not related to any numbers that may appear on the original case files.

3. For a recent example see Karen Dubinsky, *Improper Advances: Rape and Heterosexual Conflict in Ontario, 1880–1929* (Chicago, 1993). I trace the origins and development of a lesbian/gay historical practice in Canada in "In Search of 'Sodom North': The Writing of Lesbian and Gay History in English Canada, 1970–1990," *The Canadian Review of Comparative Literature/Revue canadienne de littérature comparée* 21 (March/June 1994): 117–32.

4. In referring to the subculture as "homosexual," I am describing the sexual acts or encounters within the subculture and not the sexual identities of the men who performed these acts. To help avoid the conflation of sexual behaviours in the past with modern sexual identities, I will often refer in this paper to "sex between men." For the sake of stylistic ease, however, I will occasionally refer to "homosexual subcultures" and "homosexuality."

5. Jeffrey Weeks, "Movements of Affirmation: Sexual Meanings and Homosexual Identities," in *Passion and Power: Sexuality in History*, ed. Kathy Peiss and Christina Simmons

(Philadelphia, 1989), 81. Because this historical reconstruction of the homosexual subculture of public sex is based primarily on information supplied by the police it can only be a partial one. There were undoubtedly many places within the subculture that escaped police detection. It is also important to remember that these public spaces were only several of many different sites within a series of overlapping subcultures in Toronto during this period. Alongside the lavatory and laneway, for example, sex took place in a host of more "private" settings, such as the backrooms of commercial establishments and in the rooms in which men boarded. While it is probably unwise to insist on too much of a distinction between the different layers of subcultures—no doubt many men moved back and forth between them—the distinction is useful inasmuch as the different sites of sex were subject to different forms of regulation and took on different public meanings.

6. Michel Foucault, *The History of Sexuality, Volume 1: An Introduction*, trans. Robert Hurley (New York, 1980), 24. While my subject here is what D.A. Miller would term 'policing in the streets,' my interest in surveillance and discipline has also been inspired by his work on 'policing in the closet' in his Foucauldian reading of Victorian literature, *The Novel and the Police* (Berkeley and Los Angeles, 1988). For an analysis of the psychic underpinnings of surveillance and sex between men, one based partly on historical texts see Lee Edelman, "Seeing Things: Representation, the Scene of Surveillance, and the Spectacle of Gay Male Sex," in *Inside/Out: Lesbian Theories, Gay Theories*, ed. Diana Fuss (New York, 1991), 93–116.

7. For this useful phrase to describe how I conceptualize the relationship between the subculture and policing, I am indebted to Bryan D. Palmer.

8. AO, Crown Attorney Case Files, York County, 1913, Case 9.

9. John Weaver, "The Modern City Realized: Toronto Civic Affairs, 1880–1915," in *The Usable Urban Past: Planning and Politics in the Modern Canadian City*, ed. A. Artibise and G. Stelter (Toronto, 1979), 46. See also J.M.S. Careless, "The Emergence of Cabbagetown in Victorian Toronto," in *Gathering Place: Peoples and Neighbourhoods of Toronto, 1834–1945*, ed. Robert F. Harney (Toronto, 1985), 25–45.

10. *Toronto: The Ideal Summer City—Pictured and Described* (Toronto, n.d.).

11. AO, Crown Attorney Case Files, York County, 1913, Case 11 and 1908, Case 6.

12. AO, Crown Attorney Case Files, York County, 1917, Case 27.

13. Mariana Valverde, *The Age of Light, Soap, and Water: Moral Reform in English Canada, 1885–1925* (Toronto, 1991), 134–39.

14. My description of the physical surroundings of the Albert Street Lane and the urban geography of Toronto more generally are based on details from Goad's *Insurance Plan of the City of Toronto* (Toronto, 1917) and from the bird's-eye view of downtown Toronto contained in T. Eaton Co. Ltd., *Golden Jubilee, 1869–1919* (Toronto, 1919). Guided streetcar tours of downtown Toronto, operated by the Dominion Coach Line, included several sites within the homosexual underground, including a drive by the Albert Street Lane. "Turning along Albert Street," the Coach Line's souvenir handbook indicated, "passengers get a glimpse of the factories, warehouses, garage and other buildings which are a part of the Eaton establishment." Dominion Coach Line, *Handbook of Toronto* (Toronto, 1912), Metropolitan Toronto Reference Library.

15. Weaver, "The Modern City Realized," 46.

16. AO, Crown Attorney Case Files, York County, 1918, Case 38; 1923, Case 68; 1919, Case 44. Of all the cases of public sex, the YMCA case was the only one that made mention of cash. The absence of cash within the subculture of public sex differed dramatically from cases involving sexual relations between men and working-class youth which very often were mediated by money. I take up this subject in "'Frivolous Boys' and 'Fallen Men': Danger, Desire, and Sexual Relations Between Men and Working-Class Male Youth," another chapter of my thesis.

17. City of Toronto Archives, *Annual Report of the City Engineer of Toronto* (1906), 163.

18. City of Toronto Archives, Committee on Parks, *Minutes*, 13 January 1910, item #13, RG 17, Series A, Box 9–13, 1899–1919.

19. AO, Crown Attorney Case Files, York County, 1920, Case 54 and 1928, Case 80. *Might's City Directory of Toronto, 1920.*

20. From the 113 cases, occupational information was available for 118 men.

Occupational/ Class Background	Number of Men
High White Collar	7
Low White Collar	31
Skilled	30
Unskilled	50

While I am aware of the many interpretive difficulties involved in assigning class positions to individuals, particularly the problem of inferring class position based on the occupation an individual holds at one moment in time, my designation of men as working-class (skilled and unskilled) or middle-class (high white collar and low white collar) uses occupation and residential location (as indicated on the court records and supplemented by information from city directories) and is based on a slightly modified version of the scheme developed by Olivier Zunz. See Zunz, *The Changing Face of Inequality: Urbanization, Industrial Development, and Immigrants in Detroit, 1880–1920* (Chicago, 1982),

Appendix 3, 420–33. The case of men clerks and other office workers is especially difficult when it comes to designating their class position. In most cases, I have chosen to view these men as occupying the low end of an expanding middle class. My thinking here owes much to Graham S. Lowe, "Class, Job, and Gender in the Canadian Office," *Labour/Le Travailleur* 10 (Autumn 1982): 11–37. On the occupational structure of early twentieth-century Toronto see Michael Piva, *The Condition of the Working Class in Toronto, 1900–1920* (Ottawa, 1979), 1–25.

21. AO, Crown Attorney Case Files, York County, 1919, Case 44; 1928, Case 83; 1928, Case 80. *Might's City Directory of Toronto, 1919, 1928*. The figures to compare Arthur H's income with the budget of a working-class family are drawn from Lowe, "Class, Gender and Job in the Canadian Office," 32.

22. Piva, *The Condition of the Working Class in Toronto*, 113–42.

23. AO, Crown Attorney Case Files, York County, 1921, Case 63; 1908, Case 6. *Might's City Directory of Toronto, 1920, 1921*.

24. The importance of wage labour to the historical formation of homosexual subcultures and identities is developed by John D'Emilio, "Capitalism and Gay Identity," reprinted in *The Lesbian and Gay Studies Reader*, ed. Henry Abelove, Michele Aina Barale, David M. Halperin (New York, 1993), 467–76.

25. The journey to sex has some interesting parallels with what Judith Walkowitz terms "urban spectatorship," or the imaginative and literal, often sexual exploration of the metropolis. Walkowitz maintains that for much of the nineteenth century, urban spectatorship was the privilege of bourgeois men, but by the 1880s changing material conditions encouraged a host of new social actors—striking workers, shopping ladies, charity workers, match girls and others—to lay claim

to public urban space. As the case of Toronto demonstrates, also among the new cast of urban explorers were men who searched the city's spaces looking for sex with other men. Walkowitz, *City of Dreadful Delight: Narratives of Sexual Danger in Late-Victorian London* (Chicago, 1992), 15–39.

26. AO, Crown Attorney Case Files, York County, 1920, Case 61; 1926, Case 75; 1919, Case 46. *Might's City Directory of Toronto, 1919, 1920, 1926*.

27. AO, Crown Attorney Case Files, York County, 1914, Case 13. City commissions investigating the transit system in 1912, 1914 and 1915 each reported overcrowding on Toronto's streetcars as a major problem. See Michael Doucet, "Politics, Space, and Trolleys: Mass Transit in Early Twentieth-Century Toronto," in *Shaping the Urban Landscape: Aspects of the Canadian City-Building Process*, ed. G. Stelter and A. Artibise (Ottawa, 1982), 356–81.

28. Weaver, "The Modern City Realized," 46.

29. AO, Crown Attorney Case Files, York County, 1917, Case 25. As a Salvation Army officer, Charles V's presence in the Ward was in keeping with the approach taken by the Army and religiously-based settlement houses in working directly with the poor in their own neighbourhoods. One can imagine, however, that even the Army which encouraged officers to adopt a "cheerful and even comradely attitude" in their work with "the vicious" would have frowned upon the rather intimate nature of Charles's connection with his working-class comrades. On the work of the Army and the Fred Victor Mission in "colonizing the slum" in Toronto see Valverde, *The Age of Light, Soap, and Water*, 139–54. The case of Charles V also adds a new dimension to what historians of the Army have identified as the opportunities it provided not only for salvation but also for sex. See Lynne Marks, "The 'Hallelujah Lasses': Working-Class Women in the

Salvation Army in English Canada, 1882–1892," in *Gender Conflicts: New Essays in Women's History*, ed. Mariana Valverde and Franca Iacovetta (Toronto, 1992), 67–117.

30. AO, Crown Attorney Case Files, York County, 1917, Case 30. On the immigrant Jewish communities in Toronto during this period see Stephen A. Speisman, "St. John's Shtetl: The Ward in 1911," in *Gathering Place*, 107–20 and Ruth Frager, *Sweatshop Strife: Class, Ethnicity, and Gender in the Jewish Labour Movement of Toronto, 1900–1939* (Toronto, 1992). The case files of other men contain petitions for leniency, but these took the form of letters written by individuals. In another chapter of my thesis which traces the experience of men once they entered the court, I analyze the letters as a form of resistance on the part of accused men and for what they can reveal about popular attitudes toward sex between men. I also analyze the repetitive rhetorical strategies within the letters to argue that while ostensibly about sex between men, these "pardon tales" represent instead significant moments in the ideological definition of normative male sexualities.

31. Jeffrey Weeks, *Sex, Politics and Society: The Regulation of Sexuality Since 1800* (London, 1981), 112–14. See also James Gardiner, *A Class Apart: The Private Pictures of Montague Glover* (London, 1992).

32. AO, Crown Attorney Case Files, York County, 1920, Case 53.

33. AO, Crown Attorney Case Files, York County, 1923, Case 58.

34. Toronto *Evening Telegram*, 19 May 1921, 17 and 14 September 1928, 3.

35. Toronto *Evening Telegram*, 17 June 1918, 9.

36. AO, Crown Attorney Case Files, York County, 1926, Cases 75 and 76. *Might's City Directory of Toronto, 1926*. Toronto *Evening Telegram* 1 November 1926, 17.

37. AO, Crown Attorney Case Files, York County, 1908, Case 6.

38. Chief Constable Grasett noted in his annual report in 1890 that "the caretakers of the park . . . have been sworn in as special constables." Toronto Police Department, "Annual Report of the Chief Constable, 1890," Toronto City Council, *Minutes*, 1891, Appendix C, 26.

39. AO, Crown Attorney Case Files, York County, 1922, Case 66.

40. Referring to France's Ecole Militaire, Foucault wrote that "latrines had been installed with half-doors, so that the supervisor on duty could see the head and legs of the pupils, and also with side walls sufficiently high 'that those inside cannot see one another.'" About the architecture of the Ecole more generally Foucault said that one of the reasons "for establishing sealed compartments between individuals" was to "prevent debauchery and homosexuality" among the pupils. Foucault, *Discipline and Punish: The Birth of the Prison*, trans. Alan Sheridan (New York, 1979), 173 and 172.

41. Foucault, *Discipline and Punish*, 170 and 173.

42. *Toronto Police Force: a brief account of the force since its reorganization in 1859 up to the present date* (Toronto, 1886). Toronto Police Department, "Annual Report of the Chief Constable, 1919," Toronto City Council, *Minutes*, 1920, Appendix C, 30.

43. AO, Crown Attorney Case Files, York County, 1919, Case 48.

44. Toronto Police Department, "Annual Report of the Chief Constable, 1887," Toronto City Council, *Minutes*, 1888, Appendix 82, 414. "Annual Report . . . , 1889," Toronto City Council, *Minutes*, 1890, Appendix 4, 44.

45. See John Tagg, "A Means of Surveillance: The Photograph as Evidence in Law," in Tagg, *The Burden of Representation: Essays on Photographies and Histories* (Amherst, MA, 1988), 66–102.

46. AO, Crown Attorney Case Files, York County, 1908, Case 6; 1913, Case 9; 1922, Case 66; 1921, Case 63.

47. AO, Crown Attorney Case Files, York County, 1933, Case 85.

48. AO, Crown Attorney Case Files, York County, 1908, Case 6; 1928, Case 80; 1920, Case 54; 1921, Case 63; 1921, Case 65; 1919, Case 48; 1922, Case 66.

49. George Chauncey, Jr., "The Policed: Gay Men's Strategies of Everyday Resistance," in *Inventing Times Square: Commerce and Culture at the Crossroads of the World*, ed. W. Taylor (New York, 1991), 315–28.

50. Toronto *Evening Telegram*, 22 May 1911, 6 and 19 June 1919, 19.

51. Foucault, *Discipline and Punish*, 171.

52. Michel Rey, "Parisian Homosexuals Create a Lifestyle, 1700–1750: The Police Archives," in *'Tis Nature's Fault: Unauthorized Sexuality During the Enlightenment*, ed. Robert Purks Maccubbin (Cambridge, 1987), 179–91 and Rey, "Police and Sodomy in Eighteenth-Century Paris: From Sin to Disorder," in *The Pursuit of Sodomy: Male Homosexuality in Renaissance and Enlightenment Europe*, ed. Kent Gerard and Gert Hekma (New York, 1989), 129–46.

53. This was particularly the case regarding the police use of photography. See, for example, John Tagg, "Evidence, Truth and Order: Photographic Records and the Growth of the State," in *The Burden of Representation*, 60–65 and Allan Sekula, "The Body and the Archive," in *The Contest of Meaning: Critical Histories of Photography*, ed. R. Bolton (Cambridge, MA, 1989), 343–88. For a discussion of the use of video in more recent police surveillance of men's sexual activity in public washrooms, as well as the activist deployment of video as a form of gay counter-surveillance see John Greyson, "Security Blankets: Sex, Video and the Police," in *Queer Looks: Perspectives on Lesbian and Gay Film and Video*, ed. Martha Gever, John Greyson, and Pratibha Parmar (Toronto, 1993), 383–94. For Greyson's own intervention see his film *Urinal*, the script of which is included in Greyson, *Urinal and Other Stories* (Toronto, 1993).

section

6

SPORT AND LEISURE

○

A MANLY SPORT:
BASEBALL AND THE SOCIAL
CONSTRUCTION OF MASCULINITY[*]

COLIN HOWELL

o

"Baseball is a red-blooded sport for red-blooded men," observed the immortal Ty Cobb. "It's no pink tea, and mollycoddles had better stay out. It's . . . a struggle for supremacy, a survival of the fittest."[1] For Cobb, like many young boys who came of age at the turn of the century, the baseball diamond was a testing ground for manhood, offering boys a chance to prove their masculinity to their peers. Yet Cobb's Darwinian sentiments were at odds with the ideals of many Victorian and progressive reformers when it came to defining the appropriate elements of manly character. Cobb regarded baseball as an athletic equivalent of war, playing with unregulated passion, sliding into base with spikes high, ready to bowl over and wound opposing fielders who got in his way, and willing to use all the tricks available to him whether they fell within the rules of the game or not.[2] In the opinion of many observers, however, Cobb's personal search for self-affirmation through fierce competition typified the rough and rowdy character of a sport that prior to the First World War had yet to acquire an unquestioned reputation of respectability. Although a generation of journalists, medical doctors, churchmen, child-savers, physical culturalists, and educators might agree that baseball was a crucible in which manly character could be moulded, they tended to believe that the game should balance competitiveness and individualism with a sense of teamwork and cooperation, aggressive play with respect for one's opponents, and the desire to win

[*] Reprinted by permission of University of Toronto Press Incorporated, from *Northern Sandlots: A Social History of Maritime Baseball* (Toronto: University of Toronto Press, 1995), 97–119.

with a gracious acceptance of defeat. While baseball was none the less to be played with "ginger," that is with energy and passionate intensity, it was also a game that, in true Victorian spirit, should involve the regulation of individual passion.

In the past half-dozen years or so, historians have begun to turn their attention to the ways in which notions of manhood have been constructed, just as feminist historians have been concerned with the social definition of femininity.[3] Like femininity, masculinity is culturally defined, shaped by the larger context of gender relationships and the distribution of male authority and power within the larger social order.[4] In the nineteenth century, as in our own time, there were many ways for youths to absorb what society deemed to be the appropriate standards of manly behaviour.[5] At sea, young sailors were taught to forfeit a female world of nurture for a world of social brotherhood.[6] In the workplace, apprentices were schooled in the skills of what were considered essentially male occupations, and in the process developed a respect for craft and professional traditions. In the home, young men were sometimes prematurely thrust into the role of provider upon the death of the male head of household. On the battlefield young men faced death realizing that their actions affected directly the well-being of those who fought alongside them.[7] And, finally, there was the sporting ground, where reformers sought to instil in young men the values of courage, individual initiative, teamwork, and social responsibility.

Victorian assumptions about baseball's cultivation of manly virtue developed amidst a reconceptualization of American masculinity in the nineteenth century. In his insightful work on the social construction of American middle-class manhood, Anthony Rotundo has traced the shifting contours of a discourse about masculinity from the eighteenth century into the post-Civil War era.[8] In the early republican period, he suggests, the comfortable classes defined manliness in social and spiritual rather than in physical terms. Manly virtue came to be identified with social usefulness and spiritual dedication. "The good man of the eighteenth century," Rotundo notes, "was the one who devoted himself to the good of the community while he 'lived a life of piety' and 'mild religion.'" Thus, when Johnathan Scott, an Old Light minister from Yarmouth, Nova Scotia, eulogized his late father-in-law, George Ring, he described "a humble, serene, affectionate Christian . . . and constant attendant on the Gospel and ordinances of Christ, and consequently an unspeakably *useful* member of the Church," who was also "an unspeakably *useful* member of society," and whose successful shipping business was the means by which "a number of poor people were *usefully* employed" (italics mine).

This identification of manliness and the useful life gave way after the turn of the century to an emerging language of individual or self-improvement. The first half of the nineteenth century venerated the self-made man, and idealized the sturdy, independent, and self-reliant head of the household.[9] In British North America this was an age of self-improvement societies, of mechanics institutes that tried to provide a context in which workingmen might attain greater self-understanding and government savings banks that hoped to encourage self-reliance and thriftiness among the poorer classes. In the United States, the antebellum reform impulse revealed a Christian concern with individual salvation and social improvement, and was imbued with perfectionist assumptions. In its most romantic and anti-institutional form, perfectionism cast off Christian notions of the redeemed and embraced transcendentalism, which saw all men and women capable of heroic achievement; by their work and example individuals could sweep away the obstacles to human progress. In this context, true manliness demanded a dedication to self-improvement and personal regeneration, and history itself became the product of the lives of great men.[10]

Throughout the nineteenth century these spiritual definitions of manliness increasingly gave way to a veneration of physical hardiness, so that by the time of the Civil War bodily vigour was coming to be regarded as "the wellspring of true manhood."[11] There are several explanations for this reconceptualization of masculinity in physical terms. In part, it was facilitated by a growing admiration of martial valour and physical courage that accompanied the Civil War and the subsequent age of imperial expansion. It was also a reaction to what Ann Douglas has referred to as the "feminization of American culture," which fed concerns that woman's influence in the church and the schoolroom, and in the authority they exerted over their sons at home, was contributing to social debilitation.[12] Late-nineteenth-century reformers feared the decline of society into muscular flabbiness, nervous weakness, and "effeminacy," and worried that in seeking out the comforts of life American men had become increasingly unable to withstand pain or live a virile life.[13] Distinguishing between the sexes on the basis of physical differences, these reformers ensured that "the meaning of being masculine shifted from being the opposite of childish to being the opposite of feminine."[14]

Roberta Park has recently drawn attention to the way in which images of the body became a central element in Victorian attempts to distinguish gender. The popularity of pictorial representations of the ideal male physique contributed to the consolidation of notions of male power and female softness and enhanced patriarchal dominance.[15] This preoccupation with the bodies of both sexes revealed itself particularly in the cult of physical measurement. Physical anthropologists measured the cranial capacity of female and male skulls—as well as those of various races—in order to confirm their Eurocentric and patriarchal assumptions about the mental superiority of Caucasian males.[16] Others used measurement to establish definitions of the ideal body type for both men and women. The Venus-like female was to measure five feet five inches and weigh 138 pounds. Her waist was to measure twenty-four inches, her bust thirty-four, her wrists and ankles six and eight inches respectively, and her thighs and calves twenty-five and fourteen and a half inches in turn. For those who did not conform to these guidelines, the symmetrical development of the body's parts was the objective. In James McKay's Halifax gymnasium, for example, careful body measurements accompanied McKay's exercise programs for young men which, he believed, would compensate for the overdevelopment of muscles on the right side of the body occasioned by the repetitive movements required in factory work.[17]

In this fascination for measurement there was an assumption that ideal physical development—which could be encouraged through physical-culture programs or involvement in organized sports—contributed to manly character and a healthy mental state. Arguing the importance of anthropological data in the investigation of "all classes of men," the American criminologist Arthur MacDonald undertook a study of the physical characteristics of American baseball players. The application of "scientific" principles of measurement to baseball, MacDonald argued, would improve the game, enhance gate receipts, and encourage youth to play it, thereby "developing sound bodies and sound minds, which will make them better citizens." The result of MacDonald's measurements of 140 leading major-league players, however, was nothing more than an averaging of players by height, weight and position. The average height and weight of these players was 5 feet 9½ inches and 174 pounds. The tallest by position were pitchers at 5 feet 11¾ inches and 175 pounds; the smallest were shortstops, who measured 5 feet 9⅖ inches and averaged 167 pounds in weight. Nor were any specific conclusions drawn from these findings, except that those players "less than 5'11" were in general better batters and fielders than their taller counterparts." What remained unstated was MacDonald's apparent presumption that mathematical averaging had identified the ideal baseball physique.[18]

More revealing of MacDonald's purposes were subjective judgments accompanying his published results that bore no clear relation to the statistical evidence he had amassed. MacDonald began his study by noting that criminologists were interested in baseball because it is one of the "greatest moral tonics for boys and young men," directing physical and mental energy into the "right channels," providing healthy recreation, and promoting the values of cooperation and teamwork. If the game had a weakness, however, it was the specialization of players by position, which placed fielding skills above batting. Among other things, specialization had developed "a tribe of catchers who are clumsy on their feet, usually weak at bat, poor base runners and of very little value when sent to other positions." This conclusion derived from MacDonald's belief that although specialization of labour contributed to technological advancement and material progress in the industrial state, it also encouraged mental monotony and unbalanced physical development in individuals, thus contributing to social degeneracy and mental weakness. Influenced by a generation of degeneracy theorists from Morel, Lombroso, and Maudsley to Havelock Ellis and Krafft-Ebing,[19] MacDonald became fascinated by the apparent physical, mental, and moral stigmata that branded as degenerate the "abnormal or atypical man."[20] MacDonald saw baseball as a metaphor of the larger world, where progressive and regenerative forces warred against those degenerative influences—both environmental and hereditary—that contributed to "the criminal, pauper and defective classes."[21]

Like many of his contemporaries, MacDonald applied a biological model both to the definition of appropriate masculinity, and to an understanding of society itself. Ideal manhood involved physical symmetry, mental acuity, and moral uprightness, and could only be achieved by cultivating body, mind and soul. Abnormal manhood, by contrast, bore the "bodily landmarks called stigmata."[22] Accepting this premises, William Krauss, a medical doctor from Buffalo, New York, identified eleven types of cranial deformity, twenty-three malformations of the ear, seven abnormalities of the teeth, nine of the extremities, and twenty-six conditions of the eyes that reflected stigmatic degeneracy, as well as hairy moles, "neurotic" fingers and toe-nails, deformities of the pelvis and genitalia, and malformations of the brain.[23] Physical imperfections were also thought to accompany "moral stigmata" such as acquired sexual perversions or a proclivity for degenerate pastimes, and were thought to be found more regularly in immigrants than in the native American population. In an article in the *Alienist and Neurologist*, Eugene S. Talbot, professor of dental and oral surgery in the Woman's Medical College in Chicago, reported that of 128 men that he had observed in a billiard hall, 82 possessed marked signs of degeneracy. In a larger survey of 8614 people, Talbot reported that "as compared with most foreigners, Americans exhibit the fewest signs of degeneracy," and that "the most marked degenerated types found here are imported individuals."[24]

The turn-of-the-century discourse about gender thus was connected to notions of physical and moral degeneracy, and to analogies between the natural body and the body politic. In an essay entitled "The Republic of the Body," Woods Hutchinson suggested that "the triumphs of democracy have been as signal in biology as they have been in politics." In biology, he argued, "the sturdy little citizen-cells have steadily . . . fought their way to recognition as the controlling power of the entire body-politic, have forced the ganglion-oligarchy to admit that they are but delegates, and even the tyrant mind to concede that he rules by their sufferance alone." If the individual cell, like the individual citizen of a republic, was the source of life and strength, it could also be the source of degeneracy, for the "normal activities of any cell carried to excess may constitute disease, by disturbing the balance of the organism."[25] Hutchinson pointed to numerous instances of degeneracy and moral weakness in the United States, arguing that "American lawlessness, American disrespect for authority, the dishonesty of our business, the corruption of our politics, the looseness of our marriage tie—are all matters of world-wide notoriety." Crime rates, he concluded, were higher in the United States than in Europe "except in certain trivial eccentricities such as wife-beating, burglary, ill treating children, thieving, [and] drunkenness."[26]

In their assault on degeneracy a generation of progressive intellectuals in the United States, from E.L. Godkin to William James, came to regard sport as "a social technology designed to generate and direct human energy" towards the revitalization of American republicanism and manly character. Yet, as Mark Dyerson has suggested, there was no real consensus on whether the energy that derived from the strenuous life or the field of play would lead naturally to social renewal. Although most progressives believed that sport might counteract the feminization of American culture, some felt that it might do so only by encouraging masculine pugnacity.

Dirty tricks, a lack of respect for authority, and unbridled individualism were often as much in evidence on the ball field as social cooperation, fair play, and civic responsibility. Like any other technology, sport needed to be directed towards progressive ends. Architects of a new progressive social order believed that the appropriate direction of young men towards responsible adulthood, in a regulated sporting environment, would counteract the degenerative impact of selfish individualism.[27]

The discourse about degeneracy and national weakness extended far beyond the borders of the United States. In his study of the concept of national decline in *fin-de-siècle* France, Robert Nye has demonstrated that "a language of national pathology which regarded crime, mental illness, or alcoholism as signs of national debility" was shared not only by medical practitioners, asylum superintendents, and criminologists, but also by the lay public. As in America, concern about the deteriorating health of the nation meant that sport would become a force for social and individual regeneration: in this context the body "became an ideological variable in the first burst of modern sportive nationalism."[28] The harnessing of sport to national renewal—institutionalized in the revival of the modern Olympic Games at the end of the nineteenth century—was a recurring motif in late-nineteenth-century Europe and North America.

At the same time, defeat in international competition could heighten concerns about the decline of manhood and national virility. John Nauright has shown that the defeats suffered by British rugby and cricket teams at the hands of colonial New Zealanders, Australians, and South Africans reinforced middle-class conceptions of physical decline in Britain, and raised fears about the "feminization of a British male imperial culture." Colonials in turn were lauded for their virility and robust nature. "In an increasingly competitive world the masculine qualities ascribed to colonial men were . . . qualities which British men were now believed to be sadly lacking."[29]

In Canada the notion of physical degeneracy was widespread. The editor of the *Canada Lancet* saw signs of moral degeneration everywhere: in sexual aberration, neurasthenia, and in the movement to remove "barriers hampering 'down-trodden woman,' making pleas, not for the elevation of man's morals to a higher standard, but license for woman to lower hers to man's."[30] Dr. William Bayard of Saint John thought that neurasthenia and insanity were increasing rapidly because of excessive competition, worry, compulsory education, the availability of sensational novels, and the migration from countryside to city, where the striving for existence was exhausting and sanitary surroundings unfortunate.[31] The Canadian Medical Association *Journal* attributed physical deterioration to the replacement of muscular work by machinery as industrialization proceeded. In addition, crowded streets and school-yards deprived children of natural physical outlets. School boards were therefore encouraged to provide "properly supervised play in spaces reserved as play-grounds in the crowded districts of the city" so that "inevitable physical degeneration might be avoided."[32]

In Fredericton, New Brunswick, Dr A.B. Atherton wrote extensively on the causes of degeneracy and the virtue of sports such as baseball in bringing about social regeneration and a more vigorous manhood. This was the topic of his presidential address to the Maritime Medical Association in July 1907. Atherton attributed degeneracy to the character of modern life and to unscientific approaches to marriage and reproduction. In the former category he identified the herding of people together in large cities, poorly ventillated schools and workplaces, the lack of playgrounds around city schools that would allow children to play cricket, football, and baseball, and the impact of "overstudy" on those of nervous temperament or delicate constitutions. Atherton also called for the "better breeding of the race," suggesting the need to discourage and prevent the marriage "of those who are defective in physical or mental or perhaps even moral qualities; for it is more than probable that these last are also handed down to their progeny."[33] P.C. Murphy, a Charlottetown physician and Atherton's successor as president of the Maritime Medical Association, continued in a similar vein, suggesting a program of mating the weak and strong, the tall and short, blond and brunette, stout and slight. Such a principle, Murphy believed, would create a physically balanced and symmetrical population "without any dislocation of our social system."[34]

By the end of the century, most medical doctors, asylum superintendents, social workers, and criminologists—even those who regarded degeneracy as a hereditary taint—advocated sport and exercise as a way to promote vigorous manliness and social regeneration.[35] Otis McCulley, a Saint John practitioner who shared the popular interest in the physical characteristics of degenerate manhood, was an avid sportsman and one-time president of the Maritime Provinces Amateur Athletic Association who considered sport a social tonic. His colleague Dr William F. Roberts, who would later become the first minister of health in the British Empire, wrote extensively about building manly character and physical robustness in the Canadian boy, and was the major financial backer of the Saint John Roses baseball team, one of the most competitive teams in the region during the 1890s and first decade of the twentieth century.[36] In Charlottetown, the city health officer, Dr H.D. Johnson, promoted a cleaner environment and improved athletic facilities as a way to protect young men from dissipation. A long-time member of the Abegweit Amateur Athletic Association, Johnson was elected president of the Maritime Provinces Amateur Athletic Association in 1909.

In addition to the medical profession, the churches played a critical role in the fostering of physical notions of manhood. At first, many churchmen were suspicious of baseball and were reluctant to have anything to do with it. The emergence of the "social gospel" and the tendency of the churches to subordinate theology to social regeneration resulted in a more approving attitude. Baseball seemed to be one possible solution to what social gospellers called "the young boy problem" and the declining involvement of young males in the work of the church. As sports such as baseball were increasingly seen as contributing to Christian manliness, moreover, ministers were finding it useful to employ baseball analogies in their sermons, warning their congregations not to become stranded on the third base of life. "There is no heaven, not even a newspaper notice for the player who freezes on third base," said the Reverend James W. Kramer. "Young men, it will take manhood to reach the home plate."[37] This was a common theme. "There is an analogy between a game of baseball and the game of life," another churchman wrote. "In each game there is a race to be run; and it is made by stages and beset with difficulties at every point. It would be an easy matter to get around the bases and make a home run if there were not some one at every available point to hinder you and put you out."[38] At times it seemed hard to know where traditional religion stopped and where the religion of baseball began. "To doubt the utility of the game because we ourselves cannot take part in it as we did in the simpler sport of our boyhood, is to beg the question," said one Saint John columnist who relied upon a religious metaphor to clinch his point. "Few of us feel ourselves able to occupy a pulpit, yet we do not, for that reason, cease to attend church."[39]

As Victorians became enamoured of "muscular Christianity" and genuflected at the altar of robust physicality, baseball gradually assumed the status of a civil religion for both players and spectators, for young and old, for rich and poor. The doctrine of muscular Christianity, which replaced earlier more pietistic and spiritual assumptions with a tradition of sturdy manliness and religious dedication, drew heavily upon the writings of Englishmen Charles Kingsley and Thomas Hughes, who insisted upon the "connections between a vigorously human Christ and a vigorously humane Christianity."[40] In Britain, advocates of this more physical approach to the gospel sought to merge a tradition of moral manliness with the more secular traditions of the English gentleman. In *Tom Brown's Schooldays* (1857) and its sequel *Tom Brown at Oxford* (1861), Hughes idealized public-school sturdiness and physical manliness. A blend of sports such as cricket, rowing, and rugby and appropriate Christian instruction were the fundamental ingredients in moulding gentlemanly character, and helped to counteract an earlier spiritualism that smacked of effeminacy. Norman Vance has argued that the term "muscular Christianity" is an unfortunate rendering of the Kingsleyan gospel, because it draws more attention to "muscularity" than to Christianity. While Hughes and Kingsley evoked an ideal of physical manliness, they were equally concerned about the development of Christian and gentlemanly character.[41] Their pleas for balance were not always listened to: many Victorians remained less attentive to spiritual matters than to the promotion of physical well-being.

In North America at the turn of the century the idealization of physicality became a veritable religion of its own, attached to notions of Anglo-Saxon superiority, nativist concerns about immigration from eastern and southern Europe, and a rising tide of nationalism and imperialism. In *Our Country: Its Possible Future and Present Crisis* (1885) Congregational minister Josiah Strong expressed a commonplace fear that Anglo-Saxon manhood was losing its virility, and that the greater fecundity of the lower classes and immigrant populations was leading to racial decline. Theodore Roosevelt, who came to epitomize the values of the strenuous life, having himself overcome childhood weakness through vigorous exercise, warned of the "danger of placing too little stress upon the more virile virtues—upon the virtues which go to make up a race of statesmen and soldiers, of pioneers and explorers."[42] Roosevelt advocated a physical regimen that included manly out-of-door sports such as baseball, football, boxing, wrestling, running, rowing, shooting, horseback riding, and mountain climbing. "The whole test of the worth of any sport," he declared, "should be the demand that sport makes upon those qualities of mind and body which in their sum we call manliness."[43]

This was also the message of the famous dime novels celebrating Frank Merriwell, the fictional Yale hero whose exploits on the baseball field and gridiron enthralled a generation of readers at the turn of the century. The author of the Merriwell series, writing under the name Burt L. Standish, was Gilbert Pattern, a native of Corrine, Maine, whose family's pacifism and uncompromising Adventist beliefs had moulded "a shrinking lad with a sense of inferiority." As a youngster, despite his lack of physical coordination, Patten had a passion for baseball, but was discouraged from playing the game by his parents. In making Merriwell "a paragon of manly strength and muscular coordination," Patten was compensating for his own clumsiness as a youth. In addition, Merriwell provided Patten with the chance "to preach—by example—the doctrine of a clean mind in a clean and healthy body."[44] After his marriage, Patten moved to Camden, Maine, and, having now escaped parental influence, became involved in the game that he had earlier followed from afar. During the early 1890s Patten managed the local semi-pro ball team in Maine's Knox County League, where he came into contact with a number of talented young players including eventual major leaguers William "Rough" Carrigan, Louis Sockalexis, and Mike Powers, as well as hard-bitten old pros such as "Old Nick" Nickerson and "Gramp" Morse, who threw at opponents' heads with little remorse. Patten's experiences here provided him with valuable information and anecdotes that he later incorporated in the Merriwell series.[45]

Patten introduced Frank Merriwell to American readers on 18 April 1896. After that his hero reappeared on a weekly basis in Street and Smith's *Tip Top Weekly* until the series was discontinued in 1916. The epitome of youthful masculinity, as his name implied, Merriwell blended physical ability with moral courage. "For my hero I took the given name of Frank to express one of his characteristics—open, on the level, above board, frank," Patten wrote in his autobiography. "Merriwell was formed by a combination of two words, Merry—expressive of a jolly high-spirited lad—and well, suggesting abounding physical health."[46] In many of these stories the theme was the same: Frank was engaged in a struggle against criminals and gamblers, whose evil intent often led to his being abducted before the most important game of the season.[47] At the very last moment he would escape, returning in the nick of time to lead his team to victory. In this sense Frank was an archetypical hero of the Progressive era, steadfastly opposing the corrupt practices of gamblers and speculators in a spirit reminiscent of muckraking journalists and moral reformers. Resourceful masculinity and moral toughness were also recurring elements in Patten's tales of the Maine lumberwoods, where "Bainbridge of Bangor" unravelled various timberland intrigues while on the trail of unscrupulous land grabbers.

On college campuses across the land, proponents of manly vigour tried to live out the Merriwell ideal, establishing daily regimens that included strenuous recreation and participation in manly sports.[48] In March 1903 a student at the Anglican Prince of Wales College in Charlottetown complained about the lack of gymnasium facilities at the college, pointing out that the college had an empty garret that could be used for the purpose of manly exercise. This would be a welcome alternative to the Hillsborough Rink and YMCA gymnasium in the town, and would be far less expensive than involvement in games such as hockey that required equipment and ice rental. A teacher at the college, Professor E.E. Jordan, was capable and willing to put the students through gymnasium drill and to promote the balance of mind and body. Physical exercise, he believed, helped to "nerve a man, make him manly and give him physical strength in order that he may be able to use his mind to better advantage than if his body were weak. . . . Feed the one excessively, nourish its support moderately and compensation has less power to exhaust the body for the mind. The mind has a principle of growth within itself, it has a natural power of self-development. . . . Athletics is a process artificially applied to the body, as something is artificially done to the brain, the two they call education."[49]

Manliness was also a central preoccupation of the Canadian novelist Charles William Gordon, writing under the pseudonym Ralph Connor. A Presbyterian minister, Connor saw Anglo-Saxonism, Christianity, and a robust Canadian nationality secured by a manly population who confronted the "ever rising surge of immigrants, many of whom he thought did not share those virtues as readily as they might."[50] Connor's *The Man from Glengarry* (1901) tells the story of the sturdy Scottish woodsmen of Glengarry County, Ontario, who "carried the marks of their blood in their fierce passion, their courage, their loyalty; and of the forest in their patience, their resourcefulness, their self reliance." Deep within the souls of these mighty lumbermen, whose confrontation with stern nature had bred in them hardiness of frame, remarkable endurance, and an alertness of the senses, "dwelt the fear of God." It was this combination of physical manliness and Christian humility that ensured national greatness. "For not wealth, not enterprise, not energy, can build a nation into sure greatness," wrote Connor, "but men, and only men with the fear of God in their hearts, and with no other."

The theme of many of Connor's novels was that men who made their living in this harsh northern country needed a masculine rather than a highly intellectualized and pious form of Christianity. In *The Sky Pilot*, a young minister just out of divinity school comes to a cattle camp in the foothills of the Canadian Rockies to set up his church. The initial response of the camp's brawny cowboys to this "blankety-blank, pink-and-white complected nursery kid" was lukewarm at best. Most of the ranch hands "despised, ignored, or laughed at him, according to their mood and disposition." For one thing, holding Sunday service conflicted with the weekly baseball match. One Sunday, however, the team's pitcher failed to show up, and the young minister agreed to fill in, amidst undisguised mockery and hoots of derision. What they did not know was that he was a fine athlete, having played ball for Princeton. By the end of the game it was clear that he was "the best all-around man on the field." Having now won the respect of his parishioners, he could bring them the kind of manly Christianity that appealed to "young lads, freed from the restraints of custom and surrounding," and who "stood forth in the naked simplicity of their native manhood."

Another turn-of-the-century Canadian churchman who embodied the gentleness of Christianity and the manliness associated with competitive sports was the Methodist minister Edwin Pearson, whose son Lester would later become the prime minister of Canada. Extremely popular amongst his parishioners in small-town Ontario, Ed Pearson believed that the church, the school, and the playing field all served the cause of Christianity and temperance, and rejected those who either "would crush out all amusement. . . , [or] pursue everything from which pleasure is derived."[51] Pearson's approach was a compromise, John English has observed, leading "straight to the ball field and away from the tavern."[52] The Pearson boys, Duke, Vaughan, and Lester, followed their father's lead to the baseball diamond. To Lester, whose baby-face, mildly lisping speech, and religious family background may have suggested a wimpish milk-sop, exploits on the sporting field as football quarterback, Oxford rugby star, and semi-pro baseball player stood as an assertion of his masculinity.

The desire to strike a balance between physical vigour and moral sensibility in young boys and men was a recurring theme in the religious press in Canada. The *Presbyterian Witness* believed that most young boys recognized the virtue "of bodily exercises, of . . . the gymnasium, of the ball field, of outdoor and indoor sports in general," but whatever strength was gained through rational exercise "will be impaired or lost by an unhealthy, morbid, impure mind." The young boy was admonished to show respect for his mother, to avoid wasting time instead of "striking with all his might," to associate with reputable companions, to avoid tobacco and alcohol, but above all to work vigorously, for hard work and early self-denial was the key to successful manhood. For its part the church had to present a gospel that "appeals to the manly man," faithful to the teachings of Christ, but "a live religion that expects to grow, a robust religion that is meant for work, of a virile type that is neither weak-eyed nor maudlin."[53]

The main concern of the Protestant denominations was to win young middle-class boys to the church. At an Anglican conference on "The Church, The Child and the Home," held in Halifax in September 1910, Hubert Carleton, editor of the *St. Andrew's Cross*, stressed that it was the duty of the church and parents to "win the boy," particularly "the big boy," or adolescent, who was "conspicuous by his absence, both at the services of the church and in Sunday School."[54] Many of the churches established athletic and reading clubs for adult men, young men, and boys, and though church reformers were sometimes criticized for merely providing an alternative to "worse places," such as the saloon or billiard hall,[55] athletic and reading clubs did provide an institutional framework for child-saving. Other churches established Boy's Brigades, an idea brought to North

America from Scotland in the early 1890s. In the *Canadian Magazine*, J. Castell Hopkins saw these brigades as a catalyst of a disciplined, orderly, and manly society. "We require all the discipline and habits of order which can possibly be encouraged and taught amongst the youth of our land," Hopkins opined.[56] Capitalizing upon the "martial spirit" of this period, and on what the *Presbyterian Witness* believed was the boy's "natural love of militarism," boy's brigades actively promoted military drill as a way to turn boys into men. "They come into the hall boys," said one editorial, "and the moment the company is formed they are soldiers."[57]

Although the most successful of these character-building institutions was the Young Men's Christian Association (YMCA), its reach, like that of most of these child-saving clubs and organizations, usually did not extend beyond the middle class. David MacLeod has seen character-building organizations as institutions that imposed middle-class values not upon the working class, but "upon itself, or rather upon its own young people."[58] Those involved in the YMCA, the Boy's Brigades, and the Boy Scout movement might admire "the tough virtues of the old-style, work-bound boyhood . . . and admire the vigour of sturdy street boys," but they feared the contaminating influence of lower-class delinquency. The social programs of these organizations, therefore, were "directed against the bogy of the hooligan, against working-class loafers and shirkers, and against the possibility of lower middle-class boys joining the degenerate in their idleness."[59] In turn, the rougher lads of the street, accustomed to a working-class culture of masculinity that venerated toughness and a resistance to middle-class notions of social improvement, responded to parades of scouts and uniformed members of boy's brigades with "ribald jeers, derisive songs and occasional stone-throwing."[60]

The YMCA's fourfold plan of mental, physical, social, and religious development was aimed primarily at middle-class teenagers from good families, who were thought to be susceptible to the temptations of tobacco, alcohol, and sex, and could easily be led astray by falling in with the "wrong crowd." This middle-class fear of youthful waywardness by no means implied the waning influence of the family as a moulding force of appropriate manliness. Rather it revealed a new form of adolescent dependency within the middle-class family, reflected in an extended duration of family residence, lengthier schooling, and an elevated age of entry into the workforce.[61] Within and without the middle-class family in the nineteenth century, adolescence was receiving more attention than it ever had before. YMCA gymnasiums, swimming pools, and reading rooms were thus not meant to "rival the home," said clergyman Calvin Dill Wilson, but only "to fight perilous resorts. The young men will gather together somewhere. . . . Many of them will meet in the pool room if no better place is provided as a rendezvous."[62]

Within the Y's program of physical activity, baseball did not always play a prominent role. In the cities and towns of the Maritimes and New England, the emphasis was usually upon gymnastic exercise and swimming, while in the Y-sponsored summer camps, swimming and hiking usually took precedence over ball games. There were two factions within the organization, both espousing muscular Christianity, but divided upon the virtues of baseball. One faction supported baseball as a form of manly exercise, while the other saw it as inefficient in developing physical fitness. Because of the emphasis on the confrontation of batter and pitcher, others on the field simply stood waiting and those on the bench sat idle until their turn at bat. Gymnasium exercise, by contrast, was physically demanding work that built healthy bodies and moral character. This debate was never fully resolved, however, and YMCA baseball leagues and teams were a commonplace reality throughout the region before the First World War.[63]

The idea of organizing children's play was an element in the intellectual armament of turn-of-the-century progressive reformers such as John Dewey, Jane Addams, Lester Ward, and G. Stanley Hall. Hall drew heavily upon notions of atavism in degeneracy theory, regarding childhood behaviour as an acting out of primitive impulses and instincts. He argued that the development of the individual organism, or "ontogeny," recapitulated "phylogeny," or the evolutionary process, so that a child's interest in tree climbing and swinging from branches was a vestige of his primitive ancestral origins. He proceeded to argue that playgrounds were important because through supervised play "what was morally valuable in our primitive heritage was preserved and what was inappropriate, unnecessary or disruptive was weakened or modified."[64]

By the first decade of the twentieth century, most of the major urban centres of New England and the Maritimes had supervised playgrounds. Following the lead of larger centres such as Boston and New York, civic officials in several towns in Maine and the Maritimes developed playgrounds as an alternative to street play or the use of city parks for baseball. Portland established a supervised playground at Deering's Oaks, Lewiston set up a playground in its city park, and similar plans were inaugurated in Auburn during the summer of 1908. Urban reformers, businessmen, and reform organizations such as the Local Council of Women in Halifax and Saint John or the Twentieth Century Club in Bangor, Maine, saw playgrounds as providing a healthy and safe environment for children, "free from the moral and physical dangers of the street and questionable companions," where they would be "incidentally taught to be ladies and gentlemen and learn how to handle themselves, acquiring grace and agility."[65] In Amherst, land provided by the late Senator Dickey was turned into a playground where, the *Daily News* reported, young men and boys could "congregate and indulge in those healthy sports that go to build up a sturdy and upright race of men."[66]

The fact that most of the character-building institutions of the late nineteenth century were preoccupied with elaborating an ideal of manliness to middle-class males suggests that the discourse surrounding the manly sports was part of the contested terrain of both class and gender. Unfortunately, when one begins to probe the existing literature for a discussion of working-class dimensions of the making of masculinity, both on the baseball diamond and off, one is faced with a profound silence. Most of the work on the social construction of masculinity reveals a strong preoccupation with articulate, white middle-class reformers and their prescriptions for turning youth into men. When historians have ventured beyond this mainstream constituency, they have done so, more often than not, to address issues of racial exclusivity or ethnic assimilation. As a result, we know much more about the exclusion of blacks from the game, or the extent to which ethnic minorities found sport an avenue to social mobility, than we do about how class impinged upon and shaped both baseball and the culture of masculinity of which it was a part.

In his critique of the social history of leisure, Gareth Stedman Jones warned against the tendency to elevate the study of workers' recreational time to "a subject in its own right." Concerned that writing on leisure either tended towards a "social control" interpretation that denied agency to the subordinate classes, or to a position that celebrated the victories of workers in struggles over recreation while they lost the more important war in the workplace, Stedman Jones called for an understanding of leisure as an escape from the harsher realities of the workaday world. Such an interpretation, however, overlooks the important discourse about manly labour that connected the worlds of work and play and that was rooted in changes in the labour process and the concomitant de-skilling of workers. "Manliness" was an ideal constructed within a society characterized by continuing class antagonism, a shifting relationship between capital and labour, and the emergence of new standards of gentility and ethical conduct. In this context, notions of manly behaviour carried considerable ideological force, depending upon who was employing them.

What makes this discourse difficult to unravel is the fact that the language of masculinity often transcended class divisions. On the ball field, teams drawn from different class backgrounds often employed similar nicknames, identifying themselves as exemplars of manly virtue. Team names were often chosen to indicate the essential characteristics of manliness: courage, physical alertness, and fraternal loyalty. A quick glance at the sporting press reveals the prominence of names such as the Actives, the Athletics, the Fear Nots, the Intrepids, the Invincibles, the Mutuals, the Resolutes, the Socials, and the Unions. Sportswriters lavished praise on players for their "pluckiness" and endurance, especially those like Michael Pender, catcher of the Halifax Socials, who refused to let a badly mashed hand send him to the sidelines in an important match.[67] Ballplayers were expected to bear injury "manfully," and to approach hard-hit grounders and fly balls barehanded, without any visible indication of fear. In his description of the introduction of the fly-ball rule and the elimination of the one bound out during the 1860s, for example, Warren Goldstein has demonstrated how sportswriters praised attempts to catch the ball on the fly and scorned "unmanly" players who waited to play the ball on the bounce. "No manly or skillful player will ever be guilty," said the *Clipper*, "of sacrificing the catch on the fly to the more simple effort on the bound."[68]

Although these elaborations on masculine courage seem to have had a universal appeal, bourgeois reformers and workingmen often employed the rhetoric of manliness to serve different purposes. As we have seen, the

Victorian middle class regarded strenuous athleticism, physical dexterity, and symmetrical muscularity as essential to the development of national virility and Christian manliness, and an antidote to the "feminization" of middle-class culture. Despite the ball-players' physical prowess, however, the behaviour of athletes of "lesser rank" often offended middle-class commentators. The usual bourgeois stereotype of working-class masculinity dramatized a culture of brawny physicality, heavy drinking, rough language, and sexual indulgence, which carried with it the implication of limited intellectual acumen or moral refinement. The notion that working-class athletes lacked the self-restraint to control their passions—similar to the depiction of black men as slaves to their sexual impulses[69]—was a common theme in the parables of dissipation that graced the pages of the sporting press.

Alcohol, tobacco, and illicit sexuality made up the unholy trinity of dissipation that destroyed the bourgeois ideal of true manliness and undermined the athlete's physical talents. The sporting magazines were full of references to those who had "disgraced themselves," damaged their health, and brought disrepute to the game. Editorial after editorial worried that "lushing," or heavy drinking, was doing the game "a great deal of harm," or that rowdyism and ungentlemanly behaviour was lowering "the tone of the sport" and driving respectable patrons from the parks.[70] To be sure, training rules prohibited smoking, drinking, and profane language—some clubs even required players to forfeit their salary for contracting "disease through misconduct"—but enforcement of these regulations was often lax, especially for those whose skills made them indispensable to their clubs. Outfielder Jocko Fields, a hard-living Irishman and star of the Pittsburgh club, for example, was famous for smoking cigarettes during the game. While playing for the Memphis club in the Southern League in 1895 Fields had a clause in his contract allowing him to smoke while the game was in progress.[71] Horrified by the extent of cigarette smoking, the *Sporting News* reported that "an average of three players per nine" were hooked on a habit "that shatters the nerves, debilitates the heart and the eyes, and cripples the wind apparatus." The same journal attributed the physical deterioration and death at age thirty-seven of Boston star Mike "King" Kelly to his dissolute habits. "Kelly was a cigarette fiend of the most confirmed stripe," the *Sporting News* reported, "such a slave to the habit that he would awake from a profound slumber and puff the ennervating, enticing roll of paper."[72] Kelly was also a frequent presence in the taverns and saloons of Chicago's Clark Street. When club owner Albert Spalding hired a Pinkerton detective to inquire into the after-hours exploits of his players, and presented his report to the players, Kelly offered the following amendment. "In that place where the detective reports me as taking a lemonade at 3 a.m. he's off. It was straight whiskey: I never drank a lemonade at 3 a.m. in my life."[73]

While the inability of players to restrain themselves from engaging in "degenerate pastimes" was often used to explain poor play, managers also were criticized for their inability to control their players. The *Sporting News* castigated Patsy Tebeau of the Cleveland club for his profanity and argumentative demeanour on the field, which set a bad example for his players and contributed to rowdyness and "ruffianism on the diamond."[74] It also took Bill "Scrappy" Joyce, manager of the Washington club, to task for his inability to teach players self-restraint. At issue was an incident involving Senators pitcher Win Mercer. Annoyed that his second baseman, New Brunswick native John "Chewing Gum" O'Brien, had failed to cover the bag on a double-play ball, Mercer intentionally threw the ball into centre-field to embarrass his teammate, allowing the Reds to score several runs in the process.[75] On the other hand, the *Sporting News* no doubt would have commended manager Wreath of the Augusta ball club for withholding cheques to his players on 1 July 1907 so that they would not buy too much liquor over the July 4th holiday.[76]

These parables about manly self-restraint, managerial discipline, and respectable living not only involved concerns about appropriate standards of personal behaviour, but were connected as well to the larger issue of labour-management relations and the commercialization of sport. Although baseball, like any other game, could be merely a form of amusement and healthful recreation, in its professional and semi-professional guise it was reconstituted as work. Very early in the history of the game, promoters had seen an opportunity to turn sport into a commodity, fencing grounds, erecting grandstands, charging admission to spectators, and seeking out skilful players who would attract an audience. In the larger urban centres of North America, baseball became a big business operation, often connected to urban political machines. Owners sought out the support of municipal politicians, street-railway companies, and other utilities in an attempt to reduce operating costs and increase profit margins. Even in smaller towns such as Fall River, Salem, and Brockton, Massachusetts, Dover, New Hampshire, and Lewiston, Maine, street-railway companies provided support to the clubs in the form of free grounds and cash subsidies.[77]

As baseball developed as a profitable business enterprise, the interests of players and owners often diverged. For the most part, players hoped to sell their skills in a relatively unregulated labour market, while owners attempted to keep salaries down by binding the players to their clubs contractually. The players were particularly opposed to the "reserve rule" that bound a player to a single club, and in 1885 organized a Brotherhood of Professional Baseball Players in order to protect themselves from the exploitative practices of the owners. The leader of the Brotherhood was John Montgomery Ward, a star pitcher and shortstop for the New York team in the National League, whose legal training had allowed him to draft the Brotherhood charter in 1885. Hardly a militant labour leader—Ward had spurned affiliation of the players with the Knights of Labor—he nonetheless was a vigorous critic of the reserve rule, attacking it as a modern "fugitive slave law" that "carries [the player] back, bound and shackled, to the club from which he attempted to escape."[78] In 1889 the owners, led by John Brush of the Indianapolis club, tried to consolidate and extend their authority by establishing a classification scheme that included salary limitations, and even assigned marginal players such menial tasks as tending the turnstile or sweeping out the parks after the game.[79] Ward argued that although ballplayers earned larger salaries and had shorter work hours than most skilled workers, the relationship with the owners "leaves us nonetheless workingmen." When the owners failed to soften their stance on the reserve clause and on salary limits, the Brotherhood established a rival Players' League, which operated during the 1890 season before collapsing before the 1891 campaign.

In confronting the owners, baseball workers appealed to a broader discourse about manly work, skilful production, and working-class independence that accompanied the development of late-nineteenth-century industrial capitalism. In the last quarter of the century workers on all fronts confronted employers interested in implementing new notions of scientific management and efficiency, which tended to reduce skilled to sweated labour. A number of historians, such as David Montgomery, Alan Dawley, Paul Faler, Greg Kealey, Wally Seccombe, Bryan Palmer, and Sonya Rose, have drawn attention to the attachment of the "manly" ideal to work, particularly to skilled craftsmanship. Appeals to sturdy manliness, especially in confronting unscrupulous capitalists and unmanly scab labour, was a crucial component of the artisans' attempt to defend their livelihoods. Joy Parr has argued that in the mid-nineteenth century a generation of craft-absorbed managers also asserted their masculinity through skilled work, and by so doing "obscured the differences between masters and men behind a veil of craft fraternity."[80] With mass production and scientific management, however, that relationship was altered and "the gauze of common gender identify began to tear."[81] No longer as dependent upon traditional craft skills, the new industrialist denied the notion that virility was rooted in skill and physical effort. Workingmen fought in turn to defend those traditions of skilled craftsmanship that were essential to their conception of manliness, and asserted their right to a "manly" wage. In choosing the ideal of manliness as a way of defending their class interests, however, skilled workers also contributed to the engenderment of work and the subordination of women in the workplace. As Keith McClelland has pointed out, while the foundations of the working class "rested on . . . [labour's] subjection to capital and competition within the labour market . . . they also rested on the exclusion from or subordination of women" in the workplace and their dependency within the household.[82]

As baseball developed as commercialized entertainment—both at the semi-pro and professional levels—the relationship of the player/worker to the owner/club was characterized by increasing tension and antagonism. But if the relationship of capital and labour within the baseball business was similar in many ways to that in other emerging industries in the late nineteenth century, there were some significant differences. Unlike in many factory settings where mechanization undermined traditional skills, on the baseball diamond the game was dependent upon the development and refinement of the skills that players employed. The skills of ballplayers and other athletes were more likely to be endangered by injury and advancing age than by technological or managerial assaults on their craftsmanship. The erosion of athletic skills, moreover, was readily measurable. Given baseball's fascination with statistical measurement of player performance, and because athletic skill was as much a function of age and sharp reflexes as it was of experience or strength, players knew that their careers could end quickly. As a result they often resisted the attempts of owners and managers to restrict their mobility and to control their off-field activities.

For their part, profit-seeking owners wanted to employ the most skilful players for the least amount of money and, in the hope of fielding a competitive team, to keep better players under contract and management control. The owners also realized that baseball's reputation for rowdiness hurt them at the game. Control over the extracurricular activities of players, therefore, served to enhance baseball's respectability while encouraging players to perform to the best of their abilities. Even owners like Albert Spalding and Connie Mack, who had graduated from the player ranks, demanded that players maintain a respectable and gentlemanly demeanour and defer to their authority. Having grown up in the shoemaking town of Braintree, Massachusetts, Mack turned to the ball diamond as an escape from his working-class origins.

On the issue of player autonomy and owner control, the sporting press was ambivalent. The *Sporting Life* was cautiously supportive of the players' cause, and often criticized the exploitive practices of the owners. Arguing for a reformed relationship between players and owners based upon mutual respect, it took the position that exploitation of the players made it less likely for "gentlemen" to play the game. At first it had been uncomfortable with the decision of the players to form their own league; later it saw benefits. The Players' League had undermined the monopolistic control that owners exercised, elevated salaries, and, it argued, counteracted the degradation that used to characterize baseball. High salaries put an end to the "toughs" who played the game; increasingly, players were being recruited from the "ranks of the educated, refined and well-to-do." The "toughs" had cultivated only their "animal tendencies," said the *Sporting Life*, but the bums and drunkards were being weeded out quickly. "Today questions of character are almost as potent as records of ability in securing engagement, and respectable young men may now enter the profession without feeling that they are inviting the suspicion and contempt of their friends and the general public."[83]

The *Sporting News* was not so easily convinced that high salaries would naturally result in the uplifting of the sport to respectability. For the most part it took the side of the owners, arguing for greater managerial discipline, defending the reserve clause, and attacking players for any breaches of club regulations. In so doing it believed itself to be protecting the game from those who put their own needs before those of the club. Contract jumpers, known as "revolvers," were regarded as selfish and unmanly, and were berated for being ungrateful for the opportunity that baseball had provided them to play and make a living at the same time. Revolving, The *Sporting News* argued, destroyed the stability of franchises, and undermined the attachment of fans to their local team. Without the reserve rule, it argued, the players would demand excessive salaries, and "kill the goose that laid the golden egg." How many players, it asked rhetorically, would succeed in careers outside of baseball? The implication was that few had any other real talent. "The majority of them go into the saloon business after their careers are over and most of them never save a cent of their earnings."[84]

The tug-of-war between owners and players, the issue of rowdiness on and off the field, and the continuing influence that gamblers exerted on the game all continued to plague baseball at the turn of the century. For some the solution was a return to the traditions of gentlemanly amateurism and the concomitant assumption that professional play debased the sport. For others the answer was to reform the professional game so that players and owners might exert "an earnest effort to work together harmoniously as a whole."[85] Whatever the solution, in the two decades prior to the First World War, the discourse surrounding baseball's development continued to turn upon the class question and the need to uplift the game to respectability. Gradually, however, baseball would reform itself; and as the issue of respectability carried increasingly less weight, images of class conflict that had surrounded the game gradually gave way to those of national purpose, regional loyalty, and civic pride.

NOTES

1. Ty Cobb with Al Stumpf, *My Life in Baseball: The True Record* (Garden City: Doubleday 1961), 280.

2. Charles Alexander, *Ty Cobb* (New York: Oxford University Press, 1984).

3. Harry Brod, "The Case for Men's Studies," in H. Brod, ed., *The Making of Masculinities: The New Men's Studies* (Boston: Allen & Unwin 1987), 40, 46.

4. Michael Roper and John Tosh, eds., *Manful Assertions: Masculinities in Britain since 1800* (London and New York: Routledge 1991), 7. To understand the social construction of masculinity, the authors argue, one must delve into the "mutations of male dominance over time and their relation to other structures of social power, such as class, race, nation and creed."

5. Joseph Kett, *Rites of Passage: Adolescence in America, 1790 to the Present* (New York: Basic Books 1977).

6. Margaret S. Creighton, "American Mariners and the Rites of Manhood, 1830–1870," in Colin Howell and Richard Twomey, eds., *Jack Tar in History: Essays in the History of Maritime Life and Labour* (Fredericton: Acadiensis Press 1991), 143–63.

7. See, for example, Murray E. Angus, "Living in the 'World of the Tiger': The Methodist and Presbyterian Churches in Nova Scotia and the Great War, 1914–1918," M.A. thesis, Dalhousie University, 1993; esp. chap. 2.

8. Anthony Rotundo, "Body and Soul: Changing Ideals of American Middle-Class Manhood, 1770–1920," *Journal of Social History* 16 (Fall 1983): 23–38. See also the articles by Rotundo and Roberta Park in J.A. Mangan and James Walvin, eds., *Manliness and Morality: Middle Class Masculinity in Britain and America, 1800–1940* (Manchester: Manchester University Press 1987).

9. Jacksonian democracy is often seen as embodying this self-confident individualism. Edward Pessen points out that European observers saw a rather different reality. Rather than "an inner-directed American, marching to his own music, living his life according to his own and his

family's notions as to how it should be lived," these observers saw a deficiency of moral independence and an uncommon conformity to prevailing public opinion. Edward Pessen, *Jacksonian America: Society, Personality and Politics* (Georgetown, ON: Irwin-Dorsey 1969), chap. 2. quote from p. 20.

10. John L. Thomas, "Romantic Reform in America, 1815–1865," *American Quarterly* 17 (Winter 1965): 656–81.

11. Rotundo, "Body and Soul," 27.

12. Ann Douglas, *The Feminization of American Culture* (New York: Knopf 1977).

13. T. Jackson Lears, *No Place of Grace* (New York: Pantheon 1981).

14. Clyde W. Franklin, II, *The Changing Definition of Masculinity* (New York and London: Plenum Press 1984), 8. See also J.H. Pleck and E.H. Pleck, *The American Man* (Englewood Cliffs: Prentice Hall 1980).

15. Roberta Park, "Physiology and Anatomy Are Destiny!? Brains, Bodies and Exercise in Nineteenth Century American Thought," *Journal of Sport History* 18, 1 (Spring 1991): 31–62.

16. For the craniological tradition in early anthropology, and a discussion of its connections to phrenology, see Paul A. Erickson, "Phrenology and Physical Anthropology: The George Combe Connection," *Current Anthropology* 18, 1 (March 1977): 92–93. On cranial measurement and notions of racial inferiority see John Haller, *Outcasts from Evolution: Scientific Attitudes of Racial Inferiority 1859–1900* (Urbana: University of Illinois Press 1971). For a contemporary view of cranial capacity and gender differences, see "Sex and the Brain," *Maritime Medical News* 18, 1 (January 1906): 5, which reported the findings of Marchand of Marbourg that the mean weight of the male brain was 3 pounds, 1 ounce, as compared to the female brain at 2 pounds, 10 ounces. "The disparity, if true," the report continued, "is sig-

nificant with relation to the distinct purposes for which the sexes, respectively are equipped by nature, and with reference to that other and more productive brain centre which distinguishes woman for her office and disposition. The present rage for bringing up the intellectual brain of a woman to a parity with that of man may be successful, but it can be only a transfer of the . . . womanly brain from its divine seat to a different place and function. Neither sex is gifted with vital power to grow the other sex upon itself as a double and become mentally bi-sexed." For an interesting critique of the biological determinism of cranial measurement and intelligence testing see Stephen Jay Gould, *The Mismeasure of Man* (New York: W.W. Norton and Co. 1981). "What craniotomy was for the 19th century," Gould observes, "intelligence testing has become for the twentieth, when it assumes that intelligence (or at least a dominant part of it) is a single, innate, heritable, and measurable thing" (25)).

17. Park, "Physiology and Anatomy," 48–49; M.J. Smith, "Graceful Athleticism or Robust Womanhood," *Journal of Canada Studies* 23, 1 (Spring 1988): 122–23, 128.

18. Arthur MacDonald, "Scientific Study of Baseball," *American Physical Education Review* 19, 3 (March 1919): 220–41. These measurements bring to mind Dan Sargent's attempts to create the profile of "typical" male and female students at American colleges, which one medical journal doubted "contributed anything of value to science. Park, "Physiology and Anatomy," 56.

19. Havelock Ellis, *The Criminal* (London: Walter Scott 1890); Henry Maudsley, *The Physiology and Pathology of the Mind* (London: MacMillan & Co., 1867); R. von Krafft-Ebing, *Psychopathia Sexualis, With Special Reference to Contrary Sexual Instinct, A Medico-Legal Study*, trans. Charles Gilbert Chaddock (Philadelphia: F.A. Davis Co. 1892); Ruth Friedlander, "Benedict-Augustin Morel and the

Development of the Theory of Degenerescence," Ph.D. dissertation, University of California, 1973; Enrico Ferri, *Criminal Sociology* (New York: D. Appleton & Com. 1897); Gina Lombroso Ferrero, ed., *Criminal Man According to the Classification of Cesare Lombroso* (New York & London: G.P. Putnam and Sons 1911); Daniel Pick, "The Faces of Anarchy: Lombroso and the Politics of Criminal Science in Post-Unification Italy," *History Workshop Journal* 21 (Spring 1986): 60–86.

20. A committee of the Nova Scotia Medical Society declared in 1909 that the "thorough understanding of abnormal conditions requires equally thorough understanding of the normal and the study of the normal as well as the abnormal demands very wide research. We quite accord with Dr. Macdonald's [sic] statement that "As the seeds of evil are usually sown in childhood and youth, it is here that all investigation should commence."" PANS, Nova Scotia Medical Society, Minutes of the Annual Meeting, 7 July 1909.

21. MacDonald's views are contained in his *Criminology* (New York: Funk and Wagnall's 1893). See also U.S. Senate Document 187, 58th Congress, 3rd session (Washington: 1905) and U.S. Senate Document 532, 60th Congress, 1st session (Washington: 1908). These latter sources relate to his assumptions about "man and abnormal man," juvenile criminals, the stigmata of degeneration, and the prospects for rehabilitation and reform.

22. *Canada Lancet* 2 (October 1901): 158.

23. William Krauss, "The Stigmata of Degeneration," *American Journal of Insanity* 55, 1 (July 1898): 55–88.

24. Eugene S. Talbot, "Heredity and Atavism," *Alienist and Neurologist* 19, 4 (October 1898): 628–58; and *Degeneracy: Its Causes, Signs and Results* (London: Walter Scott Publishing Co. 1909).

25. Woods Hutchinson, "The Republic of the Body," *Living Age* 2682, 7th ser., 3 (13 May 1899): 437–44.

26. Woods Hutchinson, "Are There Evidences of Race Degeneration in the United States?" *Maritime Medical News* 21, 6 (June 1909): 246–47. This paper was first presented to the American Academy of Social and Political Science, 16 April 1909.

27. Mark Dyerson, "The Moral Equivalent of War: American Ideas of Sport, the State, and National Vitality, 1880–1920," unpublished paper presented to North American Society of Sport History conference, Albuquerque, NM, June 1993.

28. Robert A. Nye, *Crime, Madness, and Politics in Modern France: The Medical Concept of National Decline* (Princeton, NJ: Princeton University Press 1984), 319.

29. John Nautright, "Sport and the Image of Colonial Manhood in the British Mind: British Physical Deterioration Debates and Colonial Sporting Tours, 1878–1906," *Canadian Journal of History of Sport* 22, 2 (December 1992): 54–71.

30. "Moral Degeneration," *Canada Lancet*, December 1895: 134–35.

31. William Bayard, "The Influence of the Mind on the Body," presidential address to the Canadian Medical Association, *Maritime Medical News* 6, 9 (September 1894).

32. "Physical Education," CMA *Journal* 1, 3 (March 1911): 265–66.

33. A.B. Atherton, "Presidential Address to the Maritime Medical Association," *Maritime Medical News* 19, 8 (August 1907): 292–96.

34. P.C. Murphy, "President's Address to the Maritime Medical Association," *Maritime Medical News* 21, 9 (September 1909): 345–48.

35. Charles Rosenberg notes that the notion that character, disease, and temperament were inherited, and that the individual inherited a constitutional tendency or diathesis, were commonplace ideas throughout the nineteenth century (*No Other Gods: On Science and American Social Thought* [Baltimore: Johns Hopkins

University Press 1976]). Until the 1840s, however, these ideas were only rarely used in the rationalization of social problems. Between the 1840s and 1870s, hereditarianism was accompanied by an optimistic confidence that man's most fundamental attributes could be moulded by individual self-control. This was the assumption of health reformers who emphasized the development of the healthful constitution. After 1870 hereditarianism became increasingly entwined with deterministic notions of degeneration, leading to the growing popularity of eugenicist arguments for sterilization and racial "upbreeding." At the same time, however, most hereditarians also argued for a reform of the urban environment in order to counter physical degeneracy and social weaknesses. In this struggle against national debility and decline, sport played a decisive role, encouraging a more robust manhood and national virility.

36. Saint John *City News*, 15 February 1938.

37. Sydney *Record*, 26 September 1911.

38. "A Sermon by the Rev. Geo. F. Degen of Nashville, Tenn. America's Need of Wholesome Recreation Supplied by Baseball," *Sporting News*, 16 June 1894.

39. Saint John *Progress*, 11 August 1888.

40. Norman Vance, *The Sinews of the Spirit: The Ideal of Christian Manliness in Victorian Literature and Religious Thought* (Cambridge: Cambridge University Press 1985), 6.

41. Although Kingsley and Hughes may have agreed with the sentiment expressed in American evangelist and former baseball player Billy Sunday's depiction of Christ as no "dough-faced lick spittle proposition," but rather "the greatest scrapper that ever lived," they would no doubt have been uncomfortable with his ungentlemanly rhetoric. Sunday attacked not only gentle pietistic approaches to Christianity, but the whole framework of institutionalized Protestantism. "Lord save us

from the off-handed, flabby cheeked, brittle boned, weak-kneed, thin-skinned, pliable, plastic, spineless, effeminate, ossified three-karat Christianity," he declared. Quoted in Michael S. Kimmel, "Baseball and the Reconstruction of American Masculinity, 1880–1920," in Alvin L. Hall, ed., *Cooperstown Symposium on Baseball and the American Culture* (1989) (Westport, Conn.: Meckler Publishing, in association with the State University of New York College at Oneonta, 1991): 285.

42. Theodore Roosevelt, "The Value of Athletic Training," *Harper's Weekly* 37 (December 1893): 156; quoted in Steven Riess, "Sport and the Redefinition of American Middle-Class Masculinity," *International Journal of the History of Sport* 8, 1 (1991), 17.

43. Quoted in Kimmel, "Baseball and the Reconstruction of American Masculinity," 286.

44. Herbert Hensdale and Tony London, eds., *Frank Merriwell's "Father": An Autobiography of Gilbert Patten* (Norman: University of Oklahoma Press 1964), 178.

45. John Levi Cutler, "Gilbert Patten and His Frank Merriwell Saga," *University of Maine Studies*, 2nd ser., no. 31, vol. 36, 10 (May 1934): 43, 86–87; quote from p. 43.

46. Quoted in Cutler, "Gilbert Patten," 87.

47. This motif can also be found in many subsequent imitators. See, for example, Robert Sherwin's sport series, which included *Strike Him Out* (Chicago: Goldsmith Publishing Co. 1931). The publisher's preface noted that Sherman's "heroes are the finest examples of sturdy American youth, lovers of sport and sportsmanship without being, in any sense of the word, 'sissies.'" Other titles in the series were *Under the Basket; It's a Pass; Interference; Down the Ice; Over the Line;* and *The Tennis Terror.*

48. Riess, "Sport and the Redefinition of American Middle-Class Masculinity." The *Bangor Commercial* of 8 July 1903

was critical of the college students' veneration of strenuousity. Most college men, it argued, care little for "artistic music, for painting or sculpture, for poetry or the higher forms of drama. . . . They know nothing of poetry and deride those who do. . . . They are all football enthusiasts and they know baseball and rowing. The spirit of college athletics is strong among them and they burn with the flame of the strenuous life."

49. Charlottetown *Patriot*, 21 March 1903.

50. Robin Winks, an Introduction to Ralph Connor, *The Sky Pilot* (Lexington: University of Kentucky Press 1970), 3.

51. Quoted in John English, *Shadow of Heaven: The Life of Lester Pearson. Volume One: 1897–1948* (Toronto: Lester & Orpen Dennys 1989), 10.

52. Ibid.

53. *Presbyterian Witness*, "Hustling Boys," 8 December 1900: 387, col. 2; "The Boy Who Didn't Care," 6 April 1901: 110, col. 5; "A Young Man and His Companions," 27 September 1902: 310, col. 4; "Smoking," 28 May 1904: 32, col. 3; "The Claims of the Ministry on Strong Men," 10 August 1907: 254, col. 2–3; "The Whole Man," 24 August 1907: 265, col. 4; "The Boy Who Takes Pride in His Work," 26 October 1907: 339, col. 3; "What is Drink," 13 June 1908: 187, col. 3; "A Young Man's Religion," 22 January 1910: 8, col. 4.

54. *Church Work* (Halifax), 22 September 1910.

55. See, for example, "Young Men's Leagues for Small Towns," *Amherst Daily News*, 4 September 1902. The Young Men's League in Amherst was open to boys from ten to sixteen from 3:30 to 5:30 p.m., and later to young men over sixteen years of age. "The reading room is filled with young men enjoying the new magazines and games," the newspaper reported. "The gymnasium has provided the needed outlet for youthful energies. The young men who had been spending many hours in saloons or pool rooms are now found daily in the quarters of the League."

56. J. Castell Hopkins, "Youthful Canada and the Boy's Brigade," *Canadian Magazine* 4, 6 (1905): 551–56.

57. "The Boy's Brigade," *Presbyterian Witness*, 11 August 1894; 215, col. 1.

58. David I. Macleod, *Building Character in the American Boy: The Boy Scouts, YMCA, and Their Forerunners, 1870–1920* (Wisconsin: University of Wisconsin Press 1983), 35.

59. Robert H. MacDonald, *Sons of the Empire: The Frontier and the Boy Scout Movement, 1890–1918* (Toronto: University of Toronto Press 1993), 163.

60. John Springhall, "Building Character in the British Boy: The Attempt to Extend Christian Manliness to Working-Class Adolescents, 1880–1914," in Mangan and Walvin, eds., *Manliness and Morality*, 60.

61. Harvey J. Graff, "Remaking Growing Up: Nineteenth Century America," *Histoire Sociale/Social History* 24, 47 (May 1991): 35–59.

62. *Amherst Daily News*, 4 September 1902.

63. William J. Baker, "Disputed Diamonds: The YMCA Debate over Baseball in the Late 19th Century," *Journal of Sport History* 19, 3 (Winter 1992): 257–62.

64. Rina Gangemi Spano, "The Social Transformation of Children's Play and Organized Activities, 1880–1990," Ph.D. dissertation, City University of New York, 1991: 121.

65. Bangor *Daily Commercial*, 9 July 1908.

66. Amherst *Daily News*, 2 August 1905.

67. *Acadian Recorder*, 3 June 1878.

68. W. Goldstein, *Playing for Keeps* (Ithaca and London: Cornell University Press 1989), 50.

69. See in particular Gail Bederman, "Civilization, the Decline of Middle-Class Manliness, and Ida B. Wells's Anti-Lynching Campaign (1892–94),"

in Barbara Melosh, ed., *Gender and American History since 1890* (Routledge: London and New York 1993), 207–39.

70. See, for example, "Bane of Baseball. Lushing Has Done the National Game a Great Deal of Harm," *Sporting News*, 8 February 1896.

71. Ibid., 28 March 1898.

72. Ibid., 12 October 1895.

73. Quoted in Benjamin G. Rader, *American Sports: From the Age of Folk Games to the Age of Spectators* (Englewood Cliffs: NJ: Prentice-Hall 1983), 121.

74. *Sporting News*, 18 July 1895.

75. Ibid.

76. *Bangor Commercial*, 11 July 1907.

77. Portland *Eastern Argus*, 18 May 1893. In Fall River the electric railway gave $350 in cash, in Brockton, free use of the grounds, in Dover, free grounds, a groundskeeper, and $300 in cash, in Salem $250 in cash, and in Lewiston "a handsome sum" was presented to the club.

78. Quoted in Lee Lowenfish and Tony Lupien, *The Imperfect Diamond: The Story of Baseball's Reserve System and the Men Who Fought to Change It* (New York: Stein & Day 1980), 31.

79. Ibid., 30.

80. Joy Parr, *The Gender of Breadwinners: Women, Men and Change in Two Industrial Towns* (Toronto: University of Toronto Press 1990), 142.

81. Ibid.

82. Keith McClelland, "Masculinity and the Representative Artisan in Britain, 1850–80," in Roper and Tosh, eds., *Manful Assertions*, 77; and Steven Maynard, "The Social Construction of Masculinity in Working Class History," *Labour/Le Travail* 23 (Spring 1989): 159–77.

83. *Sporting Life*, 9 August 1890.

84. *Sporting News*, 11 August 1900.

85. New York *Clipper*, 22 April 1876.

MASCULINITY, FRATERNITY, AND RESPECTABILITY IN HALIFAX AT THE TURN OF THE TWENTIETH CENTURY[◊]

JUDITH FINGARD

o

In common with other North American urban and semi-urban centres of the late nineteenth century, Halifax witnessed the rapid growth of male fraternal orders, mutual benefit societies, and specialized clubs, most of which were inspired by specific interests or were affiliated branches of national or international organizations. They ranged from the highly ritualistic to the relaxed and sociable.[1] They included Union Lodge No. 18, an all-black affiliate of the Grand Lodge of Ancient Free and Accepted Masons of Nova Scotia, and the Royal British Veterans' Society (RBVS), a free-standing association patronized by high-ranking military and militia officers.[2] The members of Union Lodge enjoyed masonic mystic brotherhood while the members of the RBVS basked in the military cult of manliness. At the same time, however, these fraternities were made up of two visible minority groups: men of "colour," who were of African extraction, and military veterans, who were often scarred and crippled.

An examination of these organizations enables us to appreciate why fraternal life contributed to the collective self-worth of men on the margins of society. Association helped to provide a sense of place for men who lived in hostile or unfamiliar environments. By belonging to all-male organizations that had recognized status in the community, members furthered their quest for respectability and defined their masculinity. Those attracted by the organizations's package of benefits achieved a degree of security unavailable elsewhere. For men who were in danger of being associated

◊ This article has not been previously published.

with the disparaging popular images of the happy-go-lucky "coon" of the music hall and police court, or the drunken, debauched, riotous servicemen in the streets and bar-rooms, identification with a fraternal organization established their good reputation.[3] Even if such societies tended to reinforce racial segregation and social hierarchy, they still promoted an invaluable form of legitimate fellowship for their members. This essay outlines the major features of the black lodge and the veterans' association, analyzes key membership elements in each, and explores the themes of masculinity, fraternity, and respectability in the lives of Union's lodge masters and RBVS's Crimean veterans.

The black masonic lodge was the older of the two groups, having been organized in 1856 and chartered in 1866 by the Grand Lodge of England as No. 693. It was included in the masonic merger that replaced English jurisdiction with a provincial grand lodge in 1869 when it was assigned No. 18. It survived until 1916.[4] Union Lodge attracted a cross-section of the city's black leadership, although it by no means appealed to all prominent blacks. Men of colour appear not to have been admitted to other lodges despite considerable interaction with whites at the level of the Provincial Grand Lodge of Nova Scotia. There blacks frequently served as officers, filling such positions as grand pursuivant (doorkeeper), grand steward, grand sword bearer, and grand organist. Within the Halifax district, they acted as trustees of the Freemasons' Hall.[5] This experience contrasts sharply with the American situation in which lodges of black freemasons were not recognized by the Grand Lodges.[6]

The Royal British Veterans' Society was established in 1884 and incorporated in 1899.[7] It lasted into the 1920s. Although its membership was open to any British or Canadian military veteran, a number of other veterans' organizations emerged that related to specific campaigns—most notably the Fenian Raid Veterans and the North West Rebellion Veterans' Club. The activities of these various groups challenge the recent assertion that veterans' organizations "barely existed" before the First World War.[8]

Union Lodge and the RBVS shared some characteristics but also had their differences. As a secret society, Union Lodge was far more exclusive than the Vets in its admission criteria, despite the fact that the Vets obviously had an occupational requirement for membership. Provincial Grand Lodge officials noted with approval in 1872 that Union Lodge was the most selective freemasons' lodge in Halifax, judging by the number of applicants who were rejected. Both organizations operated on the basis of fees, the collection of which seems to have been haphazard and led to Union Lodge's periodic purges of members for being in arrears.[9] In some respects, Union was a parody of a lodge. Its meetings were confined to the obligatory ones and were often short and poorly attended.[10] Although the three basic degrees of freemasonry were conferred, it seems unlikely that the elaborate masonic rituals were very closely observed except at funerals. In contrast to veterans' organizations in the United States, the Vets largely ignored initiatory and other rituals. Instead, they concentrated on organizing their meetings around song and verse, feasting, socials (including card playing) and annual events such as the New Year's Day "at home." The funeral of a member occasioned a special ritual for both the Vets and the Union, but the RBVS tended to place greater emphasis on collective funeral rites in the form of remembrance-type anniversaries to recognize the fallen of Britain's wars. The 9th of September, known as Sevastopol Day, was celebrated with ceremonial observances at the Welsford-Parker Monument in St Paul's Cemetery and, after the Boer War, Paardeberg Day was marked on 27 February at the soldiers' monument in the Public Gardens.[11]

A brief overview of the membership of the two fraternities allows us to explore their race and class dimensions.[12] In the case of Union Lodge, the analysis focuses on the thirty-two "Worshipful Masters" between 1856 and 1916. We have data on their origins, religious affiliation, marital status, and occupations. Eighteen were born in Nova Scotia, ten came from the Caribbean, one was Australian, and the birthplaces of three are unknown. Fourteen Baptists, ten Methodists, and seven Anglicans can be identified—the religion of one individual is unknown. Most of the men were married. Five of the long-lived masons were married to their wives for close to fifty years, but domestic relations varied considerably. For all of them, the marriage market was a local one, and the masters who had immigrated to the province wed Nova Scotia women, if they married.

As a group, the lodge masters pursued a range of jobs, and individuals often had to resort to occupational pluralism or job changes in order to maintain a decent existence. In broad terms, thirteen can be described as small proprietors, at least for a significant portion of their working lives. Six of the proprietors were artisans, three of them involved in the same fur and cap business as partners. Six men either came to their business pursuits from, supplemented them with, or left them for, the common black occupations of seafaring or railway portering. Five others had professional training and certification, one of whom had qualifications in the three fields of education, theology, and medicine. In addition, three were tradesmen—one a cooper and two barbers—but they do not seem to have owned businesses. The remaining eleven were wage-earners in service, clerical, and trucking occupations.

Thirty-two Crimean veterans have been identified among late nineteenth-century Halifax residents, many of whom assumed leading roles in the RBVS especially as vice-presidents, at least until after the Boer War. They formed a far more homogeneous group than the black freemasons in terms of their background and post-service occupations. All the Crimean veterans were natives of the British Isles. Many of them came to Halifax in 1856 with their regiments fresh from the war. The 62nd and 63rd regiments of foot figured prominently and accounted for at least half of the men in this sample. Both regiments served a tour of duty for over five and a half years during which many men secured their discharges and settled in Halifax and elsewhere. Four others were naval veterans who had been active in the Baltic theatre of the war with Russia. Artillerymen were also well represented. For some of the servicemen, the Crimean War had followed years of duty in garrisons and on the battlefield. Private Daniel Wilson of the 11th Hussars, for example, had enlisted in the army in 1840 at the age of eleven.[13] A few other veterans settled in the area with their families as immigrants some time after leaving the service in Britain or Canada. Others returned to Halifax with their Nova Scotia-born wives after further service elsewhere in the empire.[14]

Most of the veterans married, although, like the freemasons, a few bachelors joined the society. The majority were members of the Church of England, but their wives were often of a different persuasion. We know about the birthplaces of twenty of the wives: fifteen were born in Nova Scotia and may therefore have encouraged these servicemen to become permanent residents of the garrison-port of Halifax. The popularity of British soldiers as marriage partners for the servant girls of Halifax was well documented in the nineteenth century. The other wives were either "on the strength," that is, part of the local military complement with rations for themselves and their children, or came out from Britain after their husband's discharge.[15]

When the servicemen took their discharges, some qualified for small pensions, but very few of the thirty-two could afford to retire from waged employment. Most continued to work until they became permanently disabled or died. Their jobs as civilians were clustered at the bottom of the unskilled labour market, although they had an advantage when it came to securing jobs in military establishments. One man was caretaker of the military cemetery, two others were janitors—one in the brigade office, the other in general headquarters office. Custodial and messenger work was common, accounting for the known employment of nine men, including two church sextons. Working with horses was an appropriate form of employment for men used to riding and caring for military horses. Four veterans were described as truckmen, teamsters or expressmen: these occupations involved proprietorship in two other cases. Three men had positions in issuing, clerking, and bookkeeping. Two others held personal service jobs as butlers and coachmen, and another four returned to their probable rural origins as farmers, gardeners and milkmen. Of the remaining five, two were labourers. With such modest occupations, it is not surprising that their former military status assumed an important role in the maintenance of their self-esteem.

Accounts of the meetings and other activities of the two organizations, derived largely from the daily press, provide insight into their attitudinal and ideological underpinnings. The Royal British Veterans' Society and the freemasons defined their masculine identity and fraternity through an exclusive male membership that reflected the prevalent notion of separate spheres. Within the masculine context, their interests often turned on deeds of valour and heroism. The Vets spent much of their meeting time and special events reliving the taking of Sevastopol and the charge of the Light Brigade at Balaklava. These collective experiences, collectively recalled, amounted to group therapy for men who may have been psychologically damaged by combat. They recounted "thrilling" incidents in recitation, story, and song. They also vividly described their gallantry to the wider public. Daniel O'Connell O'Leary, a former sergeant in the 63rd Regiment, supplemented his military pension with "character" entertainments. Dressed one fine September 1892 evening in "the same glorious old, bloody and tattered suit that he had worn at Inkerman, Alma, and many other famous battles," and armed with "his good and trusty—but now, alas, very rusty—sword, with which he had fought his way up the heights of Alma," he "gave his delighted hearers graphic word pictures of the way he had FINISHED many a Russian who had presumed to bar his way up those glorious heights."[16]

The veterans were not, however, unremitting hawks by any means. They liked to recall their fraternization with the Russian soldiers between engagements, during which they played games and placed bets on the outcome of the war.[17] They also displayed sensitivity and sentimentality. It was considered perfectly natural for Aaron Tozer, who had something of a monopoly on the ritual reciting of Tennyson's "Charge of the Light Brigade," to be overcome with emotion when in 1908 he used the celebrated poem to describe an event in which he had participated as a sergeant in the Royal Artillery. Indeed his audience cheered him.[18] Notions of appropriate behaviour for men clearly depended on their age and the nature of their company. Tozer was eighty years old and, as an elderly veteran, he could openly express the feelings that for young men would normally be considered a sign of weakness—the very opposite of manliness. While Tozer's lapse occurred in front of an assembly of men and women, Arthur Wyatt was in the exclusive company of military men, including the commander-in-chief of the serving forces, when tears rolled down his cheeks during a celebration in the Halifax Citadel in 1900 marking Florence Nightingale's eightieth birthday. The seventy-one-year-old recalled for his listeners his experience as a patient of Nightingale in the hospital at Balaklava: "She was not a woman, . . . but an angel, visiting us at all hours as early as four o'clock in the morning, and administering to our comforts, when the doctors and many of their assistants were asleep, and I thank God that other women have been sent into the world to perform such good work."[19] The response produced by this nostalgic old gentleman, with his fond memories of female essentialism, was an embarrassed hush.[20]

The expression of manliness by freemasons was less specifically focused because of their diverse employment patterns, but they relished medals almost as much as the veterans did. The seafaring background, including Royal Naval service, of a large proportion of the total membership of Union Lodge meant that shipboard heroism was a cherished trait. In the commemorative reminiscences of the first fifty years of Union Lodge (published in 1906), the longest passage consists of an account of the rescue at sea of the master of a derelict vessel by one of Union's members. The chronicler was Peter McKerrow, one of the most prominent Halifax blacks and lodge master in 1872-74, who had arrived in Halifax in the mid-1850s as a seafarer from Antigua. He implied that the stature of the black mariner, recalled in the reminiscences, was further enhanced by his successful defiance of his white shipmaster in this daring exploit, as well as by the subsequent presentation of a medal from the American government in recognition of his heroism.[21]

Masculinity for both groups was very much tied up with concepts of empire and the rights of British subjects. African-Canadian freemasons, many of whom came from the Caribbean or traced their lineage through their white blood back to the British Isles, believed that they had social equality with the majority before the law of England and the dominions. This stood in sharp contrast to what they discerned as racial discrimination in the American states. They were therefore proud and keen advocates of frequent displays of loyalty to Britain. Shortly after he became master of the lodge in 1897, James Jackson appeared before Halifax city council to request permission to travel to London to act as the standard bearer of the Nova Scotia flag in the diamond jubilee procession. He claimed that he was motivated "by a desire to do honor to my queen and country, as a citizen and a British and loyal subject," as well as by "a desire to do honor to this city and credit to myself."[22] Ten years later, McKerrow wrote to his brother masons in Union Lodge that each of them

> should bend the knee in devout thankfulness and gratitude to Almighty God for his lot in having been cast in so favoured a land and under so pure and free a government with such a ruler as King Edward, our brother, under the waving of whose flag his subjects can feel themselves secure from the attack of all malicious intruders, when they themselves are law-abiding citizens.[23]

Hyperbole aside, an inclusive concept of male citizenship was crucial to black Nova Scotians' sense of self-worth.

For their part, the Vets were motivated by a patriotism that put the concerns of the British Empire first, and they avidly supported the British cause in the Boer War. In September 1900, Isaac Sallis made a speech in which he claimed:

> old Kruger had done a great act to Britain when he declared against England, and appealed to the God of battles. The message was sent to the colonies to rally about the old flag, and the response was prompt. The shedding of blood was a necessity, but British arms had come out victorious, and the empire as a consequence is greater today than it had been. It was immaterial where the Britisher resided, he was a Briton always.[24]

Given their imperial allegiances, the Vets were also in the forefront when it came to acting as a guard of honour for visiting regal and vice-regal dignitaries such as two royal princes between 1905 and 1906, and the governor-general in 1907.[25]

Fraternal masculinity was exercised in a male space, which excluded female kin. While there is no reason to believe that men who belonged to fraternal organizations had more marital problems than those who did not, male organizations enabled husbands to spend leisure time away from their wives and from the domestic turmoil that periodically characterized their married lives. Some ex-servicemen and black men had wives assertive enough to complain to the authorities about the quality of their husband's performance of their marital obligations.[26] By the 1880s, wives could turn to the Society for the Prevention of Cruelty (SPC) for aid in negotiating better support, marital separations, or improved relationships. As a result, Annie

Knight, separated wife of freemason James, succeeded in extracting funds from her estranged husband in order to discharge her debts. Ezella French and Nancy Skinner were less successful because their freemason husbands resisted their claims. John L. French denied that he had turned his wife out of the house. He had his lawyer write a letter that convinced the SPC agent that Ezella needed to try harder at making the relationship work. In 1885, Demus Skinner's wife, Nancy, charged him with physical abuse as well as neglect of his eight young children. When he responded by charging Nancy with drunkenness and neglecting her family, the SPC left them to patch up their differences.[27] Wives were not the only female influences in the lives of club men. Given their advanced years, the Vets may have felt more of a threat from their daughters than from their wives. Both Vets and freemasons were often cared for in their old age by their daughters. Not only did this tend to result in a loss of dignity, but it also signalled their displacement as head of household by the son-in-law. When women's domestic power in the private sphere usurped the primacy of male authority, the all-male environment of the masonic hall and veterans' rooms provided an escape from the challenges to traditional gender roles at home.

Homosocial relations formed a vital part of the experience of most men long before they joined voluntary male organizations. Both battalion and ship were exclusively male work spaces for servicemen; the occupations of the black leadership often existed in a male work world even when they were engaged in "women's work" as cooks and servants.[28] It was only one step further to carry the gender bonding into their leisure time. The camaraderie they enjoyed revolved around monthly meetings in which the language of brotherhood predominated; indeed the prefix "Brother" was part of the jargon of both freemasons and veterans. On these occasions new members were added, degrees of craft bestowed in the masonic lodge, and fellowship expressed in music and song.

Members also distributed funds at their meetings. The major evidence of brotherly mutual support took the form of benefits relating to sickness and funerals. The Vets contributed the standard amount of thirty dollars in 1908 to help cover the cost of the funeral of many-time vice-president John Thornton. Both Union Lodge and the Grand Lodge helped Clifford Ward after he became ill in 1913. Union paid the expenses of $47.50 for his funeral the following year.[29] The original intent of the RBVS had been broader than the disbursement of benefits. Well aware of the difficult transition to civilian life experienced by military men, the leadership in the 1880s had envisaged an organization that functioned in part as an employment agency. Their model was the corps of commissioners inaugurated in Britain several decades earlier.[30] This initial priority appears not to have been sustained, perhaps because jobs, albeit subsistence ones, were readily available to men with military connections in a military city. Instead, the preoccupation with funeral rites reigned. In 1902, William Blackman, who had served in the 1890s as treasurer and vice-president, was buried

> with fitting honors. . . . The muffled sound of drum and music added more solemnity to the scene as the cortege proceeded to the cemetery. . . . The body was drawn on a gun carriage and there was

a firing party from the 1st C.A. [Canadian Artillery]. Two bands attended. . . . There was a full attendance of the Royal British Veterans Society and the pall bearers were non-coms from the 63rd, 1st C.A. and R.B.V's.[31]

Participation in funerals also formed a major activity of Union Lodge. The obituaries of past masters such as Joseph Flint, Peter McKerrow, and Clifford Ward noted that the masonic ceremony was used in the conduct of the funeral rites.[32] We do not have a description specific to the black freemasons, but the entry in Kate Shannon's diary of 1892 relating to the masonic funeral of a man who belonged to one of the elite higher degrees of freemasonry captures the flavour of the ritual and adds a derisive female perspective. "We saw the chief features," she wrote, "some aproned and otherwise decorated creatures among them six or eight dressed in long white cloaks with red crosses on the side and crusaders' caps. They were Knights Templers [sic] I suppose and they did look funny."[33]

Like most conservative, god-fearing, law-abiding men of the period, the brethren of these organizations stood for respectability. For black people, respectability in this period was very closely tied to gaining and maintaining acceptance in the white community. They abhorred unfavourable treatment. They aimed at equal status in keeping with the masonic belief in "the equality of moral men."[34] Accordingly, the lodge masters assumed leadership roles in the struggle for school de-segregation and called for recognition of their civil rights as taxpayers.[35] They also valued formal participation with whites in religious events and secular celebrations. Limited though their success was, their occasional achievements represented a political statement against the "colour line." The lodge masters were not willing to endure racial insults. In 1891, the then master, the Reverend A.W. Jordon, prosecuted an Amherst restaurant proprietor who had refused to serve him during a visit to that town.[36] The maintenance of a segregated freemasons' lodge may have compromised the members' aims to some extent but, as pragmatists, most black leaders preferred to condone separate development if it did not involve inferior status. Freemasonry seemed to offer this opportunity. When the city's lodges participated in a procession to St Paul's church in 1878, for example, Union Lodge was not relegated to the end of the parade: it marched second in the line of twelve lodges.[37] But Union's ambivalent status also meant that black Halifax freemasons often had to cooperate with racists. In the 1880s, the influential grand secretary of the Provincial Grand Lodge was Benjamin Curren, supervisor of Halifax public schools and the leading exponent of the separate racial schooling so detested by blacks.

For their part, the Royal British Veterans received very favourable press in Halifax, in spite of the frequently disparaging comments about serving soldiers and sailors, and the reported instances of misbehaviour and crime among enlisted men. Old soldiers were associated with the glories of the past rather than the problems of the present, and their own former misdeeds were forgotten.[38] The Vets' status secured legitimization in several ways. Through the patronage of the governor-general, Lord Lansdowne, they obtained the rare privilege of carrying the Royal Standard in 1898. In 1900 the Vets received civic recognition when the Halifax city council voted to provide $100 to help them to entertain visiting members of the British Naval and Military Association of Boston. In 1906 the RBVS came second in the *Evening Mail*'s contest for identifying the most popular voluntary organization in Halifax-Dartmouth.[39] Moreover, the veterans' frequent orderly processions of men neatly dressed in dark clothing, white ties and gloves, medals, sashes, and badges, accompanied by martial music, contributed to the respectable side of street life.[40]

Nonetheless, both the Vets and Union Lodge had to grapple with some difficult issues as they forged their identity as pillars of respectability. Poverty and old age, as well as drink, were paramount concerns. With little opportunity to acquire savings for old age, the Vets could find themselves in deplorable living conditions. In 1896, Daniel O'Connell O'Leary died "in a miserable hovel" and when his body was found it had been partially eaten by rats.[41] Two years later, Patrick Early, who had been crippled in the Crimean War, and his wife perished in a fire in a tenement house on Grafton Street. A newspaper reporter who visited the small third-floor room in which they lived and died described it as "a veritable death-trap."[42]

Both Vets and Union Lodge freemasons were known to finish their days in the poor house, the resort of poverty-stricken old men, both sane and senile. Former lodge master James Jackson, one of the city's eccentric characters, who was dubbed "General Jackson" by the white press, died of Bright's disease in the poor house in 1915 after two years as an inmate.[43] One RBVS inmate of the poor house was John "Tiger" Hill, "a good old soldier with his breast covered with medals and face scarred by years of hard service under the burning suns of India, and the frozen heights of the Crimea." In his old age as caretaker of Fort Massey Cemetery he became senile and was committed to the poor house by his wife. When he died in 1906 at the age of eighty, the press was more concerned with the quality of his funeral and the care of his grave than with his final lonely months in an institution.[44] A few years later, however, the fate of another old soldier in the poor house, Albert Kerville, was avidly taken up by R.H. Murray, secretary of the SPC. Employed in Halifax as an Anglican church sexton, Kerville's removal to the poor house on 30 November 1912 occurred after he fell down a flight of stairs in the boarding house where he had lived since his wife's death, and sustained injuries that forced him to retire from his job. Murray was outraged that Kerville had been incarcerated in the insane ward of the institution with forty-eight other men on account of his slight, early symptoms of dementia. He took the RBVS to task for their failure to do something for the old Crimean veteran's welfare. Murray's protests seem to have been in vain: at the time of Kerville's death five years later, he was still an inmate of the poor house.[45]

The shift to a concern with the quality of life from a preoccupation with the celebration of death occurred in the Grand Lodge of Nova Scotia in the first decade of the century. By this time, all the affiliated lodges were working towards the common goal of establishing a home for aged freemasons, their wives, or widows. Union Lodge entered into this campaign with

enthusiasm and contributed a booth in the form of "a handsomely decorated cabin" based on a Caribbean theme to the Masonic fair in 1906 to raise
funds for the project.[46] In 1911, Thomas Arthur, a widower of sixty, applied
for admission to the Nova Scotia Freemasons' Home at Windsor. Although
no record of Arthur's application has survived in the masonic papers, the
fact that two years later he returned permanently to Barbados, the island of
his birth, suggests that his colour may have blocked his admission to the
home.[47] There was a tinge of hypocrisy to white Nova Scotians' sanctimo-
niousness when they boasted about their rejection of the colour line.

While poverty in old age might have been unavoidable for many blacks
and immigrants, excessive drinking or involvement in the liquor trade were
likely to tarnish their good names. Both fraternal organizations reached
their zenith in the period when the forces of temperance, maternal feminism, and urban reform combined against the sale and consumption of
alcohol. Members of all churches were prominent in this campaign, and the
clear message, reinforced by the press and the liquor licence inspector's
raids, was that respectable folk abstained from alcohol. By the 1880s, many
masters of Union Lodge observed this moral code both as freemasons and
as temperance workers, especially in black lodges of the Independent Order
of Good Templars, but observance was not universal. Three black freemasons were fined between 1907 and 1909[48] after attempting to offer liquor for
sale in three private clubs that they managed. Arguably, Union Lodge's dissolution in 1916 proceeded in part from the circumstances surrounding the
murder of James R. Johnston, a past master and the undisputed leader of
the black community. He was killed by his brother-in-law, Harry Allen,
who had been residing with the Johnstons. Allen was clearly a heavy
drinker and a "n'er-do-well"—indeed the very antithesis of the upright,
moral Nova Scotian.[49]

The Vets did a great deal to improve the popular image of the services
in respect to drink. In a period when even the military had temperance
organizations, much was made of the abstinence of some of the veterans.
The pitiful old poor-house inmate, Albert Kerville, was described by an
interviewer as being devoid of vices: "a non-smoker, a total abstainer, honest and industrious."[50] Aaron Tozer, known as a consistent and ardent temperance worker, liked to regale listeners with his moral superiority over his
social superiors: "an officer asked him to have a drink of whiskey; when he
replied that he did not drink, the officer said, 'Well, have a cigar,' to be met
with a courteous refusal, to which the officer replied, 'Tozer, you are too
good to live.'"[51] It is hard to imagine, however, that all the toasts proposed
at convivial gatherings to departed comrades, royal patrons, high-ranking
officers, the monarch, and Florence Nightingale were drunk in tea.
Certainly we know that the frequent "smokers" (convivial evenings held in
the Vets' rooms) involved liberal use of the "weed" at a time when the use
of tobacco was also under attack.[52]

The brotherhood that bound members across class and colour lines and
the camaraderie of shared experiences of a courageous past may well have
strengthened the accommodationist approach of men on the margins of
society. At the same time, fraternal association also helped them to cope in

difficult economic and social circumstances. Male association in freemasons' lodge or veterans' society provided an illusion of equality across racial and class lines sufficient to deflect attention away from the injustices and hardships black men and servicemen regularly encountered. There was something slightly sycophantic about the way the black freemasons cowtowed to the white, just as the rank and file veterans continued to honour the hierarchical control of military and naval officers. Black freemasons prided themselves on being complimented by their white brethren during the annual ceremony to install the new officers.[53] They were reassured by words such as those voiced by the Nova Scotia Grand Master at Union's AGM in 1905, as he anticipated a good year for the Lodge: "in whatever respects men may differ in creed, nationality, politics or otherwise, there is something in the mystic tie itself that binds them together."[54] Vets proudly presented ceremonial scarves and badges to their former officers and drank toasts to men who had regularly used enlisted men as cannon fodder.[55]

Such men were deluded into thinking that gradations of colour and rank were superseded by higher purposes of service to God or country. This attitude was neatly summed up by Nova Scotia's preeminent Victorian veteran, William Hall, an African Canadian. Hall had served in the British navy during the Crimean War and had won the Victoria Cross for his role in the relief of Lucknow during the Indian Mutiny in 1857. After he had retired on pension in 1876, he settled on a farm in Avonport, near his birthplace. In 1901 he visited Halifax as the guest of the Royal British Veterans' Society for the purpose of being presented to Prince George, the Duke of Cornwall, during his royal tour. One of the officer-members of the RBVS remarked to Hall that he had "the very great honor of being the only man in the procession to be presented to the Prince." Hall was nonplussed and saw nothing remarkable about the event for a man of his class and colour. Instead he responded: "Why shouldn't he ask for me, isn't he a bluejacket like me?"[56]

Hall's view that men stood together regardless of class or colour, that gender and cause were the primary bonds in the maintenance of interest groups, mirrored the outlook of both the Vets and the black freemasons. This perspective fostered attitudes that were uncritical of authority, patriotic in the extreme, and dedicated to traditional concepts of manliness. However important the fraternities might have been to the development of their members' self-worth, they were unlikely to act as agencies for social change.

NOTES

1. On Halifax see Janet Guildford, "Public School Reform and the Halifax Middle Class 1850–1870" (PhD thesis, Dalhousie University, 1990), ch. 6; for the major features of masonic lodge fellowship, Lynn Dumenil, *Freemasonry and American Culture, 1880–1930* (Princeton, 1984); for the appeal of ritual, Mark C. Carnes, *Secret Ritual and Manhood in* *Victorian America* (New Haven, 1989).

2. Information on Union Lodge is contained in the Masonic collection at the Public Archives of Nova Scotia (PANS MG 20, vols. 2000–3000) as well as in the *Proceedings* of the Grand Lodge of Nova Scotia, 1869–1916. For the use of correct masonic

terminology see W. McLeod, "Free-masonry, as a Matter of Fact," *Canadian Historical Review* 69, 1 (March 1988): 51–61.

The small PANS collection of RBVS papers relates to the post-incorporation period and it is therefore impossible to determine with certainty the membership before 1899 (PANS MG, vols. 541, 1527).

3. The newspapers carried frequent references to visiting performers such as the blacks who staged "A Trip to Coon Town," *Acadian Recorder* (Halifax), 4 Sept. 1902, and the "Hottest Coon in Dixie," *Acadian Recorder*, 9 Aug. 1907. For the behaviour of the military see J. Fingard, "Beyond the Barracks: The Social Context of Army Life in Victorian Halifax," unpublished W.S. MacNutt Memorial Lecture, 1984, and for black and military members of the underclass, *The Dark Side of Life in Victorian Halifax* (Halifax, 1989).

4. R.L. Reid to R.V. Harris, 5 April 1943, Harris to Reid, 13 April 1943, PANS, MG 20, vol. 2130, No. 34. The membership of master masons in Union Lodge averaged over 40 between 1885 and 1907. See *Proceedings* of the Grand Lodge of Nova Scotia.

5. *Proceedings* of the Grand Lodge of Nova Scotia.

6. See Dumenil, *Freemasonry and American Culture 1880–1930*, 9–10; William A. Muraskin, *Middle-Class Blacks in a White Society: Prince Hall Freemasonry in America* (Berkeley, 1975); Loretta J. Williams, *Black Freemasonry and Middle-Class Realities* (Columbia, MO, 1980).

7. See *Morning Chronicle* (Halifax), 1 Sept. 1884. The entrance fee was 50 cents, dues per month 25 cents, and the benefits after membership of 6 months at a rate of $3 per week minimum. In 1884 the membership was reported to be 64 (*Morning Herald* [Halifax], 6 Nov. 1884) and in 1886 about 150 (*Morning Chronicle*, 2 Sept. 1886). At least 18 of the 32 veterans included here were active members.

8. Desmond Morton and Glenn Wright, *Winning the Second Battle: Canadian Veterans and the Return to Civilian Life, 1915–1930* (Toronto, 1987), 13. On Fenian Raid Veterans, see *Acadian Recorder*, 20 Jan. 1910, 19 Sept. 1911, 10 Sept. 1914; on North West Rebellion Veterans, *Acadian Recorder*, 14 June 1890, 12 April 1905, 12 April 1913. In 1903 a veterans' federation of all the British veterans' societies of North America was proposed. *Acadian Recorder*, 7 July 1903.

9. *Proceedings* of the Grand Lodge of Nova Scotia, 1872.

10. *Proceedings* of the Grand Lodge of Nova Scotia, 1903, 1904.

11. *Act of Incorporation, Constitution, By-Laws, &c. of the Royal British Veterans' Society of Nova Scotia* (Halifax, 1906), PANS, MG 20, vol. 1527, No. 12.

12. The sources used to compile biographical information on the masons and veterans include the *Acadian Recorder*, 1890–1915, decennial federal census schedules, annual city directories, marriage bonds, licences and registers.

13. *Morning Herald*, 21 Jan. 1889. On the 1854–56 war between Britain and its allies and Russia, which emphasizes the importance of the Baltic as opposed to the better known Crimean theatre, see Andrew D. Lambert, *The Crimean War: British Grand Strategy, 1853–56* (Manchester, 1990).

14. John Hill (4th Regiment) and his Scottish-born wife arrived in Canada in 1880. Canada, *1901 Manuscript Census*, Halifax ward 1/5, p. 25, line 33. Agnes Bissett, a Nova Scotian who married Thomas Marsh in 1861, apparently accompanied her husband to Ireland and India before his settlement as a civilian in Halifax. Marriage Licence Files, Halifax County, 1861, PANS, Nova Scotia Registrar General of Vital Statistics, Series 1253, No. 49; Cánada, *1891 Manuscript Census*, Halifax ward 4, p. 39, line 21.

15. Fingard, "Beyond the Barracks: The Social Context of Army Life in Victorian Halifax."

16. *Acadian Recorder*, 19 Sept. 1892.

17. *Acadian Recorder*, 13 Feb. 1914.

18. *Acadian Recorder*, 20 Nov. 1908.

19. *Evening Mail* (Halifax), 25 May 1900.

20. A recent study which stresses the importance of the temporal dimensions of manhood but does not address old age is Donald J. Mrozek, "The Habit of Victory: the American Military and the Cult of Manliness" in J.A. Mangam and James Walvin, eds., *Manliness and Morality: Middle-Class Masculinity in Britain and America 1800–1940* (Manchester, 1987), 221.

21. "A Few Scattering Webs of Memory in the Semi-Centennial History of Union Lodge, No. 18, R.N.S., A.F.& A.M.," PANS, MG 20, vol. 2130, No. 34, 5–6; Judith Fingard, "Peter McKerrow," *Dictionary of Canadian Biography* 8: 656–57.

22. *Morning Chronicle*, 12 June 1897. For local celebratory events, see Bonnie L. Huskins, "Public Celebrations in Victorian Saint John and Halifax" (PhD thesis, Dalhousie University, 1991).

23. McKerrow, "A Few Scattering Webs," 2–3.

24. *Evening Mail*, 13 Sept., 24 Oct. 1900.

25. *Acadian Recorder*, 17 Oct. 1905, 21 April 1906, 31 July 1907.

26. Twenty years before the organization of the RBVS, Isaac Sallis was taken to court for abusing his wife. Fingard, *The Dark Side of Life in Victorian Halifax*, 67.

27. Knight, SPC Daily Journal, 3, 12 Sept., 8 Oct., 10, 22, 23, 29 Nov. 1888, PANS, MG 20, vol. 516, No. 8; French: 30, 31 Dec. 1887, 3 Jan. 1888, PANS, MG 20, vol. 516, No. 7; Skinner: 16, 17 Dec. 1885, PANS, MG 20, vol. 516, No. 6.

28. Judith Fingard, "Seafaring and Railroading: Black Transportation Workers and their Families in Turn of the Century Halifax," paper presented to the Atlantic Canada Studies Conference, St John's, 1992.

29. Warrant of Appraisement, John Thornton's estate, 21 Dec. 1909, Nova Scotia Court of Probate, file 6604; Union Lodge Minutes, 17 March 1913, 15 June and 21 Sept. 1914, PANS MG 20, vol. 2218.

30. *Morning Herald*, 6 Nov. 1884; Peter Howard Llewellyn Reese, "The Resettlement of the Soldier into Civilian Life, 1870–1914" (MPhil thesis, University of London, 1980).

31. *Acadian Recorder*, 20 Sept. 1902; Robert Blackman, "Bandmaster William Blackman: Soldier of the Queen," *Nova Scotia Historical Review* 11, 1 (1991): 118–28.

32. *Morning Chronicle*, 26 Dec. 1906, 9 Dec. 1911; *Acadian Recorder*, 3 July 1914.

33. Della Stanley, ed., *A Victorian Lady's Album: Kate Shannon's Halifax and Boston Diary of 1892* (Halifax, 1994), 26.

34. Dumenil, *Freemasonry and American Culture, 1880–1930*, 101.

35. Judith Fingard, "Race and Respectability in Victorian Halifax," *Journal of Imperial and Commonwealth History* 20, 2 (May 1992): 169–95.

36. *Acadian Recorder*, 31 March 1891.

37. *Acadian Recorder*, 5 June 1878.

38. For the career of Isaac Sallis see Fingard, *The Dark Side of Life in Victorian Halifax*, ch. 2 and "Isaac Sallis," *Dictionary of Canadian Biography* 8: 919–20.

39. *Acadian Recorder*, 10 Sept. 1898; *Evening Mail*, 22 Sept. 1900; *Halifax Herald*, 25 Dec. 1906.

40. *Evening Mail*, 19 May 1900.

41. *Acadian Recorder*, 26 Dec. 1896.

42. *Halifax Herald*, 23 June 1898. The name is reported incorrectly sometimes as Aurley or Hurley.

43. Entry, 27 Dec. 1915, City Home Register of Deaths, 1914–47, PANS, RG 35-102, 33A.29; *Acadian Recorder*, 28 Dec. 1915. The poor house was known as the Poor's Asylum until

1907 when the Women's Council succeeded in having it renamed as the City Home.

44. Register of city inmates in City Home, 1905–7, PANS, RG 35-102, 33A.23; *Acadian Recorder*, 1 May 1906; "Short Historical Sketch of the Royal British Veterans' Society of Nova Scotia" [c.1919], PANS, MG 20, vol. 1527, No. 11.

45. Register of city inmates in City Home, 1911–13, PANS, RG 35-102, 33A.26; Entry for 21 April 1917, Register of City Home Deaths 1914–47, PANS, RG 35-102, 33A.29; *Acadian Recorder*, 21 Dec. 1912, 23 April 1917.

46. *Acadian Recorder*, 25, 26 Sept. 1906.

47. Union Lodge Minutes, 20 Feb. 1911, PANS, MG 20, vol. 2218.

48. *Acadian Recorder*, 10 May 1907, 3, 4, 10 June, 1 Dec. 1908, 26, 28, 30 Jan., 16 Feb., 7 April, 9 Nov., 2, 22 Dec. 1909.

49. Barry Cahill, "The 'Colored Barrister': The Short Life and Tragic Death of James Robinson Johnston, 1876–1915," *Dalhousie Law Journal* 15, 2 (Fall 1992): 359.

50. *Acadian Recorder*, 21 Dec. 1912.

51. *Acadian Recorder*, 13 Feb. 1914.

52. *Acadian Recorder*, 24 Oct. 1901, *Morning Chronicle*, 3 Jan. 1907.

53. *Acadian Recorder*, 22 April 1910.

54. Union Lodge Minutes, 20 March 1905, PANS, MG 20, vol. 2218.

55. For example, *Morning Herald*, 6 Nov. 1884.

56. *Acadian Recorder*, 19, 26 Oct. 1901; Bridglai Pachai, "William Hall," *Dictionary of Canadian Biography* 8: 433–34.

section

7

AT WORK AND AROUND TOWN

○

"WE MAY ALL SOON BE 'FIRST-CLASS MEN'":[1] GENDER AND SKILL IN CANADA'S EARLY TWENTIETH CENTURY URBAN TELEGRAPH INDUSTRY[*]

SHIRLEY TILLOTSON

o

For most Canadians born since the Depression of the 1930s, telegraph operators are remembered only from Hollywood movies. Sometimes in a newsroom, more often at the train station in a one-horse western town, the operators in those movies seemed always to be wearing the old-fashioned clerk's eye-shade, and they were always men. Surprisingly, this stock movie-character is true to life (and not only in the costuming): press circuits and single-operator train stations tended to be staffed by men. But these were only two of the many different places telegraph operators were employed. In others, women predominated. And, in a rare exception to the longstanding rule of the gender-segregated working world, some large city offices employed almost equal numbers of both sexes.

The telegraph industry was based on the Morse electric telegraph, first used successfully in 1843. As this technology entered rapidly into commercial use, it began to transform human geography. By bringing remote points into instantaneous communication, the telegraph accelerated the conduct of commerce and politics, journalism and railroading. This transformation was accomplished by a fundamentally simple technology. A wire linked two sets of instruments, forming an electrical circuit. One set of instruments might be in Montreal, the other in Winnipeg, linked by a wire strung, pole by pole, across hundreds of miles. Each set of instruments had two basic parts. One was a hand-operated lever, called the "key," by which the opera-

◆ Reprinted with permission from *Labour/Le Travail* 27 (Spring 1991): 97–125.

tor opened or closed the circuit, thus sending short bursts of current through the wire. The other part was an electrically-operated lever, called the "sounder," whose movements in response to the electrical impulses sent by a distant operator's key made the clicking noises of Morse code, to be interpreted by the listening operator. This mid-19th century technology formed the economic and technical context for the early-20th century invention and use of wireless telegraphy and radio broadcasting. Land-line Morse telegraphy itself survived in military and railroad applications until the late 1950s, but in the industry's commercial branches, automated alternatives emerged in the 1910s and, after major improvements, entered into widespread use in the 1930s.

Although women were almost unheard of as railway operators, substantial numbers of them worked in commercial telegraphy. In Canada, there may have been some women operators as early as the 1860s; their employment in the main operating room of a large commercial firm was initiated c1870.[2] By the early 1900s, telegraphy was firmly established as one

TABLE 1   PERCENTAGE OF WOMEN ON THE OPERATOR STAFF OF PARTICULAR FIRMS *

Year	Total n	% of Women	Place	Firm
1911–12	693	13.41	Canada	CPR Tel.
1912–13	639	15.49	Canada	CPR Tel.
1913–14	521	14.35	Canada	CPR Tel.
1914–15	522	17.43	Canada	CPR Tel.
1915–16	566	21.38	Canada	CPR Tel.
1911–12	1596	2.7	Canada	GNW
1912–13	1632	3.2	Canada	GNW
1913–14	1494	4.8	Canada	GNW
1914–15	1903	4.3	Canada	GNW
1915–16	2073	7.3	Canada	GNW
1911–12	63	5.39	Ontario	N.A. Tel.✦
1912–13	65	30.76	Ontario	N.A. Tel.
1913–14	54	29.62	Ontario	N.A. Tel.
1914–15	54	29.62	Ontario	N.A. Tel.
1915–16	54	29.62	Ontario	N.A. Tel.

Source: Canada, House of Commons, Sessional Paper 20f (1913–1915). Government statistical reporting on Canada's telegraph labour began in 1911–1912; after 1917, no breakdown by firm was given.

✧ There is a substantial apparent difference in the proportion of women to men between the figures listed for GNW and CPR. CPR, however, lists only its urban office operators, whereas GNW lists its entire operator staff. The *Labour Gazette* (September 1916), p. 1547, gives a gender breakdown of GNW employees in which union members, more likely to be urban operators, are shown to be about 17 percent female. This figure is much closer to the CPR's approximately 20 percent female operators figure of the same year than it is to the aggregate GNW figure of 7 percent for that year. Although available data don't permit certainty in comparing the gender composition of the two companies' work forces, nonetheless, it seems likely that, in the cities, they both employed a large minority of women operators.

✦ North American Telegraph.

of the small number of skilled trades deemed suitable for women. Western Canadian offices seem consistently to have employed few women, but in the cities of central and eastern Canada, the proportion of women operators among main office staff-members was in some instances close to half. In 1902, 42 percent of operators in Great Northwestern Telegraph's Toronto main office were women, while the roster in Toronto of Canadian Pacific Railway Telegraph (not part of railway operations) was 28 percent female.[3] The distribution of women within commercial telegraphy itself was uneven, as is suggested by comparing aggregate figures (Table 1) with figures for specific firms (Table 2). With notable exceptions, women Morse operators tended to work in the lower-productivity branches of the industry. Only when the high-volume circuits were equipped with non-Morse instruments during World War I were women operators encouraged to work the "heavy wires."

But even though there was a degree of gender segregation within the telegraph workforce, women and men often performed the same tasks on the same equipment, working together at either end of the wire in a cooperative labour process. Telegraphy thus provides an unusual opportunity for a case study of links between gender and skill. Under this industry's special circumstances, one might perhaps expect that workers' experience would have eroded the common ideological equation of masculinity and skill. Women operators might have claimed successfully the wages to which skilled status entitled their male co-workers. The experience of shared work might even have allowed operators to see gender difference in new ways. Any indications of such developments would support arguments such as Cynthia Cockburn makes about how gender is constructed by the work people do as adults. Her point is that "work is a gendering process," one which shapes most, if not all, of adult life.[4] Conceivably, this should mean

TABLE 2   PERCENTAGE OF WOMEN ON THE OPERATOR STAFF IN PARTICULAR TELEGRAPH OFFICES

Year	Total n	% of Women	Place	Firm
1894	13	15.0	Halifax	Western Union
1894	20	5.0	Winnipeg	CPR Tel.
1902	28	28.5	Toronto	CPR Tel.
1902	52	42.0	Toronto	GNW
1902	19	5.0	Vancouver	CPR Tel.
1902	5	00.0	Winnipeg	GNW
1917	62	17.7	Winnipeg	CPR Tel.
1917	33	18.0◊	Winnipeg	GNW
1919	45	20.0✦	Vancouver	CPR Tel.

Sources: Labour Gazette; Records of the Department of Labour, Strikes and Lockouts file; *Telephone and Telegraph Age.*

◊ Department of Labour field representatives reporting on the 1917 strike described the gender composition of the Winnipeg GNW offices in various ways. The highest proportion of women operators given was 22.6 percent, the lowest 13.7 percent.

✦ All but one of the women operators in this office were automatic printer operators.

not only that sex-segregated work exaggerates gender differences, but that telegraphy's unusually integrated workplaces might have minimized them. Alternatively, if women were less respected and less well-paid than men in telegraphy as elsewhere, then the case of telegraphy can show how such differences have been reproduced, even without the support of differences in job tasks.

The case is complicated by technological changes in the early-20th century industry. But rather than muddying the analytical waters, the technology issues actually help clarify the relations of gender and skill. As the operators' union fought to control the effects of automation during World War I, operators became especially conscious of the meaning of skill. Both the strategy of the union's struggle and its outcome speak volumes about how the privileges of skill were reserved for male workers. Although the shared experience of cooperative labour had indeed challenged the myth of female incompetence, other forces, both material and ideological, had apparently confirmed it. Ultimately, only a few particles of cross-gender solidarity sifted through the male-privileging filter of the new telegraph technology. In what follows, a discussion of the telegraph labour process will provide the basis for explaining how gender differences in skilled-worker status and wage levels were constructed. A concluding section on the politics of technological change will show how the earlier links between gender and skill were remade in a new form.

THE LABOUR PROCESS

The industry in 1900 was prospering, although its future would not be as bright as its past. The two main firms, Great North Western (GNW) and the Canadian Pacific Railway Telegraphs (CPR) had about 3000 offices, there being two GNW offices to every CPR one.[5] Most of these offices—about 95 percent—employed only one operator and were located in towns or villages.[6] However, the analysis here focuses on urban offices, where both union activity and automation were concentrated.[7] Each employing as many as 100 operators, the central urban offices relayed incoming messages from "outside" points and also transmitted business originating in the city. City offices included smaller firms handling specialty business and one-operator accommodation offices similar in function to today's drug-store post-offices. Most urban operators worked in the main offices, in high-ceilinged operating rooms on the upper floors of tall buildings, far from the public they served. Wires linking the office to outside points were routed through a switchboard, then run along under the flooring and hooked up to telegraph instruments at stations on long tables. There might be 40 or 50 wires in a central office, ten to a table, with five operators on each side.[8] The scene resembled a factory more than an artisan's shop.

In spite of the work-stations' apparent homogeneity, the labour performed at each could differ considerably. One reason was that the amount of traffic on each of the wires varied. Some were constantly busy, requiring round-the-clock attendance. These were the wires on the trunk lines that connected Toronto and Montreal to each other, to American points such as Chicago or New York, and (as the western economy boomed) to Winnipeg and Vancouver. Wires connecting smaller centres or feeding into the main office from small places were called "way wires," and carried less traffic. They were likely to have full-time operators only at certain times of day. One operator might take care of several way wires at a time.[9] Trunk and way wires were often referred to as "heavy" or "light" wires, in reference to the different volumes of traffic they typically carried.

As well, some of the heavier wires were operated with special telegraph systems, either the "duplex" or the "quadruplex" (usually called the "quad"). These were circuits designed to carry signals in two directions on one wire, simultaneously. The quad was capable of carrying four messages (two in each direction) at once. Their purpose was to economize in the use of existing wires by increasing the traffic circuits could carry. Extremely sensitive to weather conditions, they were troublesome to use. Moreover, an interruption in one of the transmissions caused the others to break as well. Gradually, however, improved circuit conditions made the use of quad and duplex circuits more viable. In 1891, there were only 14 duplex circuits in Canada, most owned by CPR, and mainly used for emergencies.[10] But by 1915, their use had expanded considerably, with Canadian companies owning a total of 174 duplex and 81 quadruplex instruments, for a potential 107 circuits.[11] Most of these linked main offices.

The labour of main-office operators was subject to a close discipline. Operators were expected to stay at their keys constantly, with relief and lunch breaks often being subject to the demands of traffic.[12] Boys and girls called "check clerks" brought messages to the operators and removed finished work.[13] Operators' workload, the order in which messages were sent, and the pace of work were determined to a large extent by chief operators and supervisors. Main office operators were under constant pressure to pound out code; in the rush to extract the most work from their staff, supervisors might tear an operator away from a job, saying "I'll finish this, you take care of that one. . . ."[14] Specialty operators' work, by contrast, was subject to a kind of technical control. Both in brokerage houses and in press wire services, they faced the discipline of deadlines which created or destroyed the value of the information that was their product. Compared to main office operators or those in telegraphy's most time-sensitive branches, the accommodation office operators had much greater control over procedural decisions.

And yet, these operators were also subject to considerable pressure. In accommodation offices, a single person might juggle two or three jobs at once, with the urgency of customer's needs being brought home directly by the customers themselves, fretting or fuming at the counter.[15] And whereas the main office operator was subject to the "tyranny" of petty officials, the operator in a hotel lobby or drug-store had to put up with whatever passing tyrant chose to send a telegram.[16] The treatment operators endured in this respect no doubt resembled that experienced by other workers serving the urban public. But because a telegram was often sent in a hurry or in an anxious moment, the branch office's customers were likely to have been more difficult than, say, patrons of an ice cream parlour.[17] In different ways, the "emergency" character of the industry had its stress-inducing effect on all urban operators. In this context, pleasant relations with fellow operators would be highly valuable, and yet more difficult to sustain.

This was particularly true because the labour process in telegraphy was cooperative. Communicating a message was not an individual accomplishment; of necessity, at least two people were required. On duplex and quad systems, as many as eight operators depended on each other to keep the traffic flowing. The challenge facing those specialized operators was identical to that which every operator faced: finding the appropriate sending style and speed.

The company rule books all stated emphatically that "The sending operator must regulate the transmission of a message, to suit the ability of the receiving operator."[18] But this was more easily ordered than obeyed. The sending operator had to assess the ability of his or her receiving partner. Supposedly, the receiving operator would signal "BK" (for "break") if he or she couldn't follow the transmission. Sometimes, though, the receiver might not want to break, even though the transmission was unclear. Certain senders were known for being abusive and impatient with operators who broke too often.[19] Receivers would sometimes choose to guess at a word rather than break on such an operator's transmissions. Or a vain or insecure operator might be unwilling to admit that another operator was sending too fast for him or her to copy. Operators receiving press from a wire service knew that another half-dozen operators on the same circuit might also be receiving, and that for one to break would be to interrupt the transmission for all.[20] Operators might tire of asking for repeats from a chronically "illegible" sender, or be reluctant to make a pleasant but incompetent operator feel bad by the implicit criticism of constant breaking.[21] If for any reason operators wished to make themselves unpleasant, they could do so by sending quickly or sloppily, or by breaking unnecessarily and criticizing the receiving operator's skill. Operators even had an expression for the practice of deliberately sending too fast—they called it "giving someone a roast" or simply "roasting" someone. Sometimes roasting was just a game, but it could also be a way of putting an operator in his or her place. It was an unusual practice; operators generally observed the speed rules and enjoyed the cooperative quality of their work. Looking back over a 40-year career, an Ontario operator recalls his ability to accommodate slower operators as one of his strengths.[22] Nonetheless, cooperation also meant that interactions on Morse circuits easily could become power struggles. As another operator wrote, "Some of us obviously were not as good as some others so the potential for friction was always there."[23]

Other operating rules and descriptions of the work process further demonstrate this. "Contention for the circuit" was forbidden, reflecting the fact that operators in a hurry might try to interrupt a transmission, claiming that their business took priority. There were protocols to follow, but these required interpretation according to circuit conditions such as the size of the various offices and the characters of individuals working the wire.[24] Furthermore, particular circumstances required judgement calls. For instance, if a message was a "pink," it supposedly had priority, but operators might differ on whether an important press dispatch should be interrupted even by the pink.[25] An operator's ability to assert his or her own judgement determined the outcome of such disagreements. Operators developed their own ways of contacting and communicating with other operators in specific circumstances. A Brandon, Manitoba operator was particularly proud of his ability in managing relationships on the line:

> [I] was considered a strictly first-class man. I always did my work in the proper manner and never in my entire two years of service [in Chicago Postal telegraph] did anything on the wire which created friction between myself and operators at the other end. In fact, I had one of the best records in that office for being able to work successfully with operators who were inclined to be flighty or scrappy.[26]

In short, handling egos was as much a part of an operator's work as handling a telegraph key. Considerate, helpful operators made work easier; domineering, cavalier, or self-righteous ones made work more difficult.[27]

While all operators' jobs required that they endure pressure and cooperate in close interdependence, there nonetheless were notable differences between the responsibilities of various classes of operator. Broker work emphasized concentrated, high speed performance, and required some familiarity with a certain terminology and trade. Press, too, had a specialized code which abbreviated most English words. Press sending required steady production over long hours, and sometimes meant work at the scene of news events. Work in small offices meant handling multiple jobs, sometimes simultaneously. It also required that the operator advise inexperienced customers, and control or soothe fractious ones. Within main offices, operators' jobs were differentiated by the amount of traffic on the wires they were assigned and by the equipment they used. In the hierarchy of skill, broker operators ranked highest, followed by press operators. Within the main offices, those who worked the duplex and quad circuits were considered most skilled; working the way wires offered less status and lower wages. Lowest in stature, and least prosperous, were the branch office and hotel operators.

The available evidence permits no exhaustive specification of how women and men were distributed among the telegraph industry's branches. But evidence from union and trade journals, newspapers, telegraph schools, government documents and former telegraphers' recollections offers a clear pattern. Men were all but a few of the brokerage and press operators, while the small urban office and light wire positions were often, though not always, occupied by women.[28] This gender division of labour was constructed in ways which allow us to see the deeply rooted connections between masculinity and skill. The apparent ability of any individual operator was profoundly conditioned by the interdependent labour process.

STRUCTURAL DETERMINANTS OF WAGES AND STATUS

The gendered pattern in the operator skill-hierarchy was the product of two dynamics in the organization and conduct of the telegraph operator's work. One of these dynamics was gender relations between male owners or officials and women workers; the other was gender relations within the operators' craft culture. In part, limitations imposed by both dynamics on women operators' opportunities to acquire certain competencies produced a loose pattern of gender segregation. Wage and status differentials between women and men then proceeded from employers' skimpy rewarding of competencies exercised on low-traffic wires and in the smallest offices.[29] Women operators' wages were thus a product of both class and gender relations. Gender also shaped the intraclass, personal relations of the labour process, determining in another way the link between masculinity and skill-definition. In studying telegraphy's skill hierarchy, I have found, as did Joy Parr in her work on the hosiery industry, that "the processes that human-capital, dual-labour-market, and feminist theorists have isolated are forced to keep the same awkward company [in historical analysis as] they do in real life."[30]

The boundaries of wage determination were set by the state of the communications market. Commercial telegraph firms were still prosperous at the turn of the century, but their position was no longer as secure as it had been. Telephone systems were taking over local services, leaving mainly long-distance business to the telegraph. GNW was sufficiently unprofitable by 1915 that American Telephone and Telegraph (owners of Western Union since 1910) disposed of their controlling interest in GNW, selling it to Canadian Northern. Two years later, the financially-troubled Canadian Northern was purchased by the Dominion government.[31] Only then did the telegraphers' union have any success in edging GNW employees wages upward. The subsidized CPR telegraph was less exposed to market conditions than was GNW, and thus had kept its wage scale slightly higher.

Before the union's successes, general commercial operators' monthly incomes in 1907 Toronto ranged from $15 to $80, with women's maximum about $40.[32] This maximum was slightly higher than the 1911 Canadian average for female clerical workers. The minimum, however, was as low as the national average for all women workers in 1901, and only one dollar more per month than a female general servant's wage in 1900. The men's maximum exceeded the average wage of male clerks by about 25 percent.[33] By 1920, the range of operators' wages had been raised, although widened, with a minimum of $75 and a maximum of about $155 in central Canada.[34] Single-operator offices carried salaries of about $100 per month, while 70 percent of main office operators in Toronto were paid $142 or $149.60. These wages, if they were collected without interruption, put even men operators among the best paid of skilled workers.[35] Press and brokerage services were not much affected by telephone competition; they took full advantage of Canada's early-20th century economic expansion. In 1920, for example, press operators' monthly income ranged between $150 and $200.[36] The expanding brokerage firms could afford to pay as much as twice the scale paid to union commercial operators, so as to attract whatever operators they chose.[37]

The higher wages of the specialty operators may be attributed in part to variations in industry markets. But their wages were also linked to productivity, and within general commercial firms, productivity alone was supposedly the telegraph owner's basis for establishing wage scales. Whoever handled the most messages was producing the most revenue for the employer, and a high wage was the productive operator's reward. However, this apparently-objective standard did not prevent the power relations of gender and class from structuring workers' rewards.

The operator's level of productivity was determined partly by a complex set of operator competencies: ability to read code, orderly work habits, kinetic co-ordination, judgement about circuit conditions, and ability to work successfully with other operators and customers. But productivity also was determined by the volume of traffic to be handled and the range of tasks included in the operator's job. In these respects, the branch-office operator was at a disadvantage, with fewer messages to handle and more diverse tasks than the main-office operator. Even among main-office operators, not all operators worked under equal conditions. In telegraphy's interdependent labour process, an operator's output was not a pure reflection of his or her individual competencies. But in setting wages, the telegraph managers used simple productivity measures that reflected only the owners' economic interest. The count of messages sent, messages received, and errors made was an index of the revenue produced by the individual operator's labour. Accurate for this purpose, such measures obscured the social relationships which affected productivity; consequently, simple productivity measures distorted the definition of skill.

Officials' attitudes and beliefs about individual operators or a certain class of person could affect operators' productivity records.[38] For instance, handling the short, quick, day messages helped spruce up an operator's productivity record, but supervisors had absolute discretion as to who handled what kind of messages. Operators were not always convinced of their managers' objectivity; one wrote, "When a traffic-chief tries to convince me that I get my share of the short messages his talk sounds like a bundle of loose axe handles."[39] An operator's productivity also was determined by the quality of the circuit he or she worked. Short circuits or circuits made of copper wire were "faster" than long, iron ones. On a slow circuit, operators could send no faster than about 20 words per minute without garbling the transmission. Speeds of 40 words per minute were possible on fast circuits.[40] Which circuits an operator worked was decided by the supervisor. Therefore, although wage rates were set according to an operator's productivity record, the creation of that record was affected by power relations. In the creation of an operator's record, management practices mediated the link between competence and productivity, and in this way determined whether an operator's ability would translate into an entitlement to high wages. Depending on the place he or she was assigned in the labour process, a competent worker might not acquire a particularly good productivity record.

Operator's output depended not only on the kind of work they were given, but also on the quantity they were expected to perform. Expectations were affected by preconceptions about gender. For instance, American telegraph superintendents in the early 1890s said that "they do not call upon women to perform" at the rate of 1500 words per hour, and that they "do not expect such a service of them."[41] In 1915, a man influential in the Canadian industry told an American government commission that "Some of the most efficient, up to a certain point, of our labor, is by women; but women have not the telegraphic capacity of men."[42] During the same hearings, the international president of the Commercial Telegraphers' Union of America gave a less sexist view, emphasizing women's equal competence while noting that they usually were employed on lighter wires.[43] In fact, officials' sexist assumptions prevented most women operators from getting the experience on heavy wires necessary to increase their productivity. Even working for two weeks as a relief operator on a heavy wire could raise an operator's work from second to first class.[44] One reason, then, that women remained in low-productivity jobs was that their employers expected less of them than of men, and so denied them challenging opportunities.

Other forces shaping women's place in telegraphy are apparent in a comparison of women's and men's "career" paths. Generally, operators who grew up in cities had their earliest operating jobs in city branches or on way wires. "Star" operator Billy Gibson began at age 12 in a Montreal hotel office.[45] Successful operators would move on to heavier circuits.[46] A learner of average aptitude could handle any wire in the main office after about seven years' experience.[47] From there, the operator might advance to a supervisory position or to press or broker work.[48] But gender differences in life-cycle combined with features of the telegraph business to delay women's training, and exclude them from the industry's higher ranks.

Boys got a head start in the industry because only boys were hired as messengers. Being a messenger was the cheapest, easiest way of learning how to be a Morse operator. Boys were encouraged to learn code and practise operating in the spare time between delivering messages or after their shift. But girls were so rare as messengers that when World War I labour shortages promoted companies to take on girls, it was big news.[49] In Ottawa, the Children's Aid Society only allowed employment of girls on the condition that they have a separate entrance and their work be confined to dealings with the Imperial Munitions Board.[50] A few years earlier, American social workers had expressed concern about the dubious moral influences to which messenger boys were subject. The prospect of putting girls in the position of possibly running errands to bawdy houses was even more gruesome. Such concern prevented the employment of girl messengers, though not of young boys.[51] The definition of young girls (and, indeed, of all women) as potential victims of male lust, capable of being safeguarded only by seclusion and purity of character, worked to deprive young girls of one means to earn a living and learn a trade. Instead of starting as messengers, girls entering the urban telegraph industry usually took a course or were hired as learners, beginning at about age 18.[52] Boys' first operating jobs did not always start as early as age 12, but a boy leaving school at age 14 to work as a messenger could get a paid operating job in a year and a half or two years' time. Someone very keen and quick could acquire basic sending and receiving abilities in a year or less. As young children, boys were more likely than girls to have been encouraged to take an interest in telegraphy. Some boys even knew Morse code before beginning their first messenger job.[53] At age 23, if a male operator had worked steadily, had pushed himself, and had been expected to perform at the top of his ability, he would be as competent as possible. If he was on good terms with his supervisors and not suspected of union activity, his productivity would be high and he would be earning enough to contemplate supporting a family. A female operator of the same age might still be earning less than she needed even to live independently, because she would have had fewer years of practice, and less would have been expected of her by telegraph managers. With two operators of equal aptitude, substantial differences in performance would result from different amounts of practice. This was especially true in the first seven years of operating.[54] Differences in ability resulting from differences in amount of practice and length of career meshed with stereotypes about female inferiority to obstruct further women operators' development and hence their access to the best-paid, highest-status jobs.

The jobs deemed highly-skilled were few; only a small proportion of telegraphers could hope to get well-paid work on high-volume wires. Most operators in urban offices left telegraph operating before reaching middle age. Data showing the precise age distribution of Canadian operators is not available; however, data from a 1908 US Department of Labour inquiry show a preponderance of young operators. Seventy-eight percent of operators in four mid-sized US cities were less than 40 years of age. Fifty-eight percent were 31 or younger.[55] Representatives of the union, management, and the trade press all agreed telegraphy was a young person's occupation.[56] But advancing age did not inevitably disqualify men and women as operators. Instead, the policies of telegraph companies and sexist assumptions about gender and skill effectively reduced the number of candidates for jobs at the top of the hierarchy.

The Commercial Telegraphers' Union of America (CTUA) pointed out one way in which operators' working lives were curtailed. Up to a certain point, companies increased an operator's ratings in relation to his or her developing competencies. But when officials judged that jobs could be done by less-experienced operators who had not yet been assigned the higher ratings, older operators were laid off. In the words of CTUA president S.J. Konenkamp:

> The men find that after reaching the age of 30 or thereabouts, if they have been able to stand the treatment they received during that period, that instead of getting work, regular employment, they are assigned to the waiting list. . . . And then the higher the salary

the less the likelihood of being called. . . . [I]f they have any person receiving a rate of $50 a month that could do the same work that you are being paid $80 for doing they would call the $50 a month operator first. . . . [T]hose who have spent 15 or 20 years in the service find that they are at the bottom of the list.[57]

This picture was confirmed by the CTUA's Ottawa correspondent in 1915, in a discussion of "the determined effort of our worthy GNW traffic superintendent to reduce the top ratings all to $55.00." The correspondent wrote that operators earning more than $55 were being fired, and "With chiefs working wires regularly and 'ambitious' juniors proud of being given the chance to show that they can do a man's work (wages no object), the business gets moved some way and the company makes a little more money. . . ." Only if an operator would come back to work at the lower rating of $55 would he or she be rehired.[58] This sort of practice (against which the union had been fighting since the late 1870s) made many operators look beyond commercial telegraphy for a more stable source of income.

The telegraph companies' punitive policy towards older operators was directed primarily towards men. Konenkamp noted that women operators seemed to get steadier work.[59] A deliberate policy against top-rated operators was not necessary for women; companies needed only to invoke women operators' alleged lack of "telegraphic capacity" to justify keeping their wages down. Also, a certain proportion of female operators could be expected to leave the workforce at least temporarily (and perhaps permanently) to keep house and raise a family.[60] The companies' assumption was that the wages of women operators supported only individual women. Once a woman operator married, she would supposedly be at most a secondary wage earner. Defined by the companies as either temporary or unmarried workers, women operators were therefore believed neither to merit nor require a stable and high wage, i.e. a "family" wage. For the companies, this patriarchal definition of women workers served the same useful purpose as the policy of sidelining top-rated men.[61] Although more directly responsible for the latter practice, the companies' interests were served equally by both. Both the exclusion of women from top ratings and the laying-off of senior men reduced payroll expenses. The companies' ways of rewarding skill, and thus defining it, were structured by gender.

CRAFT STANDARDS OF SKILL

The focus on productivity to this point has meant a corresponding attention to wages and employers' standards of skill. But although operators themselves took speed seriously, it was not their sole criterion of excellence, nor were wages the only reward of skill. Operators also valued each others' work in aesthetic and social terms. Defining skill in these ways helped operators derive pleasure and self-respect from their work, maintaining standards somewhat independent of employers' material power. These standards became part of the ground from which organized workers resisted employer initiatives during the 1910s. But craft standards had another kind of importance, too. Within "the fraternity," operators themselves had a substantial measure of control over who received a certain reward of skill—that is, social status. And in determining an operator's status, issues of gender identity figured prominently. The fraternity achieved solidarity in part through excluding women from the select circle of the skilled.[62]

Craft standards had to do with the competencies of sending and receiving, and with the conduct of working relationships. Operators compared speeds of sending and feats of accurate receiving.[63] In addition, they discussed the "musical" qualities of a sender's style and the recognizable rhythms of each operator's work. They used terms like "clear," "firm," "nervous," or "staccato" to describe an operator's "fist," or style of Morse.[64] They told tales of phenomenal memory or ability to concentrate, the essential traits on which good receiving was based.[65] Long after typewriters had entered widespread use, they took an interest in "typically telegraphic" handwriting.[66] Operators also took pride in their role as carriers of vital, often-confidential information. They knew the service they provided meant at times life or death.[67] Relationships with customers were not always easy, but a good telegrapher took care to handle customers well. Good manners with the public, as well as with other operators on the wire, were noted and appreciated.[68]

The telegraph labour process gave operators considerable opportunity to enforce these standards. Their most effective tactic was simply to avoid working with incompetent operators (whom they called "plugs" or "hams").[69] "Get another op" might be the last words one operator would be willing to send another who had offended his or her standards.[70] But clearly, not everyone could avoid the bad operators all the time. Various, subtler forms of disparagement also served as sanctions. For example, an operator, driven beyond the bounds of patience, might resort to "roasting" an obnoxious receiver.[71] To hasten a laggard sender, a fast receiver might send a peremptory, "Well, well. . . ?"[72] Sometimes, all an operator could do was gently tease an inept co-worker about the illegibility of his or her sending, and hope a better effort would result.[73]

Operators also enforced craft standards in supportive ways, by encouraging good sending and receiving. Some would make a friendly game of roasting each other, when each claimed to be equally talented.[74] Warm congratulations would be conveyed to someone who had received a long transmission without breaking, or whose sending was particularly pleasant to follow.[75] Quite subtle tones of approval or disapproval could be conveyed in operators' conversation over the wires. As a result, many of the ordinary means by which people are rewarded or punished in social conversation were available to operators who never met face to face. And these sources of social rewards were supplemented by the social notes in union or trade journals, which sometimes made special mention of an operator's excellence.[76]

In urban operators' high pressure work, then, craft standards and their enforcement were the language of status and the means of its creation. Together, they formed a discourse of craft, grounded in the interdependence of operators' work, and well-suited to the formulation and expression of prejudice within the relations of daily work. For instance, judging the "musicality" of an operators' fist was to some extent a matter of personal taste. Whether or not an operator was recognized as a superior sender by such a standard could easily be determined by her fellow operators' general feelings about her personality or her sex. And those feelings could be given rich expression through the complex etiquette of telegraphy. Subtle snubs, systematic exclusions, friendly congratulations—all these and more were available as informal means of establishing status hierarchies. Through such means, operators constructed their own associations between gender and skill.

To a large extent, these associations followed the predictable schema of patriarchy. Praise and criticism were offered in gendered terms. For example, a poet operator likened the skill of a group of his fellow Montreal operators to the loyal courage of Horatio and his men defending the gates of Rome.[77] This was an image of men doing men's work, an image which situated superior accomplishment squarely in an archetypically masculine experience—armed combat.[78] The prevalence of such images indicated a shared view (among male operators at least) that skill was masculine. Even when women operators were praised, this general truth was affirmed. So, for example, women operators might be congratulated for having done "a man's work."[79] Or, a competent woman operator might be noted as an exception or an affront to the normal order. As one former operator said, "Well, I hate to admit it, but the best operator I ever worked with was a woman."[80]

This comment captures an important feature of the interplay of skill definition and gender definition: exceptions to patriarchal expectations could be acknowledged in such a way as to preserve the pattern. The fact of the woman's competence was still clear in this man's mind, when I interviewed him 40 or more years after he worked with this woman. He remembers that her work was fast, clear, and accurate. But the fact retained its special importance because of its strangeness. It was not strange by virtue of there being a woman operator at all; the same man observed that "there were women operators all over." The oddity lay in the combination of "best operator" and "woman operator." He was quite likely surprised initially when he discovered the sex of this excellent operator, and to this day, he prefaces his recollection of her with the expression, "Well, I hate to admit it. . . ." And he not only made precisely the same comment on two separate occasions. On both occasions, he followed his discussion of "the best operator" with two more stories about women operators—both of these focusing on the women's errors and ineptitude.[81]

This operator was not alone in his reluctance to link women and skill unreservedly. He spoke not only from the broad tradition of patriarchy, but also as part of the occupational culture which was expressed in telegraphy's many internationally circulated trade publications. In poems, essays, and short stories, telegraph operators reflected on the troubles and joys of their profession. These reflections often centred on admiration of skill or exasperation with incompetence. When themes such as these were developed in narratives concerning men and women, the relationship between gender and skill was addressed. For instance, the "story problem" was sometimes the contradiction between sexist ideology and women operators' actual competence.[82] Alternatively, some telegraph writers focused on the problem of gender difference being obscured in operators' work relationships. Against the assumption that men and women were different in almost every way was posed the telegraphers' experience of encountering "disembodied" co-workers, whose sex was not discernable. For some writers, this situation presented opportunities for humourous romance plots, in which laughter was to be evoked by mistaken gender identification.[83] Others insisted that criteria other than biological sex allowed them to distinguish infallibly between women and men. Some implicitly or explicitly denied the possibility of skilled women, but there also were dissenting voices and alternative visions.

An explicit example of the tensions concerning the relation of gender and skill can be found in a set of 1902 magazine articles. In *McClure's Magazine*, Mr. L.C. Hall claimed that "A woman's Morse is as feminine as her voice or her handwriting." The *Telegraph Age* editor agreed: "I have often put to the test by ability to distinguish between the Morse of a man and that of a women, and only once have I been deceived." He described that one incident, saying that the operator seemed to be a man because "his" Morse was very fast, and also "clean-clipped and musical, though it had a harsh, staccato ring which indicated a lack of sentiment and feeling in the transmitter." He was mortified, he wrote, to discover later that he had mistaken the sex of the sender. However, when he met the young woman, he was comforted to find that she was, by his categories, a "masculine" young woman. His conclusion was that "nature, and not I" had made the mistake.[84] Masculine skill had been put in a female body.

The article in *McClure's Magazine* provoked an outraged response from a woman operator in Montreal.[85] The burden of her protest, expressed in delightfully salty terms, was that men operators used distinctions between men's and women's styles of sending to impugn women operators' abilities. She expressed mock pity for men "doomed to receive unmusical feminine Morse," but speculated in tones of heavy irony as to why these men, supposedly secure "in their exalted position of super-excellence . . . use precious time and strength in attacking the less favored female race."[86] Not only did she object to the arrogance behind such attacks, but she also insisted that the supposed differences on which they were based were complete fabrications. Fundamentally, the issue was not simply whether "women's Morse" was identifiable, but whether an ideology of gender difference and male superiority would deprive women operators of one of the rewards of their work—peer recognition.

TECHNOLOGICAL CHANGE AND THE REDEFINITION OF SKILL

By the 1910s, changes in the telegraph industry affected the organization of work, supported the use of new technologies, and consequently brought skill definitions into a new focus. Telegraphy's days of rapid growth were past. In 1915, for example, GNW had only about 3000 more miles of wire than it had had in 1902, and that wire was strung between fewer points: pole mileage had dropped by half.[87] The managers' watchword was "efficiency." The priority was to cram as much signal as possible onto the circuits at any given time. Even the usual length of the spaces operators left between code elements came under scrutiny, because these constituted "dead time" on the circuit.[88] More and more, the cantankerous duplex and quad circuits came into use.

Increasing the rate at which messages were processed was another of management's priorities. Redundant elements were omitted from the conventional signals used in sending messages.[89] Typewriters, whose productivity-enhancing benefits had been embraced by operators in the 1890s, became mandatory equipment by the 1910s (and operators had to supply their own machines).[90] The pressure on operators was heightened by the more-frequent business use of "cipher" telegrams, in which numbers represented the words of the message, with some ciphers allowing the abbreviation of conventional phrases. Sending data of this sort required that operators work at half their ordinary speed, to ensure accuracy. The customer paid for fewer words, but the operator took twice as long to transmit the message. The telegraph company lost money, the customer saved, and the operator's productivity dropped.[91] Operators attempted to increase their speed by using "semi-automatic" keys, which reduced the physical labour of sending.[92] And while operators themselves attempted to maintain their productivity, they were subjected to greater monitoring and enforcement of productivity by scientific management measures such as bonus systems and time clocks.[93]

The early years of World War I also saw the first important commercial use of automatic telegraph systems in Canada. Their use was limited to the busiest, best-quality circuits. By 1917, automatic printers handled between one-third and two-thirds of GNW's traffic at Toronto, Montreal, Ottawa, Quebec, Winnipeg, and Saskatoon; CPR had a similar number of automatic circuits.[94] A small but significant new sub-group of telegraph operators had come into existence: automatic printer operators, almost all women. They operated unstable equipment on busy circuits; the machines required four operators at each end of the circuit, plus support from special mechanics.[95] With the cost of separate supervision added to their expenses, the telegraph companies needed operators who could be paid low wages. Young women and some young men were hired. Over all, they were only about two percent of the telegraph labour force, but no one could say for sure how far or how fast the use of automatic printers would grow. If anything was certain, it was that the automatics would usurp the top-quality circuits on which Morse operators had formerly performed their greatest feats of fast sending.[96]

In this context, the meaning of fast sending began to change. Morse operators could not deny that, under appropriate conditions, more messages could be handled and circuit capacity could be used best by the automatic printers. In a comparison based solely on maximum speed under ideal circumstances, the Morse system would lose to the automatic printer.[97] But Morse operators could, and very quickly did, argue that their "skill" consisted of competencies other than merely endless, high-speed key pounding. In their union journal and in conflicts with employers they argued that their most important ability was understanding the content of the messages that passed through their hands. Such understanding was the only effective way to catch the occasional inevitable errors that resulted from line problems or illegible handwriting. They believed that they noticed errors while receiving Morse, automatically fixing or checking on anything that seemed wrong. Automatics, they said, were not only more prone to introducing errors through circuit problems, but noticing errors was not an inherent part of operating the printers. The receiving operator did not interact with the sender directly, so feedback and verification could not be immediate. Instead, messages were proofread after the strips of printed tape had been glued to the message form. They claimed that errors thus either went undetected or took more time to correct. They also argued that the Morse system was more "flexible" than the automatics. By this, they meant that Morse operators were able to assess and compensate for the sudden and frequent variations in circuit conductivity, variations which would put printers out of service.[98] Thus, they claimed, in the real conditions of most offices, the Morse operators' care and judgement gave them a productivity rivalling that possible on the printer system.

The emergence of automatics was only part of the reason for operators' new emphasis on the intellectual components of craft skill. Anger at the forced pace of their work also led to questioning the value of high speed output. Even though there was a certain pleasure in pouring out a rapid torrent of fluent Morse, to be required to perform continually at top pitch pushed operators toward nervous collapse.[99] To engage in the occasional friendly "roast" was vastly different than to produce at maximum speed under the daily stresses of a job. Voices both within and outside the union decried operators' superhuman efforts. One non-union observer suggested that pride and greed were the downfall of a man who, through overwork, succumbed to tuberculosis and died at age forty-one.[100] Unionists were more sensitive to the possibility that financial need, rather than greed, might motivate operators to work two jobs and push themselves to their limit on bonus wires.[101] But thinking in collective terms, they pointed out that fast senders injured not only themselves, but other operators, too. As one press operator wrote: "Why set an exaggerated pace for himself and his fellows by sending in outlandish wire reports? . . . Why the 'bunk?'"[102]

Wanting to be a "star" no doubt explained some of the "bunk." But such a motivation was shaped by more than simply individual psyches. Telegraph companies had a substantial interest in getting the most work out of the fewest employees, so they played up to the operator's pride by publicizing exceptional feats of message handling. Noting an example of Western Union's honouring of high productivity, a Montreal unionist commented: "Did these poor simps imagine any one in Canada would be interested in their throat cutting contests?"[103] And indeed, CPR operators had succeeded in having a reasonably objective and moderate productivity standard included in their 1910 contract.[104] The critique of "speeditis"[105] was a rational one with considerable appeal to operators committed to lifelong work in the industry. But motives that led operators to drive for speed were not always rational. It is clear that high productivity and, especially, fast sending imparted a special pleasure to some operators. Many, perhaps most, of these were young men, those whom an Ottawa operator had scornfully called "'ambitious' juniors."[106] Such operators were the sort who adjusted the mechanism of the semi-automatic key at a speed greater than they could competently control.[107] They were the sort who would "roast" another operator just for "fun."[108] Undoubtedly, they were the sort who would spend their leisure time practising the set pieces used in tournaments, developing their ability to send what a senior telegrapher scornfully called "tournament Morse," distinctive for its illegibility as well as its speed.[109] In short, operators who set the fastest pace wanted to prove their superior competence more than they wanted a relaxed and cooperative working life.

While women or men, young or old, might have had such a bent, it is surely not coincidental that examples of the enthusiastic speed demon in the telegraph trade magazines and literature were all young men. Displays of skill affirmed masculinity because superior skill was understood to be based in allegedly male physical traits—nervous stamina, muscular strength. While it is certainly rational (in the sense of beneficial to one's interests) to claim masculinity in a patriarchal society, proving gender identity has an importance beyond material interests. The desire to prove oneself a man (or a woman) is often, simply, compelling. Young male operators' commitments to proving their superior gender identity must have been a formidable barrier to their accepting unionists' more purely rational critique of speed as the defining feature of skill.

For men committed to union principles, the proving of masculinity through ever-speedier work was clearly a self-destructive game; manhood could better be shown in resolute defense of one's rights to organize and to control the pace and conditions of work.[110] Unionists had rejected the gender-biased biological definition of skill, recognizing that new productivity pressures and automation made stamina no longer either a healthful or an effective basis for skill claims. From this perspective, gender differences in "telegraphic capacity" lost their importance. Both men and women could benefit from the definition of skill as a cooperative exercise in clear communication. Unionists contended that, rather than being rewarded for star performances in nervous endurance, operators deserved full-time pay for eight-hour days. In making this speed critique, unionists affirmed that what was valuable about telegraphers' work were the diverse competencies of craft, and not merely volume of output. A certain link between masculinity and skill had been abandoned.

In the course of the 1917 strike against GNW, precipitated in part by the advent of the automatic printers, the union successfully enforced their new definition of skill. The company had proposed that Morse operators' wages be based on which wires they worked, with the wires being classified by volume of business typically carried. This was essentially the old productivity standard. By contrast, the union proposed that the operators, not the wires, be classified. The basis for classification would be the "importance" of the work each class of operator could handle. "First-class men" might not work on the busiest wires, but would always be necessary to handle such wires when the printers' capacity was exceeded, or when the printers malfunctioned. The most-senior and most-competent workers were entitled, they argued, to the highest degree of job security and the best wages, regardless of the specific volume of work they might do. They were willing to negotiate on the percentage of jobs to be designated as first, second, third, and fourth class, but they insisted on their own, rather than the company's, basis of classification.[111] Morse operators had responded to automation by redefining skill as the workers' learned competencies, not the workers' productivity. Whether or not their work required full exercise of their competencies, they claimed the right to be paid for being skilled. In Cynthia Cockburn's terms, they had come to base their skill claims on "skill in the worker" instead of "skill in the job."[112]

In this new definition of skill, the link to masculinity was not the worker's stamina-based productivity but his accumulated store of knowledge. Drawing its association with masculinity in part from the fact that most of the senior operators were men, the Morse operator's work was distinguished as "skilled" and "masculine" in opposition to the labour of the new female printer operators. These women rivalled the Morse operators' productivity, but were not required to know Morse code or any of telegraphy's specialized ciphers. Underscoring this distinction was a substantial wage differential, favouring the Morse operators. Securing this differential in a wage schedule ensured the equation of masculinity and skill.

In their 1917 strike, the union failed to protest seriously the low wages printer operators were paid. Admittedly, the CTUA fought the company's attempt to exclude automatic operators from the negotiated wage schedule. However, this was clearly a strategic necessity. If the high cost of automatic systems was the chief barrier to their wider use, then maintaining some union control over automatic operators' wages would reduce any threat the technology might pose.[113] There appeared to be little danger that printer operators would become a majority of CTUA members and threaten "petticoat rule."[114] In these circumstances, a chivalrous self-interest dictated the inclusion of the automatic operators.[115] It did not, however, require demanding that the "girls" get equal pay for work of equal value. The pervasive assumption that women operators were somehow inferior made the creation of this new low-paid, low-status niche seem "natural" for women.

The conclusion, then, must be that in the telegraphers' case, the experience of shared labour did not generally and fundamentally alter either these workers' ideas about gender and skill, nor close the gap between women's and men's wages. The main reason was the degree to which gender segregation could be sustained within this complex industry. Among its diverse branches were situations where women seemed to belong, according to sexist assumptions about low stamina, lesser wage entitlements, short working careers, and patience with the public. A combination of more or less subtle dynamics guided most women operators into these apparently appropriate branches of the business. As a result, men and women might, for example, work together on a press circuit, but the women were likely to be among the many receiving operators rather than the one sender. Such working relationships presented almost no contradictions to gender stereotypes.

However, even limited evidence of female competence was clearly a source of some perplexity and tension. Male co-workers or employers responded in three ways. Female competence might be regarded as exceptional, and praised as the ability to do "a man's work." Or, women's abilities might be seen as suiting them only for certain jobs deemed (rightly or wrongly) to be less demanding. And some men in the industry used subjective aesthetic judgments to deny women operators' skills. By these means, the evidence against the equation of masculinity and skill was discounted.

For the outcome to have been otherwise, people within and outside the industry would have had to organize specifically in support of women telegraph operators. By itself, cooperative labour shared by these women and men had little effect on the meanings they made of gender. Masculinity retained its promise of higher wages and superior status. When the fulfillment of this promise was jeopardized by technological change, unionists distinguished themselves from the automatic operators, and forced employers both to reaffirm the entitlements of skill and to entrench gender hierarchy in the industry. In this new class rapprochement, Morse telegraphy became, more than ever, "men's" work.

NOTES

1. From "The Economic Objects of Unionism," *Commercial Telegraphers' Journal*, 2 (June 1904), 2.

2. McNicol Collection, Item 483, *Canadian telegraph and telegraphers*, clipping from *Maclean's Magazine*, "Great Men of the Key: Prominent Canadians Who Started as Telegraph Operators (no date), 16; Old Time Telegraphers' and Historical Association, *Proceedings*, "Reminiscences of Robert F. Easson (Toronto)," (Toronto 1920), 53.

3. *Telephone & Telegraph Age* (hereafter *T & T Age*), 19 (1 Jan. 1902), 18–19; *T & T Age*, 19 (6 Nov. 1902), 490. Re: western city offices, see *International Union of Commercial Telegraphers Journal*, 1 (March 1903), 18.

4. Cynthia Cockburn, *Machinery of Dominance* (London 1985), 168 and ch. 6 generally.

5. The CPR Telegraphs had its own staff, management, and budget, but it was a department of CPR and not an independent company. It employed about 600 operators who did nothing but commercial work, in addition to the many offices which were staffed by train operators or station agent/operators. In referring to CPR Telegraphs as simply "CPR," I follow the contemporary practice of telegraph operators. ("CP" was used to refer to Canadian Press after its formation in 1911.) On the number of offices, see John Murray, *A Story of the Telegraph* (Montreal 1905), 119–20.

6. The estimated percentage is based on the difference between the number of GNW offices covered in the 1920 union contract and the number of GNW offices listed in the 1920 Dominion Bureau of Statistics *Telegraph Statistics*. The contract covered GNW's 58 offices in Canadian cities and telegraph centres. About 20 percent of these offices employed three or more operators; more than half were in smaller centres and employed only two operators, one being the designated manager. Another 22 percent employed only a manager/operator. Out of the 2080 operators

employed by the GNW, these 58 offices would have employed at most 600 operators, assuming that the five main offices each employed about 100 operators. The remaining number of operators equals approximately the number of GNW offices not covered in the contract.

7. I have discussed the case of certain rural operators, a group which came to be composed almost equally of women and men, in "The operators along the coast: a case study of gender, the link between skilled labour and social power, 1900–1930," *Acadiensis*, 20 (Autumn 1990), 72–88.

8. McNicol Collection, Item 483, *Canadian telegraph and telegraphers*, clipping from *T & T Age* (16 October 1913), 619–20.

9. Interview #1, tape #2, side A, 141-7.

10. National Archives of Canada (NAC), Records of the Department of Public Works, RG 11, series B3(c), vol. 2859, file 1-1-1, D.H. Keeley, "Developments in Telegraphy," paper presented to the Canadian Society of Civil Engineers, 1891.

11. Canada, *Sessional Papers of the Parliament of Canada, Sessional Paper 20f* (1917), 12; McNicol Collection, Item 483, *Canadian telegraph and telegraphers*, clipping from CPR publication, 1917, states that there were 21 long distance duplex circuits in use, and another unspecified number of duplex and quadruplex services for shorter distances.

12. Questionnaire #1, answer #30; "Konenkamp Testimony" and "McElreath Testimony," *Final Report and Testimony submitted to Congress by the Commission on Industrial Relations* (hereafter *U.S. Commission on Industrial Relations*), Basil M. Manley, director, U.S. Senate document #415, 64th Congress, 1st session (Washington 1916), 9311-2, 9393.

13. McNicol Collection, Item 489, *Early telegraph rule books*, file 9, Postal Telegraph-Cable Company Rules (1903–11), 12; Marjory McMurchy,

The Canadian Girl at Work: A book of vocational guidance (Toronto 1919), 60; McNicol Collection, Item 518, *Telegraphica's Ghost*, 30.

14. *Commercial Telegraphers' Journal* (hereafter *CTJ*), 13 (1915), 142.

15. U.S. Bureau of Labor Statistics, "Displacement of Morse Operators in Commercial Telegraph Offices," *Monthly Labor Review* (March 1932), 507.

16. Graham Taylor, "The Industrial Viewpoint. Women Telegraph Operators," *Charities and The Commons*, 19 (5 October 1907), 864; Mary E. de Ginther, "The Public's Ignorance of the Telegraph," *T & T Age*, 19 (1902), 55.

17. McNicol Collection, Item 486, *Early telegraph poetry, 1896–1908*, n.p. [story contrasting the behaviour of distraught lady customer and calm, competent business-man customer.]

18. Government Telegraph Service, Department of Public Works, Dominion of Canada, *Rules* (Ottawa 1889), 18; McNicol Collection, Item 489, file 9, Postal Telegraph-Cable Company Rules (1903–11), 20; G.M. Dodge, *The telegraph instructor* (Valparaiso, Ill., 1917, 6th edition), 240. This text was written by a Western Union manager, and was intended for use in training students to work at GNW, too (60). (For Dodge's position, see *T & T Age*, 16 (November 1918), 508.)

19. Questionnaire #1, answer #28; Miss M.J. Schofield, "Wooing by Wire," *Lightning flashes and electric dashes; a volume of choice telegraphic literature, humor, fun, wit and wisdom*, 3rd edition. Comp. W.J. Johnston (New York 1882), 95. [McNicol Collection, Item 151. *Lightning Flashes* was still in print as late as 1902 (*T & T Age*, 1 January 1902, xiii.]

20. Recollections of interviewee #1, page four, unpublished typescript.

21. Questionnaire #2, answer #36.

22. Questionnaire #3, answers #35 and #26.

23. Questionnaire #2, answer #28.

24. McNicol Collection, Item 516, *Telegraph Labor strikes 1885–1922* File 10 (Reprint of Testimony of Edward Reynolds before the United States Commission on Industrial Relations, 13 April 1915), 10.

25. Interview #3, side A, 519–540; U.S. Bureau of Labor, *Investigation of Western Union and Postal Telegraph-Cable Companies* (Washington 1909), 11.

26. *U.S. Commission on Industrial Relations*, Henry Lynch exhibit on exiled operators, E.M. Wood to CTUA President S.J. Konenkamp, 17 March 1917, 9516.

27. Mrs. M.L. Rayne, *What Can a Woman Do: or, her position in the Business and Literary World* (Petersburgh, N.Y. 1893), 142; Questionnaire #2, answer #35; Interview #1, tape #1, side B, 234–241, 266–274, 415–418; Interview #3, side A, 284–294; Interview #2, side A, 367–373.

28. NAC, Records of the Department of Labour, RG 27, vol. 333, strike 57, Report of J.A. Clark, 15 September 1924; NAC, RG 27, vol. 342, strike 24, Report on Frank B. Powers, 15 May 1929; confirmed *vis-à-vis* the brokerage industry in Interview #3, side B, 152–163; U.S. *Commission on Industrial Relations*, 9307, 9318; *CTJ*, 18 (1920), 500, 502; McNicol, Item 510, file 10, clipping from *T & T Age* (16 October 1909), 725; McMurchy, *Canadian Girl*, 59–60; Interview #1, tape #2, side A, 139–147; *T & T Age*, 15 (16 Nov. 1894), 410; *T & T Age*, 14 (1 February 1894), 12; *CTJ*, 20 (1923), 398; personal communication, re: grandmother's career, from questionnaire respondent #2.

29. The determinants of wages and status in the telegraph industry's geographical periphery is considered in more detail in chapter four of my "Canadian Telegraphers, 1900–1930: A Case Study in Gender and Skill Hierarchies," MA thesis, Queen's University, 1988.

30. Joy Parr, "Disaggregating the Sexual Division of Labour: A Transatlantic Case Study," *Comparative Studies in Society and History*, 30 (1988), 512.

31. Robert E. Babe, "Telegraph," *The Canadian Encyclopedia* (Edmonton 1985), 1795; NAC, Records of the Canadian National Railway, RG 30, History of the Great North Western Telegraph Company of Canada; *CTJ*, 8 (7 July 1910), 208; Judson C. Welliver, "Will take and keep all the wire lines; cabinet favours it," [*New York Evening Globe*?], 7 July 1918 (reports A.T.&T.'s willingness to have government take over the telegraph business).

32. NAC, RG 27, vol. 557, strike 2975, "Strike To-day to be General," *Toronto Mail and Empire*, 14 August 1907.

33. Graham S. Lowe, "Class, Job, and Gender in the Canadian Office," *Labour/Le Travailleur* 10 (1982), 21; Alison Prentice, et al., *Canadian Women: A History* (Toronto 1988), 125.

34. *CTJ*, 18 (1920), 489–90.

35. As a point of comparison, see the 1921 "skilled labour" wage quoted by Bryan D. Palmer, *Working-Class Experience* (Toronto 1983), 145.

36. NAC, RG 27, vol. 333, strike 57, Report of J.A. Clark, 15 September 1924; *CTJ*, 18 (1920), 532.

37. The stock brokerage business alone expanded from 1724 people working as stock brokers in 1921 to 4873 thus employed in 1931. Before 1921, stock brokers were included with commodity and pawn brokers in one census category. This occupational category grew in number from 1251 in 1892 to 3109 in 1921. *Census*, vol. IV, Population—Occupations, 1921, 6–7, 30, 114; vol. VII, 1931, 318. On wages (for the 1920s): Interview #1, tape #1, side A, 088–095, 577–587; Interview #3, side A, 576–583.

38. McNicol Collection, Item 516, file 10, Reynolds Testimony, 25.

39. McNicol Collection, Item 517, *Telegraphers' penmanship*, 1918, Unidentified typescript, containing only the quoted sentence and a stanza of verse:

"The chief walks round the office with his pen behind his ear,
    Listnin' to the clickin' of the sounders that are near,
    He watches for the orders, as he squints beneath his specs,
    And I often wish he'd slip me more of the short ones and the blacks."

"Blacks" were day messages, as distinct from night messages ("reds"). They were charged out at a higher rate per word than were reds, and so were generally shorter.

40. Donald McNicol, *American Telegraph Practice* (New York 1913 [second impression of first edition, corrected]), 207.

41. Rayne, 137.

42. *U.S. Commission on Industrial Relations*, 9307.

43. *U.S. Commission on Industrial Relations*, 9318.

44. Interview #3, side A, 366–376.

45. McNicol Collection, Item 510, *Telegraph and radio sending and receiving contests*, W.M. Gibson to D.M. McNicol, 17 March 1917; McNicol Collection, Item 483, *Canadian telegraph and telegraphers*, Application of Milton O. Hoffman to Old Time Telegraphers' and Historical Association.

46. McNicol Collection, Item 98, clipping of article by Floyd S. Chalmers, "Great Men of the Key: Prominent Canadians Who Started as Telegraph Operators," *Maclean's Magazine*, n.d.

47. NAC, RG 27, vol. 557, strike 2975, "The Telegraph Situation and its Effect on Canadian Operators," 12 August 1907.

48. This career path is evident in the biographies of unionists and company superintendents. See *CTJ*, 20 (1923), 398; *CTJ*, 13 (1915), 130; *CTJ*, 18 (1920), 501; *CTJ*, 18 (1920), 536; *CTJ*, 18 (1920), 518; *T & T Age*, 19 (16 January 1902), 41; *T & T Age*, 19 (1 December 1902), 41.

49. *The Postal Telegraph* (December 1917), 2–7.

50. NAC, RG 27, vol. 310, strike 30, "Girl Messengers on Special Work," *Ottawa Citizen*, n.d.

51. *U.S. Commission on Industrial Relations*, 9303.

52. This difference is apparent in the biographical information given by Canadian applicants to the Old Time Telegraphers' Historical Association (OTTHA). The three women applicants started at ages 17, 18, and 19. Male applicants began as early as age 10 and half of the male applicants to the OTTHA began at age 14 or earlier. The latest starting age was 20. McNicol Collection, Item 483, *Canadian telegraph and telegraphers*. For a reference to the GNW hiring as "learners" individuals not yet finished a course in telegraphy, see George D. Perry to Dominion School of Telegraphy, 18 January 1917, reprinted in Dominion School of Telegraphy, *Prospectus* (1917), 20.

53. Interview #3, side A, 313–318; D.F. Comstock, "A Practical Home-Made Telegraphing Instrument," *Woman's Home Companion* (April 1905), 44. This article, printed on "Aunt Jane's Pages for Boys and Girls" was introduced as being for "our boys," was illustrated with a picture of a boy and described the project as being conducted by two boys.

54. Questionnaire #3, answer 28.

55. These figures were derived from data reported for Buffalo, Philadelphia, Cleveland, and Minneapolis in 1908, printed in U.S. Bureau of Labor, *Investigation of Western Union and Postal Telegraph-Cable Companies* (Washington 1909), Table III-A, 74-8, 82-94. This data describes a sample of the telegraph

workforce comprising about 20 percent of the total telegraph workforce in these cities. The proportion of men to women is greater in the sample than in the total telegraph workforce: 84 percent men in the sample, 75 percent in regular telegraph workforce.

56. *U.S. Commission on Industrial Relations*, 9321; McNicol Collection, Item 516, file 2, Clipping from *T & T Age* (1 August 1922); NAC, RG 27, vol. 557, strike 2975, "The Telegraph Situation and its Effect on Canadian Operators," 12 August 1907; *T & T Age*, 19 (1902), 168–69; *The Postal Telegraph* (August 1910), 16.

57. *U.S. Commission on Industrial Relations*, 9321.

58. *CTJ*, 13 (1915), 144.

59. *U.S. Commission on Industrial Relations*, 9321.

60. *CTJ*, 20 (1923), 398; *CTJ*, 18 (1920), 541; Interview #2, side A, 146–150, 153–161 (This operator said in a note to the author that most companies would not employ both husband and wife—one had to resign); Questionnaire #1, biographical data; "Misses" predominate among women named in staff lists: e.g. "Letters from our Agents. Toronto GNW," *T & T Age*, 19 (1902), 18–19; "Toronto CPR," *T & T Age*, 19 (1902), 490; "Notes from Halifax Western Union," *T & T Age*, 15 (1894), 410.

61. The comfortable fit between the telegraph employers' preference for young workers and the usual departure of women from paid work for marriage also meant the ongoing creation of a reserve of temporary operators. Married women were sometimes used as strike-breakers and occasional help, but seem not to have exerted a downward pressure on wages to the same degree as in the very different circumstances of the garment industry, as described by Mercedes Steedman in "Skill and Gender in the Canadian Clothing Industry,

1890–1940," in Craig Heron and Robert Storey, eds., *On the Job: confronting the labour process in Canada* (Kingston 1986), 152–76. Comparison of the two industries suggests two different ways family roles may affect gender relations in different occupations.

62. The solidarity bred in the printer's craft culture shared with the telegraphers' unity the discordant counterpoint of gender exclusion: Ava Baron, "Gender and the social construction of work in the American printing industry, 1850–1920," paper to the Social Science History Association, St. Louis, October, 1986; Cynthia Cockburn, *Brothers: Male Dominance and Technological Change* (London 1983).

63. *CTJ*, 20 (1923), 394; *CTJ*, 13 (1915), 135–35; McNicol Collection, Item 517, clipping from *Railroad Man's Magazine* (July 1918), 422–23; McNicol Collection, Item 495, file 6, Discussion on "A high-speed Printing Telegraph System," Discussant Ralph Pope, American Institute of Electrical Engineers, *Transactions* (26 June 1914), 1902; "Vancouver CPR Notes," *T & T Age*, 14 (1 January 1894), 15; Questionnaire #1, answer #35.

64. Brenton A. McNab, "Telegraphers, Rhymsters, and Poets," *T & T Age*, 19 (1 January 1902), 4; McNicol, *American Telegraph Practice*, 208–9 (an engineer's view of the rhythm of manual sending); "The Mistake Was One of Nature," *T & T Age* 19 (1 February 1902), 65; Interview #1, tape #1, side B, 299–302, Interview #3, side B, 210–222, 309–315; Thomas Raddall, *The Nymph and the Lamp* (Toronto 1963), 196–97. Raddall's first job was as a wireless telegrapher just after World War I, before voice transmission on marine radio.

65. Ned Kent, "What Came of being Caught in a Snow-Storm," in W.J. Johnston, 159; Interview #3, side A, 408–413, 417–425, 428, 443; McNicol Collection, Item 495, file 6, Discussant C.R. Underhill, 1899.

66. McNicol Collection, Item 517. This file includes reports on contests as late as 1930.

67. McNicol, Item 486, "Only a Telegrapher"; McNicol Collection, Item 98, Chalmers, 65; Interview #2, side A, 210–222; "Montreal District Council," *CTJ*, 13 (1915), 142; Questionnaire #1, answer #13; McNicol Collection, Item 410, file 11, "Telegraphy an Honorable Occupation [editorial]," clipping from *T & T Age* (16 July 1915), 331.

68. *CTJ*, 18 (1920), 498; *CTJ*, 20 (1923), 398; Questionnaire #2, answer #35; Miss J.J. Schofield, "Wooing by Wire," in Johnston, 95; Questionnaire #3, answer #39. See also note 26.

69. Interview #1, tape #1, side B, 333–344.

70. Raddall, *The Nymph*, 167–69; Interview #3, side A, 376–383; Questionnaire #2, answers #27 and #28.

71. Interview #3, side A, 448–464.

72. McNicol Collection, Item 510, file 10, Phillips, clipping from *T & T Age* (16 October 1909), 724.

73. Questionnaire #2, answer #26.

74. Interview #1, tape #1, side B, 303–307. Operators in the same office might have typing contests, too. Interview #1, tape #2, 322–327.

75. Kent, "What Came of Being Caught," 160; Raddall, *The Nymph*, 197.

76. See notes 63 to 68.

77. McNicol Collection, Item 486, *Early telegraph poetry, 1896–1908*. The poem is a direct imitation of Thomas Babington Macaulay's "Horatius" in *Lays of Ancient Rome*.

78. McNicol Collection, Item 486, *Early telegraph poetry, 1896–1908*.

79. McNicol Collection, Item 510, file 10, clipping from *T & T Age* (16 October 1909), 725.

80. Interview #1, tape #1, side B, 448–455.

81. Interview #1, tape #1, side B, 455–472, and author's notes.

82. For example, Ned Kent, "What Came of being Caught."

83. "L.C.H.," "Flirtation by Wire," *Telegraph Age*, 14 (1894), 5–6.

84. *Telegraph Age*, 19 (1902), 65.

85. This protesting voice was unique in clearly originating in Canada. Others, focusing on equal pay for equal work, sexual harassment, and "male iniquities," surfaced in American publications: Graham Taylor, "The Industrial Viewpoint. Women Telegraph Operators," *Charities and The Commons*, 19 (5 October 1907), 864; *CTJ*, 5 (August 1907), 847–48.

86. *Telegraph Age*, 19 (1902), 96.

87. CPR's pole mileage, by contrast, had increased by almost 50 percent. The GNW figures, however, reflect more correctly the change in the commercial telegraph industry, because they are not, as are CPR's, related to railway development. John Murray, *A Story of the Telegraph* (Montreal 1905), 119–20; *Sessional Paper 20f* (1913 and 1916).

88. Donald McNicol, *American Telegraph Practice* (New York 1913), 208–9.

89. McNicol Collection, Item 495, *Mechanical and printing telegraphy*, Discussion on "A High-Speed Printing Telegraph System," *Proceedings*, American Institute of Electrical Engineers, Discussant Ralph W. Pope, 26 June 1914, 1902.

90. McNicol Collection, Item 486, *Early telegraph poetry, 1896–1908* (various poems about "mills" and "sheens"—slang expressions for "typewriters"—discuss both the usefulness of typewriters and the difficulty of having to buy one); U.S. Bureau of Labor, *Investigation of Western Union and Postal Telegraph-Cable Companies* (Washington 1909). [McNicol Collection, Item 207], 38–39. American companies seem to have made this

requirement before Canadian ones did. As late as 1915, a GNW official felt it necessary to inform the Dominion School of Telegraphy that "The typewriter is taking a very prominent part in Commercial Telegraphy and it is necessary that operators be familiar with its use in order to secure good positions." Dominion School of Telegraphy and Railroading, *Prospectus* (1917), 20.

91. D. McNicol, "Speed of Morse Telegraphy," *Telegraph Age* (16 July 1907), 394.

92. These keys, called "bugs," were invented in the first decade of the twentieth century. With a bug, the dots and dashes were not produced by individual vertical movements of the key. Rather, a continuous series of dots were made by the bug's mechanism when its lever was pushed to the right, and when the lever was pushed to the left, a continuous series of dashes would be produced. The operator would hold the key to the right until the required number of dots had been sent, or to the left until enough dashes were made. Thus, for three dots or three dashes, only one operator movement would be required. Moreover, the kind of movement required was less stressful on forearm muscles than that required by the traditional Morse key, and thus protected against the paralysis of "telegraphers' wrist." The bug was widely agreed to be boon to the operator. McNicol, *American Telegraph Practice*, 208. McNicol Collection, Item 495, files 1a, 1c, and 1d.

93. On time clocks in Canada, *CTJ*, 13 (1915), 143; on bonus system in Canada, Interview #1, tape #1, side A, 304–307, 312–321; Interview #3, side A, 551–554.

94. *Labour Gazette* (hereafter *LG*), (October 1917), 793–94; McNicol Collection, Item 483, *Canadian telegraph and telegraphers*, clipping from a CPR annual report, n.p.

95. *T & T Age*, 37 (1 August 1919), 369; *T & T Age*, 38 (1 July 1920), 371;

U.S. Commission on Industrial Relations, 9397, 9409; *LG* (October 1917), 803.

96. J.F. Skirrow, "A Few Comments on Printing Telegraphs and Morse," *T & T Age* (1 April 1919), 162.

97. Even engineers who disagreed about the over-all value of printing telegraphs agreed on this point. See McNicol Collection, Item 495, file 6, John H. Bell, "Printing Telegraph Systems," Paper presented to the American Institute of Electrical Engineers, 19 February 1920, 57–79; and Skirrow in *T & T Age*, 162.

98. *CTJ*, 13 (1915), 123; *CTJ*, 13 (1915), 127; *CTJ*, 18 (1920), 522, 523; NAC, RG 27, vol. 342, strike 24, *New York Times*, 18 March 1929; Skirrow in *T & T Age*, 161.

99. For a summary of operators' stress-related health problems, see "McElreath Testimony" and "McElreath Exhibit No. 1," *U.S. Commission on Industrial Relations*.

100. *T & T Age*, 19 (16 November 1902), 479–80.

101. *CTJ*, 2 (1904), 1; *CTJ*, 18 (1920), 534–35. Union membership went from about one-seventh of all Canadian operators in 1907 to one-third by 1919. The 1907 figure for total number of operators is an estimate, *CTJ*, 17 (September 1919), 4137-8; Dominion Bureau of Statistics, *Telegraph and Cable Statistics*, 1917–1931.

102. *CTJ*, 13 (1915), 136.

103. *CTJ*, 13 (1915), 143.

104. *LG* (August 1910), 187.

105. *CTJ*, 13 (1915), 136.

106. *CTJ*, 13 (1915), 144.

107. McNicol Collection, Item 495, file 1c, J. Rosenbaum, "Adjustment of Semi-Automatic Transmitters," clipping from *T & T Age* (16 March 1920); no author, "Semi-Automatic Morse Transmitters: Adjustment and Operation," clipping from *T & T Age* (1 November 1920).

108. Raddall, 167–69; Interview #1, tape #1, side B, 303–307; Ned Kent, "What Came of Being Caught," 160.

109. McNicol Collection, Item 510, *Telegraph and radio sending and receiving contests*, file 10, clipping from *T & T Age* (1 October 1909), 676; McNicol Collection, Item 517, *Telegraphers' penmanship* (1918), George Barnes Pennock, "A Practical Telegraph Tournament," typescript.

110. I want to emphasize here that gender identity was both a means of organizing consent to individualistic productivity goals and a rallying point for union solidarity. The conflicts between union men and anti-union workers in the early twentieth century might usefully be analysed as points at which tensions within masculinity emerge in social conflict or perhaps as struggles between different masculinities.

111. *LG* (October 1917), 794–94.

112. Cynthia Cockburn, *Brothers: Male Dominance and Technological Change* (London 1983), 112–14.

113. Opinion among electrical engineers and telegraph company managers was divided as to the economies and scheduling advantages of automatic systems. Most agreed that the Morkrum automatics were the best available, but debated whether these were good enough. One of the two major American firms, the Postal (which would ultimately become International Telephone and Telegraph) abandoned the automatics entirely in 1919, after having used them for about nine years (*T & T Age*, 16 February 1920, 110). A Postal engineer concluded his critique of automatic printers with the opinion that "the Morse system will continue to be the principal reliable and economical standby for many years to come." (*T & T Age* (1 April 1919), 162).

114. The expansion of employment for women in clerical jobs and the telephone business reduced the supply of women available for telegraphy work. The phrase "petticoat rule" is taken from the telephone industry, where female takeover was a concern of the International Brotherhood of Electrical Workers, according to Jack Barbash, *Unions and Telephones: The Story of the Communications Workers of America* (New York 1952), 4, quoted by Joan Sangster, "The 1907 Bell Telephone Strike: Organizing Women Workers," *Labour/Le Travailleur*, 3 (1978), n. 85.

115. The posture of protective elder brother implicit in some telegraph unionists' tactics (for example, NAC, RG 27, vol. 307, strike 122, "Orders the workers to be taken back," *Ottawa Citizen*, 25 October 1917) resembles a similar stance by male organizers in the garment industry during the early-20th century, as noted by Steedman, "The Clothing Industry," 162–63.

MEMORIES OF WORK, FAMILY, AND GENDER IN THE CANADIAN MERCHANT MARINE, 1920–50 ◊

ERIC SAGER

o

MASCULINITY

Steamships, like sailing ships before them, were largely male workplaces. In many vessels women worked in the catering department, but only rarely were they hired elsewhere in a ship; and only in the second half of the twentieth century did women, in small numbers, become officers in Canadian merchant ships.

The transition from sail to steam actually saw a small increase in the number of women workers in shipping. In the deep-sea sailing ships of the Maritime provinces, only four out of every 1000 crew had been women.[1] In 1938, 2 percent of workers in Canadian deep-sea ships were women. Most women were kept apart from the male deckhands and stokehold crew, and most held the rank of "stewardess" or "assistant stewardess."[2] There is little doubt that the proportion of women in the industry declined during the Second World War.[3]

This male domination of the workplace was not peculiar to ships. Nor was it the result of the nature of work in steamships: although some jobs did require considerable manual strength, most jobs could be done by women, had they been given the same opportunities or the same training as were the men. In pre-industrial Canada, women worked in farming, in fishing, and in the fur trade, for instance, and their work often demanded great physical strength as well as stamina.

◊ This excerpt is reprinted with permission of the publisher from *Ships and Memories: Merchant Seafarers in Canada's Age of Steam* by Eric Sager (Vancouver: UBC Press 1993). All rights reserved by the Publisher.

In our industrial society, the separation of men and women at work deepened. Even when women were capable of doing a job, there was a deep resistance to their presence.

[Interviewer] "During the war, do you remember any women radio officers in Canadian ships?"

Never one, no. Mind you, there were lots of women went through radio school during the war. All kinds of them. Gee, I remember girls in my class.

[Interviewer] "So where did they work?"

Norwegian ships. Now, in more recent years, you find them working on oil rigs. In fact there's a friend of mine in Sarnia, she's a first class radio operator. She served on an oil rig off the coast up north. She was a first class certificate. So I'm right in saying I never met a Canadian woman radio operator in a merchant ship, but I have met them serving on oil rigs.[4]

Along with the many superstitions about women at sea, the belief persisted that women could not be trusted in certain situations. Such beliefs continued, even when women sometimes crossed the divide and performed "man's work." Among outport families operating their own small vessels, the gender divide might be a little easier to cross.

My sisters could steer just as well as I could.

[Interviewer] "Your sisters knew something about ships too?"

Oh yeah.

[Interviewer] "How did they pick it up?"

Havin' the scattered trip with us. And when they were young, they lived right alongside the wharf. Anything come alongside the wharf, they saw it just as well as the rest of us. I broke my arm once, well my sister happened to be on board the boat at the time, and my younger brother. Well, she took over the boat then, and took me to the doctor.

[Interviewer] "Who taught them?"

They just learnt it.

[Interviewer] "Would your dad take them as crew?"

No. None of 'em ever went as crew. But sometimes, say we were comin' up to St. John's, they'd come along too. They knew how to steer and so on.

[Interviewer] "Did they ever want to go as crew?"

No. Neither of them ever wanted to go as crew. It was too hard work anyway.

[Interviewer] "Could they have done the work?"

Yes. Good ears, good eyesight—that was the main thing.

[Interviewer] "Why didn't they want to go then?"

I don't know. There's very few that wants to. In the coast guard there, there's the scattered one. Not many. I don't think it's any place for a woman. It's too hard a work. . . .

We brought a young lady up from St. Anthony one time, and you could go for'ard, and hold up a board like that, and she'd put bullets through it—twenty-two bullets. You could bet your life on it. I never saw the like. She was a crack shot. If she got a gun she wasn't used to, she'd have a few shots first, after that, she was perfect.

[Interviewer] "Where did she learn that?"

Up north. Huntin'.[5]

The pressure on women to stay out of this industry—or at least to remain away from the male domains of deck, engine-room, and bridge—is clearly revealed when a woman did make it to a position of command. Captain Molly Kool was both celebrity and oddity, as the following newspaper report from 1939 suggests.

What would those hard-boiled old shipmasters, who commanded vessels out of this very spot, say to a girl being called "captain" and holding a master's ticket! I think I can feel a blueness in the air and hear the angry thump of sea boots on the quarter-deck, even from their ghosts. Many of them were so superstitious they wouldn't even sail in a ship that had a woman's name. . . .

"Molly," said I, "suppose you were married—are you going to get married?"

"Maybe." Girls are girls the world over and Molly is every inch a girl as well as every inch a sailor.

"Well, suppose you were married and your husband was first mate on the vessel you commanded?"

"I'd make him toe the mark."

I'll bet she would.

"Suppose now, he was captain and you were first mate?"

"I'd do everything he told me," said Molly firmly, "that pertained to the running of the ship."

"Can you cook, Molly?"

"Sure I can cook, but I don't do much cooking on the boat. I have to sail her."[6]

Such was the barrage of condescension and pressure that the occasional woman seafarer faced when she entered a workplace that men claimed as their own.[7]

The idea that there were such things as "man's work" and "women's work" did not begin in ships. It began on land, and was transferred to ships, long before the days of steamships. By the twentieth century, men had dominated seafaring for so long that they were very hard to displace. The skills of seafaring were their birthright, they assumed, and when jobs were scarce and promotion was difficult, they were unlikely to want to share these things. The idea that seafaring was masculine was so deeply rooted that even a woman seafarer described herself as a "seaman"—as Jessie Sauras did when reflecting on her days in lake ships.

I was the only woman. I was the first woman on those ships. One night we came in and we went down to the sailors' home, and they came to stop me at the door and said I couldn't come in, it was men only. And I said, well I'm awfully sorry but I'm a seaman too.

They said you can't be a seaman you're a woman. I said, that's all right, I'm a seaman just the same, do you want to see my papers? And they were amazed.[8]

Divisions between the sexes began ashore, but in certain specific ways seafaring reinforced those divisions. Most male seafarers, like most men ashore, assumed that married women should not normally work outside the home. Long absences at sea reinforced this assumption.

No, my wife didn't work. I didn't want her to. I said it was up to me. She spoke to me once—a friend of hers had a job in a government building and wanted to know if she wanted a job over there. I says, "Well, I'd rather you didn't. I'd like to think that when I come home, I got a wife to be able to talk to." And I figured, "It's up to me to support you, if I ask you to marry me."[9]

Even in the coastal service, a man might get little time with his wife, and so her domestic role seemed to be natural—in the interests of both man and woman.

I was on the triangle run, down to Seattle, up to Vancouver at night, down to Victoria in the morning. My home at the time was up at Moss Street and I went for four months and a half and never saw my home. You didn't have time. I'd be in the ship all that time, with no day off.

One day the chief clerk came down to me and said, "Captain Troup said you're paid for takin' tickets here, not for talkin' to your wife. He saw you sittin' in a car with her." I says, "Is that so? All the time I take off? I don't get away from here for more than ten minutes. I spend about two or three minutes with her!"[10]

Had this man's wife also held a wage-paid job, he might never have seen her at all—and so exploitation and gender stereotyping fed on each other and reinforced each other.

Seafaring, even more than most industrial labour, meant prolonged absences from women. For some, perhaps, it was a kind of escape from women, a kind of "male bonding." At sea, one was free from women, and free from the demands of mother, wife, or lover. The Lady Boats—the "love boats" of their era—and other passenger ships were something of an exception. Here contact with women passengers was a privilege of officers.

On freighters you live a very monastic life. But on passenger ships it's not so. You have female company in droves. You can live a social life. It's all sub rosa—but it's there.

The only officers permitted to have anything to do with the passengers were the captain, the purser, the doctor, and chief engineer, and the chief officer. Nobody else could even speak to them. Then you got no competition!

I remember one time in a Lady Boat, an officer was in some girl's room. And the captain heard about it, or suspected it, and sat in the rotunda where he had a view of the passageway where the officer had to emerge. So the officer peered out of the door and saw the captain. And I'd never have thought this possible, but he climbed up one side of the ship! Each port-hole was what they call an eyebrow, and he was able to crawl up there. When you consider that the ship was doing eighteen knots! And the story I heard, thereupon he walked past the captain and said, "Hello captain, how are you?" That was the story, anyway.[11]

In freighters, however, the separation from women meant that women became objects, possessing favours that might be purchased in port, and at sea they became the focus of endless yarns.

> Among my shipmates sexual images loomed large in their word pictures. These pictures were embellished—or, if the speaker lacked skill in language, degraded—by expletive. The expletive was usually used for emphasis, and talented men made it effective. The untalented were merely tiresome to listen to.[12]

If we could hear the language of the forecastle, we might know how deep-rooted was the consciousness of gender behind the language. The ship was always feminine, of course, and possessed stereotypical female attributes, as Joseph Conrad reminds us: "Your ship is a tender creature, whose idiosyncrasies must be attended to if you mean her to come with credit to herself and you through the rough-and-tumble of life. . . . Those sensitive creatures have no ears for our blandishments. It takes something more than mere words to cajole them to do our will, to cover us with glory."[13]

Seafarers lived in a society and a workplace that did little to inform (and much to corrupt) young people about their sexual natures. However ignorant, seafarers were nevertheless expected to perform sexually, as one young Canadian discovered during a voyage in a Norwegian steamer in the 1930s.

> In Adelaide, after the first night ashore, I volunteer for the job of night watchman, 10 PM to 7 AM. In theory it's to prevent intruders from boarding the ship, but in practice it's to ensure that sailors navigate the gangplank and leave their girl friends on the dock, a job demanding a certain amount of diplomacy.
>
> One night Arne staggers aboard, blood streaming from his forehead. He's had a rough going over by a gang of toughs. I wash his cuts, apply iodine, unshoe him, and dump him in his bunk. He remembers nothing the next morning.
>
> On another night a stoker from an English ship nearby blissfully walks off the dock near the stern and somersaults into the water. With a rope ladder and the help of his pal I haul him out. The two continue on their joyful way.
>
> On the first Saturday night, well after midnight, there is singing and laughter on the dock. Henry, Hans, Arne and the cook are manhandling a woman up the gangway.
>
> "You can't bring a lady on board," I say firmly.

"This is no lady," Henry says. "She hoor, beautiful hoor, see?" He shines his flashlight on her face. She's blond and two of her front teeth are missing.

"We bring her for you, Artoor!" Henry adds. "You come!"

There's no resisting Henry even when he's not in his cups. I am propelled aft, protesting, while the others follow with noisy whispers. Back in the mess the noise arouses others. A bottle of gin appears.

"The mate will hear you! You'll be in trouble!" I shout. "You've got to get this girl off!"

"Okay, okay, we take her off, okay," Arne says. "But first you got to fook her. That's why we bring her."

It takes three of them, but they push me into Arne's cabin with the woman, slam the door, and block it with a chair. She sits on the lower bunk, showing a lot of flesh.

"Come and sit down, honey," she says, smiling.

"Look miss, I've got to. . . ."

"You can call me Grace."

"Okay . . . Grace, I'm on duty, I've got to. . . ."

"Ah, come on, only take a minute!"

Blushing, I decide that honesty offers the only escape.

"Well, uh, Grace, well, as a matter of fact, I've never actually done it before and. . . ."

"You mean you're a virgin, honey? No kidding, a real one?"

"Well yes, I suppose you could say that."

"And you're scared, is that it?"

"Well. . . ." I'd heard a lot about venereal disease, but I thought it was best not to mention it.

"You don't want me to show you how, honey?"

"No thanks, not tonight. Perhaps some other time?"

She shakes her head, still smiling. "Okay, honey, you can relax." She gets up and pulls her skirt down.

"What do I tell the boys outside? They've already paid for you."

"Couldn't we pretend we did it?"

"You don't want them to know, is that it?"

"Well yes, I'd rather they didn't."

She is beside me now, hand on my arm, looking up. Her eyes are dark blue and, smiling with her lips closed, she looks pretty.

"Okay, honey, I'll do it," she says. She kisses me and her lips are warm and soft.

"Thank you," I say, meaning it. I move to the door but she stops me.

"Wait a minute, it takes longer than that!" she says, laughing.

She sits on the bunk again, bounces up and down vigorously until the springs squeak, bangs the steel wall with the heel of her shoe, and makes loud crying noises. The singing outside stops. Finally, after a prolonged moan, she gets up.

I turn to the door.

"No, wait!" she whispers.

She undoes the buttons of my shirt, unbuckles my belt, ruffles my hair. She puts my arm around her waist.

"Okay, that's better," she says. "Now don't say anything. Leave it to me."

She bangs the door and it's opened immediately. They crowd around, laughing and asking questions, but I say nothing and accept a beer.

"Now you've got to take Grace home," I say.

Before she leaves I give her a forceful kiss, pat her bottom, and say, "Thanks very much, honey."

A few minutes later they take her off. She must have kept her promise, as none of them offered me a woman again. After that, they didn't believe my stories about visiting museums and the countryside during the day, and they often joked about my "daytime woman."[14]

It would be a mistake, however, to imagine that seafarers had a "machismo" that was much different or stronger than that of men ashore. The notion that seafarers were peculiarly given to drinking, whoring, and fighting is the perspective of moral reformers and other landward types. Among seafaring workers, such activities were merely concentrated in space and time. Nobody has ever proved that they were more frequent among seafarers than among other groups, and we must remember that in the older steamships, as in sailing ships, workers were separated from women and from liquor for long periods of time.

Certainly there was a lot of drink on the waterfront. There is a lot of drink in any oppressive situation. And we come ashore, in a foreign port, and you get leave, and sure you're going to take a few drinks. I remember after a long voyage I didn't even know how to speak to a woman. I felt I had to have some drinks before I could line up and speak to some lady. . . . And seamen were not into fighting all the time! Damn it man, most seamen didn't fight! This is some kind of nonsense, the romanticism of movies, that seamen were battling with their fists all the time. No way! Most seamen were working men. This was their trade, this was the way they were earning their living. You still loved the sea, you loved the ships, yeah, but it was a way of earning a living, you didn't go around pounding it out with everybody. There wasn't any glorification of violence.[15]

On the other hand, sex was assumed to be heterosexual. The masculine culture of seafaring put its own sanctions around the relations between men themselves.

Well, this young fella we got from that family in Edinburgh, I warned him. I says, look, any time you go to take a shower, any one asks you to bend down and pick up the soap for them, don't do it. I says, there's an education in that and I told him what it was.[16]

Homosexuality, the subject of forecastle talk, promoted fear and loathing. This does not mean it never occurred: it is remarkable how many insist that it never occurred but proceed to cite an instance when it did.

> On a Swedish ship once, a second steward . . . where did we pick him up? The chief steward, he was next to the captain, four rings, you know. On Swedish ships the chief steward was a king. Then comes the first steward and second steward. This second steward, he was a young fellow, and he was caught, well, he had a young deck-boy in his bunk with him. Well, that poor guy. He landed up in hospital. The crew went to work on him, and at the next port, he was gone. That was the only one I remember.[17]

Anything that defied the heterosexual norm could become the subject of yarns, as seafarers reasserted their own masculinity, often at the expense of soldiers, officers, or naval types.

> Now here's another instance during the war. After Jerry folded I went out to the Pacific, and to India. Now when we were running to India, we had a lot of troops on board. The Black Watch was one of 'em. And I thought they was all tough people in the Black Watch, but oh Christ there was two of 'em—one called hisself Mabel and the other called hisself Maude. And in the evening— how the hell they carried it with them I don't know—but one of 'em would come out dressed in gold stuff, gold lamé or whatever, all glittering, and he'd parade up and down the alleyway. And then he'd bump into the other one and: "Helloooo Maude. . . ." "Helloooo Mabel dear! . . ."
>
> And this is the Black Watch, who's supposed to be a real first class fightin' machine? Every night they'd parade up and down the alleyways all dressed up in women's clothing, one in gold and the other in silver. And they'd make up to the fellows.[18]

Men fought and men worked. The test of manhood was how one did one's job, and he who could not do his job, or hold that job even in a depression, risked failure as a man. Masculinity was bound up with man's role as wage-earner and worker. The seaman was a worker who left his family to see the world, taking with him a masculinity which he learned ashore. Much later, an older man saw all this, and came to know much better the youth that he once was.

> Perhaps that carelessness towards the responsibility that one owes to one's partners in these fleeting love affairs was something I adopted from the ambience in which I was raised. No one in my childhood could be described as an emancipated person, and the women in the typical family were less emancipated than anyone, consigned the role as if by nature of mother, housewife, and bearer

of children. Life in these years was rather rude, and one sought out women to fulfil one's physical needs. In addition to these general attitudes, which I shared with almost everyone around me, I had a number of special reasons for avoiding entanglements. When I left home I had no intention of ever settling down: the idea was as far from my head as it could have been. I was destined to see the world.[19]

FAMILY

We all admit the importance of family in our lives, and historians spend a great deal of time and effort studying families. But fitting family into the historical process is very difficult, and it is no easier for seafarers than for any other group.

But seafarers know the subject is important. So they will raise it themselves, as one did with me: "You must interview my wife some time. Interview her! She'll tell you where the bear shit in the buckwheat."[20]

When the seafarer him or herself makes a remark such as this, the historian had better listen. So let's pursue this further, beginning with the relations between a male seafarer and his family ashore.

> First ten years of my married life, I was away 325 days a year. Second ten years, 278 days. The last ten years I was in management, and I was away about 150 days a year. Who in hell's going to run this household? Oh yeah, she ran this family. I have never seen a pay cheque! But don't forget, she's not a dictator—it's a constitutional monarchy she runs.
>
> I came home, rolls of money. I was not allowed to give money to the children. Oh no! You were disturbing the minister of supply and services if you did that. You don't disrupt. You follow the general rules of the household. There's no visible leader, but she's laid down the rules, and you pretend to ignore them only up to a point. Don't come home with pockets full of money and buy the kids bicycles and motorbikes and cars! Every once in a while that rule is brought up.[21]

And another career sailor: "This place, for instance. She was in total charge of it. She paid all the bills."[22] Such statements underestimate the power and influence of the male wage-earner, and there is plenty of evidence that husbands dictated the patterns of family life. Nevertheless, there was an ambiguity about the role and status of the husband in these circumstances, and there was additional work and responsibility for the wife.[23] The master's wife remembers much more than the bills.

> When I married him I knew he was going to sea, so I had to do the best I could. 'Course they have it a lot better now because they're only away a month and then they're home a month, which is good, you know. They're hardly away long enough to be missed.

It's almost like a single parent. They're talking about single parents so much today. I had nobody to ask what I should do. . . .

I always felt . . . the only thing I used to try and do when he was gone so long and the children were small, he was gone long enough that they'd think, well, daddy, we talk to him on the phone, but who is he? And if I saw them doing something I knew he wouldn't like, before he had a chance to say anything I'd sort of get to them first, because I didn't want them to resent this man coming home once in a while and making them do these things.

I'm still very independent which he gets annoyed at me at times, because I go and do things that normally he would do, well, probably he should do, but I just do them automatically without thinking, because I had nobody to call upon when the kids were small, you know. I used to do the painting and everything.

It wasn't all that bad. One thing, with him away so much, every time he was home it was like another honeymoon, so maybe . . . I don't know, I had a good life. I think we made out all right.

[Husband: "Well, I got a jewel to begin with so. . . ."]

Well . . . but it's a different life, too. You're sort of on your own to go anywhere. It's kind of difficult to go to mixed do's, I always found. It used to irk me to hear navy wives talking. The ships used to go out and come back in for teatime. They were called teatime ships.

It wasn't all that bad. I wouldn't mind doing it over again, really. And then when the children were older I made several trips with him which was very nice. I really enjoyed that.[24]

Many accepted long separations stoically—they were the inevitable result of the job. Some master mariners, if the employer permitted it were accompanied at sea by their wives. But for many, family was a main reason to come ashore, to "swallow the anchor," and leave seafaring to younger men. "I didn't want to go back to sea. I was still a bachelor and I wanted to live the way normal people do, with a wife and children and a home."[25]

Now my daughter was six years of age before she knew I was her father. I didn't have Christmas up till then. Finally, all I had off from the CPR, after working for them for just two weeks short of forty-eight years, was six Christmases at home. That's all I had in forty-eight years. Those were the sort of conditions.[26]

Seafaring remained largely a young man's occupation, but crews in steamships were usually older than those in sailing ships (see Table 1).[27] Here is one important change between the age of sail and the age of steam: in steamships, a larger proportion of workers stayed in the industry, or returned to it, in middle age.

The shift in age profile had important effects. For one thing, more seafaring workers were of an age to be married. It is difficult to know how many were married, because crew agreements do not give this information.

TABLE 1 AGES OF CREW IN SAILING SHIP FLEETS
OF ATLANTIC CANADA AND IN CANADIAN
STEAMSHIPS

Age	Four Atlantic Canada sailing ship fleets (1863–1912)	Canadian steamships (1938)
10–19	8.9%	5.1%
20–29	55.7	40.6
30–39	23.5	31.6
40–49	9.8	16.3
50–59	1.9	5.4
60+	0.2	1.0
Sample size	181 234	2915

But it is likely that an increasing proportion of crews in steamships were try-ing to combine marriage and family life ashore with seafaring as their regu-lar or principal occupation. A cautious estimate for CGMM crews would be that between 15 and 20 percent were married in the 1920s.[28] It is no surprise that CGMM adopted the British allotment system, whereby sailors could have a specified portion of wages sent directly to their families.

As sailing ships were replaced by steamships, it became easier to com-bine work at sea with a stable residence ashore—although one might be absent from home for long periods of time. A larger proportion of seafarers worked for liner companies, whose vessels worked to schedules on specific routes. Even cargo steamers, such as those of CGMM, were likely to return to their home port on a fairly regular basis. And, in contrast to sailing ship crews in earlier decades, the crews of steamships tended to have residences in those home ports. As if to acknowledger the growing importance of land-ward residence, twentieth-century crew agreements (unlike those for the nineteenth century) recorded each crew member's home address. In 1938, a majority of workers in Canadian deep-sea ships resided in just four places: Halifax, Dartmouth, Montreal, and/or Vancouver. Over 80 percent joined their ships in these same ports (see Table 2).[29] A similar change occurred in the British merchant marine in the shift from sail to steam: a large propor-tion of the crews in sailing ships came from inland towns or villages; in steamships a larger proportion of crews came from major port towns.[30]

Obviously, many steamship workers expected to be able to combine work with family life ashore, and this expectation had effects throughout the industry. For some, it increased the pressure to get promoted.

> Well, it was late in life when I got my mate's ticket. It was in the late 50s, 1957, I think. 'Course I had a wife and family at the time and money was scarce so I finally went and got a mate's home trade and after that I got the second mate's, foreign mate's, and a master's foreign.[31]

Some remember that prolonged absences did nothing to weaken the sense of duty to family.

TABLE 2 RESIDENCES OF CREWS IN CANADIAN DEEP-SEA SHIPS, AND PORTS IN WHICH SEAFARERS SIGNED ON, 1938

Place	% of Crew Residences	Place	% of Crew Signing On
Halifax/Dartmouth	24.4	Halifax	44.9
Other Nova Scotia	14.4		
New Brunswick	2.0	Other Atlantic	
PEI	0.7	Canada	1.4
Newfoundland	2.3		
Montreal	21.3	Montreal	34.2
Other Quebec	6.7		
Toronto	2.0		
Other Ontario	2.1		
Prairies	0.3		
Vancouver	4.8	Vancouver	4.3
Other British Columbia	1.1	Victoria	0.7
United Kingdom	1.8		
United States	1.4	United States	1.6
West Indies	10.0	West Indies	7.6
Central/South America	2.1	Central/South America	4.8
Other	2.6	Other	0.5
Total number of crew	2915		2915

Most of them, what they lacked in education, they made up in common sense. A lot of them were kind of foolish in their younger days, but very few of them stayed at sea all their life, at least in my time. When they left they kind of settled down and they'd become very stable because they'd done all their helling around. You get the roughest, toughest guys and you see them get married and they're the meekest. They put their whole thing into their family then, most of them were very good parents and good family men.[32]

For those who stayed at sea, family responsibility increased the fear of unemployment. Family was a major reason for the growing preoccupation with regularity of employment in the 1920s and 1930s. "I make good money now, but I got a wife and six kids, an' they got a bad habit—they like to eat—and I have to work."[33]

They transferred me to the *Empress of Canada*, but the thing was, I was getting employed for six weeks, and then I was off for three months. Well, you can't live off that, and I told them. Well, he says, this is how the CPR does it. Okay, I said, good-bye!
So I went on a rum-runner as second mate. The difference was ninety dollars to 350 which they were payin' the second officer of this rum-runner. Now which would you take?[34]

Many remember that the depression of the 1930s reinforced the connection to their parents and siblings.

1929 arrived. Everything came in and laid up. So I was out of a job, same as others were. They gave me a ticket home on the railroad. I was twenty-two, I guess. I had a home to go to—a lot of people didn't. So I stayed at home, and we got along. Then I got a job as a deck-hand—I was pretty lucky to get it—at sixty-five dollars a month. In the lighthouse service—now it's the coast guard. A small ship, just about ten of us altogether. I stayed there about four years. In the end I was keeping my family—my brother, my mother, and my father—that was the only money coming into the house. I'd give it to them—but I'd get a pack of tobacco once a week.[35]

This was a society which assumed that a male head of the family was the main breadwinner. And although families might grow vegetables, they lived in a society where families depended, more than ever before, on wages. Many seafarers, in both deep-sea and Great Lakes ships, returned to their families in winter. "In the wintertime they became unemployed again, and somehow they had to survive again till spring."[36]

Wage dependence—family—depression: together these things put enormous pressure on workers. The problem was that the reality differed so much from the ideal: the male "breadwinner" expected to be able to support his family on his wage, but wages were often inadequate for this purpose, and the very irregular employment in shipping often meant no wage at all. In the 1930s, average wages in seafaring fell at the same time as the shipping industry declined and fewer jobs were available. The wage of the able seaman in the CGMM steamship in the late 1920s had stood at $50 a month; ordinary seamen had been earning $35; firemen had been getting $50 a month. By the mid-1930s, all these wages had been reduced by 10 percent.[37] Table 3 offers estimates of monthly wages for selected ranks in Canadian steamships in 1938.[38] The figures indicate extreme wage differentials in a complex division of labour (the complete list of jobs contains over 200 different ranks or positions).

The averages in Table 3 conceal the enormous variation in wages for the same rank among different companies and different kinds of vessels.[39] By 1938, many of the tramp steamers that had been so numerous a decade before had disappeared from the fleet, and the large number of catering positions in Table 3 reflect the voyages of a few Canadian Pacific and CN passenger vessels. The low wages of the deck crew, firemen, oilers, male stewards, and female stewards are particularly striking. In 1938, the average male wage-earner in the manufacturing industry in Canada earned about $86 a month.[40] The majority of seafaring workers were earning much less than this. Many were earning less than half of the average manufacturing wage. Of course, seafarers received room and board while at sea, but the reality was that many were also trying to maintain a home ashore as well.

Wage dependence and unemployment were a threat to masculine pride. The fear of unemployment turned to anger and to radical ideas. The term "wage slavery" entered the political vocabulary of Canadian workers.

I was active in the unemployed movement for years during the Depression. At that time I was, you might say, pro-establishment.

TABLE 3 *AVERAGE MONTHLY WAGES,*
SELECTED RANKS, 1939

Rank	Monthly Wage	Number of Cases
Chief officer	$148.96	56
Second officer	130.30	49
Third officer	107.97	48
Chief engineer	232.05	54
Second engineer	160.76	53
Third engineer	134.57	48
Fourth engineer	111.56	47
Fifth engineer	99.45	35
Fireman	57.59	119
Trimmer	40.00	3
Oiler/wiper	51.20	49
Able seaman	54.34	407
Ordinary seaman	41.18	105
Deck-hand	24.52	50
Chief cook	85.56	27
Second cook	82.89	21
Chief steward	127.63	48
Second steward	97.07	26
Head stewardess	60.00	2
Stewardess	50.39	38
Assistant stewardess	44.22	15
Other stewards (male and female)	31.52	287
Messman	46.52	69
Waiter	30.00	76
Cabin boy	16.00	23
Purser	168.73	17
Assistant purser	100.67	18

But I was unable to find work at times during the Depression, and I joined the unemployed single men, and I even belonged to the Unemployed Married Men's Association. I was involved in several demonstrations. . . .[41]

Funny thing about the unemployed movement at that time— you were in and out of it, because you were unemployed half the time too![42]

Oh I knew there was an enemy somewhere. I mean God did not intend us to live this way.[43]

NOTES

1. Of 182 661 signatures on crew agreements of vessels registered in Saint John, Yarmouth, Windsor, and Halifax between 1863 and 1912, about 765 were signatures of women.

2. Of the 57 women crew in our sample of 2915 in 1938, 28 were stewardesses, 13 were assistant stewardesses, 2 were head stewardesses, 2 were bookstall attendants, and

there was one of each of the following: assistant cook, saloon messgirl, purser, nurse, electrician, assistant baker, shop attendant, hairdresser, and beautician.

3. A small sample of crew agreements for Canadian deep-sea vessels in 1948 has been analyzed. Of 2632 crew in this sample, only 26, or 1 percent, were women.

4. Russ Latimer interview.

5. Harry Stone interview.

6. Louis Arthur Cunningham, "Kool is the Word for Molly," *Star Weekly* (3 June 1939).

7. See also Margaret S. Creighton, "American Mariners and the Rites of Manhood, 1830–1870," in Howell and Twomey, eds., *Jack Tar in History: Essays in the History of Maritime Life and Labour* (Fredericton: Acadiensis Press, 1991), 143–63., 143–63.

8. Jessie Sauras, interviewed by Jim Green in Westville, Nova Scotia, 7 June 1980. See also Jim Green, *Against the Tide: The Story of the Canadian Seaman's Union* (Toronto: Progress 1986), 132.

9. Philip Hole interview.

10. Ibid.

11. George King interview.

12. Bent G. Sivertz, in a letter to E. Sager, 8 December 1986.

13. Joseph Conrad, *The Mirror of the Sea* (London: Dent 1923), 19, 29, 52.

14. Arthur H. Sager (Eric Sager's father), in a letter of 4 May 1990. He was in a Norwegian tramp steamer for a few voyages in the late 1930s.

15. Danny Daniels, interviewed by Jim Green in Montreal, 18 June 1980.

16. Charley Carr interview.

17. Niels Jannasch interview.

18. Charley Carr interview.

19. Gerard Fortin and Boyce Richardson, *Life of the Party* (Montreal: Vehicule 1984), 50–51.

20. A master mariner interviewed by Eric Sager in Nova Scotia, 1989.

21. Ibid.

22. Don Macfarlane interview.

23. See Valerie Burton, "The Myth of Bachelor Jack: Masculinity, Patriarchy and Seafaring Labour," in Howell and Twomey, eds., *Jack Tar in History*, 193.

24. Eric Sager's interview with Jack and Dorothy Matthews.

25. George King interview.

26. Philip Hole interview.

27. The same shift in ages occurred between sailing ships and steamships of the United Kingdom. The Atlantic Canada Shipping Project at Memorial University of Newfoundland did a computer analysis of a sample of crew agreements for non-Canadian (mainly UK) vessels between 1863 and 1900. Of crew in steamships, only 5.4 percent were aged 19 or under; 45.4 percent were aged 20 to 29; 30.3 percent were between 30 and 39; 14.4 percent were aged 40 to 49; and 4.5 percent were 50 or over. In UK sailing ships in the same decades, two-thirds were under thirty years of age. Eric W. Sager, *Seafaring Labour: The Merchant Marine of Atlantic Canada, 1820–1914* (Montreal: McGill-Queen's University Press, 1989), 254.

   In Table 1 in the text, information on workers in sailing ship fleets is from crew agreements for sailing vessels registered in Saint John, New Brunswick, and three ports in Nova Scotia: Yarmouth, Windsor, and Halifax. See Sager, *Seafaring Labour*, 139. The 1938 information is from a sample of every fourth crew agreement for Canadian-registered deep-sea ships in the microfilm collection of crew agreements held by the Government Archives Division of the National Archives of Canada in Ottawa. The file contains 2915 crew records for 58 voyages by 31 vessels. Most of these vessels were former CGMM ships, CN steamships, or Imperial Oil tankers; a minority were other tramp steamers. I am indebted to M.J. Partington for assistance in creating the computer file of information from these crew agreements.

28. This estimate is based on the "Personal Injury and Sickness Reports" for CGMM steamships contained in the Papers of Captain J.E. Faulkner, Public Archives of Nova Scotia, MG 7, vols. 83–87. These reports usually give marital status of crew who were injured or ill. Of 175 reports from the 1920s and early 1930s, 25 were for workers who were married and another four were widowers. A better way to discover marital status of seafaring workers would be to use the Canadian census returns. Unfortunately, the original enumerators' returns are not available after 1901. In another project, Dr. Peter Baskerville and I have computer files of information from the 1891 census for a 10 percent sample of all households in Halifax, Montreal, Vancouver, and Victoria. The samples contain 92 people whose occupations were seaman, able seaman, ordinary seaman, fireman, or other engine-room worker, excluding engineer officers. Of the 92, no less than 51 were married. It must be remembered, however, that this source does not allow us to distinguish deep-sea seafarers from those who worked in coastal vessels.

29. Data in the table are based on my sample of every fourth crew agreement for 1938 in the Government Archives Division, National Archives of Canada.

30. Sager, *Seafaring Labour*, 253–55.

31. Oscar Langdon, interviewed by Eric Sager at his home in Hantsport, Nova Scotia, June 1989. Captain Langdon first went to sea in 1939 in an armed merchant vessel and spent most of his postwar career in gypsum vessels operating out of Nova Scotia.

32. Morven Cox, interviewed by Eric Sager at his home in Dartmouth, Nova Scotia, June 1989. Captain Cox spent most of his career in British merchant ships.

33. Jerry Yetman, interviewed by Jim Green while driving from Halifax to Sydney, Nova Scotia, 6 June 1980. In 1980 Yetman was a senior official of the Nova Scotia Federation of Labour and a member of the Executive Council of the Canadian Labour Congress.

34. Charles Alltree interview.

35. Don Macfarlane interview.

36. Jimmy K. Bell, interviewed by Jim Green in Halifax, 5 June 1980.

37. From copies of portage bills of CGMM ships and CN steamships the *Canadian Mariner*, the *Canadian Cruiser*, and the *Canadian Skirmisher* in J.E. Faulkner Papers, Public Archives of Nova Scotia, MG 7, vols. 84–87.

38. Wages varied considerably among ships and companies, and the averages here are higher than for former CGMM ships, where wages tended to be lower than in CP or Imperial Oil ships. Particularly striking are the standard deviations for the 1938 mean wages of chief officer (standard deviation = 54.09), second officer (25.71), able seaman (8.20), chief cook (23.22), second cook (33.66), chief steward (31.43), second steward (33.19), purser (26.47), chief engineer (48.71), and fireman (9.28). One rank for which the standard deviation was low was stewardess (1.47). These results suggest that companies varied wages considerably to reward loyalty or experience—except in the case of women.

39. Note that the source in Table 3 is the same as that for Tables 1 and 2.

40. F.H. Leacy, ed., *Historical Statistics of Canada*, 2nd edition (Ottawa: Statistics Canada, 1983), series E64.

41. Jack Corrigan, interviewed by Jim Green in Vancouver, 10 December 1980.

42. Tommy Burnett, interviewed by Jim Green in Vancouver, 24 April 1980.

43. Steve Tokaruk, interviewed by Jim Green in Vancouver, 6 November 1980.

"HAVE YOU NO MANHOOD IN YOU?": GENDER AND CLASS IN THE CAPE BRETON COAL TOWNS, 1920–1926 ⬦

STEVEN PENFOLD

○

When Canadian soldiers were sent into the Cape Breton coalfields in the summer of 1922 to protect company property, they met little resistance from the striking coal miners. Instead, the soldiers encountered extensive ridicule from the women of the coal towns. The wives of striking miners brought their children to the military encampments to see "the men who were sworn to murder at the command of the ruling class of Canada." When a group of First World War veterans marched in support of the miners, the women held the soldiers guarding the collieries up to ridicule by suggesting that, by comparison, they were not "real" soldiers or "real" men—they had not fought for King and country in the trenches of France but wore their uniforms instead in the name of the Canadian capitalist.[1] This confrontation was a relatively minor occurrence in the pervasive industrial unrest in the Cape Breton coalfields in the first half of the 1920s. However, it highlights the ways that gender was woven into the fabric of class in the region and coloured the battle between the miners and their employers. The women's actions, and the gendered images they invoked, drew upon prevailing conceptions of the appropriate behaviour of men and women in the working-class community of Cape Breton. Although the women were most explicitly

⬦ Reprinted with permission from *Acadiensis* 23, 2 (Spring 1994): 21–44. For their comments and support at various stages of this project, I would like to thank Rob Kristofferson, Gerry O'Donnell, Adele Perry, Diane Swartz and the *Acadiensis* readers. At the very beginning, Adrian Shubert saved my sanity with timely advice. Since then, Craig Heron has been supportive beyond the call of duty. These interventions merit special mention.

expressing a commitment to the politics of class, the language of gender and class overlapped, and class loyalty became a test of manhood.

Such an incident was hardly the only example of women expressing their commitment to their class community. Indeed, women organized support activities, participated in crowd actions and stretched the dole to meet their family's needs during strikes. Yet the dominant historiographical view of women in Canadian coal-mining communities has placed them at home and dependent on men, if they are mentioned at all. Although scholars have illuminated important dimensions of the lives of miners in Cape Breton, including the labour process, standards of living, class identity and politics, little attention has been paid to how gender was reflected in these experiences.[2] David Frank has, in a short article, recognized the important role of the miner's wife as family financier, but he has not given any detailed examination of the important public role which women played.[3] Other studies have examined the role of women in British and American mining communities, but the public activities of Canadian mining women have thus far attracted relatively little attention.[4] Nevertheless, some historians have begun to recognize that even the efforts of non-waged women represent an important part of strike narratives.[5] In addition, it is also becoming clear that a second historiographical silence concerns the male coal miners themselves, who have not been the subject of much interest from historians exploring the gendered dimensions of men's lives.[6]

This study is an effort to integrate the analysis of gender dynamics and class conflict in the coalfields of Cape Breton in the 1920s. An "enlarged" view of strike activity is adopted in order to better integrate the actions of non-waged working-class women. Strike activity is viewed not as centred primarily in the workplace, but as a process of community mobilization. There is ample reason to adopt such a definition of strike activities in the case of the Cape Breton coalfields, since it was not just the workplace but the entire community that was, in Don Macgillivray's term, "besieged" by wage cuts, the presence of troops and company and provincial police.[7] Class drove the rhythm not just of the workplace, but of the whole community. With the establishment of the British Empire Steel Corporation (Besco) in 1921, the Cape Breton coalfield came under the control of a single corporation. The trend toward monopolization did not bring stability, however, but only served to heighten the crisis of "underdevelopment" which characterized the region. It was no surprise, given the labour-intensive nature of coal mining in the 1920s, that Besco should target wages in its efforts to rescue the consortium from financial oblivion.[8] The company's survival plan, however, met with stiff resistance from the miners, and the miners were supported by the women who lived in the coalfields. None of these women worked in the coal mines themselves.[9] Yet, working-class women engaged in a wide array of supportive class activities. Women's Labour Clubs constituted the most organized expression of women's commitment to class action, but women also played an important role in crowd actions, and the domestic labour of women itself constituted a hidden form of strike support. This study is concerned to map the discourses of gender, mainly as they relate to class and labour militancy in the working-class community, and in doing so to write women back into the well-established narrative of class conflict in the coalfields.[10]

Until recently, paying attention to gender meant nothing more than discussing women. But under the influence of postmodern theorists, historians (even those who would reject much of postmodern philosophy) have begun to advance a more complex understanding of gender which focuses on the interplay of ideals of femininity and masculinity. Joan Scott has been particularly vocal in her call for a more creative use of the concept of gender, demonstrating how it was often used to give a "natural" appearance to the construction of differences based on class, ethnicity or citizenship.[11] Gender biases penetrated the core of Cape Breton's class ideology, which depended on the discursive opposition of masculine and feminine to legitimize the opposition of worker to capitalist. But masculinity was not linked only to class. Indeed, it played itself out across a wide range of practices, only a few of which are discussed here. For analytical purposes, notions of manhood adopted by the miners will be grouped into three broad categories: one tied to work, one to family and one to class.[12] Obviously, the distinctions are to some degree false, as the different aspects of masculinity were lived simultaneously, and conflicting discourses intersected within each of those categories. Masculinity and femininity were not, after all, neat categories, but were practices often involving conflicting and contradictory ideas.[13]

Certainly the work culture of the mine was deeply imbued with gendered images. The mine itself was often referred to as a "she," and while officials were called "officials" and non-miners referred to as "citizens," the miners were referred to (and referred to themselves) as simply "the men."[14] Not all mine workers were seen as "men," however. The mines contained a variety of boy labourers in this period, who were socialized into manhood as they moved through the hierarchy of jobs underground. As Robert McIntosh has pointed out, the hierarchy of tasks in the 19th-century coal industry depended not so much on acquiring skill as acquiring certain gender traits: "The pit boy could expect to become a miner on reaching physical maturity. If most boys' work in the mine did not contribute directly to the acquisition of the technical skills of the miner, it did constitute . . . a process of 'pit-hardening,' the development of qualities of 'toughness, manhood and fatalism' associated with the collier."[15] It was not just skills that were taught, then, but manhood—which in the case of the miner included courage and stoicism in the face of constant danger and a sense of independence derived from being a tradesman. Completing the process of moving up through this gender hierarchy meant reaching "a man's estate." This socialization process included not just work-related education but initiation rituals as well. Pit boys complained of being the butt of practical jokes and the targets of spitting by tobacco-chewing adult miners. Key to this process of going up through the ranks was often the supervision of work by kin. Indeed, many boys were originally brought into the mine as helpers for their father.[16] By the turn of the century, mechanization of the cutting of coal had compromised the traditional place of boy labour in Nova Scotia mines by pushing mining toward what McIntosh describes as a "uniform semiskilled workforce of machine operators." At the outbreak of the First World War, only six percent of Nova Scotia mine workers were boys, down from 20 percent in the late-19th century.[17] Nevertheless, the sense of independence gained from this procession to manhood was a vital part of the gender identity of adult miners, and as late as the 1920s, the miners' sense of independence retained a structural basis. The physical conditions of the workplace made supervision difficult and placed a premium on the initiative and judgement of the individual miner of the "bords." While some miners guarded their independence, the physical conditions of the mine also led to a feeling of cooperation and common interest with fellow miners. A sense of mutual respect was even extended to underground foremen, whose judgement was preferred over the "checkers" brought in by Besco.[18]

The image of the male breadwinner was another important aspect of manhood, and it was often invoked for the ends of working-class struggle. "The first duty of a worker is to his family," a *Maritime Labor Herald* heading proclaimed in 1923.[19] The statement crystallized a common theme in the rhetoric of the Glace Bay labour newspaper, as well as that of union leaders and the miners themselves. Indeed, working-class grievances on a whole array of issues were defined in terms of the miner's concern for family and his role in it as sole breadwinner. The image of the male breadwinner was most forcefully expressed, logically enough, on the issue of wages. Miners consistently blamed the strife in the region on the fact that "we are not making enough money to live on, to support our families." The miners claimed a right to a "living wage," which, as David Frank has pointed out, entailed a level of comfort above mere subsistence.[20] The living wage was also based on the idea that the man's wage would constitute the only income for a family. As such, Alex Stewart told a royal commission in 1925, it "must . . . allow Canadian citizens, hardworking, honest heads of families, to live in peace and comfort and to have happy and well fed and well clothed children to comfort them in the hours after their day of toil." The living wage, then, had to be enough to prevent the necessity of a wife working to supplement the husband's income. Stewart was annoyed by the fact that his wife had to work while he was off at war: "the wife was forced and compelled to take a job. . . . That was the recompense I got for it [going to war]. She had to get out and labour too."[21]

But the living wage was not just an abstract definition or ideal, it was a concrete measure of a standard of living. As such, the union was quick to invoke this notion during periods of wage negotiation. When Besco argued before the Gillen Conciliation Board in 1922 that wage cuts were necessary because of the pressures of international competition, union leader J.B. McLachlan produced several wage slips "that did not allow a miner to support his family."[22] That the union would produce wage slips to support its demands for a living wage is instructive. The living wage was, after all, primarily a monetary standard, and it did not fully integrate the important role of the wife's labour to family support. Certainly miners recognized that without women's labour, they could never support the family—McLachlan, after all, had called the working-class woman the "best financier in the world." But McLachlan made the statement before a conciliation board, and he was really making a point about the level of men's wages, not the significance of women's domestic labour to the working class.

The male breadwinner ideal was not the exclusive property of the working class. The image could also be used in the rhetoric of anti-strike or pro-capitalist forces. During idle times, it was the advertised policy of the company to provide employment for married men if possible (it is not clear if they actually did so), a claim the company was quick to exploit during strikes. In 1922 the *Sydney Post* attributed the very existence of strikes to the lack of "domestic responsibilities" on the part of the strike leaders. The *Post* also appealed to the miners' breadwinner identity to try to convince them to stay on the job. In one case the paper argued that preparations for a strike constituted a "conspiracy to deprive 12 000 breadwinners of the opportunity of supporting their families." The *Sydney Record* echoed such appeals to male breadwinner ideology by editorializing during the 1925 strike that although the union executive had caused the work stoppage, it was "the miners' families . . . who will suffer."[23]

Because manhood was tied to the mine, to the labour process and to wages, a propensity to act in class ways was an important test of manhood for miners.[24] In this context "real men" were defined as those who maintained solidarity with their fellow workmen. "Real men," argued the *Maritime Labor Herald*, were not afraid "to oppose Besco at all times without slavish regard for the legal taboos set up to make the hearts of cowards quail." On another occasion, the *Labor Herald* suggested that weak or timid leaders ought to be replaced so that "men" were doing the "job of men." The rank and file apparently adopted this type of language as well. In 1923 picketers taunted a truck driver who was crossing picket lines, urging him to join their strike against Besco: "Jump out. You're a working man. These fellows have no hold on you. Be a man."[25] Ideals of manhood were used not only against union men, but could be used also to appeal to a wider definition of justice. Nova Scotia Premier George Murray was rhetorically asked "Have you no manhood in you? . . . Will you stand by the people of this province or will you stand by the stock gamblers of Montreal?"[26] Provincial policemen were ridiculed as unworthy of female affections, while class conscious miners were described as worthier mates than princes.[27] The importance of courage in the face of legal and company sanctions was articulated neatly in a letter to the *Labor Herald* from a miner who placed labour militancy in opposition to cowardice: "We workers are all Red, not yellow."[28]

The other side of this class definition of manhood was the use of feminine images to describe class enemies. A miner who was complaining about his small pay packet but admitted not voting for the Independent Labour Party was told by his mates to give his wife "the pants, and you go home with the children and wear the skirt."[29] The strongest use of feminine symbols was reserved for scabs. J.W. MacLeod, president of District 26 of the United Mine Workers of America in 1925, told the *Post* that picketers would prevent any "weak sisters members of the U.M.W. from going to work."[30] In a particularly dramatic style, scabs were described as being victims of "feminine domination," a circumstance which was bad enough in the home, but inexcusable in matters of class: "Where symptoms of feminine domination prevail and 'Eve' takes charge of the garden, mi-lord and master is deserving of pity, but when the feminine gender assumes the dictatorship in matters of industrial struggles, mere man becomes a worm." In such cases the assumption always existed that "a real man is never a scab."[31]

Opponents of working-class militancy also used gendered symbols to describe class behaviour. In this case, however, a disposition toward class cooperation was the important test. The general line of anti-strike newspapers was that strikes were caused by red agitators who stirred up trouble to benefit themselves. If the rank and file followed these leaders they were said to be displaying the "moral cowardice which compels people to follow the crowd, even when they know the crowd to be blatantly wrong." Strikes caused by the manipulations of these agitators were considered "unmanly."[32] Alexander MacNeil, general superintendent of coal mines for Besco, argued that it was precisely those positive gender traits of Cape Breton miners that allowed "weak leadership" to manipulate them: "The Nova Scotia miner is highly intelligent, courageous and independent. If left to himself he will play the game with his employer, but under weak leadership he is apt to go astray. His very fidelity to his leader causes him to follow where reason often forbids." MacNeil went on to contrast the sorry state of labour relations under the U.M.W. with the "gentlemanly" relations which existed under the Provincial Workmen's Association.[33]

Masculinity was clearly linked to class ideology, but there was no automatic relationship between manhood and class. Indeed, gender definitions and their implications were highly contextual, and different conclusions could be drawn from similar premises. Masculinity, after all, was not a rigid set of categories, but a practice. It is important, then, to examine the ways various definitions could collide and overlap in specific situations. While it is impossible in this space to explore the entire range of conflicting masculinities, two examples can help us understand how masculine norms were played out in practice.

In March 1922 Cape Breton miners overwhelmingly rejected a new agreement negotiated by the officers of District 26. The next step was not clear, but it was obvious that a strike was unrealistic. Indeed, the president of District 26, Robert Baxter, had recommended acceptance of the agreement partly because there was no money available for a strike. On the other hand secretary-treasurer J.B. McLachlan recommended a "strike on the job," where miners would work and collect pay, but restrict their output.[34] A debate ensued over whether this was the proper course. Part of the conflict was over tactical questions, but disagreements also revolved around the moral question of the propriety of the tactic, a debate which hinged on gender definitions.

Three basic positions emerged. Robert Baxter took essentially a tactical position, arguing that the strike on the job would not work and would probably lead to dismissal or a lockout. But he also expressed his opposition to striking on the job in gendered terms. Baxter argued that the miners should ignore McLachlan's "rantings" and that they should have the courage to admit they were not strong enough to win and that a strike would make it even harder to support their families. Admitting these were the facts, Baxter believed, would lead the miners to accept an "honourable retreat." McLachlan responded that there was no honour in giving in: the choice was between the organized miners who were "fighting for a living for your wife and family" while the "stock gamblers are fighting for profits on watered stock." Both Baxter and McLachlan tried to invoke the bread-winner role of miners, and both tried to argue that they had staked out the "honourable" position. This points to the third position, that of Minister of Labour James Murdock, who appealed to ethnic and gender definitions of "honour." Murdock sent a telegram to McLachlan which argued that the tactic was "unBritish, unCanadian and cowardly," because it was "in effect declaring to the world that only partial, grudging service will be given." The "strength of labour," he argued, was not to be found in such "under-handed dealings," but in "straight and honest dealings, each worker giving the best that is in him for the wages agreed upon." He preferred that "men quit like men and walk off the job when unwilling to work for wage rates or conditions offered." McLachlan responded angrily to Murdock's charges, telling a meeting of the unemployed that many of the miners who were striking on the job learned such tricks while serving their country in France.[35] Competing and overlapping definitions of manhood, then, were crucial to this debate.

Three years later, when Besco vice-president J.E. McLurg flippantly told a Canadian Press reporter that the miners would eventually come crawling back to the company because "they can't stand the gaff," he uttered what became probably the single most (in)famous line in Maritime labour history.[36] The statement became something of a rallying point, with miners greeting each other with the question "how are you standing the gaff?" The statement retains a resonance even today, and is typically por-trayed as a symbol of the heartlessness of the company. The statement also had resonance because it spoke to important gender definitions in the com-munity, and the reaction to the statement was expressed in gendered ways. A letter to the *Post* from a New Waterford miner objected in these terms: "The miners can stand the gaff far better than their wives and little children can."[37] Within this discourse women and children appeared as victims, while the statement also asserts that the miners are courageous enough to withstand the misery of a prolonged strike—that they can in fact "stand the gaff." When read in light of the connection between class solidarity and manhood, it becomes clear that McLurg had effectively closed off compet-ing discourses of manhood (and ethnicity) that were typically invoked by the government and the company as resources in class struggle (breadwin-ner ideology, honouring a contract, communist agitators as unmanly, union organizers as outsiders). McLurg had in effect questioned the miners' courage and, by extension, their manhood. By explicitly tying the success of the strike to the miners' courage and resolve, he reinforced the masculinist definitions of solidarity adopted by the miners.

The enforcement of such masculinist ideals of solidarity was in part dependent on the activities of women. Women often violently confronted scabs, policemen and soldiers. They had, however, something of an ambiguous relationship to class ideology. The miners were generally proud when women acted in class ways, and several examples of positive portrayals of the activities of working-class women can be found in the statements of labour leaders. But even in these cases, a class-conscious woman was never considered as valuable as a class-conscious man. Even then, women's class action was seen as something of a bonus, and recognition of it was usually an afterthought. The *Maritime Labor Herald*, for example, celebrated the fundraising efforts of radical women in 1924, but used gendered language which suggested that men ought to "speak in a louder voice."[38]

Yet many images of femininity warned against the dangers women posed to class solidarity. The image of woman-as-seductress, for example, was used to show how capitalists could use prostitutes and alcohol to corrupt class-conscious men. The *Maritime Labor Herald* warned miners that the capitalists had learned this trick from the Germans, who employed women as "spies": "The sirens would use their charms to get British officers drunk and babbling. Then the information given in drunkenness was used against the allies." Besco used similar tricks, the article warned, employing women in booze joints to seduce careless miners. The article warned miners to "beware of women who want to take you for a drink."[39] Another working-class image of womanhood was that of the "nagging wife." "If you cannot get a labor men through himself," the *Maritime Labor Herald* warned, "get him through his wife." If capitalists were unable to corrupt the radical labour leader, the article continued, they would attempt to corrupt his wife by inviting her to exclusive affairs and parties. Once the wife became accustomed to her new social circle, she would be told that "her husband is making too many enemies" and then—"The nagging then begins at home." The solution to this problem was to "educate the working-class women in the facts of the class struggle."[40]

Such images of women in working-class discourse point to the gendered hierarchy of class ideology which existed in the coal towns. Masculinity was thought to dispose one naturally toward loyalty to the working class, and no one with the attributes of true manhood was thought to be a threat to working-class solidarity. This was not the case with femininity. Though women were recognized as potentially class-conscious, many attributes associated with femininity were thought to constitute a threat to working-class solidarity. A man who was not class-conscious was acting in a way unnatural to his gender, while a women behaving the same way was not. It is clear, then, that the miners did not fully integrate the radical efforts of women into their view of class militancy. This was no doubt because of the importance of discourses of masculinity to the waging of class conflict in the region and the fact that the "naturalness" of viewing women as either conservative influences or passive victims of distress had already been constructed.

Chronic insecurity of income was a distinguishing feature of the Cape Breton mining communities, and the situation was especially severe during the industrial conflict of the 1920s. The combination of low wages and idle times increased the importance of careful budget management for the family. Although each family had different arrangements for domestic work, the responsibility for budget management fell most often on the women. Many of the miners who testified before the Duncan Commission in 1925 professed ignorance of the household accounts, and one even suggested that the union ought to call miners' wives to testify to the inadequacy of the wages paid by Besco.[41] J.B. McLachlan recognized women's role when he told the Gillen Conciliation Board that "the ordinary working man's wife is the best financier in the world—honest financier—I do not mean the other kind." McLachlan went on to note that the task was nevertheless impossible to fulfill under the present rate of wages.[42] Women obviously had a sense of the impossibility of the task they faced. When requested, they produced elaborate family budgets, and noted how the existing wages could not possibly cover all the expenses. One women described her role as trying to "make one dollar do the work of two."[43]

But careful budget management could not make up for the fact that there was often no money to manage, and part of the woman's role as financier and consumer consisted of waiting in line for relief. Although men did visit the relief stations, women appeared to predominate in relief lines. Observers noted that the relief provisions were not sufficient to feed the entire family and often provided only one or two meals a day. Relief was often unavailable as well, especially between the end of a strike and the first payday.[44] In this context, an extra burden was placed on women to make ends meet. Of course, making ends meet during strikes was a family affair, with men taking up fishing and digging coal for family use. Some families were fortunate enough to have a son or daughter working, which provided extra cash during difficult times. But many of the duties associated with making ends meet fell on the woman. Some of the company homes had small plots, and a few families took advantage of this land to garden. Many women raised chickens as a source of eggs and meat. Some families kept cows and pigs as well. Families also had to rely on careful preparation to stretch the food dollar, often reusing staples such as soup bones over several successive days.[45] Clothing was expensive and always in short supply, especially during strikes. Women used considerable inventiveness in improvising items. The sleeves of old sweaters, for example, were converted into stockings for children. Bedding supplies were improvised from old potato sacks, and one report even mentioned that children were wearing clothes fashioned from discarded cement bags.[46]

When a strike or lockout was the cause of shortages, "making ends meet" became an important aspect of labour militancy. The U.M.W. required the district offices to finance relief for the first 30 days of a strike, but the international union could delay providing relief considerably longer. This was the case in 1925 , when international president John L. Lewis made District 26 wait almost two full months before he promised any money for relief. Even then, the funds Lewis forwarded were inadequate to the task at hand, amounting to less than one dollar per week for each man on strike.[47] The fact that District 26 was so often at odds with the international office made Lewis's control of strike funds especially pernicious and concurrently made women's survival strategies that much more important.

Crowd actions were another example of the working class defending its interests against the actions of the company and its allies in government, and these were another important arena of women's activities. Crowds looted company stores during times of dearth, attacked and harassed scabs during strikes, and battled the police and soldiers who were sent to the area to protect the company's property. Both men and women participated actively in these types of crowd violence, though each gender seemed to have its own specific role in certain aspects of the working-class "repertoire of collective violence."[48]

In his classic study of English foods riots, E.P. Thompson has identified the basic tenets of what he called the "moral economy of the poor." First, the plebeians believed that the link between consumer and producer ought to be as direct as possible. They also believed that in times of dearth, hoarding should be avoided, since this represented an illegitimate attempt to "profiteer" rather than a legitimate attempt to "profit." If local authorities turned a blind eye to such practices, the plebeian moral economy deemed it legitimate for the people themselves to suspend the market imperative and to enforce a "fair price." Crowds often compelled producers to sell their goods at what was considered a reasonable price, a level which was based mainly on custom.[49]

Food riots in Cape Breton also displayed a commitment to such a "moral economy," although it was adapted to the specific consumer experience in the district, which was defined to a large extent by the inequities of the company store credit system. The company store piled one humiliation on another. Not only did it force families into debt, but the system allowed the company to control both how much and which items each family purchased in a given week. The latter power was especially pernicious, since it allowed the store manager to refuse what he considered "luxury" goods in favor of cheaper and less desirable "necessities." Staples such as milk, butter, fruits and vegetables were often refused (or sold in tiny quantities), while cornmeal and molasses were considered appropriate for credit customers. Such decisions operated within a cultural nexus where, in Thompson's words, food "involved feelings of status over and above their dietary value."[50] In 1922 the *Maritime Labor Herald* contrasted items sold on credit to an expectant mother to the rations handed out to the troops who came to the area to keep the peace:

The manager of the store dictated to her what the coal company would let her have, just like the slave masters of the Southern slaves used to dictate what the slaves should eat. . . . Cornmeal and molasses, that was fitting food for the mother of one of Canada's future citizens. . . . To the mothers of Canada's working-class children, hunger and want or cornmeal and molasses, flung at them in scorn; to the soldiers protecting the legalized stealings of the

Wolvin's and MacDougall's, choice chicken and lamb, bread and condensed milk, so plentiful that they throw the surplus out of the car windows.[51]

To be denied goods, then, was considered a degradation, and because it occurred in the company store, the humiliation was interpreted in a class manner. But the account is also replete with gender and ethnic (or nationalistic) language. Most strikingly, the victims in this account were a woman and her unborn child, not the miners themselves. But the symbolic role of the mother and the child was not identical. The account presents the woman's claim to justice as derived mainly from her role as a mother, while the child's claim is derived from its status as a (future) citizen.

Within the local moral economy, it was considered unacceptable for the corporation to withhold credit at its stores during periods of widespread idleness, a demand that U.M.W. vice-president Joseph Nearing at least did not feel should be extended to private merchants:

if it is a cause of unemployment, and a man has given all his earnings to a store, that is to the Corporation who he is working for, when that man is out of work he should not be turned down. Any man that works for a living should have food while there is work and if there is no work he should be protected. . . .
Question: Would you expect a private individual to go on giving credit?
Answer: No, Mr. Chairman, I put a private concern altogether in a different category.
Question: You think a company store should be on a different footing?
Answer? Yes. . . .[52]

Following such logic, crowd actions typically occurred after Besco had cut off credit at its stores, and company stores were the specific targets. On 22 January 1922, three riots occurred at a single company store. Between 11 June and 22 June 1925, there were a total of 16 raids on company stores and warehouses. During the same period, five or six privately owned stores were sacked, and most of these raids occurred after the first three days of looting, by which time the company stores had been completely cleaned out.[53]

The press reported the presence of men, women and boys in the crowds which looted stores in 1922 and 1925.[54] Often men and women rioted side by side. During the raid on the Scotia company store on 11 June 1925 "women helped their male accomplices in rolling out the goods, and worked just as hard as the latter." In other instances, however, the crowds adopted an interesting division of labour. The men would enter the store, remove the goods and haul them to a nearby vacant lot (during one raid, a skating rink was used). The female participants would then carry the loot away from the improvised depot.[55] This division of labour seemed to build on idealized gender roles in the community. The men performed the "rough" work of breaking into the store, while the women played the role of "consumer," waiting outside to select whatever goods were needed in their own household. In the first food riot in 1925, which was presumably the most spontaneous (the crowd having had little time to plan specific roles for its members), men and women acted in similar ways. Both the men and women entered the store and apparently carried off the goods together. Subsequent riots, however, displayed the gendered division of labour, where women did not enter the store, but remained outside to carry off the goods.[56]

The "repertoire of collective violence" also extended to the use of violence to enforce solidarity during strikes. Women participated by harassing scabs in the streets and participated in other actions as well. During the strike of 1923, a crowd of women, men and children stood in front of a troop train as it entered the mining district. The train was searched, and the crowd dispersed when no scabs were found on board. In both 1922 and 1925, women gathered alongside the railway tracks to greet the arriving soldiers with a barrage of rocks. In 1925 the crowd which burned the barn and house of Dan McNeil, a Besco stableman, contained several women.[57] On another occasion, a crowd of men and women surrounded Charlie Campbell, a maintenance man at No. 11 colliery who was "scabbing" at the mine. The crowd "hooted and jeered and endeavored to induce Campbell not to go back to work." Before Campbell could be physically assaulted, however, two mounted policemen came to his rescue. The crowd then turned its fury on the policemen, who were stoned until four other officers arrived on horseback to disperse the crowd. The men and women continued to jeer the policemen from the back yards of houses.[58]

Women also played a prominent role in the violence which followed the killing of William Davis in 1925. The incident occurred after a crowd of miners marched to the New Waterford power plant to attempt to reinforce the union's pickets. The company police anticipated the crowd's arrival, however, and were "formed up awaiting them." Before a spokesman for the miners had a chance to talk, the police charged, shooting randomly into the crowd. Davis was shot through the heart and killed. The crowd overwhelmed the policemen, however, who were dragged off their horses and severely beaten. The crowd then turned on the power plant, beating policemen and removing carloads of food that had been brought in by the police. The miners then returned to the beaten policemen, dragging them back to the town of New Waterford. The captured police were laid down in the street, where several women "belaboured them with their fists and sticks and other weapons." The women were so "vicious" in their attacks that the company police were eventually held in a town jail for their own protection.[59]

Violent activities on the part of women were largely ignored by local authorities and newspapers. Following the food riot in 1922, for example, 12 men, perceived to be the "ring leaders" were arrested, tried and convicted of theft in a case that attracted a great deal of public attention. Despite the sensationalist reports splashed across the front pages of the Sydney newspapers, the only mention of women's participation in the crowd appeared in the initial report. Indeed, the only time women entered the latter story at all was when one of the defendants appealed for clemency on the grounds that he was a breadwinner with a family to support.[60] The lack of attention afforded to women in crowds was repeated in June 1925. Although almost 200 men were arrested during the two weeks of violence, there were no reports of women being charged with offences. Women were not, however, totally immune from prosecution. "Mrs. Madigan," the head of the Women's Auxiliary of the steelworkers' union became, in the words of the *Post*, the "first English-speaking woman" arrested on a charge of assault, apparently after a picket line confrontation with James MacNeil during the 1923 steel strike in Sydney. This report sheds some light on the gender and ethnic prejudices behind the apathy of authorities to women's violence.[61] The notion that women could be violent class fighters was largely absent from mainstream political and journalistic discourses about the coalfields. Indeed, working-class women were most often coupled with children and portrayed as passive victims of injustice, either at the hands of an uncaring company and an impotent government or of misguided communist labour leaders.

When used this way, gender could become an important resource in the area of traditional politics. In 1925, for example, the discourse of women-as-victims was used by the Conservatives against the Liberal government. Key to this strategy was linking images of the victimized women and children with images of a heartless company and apathetic government. The *Halifax Herald* splashed dramatic headlines across its front page: "Women and Children Are Starving," "Women and Children Are Destitute," "Mothers and Children are Facing Starvation" and "Government Defeats Motion To Send Relief to Hungry Women and Children." The *Herald* and the *Post*, both associated with the Conservative Party, described in great detail the deplorable conditions in the colliery districts, and women and children featured prominently in these descriptions. Graphic illustrations and pictures were also used to convey images of women suffering at the hands of a vicious company and apathetic government. In one drawing, the figure of "hunger" was shown reaching out to scoop up fleeting women and children.[62] The triad of victimized women, heartless corporation and apathetic government was expressed most clearly on the front page of the 18 March 1925 edition of the *Herald*. Between the captions "They Can't Stand the Gaff" and "Nothing to Say: Why is There no Action from the Provincial Government" was a drawing of a weather-beaten woman clutching a baby in one arm and holding a blanket over herself with the other.

This women-company-government triad could be so powerful because it was essentially a distancing discourse. The intention of the images was not to promote a genuine understanding of the issues of the dispute, nor to advance the miners' cause. Rather, by using such images, the opposition was attempting to take advantage of the existence of distress and strife in the coalfields without fully addressing the issues which had caused it.[63] Women and children were key to this strategy because focusing on the miners' plight would have allowed the government to use the history of labour militancy in the coal industry and undercut criticism by using red-baiting rhetoric. Opposition attacks were even phrased in a way so as to distance themselves from the miners' grievances. The *Herald* editorialized under the headline "The Government Duty" that "no matter who is right or who is wrong, women and children should not be allowed to suffer." Responsibility was placed on the Liberal government: "it is the duty and responsibility of the government to make adequate provision at once for these helpless people." Conservative politicians also adopted this approach: "leaving aside the merits of the dispute between the corporation and the men, should the government permit women and children to suffer the pangs of hunger?" Disarmed by the use of women and children as images of distress, the government was never able to mount an effective counter-strategy. Instead it fluctuated between saying the reports of starvation were exaggerated and pointing out that the opposition was merely using the existence of distress to its own partisan advantage.[64]

The silence of the authorities should not blind us to the important role women played in the crowd actions which defended the interests of the working-class community. They helped to enforce solidarity during strikes and to provision families in times of deprivation. While important to the class struggle, such actions did not necessarily reflect a long-term and coherent commitment to the politics of class. A smaller group of women did display such a commitment, and pursued more organized efforts in the name of their class community. By early 1924 Women's Labour Leagues appeared in the colliery communities. It is likely that the first leagues were organized in New Aberdeen and New Waterford, but chapters were soon added in Dominion No. 4, Dominion No. 6 and other communities.[65]

The formation of the Women's Labour Leagues across Canada was linked to the activities of the Canadian Labour Party and to Florence Custance's work in the Women's Department of the Communist Party of Canada. The Cape Breton Leagues obviously had ties to the Canadian Labour Party, but their educational efforts and the activities of their most vocal member, Annie Whitfield, suggest a strong Communist influence.[66] In addition, the mining women were probably at least partly inspired by the earlier organization of the Ladies' Auxiliary of the steelworkers' union, which was formed in Sydney in March 1923.[67]

The Labour Leagues could be seen as little more than organized extensions of the traditional strike activities of working-class women in the region, but organization not only formalized the women's activities, but also expanded them. Unlike the earlier sporadic and spontaneous efforts, women in the Leagues began to take a more ongoing role in class and union politics, focusing their efforts on four broad areas: social events, fundraising, educational work and union politics.[68] The women of the district engaged in important activities in the name of the organized branch of their class community. They operated much like Women's Labour Leagues in other areas, concentrating on union support work, self-education and fundraising, but they also availed themselves of a degree of autonomy to map out areas of particular local concern. Following the ideology of the Communist Party, they identified the owners of Besco as their primary enemy, and they worked in the name of their community against the company's wage policies. These were activist women, and as such, they obviously had a more coherent and stable allegiance to class than the majority of women in the region.

The Leagues organized a wide array of socials, including dances, concerts, bake sales and box dinners. The gatherings usually had educational motives, but often were no more than an opportunity for working-class women to "get to know each other" and to have a welcome respite "from the eternal grind that is the usual thing in the life of the ordinary working class wife and mother." Such social gatherings were extensions of the "kitchen talk" networks which had formed in the region, where women gossiped, traded recipes and techniques to make ends meet and discussed the various "goings on" in the community.[69] But the social events were rarely used for purely social purposes. They also carried out fundraising and educational work. By organizing socials, the Leagues raised considerable sums of money to aid other class institutions, such as the Canadian Labour Defence League (C.L.D.L.) and working-class relief organizations. Such activities should not be trivialized. Entertainment functions constituted the primary source of income for the Nova Scotia branch of the C.L.D.L. Women's organizational energy was particularly important in the context of declining wages and employment, when steady incomes could not be counted upon to fill the coffers of working-class organizations. The clubs were especially generous toward the cash-starved *Maritime Labor Herald*. Between April and October 1924, the New Aberdeen League donated more than $300 to the paper. Not to be outdone, the Dominion No. 4 League collected $105 in one week.[70] The labour press often received more financial support from the clubs than from the union locals, and the paper used this fact to urge the miners to do more for the paper: "What are the Miners' Unions going to do about it? . . . This paper is your paper, if you want us to live let us hear from you, in the same kind of language that the women have spoken, only in a stronger voice as becomes men."[71]

Social events also overlapped with the educational work performed by the Women's Labour Leagues. Most of the Leagues met once a week, with one evening per month devoted to education. On this evening, an active member of the labour movement would lecture on some subject connected with organizing and maintaining the labour movement. The Leagues often invited prominent women to speak at their meetings. The New Aberdeen Club, for example, hosted a lecture by Communist Party activist Annie Buller of Toronto in May 1924. On other occasions, two or more Leagues would pool their resources to secure a speaker to address a joint meeting. The speakers, or at least those reported on in the *Labor Herald*, often discussed the position of women in society, although they tended to privilege class analysis over any discussion of the special place of women in working-class communities. One speaker, Mrs. William MacKinnon, for example, gave an address on how the evolution of capitalist industry was forcing women to work outside the home and was making it imperative that women educate themselves "to grasp the real meaning of the class nature that had developed in society. . . ."[72]

If such educational efforts privileged class over gender, the tendency corresponded to public expressions of allegiance on the part of working-class women in the coalfields. Indeed, many of the women in the mining communities eloquently expressed their commitment to the working-class community through letters and statements to the press. Most often, women's statements related to issues of close proximity to the experience of women in the community. Wages and household budgets, for example, were common themes in women's statements. In 1923 a reporter for the *Sydney Post* was unable to find any women in the coalfields who were willing to admit that "the men folks were not justified in going out on strike. Invariably, the hardships of the past two winters are cited. . . ." A letter signed "Red sister" attacked Besco for "paying a wage that looks like telling our children to go and eat grass, while the children of Besco bosses live on the best." A letter signed only "A Miner's Wife" complained that her husband "will go to work five days a week" but will not "make one decent day's wage out of the five." Mrs. Burt Boone of New Aberdeen urged women to organize "to help our men get a better and higher living wage." Housing conditions were another common theme. League member Annie Whitfield was a frequent correspondent to Communist Party publications, writing to the editor of *The Woman Worker* that the company houses were "so old and broken down that it would cost as much to repair them as it would to build new ones."[73]

Activist women did not confine their activities to extensions of their domestic role. The Leagues played prominent roles in marches, demonstrations and meetings. They sent delegates to the annual meeting of the Canadian Labour Party, as well as attending the regular local meetings. Delegates from the Leagues also attended the 1924 District 26 Rank and File Convention, where they sponsored their own resolution.[74] The Leagues were also prominent in May Day celebrations. The women marched with the men, and worked energetically behind the scenes as well, training the children's choir, preparing and serving the food, selling tickets, cleaning up and washing dishes. "On the labours of these miners' wives was this day of joy built," the *Labor Herald* noted following the 1924 May Day celebrations.[75]

The Leagues also became involved in activities relating to wages and unemployment in the coalfields. According to the *Labor Herald*, the Leagues were cautious in these areas, however, since they conspicuously sought to avoid interfering with the efforts of the district executive and the various union locals: "the women want to do their part, but it is sometimes hard for them to find the proper part to play. They try to avoid running counter to anything done by the local union, and this carefulness very often keeps them back." In late 1924, after "several weeks" of trying to decide what kind of role they could play in bringing the unemployment question "before the powers that be" without interfering in union affairs, the New Aberdeen Club decided to circulate a petition among people who were "not in any way connected with organized labor, asking them to get after the government to do something for the idle miners."[76]

It is possible that the *Labor Herald's* account of the women's caution was exaggerated, since the Women's Labour Leagues intervened vigorously in alerting British miners to local conditions. In the summer of 1924, Besco had placed advertisements in several British newspapers and had contacted several British employment agencies, promising steady work and high wages to any British miners willing to make the trip to Cape Breton. The promises were empty, since several collieries had been idle for long periods in the previous few months. In the face of union inaction, the Women's Labour League of New Aberdeen organized a letter-writing campaign to British labour newspapers to edify unemployed miners as to the real conditions in Cape Breton and to warn the miners that the transatlantic journey would be unprofitable. The Leagues picked up the issue with a vengeance, introducing resolutions on the subject at the conventions of both the Canadian Labour Party and the district union. The resolutions condemned Besco's false promises and urged the governments of Canada and Great Britain to take immediate action to remedy the situation.[77]

The Women's Leagues engaged in other activities of importance to the working-class community. In the early spring of 1925, for example, the Leagues participated in the operation of soup kitchens. Conditions in the area were already dire before Besco cut off credit to unemployed miners at its company stores at the beginning of March. Starvation and want quickly grew to crisis proportions. Relief came from a variety of sources, including the Salvation Army, the Anglican and Catholic churches, and a Citizens' Committee formed specifically to meet the tremendous need. An early relief effort, however, was a soup kitchen organized as a joint venture of the New Aberdeen Women's Club, the British Canadian Cooperative and the Phalen local of the U.M.W. The soup kitchen provided one meal per day to children so that they might attend school properly nourished. The efforts of the women were particularly important, since they were responsible for preparing and serving the food.[78]

A relief controversy erupted in 1925 when the Moscow-based Red International of Labour Unions (R.I.L.U.) attempted to donate $5000 to the Glace Bay Citizens' Committee. The Citizens' Committee, made up of merchants, clergymen, professionals and businessmen, rejected the money, arguing that accepting the donation would "be construed in certain quarters as Russian propaganda."[79] The New Aberdeen Women's Labour Club immediately condemned the action, arguing that the Citizens' Committee had declined to accept the donation because it was "real working class money." In the opinion of the New Aberdeen women, there was something wrong with a group of well-fed, middle-class philanthropists refusing relief money on the basis of their own political prejudices regarding its source: "only those who are neither miners nor the wives of miners, and therefore have no right to speak in the name of mine workers, have tried to block acceptance of this relief money." The precise wording of the protest was significant, as it implied that, at least on this issue, the wives of miners had some legitimate right to speak for the mine workers. The Leagues continued to take great interest in this issue. One week later, the Club at Dominion No. 4 appealed to J.B. McLachlan, the influential former secretary-treasurer of District 26, to ensure that the donation was used to buy flour for their impoverished families. Significantly, the Club hoped to control the actual distribution of the flour.[80]

The episode brought into clear focus the line that divided activist working-class women from their middle-class counterparts and thus points to the influence of class identity among organized women in the coalfields.

Although both middle-class and working-class women were confined by a patriarchal ideal which stressed their domesticity, the women in the Leagues felt the pull of class over that of gender. In addition, the R.I.L.U. controversy demonstrated that women were considerably more confrontational in approaching the issue of relief than on other issues of importance to the working-class community, and the *Labor Herald* was more accepting of their militancy in this area as well. Although the paper had earlier stressed the caution of the Leagues vis à vis the union locals, it fully reported the demands of the women on this issue. There is no doubt the women felt they were speaking with a special authority in this area, since the distribution of relief touched directly on their primary function as family financier and consumer in the working-class family. It is significant in this regard that the women made reference not to the shortage of flour in the community as a whole, but to its scarcity in their own households: "we do not get enough flour with our rations to bake with."[81]

The close attachment to the relief issue manifested itself again in 1926. When it was reported that the family of William Davis, the miner shot and killed by company police a year before, was suffering from "dire poverty," the Women's Leagues energetically seized on the issue. The New Aberdeen League took the district executive to task for its inaction, who they believed had "stated publicly in convention and elsewhere that his family was to be properly provided for." The League reminded the district executive of its promise that no contract would be accepted unless it provided for the maintenance of the Davis family. If the union could not compel Besco to take responsibility for its actions, the women suggested that "a levy be put on every member of the U.M.W. of A for the benefit of this family."[82] Since women in the Cape Breton coal communities rarely worked for wages outside the home, they could not be sure of a secure income in the event of the death of their "breadwinner" (whether husband, father or son). They were understandably incensed at the fact that the widow of a class martyr was not being supported by the union. But while their concerns were based on the particular position of women, they did not explicitly frame the issue in gendered terms. Indeed, the language they used made reference to the male union leaders' lack of class militancy, rather than their insufficient attention to gender: "It appears to us by your inactivity in this case . . . that you are at least willing to cooperate with Besco in watching this family suffer instead of coming and cooperating with the workers for their protection."[83]

Scholars have expended a great deal of time and energy trying to locate women's unpaid domestic labour in its proper place within capitalist productive (and reproductive) relations. This project, referred to as the "domestic labour debate," is too nuanced to summarize in a few sentences. At its most basic level, women's domestic labour has been characterized as providing capitalism with an important support mechanism.[84] Jane Humphries has attempted to reframe the debate by pointing out that the family as an institution was functional to the working class, not capitalism, by providing a way both to support unwaged kin and to regulate the labour supply through male breadwinner ideology.[85] What is seldom mentioned is that unions, like capitalists, have relied on the domestic labour of women to pursue their class goals. Since household goods were particularly scarce during strike periods, the labour of women in the home became an important element in working-class survival. In this sense it can be said that the union movement relied on the domestic labour power of the woman to "produce and reproduce the picketer." From this perspective women's domestic labour constituted an important, but hidden, support mechanism for the union movement in Cape Breton.[86]

The domestic labour of women constituted one of the foundations of class struggle in the coal communities, and working-class women raised both their voices and their fists in the name of their class community. Since most women in the coal towns were economically dependent on men, the gendered division of labour in the community forced women to tie their material security to class battles over men's wages and men's employment. But the actions of women in the coalfields in the 1920s demonstrated that they did not simply adapt themselves to male categories, as they rejected mainstream and radical constructions of women as passive victims or conservative influences. Ultimately men controlled the production of class discourses in the region, and the discourse of class struggle continued to privilege the masculine class actor over the feminine. Masculinity and femininity were used as resources to legitimize class distinctions. But gender was also a lived experience, and it was therefore embedded in such diverse spheres as the workplace, the union and the home. The story of class in the Cape Breton coal towns in this important period of Maritime labour history was intimately connected to overlapping and conflicting gender discourses and experiences, and while much still needs to be learned it is clear that our understanding will be enriched by increased attention to the role of gender in the Maritime working-class experience.

NOTES

1. The incident is described in the *Maritime Labor Herald [MLH]*, 23 September 1922.

2. For otherwise excellent studies which nevertheless ignore women, see David Frank, "Coal Masters and Coal Miners: The 1922 Strike and the Roots of Class Conflict in the Cape Breton Coal Industry," M.A. thesis, Dalhousie University, 1974; Frank, "Class Conflict in the Coal Industry: Cape Breton 1922," in G.S. Kealey and P. Warrian, eds., *Essays in Canadian Working-Class History* (Toronto, 1976), 161–84; Frank, "The Cape Breton Coal Miners, 1917–1926," Ph.D. thesis, Dalhousie University, 1979; Ian McKay, "Industry, Work, and Community

in the Cumberland Coalfields, 1848–1927," Ph.D. thesis, Dalhousie University, 1983; and Paul MacEwan, *Miners and Steelworkers: Labour in Cape Breton* (Toronto, 1976).

3. David Frank, "The Miner's Financier: Women in the Cape Breton Coal Towns, 1917," *Atlantis*, 8, 2 (Spring 1983), 137–43. Women occasionally appear in John Mellor's narrative history *The Company Store* (Toronto, 1983), but their presence is peripheral. Robert McIntosh and Ian McKay also discuss women, but largely in the context of the family: see McIntosh, "'Grotesque Faces and Figures': Boy Labour in the Canadian Coalfields," Ph.D. thesis, Carleton University, 1990, esp.

91–125; and Ian McKay, "'The Realm of Uncertainty': The Experience of Work in the Cumberland Coal Mines, 1873–1927," *Acadiensis*, 16, 1 (Autumn 1986), 23–25. Michael Earle's work touches on the auxiliary efforts of radical women: see his "The Coal Miners and Their 'Red' Union: The Amalgamated Mine Workers of Nova Scotia, 1932–1936," *Labour/Le Travail*, 22 (Fall 1988), 103.

4. In an American context, see Elizabeth Jameson, "Imperfect Unions: Class and Gender in Cripple Creek, 1894–1904," in Milton Cantor and Bruce Laurie, eds., *Class, Sex, and the Woman Worker* (Westport, Conn., 1977), 166–202; Ann Schofield, "An 'Army of Amazons': The Language of Protest in a Kansas Mining Community, 1921–1922," *American Quarterly*, 37 (Winter 1985), 686–701; and Priscilla Long, "The Women of the Colorado Iron and Fuel Strike, 1913–14," in Ruth Milkman, ed., *Women, Work and Protest: A Century of U.S. Women's Labor History* (New York, 1985), 62–85. Angela John, *By the Sweat of their Brow: Women Workers in Victorian Coal Mines* (London, 1980) discusses women in British coal communities. The pioneering Canadian work on women in mining towns is Meg Luxton, *More Than a Labour of Love: Three Generations of Women's Work in the Home* (Toronto, 1980).

5. See, for example, Mary Horodyski, "Women and the Winnipeg General Strike of 1919," *Manitoba History*, 11 (Spring 1986), 28–37; and Linda Kealey, "'No Special Protection, No Sympathy': Women's Activism in the Canadian Labour Revolt of 1919," in Deain Hopkin and Gregory Kealey, eds., *Class, Community and the Labour Movement: Wales and Canada, 1850–1930* (St. John's, 1989), 134–59. See also Ava Baron, ed., *Work Engendered: Toward a New History of American Labor* (Ithaca, 1991).

6. Some examples of recent work on working-class masculinity can be found in Baron, ed., *Work*

Engendered, esp. essays by Baron, Blewett, Boris and Hewitt; Elizabeth Faue, "'The Dynamo of Change': Gender and Solidarity in the American Labor Movement of the 1930s," *Gender and History*, 1, 2 (Summer 1989), 138–58; Ava Baron, "Acquiring Manly Competence: The Demise of Apprenticeship and the Remasculinization of Printers' Work," in Mark Carnes and Clyde Griffin, eds., *Meanings For Manhood: Constructions of Masculinity in Victorian America* (Chicago, 1990), 152–63; and Mary Blewett, "Masculinity and Mobility: The Dilemma of Lancashire Weavers and Spinners in Late-Nineteenth-Century Fall River, Massachusetts," also in *Meanings For Manhood*, 164–78. In a Canadian context, see Joy Parr, *The Gender of Breadwinners: Men, Women and Change in Two Industrial Towns* (Toronto, 1990); Shirley Tillotson, "'We may all soon be first class men': Gender and Skill in Canada's Early Twentieth Century Urban Telegraph Industry," *Labour/Le Travail*, 27 (Spring 1991), 97–125; Mark Rosenfeld, "'It Was a Hard Life': Class and Gender in the Work and Family Rhythms of a Railway Town, 1920–1950," *Communications historiques/Historical Papers* (1988), 237–78; Christina Burr, "'Defending the Art Preservative': Class and Gender Relations in the Printing Trades Unions, 1850–1914," *Labour/Le Travail*, 31 (Spring 1993), 47–73.

7. Don Macgillivray, "Cape Breton in the 1920s: A Community Besieged," in B.D. Tennyson, ed., *Essays in Cape Breton History* (Windsor, N.S., 1973), 49–67.

8. On the "underdevelopment" of the coal industry and creation of Besco and its financial problems, see Frank, "The Cape Breton Coal Industry and the Rise and Fall of the British Empire Steel Corporation," *Acadiensis*, 7, 1 (Autumn 1977), 3–34.

9. For a discussion of women's waged labour in Sydney Mines and other communities, see Del Muise, "The Industrial Context of Inequality:

Female Participation in Nova Scotia's Paid Labour Force, 1871–1921," *Acadiensis*, 20, 2 (Spring 1991), 3–31.

10. For a detailed study of the operation of gender in one Maritime working-class community, see Suzanne Morton, "Men and Women in a Halifax Working-Class Neighbourhood in the 1920s," Ph.D. thesis, Dalhousie University, 1986.

11. See Joan Scott, *Gender and the Politics of History* (New York, 1988).

12. The scope of this paper does not allow a discussion of manhood as it relates to sexuality.

13. My thinking in this area was influenced greatly by Blye Frank, "Masculinity: Challenging Ourselves," paper presented to Halifax Men For Change, Dalhousie University, 24 March 1993.

14. See, for example, Province of Nova Scotia, Royal Commission To Inquire Into the Coal Mining Industry, "Minutes of Evidence" [Duncan Commission], 833, 883, 1749.

15. McIntosh, "Grotesque Faces," 158.

16. Duncan Commission, 72–3, 441. The question of kin socialization was complex by the 1920s. Although it continued to have important resonance in the community, it was the company that was loudest in its calls for this type of recruitment. For Besco, this process of kin socialization ensured an ample supply of local labourers.

17. McIntosh, "Grotesque Faces," 156, 162, 44, 12, 78.

18. For examples, see Duncan Commission, 270–76, 403, 411, 575. For the labour process of coal mining in this period, see David Frank, "Contested Terrain: Workers' Control in the Cape Breton Coal Mines in the 1920s," in Craig Heron and Robert Storey, eds., *On the Job: Confronting the Labour Process in Canada* (Kingston/Montreal, 1986), 102–23.

19. *MLH*, 17 March 1923.

20. See, for example, Duncan Commission, 140, 315, 390, 434; Frank, "Coal Masters and Coal Miners," 91–96.

21. Duncan Commission, 595.

22. *MLH*, 13 May 1922. See Frank, "The Miner's Financier," and Wally Seccombe, "Patriarchy Stabilized: The Construction of the Male Breadwinner Wage Norm in Nineteenth Century Britain," *Social History*, 11 (January 1986), 64.

23. *Sydney Post* [*Post*], 16 August 1922, *Post*, 29 July 1922, *Sydney Record*, 4 June 1925.

24. Many recent studies have linked class ideology to masculinity. See, for example, Elizabeth Faue, *Community of Suffering and Struggle* (Chapel Hill, 1991); and Michael Yarrow, "The Gender-Specific Class Consciousness of Appalachian Coal Miners: Structure and Change," in Scott McNall, Rhonda Levine, and Rick Fantasia, eds., *Bringing Class Back In: Contemporary and Historical Perspectives* (Boulder, Col., 1991), 285–310.

25. *MLH*, 12 May 1923, 12 August 1922, *Record*, 15 February 1923.

26. *MLH*, 16 September 1922.

27. *MLH*, 11 October 1924, 17 May 1924, *Post*, 13 June 1925.

28. *MLH*, 19 May 1923.

29. The incident is described in the *MLH*, 15 April 1922.

30. *Post*, 1 May 1925.

31. *MLH*, 26 July 1924.

32. *Post*, 17 February 1923, 29 July 1922.

33. Duncan Commission, 2453.

34. The tactic appears to have originated often among boy labourers in the mine, most likely because of their strategic position within the system of underground haulage. See McIntosh, "Grotesque Faces," 174.

35. *Post*, 15, 18, 22 March 1922, *Record*, 13 March 1922, *Glace Bay Gazette*, 5 April 1922, *Halifax Evening Mail*, 3 April 1922.

36. McLurg later insisted that the statement had been off the record, and that he had been referring to the union executive, not the mass of miners and their families. Even if this qualification were true, by this time the statement had taken on a life of its own. For McLurg's explanation, see Duncan Commission, 3350.

37. *Post*, 4 April 1925.

38. *MLH*, 18 October 1924. For other examples of positive portrayals of class-conscious women, see *MLH*, 3 March, 21 July 1923, 9 February, 14 June, 8 November 1924.

39. *MLH*, 6 May 1922.

40. *MLH*, 3 February 1923.

41. Duncan Commission, 240, 470–72, 489, 513, 520, 548. The suggestion that women be invited to testify was made by Arthur Petrie (p. 513). The union did not follow through on his suggestion.

42. *Post*, 20 January 1922. As pointed out above, McLachlan's statement was as much a claim about men's wages as it was a recognition of women's work.

43. *MLH*, 3 May 1924. For examples of women's budgets, see Frank, "The Miner's Financier."

44. *Post*, 23 March, 8 April 1925, *MLH*, 1 March 1924.

45. Duncan Commission, 97, 449; *Record*, 26 March 1925; Frank, "Cape Breton Coal Miners," 324–26; Interview with Katie Flora MacKenzie, Tape 2386, Beaton Institute of Cape Breton Studies, Sydney; *Post*, 3 March 1925.

46. *Post*, 23 January 1925, *Record*, 5 March 1925. A miner admitted before the royal commission that his children wore cement bags as clothing: Duncan Commission, 174.

47. See *Post*, 23 April 1925, and MacEwan, *Miners and Steelworkers*, 137.

48. The phrase is taken from Charles Tilly, "European Violence and Collective Action Since 1700," *Social Research*, 53 (Spring 1986), 176.

49. E.P. Thompson, "The Moral Economy of the English Crowd in the Eighteenth Century," *Past and Present*, 50 (February 1971), 79, 85–87, 98, 100–104.

50. E.P. Thompson, *The Making of the English Working Class* (New York, 1980 [1963]), 349. To circumvent the credit system, women were encouraged to shop at cash stores, especially the British Canadian Cooperative. Many families dealt with private merchants and resorted to the company store only when their debt to other merchants had reached an intolerable level. Chronic insecurity of income made it impossible for all miners to completely reject the company store. See Duncan Commission, 130, 149, 162–63. For an example of an organized objection to the credit system, see *MLH*, 7 March 1925.

51. *MLH*, 26 August 1922. The *Record*, a notoriously pro-company paper, denied that the troops had been issued anything but standard military rations: *Record*, 23 August 1922. The disagreement between the two accounts does not nullify the point about the cultural importance of food. A miner told a similar story before the Duncan Commission, although he alleged his pregnant wife was denied clothes for their children: Duncan Commission, 253.

52. Duncan Commission, 1492.

53. *MLH*, 28 January 1923, *Post*, 23 January 1922, *Post*, 12–17 June 1925; *Record*, 13–23 June 1925. The *Record* provided a detailed summary of each night's raids.

54. *Post*, 23 January 1922, 15 June 1925; *Record*, 23 January 1922, 13 June 1925. Thompson assumed the crowd existed as a single entity and shared a community of values, and he did not attempt any detailed examination of gender dynamics within food riots. For an intelligent discussion of this point, see Suzanne Desan, "Crowds, Community, and Ritual in the Work of E.P. Thompson and Natalie Davis," in Lynn Hunt, ed.,

The New Cultural History (California, 1989), 47–71. For women in crowds, see John Bohstedt, "Gender, Household Economy and Community Politics: Women in English Riots, 1790–1810," *Past and Present*, 120 (August 1988), 88–112.

55. *Post*, 15 June 1925, *Record*, 13, 14 June 1925.

56. Dana Frank has described in detail organized food boycotts in New York which relied on violent activities of women for enforcement. In a Canadian context, Ruth Frager has uncovered evidence of similar actions by women in Toronto. But these were crowd actions of a different sort and appeared to be tied more closely to a new type of consumerism than an older community-wide definition of a moral economy. Meat boycotts tended to be exclusively female and were conducted under the rubric of organized boycotts of specific products or merchants. In the case of Cape Breton, the riots were more spontaneous and less organized, although some type of informal planning was clearly involved. Another important distinction was the specific targeting of company stores. See Dana Frank, "Housewives, Socialists, and the Politics of Food: The 1917 New York Cost-of-Living Protests," *Feminist Studies*, 11, 2 (Summer 1985), 255–85; Ruth Frager, "Housewives in the Jewish Communist Movement" in Linda Kealey and Joan Sangster, eds., *Beyond the Vote: Canadian Women and Politics* (Toronto, 1989), 258–75.

57. J.S. Woodsworth, "Echoes of the Miners' Strike in Nova Scotia," *Canadian Forum* (January 1923), 107, *Post*, 15–19 August 1922, 16 June 1925, *Record*, 12 June 1925.

58. *Post*, 21 July 1923.

59. *Record*, 16 June 1925; *Post*, 12 June 1925; *Halifax Herald*, 13 June 1925.

60. *Halifax Mail Star*, 13 March 1922.

61. *Post*, 26 July 1923. Contrast this with Ann Schofield, "An 'Army of Amazons.'"

62. *Herald*, 7 March 1925, and other issues of this month.

63. I am indebted to Gerry O'Donnell for pointing out how reports can be manipulated to give the impression of concern while actually distancing the reader from the issues in a dispute.

64. *Herald*, 2, 28 March 1925, *Halifax Chronicle*, 20 March 1925.

65. *MLH*, 14 April 1924. The *Labor Herald* always referred to the organizations as Women's Labor Clubs. Because the women themselves appeared in public with Labour League on their banners, I have in most cases used this name. For a description of such a banner, see Duncan Commission, 3223. The League had originally existed as extensions of sewing circles among Finnish socialist women before the First World War. Leagues inspired by the WLLs of the British Independent Labour Party had also been active before the war in Toronto, Winnipeg and Port Arthur. Thanks to efforts of the Women's Department of the Communist Party, the inaugural meeting of the reborn Toronto League was held in 1923, and a federal umbrella organization was formed in September of the following year. On the formation of the WLLs, see Joan Sangster, *Dreams of Equality: Women on the Canadian Left, 1920–1950* (Toronto, 1989), ch. 2; and Sangster, "The Communist Party and the Woman Question, 1922–1929," *Labour/Le Travail*, 15 (Spring 1985), 25–56.

66. *MLH*, 31 May 1924, 7 February 1925.

67. *MLH*, 7, 14 April 1923, *Record*, 20 June 1923. It is possible that the Women's Labour Leagues were organized before the spring of 1924, but this is the first mention of them located in the sources. It is unlikely that the Leagues were organized before the 1923 strike, however, since they do not appear in accounts of the strike, while the steelworkers' auxiliaries do. For more detail on the links between the steelworkers' and miners' organizations, see Craig Heron, *Working in Steel: The Early*

Years in Canada, 1883–1935 (Toronto, 1988), ch. 4.

68. These broad areas of concern were similar to those of WLLs in other mining areas, such as the Crowsnest Pass region of the West. See Sangster, *Dreams of Equality*, 48.

69. *MLH*, 15 April, 17 May 1924.

70. *MLH*, 15 April 1924, 12 July 1924, 18 October 1924, 13 February, 10 April 1926.

71. *MLH*, 18 October 1924.

72. *MLH*, 23, 31 May 1924.

73. *Post*, 22 August 1923, *MLH*, 1 March, 3 May 1924, *The Woman Worker* (July 1926), 6. For another example of Whitfield's correspondence, see Sangster, "The Communist Party and the Woman Question," 45.

74. *MLH*, 31 May, 28 June 1924; *Post*, 4 February 1924, *Proceedings of the Special Rank and File Convention of District No. 26, UMWA, New Glasgow, May 15–16, 1924* (Glace Bay, 1924).

75. *MLH*, 3 May 1924. See also *MLH*, 18 April 1925.

76. *MLH*, 27 December 1924.

77. *MLH*, 7, 14 June 1924, 5 July 1924; *Proceedings of Rank and File Convention*, 6–7.

78. See the *Post* and the *Record*, March–June 1925; Interview with Katie MacKenzie, Beaton Institute; *MLH*, 14 March 1925, *Post*, 5 March 1925.

79. *Post*, 23 March 1925. On the composition of the Citizens' Committee, see *Post*, 6 March 1923.

80. *MLH*, 4, 11 April 1925.

81. *MLH*, 11 April 1925. For other relief activity, see *Post*, 5, 6, 9 March 1925, *Record*, 24 March, 4 April 1925.

82. *MLH*, 17 April, 19 June 1926.

83. *MLH*, 19 June 1926.

84. Some of the major articles in the domestic labour debate are collected in Roberta Hamilton and Michele Barrett, eds., *The Politics of Diversity: Marxism, Feminism and Nationalism* (Montreal 1987).

85. See Jane Humphries, "The Working Class Family, Women's Liberation, and Class Struggle: The Case of Nineteenth Century British History," *Review of Radical Political Economics*, 9, 3 (Fall 1977), 25–41. For more on domestic labour and its relationship to family and class, see Veronica Strong-Boag, "Keeping House in God's Country," in Heron and Storey, eds., *On the Job*, 126–28; Meg Luxton, *More Than A Labour of Love*; Batya Weinbaum and Amy Bridges, "The Other Side of the Paycheck: Monopoly Capital and the Structure of Consumption," in Zillah Eisenstein, ed., *Capitalist Patriarchy and the Case for Socialist Feminism* (New York, 1979), 190–205; Zillah Eisenstein, "Some Notes on the Relations of Capitalist Patriarchy" in Eisenstein, ed., *Capitalist Patriarchy*, 48–52; Bonnie Fox, ed., *Hidden in the Household* (Toronto, 1980), and Wally Seccombe, "Patriarchy Stabilized," 56–59.

86. For a fuller discussion on women's unpaid labour in the home, see McIntosh, "Grotesque Faces," 99–116 and (for a different mining town), Luxton, *More Than a Labour of Love*, 81–160.

section 8

THE BODY POLITIC

○

FAMILIES, PRIVATE PROPERTY, AND THE STATE: THE DIONNES AND THE TORONTO STORK DERBY[*]

MARIANA VALVERDE

o

In the middle of the Great Depression, a number of state institutions in Ontario (the legislature, the judiciary, the Attorney-General's office) felt called upon to administer two sets of "problem" families. One was the Dionnes, the other those competing in the Toronto Stork Derby. The former "group" was perceived by the Hepburn government as two distinct families: the Quintuplets on the one hand, and their five siblings and parents on the other. In 1934, the Ontario government declared itself the true parent of the newborn Quintuplets and made a complete physical as well as legal separation between them and their kin. Eventually the Quints were legally and physically reunited with the other Dionnes, at a time when their fame and fortune had in any case been rather exhausted, and control over their trust fund was no longer a source of wages to many retainers and of tourist revenue to the province. A close analysis of the government documents of the Dionne case reveals that the Quintuplets were not dealt with as children in need of state protection: the Children's Aid Society was not involved.[1] Rather, they were managed as natural resources or scenic wonders requiring nationalization. In other words, the guardianship of the five little girls had very little to do with child welfare or family policy; rather, it became an aspect of provincial economic policy. Just as the "natural beauty" of Niagara Falls has been sold to tourists and exploited by Ontario Hydro, so

[*] Reprinted with permission from *Journal of Canadian Studies* 29, 4 (Winter 1994–95): 15–35. This paper overlaps somewhat with my article, "Representing Childhood: The Multiple Fathers of the Dionne Quintuplets" in Carol Smart, ed., *Regulating Womanhood* (London: Routledge, 1992).

too the apparently priceless Quintuplets were economically exploited by their legal father, the government of Ontario.

The unusual degree of government intervention in the Dionne case stands in contrast to the more laissez-faire position taken by the same government in another regulatory dilemma, namely the so-called Toronto Stork Derby of 1926–38. The Stork Derby was occasioned by an eccentric lawyer's will leaving a very large amount of money to the Toronto woman giving birth to the largest number of children over the subsequent 10 years. Immediately after the will was probated, in December of 1926, the Conservative government at Queen's Park attempted to declare the Stork Derby clause invalid on the grounds that it was "disgusting" and against the public interest. However a public outcry, mostly from women's groups, managed to reverse the government's decision: both Premier George Henry's government and the subsequent Hepburn government let the various mothers and other potential heirs fight the case out in the courts, with little political interference. The courts, concerned with safeguarding the principle of the autonomy of property owners, decided to uphold the will against the claims of distant relatives, but only after resolving tricky issues regarding the moral and legal status of both children and mothers.

A comparison of these two cases raises some interesting questions about the role of the state in the administration of reproduction. The relationship between the state and mothers and children is always analyzed under the rubric of family policy or social policy, but the present study shows that at least some children and mothers were managed and administered through processes normally associated with the regulation of the economy. Property, rather than family, is the central category in both the Dionne and the Stork Derby cases, casting some doubt on historians' generalizations about the 20th century's view of childhood as a sentimental, non-economic category. At a theoretical level, this study shows that instead of assuming the family and the economy to be fixed realms with unchanging boundaries, they might be better regarded as categories in flux, which the state can invoke with astonishing flexibility.[2] What is and is not a family question and, even more surprising, what is or is not a child, turns out to be largely a matter of which administrative techniques are brought to bear on a particular situation.

"A HUMAN GOLDMINE TO THEIR PROVINCE": THE PATERNAL STATE AND THE DIONNE QUINTUPLETS

Elzire Dionne, a 25-year-old francophone farm woman living in the village of Corbeil near North Bay, Ontario gave birth to five identical girls in May of 1934. The attending anglophone doctor, Dr. Allan R. Dafoe, did not believe the tiny babies would survive, and most probably neither did the parents. Oliva Dionne, their father, signed a contract—which the mother, extremely sick as she was, refused to co-sign—with Chicago World Fair promoters, promising to let the girls be exhibited if and when they were sufficiently healthy. In the late 20th century public displays of unusual human beings have virtually disappeared under the weight of ideas about "privacy," but such displays, either in freak shows or in the sanitized displays of modern science, were still relatively common in the 1930s. Nevertheless, both Canadian and American press reports painted the parents as ruthless baby-sellers. The negative publicity prompted the Ontario government to obtain a judicial order taking the children away from their parents' custody and control. The *Globe* reported: "Acting in his function as *parens patriae*—father of the people—[Attorney-General] Mr. Roebuck has obtained . . . a judicial order appointing guardians for the quintuplets, and so defeated the 'perfidious contract.'" Roebuck, posing as the chivalrous defender of a feminized Canadian nation, stated that "If exploiters from American cities come to Canada to pull off this sort of racket, they need not expect the Attorney-General's office or the courts to stand idly by."[3]

The guardians named were all male and all Liberal, and included Dr. Dafoe but excluded both parents. The records of this first guardianship were removed from the government records by then Minister of Public Welfare, David Croll.[4] That extant evidence, however, clearly shows that Dr. Dafoe behaved as if he were the only guardian, signing commercial contracts involving the Quintuplets as well as his own increasingly famous self.

The government had a shiny new hospital built across the road from the Dionne farm. The babies were placed there under the care of nurses, and Dr. Dafoe put very strict restrictions on the Dionne family's right to visit them. Louise de Kiriline, Dafoe's second in command, later admitted that she had treated the parents and five older Dionne siblings as nothing but unhygienic nuisances.[5] The parents complained that they had to put on surgical masks when in attendance, while famous visitors, including provincial politicians, were photographed holding the babies without any fear of germs.

The hospital's widely publicized medical equipment, including the new reproductive technology of incubators, created the impression that the children were very delicate and needed to be away from the family home, when in fact the babies had survived their crucial first weeks with minimal technology. To polish even further its paternal image, the government claimed that it had spent $20 000 on the hospital, when in fact the funds had come from the Red Cross and private donations.[6]

In March of 1935, when the Quintuplets were 10 months old, the government sought to regularize the guardianship through a special law making the girls wards of "His Majesty," with the Crown's authority vested in David Croll, head of the new Ministry of Public Welfare. The crucial clauses of the law were No. 4, by which the province assumed direct control over any commercial contracts involving the Quints (thus marginalizing the enterprising Dr. Dafoe), and No. 6, by which the estates of the Quintuplets were vested in the minister of welfare.[7] In a change of policy, however, the father was also named as a guardian, though his opinion was to be subject to "the jurisdiction and direction of the said Minister." The mother was not included, either at the time or later when she requested that she and the other mothers be added to the board of guardians.

During the debate on this bill, the government revealed that it was by no means rejecting the father's original idea of displaying the sisters: "the government is also considering improvements to the Dafoe hospital that may include a large glass-covered solarium where tourists and visitors would be able to see the quintuplets."[8] The solarium eventually expanded to include a whole complex of buildings, complete with a parking lot for 1000 cars and several souvenir shops (one owned by the midwives who had attended the Quintuplets' birth, and one owned by Oliva Dionne).[9] Quintland, as this attraction was predictably named, soon drew as many tourists as Niagara Falls. Speaking before the Canadian Association of Tourist and Publicity Bureaus, Dr. Dafoe boasted that his "winsome charges" had attracted 400 000 tourists to North Bay in 1938 alone, whereas the snowy peaks of the Rockies had only managed to draw 200 000 to Banff.[10]

The Quintuplets were exhibited to tourists twice a day. The crowds were supposedly contained behind one-way glass, but the girls later said that although the glass did not allow them to see their visitors well, they were aware of them and "performed" accordingly. It is, of course, not possible to generalize about the motives of the hundreds of thousands of people who used the relatively new leisure activity of motoring to visit Quintland.[11] One can nevertheless speculate that the Quintuplets offered North American middle-class families on holidays a certain Shirley Temple cuteness combined with a uniquely Canadian emphasis on scenic rural ruggedness (symbolized by the stained logs covering the exterior of the nursery building).

In addition, Quintland seemed to have functioned as a post-Christian fertility shrine. Every day in the summer, trucks from the Ontario Department of Public Works delivered pebbles from nearby Lake Nipissing to Quintland. Made available to tourists as "stones from the quints' playground," these seem to have been popularly regarded as fertility amulets.[12]

Misleading information about public funds spent on the hospital was part of a larger government strategy. Very few people seemed to know that the doctor, the parents, the nurses, the business manager and the security guards were all paid out of the Quints' own money (the trust fund controlled first by the minister of public welfare and later by the official guardian, P.D. Wilson). The business manager was the highest-paid employee of the trust fund, which reveals something of the guardianship's character. The trust fund's function as a fiscal goose laying golden eggs, reversing the usual flow of welfare state expenditures on children, is further demonstrated by the fact that quite a number of provincial officials, including the Ontario Provincial Police posted in Quintland, were paid out of the children's money, instead of the government payroll. The government's records contain many letters from Ontarians hoping to obtain employment in the privately funded but publicly controlled Quint enterprise. People offering their services as teachers or general help often mentioned their commitment to the Liberals as a job qualification, in keeping with the patronage practices of the time.

During the relatively profitable year of 1938, expenses billed to the trust fund included $8737 for administrative salaries, $4900 for legal fees, $2918 for medical fees, $4748 as parents' allowance, and $4019 paid to private security and public police. Although complete financial records do not exist for every year, there are enough records to suggest that the 1938 level of expenditures was typical. (For comparison purposes, the excess of revenue over expenditures for 1935–36 was $162 969, and for 1936–37 was $359 524; the largest source of revenue was Hollywood movie contracts.)[13]

In later years, this pork-barrel effect was compounded by the curious fact that both the judge who oversaw the trust fund's accounts and the official guardian decided to pay themselves for going over the accounts.[14] P.D. Wilson clearly had become used to seeing the Quints' trust fund as the province's, and hence his own, money. Every conceivable expense, from trips to New York to meet with legal counsel to the fish and chips Wilson regularly ate in North Bay hotels, was charged not to his government department but to the trust fund. Despite this reality, David Croll misled the legislature about the direction of the flow of dollars, reassuring the opposition that the government was not squandering public money on the Quints: "We regard what the province has done as a whole-hearted contribution from all the people of the province."[15]

The trust fund paid for at least some of the expenses of Canada's leading child psychologist, Dr. William Blatz, whose research assistants studied the girls' physical and behavioural characteristics in obsessive detail. Billing one's research subjects is, needless to say, not a common practice among psychologists, but once again powerful men did not hesitate to dip into the fund set up for the "protection" of the girls.[16] Blatz's actions were not, however, simple researcher's greed. In his view they were fully justified by the Quintuplets' status as servants of science. In a remarkable passage in his popular book on the girls, he expresses pleasure at the fact that in the management of the Dionne family, "no petty consideration of individual rights" has been allowed to intrude. The whole passage is worth quoting as an example of the discourses—scientific in this case, but similar to those employed by the media and by the government—that constructed the girls as indebted to the very people who exploited them. Using the language of capital investment in a way that would have warmed the business manager's heart, he wrote:

> It will be their responsibility to show some day that the care and effort that is expended on childhood returns dividends in the form of a happily adjusted adult. This is the first price which the children have to pay. It is needless to emphasize the responsibility of the Guardians in this connection. Happily, to date no petty consideration of individual rights have been permitted to interfere with the carrying out of this trust.[17]

It is curious that, in Dr. Blatz's narrative, the five children are envisaged as turning into one "happily adjusted adult," rather than five adults. And indeed, neither Blatz's management of scientific objects nor the official guardian's practices reveal any concern for the psychological growth of the girls as individuals. In the thousands of pages of documents in the official guardian's files, it is difficult to discover the Quintuplets' names. They are always treated as a single entity—with the significant exception of the "Income tax" file (by far the fattest in the collection). Wilson thought that if the girls were considered to be individuals for income tax purposes, then the trust fund would be subject to a lower rate of income tax. He fought a long battle with Ottawa on this point, since Ottawa considered the trust fund a single income. Eventually Wilson won: the five identical income tax returns filed every year are the only official document in which they are consistently individuated.[18]

Unconcerned with the effect on the girls of always showing them as a group and never for a moment separating them, the guardians were equally unconcerned about the possible ramifications of their "performer" status. When some press reports suggested that the daily exhibitions of the girls might not be good for their mental health, the guardians quickly called in Canada's leading pediatrician, Dr. Alan Brown. After playing with the girls for a short time he had no hesitation in submitting a very brief and very general report stating that the girls were psychologically healthy. No stranger to the commercial world since leading a team that invented the baby cereal Pablum, the chief physician of Toronto's prestigious Hospital for Sick Children wrote: "the showing of the children under the present plan appears to have had no effect upon them either mentally or physically, and in fact, I believe that if necessary the time could be extended to one hour."[19] Dr. Brown's advice appears to be a prescription to improve the health of Ontario's tourist industry rather than to benefit the girls.

The most graphic evidence of the government's perception of the Quintuplets as a godsend for the provincial coffers is found in the documents regarding the province's effort to have the federal parliament pass a special "Quintuplet" trade mark law in early 1937. This act to copyright the word "Quintuplet," its synonyms and French translations, was sought in order to prevent manufacturers from using references to the Quints in advertising without paying royalties to the trust fund. Expensive lawyers in the United States as well as on Bay Street concurred that the peculiar law, effectively copyrighting a common noun, would not stand judicial scrutiny, since only names of products could be trademarked. The lawyers had to tell the guardians that the Quintuplets were not exactly products in the eyes of the law.

Nevertheless, the provincial Attorney-General's department, acting on the assumption that even if the Quintuplets were not legally products they could be administered as such without political repercussions, proceeded to obtain from Ottawa a badly drafted law. In this the provincial government was influenced by legal opinions highlighting the scarcely legal but importantly symbolic value of making the children into products with registered trade marks. New York lawyer Arthur Garfield Hays put if frankly:

> The obtaining of some trade-marks, the licencing of the names and the reputation of the Quintuplets has resulted in a general public belief that these terms should be regarded as a monopoly. Business men hesitate to infringe when threatened with a law suit. We have on occasion been hard put to it to lay a foundation for legal rights

when we have been squarely faced with the question, but we have not yet failed in persuading any such user to cease his unfair use. The argument that a law suit for infringement would publicize the user as one who is attempting to take money from babies, has usually been effective as a deterrent.[20]

Meanwhile, of course, Mr. Hays himself was collecting thousands of dollars from the babies' trust fund.[21] Like so many other people, most of them professional men, he was no doubt glad to obtain such credit-worthy customers in the middle of the Depression.

The final irony is that the government's attempt to protect its monopoly over the valuable word "Quintuplets" was couched in the language of chivalrous protection. The Quintuplet copyright act read: "Whereas it has been, by petition, represented that it is in the interests of the above named quintuplets and of the people of Canada that a special Act be passed to protect the said quintuplets against exploitation. . . ."[22]

There is evidence that by the early 1940s some people began to suspect that the rhetoric of state benevolence was but a cover for public greed. In an influential article in an American magazine, Lillian Barker noted in 1941 that the Government of Ontario could not have foreseen "that such human mites would soon become a human gold mine to the province."[23] But by then, the government's paternal image was in any case tarnished, due partly to the efforts of Catholic leaders in both the US and Canada to "reunite the family," and most importantly to Oliva Dionne's ultimately successful mobilization of Franco-Ontarian interests on his behalf. Oliva Dionne began to work closely with the Association Canadienne-Française de l'Education de l'Ontario (ACFEO), and found in this association a useful ally in his battle against Dr. Dafoe for control of the girls. The ACFEO in turn saw the Quintuplets, and specifically their education, as an important site for the ongoing battle for francophone education rights. But what was for the ACFEO an issue of language politics appears, in the minutes of the guardians' meetings, as a purely financial issue. Business manager Keith Munro, expressing no opinion at all on the merits of French vs. English education, constantly reminded the guardians that the commercial value of the children would be raised considerably if they learned to speak English. The other guardians, including Oliva Dionne, quite agreed. On one occasion Munro deplored the "loss of revenue" that was taking place due to the girls' poor English, and so Oliva Dionne agreed to cooperate with his adversary Dr. Dafoe in writing the government yet again to request an English teacher.[24] From outside the guardianship, Munro was supported and pressured by manufacturers holding Quintuplet contracts, as shown in a letter from the American Grocers' Association: "Everyone with whom I talked tells me that the children are going to be much more valuable from an advertising standpoint after they have learned to speak English. . . . This is straight from the shoulder, Keith. But they [advertising executives] informed me: 'Get these kids speaking English, and they'll have great advertising value!'"[25] The government also wanted to increase the advertising and tourist value of the Quintuplets, but Dionne's actions as a committed Franco-Ontarian (as distinguished from his rather different actions as a guardian) had caused political headaches at Queen's Park. Eventually Wilson resigned himself to losing some potential financial benefits for the sake of political peace. His resistance worn down by constant harassment from Dionne and from the ACFEO's legal counsel, Wilson wrote an exasperated memo to the Attorney-General recommending that the Quints' education be entrusted to French-speaking nuns, since "the parents would, perhaps, be more amenable to their authority, or at least more amenable to them than to any other authority."[26]

In any case, by 1940–41 the commercial value of the Quintuplets was on the wane. Even if the business agent had been able to maximize their modest acting talents and their fluency in English, this would not have sufficed to maintain the previous level of revenues. The children were no longer babies, but rather ordinary looking girls; they were no longer associated with the "medical miracle" imagery which defined their identities as babies; and the war had turned the public's attention to other matters. Thus, the campaign by francophone groups to return the Quintuplets to their parents could be allowed to succeed without serious harm to the provincial treasury, and with some benefit to the provincial government's legitimation problems vis-à-vis francophones. The Depression was in any case over, and many of those who had fed the Quintland trough moved on—business manager Keith Munro, for instance, set up his own advertising firm on Madison Avenue.

By 1942 Wilson worried that the Quintuplets might lose their commercial value altogether: "It must ever be kept in mind, in view of the general conditions, of the possibility of the earning power of the quintuplets falling below their necessary expenditures. In other words, the time will come when the capital will have to be drawn upon for their maintenance. . . ."[27] Until then, the fund had generated so much revenue every year that capital accumulated despite the numerous drains on the fund. After reaching somewhat over half a million dollars, however, revenues began slowly to decline. The prospect of financial decline gradually led Wilson to accept the plan of returning the girls to their parents, which was done through the 1940s.[28]

The government went so far as to build a large new home for the parents and both sets of siblings. At a high-level meeting to plan a site for this home, the Attorney-General stressed that the parents had the duty to continue to foster tourism. Wilson stated that the government was quite willing to give up guardianship rights as long as the children were still used "by way of attracting tourists to the province."[29]

In the protracted power struggles between the biological father, the doctor, the provincial government, and other "paternal" claimants such as the media and the scientific establishment, maternal voices are conspicuously absent. This was not due to any reticence or passivity on Elzire Dionne's part.[30] On several occasions she mobilized political support for her claims as a mother as successfully as a rural francophone woman speaking little or no English could be expected to do. In 1935, the Fédération des Femmes Canadiennes-Françaises happened to be meeting in North Bay,

304 THE BODY POLITIC

and Mrs. Dionne attended this meeting to plead her case: "Mrs. Dionne said she is anxious the board of guardians include herself and two other women, both mothers, who could understand her longing to be with the babies as much as possible." Since there were three active guardians at this time, the addition of three women would have created gender parity. The politics of this request are thus quite sophisticated, and go beyond a simple "mother's plea." The federation's president supported Mrs. Dionne, but the North Bay convention, possibly unwilling to antagonize the Liberal government given traditional French and Catholic support for the Liberal Party, merely expressed pious hopes that Mrs. Dionne would soon be able to spend more time with her daughters.[31] (It is interesting, incidentally, that the recent film *Million Dollar Babies* paints a sexist portrait of Elzire Dionne as a weak and passive character with no connection to women's organizations.)

Having lost the fight to become guardian to her children, Mrs. Dionne still tried to retain some control and some maternal dignity. Two years later, she managed to obtain the support of the provincial ruling party's own women's wing for a new demand: equal schooling for her non-famous children. Mrs. M.J. Poupure, French vice-president of the Ontario Women's Liberal Association, met with Mrs. Dionne and wrote a long and eloquent report that caused discontent at Queen's Park. Mrs. Poupure began by covertly attacking the male guardians' authority by describing her talk "in my own language as a French woman, as one Northerner to another, and as one mother to another." She stated that Mrs. Dionne appreciated the educational opportunities being given to the Quintuplets, but complained that her other children were "getting a rural education without any opportunity of gaining culture, and in the French language only, when English too is imperative." Thus the Quints' better education would "create a barrier between the two family groups. . . . It might make for an inferiority complex on the part of her other children. . . ." Mrs. Poupure then movingly described Mrs. Dionne's exclusion from the maternal tasks of putting children to bed, having them say their prayers, and choosing their clothes, and concluded by putting her finger on the delicate question of revenue, saying "when we think how much the Province of Ontario gained from tourist trade by the publicity the Quints have given the province . . . [Mrs. Dionne's] request for a private school for her family would be only a small consideration."[32] Contrary to the newspapers' portrayal of her as a peasant with purely instinctual mothering practices, Mrs. Dionne clearly wanted her other children to share the benefits of the sudden modernity foisted on the Quintuplets, and was able and willing to engage in sophisticated political tactics.

Mrs. Dionne's political efforts were all unsuccessful. This could be attributed to the fact that francophone interests tended to rally behind their own image of a patriarchal family, while most of the women who might have had influence at Queen's Park probably shared the media's contempt for the "peasant" woman who had had 10 children by age 26 and had only a grade 3 education. Excluded from public power struggles, Elzire Dionne was reduced to very undignified battles with the Dafoe-appointed nurses for control over the daily details of the nursery, from prayers to hair styles.

A log kept by a Dafoe Hospital nurse during the summer of 1939 records the painful and almost daily squabbles between the mother and the nurses, squabbles in which the children seemed to have played one woman off against another.[33] The mother's visits to her children often ended in tears. Blamed by the nurse for interrupting the children's highly orchestrated activities, Mrs. Dionne must have been perpetually anxious about her children's loyalty.

The exclusion of Mrs. Dionne, and the relative absence of an outcry by women, is in contrast to the Stork Derby case, which saw a successful protest by organized and unorganized women against the province's attempt to invalidate Charles Millar's will and hence deprive mothers of numerous children of their share in the eccentric lawyer's estate. One wonders to what extent the Quintuplets' *sui generis* status as a scenic wonder, compounded by their media presentation as medical rarities, disqualified them for child status altogether, hence disqualifying their mother from motherhood. As we shall see below, the Stork Derby mothers could only qualify as legitimate mothers if their children met a number of specifications, among which being a *legal* child was the primary one. The disjunction between natural and legal children is one of the key features of the Stork Derby case. The Dionne Quintuplets, whose legitimacy was never in doubt, ran no risk of being construed as "natural" in the sense of illegitimate or non-legal; on the contrary, they verged on the supernatural. They were celebrities, medical miracles, and tourist attractions, and as such members of categories superseding childhood.

The Dionne Quintuplets' tragedy is that, while their mass-produced photographs are still considered to be the ideal representation of 1930s childhood, they were not themselves considered to be children. Like Mickey Mouse in Disneyland (who represents animals but is not an animal), the girls in Quintland were icons of "modern" childhood who were not treated as children. Therefore, they were not seen as requiring a mother, and nobody thought it odd that they were cared for by a series of nurses under Dafoe's paternal eye.

To continue the analysis of the ways in which "natural" mothers and "natural" children might or might not be certified as such by legal and media discourses, let us then turn to the Toronto Stork Derby.

VALUABLE BABIES AND ILLEGITIMATE MOTHERS: THE TORONTO STORK DERBY, 1926–38

A study of newspapers and judicial decisions reveals that, for the men generating both the "expert" and the media opinions, the issues involved in the Stork Derby case did not include the situation of mothers with numerous offspring during Canada's worst economic depression.[34] Rather, the themes outlined in dominant discourses were the following: the right of testators to defy common sense in the disposition of their property, the right of the government to interfere with private property, the eugenic theme of poor mothers having "excess" offspring and, finally, the norms of reproductive conduct. When focusing on reproductive morality, the prime object of discussion was the dubious morality of poor women, accused of recklessly getting pregnant for the sake of a prize; but moral aspersions were also cast on the male lawyer whose will produced the spectacle in the first place.

From the legal standpoint, morality was a side issue; the case centred more on the respective rights of testators and government regulatory authorities. The judgements, from the lowest to the highest court, were consistently included in the *Dominion Law Reports* for the sake of clarifying the situation of unusual wills, and were apparently regularly taught in wills and estates courses in Ontario law schools for decades afterwards. Nevertheless, to discuss the case simply as an interesting precedent in the history of estate law would be to miss some very important social dimensions. The state's right to regulate private property (the estate) was in this case inextricably linked to the moral and legal regulation of family and reproduction. That private property, family and the state should be so intertwined (as Frederick Engels pointed out in a different context) meant that many Toronto women and children had their lives organized by a peculiar combination of the law of wills and estates and the dominant norms regulating reproductive conduct.

When Charles Millar's will was probated in November of 1926, the clause leaving most of the estate to the Toronto mother who would have the most children in the 10 years after his death caused much consternation. A headline in the *Toronto Star* raised the possibility that the controversial clause might be judged to be "not in [the] public interest," hence invalidating the will. Unnamed people questioned the immorality implicit in Millar's wording, particularly since it did not specify that the prize ought to go to a married woman with the most number of children, although as a lawyer he knew full well the difference between married and unmarried mothers.[35] But the neglected distant relatives, who had a financial interest in declaring the will against the public interest, took almost a year to get organized to contest the will and claim their share of over $300 000 in the estate. The story simmered, and the *Toronto Star* tried to keep it alive by sending reporters to hunt down possible prizewinners and sign them up for exclusive interviews.[36]

The first set of long-lost cousins launched a case in November of 1927, with their lawyer arguing "... that the said clause is void on the ground that it is against public policy and the provision therein contained tends to the propogation [sic] of illegal children and promotes competition among the women of Toronto in sexual matters and tends to place a premium on immorality...."[37] This case was thrown out, not because of the appalling grammar and logic of the lawyer's argument, but because the cousins launching the suit were not next of kin. This initial attempt to brand certain children as illegal and certain mothers as immoral, however, was to be continued by others in later years.

A recently deceased half-aunt was in fact the next of kin, and the executor of her estate now made a more credible attack on the will. Even though the nationality of the executor (who was also a partial heir) was of course legally irrelevant, his status as a US citizen harmed his claim, in the opinion of a patriotic and Depression-ridden public, and an equally patriotic and equally Depression-ridden provincial government. The Attorney-General, William Price, introduced a bill to "escheat" or invalidate the Millar estate and give the money to the University of Toronto, which had been the main beneficiary in an earlier Millar will.[38] The government's actions may have been prompted by a desire to keep the money in the country. It may also have been influenced by the kind of sentiment expressed by the distant cousins' lawyer regarding the immorality of reckless breeding: the spectre of the eugenically unfit was repeatedly applied to the Millar estate case by a clergyman leading the publicly visible movement for birth-control clinics.[39] (The last judicial decision in the Derby case was made in the middle of the much-publicized Dorothea Palmer birth-control case.)

The *Star*, whose reporters had combed the city of Toronto for possible winning mothers, chivalrously leaped to the defence of wounded motherhood. A mother of 27 philosophically said, "Maybe it's just as well if we don't get the money. . . . If we were rich, some might kidnap little Jean . . . here, like they did with Lindbergh's baby."[40] But other women, whether participating in the contest or not, were less resigned to seeing the prize money disappear. Women of the Liberal Party said the government had "cheated," and the *Globe* reported that women were threatening to make the will an election issue.[41] The same day, the *Globe* took the opportunity to chastise the government on the Millar will issue. In keeping with the newspaper's politics, its main complaint was the right of testators to dispose of their money at will, not the raised hopes of poor women:

> The Ontario government will have serious difficulty in convincing the people of the Province that it has any justification whatsoever for setting aside, by legislation, the will of a wealthy citizen, and diverting the proceeds of the estate to provincial purposes. . . . It is a dangerous precedent for any Province to set up in these days when the right to hold and dispose of property is being challenged in many quarters.[42]

Faced with this anti-statist, anti-regulatory sentiment, the Attorney-General quickly withdrew the contentious bill and allowed the courts to dispose of the estate.

Despite the *Globe*'s attempt to make property the central issue, the unusual activism of women forced the conservative newspaper to acknowledge women's role in the reversal (though in a somewhat offensive tongue-in-cheek prose). The *Globe*'s headline was: "WOMEN HALT MILLAR ESTATE ESCHEATMENT ATTEMPT," and the article is worth quoting at length:

> Womanhood—indignant, outspoken womanhood—asserted itself in the political arena yesterday. . . . Both yesterday and the day before the articulate indignation of women could be heard in every phase of daily life. On the street cars they could be overheard denouncing as "thievery" the proposed action of the government

in escheating the half million dollar estate. . . . In the department
stores and from the small corner grocers the feminine customers
raised their voices in an equally protesting vein. Newspaper offices
were bombarded with salvos of feminine protestations. . . .[43]

The following day the *Star*, taking its cue from the earlier *Globe* editorial
decrying state intervention in the economy, accused Attorney-General Price
of "resort[ing] to Communism in the raw when he contemplated, regardless
of the courts, to set aside a man's last will and testament by statute."[44] Price,
who had been responsible for the jailing of Communist leader Tim Buck,
was probably infuriated by this editorial, as well as by a *Star* editorial car-
toon a few days later portraying him taking a bag marked $500 000 from a
woman pushing a pram full of babies. From this moment on, no provincial
politician, however distasteful he found the contest, dared to interfere with
the judiciary's decisions.

In October 1936, newspaper readers with an interest in reproduction
could have followed two high-profile stories running in the front pages of
the Toronto press: the closing days of the Stork Derby, and the Dorothea
Palmer birth-control trial. At issue in the trial was not so much women's
right to control their own bodies as the fear that the poor and "unfit" were
reproducing more than the middle classes. The eugenic views of A.R.
Kaufman, a Kitchener manufacturer sponsoring the birth-control clinic
being prosecuted, have been outlined in detail by Angus and Arlene
McLaren and need not detain us here.[45] What should be noted is that expert
witnesses in favour of population control literally went from one courtroom
to another and related the two cases in interesting ways. The Stork Derby
was ominously cited by the magistrate in the birth-control trial as an example of the consequences of unregulated reproduction. He went on to invoke
the spectre of fascist pro-natalist policies in order to justify finding Dorothea
Palmer not guilty despite the fact she had clearly broken the law banning
contraceptive information.[46]

Meanwhile, back at the Stork Derby trial, the pro-eugenic expert witnesses borrowed from the contraception case did not manage to persuade
the courts to declare the will invalid, but they heaped moral and social
stigma on the contesting mothers. Their eugenic views were at this time
widely accepted: in the fall of 1936 the Ontario Liberal Party passed a resolution in favour of the compulsory sterilization of the "feeble-minded."[47]

Eugenic fears were clearly fuelled by the fact that many of the contesting mothers (and most of the ultimate winners) were on welfare. Nevertheless, some people offered a different interpretation of the eugenic gospel,
arguing that pro-natalism was useful to make sure that Ontario anglo-
phones were not overtaken by the French in Quebec. A bachelor writing to
the *Star* stated that "The shade of Theodore Roosevelt could delight in the
pictures of large healthy families, rather than race suicide. Is Ontario to suffer in comparison with Quebec? There large families are very common."[48]
The fact that several of the leading contestants had Italian names probably
diminished the popularity of this writer's selective pro-natalism. Although
the newspaper coverage does not make explicit reference to the women's

ethnicities, the over-representation of Italians or Italian-Canadians had to be, given the context, yet another sign that the Stork Derby babies were not the kind of "stock" favoured by ruling groups. Even those who favoured giving the Millar money to poor mothers did not always view them as deserving. Some of the people writing to the government to express their views opined that although the mothers should never have been encouraged to have so many babies, the money should be apportioned out among them in order to support the Derby babies, described by one writer as "victims of avarice."[49]

While prevalent views about population control, about the worthiness of the poor, and about sexual morality could not suffice to overturn the will in the face of a strong sentiment against government regulation of private property, they did have some influence on judicial decisions about exactly which mothers were entitled to the money. The Derby officially ended 10 years after Millar's death, on Hallowe'en night 1936. A few days later, a senior judge about to retire, Justice Middleton, was called upon to adjudicate the prize. Undaunted by affidavits against the will filed by Rev. Charles Silcox of the Social Service Council of Canada (who had just testified in favour of population control at the Palmer birth-control trial), and by a prominent obstetrician who believed that the will encouraged dangerous numbers of births, Middleton said: "I don't see that the reproduction of the human race is contrary to public morals."[50]

But Middleton now had to make decisions that would give precise legal content to the suddenly vague words "mothers" and "children." In respect to children, Middleton did not hesitate to specify that despite the indiscriminate wording of Millar's will, only legitimate children could be counted. As we shall see shortly, there were various ways in which the line between having a child and not having a child could be blurred, but the most important distinction made both by Middleton and by subsequent higher courts was that between the legitimate and the illegitimate.

There were no "really" illegitimate children in the contest. One of the leading contenders, however, had had five children by her husband and five by another man. Although she was still married, and hence her second set of children was by the letter of the law legitimate, Middleton eventually disqualified the mother on the basis that some of her children had been conceived in "open adultery."[51] Having made this questionable ruling on the children's legitimacy status, Middleton then proceeded to the most questionable feature of his decision. In a judgement later endorsed by the Supreme Court of Canada, Middleton argued that although it was the mothers, not the children, who were inheriting (and hence it should have been the mothers' own legitimacy status that counted, not that of their children), the children's status somehow rubbed off on their mothers: "'Children,' when used in any testamentary document, always means legitimate children and I can find no foundation for the contention that this is only in gifts to the children. I think it applies equally, perhaps *a fortiori*, to gifts to the mother of the children."[52] The mother of the 10 children by two different biological fathers, Mrs. P.C., was thus branded as an illegitimate mother by Middleton. The Court of Appeal agreed that to include illegitimate children in the head count would be "against public policy," and this was reaffirmed by the Supreme Court.[53]

By the beginning of 1938 when the case, having gone up to the Supreme Court, was referred back to Middleton for the adjudication of the prize among various possible winners, the issue of legitimacy had been settled. But this did not put an end to the difficulties of specifying exactly who counted as a legal child. There were two further issues which made a difference to some of the contesting mothers. One was the distinction between stillbirths (which according to Middleton did not count as children) and live births of children who died very quickly. Many of the mothers, from whose point of view a child born dead was still a child, took a dim view of the ruling; one of the top contenders, Mrs. H.G., wrote to Premier Hepburn that she had had a child born dead five years earlier, and that she found it odd that a minister had now ruled that the dead child did not count.[54] In court, Middleton listened to lengthy medical testimony on the fine line separating babies who do not breathe at birth and are not baptized and those who die but appear to have been born alive. Although the court was cleared during the medical testimony, the doctors' graphic descriptions of the births, the efforts to make the babies breathe, and the death throes of the newborns were reported at length in the newspapers.[55]

The second point of contention between mothers and the law was that women believed that all physical children counted, whereas the state insisted that only babies whose births had been legally registered counted. Not surprisingly, some of the women with the most children had not complied with the requirement of registering all births within the time limit. A Mrs. K., for example, had two unregistered children as well as nine registered ones, and since she expected to give birth a day or two before the will's deadline, she was counting on walking away with the prize (no other mother had more than 10 eligible children).[56] The birth registrar's official records were deemed more authoritative than her experience and she was disqualified. As Elizabeth Wilton points out in her thesis on the topic, the mother's lawyer tried to get the provincial government to register retroactively the children, something which was commonly done when parents suddenly experienced the need for official documents. But the government, undoubtedly aware of the fact that Mrs. K. was Italian and her husband was Irish Catholic, refused to issue the certificates, hence throwing Mrs. K. out of the competition.[57]

Finally, on Mar. 19, 1938 Middleton ruled that the prize money should be divided between four mothers who all had nine eligible children. The prolific Mrs. K. was disqualified because she had had two stillbirths and two unregistered children, while Mrs. C., whose last five children were fathered by her new commonlaw husband rather than by her legal husband, was also disqualified in a slanderous ruling that intimated that Mrs. C. may have been sleeping with both men simultaneously.[58] Subsequently, however, counsel for Mrs. K. and Mrs. C. pressed Middleton and the executors of the will, and were able to obtain a kind of consolation prize of $12 500 for each of their clients.

The municipal welfare department, in a move of questionable taste as well as dubious legality, sent out a press release showing that 11 of the Stork Derby finalists had received a total of $28 956 in relief and medical care. The names of all these people, losers as well as winners, were published, and the city insisted that the winners should repay them. Two out of the four winners had been on relief, and pressure was put upon them to repay, which they did. Mrs. C., who had received one of the small consolation prizes, thought better of it and simply disappeared with her money.[59]

The winners enjoyed a brief moment of celebrity. In a pale reflection of the Dionne Quintuplets' fame, three out of the four winning families appeared in advertisements for corn syrup and signed various contracts to appear in public. Earlier on, three hopeful mothers had done a vaudeville tour in the US.[60] The mothers, however, were not simply exploiting the situation; there is plenty of evidence to suggest that although they certainly enjoyed both the money and the fame, they also showed remarkable solidarity with one another. Mrs. H.G. (an early leader eventually disqualified) asked Premier Hepburn to divide the money equally rather than to force a competition, a sentiment echoed by other mothers. Mrs. G. also gave blood for the baby of another contestant.[61] The *Star* recorded various acts of sisterly solidarity among the women, particularly those on relief, and remarked on "the spirit of camaraderie which has lately grown up among the maternity contest mothers" even though this spirit undermined the horse-race metaphor promoted by the newspapers.[62] Although the mothers obviously saw a need to maintain an image of respectability and good citizenship (as evidenced in the voluntary payback of relief money to the city), they nevertheless stood their ground and made their views known, going so far as to defy Premier Hepburn when he publicly described the Stork Derby as "disgusting and revolting." "MOTHERS OF BIG FAMILIES DON'T AGREE WITH HEPBURN" was, perhaps, the headline that pointed to the heart of the Stork Derby controversy.[63]

CONCLUSION: DILEMMAS IN STATE REGULATION

The Stork Derby ended up financially benefitting some Toronto mothers. Unlike the disenfranchised Elzire Dionne, at least some of the Toronto mothers obtained a reward—although the money was won at the cost of having the details of private lives, from medical histories to finances, publicly broadcast, as well as the less direct cost of further stigmatizing poor mothers of large families. The reason for their somewhat tarnished victory was, however, that their cause happened to be tied to the interests of private property. The Star expressed the dominant opinion: "it may have been a foolish will, but in law a man has a perfect right to do foolish things as concerns the disposition, in life or in death, of his property."[64]

Mrs. Dionne, by contrast, was not able to appeal to the right of "a man" over his property in order to buttress her case. She tried to invoke the accepted idea that mothers have a natural relationship to their children, but this appeal to biology and to natural right was no match for the state's desire to control the estate of the Quintuplets. The Quints had in any case been constructed by the media as peculiar entities located at the intersection of tourism and science, having nothing in common with ordinary children.

Thus, one can see that the fortunes of motherhood depend not only on the social and legal standards regulating motherhood and family life at any particular time. They can also depend to a large extent on other factors—the interests of private property, for instance—which may appear as external but which become internal organizing principles for at least some women's experience of motherhood.

And what can one say about the role of the state in the regulation of childhood? We saw that Attorney-General Arthur Roebuck had declared himself to be the legal father of the Quintuplets in his capacity as *parens patriae*, although why the paternal qualities of the state ought to devolve on the Attorney-General in particular was never explained. In the Derby case, Roebuck was moved to repeat the high-sounding phrase: "I am watching in my capacity as *parens patriae*, a term which literally means father of the people, but which actually means more or less official guardian."[65] Roebuck was clearly torn between his parental/patriarchal desire to regulate, on the one hand, and the laissez-faire principles of estate law and property on the other. The structural contradiction between the two opposing principles (paternalism and liberalism) manifested itself as political wavering, as is obvious in the following report:

> Attorney-General Arthur Roebuck was understood to be lukewarm to any legislative tampering with the will, but yesterday pointed out that the Government had stepped in to save the Dionne quintuplets from harm. . . . If the Dionne case is taken as precedent, the Government may see fit to split the prize money, set it up in a trust fund, or otherwise act for the public welfare.[66]

Whatever the noble intentions of this statement, the precedent of the Quintuplet trust fund suggests that the well-being of poor children and mothers would not have been the government's first priority if it had taken over the half-million-dollar Millar estate. The publicity and commercialism decried by Premier Hepburn, when engaged in by parents, would not have been so distasteful if the estate had been nationalized by the province as the Quintuplets had been.

Both Roebuck and his predecessor were forced to take a more laissez-faire attitude in the Derby case than with the Dionnes, since the right of a man over his property was deemed by the courts to be the overriding factor in the case. And yet, the requirements of a capitalist marketplace, though tending to uphold the validity of the Millar will, do not suffice to explain the specific outcome. In order to adjudicate the prize Justice Middleton had to make a series of extra-economic decisions about the legal and moral legitimacy of both children and mothers.

Moral regulation, economic regulation, and certain local political questions (such as the issue of francophone rights, which ultimately weighted the balance against the state in the Dionne case) were all involved in determining the fates of the two sets of people whose administration is analyzed here. In future studies of cases involving families and the state it may therefore be useful to avoid the assumption that what is at stake is the history of child welfare or the relation between the public state and the private family. The social world is not always best understood through taken-for-granted, mutually exclusive categories dividing economics from sexuality, estate law from birth control, tourism from family policy. Why certain children were treated by the state as though they were not children is perhaps as important a question as determining the state's policy toward official children. Examining the "exceptional" cases can provide new insights into the ways in which categories such as "child welfare" (or for that matter "children") were constructed. Revealing the fractures in the exercise of power, the slippages from one category to another is as important as outlining the basic lines of the development of economic regulation or family policy.

NOTES

1. In keeping with Pierre Berton's *The Dionne Years*, her main source, Veronica Strong-Boag portrays the Dionne parents as victims of an interventionist state and a powerful group of experts. (V. Strong-Boag, "Intruders in the Nursery," in J. Parr, ed., *Childhood and Family in Canadian History* [Toronto: McClelland and Stewart, 1982], esp. 173–78). Strong-Boag's general thesis on the growth of government and professional regulation of family relations is undoubtedly correct, but I want to show here that the Dionne case and the Stock Derby case make it clear that not all children being regulated by the state are regulated as children.

2. For a relevant theorization of the family/market/state triad, see Frances E. Olsen, "The Family and the Market: A Study of Ideology and Legal Reform," *Harvard Law Review* 96 (1983), 1497–1578.

3. "Roebuck breaks Chicago Contract," *Globe*, 27 July 1934. The next day's *Globe* had an editorial praising Roebuck's action. The text of the contract between Mr. Dionne and the Chicago Fair promoters can be found in "Agreement between Oliva Dionne and Chicago World's Fair Promoters," dated 31 May 1934, in vol. 1, series C, Dafoe Papers, Public Archives of Ontario (This collection will be cited simply as Dafoe Papers).

4. When the second guardianship was established under the provincial official guardian, P.D. Wilson, he made repeated requests to Croll for the files on the first guardianship, even visiting Croll in his Windsor law office. But Croll refused, writing to one of the later guardians: "I cannot possibly let you have the quintuplet file. . . ." (Croll to K. Munro, 7 July 1937; letter in Croll file, Box 2 of Dionne Quintuplet Guardianship papers, RG 4, Series 4-53, Public Archives of Ontario [This 12-box collection will be cited simply as DQG papers]).

5. See Pierre Berton, *The Dionne Years* (Toronto: McClelland and Stewart, 1977), 71–73.

6. For the government's claim see "Province plans full care for the whole Dionne family," *Toronto Star* 27 March 1935, 23, But the documents in the "Reports of the Official Guardian" file, Box 8 DQG papers, show that the Dafoe Hospital was built by the Red Cross with $5000 of its own money plus an equal amount from private donations. The government may have paid the $4000 that was later given to local landowners in compensation for land expropriated for the Quintland complex, but Queen's Park specifically refused to pay for the buildings; David Croll said the government had "done

plenty" (undated report c. late 1938, "Reports of the Official Guardian," Box 8 DQG papers).

7. An Act Respecting the Guardianship of the Dionne Quintuplets, 1st session, 19th legislature of Ontario, 25 George V, 1935.

8. "Dionne family to get care," *Mail and Empire* 27 March 1935, 11.

9. For a full description of Quintland and of the tourist industry it sparked in nearby towns, see Berton, *The Dionne Years*, chapter 10.

10. For Dafoe's speech, see clipping in "New site and reunion of family" file, Box 7, DQG; the Niagara Falls comparison is from Berton, *The Dionne Years*, 9.

11. On Quintland see Berton, *The Dionne Years*, 5–9; see also the ghost written autobiography by James Brough, *We Were Five* (New York: Simon and Schuster, 1965).

12. Berton, *The Dionne Years*, 6.

13. See auditor's reports in "Reports of the Official Guardian" file, Box 8, DQG papers.

14. Detailed financial information is found in the file marked "Surrogate Court Audits" in Box 9, DQG papers. Copies of annual expense reports for the early years also exist in Vol. 2, Series C of the Dafoe papers.

15. "Dionne Bill Being Aimed at Chisellers," *Globe*, 12 March 1935.

16. For Blatz's expenses, see minutes of the guardianship for January 1938, in "Minutes" file, Box 5, DQG papers.

17. William Blatz, *The Five Sisters* (Toronto: McClelland and Stewart, 1938), 203.

18. See "Income Tax" file, Box 4, DQG papers.

19. Dr. Alan Brown, report dated 2 July 1938, in "Reports" file, Box 8, DQG papers.

20. A.G. Hays to P.D. Wilson, 28 Jan. 1938, "Trade Mark" file, Box 9, DQG papers. This file also contains information about the province's negotiations with the Ottawa office in charge of trade marks.

21. From July 1937 to July 1938, Hays's firm in New York billed the guardianship for $5815 (information from the "Minutes" file, Box 5, DQG papers).

22. An Act for the Protection of the Dionne Quintuplets, 2nd session, 18th parliament, 1 George VI, 1937.

23. Lillian Barker, "Dionne wins back the Quints," *America*, 25 October 1941, 65.

24. Minutes of January 1940 meeting of guardians, "Minutes" file, Box 6, DQG.

25. Darius Benham Inc., NY, to Keith Munro, 11 July 1941, in general correspondence file, Box 2, DQG papers.

26. Wilson's memo (probably to Attorney-General) of 20 June 1941, Reports of the Official Guardian file, Box 8, DQG papers.

27. Wilson to Munro, 19 Jan. 1942, "Paramount" file, Box 8, DQG papers.

28. There is no reliable information on how the remaining trust fund money was spent. The surviving Quintuplets have consistently claimed that they never got their rightful share of the fund upon reaching the age of majority, and on occasion have made allegations against both their father and the Ontario government. No legal case for fraud or misappropriation of funds has ever been heard, however.

29. See Wilson's "Memo of a discussion re guardianship on 7 March 1941," in "Religious" file, Box 8, DQG papers.

30. Pierre Berton consistently portrays Elzire Dionne as a simple-minded woman with no political savvy whatsoever; he even writes that "childbearing was for her as natural a process as eating" (*The Dionne Years*, 24).

31. "Mother of Quints voices complaints," *Globe*, 28 March 1935, 12.

32. "Looking into the future with Mrs. Dionne," Report in "Mrs. Dionne" file, Box 2, DQG papers.

33. Nurse's log, June–September 1939; unnumbered file, Box 11, DQG papers. See also "Mrs. Dionne" file in Box 2 for complaints from the mother transmitted to Queen's Park via the ACFEO's lawyer, Henri St-Jacques.

34. A similar point is made by Elizabeth Wilton in her MA thesis on the Stork Derby (Dalhousie University, History Department, 1994). I thank Elizabeth Wilton for allowing me to read a draft of her thesis.

35. The question of married vs. unmarried mothers is raised in a front-page article, "Attempt may be made to break Millar's will," *Star*, 7 Dec. 1926, 1 and 8; for information about the estate see *Globe*, 7 Dec. 1926, 1 and 17.

36. See Mark M. Orkin, *The Great Stork Derby* (Don Mills: General Publishing, 1981), 77. Orkin's book is an uncritical exposé, focusing mainly on the careers and personalities of the legal personnel involved in decision-making, but providing some useful information.

37. Quoted in Orkin, *The Great Stork Derby*, 86.

38. Orkin, *The Great Stork Derby*, 91–93; and two stories in the *Star*, 24 March 1932, 2.

39. The Rev. A.H. Tyrer, quoted in "Millar will is withdrawn by Price," *Star*, 24 March 1932, 2.

40. "Mother of 27 children proposes legal fight," *Star* 23 March 1932, 2; articles referring to the kidnapping of US aviator Charles Lindbergh's small child appeared around this time in the *Star*, and in this same issue of the *Star* there was an article reporting a sighting of the Lindbergh baby.

41. "Legatee 'Cheated,' say Liberal Women," *Globe*, 24 March 1932, 1.

42. Editorial, *Globe*, 24 March 1932, 4.

43. "Women halt Millar estate," *Globe*, 25 March 1932, 1–2.

44. Editorial, *Star*, 26 March 1932, 4.

45. Arlene and Angus McLaren, *The Bedroom and the State* (Toronto: McClelland and Stewart, 1986), chapter 5.

46. See especially "Eastview charge reduced by court," *Mail and Empire*, 28 October 1936, 1–2; but also stories in all Toronto papers during the month of October.

47. *Globe*, 7 November 1936, 1.

48. Letter, *Star*, 31 October 1936, 6; as part of the same discussion on reproductive politics, another letter writer opined that Millar should have left his money to a birth-control clinic (*Star*, 29 October 1936, 6).

49. Public Archives of Ontario, Hepburn papers, RG 3, Box 259, unnumbered file. There appear to be no records of public input into the earlier government decisions of 1926 and 1932, but the records of all decisions in the Attorney-General's department are very badly documented up to 1935.

50. "Judge refuses to agree frequent births an evil," *Star*, 16 November 1936, 1–2; for Dr. Silcox and Dr. Hendry's affidavits, see "Two affidavits," *Globe*, 13 November 1936, 1, section 2.

51. Middleton, quoted in "Four mothers share . . ." *Star*, 19 March 1938, 1 and 3.

52. Re Millar, Ontario Supreme Court, Middleton J.A., Nov. 16, 1936; Dominion Law Reports (1937), 135.

53. For Appeal Court ruling, see "Appeal Court rules . . ." in *Star*, 23 February 1937; for Supreme Court, see "Legitimate children alone are eligible," *Star*, 22 December 1937, 1. The Supreme Court ruling is: Re Millar (Estate of), (1938) S.C.R. 1; it is almost wholly concerned with the question of the rights of testators, and on issues concerning legitimate or illegitimate mothers it simply confirms Middleton's decision.

54. Mrs. H.G. to Premier Hepburn, 28 October 1936, in Public Archives of Ontario, Hepburn papers, Box 259, "Millar" file.

55. "Babies didn't breathe though heart beat," *Star*, 25 February 1938, 1–2.

56. "Mrs. K. expects baby's birth today," *Star*, 29 October 1936, 1.

57. Elizabeth Wilton, "The Toronto Stork Derby."

58. See the details of Middleton's judgement in Orkin, *The Great Stork Derby*, 297–99.

59. Orkin, *The Great Stork Derby*, 301–2; also "Two Stork Derby winners will gladly repay city," *Star*, 21 March 1938, 2.

60. See for instance ad for Edwardsburg Corn Syrup, including the statement "Money can't buy a more healthful food," in *Star*, 21 March 1938, 7; for vaudeville tour, see *Globe*, 14 November 1936, 1.

61. Letter from H.G. to Hepburn, 28 October 1936, in Public Archives of Ontario, Hepburn papers, Box 259, "Millar" file; see also "Millar will contenders offer one another aid," *Star*, 23 October, 1, 2.

62. "Millar will contenders offer one another aid," 1.

63. "Mothers of big families . . ." *Star*, 24 October 1936, 2.

64. Editorial, *Star*, 26 March 1932, 4.

65. *Star*, 23 October 1936, 3.

66. *Star*, 24 October 1936, 1, section 2.

THE QUEER CAREER OF
HOMOSEXUAL SECURITY
VETTING IN COLD WAR CANADA ✧

DANIEL J. ROBINSON
DAVID KIMMEL

o

The Cold War is over but the historical assessment of its impact on postwar Canadian society has scarcely begun. Recent studies suggest that Canada's "home front" was not entirely spared the ignominy of civil rights abuses commonly associated with Cold War America.[1] Although in Canada no McCarthyesque figure or televised loyalty board hearings captured the public spotlight, there were many groups and individuals—among them Communists, labour leaders, academics, immigrants, and artists—whose varied left-wing political views or affiliations subjected them to state persecution and other organized forms of "red-baiting." Jobs were lost, careers ended, and lives ruined, the most notable example being Canadian diplomat Herbert Norman who committed suicide in 1957 when the United States Senate reopened an investigation of his political loyalty.[2] While scholarly work has elucidated Ottawa's handling of political and ideological threats during the Cold War, another important subject has received only passing notice: the federal government's security investigation and subsequent firing of homosexuals during the 1950s and 1960s. When the episode was brought

✧ Reprinted by permission of University of Toronto Press Incorporated, from *Canadian Historical Review* 75, 3 (Sept. 1994): 319–45. An earlier version of this paper was presented to a conference called "Canada at the Crossroads: The Critical 1960s" (York University, May 1993, and Ruhr-Universitat Bochum, December 1993), organized by J.L. Granatstein and Gustav Schmidt. The authors wish to thank Professor Granatstein and Reg Whitaker for their helpful commentary while this paper was in preparation. Daniel Robinson gratefully acknowledges the financial assistance of the Canada-U.S. Fulbright Program.

to public attention in 1992, Prime Minister Brian Mulroney denounced it as "one of the greatest outrages and violations of human rights" which even "the passage of time . . . [has not made] any less odious."[3]

This "odious" event was a peculiar product of Cold War era "insecurities." Government officials maintained that homosexuals (almost exclusively males) fearing public exposure were security risks owing to their susceptibility to blackmail by hostile intelligence agencies. Along with political subversives and foreign spies, they were considered legitimate targets of investigation. The Royal Canadian Mounted Police (RCMP) took up the challenge wholeheartedly. A separate unit was formed to deal with the homosexual issue. And by the late 1960s the total number of RCMP files concerning homosexuals reached roughly 9000, only one-third of which involved government employees. In conjunction with this investigation, the federal government sponsored a research project that sought to "detect" homosexuality through the photographic measurement of eye movements of people shown hetero- and homoerotic pictures. The research was headed by Carleton University professor Robert Wake and was backed by officials from a number of federal departments. Dubbed the "fruit machine" by the Mounties, the project amounted to a four-year effort to enlist science in the cause of state security.

How this investigation and research project could reach such advanced and, to the modern reader, disturbing degrees is the result of many factors. The government's internal security system, soon after its founding in 1946, institutionalized procedures that provided both the security rationale and the investigative means for later anti-homosexual campaigns. These consisted of the government's early preoccupation with employee "character weaknesses" as a security concern, the predominant role of the RCMP in the security vetting process, and the importance of appeasing American security interests in Canada. As well, Canadian officials adopted some features of Washington's early 1950s efforts to root out homosexuals from federal offices, efforts that advanced far beyond a security rationale and into outright homophobia. Yet another example of US influence was the reliance of Dr Wake on the American psychiatric community for information concerning homosexual-detection methods. Throughout the period the most vehement opponents of the employment of homosexuals in any government capacity were the RCMP and the Department of National Defence (DND). Their common position derived in large measure from each organization's internal policy of automatically discharging all discovered homosexuals. Not all government officials, though, were as prejudiced as their police and military counterparts. As a result, the debate over the homosexual security issue was characterized by liberal-versus-hardliner disagreement.

The story is bitterly ironic. When the Canadian government earnestly turned its attention to the homosexual security question in 1958, it was to inquire whether security policies and procedures regarding "character weaknesses" might be moderated. The phenomenon that culminated the RCMP's 9000-name homosexual index and the fruit machine was, in part, the unintended consequence of a liberal initiative.

ɔ

While the Canadian government's investigation of homosexuals began in the late 1950s, the origins of this policy date back to an early Cold War development, the September 1945 defection of Igor Gouzenko. The ensuing royal commission, after concluding that a number of ideologically motivated public servants had passed on state secrets to Soviet agents, recommended the adoption of a more systematic and stringent approach to government security.[4] In May 1946, before the release of the commission's report, the Security Panel was established, consisting of an interdepartmental committee under the auspices of the Privy Council Office (PCO) and chaired by the secretary to the cabinet. Its permanent representatives were from the Department of External Affairs (DEA), the RCMP, the Defence Research Board, and the three branches of the armed forces. A senior mandarin body—by 1953 all members were deputy ministers or their equivalents—its terms of reference were to "advise on the co-ordination of the planning, organization and execution of security measures which affect government departments" and to offer advice to cabinet on these matters. In May 1947 the panel issued a Security Booklet that described the handling and classification of government documents as well as measures to ensure the physical security of public buildings. A cabinet directive on security (CD no. 4) was issued in March 1948 stating that "maximum care" be used "to ensure that government employees are completely trustworthy."[5]

The investigative task outlined in CD no. 4 fell to the RCMP, which conducted two types of security probes. For government employees seeking the lower-level "confidential" or "restricted" security clearances, a simple record check was done. This process involved a criminal record check and a search of RCMP files for any links to "known subversive organizations." For "secret" and "top secret" clearances, along with the record check, a "field investigation" involving a "full enquiry into the antecedents of the employee" was conducted. Former employers and others "closely connected with the person" were contacted and interviewed.[6] While the Mounties conducted the investigations and compiled "adverse" reports on employees where evidence warranted, the authority to grant or deny a security clearance—or in fact take any other course of action with respect to the employee—rested with the respective deputy minister.[7] The separation of fact-finding and decision-making functions was supposed to ensure that an overzealous RCMP did not unnecessarily deny security clearances. The most thorough study of the Security Panel's early years, however, suggests that this separation was more nominal than actual. Deputy ministers were largely unfamiliar with security issues and often deferred to the RCMP's more experienced judgment in these matters. The result, according to Reg Whitaker, was "a procedure by which the police would not only gather information, but would themselves evaluate it and in effect make recommendations on whether individuals were security risks."[8] C.W. Harvison, who as RCMP commissioner represented the force on the Security Panel from 1960 to 1963, partially confirms this conclusion in his memoirs. He notes that deputy ministers and other panel members "attempted to have police reports advance some comment" on whether certain employees represented security threats.[9] In the late 1940s the RCMP were conducting some 2000 security checks a month; by the mid-1950s this number had climbed to nearly 5000.[10]

Along with the RCMP's central role in the security vetting process, three other aspects of the Security Panel's operation are significant to the later targeting of homosexuals as risks. First, extreme secretiveness surrounded the security screening process. Second, the matter of "character weaknesses" was of increasing concern. The third aspect was Canada's sensitivity to American concerns when formulating its own security policy.

Unlike the United States, where government security systems were more open and allowed for appeals (albeit of a very limited nature), Canada's procedure was a closed-door affair without review provisions.[11] This undisclosed approach was viewed favourably by officials overseeing the system.[12] They argued that government employees secretly deemed security risks were spared the public humiliation and "black-listing" characteristic of American loyalty board hearings. In Canada, discreetly released public servants would not have their reputations smeared and their careers ruined. Thus they would be better placed to find other employment. Of course, this approach was something of a mixed blessing. Unlike the United States where the Attorney General's Office published a list of "subversive" organizations, in Canada the RCMP secretly dubbed many clubs and organizations "communist fronts," and suspicions were cast on members even if they had no way of knowing which associations were "acceptable" and which were not. Indeed, Canadian civil servants were most likely unaware that security reasons were to blame for a firing, transfer, or demotion. CD no. 4 stipulated that such matters be dealt with not on the basis of security, but rather "personal unsuitability."[13] This situation was callously evidenced in February 1949 by RCMP Assistant Commissioner L.H. Nicholson's advice to F.W.T. Lucas, secretary of the Security Panel, regarding an "unreliable" employee:

> Before precipitating a complaint and publicity the departmental head should exhaust all means of releasing the employee without letting him become aware that his loyalty is suspect. Should the employee voice his suspicion as to the real grounds for his removal then every effort should be made to dispel that suspicion. Depending on circumstances, it is at times possible to effectively camouflage the reason for action.[14]

This furtive and evasive approach, advocated by the Mountie who, from 1951 to 1959, represented the force on the Security Panel, becomes more troubling from a civil liberties perspective when viewed alongside the content of RCMP security reports. The first batch of RCMP security investigations, dated 1949, revealed that of 213 adverse reports, only twenty-seven involved political subversion. The remaining 87 percent comprised "character" or moral flaws such as gambling, adultery, drinking, or women having illegitimate children. No cases of homosexuality were cited. While Lucas was initially disturbed by these results, other civilian members of the panel soon accepted the Mounties' rationale for this comprehensive approach: individuals engaging in socially stigmatized behaviour were subject to blackmail because they had something to hide. In light of these developments a new classification category covering "character weaknesses" was created. It entailed the following notice being placed in an individual's file: "information at hand, although not bearing directly on security, may be considered to affect the suitability of this person for employment in the public service." Thus the handling of character weakness became a routine feature of the internal security process. Though the frequency of "character weakness" entries declined in the early 1950s, they still comprised twice the number of "political" adverse reports.[15] It would seem, therefore, that Justice Minister J.L. Ilsley's assurances in the Commons on 22 June 1948 that government security screening would not devolve into "any irrelevant inquiry into the private lives of individuals" were in fact premature.[16]

The final significant feature of Ottawa's internal security system was its vulnerability to American pressure. When in 1920 the RCMP began collecting security intelligence, its covert operations were restricted to Canadian territory. This practice continued into the post-1945 period. Hence Canada, unlike Britain and the United States, lacked its own means of gathering foreign-based intelligence affecting the national interest.[17] Accordingly the RCMP depended on "friendly" security agencies like the Federal Bureau of Investigation (FBI) and, after 1947, the Central Intelligence Agency (CIA) for help in these areas. The FBI representative at the American Embassy in Ottawa actually worked out of RCMP headquarters until the mid-1950s. As well, the Mounties were in the habit of giving the FBI information on Canadian political subversives to which even federal cabinet ministers were denied access.[18] Compounding the asymmetrical relationship of the two countries' intelligence agencies was a larger structural dependence resulting from Canada's accelerating economic and defence integration with the United States after 1945.[19]

Hence it is not surprising that American security considerations weighed heavily on Security Panel decisions. A 6 April 1948 panel meeting noted that the United States War Department was willing to share classified information with DND and other government agencies provided that "all personnel handling such material had been cleared from a security standpoint." The panel therefore recommended that "full security precautions" in certain government branches be undertaken to accommodate this information transfer.[20] American security concerns also lay behind the Canadian government's decision in 1951 to launch security investigations of merchant seamen on the Great Lakes.[21] This close interconnection between internal security and international intelligence links is underscored by the following excerpt from a government report on the topic:

> There is more than just an internal need for a security intelligence agency. Canada's international alliances require that it be able to assure its allies, with whom it participates in common defence

arrangements, that it has a sound system of internal security. Allied countries will not entrust Canadian officials and political leaders with secret information unless Canada has in place effective structures and procedures for detecting and preventing foreign espionage.[22]

Logic indicates, therefore, that the security preoccupations of the senior partner were likely to become those of the junior partner seeking to preserve access to the former's intelligence secrets.

With these factors in mind we turn to the American government's security vetting of homosexual public servants in the early 1950s. "It is the opinion of this subcommittee," a December 1950 United States Senate report concluded, that homosexuals "are unsuitable for employment in the Federal Government" because their "degraded," "illegal," and "immoral" activities rendered them innately unreliable.[23] Since it was also an "accepted fact" that homosexuals were "prime targets" of blackmail by hostile foreign agents, such "sex perverts" constituted high-level security risks.[24] Testimony from "eminent [though unnamed] psychiatrists" and an "abundance of [undocumented] evidence" confirmed the homosexual's depraved, pitiful, and socially abhorrent condition. Moreover, these persons were a physical threat to other employees: "[Homosexuals] will frequently attempt to entice normal individuals to engage in perverted practises. This is particularly true in the case of young and impressionable people who might come under the influence of a pervert. . . . It is particularly important that the thousands of young men and women who are brought into Federal jobs not be subjected to that type of influence while in the service of the Government. One homosexual can pollute a Government office." The report's recommendation that the government not "pussyfoot" about or adopt "half measures" regarding this issue was in fact preaching to the recently converted.[25] By early 1950 Washington had already stepped up its efforts to remove homosexuals from the federal payroll. While between 1947 and April 1950 an average of five homosexuals per month were dismissed from civilian positions, during the next year the total jumped to more than sixty. The "lavender scare" became a frequent topic of concern for congressional leaders throughout 1950. The FBI took a prominent role in internal investigations, even opening a file on presidential candidate Adlai Stevenson's "alleged homosexuality." In March 1953 the State Department revealed that 425 of its employees had been released as a result of homosexual probes. The next month the Eisenhower administration issued Executive Order 10450 which specified that "sexual perversion" was definite grounds for dismissal from public positions. As a result, an average of forty homosexuals per month were released in the following year.[26] At the same time Alfred Kinsey, whose widely read 1948 study on male sexuality argued that homosexual behaviour was more common then previously thought, was denounced as a communist by newspapers and the Catholic Church. By 1954 much of his private and federal research funding had been withdrawn.[27]

The influence of the American preoccupation with the homosexual security question manifested itself in amendments to Canada's immigration laws. A government committee overseeing revision of the Immigration Act met on 20 December 1950 (five days after the release of the above Senate report) and added "homosexuals, lesbians, and persons coming to Canada for any immoral purpose" to the list of prohibited classes. The proscription on homosexuals remained in the version that went before a Commons committee in June 1952 and which soon after became law. At no point during this committee or parliamentary debate did the subject elicit any comment. Thus the first time an Act of Parliament referred to "homosexual" as "a status or a type of person" (as opposed to specific "homosexual acts") passed unnoticed.[28] The law barred homosexuals from visiting Canada and applying as immigrants or permanent residents. As seen earlier in a different context, people denied entry to Canada on security grounds were also not informed of the actual reasons for this action.[29] Philip Girard argues that the principal backer of the homosexual exclusion was the RCMP, which oversaw the drafting of the new lists of prohibited categories. As well, Girard attributes the impetus for the homosexual ban to "American concern about the alleged laxity of Canada's security system," which was conveyed to Canadian officials via the RCMP and DND.[30]

Shortly after the passage of the Immigration Act, a new cabinet directive on security was issued. Among the October 1952 provisions was the recommendation that reliability from a security viewpoint take account of "defects of character" that might cause an employee to be "indiscreet, dishonest or vulnerable to blackmail."[31] Three years later a more detailed cabinet directive (CD no. 29) reaffirmed this policy position.

It also remains an essential of Canadian security policy that persons who are unreliable from a security standpoint, not because they are disloyal, but because of defects in their character which may lead to indiscretion or dishonesty, or may make them like subjects of blackmail, must not be employed in any position where they have access to classified information. Such defects of character may also make them unsuitable for employment on grounds other than security.[32]

"On grounds other than security" clearly echoed American policy in which the "general unsuitability" of homosexuals justified their exclusion from federal offices irrespective of security considerations. When cabinet met on 21 December 1955 to consider CD no. 29—which had been drafted by the Security Panel—it deemed the directive "eminently reasonable" and passed it without any discussion of the character weakness clause.[33]

o

While the character weakness provisions of internal security did not appear to concern the Liberal St Laurent government, such was not the case for its Tory successor. John Diefenbaker's twin election victories in 1957 and 1958 brought to the prime minister's office a man with a long-standing reputation as a civil rights advocate who had voiced concerns about government security screening as early as 1948.[34] In June 1958 Diefenbaker requested that security procedures affecting character weaknesses be re-examined with a mind to adopting a more liberal approach. G.F. Frazer of the Privy Council Office was charged with drafting a memo for consideration by the Security Sub-Panel, the interdepartmental body formed in 1953 to supervise much of the preparatory work for the Security Panel.[35] Frazer's memo noted that on only one occasion had a matter of character weakness "rendered an employee untrustworthy for access to classified information." That case involved a civilian employee of the Royal Canadian Air Force who in 1956 passed low-grade information to a Soviet official while inebriated. The incident was not thought serious and Frazer argued that character weaknesses as a whole were less sensitive than subversive threats. He therefore called for a "greater measure of fairness" when dealing with individuals whose loyalty was not in doubt. A more "sympathetic" handling of the matter was both possible and desirable.

> For example, where there is evidence of character weakness, an employee, or prospective employee, might be taken into the confidence of the employing government department or agency. It might be indicated to him with the greatest possible tact that the department is aware that he may have a character weakness which could affect his career. The employer could point out to him the possibility that he might be made the object of blackmail, and emphasize the duty to report any such approach with the assurance that he will receive the full cooperation of his employer and the security authorities.[36]

This liberal approach would have sharply differentiated Canadian character weakness security policy from that of the United States.

This sympathetic impulse proved short-lived. Frazer's memo was not received enthusiastically when the Security Sub-Panel convened on 8 July (the first comprehensive discussion of character weakness in a security forum). DEA representative J. Timmerman described how on at least four occasions Soviet intelligence agents had (unsuccessfully) attempted to exploit character weaknesses by blackmailing Canadian personnel serving abroad. While he did not say specifically whether these cases involved homosexuality, he advocated the maintenance of current security regulations regarding "character weaknesses in general, and homosexuality in particular." F.H. Watkins, the DND representative, remarked that the military dismissed all discovered homosexuals as a matter of personnel policy regardless of security considerations. K.W.N. Hall of the RCMP emphasized the security aspect of the homosexual issue and noted the difficulties present in investigating such cases. In sum, rather than moderating the character weakness provisions of CD no. 29, the meeting endorsed actions to enhance counterintelligence measures: American and British governments' handling of the homosexual question would be consulted; departmental case histories of character-weakness blackmail attempts would be compiled and made available to the Security Panel; and the RCMP would contact the morality squad of the Ottawa Police Department to examine the latter's handling of related criminal cases. Don Wall, the Security Panel secretary, was charged with preparing a report on the subject encompassing the "full context of problems of personnel administration as well as problems of security."[37] Frazer's earlier progressivism now seemed sidetracked.

When completed nine months later, Wall's report confirmed the conservative position advocated by the Security Sub-Panel.[38] His paper discussed the 1955 Australian Royal Commission on Espionage and its conclusion that Soviet intelligence agencies were recruiting fewer ideological agents and instead targeting for blackmail government officials with character weaknesses. Furthermore, DEA had recently received a copy of a Soviet intelligence training manual describing techniques of blackmail to exploit the "human weakness[es]" of influential civil servants. Wall also compared British and American approaches to the subject, paying special attention to the conclusions of the 1950 Senate report described above. Lengthy quotations from the 1950 congressional testimony of then CIA director Admiral Roscoe Hillenkoetter were included:

> The moral pervert is a security risk of so serious a nature that he must be weeded out of government employment wherever he is found. . . . In addition, homosexuality frequently is accompanied by other exploitable weaknesses, such as psychopathic tendencies which affect the soundness of their judgement, physical cowardice, susceptibility to pressure, and general instability. . . . Lastly, perverts in key positions lead to the concept of a government within a government. . . . One pervert brings other perverts. They belong to the lodge, the fraternity. . . . [T]hey move from position to position and advance themselves usually in the interest of furthering the romance of the moment.

British practices, Wall noted, were decidedly more liberal. A 1956 Conference of the Privy Councillors on Security, while recognizing that homosexuals were potential subjects of blackmail, concluded that their employment posed "no greater threat than any other deviation from the straight and narrow path of virtue." Wall also mentioned the 1957 Wolfenden Report, which recommended the decriminalization of homosexual acts between consenting adults.[39]

His conclusions, however, owed far more to Washington than London. The threat of blackmail, coupled with Hillenkoetter's assessment of homosexuals' natural propensity towards "instability, willing self-deceit, and defiance towards society," engendered both security and personnel-administrative reasons for their exclusion from public positions. In support of this view Wall referred to the DND submission to his study which advocated a ban on homosexuals from all government positions. It found that such persons were intrinsically "unreliable" and thus "unsuitable for employment from the point of view of good personnel management, quite apart from the security considerations."[40] Not surprisingly, Wall's final advice was against softening the character weakness provisions of CD no. 29.

When the Security Panel met on 6 October 1959 to discuss Wall's report, it became clear that a can of worms had been opened.[41] Within the panel, liberal-conservative divisions had begun to take shape. Among the liberals were Robert Bryce, secretary to the cabinet and panel chairman; Norman Robertson, undersecretary of state for external affairs; and Paul Pelletier of the Civil Service Commission. While Bryce acknowledged that the threat of blackmail would in most cases preclude homosexuals from gaining access to classified information, these persons could be transferred to "less sensitive departments." Robertson, claiming that Wall's report exaggerated the security risk presented by homosexuals, stressed that an individual's reliability involved a "mixture of considerations"; a homosexual's "great discretion" and "brilliant capacity for public service" might very well "neutralize" the security risks stemming from his sexual orientation. Like Robertson, Pelletier criticized Wall for overemphasizing the homosexual security danger and underscored the fact that never had a federally employed homosexual been successfully blackmailed into disclosing state secrets. Opposing these views were RCMP Commissioner Charles Rivett-Carnac and F.R. Miller, deputy minister of national defence. Rivett-Carnac reiterated the RCMP's position that homosexuals were a serious and widespread security threat. Miller sounded the familiar DND refrain that no homosexuals be allowed "in any capacity" within the public service. Split by such differences, the panel was unable to recommend to cabinet a course of action on the matter. Diefenbaker's original desire to reconfigure CD no. 29 appeared stymied.

National Defence's and the RCMP's extreme opposition to the employment of homosexuals was in fact a reflection of each organization's internal handling of the matter: all detected homosexuals, irrespective of security concerns, were discharged. This policy became a routine aspect of military operations during the Second World War, when enlistees and soldiers were given psychiatric examinations to determine their suitability for armed service. Homosexuals were classified as "psychopathic personalities" and promptly discharged, which, considering the army's definition of this pathology, is hardly surprising:

> Men with this disorder are unable to meet the usual adult social standards of truthfulness, decency, responsibility and consideration for their fellow associates. They are emotionally unstable and absolutely not to be depended upon. They are impulsive, show poor judgement and in the Army they are continually at odds with those who are trying to train and discipline them. . . . Among this group are many homosexuals, chronic delinquents, chronic alcoholics and drug addicts. All such men should be regarded as medically unfit for service anywhere *in any capacity*.[42] [author's emphasis]

Because homosexuals were thought incapable of functioning in an organizational and hierarchical setting, they constituted a threat to military authority and general troop morale. This "psychopathic" categorizing of homosexuals during the war, Gary Kinsman argues, helped "lay the basis for the anti-homosexual purges" of the postwar period. Not until 1992 did the Canadian Armed Forces end its policy of summarily dismissing discovered homosexuals.[43]

Similarly, the RCMP as a "quasi-military organization" had a hierarchical and rigid command structure. New recruits, usually straight out of high school, underwent a period of basic training. While in the force, Mounties' personal lives were subject to many controls. For example, recruits had to remain single during the first few years of service, and cohabitation with unmarried women was prohibited. Violators of the RCMP's internal discipline code were subject to harsh discipline, including what Mann and Lee record as "degradation rituals." Such moralistic measures contributed to the McDonald Commission's assessment that the RCMP "through its recruiting, training and management practices, engulfs its members in an ethos akin to that found in a monastery or religious order." Religious symbolism also conformed to the popular myths promulgated by Hollywood films and pulp fiction surrounding the men in scarlet as virtuous archetypes of public morality and defenders of the social order.[44] While no official written policy barred gays from the force, in practice they were routinely dismissed when discovered. This policy persisted until the late 1980s.[45]

The RCMP's direct involvement in investigating homosexuals in other government departments began in 1959. On 29 April 1960 J.M. Bella, director of the RCMP's Security and Intelligence Branch, issued a report concerning the ongoing probe of federally employed homosexuals.[46] As a justification for the investigation, Bella referred to Wall's report, especially its conclusion that "homosexual characteristics" like "instability [and] willing self-deceit" constituted *prima facie* evidence of employee unreliability and of security risk. During the past year the force had uncovered 363 confirmed, alleged, and suspected homosexuals in thirty-three government departments and agencies.[47] These included such low-level security offices as the Central Mortgage & Housing Corporation, the Department of Public Works, and the Unemployment Insurance Commission. The largest totals were within the navy (199 of 363) and External Affairs (59 of 363).[48] Of the 363, 156 were classified as "confirmed" cases. Since 116 employees were listed as being either released or resigned, retired or deceased, it would seem that roughly 75 percent of the "confirmed" group were no longer on the government payroll. But these numbers were only half the story. About 350 homosexuals outside the public service had also been investigated in order that, Bella wrote, "the most complete picture possible might be obtained." These persons warranted investigation because they might later seek government employment and, more importantly, because they were necessary sources of information for tracking down federally employed homosexuals. Record checks almost never uncovered "evidence of homosexuality," so to widen the security net the Mounties depended on the "opinions or knowledge expressed by friends and acquaintances, usually homosexual, of the person concerned." Homosexuals, while untrustworthy as government employees, were paradoxically considered reliable police informants.

Interviewing homosexual government workers, however, was problematic for the RCMP because, as noted above, official policy prohibited the disclosure of security grounds for any employee investigation. The RCMP was uncertain whether it had the proper terms of reference to interview homosexual civil servants. The force was also stymied by regulations that obligated it to disclose employee security information to the respective deputy minister. "We have already experienced difficulties arising from departments discharging homosexuals who have admitted their weakness," Bella lamented, and "we firmly believe that if it becomes a general practice to discharge homosexuals who co-operate with us these people will refuse to talk, and without their assistance this type of investigation cannot achieve complete success." To ensure the operation's viability, Bella recommended charges to CD no. 29 to facilitate the questioning of homosexuals and to restrict deputy ministers from launching disciplinary measures against employees until after the RCMP completed its investigations. Ironically, both liberals and conservatives were now seeking charges to CD no. 29. Finally, and of particular note, Bella reported that the RCMP had received the "necessary ministerial authority" to continue its investigations in "sensitive and non-sensitive" government departments and agencies.[49]

When the Security Panel met again on 24 June 1960 to discuss the issue with specific reference to Bella's memo, there were more notable differences of opinion.[50] Harvison, now RCMP Commissioner, discussed how the security problems associated with homosexuality were escalating, as witnessed by the force's list of homosexual names "growing with each new enquiry." To confront this security challenge, a "clear directive" from the government was needed as Bella recommended. But other committee members were far less alarmist. Robertson criticized the Mounties' "statistical approach" that devolved into "a sociological survey in which the security aspects were lost sight of." He suggested that RCMP inquiries be limited to the security implications of employing homosexual civil servants. S.H.S. Hughes, chairman of the Civil Service Commission, maintained that too much of the RCMP investigation was based on suspicion alone. He underscored the importance of assessing the matter strictly on security grounds and on a case-by-case basis. Furthermore, he noted that there had been no evidence to date of any successful blackmailing of government homosexuals. Bryce also concurred that security investigations should be limited to employees who were susceptible to foreign intelligence exploitation. When possible these persons should be transferred to non-classified positions. Finally, any decision concerning changes to CD no. 29 was postponed until a meeting with the prime minister and Justice Minister Davie Fulton could be arranged.

Over six months would elapse before a memo outlining the Security Panel's recent handling of the homosexual issue was sent to Diefenbaker and Fulton.[51] The brief, written by Bryce, raised a number of points suggestive of the panel's liberal spokesmen. Security investigations of homosexuals "should not be widespread" but restricted only to those employees susceptible to foreign intelligence blackmail. Cabinet approval for several courses of action was requested. Government departments with overseas missions were asked to compile a list of personnel with access to security-sensitive information. Afterwards, internal and RCMP investigations would determine if any of these employees were vulnerable to blackmail. Lastly, all cases of discovered homosexuals would be referred to the Security Panel secretary before departmental actions were taken. Clearly, the narrow focus on the homosexual security implications centred mostly on employees subject to foreign posting ran counter to the RCMP's calls for a wider investigation. But not all was lost for the Mounties. The report also recommended that a research program to "devis[e] tests to identify persons with homosexual tendencies" be undertaken. In commenting on this development, Harvison noted that such tests could be used to disqualify homosexual candidates for public service positions on the grounds that they were "practising criminals" under sections 147 and 149 of the Criminal Code.[52]

This research project was that of Carleton University psychologist, Robert Wake, who with Don Wall's backing had written a preliminary report in June 1960 on the issue of homosexuality and government employment for the Security Panel. The paper outlined various approaches to managing the issue and recommended that a "fully considered research program" be established to "develop suitable methods of selecting personnel for sensitive positions."[53] Wake planned to spend his 1961–62 sabbatical year in the United States studying "sex deviates" and subsequently secured $5000—an appreciable sum in 1961—from the Department of National Health and Welfare to assist his research.[54]

That government officials would turn to psychiatric and psychological specialists for solutions to the "problem" of homosexuality is understandable. Since the early twentieth century, and especially after 1945, the epistemology of homosexuality had moved from a "moral-religious" framework to a "medical-scientific" one. Influential in substituting the "concept of illness for that of sin"[55] were the rising cadre of psychiatric professionals. From Sigmund Freud to Charles Socarides in the 1960s, a consensus within psychiatry maintained that homosexuality constituted a pathological disorder. The scientific and objective mantle of the psychiatry profession's authority did not shield its practitioners from the cultural beliefs and social attitudes of their day; "value neutral" diagnoses of homosexuality were all too uncommon.

A few Canadian examples illustrate this point. Writing in a medical journal in 1950, S.R. Laycock described the varied psychiatric and psychological methods at hand to develop the "heterosexual aspects" of homosexuals, especially among those who realized "that it [was] fun to be reasonably normal and that it pa[id] great dividends." For "confirmed" homosexuals unable to make the transition he advocated fraternization with heterosexuals and a channelling of their sexual energy into "worthwhile" endeavours such as art, literature, music, and community work. Another writer in the *Canadian Journal of Psychology* reported that because homosexuals were torn between a longing for social acceptance and their own sexual desires they were often prone to "sadistic behaviour," paranoia, "neurotic and/or psychotic tendencies such as extreme anxiety," and "schizoid thinking." They were also more likely to use drugs and alcohol. In a 1959 article pandering to homosexual-child molester stereotyping, P.G. Thomson examined homosexual formation during adolescence. While a homosexual phase during childhood and puberty was usually a temporary phenomenon, any "seduction" by an "adult homosexual" could "crystallize trends already present and make them irreversible." As a final example, from 1960 to 1962, 40 percent of diagnosed cases of "sexual deviation" at the Forensic Clinic of the Toronto Psychiatric Hospital—by far the largest single group—were homosexuals.[56]

On the surface, Ottawa's choice of Wake as a psychological expert of homosexuality would seem odd. He had no publication record on the subject.[57] He had, however, become known to federal officials through his work as research consultant to a 1958 royal commission on criminal sexual psychopaths.[58] The brief reference to homosexuality in the commission's report was unflattering. While the commission did not recommend, as some witnesses advocated, that "all those convicted of homosexual offenses" be considered for indeterminate prison sentences, it did find that there were "profound problems raised by homosexuality."[59]

His sabbatical year in the United States complete, Wake submitted a report to the Privy Council Office in December 1962.[60] The paper begins with a discussion of the research of Evelyn Hooker and Alfred Kinsey, two dissenting voices within the psychiatric community who challenged orthodox views linking homosexuality with disturbed personalities.[61] The "abnormal" label affixed to homosexuals was a carry-over from earlier religious-moral condemnation of non-procreative sex practices. To comprehend homosexuality fully in its scientific setting it was necessary, Wake argued, to do away with crude stereotypes and "divest [one]self of prejudice." But Wake's initial progressive thrust gets lost in the remainder of the report. Kinsey's and Hooker's findings that male homosexuality was more common than previously thought meant, for Wake, that "the numbers are sufficiently large to be of concern to anyone interested in the problem of suitability." He then discussed homosexual "cure" methods (a concept anathematic to Hooker and Kinsey) such as anti-depressant drugs and aversion therapy. The latter technique, in which induced nausea coincided with a patient's viewing of homoerotic pictures, Wake concluded to be a "somewhat extreme" method, although "the fundamentals—a deconditioning-reconditioning approach—[were] sound."[62]

The bulk of the report, however, dealt with the "battery of tests" available to assess and detect homosexuality. Such methods included psychiatric interviews, medical exams, and projective, polygraph, plethysmograph (electronic or pneumatic measurement of blood volume in the finger), and palmar sweat tests. Examples of word association and masculinity-femininity tests were included in the annex of Wake's report. In the first set of tests, individuals linked to a polygraph or plethysmographic device heard a series of words, some of which contained double meanings known to homosexuals.[63] Nervous reactions to these words would, it was theorized, pinpoint gay subjects. In the masculinity-femininity tests people would respond affirmatively or negatively to such statements as "I like mechanics magazines," "I would like to be a nurse," or "I liked 'Alice in Wonderland' by Lewis Carroll." As

Wake noted, an obvious methodological problem was the fact that the test's purpose was easily discernible and respondents could then lie to beat it.

The most promising method, however, was the Pupillary Response Test developed by E.H. Hess and J.M. Polt at the University of Chicago in 1960. While Wake had not seen the test in operation, he regarded it as a "relatively uncomplicated mechanism." Test subjects peered through an opening in a box and were shown pictures while a camera photographed pupil dilation and eye movement at half-second intervals. Allan Seltzer, one of Hess's graduate students, had successfully employed the test to differentiate between homosexual and heterosexual subjects based on their reactions to nude imagery. The merits of this method were that subjects remained unaware of the test's purpose, their reactions were involuntary, the results were available as soon as the film was developed, and the necessary equipment was relatively cheap and easy to assemble. Such a device, Wake argued, had research applications beyond homosexuality and could also be used "to detect alcoholism and other 'frailties'" among civil servants. Accordingly, Wake recommended that the federal government sponsor a research program to develop a Canadian version of the Pupillary Response Test. The project would require a part-time senior social scientist and a full-time masters-level clinical psychologist, and between $5000 and $10 000 of annual funding. A board of federal officials, including the RCMP, would oversee the project.[64] In early 1963 the Security Panel (with Minister of Justice Donald Fleming present) approved the project.[65]

What concerned panel members most during this 28 February meeting was the prospect of making changes to CD no. 29 in light of a report prepared by Wall examining security screening practices in the United States.[66] In October 1961 and June 1962 Wall had met with his government security counterparts in Washington and had come away impressed by the professionalism and thoroughness of the American system. Most security investigations there were done by university graduates (unlike in Canada where few Mounties had post-secondary training) who displayed balanced judgment and possessed a broad understanding of human behaviour. Significantly, Wall also noted that the Americans' approach to the "character weakness" question had changed substantially since the early 1950s:

> The [Civil Service Commission] indicated that it would be neither wise nor feasible to attempt to exclude all homosexuals from the public service. . . . In addition there was general agreement that employees found to have some character defect should be treated fairly, objectively and privately, and to the greatest extent possible without jeopardy to their future careers elsewhere. Each case had to be considered on its own merits.[67]

In characteristic fashion Harvison expressed opposition to this "rather permissive attitude," while Robertson, Pelletier, and Bryce voiced varying degrees of support for a compassionate, case-by-case treatment of the subject. While homosexuals should be excluded from certain positions requiring Secret and Top Secret security clearances, they should wherever possible be transferred to "less sensitive positions." Paradox and irony were now aligned. The same meeting that approved the Orwellian-like Wake project also saw a majority of members express support for a flexible and liberal approach to the homosexual question. None of the committee members appeared to realize that American security practices in the early 1960s were now charting a liberal course for Canadian policy makers.[68]

The influence of Wall's characterization of liberal American practices appeared in the new Cabinet Directive on Security issued in December 1963 (CD no. 35). For the first time "illicit sexual behaviour" was stated explicitly as an element of character weakness. Individuals demonstrating such behaviour would, under the new policy, normally be denied access to classified information "*unless* [original emphasis] after careful consideration of the circumstances, including the value of their services, it is judged that the risk involved appears to be justified."[69] This proviso allowed government officials to assess each situation on a case-by-case basis. Absent from CD no. 35 was any mention of character weaknesses to serve as a basis for denying employment "on grounds other than security," as was the case with CD no. 29. For Security Panel officials the matter now appeared settled; no subsequent meetings dealt with the homosexual issue.

But for the RCMP the issue was far from resolved. As noted earlier, in 1959 the Mounties launched an investigation of homosexuals both inside and outside the civil service. Annual reports of the Directorate of Security and Intelligence (DSI) reveal how quickly these investigations progressed. By 1960–61 some 560 federal employees had been identified, many of whom had "subsequently obtained employment elsewhere." This took place despite the fact that "owing to lack of evidence or corroboration" not all these 560 could be positively identified as homosexuals. The following year approximately 300 additional government employees were identified and, by this time, the "Directorate Index System" contained the names of some 2000 non-government homosexuals. In 1962–63 the RCMP complained that its investigators were "hindered by the lack of cooperation on the part of homosexuals" and, to compensate, the force was establishing contacts with the morality squads or urban police forces. By 1964–65 some 6000 homosexuals were on RCMP file. The next year this number climbed to 7500. And there were ninety-seven homosexual adverse reports issued to government departments, a 117 percent increase from the year before.

By 1967–68 continued interviewing and collaboration with other police agencies had brought the total number of files to some 9000, of which roughly only one-third were federal public servants.[70] Justice Minister Pierre Trudeau's proposed changes to the Criminal Code (1967) to legalize consensual gay sex did not worry Mountie investigators: "it would appear that as long as the social stigma of homosexuality remains, the element of its use for blackmail will exist and so, therefore, will the security risk factor." The annual reports discuss frequently the force's concern about its continuing lack of a "clear directive" from cabinet regarding homosexual investigations.[71] The RCMP never did receive one and, as a 1969 PCO document reveals, their operational guidelines for these investigations remained ill-defined: "In order to operate, they have adopted procedures which appear to fall within the context of the views expressed by Panel members."[72] It would seem that the "context of views" of most importance to the RCMP were its own and those of DND's representatives on the Security Panel.

The Wake project, however, did not advance as far as the RCMP investigations. The DSI annual reports discuss briefly the ongoing difficulties it encountered. The Mounties were unable to recruit sufficient numbers of homosexuals as test subjects, and there was also reluctance among "normal males" within the force to volunteer. Research moved along fitfully; the annual report for 1964–65 recorded that tests on fifty-one subjects had proven "inconclusive." The following year the "lack of suitable subjects" again impaired the program's progress. The final reference to the study in 1966–67 noted that, while some headway had been made, conclusive means to identify homosexual subjects were still out of reach.[73] In the end, methodological obstacles shut down the fruit machine, concluding one of the most distasteful federal undertakings in recent history.

o

A number of domestic and external factors help explain the Canadian government's security investigation of homosexuals during the Cold War. Well before Ottawa turned its attention to the matter in the late 1950s, the Security Panel had adopted procedures which facilitated the latter anti-homosexual campaigns. The *sub rosa* nature of the internal security system, in addition to removing any appeal possibilities for homosexuals, allowed the RCMP to widen its investigation without concern over public criticism. The panel's initial emphasis on character weaknesses like gambling and alcoholism established the precedent and investigative tactics for the homosexual purges. The RCMP's central role in the security vetting processes, which exceeded its mandated fact-finding function, also expedited the process; the force, like DND, had strict anti-gay policies in its own department and sought to extend these to the wider public service. The panel was also highly sensitive to American security concerns. When in the early 1950s the United States stepped up its campaign to purge homosexuals from federal offices, Canada followed suit, first with changes to immigration legislation, and then a few years later with the RCMP investigation. The extent of American influence was ironically displayed in the early 1960s when Canada followed Washington's liberal lead and relaxed its own security provisions for character weaknesses.[74]

As evidenced by this study, considerable differences of opinion characterized the Security Panel's handling of homosexual security vetting. The panel's liberal-minded representatives like Robertson and Pelletier sought to restrict security probes only to those individuals privy to classified information. National Defence and RCMP officials, citing the "general unsuitability" of homosexuality within an organizational setting, lobbied to bar gays from all government positions irrespective of security considerations. Both moderates and hardliners, however, supported the Wake project and its promise of a scientific solution to this administrative and security problem. The tempering of the character weakness provisions of CD no. 35

(1963) indicates a policy triumph for the panel's liberal spokesmen. But the Mounties' continued and widespread investigation of homosexuals after 1963, largely beyond the purview of the Security Panel, suggests a practical victory of sorts for the panel's conservatives. Of course, for the many homosexuals affected by Ottawa's actions there was only defeat, accompanied, in all probability, by prolonged anguish.

NOTES

1. Reg Whitaker has written extensively on this subject. See "Origins of the Canadian Government's Internal Security System, 1946–1952," *Canadian Historical Review* 65, 2 (1984): 154–83; "Fighting the Cold War on the Home Front: America, Britain, Australia, and Canada," in Ralph Miliband et al., eds., *Socialist Register 1984* (London: Merlin Press 1984), 51–67; "Official Repression of Communism," *Labour/Le Travail* (1986): 135–66; "Left-Wing Dissent and the State: Canada in the Cold War Era," in C.E.S. Franks, ed., *Dissent and the State* (Toronto: Oxford University Press 1989), 191–210; *Double Standard: The Secret History of Canadian Immigration* (Toronto: Lester & Orpen Dennys 1987). Also see Irving Abella, *Nationalism, Communism, and Canadian Labour: The CIO, the Communist Party and the Canadian Congress of Labour, 1935–1956* (Toronto: University of Toronto Press 1973), chap 5; Cameron Smith, *Unfinished Journey: The Lewis Family* (Toronto: Summerhill Press 1989), 242–53, 299–326; Len Scher, *The Un-Canadians: Stories of the Blacklist Era* (Toronto: Lester Publishing 1992); and Frederick W. Gibson, *Queen's University, 1917–1961: "To Serve and Yet Be Free"* (Montreal: McGill-Queen's University Press 1983), 273–96.

2. Roger W. Bowen, *Innocence Is Not Enough: The Life and Death of Herbert Norman* (Toronto: Douglas & McIntyre 1986).

3. Dean Beeby, "Mounties staged massive hunt for gay males in civil service," *Globe and Mail*, 24 April 1992; Beeby, "RCMP was ordered to identify gays," *Globe and Mail*, 25 April 1992. Earlier accounts appeared in two books by John Sawatsky, both based on unattributed sources: *Men in the Shadows: The RCMP Security Service* (Toronto: Doubleday 1980), 124–37; *For Services Rendered: Leslie James Bennett and the RCMP Security Service* (Toronto: Doubleday 1982), 171–84. The first official government acknowledgement of this event was reported by the Commission of Inquiry Concerning Certain Activities of the Royal Canadian Mounted Police [McDonald Commission], *Freedom and Security under the Law: Second Report* (Ottawa: The Commission 1981), vol. 2, 782. Also see Robert Winters, "Civil service homosexuals fired as 'security risks,'" *Montreal Gazette*, 23 Feb. 1985. On Mulroney see "PM denounces 1960s purge of homosexual civil servants," *Globe and Mail*, 28 April 1992, and Bruce DeMara, "The persecution of the gays," *Toronto Star*, 9 Aug. 1992.

4. Canada, Royal Commission to Investigate the Facts Relating to and the Circumstances Surrounding the Communication by Public Officials and Other Persons in Positions of Trust of Secret and Confidential Information to Agents of a Foreign Power, *The Report of the Royal Commission* (Ottawa: King's Printer 1946).

5. See Whitaker "Origins", especially 157–58; J.L. Granatstein, *A Man of Influence: Norman A. Robertson and Canadian Statecraft 1929–1968* (Ottawa: Deneau Publishers 1981), 181–82, 272–76; McDonald Commission, vol. 1, 89; National Archives of Canada (NA), Privy Council Office (PCO), series 18, vol. 103, file

S-100-D, Barclay to Cabinet Defence Committee, 4 May 1946; file S-100, Heeney to Pearson, 2 June 1948.

6. PCO, series 18, vol. 189, file S-100-I, Heeney to deputy ministers, 23 Feb. 1949.

7. McDonald Commission, vol. 1, 61.

8. Whitaker, "Origins," 159.

9. C.W. Harvison, *The Horsemen* (Toronto: McClelland and Stewart 1967), 217. Harvison does note that the RCMP routinely "resisted such pressures" when they arose.

10. Whitaker, "Left-Wing Dissent," 196.

11. See Richard M. Freeland, *The Truman Doctrine and the Origins of McCarthyism: Foreign Policy, Domestic Politics, and Internal Security, 1946–1948* (New York: New York University Press 1985), sections 3, 5, and 7, and especially 117–34; Walter Goodman, *The Committee: The Extraordinary Career of the House Committee on Un-American Activities* (New York: Farrar, Straus, and Giroux 1968), chap. 5, especially 125ff, 135, 142; Alan D. Harper, *The Politics of Loyalty: The White House and the Communist Issue, 1946–1952* (Westport, Conn: Greenwood 1969).

12. See Brooke Claxton's letter to Dean Acheson, 7 Dec. 1950, cited in Whitaker, "Origins," 180–81.

13. "Security Investigation of Government Employees," 5 March 1948, cited in Whitaker, "Origins," 162.

14. PCO, series 18, vol. 189, file S-100-I, Nicholson to Lucas, 23 Feb. 1949.

15. Whitaker, "Origins," 167–68, 176–77, and Granatstein, *Man of Influence*, 274.

16. Canada, House of Commons, Debates, 22 June 1948, 5630.

17. McDonald Commission, vol. 1, 60.

18. Sawatsky, *Men in the Shadows*, 14; Harvison, *Horsemen*, 209; Whitaker, "Fighting the Cold War," 56.

19. Robert Cuff and J.L. Granatstein, *Ties That Bind: Canadian–American Relations in Wartime, from the Great War to the Cold War* (Toronto: Samuel Stevens Hakkert 1977), 113–29.

20. PCO, series 18, vol. 103, file S-100-M, Security Panel Meeting, 6 April 1948.

21. Whitaker, "Origins," 170–71.

22. McDonald Commission, vol. 1, 41.

23. U.S. Congress, Senate, Committee on Expenditure in Executive Departments, *Employment of Homosexuals and Other Sex Perverts in Government* (Washington 1950), reprinted in Jonathan Katz, ed., *Government versus Homosexuals* (New York: Arno Press 1975).

24. The report cited only one example, the pre-First World War case of Alfred Raedle, a homosexual who, while head of the Austrian counter-intelligence service, had been blackmailed into divulging information to Russian agents.

25. *Employment of Homosexuals*, 4–5, 21.

26. John D'Emilio, *Sexual Politics, Sexual Communities: The Making of a Homosexual Minority in the United States, 1940–1970* (Chicago: University of Chicago Press 1983), 44. Also see his *Making Trouble: Essays on Gay History, Politics, and the University* (New York: Routledge 1992), 17–56; Gerard Sullivan, "A Bibliographic Guide to Government Hearings and Reports, Legislative Action, and Speeches Made in the House and Senate of the United States Congress on the Subject of Homosexuality," *Journal of Homosexuality* 10, 1/2 (Fall 1984): 135–51; Geoffrey Smith, "National Security and Personal Isolation: Sex, Gender, and Disease in the Cold-War United States," *International History Review* 14, 2 (May 1992): 321–22; Ralph S. Brown, *Loyalty and Security: Employment Tests in the United States* (New Haven: Yale University Press 1958), 258.

27. Alfred C. Kinsey, *Sexual Behavior in the Human Male* (Philadelphia: W.B. Saunders 1948), chap. 21. See Ralph Slovenko, "The Homosexual and Society: A Historical Perspective," *University of Dayton Law Review* 10, 3 (Spring 1985): 488. On Kinsey see

Cornelia V. Christenson, *Kinsey: A Biography* (Bloomington: Indiana University Press 1971), 163–66.

28. Philip Girard, "From Subversion to Liberation: Homosexuals and the Immigration Act 1952–1977," *Canadian Journal of Law and Society* 2 (1987): 7. See also Whitaker, *Double Standard*, 37–38.

29. Granatstein, *Man of Influence*, 273.

30. Girard, "From Subversion," 6.

31. Cabinet Directive no. 24, 16 Oct. 1952, cited in McDonald Commission, vol. 2, 782.

32. Department of External Affairs (DEA), file 50207-40, Cabinet Directive no. 29, "Security Screening of Government Employee," 21 Dec. 1955. We would like to thank Reg Whitaker for providing us with this document.

33. PCO, vol. 2659, Cabinet Conclusions, 21 Dec. 1955.

34. House of Commons, Debates, 19 June 1948, 5488. Diefenbaker also spoke out against the American government's handling of the Herbert Norman affair. See *Debates*, 15 March 1957, 2349; 10 April 1957, 3359; and 12 April 1957, 3493-9.

35. McDonald Commission, vol. 1, 89.

36. DEA, Access to Information Request (AIR) A-2321, Frazer to Security Sub-Panel, 2 July 1958.

37. DEA, AIR A-2321, Security Sub-Panel Meeting, 8 July 1958.

38. Canadian Security and Intelligence Service (CSIS), AIR 91-088, Wall to Security Panel, 12 May 1959.

39. On the Wolfenden Report's impact on the campaign for homosexual law reform in Britain see Jeffrey Weeks, *Coming Out: Homosexual Politics in Britain, from the Nineteenth Century to the Present* (London: Quartet Books 1977), 162–82; Allen Horsfall, "Battling for Wolfenden," in Bob Cant and Susan Hemmings, eds., *Radical Records: Thirty Years of Lesbian and Gay History, 1957–1987* (London: Routledge 1988), 15–33; and Stephen

Jeffery-Poulter, *Peers, Queers, and Commons: The Struggle for Gay Law Reform from 1950 to the Present* (London: Routledge 1991), 28–89.

40. CSIS, AIR 91-088, Wall to Security Panel, 12 May 1959.

41. Ibid., Security Panel Meeting, 6 Oct. 1959.

42. Cited in J.T. Copp and Bill McAndrew, *Battle Exhaustion: Soldiers and Psychiatrists in the Canadian Army, 1939–1945* (Montreal: McGill-Queen's University Press 1990), 166, 8, 19. For the American experience see Allan Bérubé, *Coming Out under Fire: The History of Gay Men and Women in World War Two* (New York: Free Press 1990), 149–74.

43. Gary Kinsman, "Official Discourse as Sexual Regulation: The Social Organization of the Sexual Policing of Gay Men" (PhD dissertation, University of Toronto 1989), 57, 88–89; Thomas Claridge and Geoffrey York, "Forces agree to end anti-gay policies," *Globe and Mail*, 28 Oct. 1992.

44. See Richard French and André Béliveau, *The RCMP and the Management of National Security* (Toronto: Butterworth 1979), 46–47; W. Edward Mann and John Alan Lee, *RCMP vs. the People: Inside Canada's Security Service* (Don Mills: General Publishing 1979), chap. 9, especially 123, 126, 140–41; Lorne and Caroline Brown, *An Unauthorized History of the RCMP* (Toronto: James Lewis & Samuel 1973); McDonald Commission, vol. 1, 102; Keith Walden, *Visions of Order: The Canadian Mounties in Symbol and Myth* (Toronto: Butterworth 1982), 38–39.

45. See House of Commons, Sub-Committee on Equality Rights, *Equality for All: Report of the Parliamentary Committee on Equality Rights* (Ottawa: Queen's Printer 1985), 30–31. For the testimony of RCMP commissioner R.H. Simmonds see *Minutes of Proceedings and Evidence of the Sub-Committee on Equality Rights of the Standing Committee on Justice and Legal Affairs*

(Ottawa: The Committee 1985), 6:4–29, especially 8–12. See too Stephen Bindman, "Homosexual Mountie gets badge back in out-of-court deal," *Ottawa Citizen*, 19 July 1988.

46. CSIS, AIR 92-008, Bella to RCMP commissioner, 29 April 1960.

47. Confirmed cases were defined as "those who have been interviewed and admitted being homosexuals or who have been convicted in court on a charge of sexual deviation with another male." The "alleged" and "suspected" categories seem indistinguishable. The former were "those who have been named as homosexuals by a source or sources whose information is considered to be reliable." The latter were "those who [were] believed to be homosexuals by a source or sources whose information is considered to be reliable." Ibid.

48. The documents give credence to John Sawatsky's account—based on unattributed interviews—of an RCMP investigation begun in late 1959 in which many homosexual employees of DEA were fired, including David Johnson, Canada's ambassador to Moscow (1956–1960). See *For Services Rendered*, 172–74. It was later revealed that John Holmes, another DEA senior official, also resigned in 1960 when his homosexuality was discovered. See Beeby, "RCMP was ordered." The case of John Watkins, who when ambassador to Moscow in 1955 was photographed by the KGB during a homosexual encounter, was not known to the RCMP until 1964. See *For Services Rendered*, 175–83, and Dean Beeby and William Kaplan, eds., *Moscow Dispatches: Inside Cold War Russia* (Toronto: James Lorimer 1987), xiii–xxxii.

49. CSIS, AIR 92-008, Bella to RCMP commissioner, 29 April 1960.

50. CSIS, AIR 91-088, Security Panel Meeting, 24 June 1960.

51. Ibid., Bryce to Diefenbaker and Fulton, 26 Jan. 1961.

52. Ibid. Section 147 of the Criminal Code dealt with "buggery or bestiality" and carried a maximum sentence of fourteen years. The maximum penalty for "gross acts of indecency," as outlined in section 149, was five years. See the *Report of the Royal Commission on the Criminal Law Relating to Criminal Sexual Psychopaths* (Ottawa: Queen's Printer 1958), 5–6, and Alex K. Gigeroff, *Sexual Deviations in the Criminal Law* (Toronto: University of Toronto Press 1968), 71–82.

53. CSIS, AIR 92-008, Wake to Wall, nd.

54. CSIS, AIR 91-088, W.H. Kelly, Directorate of Security and Intelligence internal memo, 8 June 1961; and Dean Beeby, "RCMP hoped 'fruit machine' would identify homosexuals," *Globe and Mail*, 24 April 1992.

55. Ronald Bayer, *Homosexuality and American Psychiatry: The Politics of Diagnosis* (Princeton: Princeton University Press 1987), 18, 10. Also see Kenneth Lewes, *The Psychoanalytic Theory of Male Homosexuality* (New York: Simon and Schuster 1988).

56. S.R. Laycock, *Canadian Medical Association Journal* 63 (Sept. 1950): 245–50; John K. McCreary, "Psychopathia Homosexualis," *Canadian Journal of Psychology* 4, 2 (June 1950): 73; P.G. Thomson, "Sexual Deviation," *Canadian Journal of Psychology* 4, 2 (June 1950): 73; P.G. Thomson, "Sexual Deviation," *Canadian Medical Association Journal* 80 (1 March 1959): 381–89; J.W. Mohr and R.E. Turner, "Sexual Deviations, Part I," *Applied Therapeutics* 9 (Jan. 1967), reprinted in W.E. Mann, ed., *Social Deviance in Canada* (Toronto: Copp Clark 1971), 354.

57. Directories of psychologists list Wake's areas of expertise as follows: adolescence and youth, aging, and health psychology. A search of *Psychological Abstracts* (1950–70) reveals that his published research was mainly concerned with juvenile delinquency and physical cruelty.

58. *Report of the Royal Commission on the Criminal Law Relating to Criminal*

Sexual Psychopaths. For an examination of the commission's work see Gary Kinsman, *The Regulation of Desire: Sexuality in Canada* (Montreal: Black Rose Books 1987), 126–29. On the state's part in restoring traditional gender and sexuality roles and family relations after the Second World War see Annalee Gölz, "Family Matters: The Canadian Family and the State in the Postwar Period," *left history* 1, 2 (Fall 1993): 9–49; Yvonne Mathews-Klein, "How They Saw Us: Images of Women in National Film Board Films of the 1940s and 1950s," *Atlantis* 4, 2 (Spring 1979): 20–33; Ruth Roach Pierson, "'Home Aide': A Solution to Women's Unemployment after World War II," *Atlantis* 2, 2 (Spring 1977): 85–97; and Veronica Strong-Boag, "Home Dreams: Women and the Suburban Experiment in Canada, 1945–60," *Canadian Historical Review* 72, 4 (Dec. 1991): 471–504.

59. The only cited testimony on the subject of homosexuality was that of John Chisholm, chief constable of Metropolitan Toronto. Homosexuality, he said, "is a constant problem for the Police in large centres, and if the Police adopt a laissez-faire attitude toward such individuals, City parks, intended for the relaxation of women and children and youth recreation purposes, will become rendezvous (sic) for homosexuals. . . . The saddest feature of all, however, is that homosexuals corrupt others and are constantly recruiting youths of previous good character into their fraternity." *Report of the Royal Commission*, 27.

60. CSIS AIR 91-088, "Report on Special Project by Dr. F.R. Wake," 12 Dec. 1962.

61. Hooker's studies, rather than being based on a clinical population, used the membership list of the Mattachine Society, a US homophile organization founded in the early 1950s. Bayer, *Homosexuality*, 49–53, and Richard D. Mohr, *Gays/Justice: A Study of Ethics, Society, and Law* (New York: Columbia University Press 1988), 23.

62. CSIS, AIR 91-088, "Report on Special Project."

63. Such words included "queen," "circus," "gay," "bagpipe," "bull," "camp," "cruise," "blind," "drag," "fruit," and "trade."

64. CSIS, AIR 91-088, "Report on Special Project."

65. PCO, AIR 9293070, Security Panel Meeting, 28 Feb. 1963.

66. Ibid.

67. Wall also criticized RCMP investigators for overstepping their fact-finding function and advising on security risks. See CSIS, AIR 91-088, Harvison to DSI, Annex "A Summary of the Salient Points in United States Security Procedures," 4 March 1963.

68. PCO, AIR 9293070, Security Panel Meeting, 28 Feb. 1963.

69. Cabinet Directive no. 35, "Security in the Public Service of Canada," 18 Dec. 1963. From documents provided by Reg Whitaker.

70. CSIS, AIR 91-088, DSI Annual Reports, 1959–60 to 1967–68; Beeby, "Mounties staged massive hunt." After 1960 the DSI reports do not indicate how many government homosexuals were fired or resigned.

71. CSIS, AIR 91-088, DSI Annual Reports, 1959–60 to 1967–68.

72. PCO, AIR 9293070, PCO memo to Wall, 24 Dec. 1969.

73. CSIS, AIR 91-088, Bordeleau to Wall, 25 Jan. 1963; and DSI Annual Reports, 1963–64 to 1966–67.

74. However, immigration was one important policy area where Canadian and American thinking diverged. In the 1960s Ottawa began moderating immigration policies with respect to homosexuality, while the United States strengthened its anti-gay proscriptions. See Girard, "From Subversion," 17.

section

9

LIFE COURSE

○

ELDERLY MEN AND WOMEN IN A HALIFAX WORKING-CLASS SUBURB DURING THE 1920s [*]

SUZANNE MORTON

o

Inside many of the modern homes of this up-to-date subdivision lived men and women who had grown up in a colonial city when Queen Victoria was on the throne and her army stationed at the Citadel. By 1921, one in every four residents of Halifax had been born before 1881 and had witnessed tremendous change in the first forty years of his or her life. Between 1881 and 1921 the population of the city increased from 36 100 to 58 371[1]—not a tremendous level of growth compared to other cities in Canada, but sufficient to encourage population expansion into the northern section of the peninsula. More striking than the change in size and geographic boundaries of the city was the change in Halifax's physical appearance. The combination of the passing of time and the explosion was, according to one visitor, so great that the North End had altered beyond recognition.[2] But even the magnitude of local change must have appeared insignificant in light of the changes occurring nationally and internationally. Concepts as basic as time and space were in flux, with such technological innovations as air travel, the automobile, the moving picture, and the radio transforming the way in which people conceived their world. As the physical world changed, so did its ideological foundations. Basic values across North America were challenged by what one historian has referred to as a crisis in cultural authority, in which politics, religion, economics, gender roles, and the psychic composition of the individual all came into question.[3]

---

[*] Reprinted by permission of University of Toronto Press Incorporated, from *Ideal Surroundings: Domestic Life in a Working-Class Suburb in the 1920s* (Toronto: University of Toronto Press, 1995), 51–66.

In the very midst of this metamorphosis, the proportion of Haligonians who remembered the older city and an older world was increasing. In fact, the national trend of an aging population was reflected in Halifax to such a degree that in 1931 the age distribution of the population matched the Canadian average better than that in any other census district in the country.[4] An important characteristic of twentieth-century Canada was an aging population; and Halifax, as a long-established city in a region generally suffering from outmigration, reflected this trend earlier than other urban centres. While Canadian cities generally had a more youthful population than rural districts, urban centres in the Maritimes exhibited overall national demographic trends of aging. Since its demographic breakdown foreshadowed general Canadian population trends in the twentieth century, Halifax is thus an excellent place to investigate an aging population.

Haligonians of different ages not only shared the city and the same neighbourhood, but in many cases they cohabited within the same household. Under a single roof, individuals coexisted with varying self-definitions, partially rooted in generational differences. Class and gender were experienced differently according to age, since identities formed in youth resonated in an individual's world-view throughout his or her life. Men and women who came of age in the 1870s or 1880s experienced and interpreted class differently from their grandsons and granddaughters who entered the workforce in the 1920s. The meaning and definition of gender underwent a similar historical transition. Recognition of the role of generation in the formation of an individual's identity can prevent us from making careless generalizations about uniform and universal values.

The approximately 6 percent of the population of Halifax over the age of sixty-five was central to the balance between change and continuity, yet this group has often escaped the notice of historians. The elderly of Richmond Heights were generally pushed to the margins of society during the 1920s, but the glimpses of their lives that remain reveal their efforts to maintain independence and participation in the labour market. Their presence in the households of Richmond Heights offered an immediate and personal link to the past as well as a measure to evaluate change.

It is difficult to define precisely the aged as a distinct segment of the population. Without access to the manuscript census, it is impossible to determine the actual age distribution within Richmond Heights, but qualitative evidence suggests that age played a critical role in the way individuals experienced home and the workplace. In some ways the definition of "old" differed for men and women because it was based on a variety of economic, biological, life-circle, or cultural criteria that differed by sex. In accordance with the definition of masculinity, men were old when they were no longer able to support their families financially. Most men continued to work as long as they were able and experienced a gradual decline in their incomes.[5] On the other hand, women were judged by biological criteria connected to their reproductive roles. Menopause was a common boundary for women, as medical or biological tradition held that after its onset women ceased their reproductive roles, rejected sexual desire, and began a long period of illness or decline.[6] The use of menopause as the start of old age fostered the belief that women aged earlier than men despite the fact that they lived longer. The discrepancy between the economic definition of old age for men and the biological definition for women was exemplified in the difference in the ages at which men and women could retire under the pension plan of Maritime Telephone and Telegraph (MT&T), the local telephone company. Although women were likely to live longer than men, women could retire five years earlier with a full, Class-A pension.[7] Another important marker for women was life cycle. As women had fewer children and these children were spaced more closely together, women were increasingly likely to be middle-aged grandmothers, with their own children grown. The image of a grandmother as "aged" could conflict with the reality. In other cases, old age was signalled by widowhood, a common experience among women who lived long enough.[8] Finally, old age could also be generally associated with women, since they numerically dominated the age group. Chris Gordon has claimed in his study of London's working-class elderly during the 1930s that when we speak of the elderly, "we are talking mainly about women in later life."[9]

While many factors were responsible for the different definitions assigned to men and women, there were some categorizations that measured age in gender-neutral terms. Both men and women were classified by an arbitrary bureaucratic definition of old age as beginning at seventy years of age. This chronological point was used by the Nova Scotia government in its study of the old-age pension and its collection of statistics under the provisions of the Workmen's Compensation Act, and by the federal government in its introduction of an old-age pension. James Struthers has recently made the important argument that the old-age pension was Canada's first "'gender inclusive' social program," since payments were to be awarded equally to both men and women at the same age.[10] The fact that "gender inclusive" legislation was first associated with the elderly was surely not a coincidence. Despite the differences in the ways that men and women experienced old age, their vulnerability and perceived redundancy emphasized and highlighted a number of shared characteristics that could overcome important gender distinctions.

Of all the groups in the community the aged were the most invisible to the social historian. Older people were more likely to be housebound by poor health and inclement weather, and so were less likely to be involved in activities outside the home that left historical evidence. In the 1920s in Halifax, the elderly were not yet considered to have any particular residential, social, or consumer needs. Glimpses of their lives can be caught in the rare announcement of a golden or diamond wedding anniversary, or the family celebration of an important birthday. The elderly in Halifax appeared most visibly at death, in obituaries that indicated age, marital status, religious affiliation, number of children, and their children's place of residence, and in accounts of funerals. The difficulty of capturing historical insights into the lives of older men and women is compounded by the difficulty of classifying them in other than broad chronological terms. Because of the variance in the definitions of old age, the category included a wide and heterogeneous group. The use of a broad chronological category, therefore, has methodological advantages; for example, as Tamara Hareven has noted, "transitions of the later years—the empty nest, widowhood and loss of household headship—followed no ordered sequence, were not closely synchronized and took a relatively long time to complete."[11]

The vague historical and disparate contemporary methods of classifying old age contrast with the intense interest in the aged that developed in the early twentieth century. Some American historians have claimed that between the First and Second World Wars, old age was increasingly regarded from a negative perspective and eventually came to be seen as a "national problem." Those who have wished to emphasize long-term continuity rather than change in the devaluation of the elderly have also focused on the early twentieth century as an especially important period in their research.[12]

In Halifax, as elsewhere in Canada in the early twentieth century, interest in the elderly centred on an awareness of their poverty. The Halifax Labour party actively supported the introduction of the old-age pension as part of its platform, a goal later adopted by both the Liberal and Conservative parties.[13] Concern expressed by the Labour party contained at least some degree of immediate self-interest, since many workers faced the expense of caring for elderly parents. In Labour's promotion of an old-age pension during its 1925 campaign, it claimed that a pension would not only "keep the worker that is thrown on the scrapheap by industry from going to the poorhouse," but also prevent him "from becoming a charge of his dependents." Political groups were not the only associations to notice the condition of the elderly. The local Society for the Prevention of Cruelty specified "old people" as a segment of the population that needed the "attention of our officers."[14] Research conducted by a government commission into the introduction of an old-age pension in 1929 confirmed the widespread poverty among those in the population over the age of seventy. The financial and living conditions of the 929 Haligonians interviewed were shocking. More than one-third reported having no income at all, and more than half had an income of less than $199 per annum. Poverty among aged Haligonians would have been much more severe than for their rural counterparts, as the 1930 Commission on Old Age Pensions noted the importance of informal sources of income and home production such as the raising of hens and pigs and the cultivation of vegetable gardens; such activities did occur in the city but were more feasible in rural areas. The commission concluded that the province's aged had either successfully accumulated a moderate income and found themselves able to live off savings or were "practically destitute and dependent" on others.

Poverty among the elderly had several roots. Explanations can be found in the lack of employment opportunities for older women, the death or illness of a wage-earning husband, and the gradual withdrawal of men from the workforce. American historian Andrew Achenbaum has linked deteriorating economic conditions for the elderly in the early twentieth century with the forced withdrawal of older men from the workforce. But according to Brian Gratton, caution is required in any discussion of workforce participation, since the level of employment among the elderly declined very gradually, with the result that scholars have exaggerated the poverty and dependency of the aged prior to the creation of the welfare state. This discrepancy between the very real poverty of the aged and the important role many elderly men continued to play in the workforce was reflected in Halifax in the 1920s.[15]

The question of the place of elderly men in the workforce was part of a general discussion that emerged across North America concerning the suitability of older male workers as employees. In the nineteenth century, workers had expected to have been employed as long as they were able to work. Despite the fears of older workers and the presence of efficiency experts, old age did not result in widespread dismissals. Fifty-five percent of males aged sixty and above had some type of income from wage earnings in 1921, while the remaining 45 percent had no access to such revenue. Comparable statistics for 1931 are not available, but men over the age of sixty-five continued to compose approximately 5 percent of the total male population and approximately the same percentage of men over the age of ten who were gainfully employed. Although large numbers of men continued to work, the fear of job loss was not unfounded. Many older male employees found themselves working at different, less lucrative jobs as watchmen, janitors, and sweepers—less physically demanding work that they were judged still able to perform. Factory workers and industrial labourers who were less likely to keep their jobs probably composed the bulk of men in these occupations for "old men." Of the 608 men over the age of sixty-five listed in the 1921 Halifax census as still working, nearly half were employed in the trade, service, and finance sectors. Examination of the city's manufacturing sector in 1921 reveals few opportunities for older working-class men, since nearly 40 percent of men over sixty-five were listed as owners, managers, and superintendents.[16]

Local economic conditions, with high levels of unemployment and underemployment, may have made keeping a job particularly difficult for older men. During the Halifax Shipyards strike of 1920, a prominent elderly socialist ignored the strike call and crossed the picket lines to continue working. A younger contemporary looking back with the advantage of more than fifty years of hindsight analysed his motivation by referring to his age, attempting to reconcile the elderly man's socialist politics and his strikebreaking activity. He noted "for a man of his age to have any job, let alone a rather good job was unusual. Did he fear that he would be fired and never get another?"[17] This was a relevant question for aging workers across the country.

The impact of limited economic opportunities was exacerbated by illness or declining health, thereby accelerating aging workers' shift to less demanding and less lucrative positions. Patrick Ross of 27 Stairs Street spent fifteen years as a groundman, lineman, and finally loop crew foreman with MT&T before becoming a janitor at its central office in 1921. Ross worked only three years in his new position of janitor before his death at the age of fifty-nine.

Occupational adaptability was an important factor in survival. An army pensioner was able to support himself and his wife by supplementing his pension with earnings from his position as caretaker at Joseph Howe School. John and Barbara Green, an aged couple who owned a house at 60 Stairs Street, made their living by taking in boarders. Others, such as sixty-four-year-old David Schultz, who was crippled, may have felt they had no option except illegal activities. Schultz, a Richmond Heights resident, pleaded guilty in February 1924 to keeping a gaming house at the corner of Agricola and Almon Streets. The newspaper report of the sentencing condemned his actions in terms of his having encouraged "young men going into the house and gambling away earnings." But after years as a boilermaker and ironworker at the Halifax Graving Dockyard, he may have felt entitled to some of the employed young men's money. Older men in Richmond Heights rarely formally retired. During the entire decade, not one name in the city directory listed occupation as retired, and only six retired men were recorded on the municipal voters' list.[18]

The most obvious explanation for avoiding formal retirement was the economic consequence. Some workers at both Canadian National Railways (CNR) and MT&T were eligible for retirement or pension programs, but these programs were not generous, nor were they guaranteed. Harry Walters had been employed with the railway for more than twenty years, yet found himself at the age of sixty-nine working as a caretaker at one of the waterfront piers.[19] Railway pensions varied according to position, length of service, and age of retirement. Engineman Norman Prince, a homeowner at 19 Kane Street, was employed intermittently with the Intercolonial, Canadian Government Railways, and the CNR from August 1890 until his retirement in March 1934 at the age of sixty-one years after a total of thirty-three years with the railway. His length of service, occupational classification, and age entitled him to a generous pension of $96.24 a month. Less fortunate was co-worker James Karl of 39 Livingstone Street whose poor health forced him to retire early on a pension of only $44 a month.[20]

Employees at MT&T received 1 percent of their average annual pay for ten years multiplied by the number of years of employment. There was a minimum monthly pension of $25 for men and $20 for women, but this did not apply to employees who had worked for less than twenty years. The pension was also at the discretion of the Employee Benefits Committee, which was capable of suspending pensions to any employee it judged to be involved in activities "prejudicial to the interests of the Company." MT&T admitted to the inadequacy of its pension program when it introduced an Employees Stock Savings Plan in 1927 with the dual purpose of encouraging thrift and providing "competence for old age."[21] Poor private pensions and limited opportunities to save meant that voluntary retirement was a luxury that few people achieved.

Pension plans were an important component of the corporate welfare policies that flourished in Canada during the 1920s. Craig Heron has connected the steel industry's need to secure a dependable and stable labour force to the introduction of pension plans in that industry in the early 1920s. Similarly, Joy Parr in her study of the workforce in an Ontario knitting mill noted that the knitting company introduced "a discretionary pension plan" around 1922. Parr claimed that the unstructured and arbitrary nature of this pension plan placed long-term employees with a potential stake in pension earnings in a particularly vulnerable situation that required "aging employees and their kin" to take care not to jeopardize good relations with the company.[22] Personal and arbitrary pension plans bound long-term employees to the subjective whims of their employers as they approached the most vulnerable stage of their lives.

When private industry was newly experimenting with pension plans, the federal government had long attempted to encourage saving for old age through Canadian Government Annuities. This savings program was, significantly, transferred from the Post Office to the Department of Labour in April 1923, but was largely unsuccessful despite its claim to provide safe old-age pensions. Throughout the early 1920s, only several hundred Canadians undertook contracts; but a Department of Labour advertisement campaign through newspapers, periodicals, and radio talks increased sales to more than a thousand in 1928 and 1929.[23] The "hard-sell" nature of this campaign is illustrated by an item in a Halifax newspaper that played upon the working-class fear of unemployment among the elderly with a drawing of a rejected older man and the caption: "Everywhere they say too old. What a tragedy—to be turned away from all chance of earning one's living."[24]

The attempt to play on fear of unemployment was obviously directed at male workers, for female employment opportunities diminished much earlier with marriage or motherhood. Employment for elderly Richmond Heights women did not differ from that of their middle-aged neighbours. The loss of youth-defined by physical attractiveness, marriage, or reproductive capacity—meant that employers discriminated against them. Their choices were often limited to domestic service or low-wage work that could be conducted from their own homes such as dressmaking, washing, or operating a rooming-house.[25] Few women over sixty-five were engaged in waged employment in Halifax in 1921, less than 7 percent of the total age group, reflecting similar circumstances across the country.[26] The limited role of women in the paid workforce did not mean that old age brought relief from work. Women with homes continued to work within their houses and contribute domestic labour as long as they were able. In this respect old age was experienced differently by men and women. Men gradually withdrew from the workforce, while the work of women continued.

While the approach of old age for men was associated with a withdrawal from participation in the labour force, the greatest change in most women's lives was the death of the husband. The 1930 report on old-age pensions in Nova Scotia found that men over the age of seventy were much more likely to be married than women. Based on research gathered in the city of Halifax and the counties of Cape Breton, Richmond, and Shelburne, the report concluded that 55.7 percent of men compared to 25.1 percent of women were likely to have a spouse living.[27] This dramatic difference was explained by the dual impact of women's longer life expectancy and the tradition that men married younger women. For example, those over seventy who had a spouse under seventy accounted for 19 percent of the men interviewed and only 2.3 percent of the women.[28] This meant that the loss of a spouse was a more common experience for women.

The death of either spouse could mean the loss of household independence, since most women depended on a male wage to operate their home and men depended on unpaid female domestic labour. A rare glimpse of a woman who did not want to give up operation of her own home was evident in an enterprising widow's 1922 classified notice advertising for "correspondence with gentleman 50 years of age or more. Protestant preferred."[29]

American scholars have suggested that elderly men were more likely to face institutionalization than women.[30] A study of a slightly later period in Ontario by James Struthers, in contrast, has found that while men predominated in institutions in rural districts, women formed the majority in urban institutions.[31] Findings for Halifax are similar to American models. In Halifax, the impoverished aged were admitted to the City Home, where they composed a substantial proportion of the residents. An analysis of the number of deaths of residents at the City Home who were over sixty showed that, although women composed a greater percentage of the general population over that age, more older men than older women died in the City Home. These older men were not transient labourers or itinerant seafarers without local kin. Among those admitted to the Halifax City Home during the 1920s were five men from Richmond Heights but not a single woman. All these men, who were between the ages of fifty-six and seventy-seven, listed sons and/or wives who continued to live in the subdivision, with their families divided between the tenants in the Hydrostone District and the residents of the owner-occupied wooden homes on the extension streets. Their religious affiliations also reflected the neighbourhood's composition. Three of the five men were Roman Catholic, one was Anglican, and one was Presbyterian. In fact, the only unusual feature of this group was that four of the five were born in either Ireland or England, thereby making them somewhat atypical of the native-born majority of Haligonians.[32]

Why did more old men find themselves in the City Home than women? This discrepancy was probably the result of a number of factors. Most obviously, women in good health continued to make a valuable contribution to the household through their domestic labour. Older women babysat, cooked, and cleaned. Secondly, in a culture that sentimentalized motherhood, there may have been more social pressure on adult children to keep their mothers from the poorhouse than their fathers.[33] Finally, examples of Richmond Heights men who resided in the City Home may reflect individual circumstances. Institutionalization may have been the result of deteriorating mental or physical health rather than financial exigency, as their families may have been unable to cope with senility or provide full-time care.

For households dealing with this problem, there were few institutional options for working-class Haligonians apart from the poorhouse. In addition to the City Home, local charities operated the Home for Aged Men and the Old Ladies Home on Gottingen Street, but the clients of these institutions were elderly middle-class people in declining circumstances. The Sisters of Charity opened a home for aged women in 1886, but this institution evolved into the city's Catholic hospital. Apparently the work of the Sisters locally among the elderly must have been limited, since Roman Catholic women resided in the City Home, and the Catholic benevolent society, the St Vincent de Paul, regularly cooperated with admissions to the secular civic institution.[34] In fact, the St Vincent de Paul Society agitated for reforms within the City Home, including provision of married couples' quarters. The society claimed that it frequently had to maintain, for long periods of time, "old married couples who when advised to enter the City Home, refuse to do so because it would entail their separation."[35] In the absence of alternative institutional structures, at least some people preferred the insecurity of accepting direct charity, if it meant staying with their spouses and maintaining their own homes.

Many older people surveyed by the commission did manage to keep their homes and maintain residential independence. Of the 2767 persons who were over the age of seventy and had incomes of less than $400 a year, nearly half lived in their own home and more than a third lived with their children. The remaining 17 percent, in declining order of frequency, lived with relatives or friends, in charitable institutions, and as boarders.[36] Once again, without a manuscript census, it is impossible to determine the exact household composition in Richmond Heights. Certainly, the relatively small houses of the neighbourhood did not encourage multigenerational co-residency. Nevertheless, many elderly people resided with their children. We do not know if elderly parents were more likely to stay with the eldest child than with the youngest, if daughters had more responsibility than sons, if those who stayed in Nova Scotia had more responsibility than those who left, or if there was any difference based on rural or urban origins. Based largely on obituaries, we do know that many parents and in-laws lived with their adult sons and daughters in Richmond Heights.

Living with an adult child could take a large variety of forms. Sometimes the accommodation was seasonal, as in the case of the Hennessey Place retired military man and his wife who spent the winters with their son in Massachusetts. It could also be permanent, as in the case of Richmond Heights resident John Ryerson, who was "unable to earn a living through age" and whose only option was that of moving in with his married daughter's family a few blocks over.[37] The experience of those who had grown old in Halifax was different from that of those who moved into the city when they were unable to maintain their independence elsewhere. Moving in with an adult son or daughter may have been a terribly lonely and bewildering experience, as people were uprooted from the place where they had lived most of their lives. In 1922, at the age of eighty-five, George Milroy moved from Newfoundland to live with his son at 27 Columbus Place, where he died five years later. The impression that the stay in Halifax was only temporary and quite separate from their past was also suggested by the number of older men and women who died in Richmond Heights but were buried in outlying fishing villages such as Terrence Bay or Ketch Harbour.[38]

The loss of household independence in some situations was averted through the generosity of adult children. An elderly couple on Duffus Street was able to get by, since the husband earned $10 a week and their son paid their rent.[39] While some of the elderly managed by drawing on the principal of their savings or generating income from property, the report of the Nova Scotia government concluded that "by far the greatest number were supported by their children" (see table 1). The importance of adult children as providers of financial support to the elderly raised fears that the declining birth rate would place the same responsibility on fewer family members.[40] More than half of the sample group received full support from their children—with the likelihood of full support increasing with the number of children living (table 2). This conclusion conforms with

TABLE 1   *SOURCES OF SUPPORT AND INCOME OF PERSONS OVER SEVENTY YEARS OF AGE IN THE CITY OF HALIFAX AND THE COUNTIES OF CAPE BRETON, SHELBURNE, AND RICHMOND*

	Number of people	Percent		Percent others			
		Self-support	Others	Children	Relative	Friend	Charity
Total elderly	2767	29.7	70.3	71.2	13.2	8.0	7.6
Total annual income ($)							
300–399	228	78.5	21.5	91.8	4.1	4.1	0.0
200–299	306	80.4	19.6	78.3	15.0	5.0	1.7
100–199	469	62.2	37.6	73.5	10.7	7.9	7.9
< 100	385	27.0	73.0	63.7	11.7	9.3	15.3
none	1379	0.0	100.0	71.4	14.1	8.0	6.6

Source: Nova Scotia, *Journal of the House of Assembly,* 1930, Appendix 29, "Report of Commission on Old Age Pensions," 7, 9, 11. All numbers are based on people seventy years of age and over with incomes less than $400 per annum and living in the sample areas of Halifax city and the counties of Cape Breton, Richmond, and Shelburne.

TABLE 2   *SOURCES OF SUPPORT AND NUMBER OF CHILDREN OF PERSONS OVER SEVENTY YEARS OF AGE IN THE CITY OF HALIFAX AND THE COUNTIES OF CAPE BRETON, SHELBURNE, AND RICHMOND. EXTENT CHILDREN CAN AID AS A PERCENTAGE*

	Full	Partial	None	Unstated
Total	51.0	13.4	32.4	3.2
1 child	51.4	27.2	17.4	4.0
2 children	70.7	16.3	8.7	4.3
3 children	69.2	15.0	8.6	7.2
4 children	75.3	15.9	6.3	2.4
5 children	70.7	16.5	7.8	5.0
6+ children	72.7	16.6	7.8	2.9
none	—	—	100.0	—

Source: Nova Scotia, *Journal of the House of Assembly,* 1930, Appendix 29, "Report of Commission on Old Age Pensions," 7, 9, 11. All numbers are based on people seventy years of age and over with incomes of less than $400 per annum and living in the sample areas of Halifax city and the counties of Cape Breton, Richmond, and Shelburne.

traditional wisdom that children formed the best old-age policy, but casts doubt on the findings of American historian Daniel Scott Smith, who concluded that in 1900 the number of children did not affect the likelihood of support in old age in America.[41] Family commitment in Nova Scotia to the elderly may have been higher than elsewhere in Canada. After Saskatchewan, Alberta, and British Columbia, Nova Scotia had by far the lowest ratio of institutionalized elderly to overall population, despite its older population and the existence of county and municipal poorhouses.[42] Care for an elderly parent or family member may have been required by the definition of Maritime respectability. In L.M. Montgomery's *The Tangled Web*, eighty-five-year-old Aunt Becky lived on her own in two rooms she had rented within a friend's home. Montgomery wrote that this housing arrangement had been Aunt Becky's own choice, for the homes of any number of her relatives "would have been open to her, for the clan was never unmindful of their obligations."[43]

But children were not always available to give the needed assistance. Approximately one in four of the septuagenarians interviewed had no children living, and in the remaining group, nearly a third of their adult children had left the province.[44] While many of these adult children may have provided material support through remitted wages, they would not have been immediately or regularly available for physical assistance. Care and support for elderly parents fell hardest on single-child families, and this appears to have influenced the life options of these children in adulthood. Even in large families, however, responsibility could fall unevenly on one or two adult children, since the size of a family appears to have been connected to the overall likelihood of sibling outmigration. Children in large families were more likely to have siblings living elsewhere in Canada or the United States (table 3).

TABLE 3	SIZE OF FAMILY AND PLACE OF RESIDENCE OF ADULT CHILDREN FOR PERSONS OVER SEVENTY YEARS OF AGE IN THE CITY OF HALIFAX AND THE COUNTIES OF CAPE BRETON, SHELBURNE, AND RICHMOND					
Families	Number of families	Nova Scotia (%)	Elsewhere in Canada (%)	United States (%)	Other (%)	Total number of children
1 child	313	86.6	2.9	10.5	0.0	313
2 children	346	77.5	3.3	19.2	0.0	692
3 children	320	69.4	4.7	25.7	0.2	960
4 children	306	69.4	6.3	23.7	0.6	1224
5 children	184	65.0	5.2	29.5	0.3	920
6+ children	319	64.6	4.4	30.7	0.3	2270

Source: Nova Scotia, *Journal of the House of Assembly*, 1930, Appendix 29, "Report of Commission on Old Age Pensions," 7, 9, 11. All numbers are based on people seventy years of age and over with incomes less than $400 per annum and living in the sample areas of Halifax city and the counties of Cape Breton, Richmond, and Shelburne.

Adult sons and daughters regularly assisted their elderly parents, but occasionally this relationship was reversed. In at least three cases in the neighbourhood, mothers financially or materially assisted their married daughters and grandchildren. Thea Buckles married a man with an "indisposition to work, a state of matters which has existed since her early married days." As a result, she and her four small children relied on the generosity of her mother to supply the family with coal and fuel.[45] Another example of a mother who offered material support to a married daughter became evident when the Halifax Relief Commission was unable to place a lien on William O'Reilly's furniture, since it was not his own and had been loaned to him by his mother-in-law.[46] Probably, the most common means of support was offering shelter to a married daughter moving home with or without her husband. When Edna Farmer left her husband shortly after her marriage in 1919, she moved into her parents' Duffus Street home.

Examples of couples living with parents could be more complicated, since the balance of who was supporting whom shifted over time. Young newlyweds who could not afford either separate housing or the expense of setting up housekeeping occasionally moved in with parents. In the case of those families in the extension streets who owned their own homes, this pattern was prevalent, and appears to have been worked out in intergenerational negotiations in which housing was exchanged for regular contributions of money to the household.

The economic vulnerability of the elderly and their sometimes dependent state meant that the aged, along with widowed mothers and orphans, were at the forefront of the development of the welfare state. The federal Old Age Pension Act of 1927 provided the possibility of an income of not more than $20 a month to British subjects seventy years of age and over who did not have an annual income of more than $365, who had lived in Canada for twenty years and in the province for the preceding five years before payment. The pension act was a shared-cost program between the federal and provincial governments that Nova Scotia could not afford to enter into until 1934. When Nova Scotia began issuing cheques in March 1934, 11 685 Nova Scotians received an average monthly grant of $14.10. The hens, pigs, and woodlots were still needed, since poverty was not eliminated even from the lives of those who qualified.[47]

Gender was experienced in old age differently from how it was lived in youth or middle age, and younger men and women did not generally hold up the elderly as role models for gender-appropriate behaviours in their own lives. There were, of course, exceptions. The local Catholic church, which engaged in a battle against modern forms of sexuality as expressed in dancing, regularly hosted such events as "old time" dances like those of "grandmother's day." Similarly, some union men clung to the probably false notion that their grandfathers had been better able to support their families than they could now. More typical were the complaints of local public-health officials about the detrimental influence of old women on efforts to modernize child-care practices.[48] Michael Roper and John Tosh have recently noted with regard to masculinity that "one of the most precarious moments in the reproduction of masculinity is the transfer of power to the succeeding generation."[49] For the elderly men of Richmond Heights, with this abdication through the loss of the status of breadwinner, the albeit limited social power they possessed as men was gone.

Men and women experienced old age differently, though they shared a common vulnerability and dependency on children. As with most women, old men were often caught in inferior and low-paying jobs. Old age, like gender, influenced the employment options that were available and limited the possibility of economic independence.[50] Just as old age took away those characteristics that defined men—their physical strength and their ability to support a family—so it defeminized women. Women reaching menopause lost some of the physical traits that society used to define women as feminine. Older women looked different, a change that went beyond natural attributes such as grey hair, stooped posture, wrinkled skin, and false teeth. Peter Stearns notes that the dress of older women was distinct—shapeless and black and often covered with shawls, in sharp contrast to the colourful fabrics of youth.[51] In the 1920s, this contrast must have been particularly visible with the increased cultural emphasis on youth. Older women also occasionally wore their hair short, but without the disapproval that marked the discussions about young girls who cut their hair short in the fashion of the 1920s.[52] Perhaps short hair on older women did not matter, since in many ways they were no longer considered to be feminine. Older women, however, remained entitled to be female through their roles as mothers and grandmothers. The Mother's Day attention paid by a local newspaper to Livingstone Place resident Mrs Fleck, the proud grandmother of 105 grandchildren, offered one example of a positive portrayal of old age.[53] Because old age was associated with dependency and vulnerability, gender connotations were less relevant. Men and women were perhaps equally disadvantaged by the scarcity of pensions and exclusion from the formal labour market. It is ironic that, in the final years of their lives, the men and women who probably possessed the clearest polarized and class-based understanding of male and female gender ideals were treated and perceived as very much the same.

NOTES

1. Canada, *Census*, 1881, vol. 1, T. 1, 9; 1921, vol. 1, T. 16, 254.

2. James Seth, "Halifax Revisited," *Dalhousie Review* 1, no. 4 (Jan. 1922): 338–39.

3. Jackson Lears, *No Place of Grace: Antimodernism and the Transformation of American Culture, 1880–1920* (New York 1981).

4. M.C. MacLean, "The Age Distribution of the Canadian People," *Census*, 1931, vol. 12, 768.

5. Canada, *Census*, 1921, vol. 4, T. 40, 200–3.

6. Peter N. Stearns, "Old Women: Some Historical Observations," *Journal of Family History* 5 (Spring 1980): 44–45. In *The New Day Recalled: The Lives of Girls and Women in English Canada, 1919–1939* (Toronto 1988), Veronica Strong-Boag uses the age of forty to mark the final life stage. For a critique of the history of older women, see Marjorie Chary Feinson, "Where Are the Women in the History of

Aging?" *Social Science History* 9, no. 4 (Fall 1985): 429–52.

7. DUA, MS 4, 180, H 301, Maritime Telephone and Telegraph Personnel Benefits; Stearns, "Old Women," 45.

8. Tamara Hareven, *Family Time, Industrial Time: The Relationship between the Family and Work in a New England Industrial Community* (Cambridge 1982), 173; Howard Chudacoff and Tamara K. Hareven, "From the Empty Nest to Family Dissolution," *Journal of Family History* 4, no. 1 (Spring 1979): 59–63.

9. Chris Gordon, "Familial Support for the Elderly in the Past: The Case of London's Working Class in the Early 1930s," *Ageing and Society* 8 (1988): 309.

10. James Struthers, "Regulating the Elderly: Old Age Pensions and the Formation of a Pension Bureaucracy in Ontario, 1919–1945," *Journal of the Canadian Historical Association*, New Series, 3 (Charlottetown 1993): 237. Struthers carefully notes that, although the program's intent was inclusive, "gender played an important role in limiting and constraining the entitlement of women to state support in their old age."

11. For examples of birthdays and anniversaries see *Evening Mail*, 24 Nov. 1921, 13 Sept. 1923, 26 Sept. 1929; Hareven, *Family Time*, 180.

12. See W. Andrew Achenbaum, *Old Age in the New Land: The American Experience* (Baltimore 1978), ch. 6, "Old Age Becomes a National Problem," and David Hackett Fischer, *Growing Old in America* (Oxford 1978), ch. 4, "Old Age Becomes a Social Problem." Also Carol Haber, *Beyond 65: The Dilemma of Old Age in America's Past* (Cambridge 1983); Brian Gratton, *Urban Elders: Family, Work and Welfare among Boston's Aged, 1890–1950* (New York 1986), and "The Labor Force Participation of Older Men, 1890–1950," *Journal of Social History* 20, no. 4 (Summer 1987): 689–710; N. Sue Weiler, "Industrial Scrap Heap: Employment Patterns

and Change for the Aged in the 1920s," *Social Science History* 13, no. 1 (Spring 1989): 65–88, and "Family Security or Social Security? The Family and the Elderly in New York State during the 1920s," *Journal of Family History* 11, no. 1 (1986): 77–95.

13. E.R. Forbes, "Prohibition and the Social Gospel in Nova Scotia," *Challenging the Regional Stereotype: Essays on the Twentieth-Century Maritimes* (Fredericton 1989), 36–37; *Citizen*, 17 Jan. 1920, 29 June 1923, 19 June 1925.

14. *Citizen*, 19 June 1925; PANS, MG 20, vol. 517, no. 1, Minutes of the Society for the Prevention of Cruelty, President's Report, 31 Mar. 1921.

15. Nova Scotia, *JHA*, 1930, App. 29, "Report of Commission on Old Age Pensions," 6. The Halifax statistics found that 41.7 percent had incomes over $400, 3.9 percent $300 to $399, 4.3 percent $200 to $299; 7.3 percent $100 to $199; 8.5 percent less than $100, and 34.6 percent no income at all. The elderly in Halifax had a greater opportunity to accumulate wealth in the city than in the rural counties (4, 7). Achenbaum, *Old Age*, 115; Gratton, "Labor Force Participation," 689, 703; Brian Gratton, "The New History of the Aged: A Critique," in David Van Tassel and Peter N. Stearns, eds., *Old Age in a Bureaucratic Society: The Elderly, the Experts, and the State in American History* (New York 1986).

16. Howard P. Chudacoff, "The Life Course of Women, Age, and Age Consciousness, 1865–1915," *Journal of Family History* 5, no. 3 (Fall 1980): 290; Canada, *Census*, 1921, vol. 4, T. 5, 382–99; Canada, *Census*, 1931, vol. 3, T. 15, 134–35, and vol. 7, T. 5, 7.

17. DUA, MS 10, 2, A.1, Correspondence: Fred W. Thompson to J. Bell, 9 Aug. 1976, 8–9.

18. *Evening Mail*, 13 June 1924; *Monthly Bulletin* (Halifax, Maritime Telephone and Telegraph), June 1924; PANS, MG 36, HRC, R.1361, 25 Sebastian Place, and A.79, Correspondence re: claims, John and Barbara Green, property; *Evening*

Mail, 27 Feb. 1924; Halifax City Directory, 1904–14; 1920–29; PANS, RG 35, vol. 102, City of Halifax, 8A, 1920s. The voters' list included a total of 448 men.

19. *Evening Mail*, 26 Sept. 1929.

20. NAC, RG 43, Department of Railways, vol. 291, 3871.

21. DUA, MS 4, 180, Maritime Telephone and Telegraph, H 302, Employee Benefits. See also James Stafford, "The Class Struggle and the Rise of Private Pensions, 1900–1950," *Labour/ Le Travail* 20 (Fall 1987): 147–71.

22. Craig Heron, *Working in Steel: The Early Years in Canada, 1883–1935* (Toronto 1988), 102; Joy Parr, *The Gender of Breadwinners: Women, Men and Change in Two Industrial Towns, 1880–1950* (Toronto 1990), 48.

23. Canada, Department of Labour, *Labour Gazette*, July 1923, 704; Feb. 1929, 170; Oct. 1929, 1123.

24. *Daily Star*, 9 Mar. 1927.

25. Joanne J. Meyerowitz, *Women Adrift: Independent Wage Earners in Chicago, 1880–1930* (Chicago 1988), 37, and Strong-Boag, *New Day Recalled*, 182.

26. Canada, *Census*, 1921, vol. 4, T. 5, 382–99.

27. Nova Scotia, *JHA*, 1930, App. 29, "Report of Commission on Old Age Pensions," 14.

28. Ibid. The report was based on research in Halifax city and the counties of Cape Breton, Richmond, and Shelburne.

29. *Evening Mail*, 16 June 1922.

30. See, for example: Haber, *Beyond 65*, as cited in Feinson, "Where Are the Women?" 433; The 1931 census listed 126 men and 165 women over the age of sixty in Nova Scotia who resided in charitable or benevolent institutions. Although women outnumbered men in the province's institutions, the circumstances of their residence were remarkably different. In 23.8 percent of the cases for men and 51.4 percent of the cases for women, someone was paying the full or partial cost of their maintenance. Canada, *Census*, 1931, vol. 9, T. 14, 286–87.

31. Struthers, "Regulating the Elderly," 238.

32. PANS, RG 35, vol. 102, City of Halifax, 33, 31.A, City Home, Inmates Admitted and Discharged, May 1919–May 1929; 36, City Home, City Inmates, 1919–29.

33. Michael Katz, "Poorhouses and the Origins of the Public Old Age Home," *Milbank Memorial Fund Quarterly* 62, no. 1 (1984): 134.

34. PANS, MG 1, vol. 315, no. 2, Diary of George Morton; Sister Maura, *The Sisters of Charity of Halifax* (Toronto 1956), 32; Bettina Bradbury, "Mourir chrétiennement: La vie et la mort dans les éstablissements catholiques pour personnes âgées à Montréal au XIXe siècle," *Revue d'histoire de l'Amérique française* 46, no. 1 (Summer 1992): 143–75.

35. *Daily Star*, 14 Feb. 1927.

36. Nova Scotia, *JHA*, 1930, App. 29, "Report of Commission on Old Age Pensions," 12. It is interesting to note that the Canadian census did not differentiate between elderly parents and other dependents within a household, despite the fact that this specific group were supposedly regarded as a social problem.

37. PANS, MG 36, HRC, R.748, 2 Hennessey Place; R.1854, Vacated Balances, Rent Ledger, 1919–25.

38. *Daily Star*, 26 Jan. 1927, *Acadian Recorder*, 29 Dec. 1919; *Daily Echo*, 14 May 1920; *Evening Mail*, 28 Jan. 1925.

39. PANS, MG 36, HRC, R.1854, Vacated Balances, Rent Ledger, 1919–25.

40. Gratton, *Urban Elders*, 177.

41. Daniel Scott Smith, "Life Course, Norms, and the Family System of Older Americans in 1900," *Journal of Family History* 4, no. 3 (Fall 1979), 285–98.

42. Overall in Canada, 208.7 per 10 000 over the age of seventy were institutionalized compared to 91.5 in Nova

Scotia, 199.7 in New Brunswick, 378.5 in Quebec, and 193.3 in Ontario. Canada, *Census*, 1931, vol. 9, T. 9, 280–81.

43. L.M. Montgomery, *The Tangled Web* (Toronto 1931 [1972]), 3.

44. Nova Scotia, *JHA*, 1930, App. 29, "Report of Commission on Old Age Pensions," 10.

45. PANS, MG 36, HRC, R.1411, 30 Stairs Place.

46. PANS, MG 36, R.1365, 29 Sebastian Place.

47. Nova Scotia, *JHA*, 1935, App. 32, Old Age Pensions, 7–8.

48. *Evening Mail*, 21 Nov. 1928; *Citizen*, 17 Nov. 1922; Jessie L. Ross, "Attacking Infant and Maternal Mortality. A Group of Papers Read before the Canadian Council of Child Welfare, Toronto, Ontario, Sept. 1922. 1. In a City. The Halifax Experiment," *The Public Health Nurse* (Mar. 1923): 126.

49. Michael Roper and John Tosh, "Introduction," *Manful Assertions: Masculinities in Britain since 1800* (London 1991), 17.

50. Gratton, *Urban Elders*, 76, 96.

51. Stearns, "Old Age," 48.

52. PANS, MG 27, vol. 1, 285, "Some Details That May Assist in the Identification of the Hundreds of Unclaimed Bodies Which Have Been interned," 1917–18, 114, 183.

53. *Evening Mail*, 12 May 1928.

FATHERHOOD AND THE SOCIAL CONSTRUCTION OF MEMORY: BREADWINNING AND MALE PARENTING ON A JOB FRONTIER, 1945–1966 ◇

ROBERT RUTHERDALE

○

After the Second World War, Sam Taylor returned to Prince George, a small city in northern British Columbia destined to grow during Canada's postwar resource-sector boom. He was a veteran and a husband, and within a year would be a father. Taylor and his wife went on to raise six boys. The ample employment and business opportunities at the time provided men like Taylor with relatively secure and growing incomes. But his work later stood out in memory as something that had robbed him of closer contact with his sons. "I had no time for them. I had no patience with them. And its amazing that they turned out so well."[1]

Born and raised in Vancouver, Jim Kane moved to Prince George shortly after Sam Taylor's return. He became a successful grocer, establishing a small chain of stores. During the mid-fifties, he and his wife adopted three children, two boys and a girl. Like Taylor, Kane remembered how work and community service pulled him away from his family and role as a parent. He later claimed this as his "single biggest regret."[2]

At about the same time, Olaph Christensen, another veteran, arrived in Prince George with his wife, in search of a freer lifestyle. They had dreamed of somewhere rustic and northern—a place where they could enjoy the outdoors. They bought a woodlot just outside the city limits and built on it.

◇ This article has not been previously published. The author would like to thank Carol McKee at the University of Northern British Columbia for her able assistance in research. The advice and encouragement of Bridget Moran and Myra Rutherdale proved invaluable. This paper is drawn from a larger project, in progress, on fatherhood in the postwar period.

Christensen worked full-time in town as a mechanic, and logged part-time. After a son, born at the end of the war, three daughters arrived during the peak years of the baby boom. Christensen remembered fatherhood as an engaging experience. He claimed to have taken an active part in parenting. And yet he recalled that many things seemed predetermined in his role as a father during those years that kept him from active parenting.[3]

As part of a new generation of postwar families across Canada, the Taylors, Kanes, and Christensens faced the dual tasks of domestic labour and breadwinning in an expanding consumer-based economy. How did they, or others like them, negotiate gender boundaries or construct family roles? For men, how was male parenting perceived? How did fatherhood as a role extend into the community? The following study attempts to address these questions using oral history. The conclusions, given the paucity of related literature, are offered as preliminary directions for further inquiry rather than definitive answers. It is hoped that they might inform further studies of Canadian fatherhood since 1945.

An attempt has been made to determine some important contours that tend to shape perceptions of fatherhood in memories of this period. What was told to me during my interviews was related through many levels of perception. Periodically, oral evidence appeared to be influenced by partial understandings, archetypes, or myths that may reflect recurrent self-perceptions among fathers of this era. At other times, perspectives unique to the subject or circumstance emerged. Throughout, my interest remained focused on relationships between the experiences and practices of postwar fathers and the socially constructed frameworks of perception their narratives depended on. Studies that use oral history might benefit from approaches that treat individual memories as subjective products of social relations rather than as objective records of personal pasts.

This work also seeks to draw attention to a relatively uncharted period in Canadian family history. Though Canadian historians have considered many aspects of family history for earlier periods, attention might now turn to the baby boom years, since that era has gained sufficient distance from our own. As well, gender historians need to consider men's experience at that time. Though families are certainly not the only place to look, the significance of high marriage and fertility rates, increased household formation, and changing consumption patterns, after a prolonged period of depression and war, all underscore the importance of this topic. The following approach to oral history, with all subjects drawn from a single locale, is but one of many research strategies that could be applied to the study of fatherhood in this period.

METHODS AND CONCEPTUAL APPROACHES

I interviewed twenty-one men who spent most of their lives as parents in or near Prince George from the end of the Second World War to the mid-1960s. In certain features, this group was unique. Their long-term residency contrasted with the high degree of transience in Prince George during the period. But, the fact that they became stakeholders in one community does not necessarily mean that their experiences were particularly atypical. Much more important, given their diverse occupations and socioeconomic backgrounds, was the emergence of comparable perspectives on breadwinning, community service, and parenting. What they shared as fathers proved significant enough to form the basis of a coherent historical sample.[4]

The questioning strategy used in the interviews was intended to be sensitive to the dynamics involved in the construction of spoken narratives. Oral narratives are not constructed simply through exchanges directed by the researcher and the teller; many influences are involved. The social basis of memory is a crucial concern. Although many of the men interviewed believed that they had led self-directed lives or had formed their opinions independently, their beliefs were assessed for both internal and comparative consistencies. Factors that appeared to influence perceptions of fatherhood were closely inspected.

Oral historians have recently turned much of their attention to the social construction of memory. Although much work remains to be done on constructions of gender and family practices in the period, many significant contours—some related to fatherhood—have been mapped out, constituting a general backdrop for my locally based research.[5] With respect to familial power relations, the concept of a "gender regime" in family life proved useful for interpreting patterns that displayed stability across my sample. So did the related ideology of male breadwinning, further explained below, when concurrent attitudes and beliefs concerning work, family life, and father's self-perceptions were expressed.

Gender is approached here as a socially constructed response to sexual difference, experiences that produced boundaries delineated in part by the complex and multilayered politics of family relations. Given that *constructions* of gender through time serve as a primary link between the salient practices of a given society and its institutions, including the family, the need to situate those practices in historical dimensions seems clear.[6] Nonetheless, some key sociological approaches, skillfully delineated by R.W. Connell in *Gender and Power*, informed my interpretations. Gender, Connell states, is a "linking concept." It concerns "the linking of other fields of social practise to the nodal practises of engendering, childbirth and parenting."[7] In industrialized countries, as an abundant literature demonstrates, the political economy of masculinity and fatherhood has had crucial implications for those studying family practices. Much of this work establishes how family relations are negotiated in large part to accommodate hegemonic demands of production and reproduction in societies where gender connects many societal fields with family life.[8]

It is through such links that the ideology of male breadwinning has become one of the most crucial exigencies placed on families, particularly in urban, industrial contexts. And yet, next to an emerging social scientific literature on fatherhood, a lamentable dearth of historical work exists, with the exception of Robert L. Griswold's recent survey of American fatherhood since 1800.[9] Griswold affirms the significance of breadwinning in terms that transcend the spatial bounds of his study:

> Despite men's differences, breadwinning has remained the great unifying element in father's lives. Its obligations bind men across the boundaries of color and class, and shape their sense of self, manhood, and gender. Supported by law, affirmed by history, sanctioned by every element in society, male breadwinning has been synonymous with maturity, respectability, and masculinity.[10]

He also stresses the fact that as an ideological system, male breadwinning justified a limited commitment among fathers to nurture their young children.[11]

My approach to memories of family life and male breadwinning also considered how cultural perceptions are enacted through language to help reconstruct gender relations from one generation to the next. In *The Lenses of Gender*, Sandra Lipsitz Bem develops the idea of a gendered masculine consciousness, a metaphorical lens that distorts, reconfigures, or even omits the presence of women in male-dominated societies. Though she points out that this kind of thinking, or androcentrism, has long dominated men's perceptions of society in America, the concept helps clarify how discursive strategies are employed to validate male breadwinning and the gender regime of particular families. As a relatively stable force, Bem maintains, "hidden assumptions about sex and gender remain embedded in cultural discourses, social institutions, and individual psyches that invisibly and systematically reproduce male power in generation after generation."[12]

Oral historians are particularly well situated to consider how gendered family regimes, structured in part to accommodate male breadwinning, reflect such modes of awareness (or unawareness!). This is because subjective viewpoints offer clues concerning the social origins of perception and memory.[13] As men like Sam Taylor, Jim Kane, or Olaph Christensen recalled the various roles of their lives, they produced narratives embedded in what Clifford Geertz has conceptualized as a "native consciousness." That is, they could not readily distinguish between what they experienced and how their society construed what they experienced. During my fieldwork, perceptions of reality often seemed, as Geertz has put it, "indissoluble" from the forces that shaped them. For instance, subjects were apt to refer to "women's work" as something inherent in the female condition rather than a depiction of a cultural construct.[14] In the process, they revealed a host of understandings and sensibilities embedded partly in myths.

Myths are not always approached here in the typical way that many historians have considered them—as stories that are not true. Instead, periodic references in my interviews to behaviours, beliefs, or ideas that collectively form identifiable stereotypes are assessed as mythical constructs. If there was strong concurrence on a given aspect of fatherhood, the appropriateness of approaching it as a perception informed by partial, or "mythical," understandings was considered. "There are occasions," as Peter Burke has put it, "when we can observe the process of 'mythification' at work, in a series of accounts of the past which come closer and closer to an archetype."[15]

As something that happens when stories are told, rather than something that actually happened in the past, myth then becomes a structuring device of both memory and self-awareness.[16] As Raphael Samuel and Paul Thompson contend, life stories can "become a vital document of the construction of consciousness, emphasizing both the variety of experience in any social group, and also how an individual story draws on a common culture."[17] The "culture" of fatherhood, like any other human experience transmitted across generations, both creates and relies on its own sense of the past. Interpreting subjective evidence is far from an exact science. But examining some key aspects of fatherhood, such as breadwinning, parenting, and community service, with attention paid to how particular narratives are generated within a cultural context, certainly places us on safer ground.

BREADWINNERS

Gender/power relationships in families were supported by the comparative advantages male breadwinners enjoyed in a male-dominated work force and economy. Employment opportunities, from professional to unskilled occupations, were relatively high during this period, particularly in resource-based centres like Prince George. But since many jobs were available only to men, who also enjoyed higher earnings, wives and mothers were not normally expected to engage in paid work. Certainly the participation of married women in the work force increased dramatically from the mid-1950s to the mid-1960s. But significant attitudinal changes did not occur in my sample, although opinion often divided over the issue across Canada.[18]

With living standards rising during the postwar decades, new fathers were far more able than their fathers had been to assume what they saw as respectable and mature places within families of their own. Striving for self-fulfillment through breadwinning was not only revived as a compelling pursuit, it was amplified by a growing economy. Anecdotal evidence invariably confirmed the impression that employment availability and wage rates in Prince George were capable of supporting single wage-earning families at the time. Roy Gibson, an unskilled worker, recalled that when he and his wife came up from Vancouver in 1951, jobs could be had on the spot: "So we arrived here on Sunday afternoon. Monday morning I walked down George Street, over to Strom's Planer, across the tracks. Got a job there, came back and stopped at Roger Motors ... and got a job in the garage there. So I went to work there." As he put it, "there was no such thing as "you couldn't get work."[19] Others in the trades, service, and professional sectors confirmed his description.

Male breadwinning, self-identity, and the family's survival were inextricably linked in a series of comparable narratives. Moreover, noticeably similar themes were conveyed across age and class lines. Breadwinning was described as an onerous obligation. It combined a sense of duty and responsibility with memories of its burdens and demands. "Everything was on my shoulders," one said of supporting five children.[20] "I had to look after the whole thing,"[21] claimed another. "It was mostly on my hands. . . . I was always out working."[22] Clichés like "putting bread on the table" or "keeping your nose to the grindstone" cropped up regularly.[23]

However, one informant's terse summation, "I gave her the money—and she spent it," suggested more than a simple obligation fulfilled. Within families, breadwinning was an enormously empowering role. An implicit assumption contained in references to it was the prerogative men "earned" to leave most domestic chores to their spouses. Though several marriages were described as equitable partnerships, most fathers saw themselves as the "head" of their households because of their economic function. Carrying "everything" on their shoulders or looking after "the whole thing" fed into notions of fathers as leaders, a persona many proudly embraced.[24] "A father first of all," Sam Taylor said, "has to be a leader. Somebody has to be a leader. If the woman is a leader, the other men laugh at the father, don't they?. . . 'Oh hell, you know who wears the pants in the family,' y'know. And this is what you hear. And even if you know, and the father knows, he's not really leading, at least act it out. Give the guy a little respect."[25]

If memories of spouses working outside the home before marriage were devalued, they could be recalled as unthinkable once children began to arrive, even if the possibility of a career seemed open. In one case, the wife of a former truck driver had been promoted to a management position in a department store before the birth of her first child. Motherhood ended that. "No—there was no way she was going to work with a baby around the house. . . . Nope, mother's gotta be home." His stubborn attitude was attributed to an incident recalled as a kind of failed experiment. Curiously, it took place long after the first-born, and two other children, had passed infancy: "Over the years, occasionally, she'd go out and do some house-cleaning or something like that, y'know, when the kids were away from school. And it just happened about once or twice that the kids said: 'Mom, I don't like us to come home when you're not here.' So that settled it. . . . It was just one of those things."[26] Although the details seem fuzzy, with something happening "about once or twice" settling an important issue apparently on the spot, he recalled coming to terms with "one of those things": a gendered role for his wife epitomized by his simple adage "mother's gotta be home." Others expressed it in less adamant language, but the gender power and division of labour reflected in these stories seemed quite clear. "We never had anyone come in," one said of house-work, something he referred to explicitly as "women's work," and "fundamentally" his wife's responsibility.[27]

A normative ideology of containment and, for many fathers, shift work requiring travel, underscored expectations that mothers could not enter the paid work force.[28] Nearly half the men I interviewed worked outside town for long stretches. When asked about parenting, Ralph Monahan, a former diesel mechanic, offered a typical reply: "Nancy [was often] left alone, she used to, more or less, look after the girls because I was away so much, really. I was out on jobs all over the country."[29] Again, his wife's full-time commitment to nurturing is somewhat downplayed as a "more or less" activity, when it was clearly more than less. Monahan's job certainly required travel, although not as far from home as he suggested. His territory seldom went beyond the Prince George Forest District. Nonetheless, for many fathers, comparable stints of out-of-town work, generally for a week at a time, restricted contact with domestic life and, in the process, reinforced a rigid sexual division of labour.

A sense of the social stigma attached to working mothers can be gleaned from the marked unease expressed by Robert Lewis when he recalled his feelings at the time his wife returned to nursing after the arrival of their second of six children. "At that time," Lewis recalled, "I didn't really want her to work." Given their situation, though, it seemed an unavoidable necessity.

> She sort of talked [to] me, and wanted to know if it would be a good idea to go to work. I didn't really want her to work. I didn't want [her] to work because of the kids, at the start. I didn't think, y'know, I thought it was tough to get, I was always under the impression [it] wasn't a good idea to work if you didn't have to work. But it got so that, I guess, that the financial need was there.... I thought it wasn't fair to the, well it wasn't just me—it was her too—figured it wasn't fair to the children. It sort of neglected a bit from not being, from not being—the mother—not being around, or somebody, here all the time.[30]

In this segment, incomplete sentences, frequent hesitation throughout his delivery, and concern with the impact on children of their mother in the paid work force, all suggest an informant ill at ease with this particular memory. Terms like "tough," "fair," and "neglect" seem indicative of the hard edges on which this issue resided in Lewis' sense of a personal past.

Others in this study seemed proud to recall what they considered hard-won successes as breadwinners, which included supporting a wife at home. But a curious paradox often crept into these narratives. While domestic labour was repeatedly devalued as "women's work," with prepositions like "just" or "only" attached to it, such terms were usually employed in relation to a father's paid employment to stress perceptions of the high status accorded the male breadwinning function. But when attention turned to consider wives as chief caregivers—the mother of the family—a mythical archetype emerged in which they were adored. Even though housework and even child rearing may have held little esteem next to breadwinning, conspicuous tributes appeared time and again, exalting spouses as nurturers and unpaid domestic servants. This might be called the wife on-a-pedestal myth. Although a wife's cooking and what was often seen as her unique talent for household crafts or "handiwork" were frequently commended, a commitment to nurturing was given a special place as her paramount virtue, selflessly expressed. "Her whole life was in those boys," Sam Taylor told me. "She's an excellent mother—excellent mother. She just lives for her children."[31] In one interview after another, tasks and responsibilities from cooking to nurturing were identified with pride as something "the wife" was particularly gifted at.

Myths, as Claude Lévi-Strauss argued, serve to "provide a logical model capable of overcoming a contradiction."[32] These men's comments suggest how the construction of stereotypical portraits of motherhood, fashioned from the pedestal myth, helped to rationalize gender inequality at home. Contradictions between the past as actually lived and memory as a subjective perspective prompted reconciliation through other myths as well.

Many fathers expressed a sense of loss over the time away from home their jobs demanded. "That's the part that hurts," Ken Wilson said when asked how he felt about his children's upbringing during the most hectic stretch in his business.[33] Shift workers like Roy Barker, who used to think about shift work as a repressive constraint on family life, may very well have preferred more time with their children and wives.[34]

Nonetheless, their achievements as providers seemed to entitle most to time away from the family—leisure time that was considered legitimate because it was seen as having been earned. "She was supportive," Barker added, recalling his wife's attitude towards his Lion's Club activities. "She knew that I had to have an outlet."[35] "I didn't mind being cooped up in the building," James McAndrew said of his practice, "as long as I knew I could get out and play golf. Didn't play that much with my children as far as their sports were concerned."[36] When McAndrew attended community functions, he delegated the chore of getting his children to sleep to his wife. "When I think back on it, I guess maybe I let her do more of that than I did," he confessed. "I belonged to organizations and I'd go out to meetings."[37]

Alongside breadwinning demands, all interviewees recalled a high commitment to their family's well being, although many lamented the constraints that they believed their work placed on family life. Yet time was often reserved for peer companionship, whether on the golf course, at a service club meeting, or even out with "the boys" for a beer after work. Paul Atkinson imagined a moral boundary between male social drinking and poor parenting:

> I've seen quite a few [bad fathers]. . . . Guys [that] spend more time in the bar than what they would at home. And that's not right. I mean like us—if we went out, we always went together. Once in a while I'd join the boys and go right from work and have a beer or two. But to come home out of your mind? And don't know where your wife and kids were? That wasn't my style.[38]

Boundaries between leisure and family responsibilities appeared to vary among the husbands I interviewed and also tended to shift during each family's life cycle. But expressions of regret for time spent breadwinning, given so many distinct memories of activities pursued without the family, need to be explained. Even when conveyed as "the part that hurts,"[39] or as Jim Kane put it "my single biggest regret,"[40] these and similar claims may constitute a recurring and significant myth in fatherhood narratives, summoned to rectify a contradiction between time away from the family and what was perceived as a more ideal situation—father at home. It appears that power gained through gendered access to earning money, contributed to a male prerogative—a degree of socially acceptable personal freedom. This we might call the time-away myth, a recurring lament blamed on work demands. While breadwinning was remembered as having placed a regrettable burden on family time, fathers also earned a "right" to some exemption from domestic responsibilities, duties that were not considered the primary responsibilities of fathers.

COMMUNAL FATHERS

Leisure time could either be consumed in recreational self-indulgence, or be donated to community service. If family life proved too restrictive for masculine assertiveness, the community as a whole presented varied and expansive fields for masculine affirmation. In E. Anthony Rotundo's study of American manhood, he invokes the term "communal manhood" to describe how a man's identity was considered "inseparable from the duties he owed to his community." While he was referring to the "densely woven social world of colonial New England," its applicability to other historical contexts involving families and social interaction in local communities seems apt.[41] Communal fatherhood is used here to describe non-paid pursuits at the local level in which fathers participated in activities of benefit to families, particularly to other parent's children. The term could be applied to innumerable endeavours, from organized community service to political involvement. Voluntarism was embraced, but so was any locally based activity related to male parenting and the good of the local community.

A strong sense of communal fatherhood, of the value of serving others in Prince George, shaped the memories of many interviewees. Of the twenty-one men interviewed, eight participated in a formal association in Scouts, Cadets, sports teams or other community groups that involved them directly in community service. All recalled, at least in informal roles, some aspect of this experience, and could hardly avoid doing so as parents. Although not every father sought community-based roles, these kind of pursuits were an important facet of male parenting in this period.

To explore how this role was perceived in memory, I addressed three relationships: how childhood memories of communal fatherhood may have influenced what my informants later did themselves; how the lack of related services and programs in Prince George in the 1950s and early 1960s affected the degree and nature of their involvement; and finally, how performance as communal fathers reflected perceptions of gender and parenting at home.

Curiously, the most active fathers recalled responding to their own childhood circumstances in one of two ways. Either they carried on a tradition set down for them by their fathers, or they reacted against perceptions of a woeful neglect on their own father's part.

Charley Farrow stressed the link between his father's dedication to community service and his own contributions years later. Among the many causes that his father led or took part in during the 1930s, rural electrification and organizing a local community association stood out. Farrow set the scene for his father's departure with the Canadian forces in 1940 as a lifelong impression: "One of the important things that he told me just before he went overseas . . . was when you grow up—do your share for your community." After moving to Mud River in 1957, Farrow organized the local drive for electrification in his district, just like his father.[42] The father-to-son tradition of community service was an important theme in Farrow's life story.

Ken Wilson also carried on a communal-oriented custom practised by his father, but it entailed something quite different and generally more informal: the telling of stories about local history. Wilson described his father as one of the "new pioneers" of Prince George. He had settled permanently in 1906, after several seasons work with the pack trains for river barges that made their way to what was then Fort George. With a partner, he set up a drug dispensary that took him into general retailing. Some years later, once established, married, and a father, he occasionally joined other veterans of the pack train days to reminisce about their youth. They told stories of exploration, danger, and discovery—tales of masculine adventure set in northern British Columbia sometime before the First World War. "I listened to the stories for years," Wilson recalled,[43] remembering how he and other children gathered to hear these tales at neighbourly picnics on the banks of the Fraser River.

In the early 1950s, Wilson's turn came. Steeped in local lore, and a father with school-aged children, he made a special effort to impart his sense of Prince George's "pioneer" past, especially in the schools. "Carousels were my first effort," he said. "What pictures! Most of them would be passed on to me for redoing, or recopying." Wilson's historical slide show formed the backdrop for a brand of story telling he recognized as heavily influenced by his father. Wilson usually addressed children in grades five to seven who also passed around photographs while he told stories.[44] As a communal father, Wilson both acted out a tradition as a storehouse of local lore and carried one on by assuming his father's role as story teller.

As fathers like Wilson went out into the community, they crossed a boundary—the family threshold. What seems most significant is the noticeably loose demarcation between fatherhood at home and communal fatherhood. Memories of being *in loco parentis*, in particular, often included stories that reflected efforts made to transmit principles practised at home to groups of boys (and occasionally girls) drawn from the community.

Roy Gibson distinctly remembered his community service as a Scoutmaster this way. His leadership philosophy seemed influenced by a Depression-scarred childhood. Gibson's father died when he was nine, leaving him, his sister, and his mother nearly destitute on a small farm in Saskatchewan. As he explained, "I . . . shouldn't say that I felt I was head of the family, but I felt a responsibility. . . . There was no asking for it—put it that way." Later he said, "growing up in the depression—there was no room for arguing. You had to look at the facts and take what was there and go from there." Both as a father and a Scoutmaster, Gibson felt that self-reliance, more than anything, had to be instilled in boys. He remembered hoping that his hard lessons might serve as their best example. "You were in a corral" he said of his childhood, "and within that corral certain things had to be done and that was all there was to it. Whether you liked it or not, you did it. Now that's—my years with the Scouting movement—this is what I put across to the boys."

His three sons all joined Scouts. He claimed to show no favouritism. More significantly, he suggested strong consistencies between the values he espoused as a parent and those upheld as a Scoutmaster. When asked in a general way what good fatherhood was all about, Gibson replied:

> teaching the kids to paddle their own canoe. . . . If you can't take care of yourself nobody else is going to. And yet, they're teaching in the schools, and this I found very difficult to counter in Scouting—I was teaching one set of values and they would see another set. And they couldn't make up their minds as to who was right. And it was the older group of boys, basically after they left my group—where they went in Venturers—where you'd see it finally, where the boy made up his mind. And he fell off the fence one way or another. And, if they fell off on my side of the fence, OK, they're still around the community. They're members of the community—some of the others are in jail![45]

Communal fatherhood provided fields of activity where male parents as role models, group leaders, or experts could contribute to what they regarded as useful familial influences to the whole community. As this took place, partial understandings or certain life myths they held influenced their approach to youth both inside and beyond the home. Roy Gibson's strong sense of suffering and survival during the Depression translated into a code of conduct for personal responsibility.

Sam Taylor's lifelong struggle to overcome childhood scars and become an effective parent was reflected in his stories of coaching minor hockey. Taylor remembered struggling to come to terms with the fact that competition should not interfere with his young players simply having fun. Remembering vividly the poor example set by his own domineering father, Taylor described a moment he faced behind the bench when one of his players pleaded with him to let up with his scolding. "I'm trying to do what you say, coach, but I'm only an eleven year old boy."[46] Communal fatherhood, for Taylor, was described in terms of enormous contrasts between himself and his father. He also claimed to have tried to bring to coaching the same sense of fairness that he applied to his six boys at home.

There was some indication given by two professionals in this study that middle-class fathers took a dimmer view of getting involved at the level of Scoutmaster or coach. "I didn't go out there with the rest of the mob," Roy Miller stated. "If the kids wanted to play—fine they did it. . . . Everything was close by."[47] James McAndrew was equally happy with new and close facilities, but more so with the fact that what he described as excellent coaching was also available. He felt he wasn't needed and that his time was too limited.[48]

Communal fatherhood was recalled as a complex experience. Its inspiration could come from positive or negative examples. How these men remembered their efforts seemed rooted in their childhood and was reflective in subsequent understandings of responsible fatherhood. Being a principled father in the community meant recognizing a link between the family's stake in the community and the father's role in maintaining it. In this way communal fatherhood reflected masculine notions of community building. Since much of communal fatherhood involved leading boys, many men readily recalled themselves as manful role models. Attitudes toward gender, military life, masculine adventure, competitiveness, sportsmanship, and the hardship of the Depression, to name just a few, were readily apparent. When fathers were taking community roles, their wives were likely at home doing the primary parenting. And even if some duties could be avoided or even shunned, every father recalled co-operative parenting situations with other families. From there, they often moved on to recall how they parented.

Memories of parenting constituted an ambivalent terrain. The degree of actual involvement was difficult to determine with any certainty. In many instances memories appeared to have been coloured far more by what was considered ideal than by reality. Accounts of this type displayed their own set of archetypes used to structure the narratives of many informants.

PARENTS

When Olaph Christensen was asked about work demands cutting into home life he replied, "I think it's all *involved*: you gotta be a breadwinner and you gotta be a parent." He went on to criticize fathers whom he imagined had spent too much time chasing the "almighty dollar."[49] Breadwinning and parenting usually conflicted. Christensen's ambiguous notion of them being "all involved," on one hand, while divided into "gotta be a breadwinner" and "gotta be a parent," on the other, touched on a basic quandary fathers faced. One way to conceptualize male parenting is to consider the broad spectrum of commitment from which its memories are drawn. At one end was the highly involved, nurturing father; at the other, stood a totally absent figure. My informants appeared to operate somewhere in the middle as they constructed or abandoned a variety of new, old, or changing roles. While breadwinning was recalled through myths of self-identification, spousal idealization, and regret, memories of parenting opened many more paths and mythical understandings. Consistently, my informants recalled positive attributes or placed themselves within involved parental roles.

At the same time, many narratives reflected androcentric understandings of ideal behaviour. Mothers were described as the primary caregivers by every informant. Fathers' parenting functions were portrayed as complementary or secondary, though their importance as teachers, counsellors, and benefactors seemed to increase as children grew.

One of the most commonly expressed purposes of male parenting was father as progenitor. Some considered its strictly genealogical form, as when Ken Wilson spoke of the importance of "my family's production of the lineage."[50] Others combined this with notions of memorializing a father's place within a patrilineal chain. "The first thing is that I feel that I never die," Sam Taylor claimed, adding "I have my own son and he's going on. And somewhere in the future—'Oh! You're one of Sam Taylor's boys, or grandson,' or whatever."[51] As a patrilineal legacy, fatherhood was not only recalled as something one left behind. Memories of birth, too, often drew on some variant of the progenitor myth. "I was proud as hell that the first born was a son," related David Benson, then a timber cruiser. "And the joke was on. Give'm a mainline cable and send him to the bush. He's big enough to go to work."[52] Perceptions of father as progenitor took many forms, from a simple notion of reproducing the lineage, to the suggestion of a family stamp, "one of Sam Taylor's boys" to impressions of the father as a model or perhaps teacher—"he's big enough to go to work," just like dad. Andro-centric perspectives were obvious; but so too was the sense, however mythical, of stem families delineated by patrilineal descent.

Father as benefactor was another discernible construct, again one informed by a prevalent notion of ideal parenting. Here, sons were not always favoured since some fathers were committed to furthering the education of every child. And in school performance, daughters often outshone brothers in achievement or ambition. An inability to provide for postsecondary education might also draw on the benefactor archetype: "Karen was always good in school," Charley Farrow told me. "She graduated in June of '66 and she won several scholarships for going to university. And she went to university. She worked in the summer as a telephone operator. And she got her first two years. . . . Then, she ran out of money. Of course, I couldn't help her on my wages. I wouldn't wanted nothing better."[53] In this case, Farrow failed, and painfully so he recalled, to become his daughter's benefactor. Several times he returned to this story, which suggested its importance as a lifetime regret.

Father as teacher also emerged as a common structuring device. Transmitting values to both sons and daughters was often recalled in circumstances related to other roles, such as father as moral guardian, guidance counsellor, or disciplinarian. This multifaceted framework of fatherhood was occasionally said to rest on a basic standard, sometimes expressed as the "right way" to bring up children. David Benson's sense of this seemed particularly telling because he connected it to the challenge he faced as a parent in the sixties, a period many recalled in terms of cultural and moral upheaval.[54] He also considered how perspectives appeared to change from his generation to the next:

> We always had a problem, y'know, after the flower children days, and so forth—the "freedom of sex." Sex freedom and, y'know, sleep with anything you can and whenever you can and whatever. This wasn't in our generation and it wasn't in our bringing up, eh? And trying to instill that into our sons, y'know, when they're in their prime, y'know. My influence on them was that: "hey mister—be careful who you take out," y'know. "If she's good enough to take her to bed you'd better be thinking about marrying her—because that's the way its done and that's the right way." So that, that's the thing that raised my family, and how I was raised.[55]

Apart from the obvious objectification of women, Benson recognized a standard or code of conduct that may have defined many behaviours and served to integrate different parenting roles. Many fathers, particularly when recalling how they influenced children's behaviour, offered similar notions of proper conduct as something fixed and absolute. As James McAndrew claimed, "I had to teach them whatever it was—fairness and, y'know, the precepts that there's a good way to live, and a bad way."[56]

Memories of parenthood tended to be conveyed through a series of ideal visual images. In memory, male parenting can have its own photograph album, suggesting the place of pastoral mythologies. Herb Brunell, for example, pictured his nine-year-old son rambling about the fields of their Manitoba farm, home to his family before they moved to Prince George in the mid-1950s. While Brunell often portrayed life there as harsh and ultimately a financial failure, this excerpt recalled the simple joy of being outdoors as if seen through his son's eyes. "They were happy," he began, referring to all his children. "Joey . . . liked to [watch] the cattle, and here was a fence, and there was the hay. He'd take the hay—little guy, about maybe twenty below—he'd take the hay from here and the young calf come up and he'd feed him. Right against the sun in February, maybe March. And he was so happy."[57]

As Brunell visually recalled a scene of simplicity and contentment drawn from this period, he also spoke from a very common context for male parenting—father as audience. Often children were described as growing up under dad's watchful eye. They were placed in settings in which he stood on the sidelines while children performed, competed, or presented some accomplishment. Collectively, such scenes and situations tended to extend the role of father as audience to embrace notions of the concerned, involved parent. But as long as certain boundaries were not crossed, fatherhood was not portrayed as an intrusive, interfering kind of parenting. "I was interested in what they were doing," Olaph Christensen related. "Well that's only a father's duty. Yeah, you want to know what they're doing and that. And ask them, like when they come from school, 'how'd you make out this year?'"[58]

Christensen's point takes us back to the original muddle he began with. Breadwinning and parenting were not "all involved." They conflicted, unless on a few rare occasions paid work was done with the help of children. But the time and energy men spent raising their children appears to have drawn on fairly well-established understandings of how male parenting should be done. Each informant tried to locate stories of child rearing within a fairly common perception of ideal male parenting. While, as breadwinners, many lamented time away from home, all seem to know where they ought to have been and what a good father should do. The recurring archetypes that emerged seemed to reflect broad cultural understandings of fatherhood. Fathers as progenitors, teachers, or audiences suggests a socially constructed framework from which memories of family life, cast in diverse narratives, are organized. Embedded within this schemata were notions of the proper way to raise one's children. But where might we historically situate recurring patterns in fatherhood narratives, however ideal or mythical their depictions?

MASCULINITY, FATHERHOOD, AND MEMORY

E. Anthony Rotundo has traced what he calls the "modern mode" of father-hood to the rise of urbanization and industrialism in the early nineteenth century. Its emergence, he argues, has been part of structural changes in industrialized countries to the near-present. The extent of paternal involve-ment in parenting was a perennial conundrum, given that gender and eco-nomic power were so highly integrated.[59]

At the same time, constructing cultural ideals for fatherhood drew on massive diffusion of middle-class values, attitudes, and beliefs. Rural out-migration, urbanization, and the development of gender power in the workplace were essential trends that set the stage; changes in the practices of new immigrants also shaped the process. Rotundo has concluded that

> modern fatherhood came to large new groups outside the middle class. Of course, the economic pressures of working-class life and the variety of ethnic values produced many variations on the basic form among the different immigrant groups. But modern father-hood became the norm, the cultural ideal toward which all styles of fathering tended.

Many of the stories I collected reflected the enormous influence of this ideal, particularly with respect to parenting.

For generations, families have struggled to come to terms with a basic problem concerning their responses to gender power—conflicts between male breadwinning and parental involvement. For the men in this study, the postwar years may have produced only mixed results. But the evidence also suggests that many fathers had fairly consistent notions of what was expected of them as concerned, involved parents, as well as husbands and community members.

Oral history has certain advantages, notwithstanding its limits as a reli-able record of actual rather than perceived pasts. Primary among its strengths is the light it sheds on the frameworks of perception that shape oral narratives. Memories of breadwinning produced several recurring myths, or partial understandings, that served to structure story telling. Wives at home lacked status in memory compared to breadwinning hus-bands, yet they were often portrayed in elevated positions as homemakers and nurturers. Time away at work was lamented in memory, though many outlets for leisure were also described. Among them, communal fatherhood was cast as an important vehicle for manful assertiveness and served as a channel connecting personal pasts and home life to community service. Fatherhood was recalled through a common understanding of what good fathers should do. Roles seemed determined by recurrent archetypes, and many perceptions were distorted by androcenticism. They also combined to create similar models of ideal male parenting.

What Rotundo has called the modern mode of fatherhood was often referred to by family experts as far back as the 1920s as the "new father-hood." "Good fathering" emerged from many efforts to overcome the anachronisms of a patriarchal ideal fashioned in cultures that had long since been displaced by industrialization, urbanization, and conformity to corresponding consumption, work, and leisure practices.[60] Paradoxically, lines between home and work became more sharply drawn; but the fruits of male labour were supposed to be redistributed in homes where fathers were more engaged in domesticity, even if this did not always occur. Emerging trends reflected new relationships between fathers and families. Homes were more child-centred, fathers more home-bound, more domesticated. As Robert L. Griswold has observed, "this new mode of masculinity and fatherhood—'masculine domesticity,' as one historian called it—had great implications for twentieth century manhood and family life."[61]

The years of depression and war interrupted this trend but did not change it. After 1945, the return of peace, prosperity, and changes in family demography should not lull us into simplistic view of blissful family lives, but home-based consumerism, the baby boom, and the growth of local youth programs did appear to revitalize forms of masculine domesticity encountered in my fieldwork.[62]

It is true that when men were asked about breadwinning, they seemed to recall something far beyond the home: portraits of hard-working loggers, truckers, mechanics, businessmen, or professionals were drawn time and again. Times were good and work was available. But virtually every informant shared a general understanding of what the responsibilities and duties of fatherhood entailed.

Narratives of communal fatherhood also revealed the appeal of masculine domesticity. Masculine roles, or role modelling, that transcended family thresholds, yet respected family life, were described. Many elements of masculine domesticity in Prince George's homes of the 1950s and early 1960s were taken into the community, especially to instill notions of masculine behaviour among male youths. The rise of communal fatherhood was influenced by new forms of masculine domesticity, forms we might associate with the postwar booms in fertility and prosperity.

Styles would change once again with the "flower children days" that David Benson and many others remembered as radical departures. In memory, their era as fathers ended abruptly with the coming of the sixties. But personal pasts are simultaneously embedded in social pasts with much longer histories. From the viewpoint of the men interviewed, change seemed more apparent than continuity, the family life of a preceding generation more foreign than familiar. Further consideration of the historical expanse, however, may suggest quite the opposite.

NOTES

1. Interview #4 (Part I), 9 March 1995. Pseudonyms are used to identify all subjects.

2. Interview #1, 18 Jan. 1995.

3. Interview #9, 30 March 1995.

4. Of the men interviewed, eight were labourers, five were salespersons and/or retailers, three were managers, and five were professionals. The oldest was born in 1919, the youngest in 1943. All, however, had

children born between 1948 and 1963.

5. Some Canadian historians are beginning to turn their attention to family and gender studies situated in the 1950s. Challenges faced by women in paid employment are evaluated by Veronica Strong-Boag in "Home Dreams: Women and the Suburban Experiment in Canada, 1945–60," *Canadian Historical Review* 72 (1991): 471–504, and in "Canada's Wage-Earning Wives and the Construction of the Middle Class, 1945–60," *Journal of Canadian Studies/Revue d'études canadiennes* 29 (1994): 5–25. For a comprehensive assessment of how gender/breadwinning boundaries were constructed in two southern-Ontario locales in an earlier period see Joy Parr, *The Gender of Breadwinners: Women, Men and Change in Two Industrial Towns, 1880–1950* (Toronto: University of Toronto Press, 1990). On the experience of men, work and family life see Mark Rosenfeld, "'She Was a Hard Life': Work, Family, Community and Politics in the Railway Ward of Barrie, Ontario 1900–1960" (PhD thesis, York University, 1990). Recent studies in the United States include Elaine Tyler May, *Homeward Bound: American Families in the Cold War Era* (New York: Basic Books, 1988) and Robert L. Griswold, *Fatherhood in America: A History* (New York: Basic Books, 1993). An extensive sociological literature on American fathers and family life is also available. See, for example, Mirra Komarovsky, *Blue Collar Marriage* (New York: Random House, 1962), Barbara Ehrenreich, *The Hearts of Men: American Dreams and the Flight From Commitment* (Garden City: Anchor Press, 1983) and Kathleen Gerson, *No Man's Land: Men's Changing Commitment to Family and Work* (New York: Basic Books, 1993). See also Thomas Dunk, *It's a Man's World: Male Working-Class Culture in Northwestern Ontario* (Montreal: McGill-Queen's University Press, 1991) for an anthropologist's interpretation of male culture in Thunder Bay, Ontario.

6. See R.W. Connell, *Gender and Power: Society, the Person and Sexual Politics* (Stanford: Stanford University Press, 1987), esp. ch. 7. On relationships between praxis, socialization, and memory see Tonkin's approach to "habitus" in Elizabeth Tonkin, *Narrating Out Pasts: The Social Construction of Oral History* (Cambridge: University of Cambridge Press, 1992), 106–9.

7. Connell, *Gender and Power*, 140.

8. For consideration of methodological problems in crossing family thresholds through qualitative methods see Kerry Daly, "Reshaping Fatherhood: Finding the Models," *Journal of Family Issues* 14 (1993): 510–30, and "The Fit Between Qualitative Research and the Characteristics of Families" in Jane F. Gilgun and Kerry Daly, eds., *Qualitative Methods in Family Research* (Newbury Park, CA: Sage Publications, 1992), 3–11. Critiques and applications of subjective evidence in oral sources are found in Raphael Samuel and Paul Thompson, eds., *The Myths We Live By* (London and New York: Routledge, 1990). Theoretical discussion has been further advanced in Tonkin, *Narrating Our Pasts*. A useful guide to interviewing techniques, potential problems, and interpersonal dynamics during research is provided by Valerie Raleigh Yow, *Recording Oral History: A Practical Guide for Social Scientists* (Thousand Oaks, CA: Sage Publications, 1994). Paul Thompson's *Voice of the Past*, 2d ed. (Oxford: Oxford University Press, 1988) is an excellent standard guide. Ch. 5, "The Memory and the Self," is particularly useful on problems concerning subjectivity and oral evidence.

9. For a recent review of such studies see William Marsiglio, "Contemporary Scholarship on Fatherhood: Culture, Identity and Conduct," *Journal of Family Issues* 14 (1993): 484–510. For historical profiles drawn from the American experience see John Demos, "The Changing Faces of Fatherhood: A New Exploration in Family History" in Stanley Cath, Alan

Gurwitt, and John Munder Ross, eds., *Father and Child: Development and Clinical Perspectives* (Boston: Little, Brown, 1982): 425–50; E. Anthony Rotundo, "American Fatherhood: A Historical Perspective," *American Behavioral Scientist* 29 (1985): 7–25; and Joseph Pleck, "American Fathering in Historical Perspective" in Michael Kimmel, ed., *Changing Men: New Directions in Research on Men and Masculinity* (Newbury Park, CA: Sage Publications, 1987): 83–97.

10. Griswold, *Fatherhood in America*, 2.

11. Ibid., 3.

12. Sandra Lipsitz Bem, *The Lenses of Gender: Transforming the Debate on Sexual Inequality* (New Haven: Yale University Press, 1993), 2.

13. Recent studies of subjectivity in oral reconstructions of the past abound. In addition to some excellent examples in Samuel and Thompson, eds., *The Myths We Live By*, and poignant discussion of its many aspects in Tonkin, *Narrating Our Pasts*, see Ronald J. Grele, ed., *International Annual of Oral History, 1990: Subjectivity and Multiculturalism in Oral History* (New York: Greenwood Press, 1992). One of the most promising new areas in the study of subjectiveness in oral narratives concerns the place of myth in narratives. As Tonkin points out, the conventions of oral historical discourse structure narratives at many levels. "Historians have labeled as 'myth' what seem unrealistic ways of representing the past, but it can sometimes be shown that mythic structures encode history, that is they register actual happenings or significant changes." See Tonkin, *Narrating Our Pasts*, 8. See also Alexander Freund and Laura Quilici, "Exploring Myths in Women's Narratives: Italian and German Immigrant Women in Vancouver, 1947–1961" (*BC Studies*, forthcoming) for a recent application of myth and self-perceptions set in Canada.

14. Clifford Geertz, *Local Knowledge: Further Essays in Interpretive Anthropology* (New York: Basic Books, 1983), 58.

15. Peter Burke, *History and Social Theory* (Cambridge: Polity Press, 1992), 103.

16. Tonkin, *Narrating Our Pasts*, 67. Researchers are prone to communicate their own perspectives or expectations during interviews. For perceptive commentaries on the multifaceted nature of authoring in oral history see Michael Frisch, *A Shared Authority: Essays on the Craft and Meaning of Oral and Public History* (Albany: State University of New York Press, 1990). A useful caveat concerning leading questions is offered by Thompson, *The Voice of the Past*, 202. Researchers, he argues, need to balance coherence with non-interference. Non-directed interviews, where subjects choose their own topics, simply provide a poor basis for comparison. Excessive structure, on the other hand, tends to stifle useful story telling and reflects the interviewer's *a priori* agenda. As well, informants often wish to revise their statements after they have read written transcripts. This offers some measure of distances between imagined and desired pasts. On this point, see Luisa Passerini, "Mythbiography in Oral History" in *The Myths We Live By*, 52–53.

17. Samuel and Thompson, eds., *The Myths We Live By*, 2.

18. In addition to Strong-Boag, "Home Dreams" and "Canada's Wage Earning Wives," cited above, see Annalee Gölz, "Family Matters: The Canadian Family and the State in the Postwar Period," *left history* 2 (1993): 9–50, for an analysis of government strategies and family life.

19. Interview #11, 4 April 1995.

20. Interview #2, 28 Feb. 1995.

21. Interview #4 (Part II), 15 March 1995.

22. Interview #8, 22 March 1995.

23. Interview #9, 30 March 1995.

24. Interview #1, 18 Jan. 1995; Interview #7, 22 March 1995; Interview #8, 22 March 1995.

25. Interview #4 (Part II), 15 March 1995.

26. Interview #7, 22 March 1995.

27. Interview #10, 30 March 1995.

28. The "ideology of containment" used here draws on the concept of a "closed" nuclear family discussed by Elaine Tyler May in *Homeward Bound*. Though a more common usage of "containment" in the Cold War era refers to American-led policies to restrict the spread of communism, May gives it a double meaning by applying it to the notion of breadwinning husbands providing for housewives and children "contained" within single-family households. This idealized view of family life as a "contained" experience was also reflected in my sample.

29. Interview #18, 12 April 1995.

30. Interview #12, 5 April 1995.

31. Interview #4 (Part II), 15 March 1995.

32. Claude Lévi-Strauss, *Structural Anthropology* (London: Allen Lane: Penguin Press, 1958), 229.

33. Interview #5 (Part II), 28 March 1995.

34. Interview #10, 30 March 1995.

35. Ibid.

36. Interview #3, 6 March 1995.

37. Ibid.

38. Interview #8, 22 March 1995.

39. See interview #5 (Part II), 28 March 1995.

40. Interview #1, 18 Jan. 1995.

41. See E. Anthony Rotundo, *American Manhood: Transformations in Masculinity from the Revolution to the Modern Era* (New York: Basic Books, 1993), 2.

42. Interview #2, 28 Feb. 1995.

43. Interview #5 (Part II) 14 March 1995.

44. Ibid. (Part III), 13 April 1995.

45. Interview #7, 22 March 1995.

46. Interview #4 (Part II), 15 March 1995.

47. Interview #13, 6 April 1995.

48. Interview #3, 6 March 1995.

49. Interview #9, 30 March 1995.

50. Interview #5 (Part III), 13 April 1995.

51. Interview #4 (Part I), 15 March 1995.

52. Interview #11, 4 April 1995.

53. Interview #2, 28 Feb. 1995.

54. For historical approaches to social memory, see James Fentress and Chris Wickham, *Social Memory* (Oxford and Cambridge: Blackwell, 1992).

55. Interview #11, 4 April 1995.

56. Interview #3, 6 March 1995.

57. Interview #6, 21 March 1995.

58. Interview #9, 30 March 1995.

59. E. Anthony Rotundo, "Patriarchs and Participants: A Historical Perspective on Fatherhood in the United States" in Michael Kaufman, ed., *Beyond Patriarchy: Essays by Men on Pleasure, Power, and Change* (Toronto and New York: Oxford University Press, 1987), 70.

60. Griswold refers to this as the "invention" of new fatherhood. Discernible evidence of comparatively new patterns of family-centred fatherhood, measured through evidence generated in social scientific research, was situated in the interwar period. See Griswold, *Fatherhood in America*, ch. 6.

61. Ibid., 89. The historian, Margaret Marsh, has traced the emergence of masculine domesticity in America as far back as the 1870s. This is understandable given its origins in the rise of cities, suburbs, and industrial work patterns. For two essays on this theme, see Margaret Marsh, "Suburban Men and Masculine Domesticity, 1870–1917," *American Quarterly* 40 (1988): 165–86, and by the same author, "From Separation to Togetherness: The Social Construction of Domestic Space in American Suburbs, 1840–1915," *Journal of American History* 76 (1989): 506–27.

62. In addition to Strong-Boag's work on suburban and middle-class women, cited above, a useful set of studies on women who did not fit the prevailing reproductive consensus or domestic containment May describes in *Homeward Bound* is found in Joanne Meyerowitz, *Not June Cleaver: Women and Gender in Postwar America, 1945–1960* (Philadelphia: Temple University Press, 1994).

FURTHER READING

○

THEORY AND METHOD

Brod, Harry and Michael Kaufman, eds. *Theorizing Masculinities*. Thousand Oaks: Sage, 1994.

Butler, Judith. *Gender Trouble: Feminism and the Subversion of Identity*. London: Routledge, 1990.

Canning, Kathleen "Feminist History after the Linguistic Turn." *Signs* 19, 2 (Winter 1994): 368–404.

Connell, R.W. *Masculinities*. Berkeley and Los Angeles: University of California Press, 1995.

Connell, R.W., *Gender and Power*. Stanford: Stanford University Press, 1987.

Fraser, Nancy and Linda Gordon. "A Geneology of *Dependency*: Tracing a Keyword in the US Welfare State." *Signs* 19 (1994): 309–36.

Journal of Women's History 5, 1 (Spring 1993). Special section, "Women's history/gender history: is feminist scholarship losing its critical edge?"

Nicholson, Linda. "Interpreting Gender." *Signs* 20 (1994).

Morgan, David. *Discovering Men*. London: Routledge, 1992.

Riley, Denise. *"Am I that Name?: Feminism and the Category of Woman in History*. Minnesota: University of Minnesota Press, 1988.

Scott, Joan. *Gender and the Politics of History*. New York: Columbia University Press, 1988.

Scott, Joan. "The Evidence of Experience," *Critical Inquiry* 17 (Summer 1991): 773–97.

Shapiro, Ann-Louise. *Feminists Revision History*. New Brunswick: Rutgers University Press, 1994.

Theory and Society 22, 5 (Oct. 1993). Special issue on masculinities.

Weedon, Chris. *Feminist Practice and Poststructuralist Theory*. Oxford: Basil Blackwell, 1987.

SELECTED NON-CANADIAN WORKS

Baron, Ava. *Work Engendered: Toward a New History of American Labor*. Ithaca: Cornell University Press, 1991.

Carnes, Mark C. and Clyde Griffen. *Meanings of Manhood: Construction of Masculinity in Victorian America*. Chicago: University of Chicago Press, 1990.

Chauncey, George. *Gay New York: Gender, Urban Culture and the Making of the Gay Male World, 1890–1940*. New York: Basic Books, 1994.

Davidoff, Leonore and Catherine Hall. *Family Fortunes: Men and Women of the English Middle Class 1780–1850*. Chicago: University of Chicago Press, 1987.

Faue, Elizabeth. *Community of Suffering and Struggle*. Chapel Hill: University of North Carolina Press, 1991.

Gordon, Linda. *Heroes of Their Own Lives: The Politics and History of Family Violence*. New York: Viking Penguin, 1988.

Hall, Catherine. *White, Male and Middle-Class: Explorations in Feminism and History*. New York: Routledge, 1992.

Hearn, Jeff. *Men in the Public Eye*. New York: Routledge, 1992.

Kimmel, Michael S. *Changing Men: New Direction in Research on Men and Masculinity*. Newbury Park: Sage, 1987.

Mangan, J.A. and James Walvin, eds. *Manliness and Morality: Middle-Class Masculinity in Britain and America, 1800–1940*. Manchester: Manchester University Press, 1987.

Melosh, Barbara. *Gender and American History Since 1890*. London: Routledge, 1993.

Nye, Robert. *Masculinity and Male Codes of Honor in Modern France*. New York: Oxford University Press, 1993.

Osterud, Nancy Grey. *Bonds of Community*. Ithaca: Cornell University Press, 1991.

Peiss, Kathy. *Cheap Amusements: Working Women and Leisure in Turn-of-the-Century New York*. Philadelphia: Temple University Press, 1986.

Peiss, Kathy and Christina Simmons. *Passion and Power: Sexuality in History*. Philadelphia: Temple University Press, 1989.

Phillips, Jack. *A Man's Country? The Image of the Pakeha Male: A History*. Aukland: Penguin, 1987.

Poovey, Mary. *Uneven Developments: The Ideological Work of Gender in Mid-Victorian England*. Chicago: University of Chicago Press, 1988.

Roediger, David R. *Toward the Abolition of Whiteness: Essays on Race, Politics and Working Class History*. London: Verso, 1994.

Roper, Michael and John Tosh. *Manful Assertions: Masculinities in Britain since 1800*. London: Routledge, 1991.

Rose, Sonya. *Limited Livelihoods: Gender and Class in Nineteenth-Century England*. Berkeley: University of California Press, 1992.

Rotundo, Anthony. *American Manhood: Transformations in Masculinity from the Revolution to the Modern Era*. New York: Basic Books, 1993.

Sinha, Mrinalini. *Colonial Masculinity: The "Manly Englishman" and the "Effeminate Bengali" in the Late Nineteenth Century*. Toronto: McClelland & Stewart, 1995.

Wajcman, Judith. *Feminists Confront Technology*. University Park, PA: Pennsylvania State University Press, 1991.

Walkowitz, Judith. *City of Dreadful Delight: Narratives of Sexual Danger in Late-Victorian London*. Chicago: University of Chicago Press, 1992.

CANADIAN MONOGRAPHS

Barman, Jean. *Growing Up British in British Columbia: Boys in Private School.* Vancouver: UBC Press, 1984. Esp. "Realizing the Ideal," 78–106.

Bradbury, Bettina. *Working Families: Daily Survival in Industrialising Montreal.* Toronto: McClelland & Stewart, 1993.

Dubinsky, Karen. *Improper Advances: Rape and Heterosexual Conflict in Ontario 1880–1929.* Chicago: University of Chicago Press, 1993.

Dunk, Thomas. *It's a Working Man's Town: Male Working-Class Culture in Northwestern Ontario.* Montreal: McGill-Queen's University Press, 1991.

Fingard, Judith. *The Dark Side of Life in Victorian Halifax.* Halifax: Potters Field, 1989.

Frager, Ruth. *Sweatshop Strife: Class, Ethnicity and Gender in the Jewish Labour Movement of Toronto, 1900–39.* Toronto: University of Toronto Press, 1992.

Gruneau, Richard and David Whitson. *Hockey Night in Canada.* Toronto: Garamond, 1993. Esp. "Violence, Fighting and Masculinity," 176–95.

Howell, Colin. *Northern Sandlots: A Social History of Maritime Baseball.* Toronto: University of Toronto Press, 1995.

Iacovetta, Franca. *Such Hard-working People: Women, Men and the Italian Immigrant Experience in Postwar Toronto.* Montreal: McGill-Queen's University Press, 1992.

Kaufman, Michael. *Cracking the Armour: Power, Pain and the Lives of Men.* Toronto: Viking, 1993.

Kinsman, Gary. *The Regulation of Desire.* Montreal: Black Rose, 1987.

McLaren, Angus. *Our Own Master Race: Eugenics in Canada 1885–1945.* Toronto: McClelland & Stewart, 1990.

Morton, Suzanne. *Ideal Surroundings: Domestic Life in a Working-Class Suburb in the 1920s.* Toronto: University of Toronto Press, 1995.

Parr, Joy. *The Gender of Breadwinners: Women, Men and Change in Two Industrial Towns 1880–1950.* Toronto: University of Toronto Press, 1990.

Ross, Becki. *The House the Jill Built.* Toronto: University of Toronto Press, 1995.

Sager, Eric. *Ships and Memories.* Vancouver: UBC Press, 1993. Esp. "Masculinity," 106–17, and "Family," 97–105.

Sangster, Joan. *Earning Respect: The Lives of Working Women in Small-Town Ontario 1920–1960.* Toronto: University of Toronto Press, 1995.

Strange, Carolyn. *Toronto's Girl Problem: The Perils and Pleasures of the City, 1880–1930.* Toronto: University of Toronto Press, 1995.

Valverde, Mariana. *The Age of Light, Soap and Water.* Toronto: McClelland & Stewart, 1991.

CANADIAN COLLECTIONS

Axelrod, Paul and John Reid. *Youth, University and Canadian Society.* Montreal: McGill-Queen's University Press, 1989.

Backhouse, Constance. "White Female Help and Chinese-Canadian Employers: Race, Class, Gender and Law in the Case of Yee Clun, 1924." *Canadian Ethnic Studies* 26, 3 (1994): 34–52.

Bradbury, Bettina, ed. *Canadian Family History*. Toronto: Copp Clark, 1992.

BC Studies Nov. 1995. Special issue on gender history.

Dodd, Diana and Deborah Gorham, ed. *Caring and Curing: Historical Perspectives on Women and Healing in Canada*. Ottawa: Carleton University Press, 1994.

Guilford, Janet and Suzanne Morton, ed. *Separate Spheres: Women's Worlds in the 19th Century Maritimes*. Fredericton: Acadiensis Press, 1994.

Howell, Colin and Richard J. Twomey, ed. *Jack Tar in History: Essays in the History of Maritime Life and Labour*. Fredericton: Acadiensis Press, 1991.

Iacovetta, Franca and Mariana Valverde, ed. *Gender Conflicts: New Essays in Women's History*. Toronto: University of Toronto Press, 1992.

Journal of Canadian Studies. Winter 1994–95 special issue on the Dionne Quintuplets.

Kaufman, Michael, ed. *Beyond Patriarchy: Essays by Men on Pleasure, Power and Change*. Toronto: Oxford University Press, 1987.

Samson, Daniel, ed. *Contested Countryside: Rural Workers and Modern Society in Atlantic Canada, 1800–1950*. Fredericton: Acadiensis Press, 1994.

Strong-Boag, Veronica and Anita Clair Fellman, ed. *Rethinking Canada: The Promise of Women History*. 2nd ed. Toronto: Copp Clark, 1991.

CANADIAN JOURNAL ARTICLES

Baskerville, Peter A. "She Has Already Hinted at Board: Enterprising Urban Women in British Columbia, 1836–1896." *Histoire sociale/ Social History* 26, 52 (Nov. 1993): 205–27.

Bennett, Paul. "Taming 'Bad Boys' of the 'Dangerous Class': Child Rescue and Restraint at the Victoria Industrial School 1887–1935." *Histoire sociale/Social History* 21, 41 (May 1988): 71–96.

Burr, Christina. "Defending 'The Art Preservative': Class and Gender Relations in the Printing Trade Unions, 1850–1914." *Labour/Le Travail* 31 (Spring 1993): 47–73.

Fingard, Judith. "The Problem of Cruelty, Marriage Breakdown and the Rights of Wives in Nova Scotia, 1880–1900." *Acadiensis* 22, 2 (Sept. 1993): 84–101.

Frank, Blye. "Hegemonic Heterosexual Masculinity." *Studies in Political Economy* 24 (Autumn 1987): 159–70.

Hobbs, Margaret. "Rethinking Feminism in the 1930s: Gender Crisis or Workplace Justice." *Gender and History* 5, 1 (Spring 1993): 4–15.

Kinnear, Mary. "'Mostly for the Male Members': Teaching in Winnipeg, 1993–1966." *Historical Studies in Education* 6, 1 (Spring 1994): 1–20.

Kinsman, Gary. "'Character Weakness' and 'Fruit Machines': Towards an Analysis of the Anti-Homosexual Security Campaign in the Canadian Civil Service." *Labour/Le Travail* 35 (Spring 1995): 133–62.

Jasen, Patricia. "Romance, Modernity and the Evolution of Tourism on the Niagara Frontier 1790–1850." *Canadian Historical Review* 72, 3 (1991): 283–318.

Morgan, Cecilia, "'In Search of the Phantom Misnamed Honour': Duelling in Upper Canada." *Canadian Historical Review* 76, 4 (1995).

Murray, Sylvie. "Quand les menageres se font militantes: La Ligue auxiliaire de l'Association internationale des machinistes, 1905–1980." *Labour/Le Travail* 29 (Spring 1992): 157–86.

Pierson, Ruth Roach. "Gender and the Unemployment Insurance Debates in Canada, 1934–1940." *Labour/Le Travail* 25 (Spring 1990): 77–103.

Porter, Ann. "Women and Income Security in the Post-War Period: The Case of Unemployment Insurance, 1945–62." *Labour/Le Travail* 31 (Spring 1993): 111–44.

Strong-Boag, Veronica. "Canada's Wage-earning Wives and the Construction of the Middle-Class, 1945–60." *Journal of Canadian Studies* 29, 3 (Fall 1994).

Struthers, James. "Regulating the Elderly: Old Age Pensions and the Formation of a Pension Bureaucracy in Ontario, 1919–1945." *Journal of the Canadian Historical Association* NS 3 1993.

Yee, Shirley. "Gender Ideology and Black Women as Community-Builders in Ontario, 1850–70." *Canadian Historical Review* 75, 4 (1993): 53–73.

BIBLIOGRAPHIES

Canadian Historical Review. "Recent Contributions" section by subject area in each issue.

Canadian Committee on Women's History. *CCWH Newsletter* "CCWH Bibliography" in each issue.

Journal of Women's History Guide to Periodical Literature. Compiled by Gayle V. Fischer, foreword by Christie Farnham, introduction by Joan Hoff. Bloomington: Indiana University Press, 1992.

Pederson, Diana. *Changing Women, Changing History.* Toronto: Green Dragon, 1992.

Sutherland, Neil, Jean Barman and Linda Hale. *History of Canadian Childhood and Youth: A Bibliography.* Westport, CT: Greenwood Press, 1992.